Teaching Communication:
Theory, Research, and Methods

Teaching Communication:
Theory, Research, and Methods

Second Edition

Edited by

Anita L. Vangelisti
John A. Daly
University of Texas at Austin
and
Gustav W. Friedrich
Rutgers University

 LAWRENCE ERLBAUM ASSOCIATES, PUBLISHERS
1999   Mahwah, New Jersey   London

Lawrence Erlbaum Associates, Inc., Publishers
10 Industrial Avenue
Mahwah, NJ 07430

Cover design by Kathryn Houghtaling Lacey

Library of Congress Cataloging-in-Publication Data

Teaching communication : theory, research, and methods / edited by Anita L. Vangelisti, John A. Daly, Gustav W. Friedrich. —
2nd ed.
   p. cm.
Includes bibliographical references and indexes.
ISBN 0-8058-2835-4 (alk. paper). — ISBN 0-8058-2836-2
(pbk. : alk. paper)
   1. Communication—Study and teaching (Higher)   I.
Vangelisti, Anita L. II. Daly, John A. (John Augustine), 1952– .
II. Friedrich, Gustav W.
   P91.3.T43   1999
   302.2'071'1—dc21   97-49374
                                                                  CIP

Books published by Lawrence Erlbaum Associates are printed on
acid-free paper, and their bindings are chosen for strength and dura-
bility.

Printed in the United States of America
10 9 8 7 6 5 4 3 2 1

Contents

Introduction

The field of communication was founded, in part, because of a felt need to make people better communicators. That meant teaching them how to communicate more effectively, whether it be in public settings (e.g., public address, groups) or in private (e.g., interpersonal). Most of that teaching has happened within the classroom and many professionals have spent their lives instructing others on various aspects of communication. Yet, in the 70 years or so that the field of communication has existed, very little integrated attention has been paid to the methods involved in teaching communication. Although there have been journal articles on techniques, and classes on instruction in communication, there have been few attempts to integrate the many issues and concerns that face teachers. This book attempts to do that.

Who is this book for? Many readers should find it especially useful when they start their careers as communication educators. One of the toughest parts of graduate school is moving from one side of the desk to the other with little or no preparation or guidance. There are few fields of endeavor in which people expect so much quality so quickly, yet provide so few resources. At best, most beginning graduate students are hired to teach undergraduate courses (at paltry rates) and receive a single 3-hour class in teaching. Many times these beginning teachers do not even receive credit for the course and are forced to fit that course in with more so-called substantive classes. This book is for them. One of the prime motivations for compiling this volume was to provide a useful reference for beginning teachers in communication—whether they be graduate students or, perhaps, beginning faculty members who have not yet faced an audience of 20, 30, or even 500 inquiring, demanding pupils.

Another audience for this book is the individual teacher who has, perhaps for many years, taught communication. The editors of this volume often find themselves sharing and listening to stories about teaching. Learning to teach is not a one-time effort. It is a continual growth experience. Good teaching requires more than knowledge about a topic area. It demands an understanding of instructional processes, learning, and constant refining of skills. Hopefully, this volume will offer new insight and fresh perspective for even the most experienced of teachers.

Who else might use this book? Aside from Gus' son, Anita's mother, and John's children, we hope that department chairs and deans will offer it to new faculty members in both 2-year and 4-year colleges, that directors of basic courses and multisection courses will give it to the instructors they supervise, and that directors of graduate studies and instructors of courses in communication education make regular use of it in their classes.

In thinking about the organization of this volume, we identified six major concerns that face any communication educator and asked some of the best people in the discipline to write chapters elaborating these concerns.

The first issues addressed in this book, examined in Part I, focus on the goals of communication education. In five chapters, authors describe the nature of the communication discipline and the goals for communication instruction that derive from it. With the goals of communication education identified, Part II focuses on the preparation of specific communication courses. Rather than examining every potential course that could be developed, this section offers descriptions of a smaller sample of topics such as public speaking, persuasion, and intercultural communication. The chapters provide hints from experts on how to prepare relevant class materials. Page limitations precluded the inclusion of equally important subjects (e.g., interpretation, political communication, language). Hopefully, even if a reader's favorite course is left unmentioned, he or she will be able to garner ideas and perspectives from other course areas as well as from the chapter that covers issues associated with teaching special topics. Part III assists the instructor in organizing the instructional context. Within this section, the emphasis is on classroom roles of teachers and students, classroom management, and organizing the first day of a class. Part IV, then, focuses on using instructional strategies and tools. This section is concerned with both global issues (e.g., interaction skills) and more specific tools (e.g., writing, class activities). In addition to describing various instructional tools and criteria for their selection, the chapters in this section offer ideas on evaluating both the processes and the products of instruction. In Part V the emphasis is on unique teaching assignments that readers of this book may sometimes encounter. For instance, it is not uncommon for new assistant professors to direct a basic course, whether it be "the" basic course or multiple sections of the basic public speaking course. It is also not uncommon to be asked to prepare instructional material for continuing education. Each of these responsibilities requires particular skills. Additional assignments discussed in this section are teaching in the 2-year college, directing forensic programs, distance education, and consulting. The final section of this book, Part VI, explores important professional issues that face both the new and experienced communication instructor. One chapter involves ethical concerns—issues connected to both day-to-day instructor–student interaction (e.g., plagiarism) and issues that relate to the content of communication instruction (e.g., freedom of speech). The other chapter focuses on political and ethical issues that may arise as instructors join a department. It includes, among other things, practical advice on how to deal with the sometimes perplexing rules and procedures that characterize many academic departments.

This is the second edition of *Teaching Communication*. The first edition, according to the publisher, was a steady seller with few secondhand sales. In part, this is a compliment to the fine group of authors who contributed to the first volume, but it is also much more. It represents the palpable commitment of our discipline to teaching. The prior edition offered the first integrated text in the field of communication that specified the conceptual as well as the practical issues related to communication instruction. We hope this book continues in the same tradition.

—*Anita L. Vangelisti*
—*John A. Daly*
—*Gustav W. Friedrich*

I

Thinking About the Goals
of Communication Education

1

The Communication Discipline

Gustav W. Friedrich
Rutgers University

Don M. Boileau
George Mason University

THE BEGINNINGS

Gray (1949) persuasively argued the case for studying the history of communication education in the United States:

> A more complete examination of the route we have traveled in coming from our beginning ... to our present position is well worth the undertaking.... It will give us a still deeper understanding and appreciation of that position, in the same way that any study of history may provide the basis for a better orientation as an aid in determining the direction we should proceed. (p. 156)

Based on Gray's premise and the need to provide a context for understanding the diversity of tasks that face the communication educator, this chapter surveys the development of the communication discipline in the United States and then explores its current status in terms of goals and structure.

The starting point for the field of communication in this nation was 1636, 16 years after the Pilgrims landed in America, with the founding of Harvard

University by the Massachusetts legislature. Because Harvard's mission, as was true of the other New England colleges soon to follow, was to train ministers of the gospel with a curriculum modeled on medieval universities, instruction in the practical discipline of communication (Craig, 1989) was needed.

An important goal of ministerial schooling was to produce clerics who were able to defend the church with well-crafted arguments. Because Latin was the language of educated people, the pedagogy for developing presentational and dialectical skills was the Latin syllogistic disputation. A tutor (usually the college president) selected a student to defend the "truthful" side of a question from one of the arts or sciences taught in the college. This student, utilizing a format specified by the divisions and dichotomies of Ramistic logic, opened the disputation by reading a carefully worded Latin discourse that: (a) stated the thesis, (b) defined and delimited the question, and (c) used the format of a syllogism to present the arguments supporting the thesis. At the conclusion of this presentation, the other students in the class raised objections, also in syllogistic format, either by disagreeing with the definitions or by denying the major or minor premises. As objections were raised, the disputation's author was provided the opportunity to reestablish the original arguments. During this whole process, the tutor actively assisted students who experienced difficulty in the use of either Latin or logic (Potter, 1954).

As the mission of higher education expanded to include other professions, English replaced Latin and students received instruction in persuasion in addition to argumentation. As this happened, college presidents and tutors were replaced by specialists in rhetoric, elocution, and speech as providers of communication instruction.

EMERGENCE OF DEPARTMENTS

Although communication instruction was a part of higher education from the beginning, separate departments of communication were not the original providers of training in the subject. In fact, as recently as 1900, there was no such entity as a department of communication. In his description of the origin and development of departments of speech, Smith (1954) pointed out that college departments, as we know them, did not exist until late in the 19th century when the structure of higher education responded to tremendous expansion. Smith identified four interrelated pressures that produced a departmental structuring of higher education: (a) a flood of new know- ledge, (b) the development of specialization within numerous and narrowly defined segments of the curriculum, (c) the inclusion of useful and practical knowledge (e.g., agriculture and engineering) within the college curriculum, and (d) college enrollments that more than doubled in the last quarter of the 19th century. In short:

> The modern college department ... was born out of the pressures of new knowledge, specialization, new utilitarian concepts of the functions of education, and swelling enrollments. It judged the fitness of course offerings, the relationships of courses to one another; it set up prerequisites, and programs for majors and minors; it cultivated the expansion of knowledge in its own segment of the academic globe, and looked anxiously to unoccupied territory between itself and neighboring departments; it sought money and equipment, and made recommendations for appointments, promotions, and salary changes. (p. 449)

The departmentalization of U. S. higher education proceeded rapidly between 1860 and 1900. Although it was possible to form autonomous departments of communication during this period, and this occurred in some institutions, the general trend saw departments of English language and literature take responsibility for most communication instruction. Smith (1954) believed that this occurred for two reasons: (a) the fact that both communication and English literature trace their historical roots to the study of rhetoric, which, with its traditional concern for the arts of both oral and written discourse, has been an established part of the curriculum since medieval times; and (b) " a certain lack of independent vitality within the area of rhetoric" (p. 451). In short, "neither the practice of rhetoric nor the practice of elocution, as it was conceived in the colleges in the last half of the nineteenth century seems to have possessed the status necessary for the general emergence of a department separate from English literature" (p. 453).

The bonds between communication instruction and the English department, however, were from the beginning very fragile. Smith (1954) identified four pressures that provided early impetus for the establishment of independent communication departments:

1. Pressure created by the specialization of interest within English. As English developed as an academic specialty, it defined its uniqueness and academic respectability in terms of intensive literary study and linguistics—a move that left little room for teachers of speaking and writing.

2. The outspoken discontent of speech teachers working in departments of English. Individuals who believed strongly in the importance of providing instruction in the practical skills of discourse were quickly disillusioned by their location in a department with a budget controlled by individuals with different enthusiasms. The first important public demand for the separation

of speech and English came on March 25, 1913, at the Public Speaking Conference of the New England and North Atlantic States.

3. The claims of distinctiveness in subject matter—claims that had their origins in two sources. First, teachers of public speaking asserted that their subject matter possessed a heritage (the rhetorical tradition) that was equally as classical as that of literature. Second, they argued that the modern sciences, and particularly psychology, provided them with new knowledge that was both foreign to the interests of English departments and worthy of independent departmental status.

4. The demand of students. The influence of student interest and pressure on the formation of communication departments is illustrated by the following editorial in *The University of Oklahoma Magazine* ("Great Need," 1912):

At the time we are writing our editorials it is rumored that a movement is on foot, backed by some one hundred and fifty students of the University who are members of literary societies to petition the State Board of Education to establish a Department of Public Speaking with a full-paid professor with special training in that line in charge. It is hoped that the Board will give the matter very careful consideration, as the need for such a department here is extremely urgent.

It is not enough to have a student as a debating coach, giving in addition one or two courses in public speaking. Such a plan does not meet the needs at all. During the past two years we have had Paul Walker at the head of this work. The Board will have to look a long time before it will find a man with Walker's qualifications willing to work for what Walker has been working for. He could afford to do it because he wanted to study law and the work afforded him the opportunity. He had had previous training in the work and he was specially fitted for the job. But even the work he has been able to do has not met the need. The need requires the full time of a trained professor.

There are about one hundred and fifty students in the University who are engaged in active literary society work. Every one of them would like to have some training in public speaking. Most of them consider it a waste of time to enter classes taught by one of their fellow students. Teaching public speaking is not like any other teaching. After one has studied well a subject in mathematics, or geology, or some kindred subject, where the accumulation of facts, rules, laws, etc., is the main thing, all of which can be done in one year's application to a given course, any student ought to be qualified to teach that subject. But in public speaking the ability to teach it cannot be learned by merely studying a textbook, nor can one teach it by merely knowing a few rules, or laws, or facts. A good teacher of public speaking must be a good speaker himself.

Ever since we have been at the University we have heard the complaint frequently made that not enough attention is given to public speaking. The English Department gives some courses in debating, which is only one phase of public speaking. The debating coach gives a course each semester in debating. Aside from the training given by the expression department that is the extent of instruction the University offers at present in public speaking. The training in the expression department does not properly come under what we are discussing. Someone has said: "Whistle to a dog and he comes—that's oratory; speak to him and he runs away—that's elocution." Well, it's the whistling that we're discussing.

If a student wants training in how to be at ease on the stage, or how to hold his hands (not her's), or how to make a graceful appearance, or how to control his gestures so as to make them effective, or how to train his voice so as to make his speech smooth and eloquent—his only resource is the downtown preachers, and some of them need a little of that training themselves. In the Kansas–Oklahoma debate this year our boys clearly excelled in argument, but the Kansas boys had been trained in these things; our boys showed that they had not. Now suppose that Kansas had put up as good an argument as our boys did they would have won the debate in spite of everything, because they were better speakers than our boys were.

One hundred and fifty students asking for a strong Public Speaking Department ought to be sufficient to warrant the Board in giving it to us. Now is a good time to ask for it, too, for a new coach will have to be selected for next year to take Paul Walker's place, and why not just have a full-time man who can give us a little more than training in debating. There are other phases of public speaking that are just as important—indeed, if not more so. (pp. 17–18)

As a result of the pressures just described, independent communication departments began to emerge in significant numbers shortly after the turn of the century. Although the titles of these departments were varied, a common one was Department of Public Speaking. This title began to change to Department of Speech after 1920, to Department of Speech Communication in the 1960s, and, most recently, to Department of Communication.

In the beginning, departments focused their instructional efforts on developing the skills of formal, public discourse through courses with such labels as Forensics, Declamation, Elocution, Oratory, Logic, Rhetoric, Extemporaneous Speaking, Debate, Dramatic Interpretation, and Public Speaking. Course work in drama was present from the beginning, theater production courses were added in the 1920s, the addition of speech science and training for speech therapists developed after 1920, and course work in radio developed after 1935. During the 1950s, departments began to develop course work in less formal modes of discourse as the field started to expand the focus of investigations. Haiman's (1951) *Group Leadership and Democratic Action* was the first book to focus on the concepts, developments, and research findings in group dynamics, leadership, and interpersonal communication. The first text to focus completely on interpersonal communication was Wiseman and Barker's (1967) *Speech-Interpersonal Communication.*

As this discussion suggests, departments of communication were founded to serve utilitarian and pedagogical ends. Although our founding fathers called for research (as a means for achieving academic respectability), much of the early research was directed toward pedagogical ends. This changed rapidly, however, as scholars rediscovered the classical and modern rhetorical traditions and as they explored the applicability of social scientific research methods to communication phenomena. For excellent treatments of the history of our research traditions, see Chaffee and Rogers (1997), Cohen (1985, 1994), Delia (1987), Pearce (1985), and Rogers (1994).

CURRENT STATUS

Currently, the field of communication is both broad and diverse—encompassing teacher-scholars housed in departments with varied titles (e.g., Communication, Speech Communication, Mass Communication, Journalism) that are, in turn, located in various colleges (e.g., Arts & Sciences, Humanities, Social Sciences, Fine Arts, Communication). It is possible, therefore, to define the communication discipline in multiple ways. This chapter adopts (with minor exceptions) a position articulated by Craig (1989), who argued that communication is best conceived as a practical discipline with the essential purpose of cultivating communication as a practical art through critical study. For Craig (1989) and for us, the defining characteristic of the communication discipline is "the intimate tie that exists between the discipline's work and practical communicative activities" (p. 2). As such, the communication discipline views communicative behavior as basic to human activity—to individual development; to interpersonal and social relationships, and to the functioning of political, economic, cultural, and social institutions. Thus, communication professionals study communicative behavior with the dual goal of (a) understanding the structure, patterns, and effects of human communication; and (b) facilitating a higher quality of communication both for individuals and for society.

Across a diversity of levels and focus, communication professionals share three key assumptions that are reflected in the nature of the courses we teach and in the nature of our scholarly research.

The first assumption is a belief that communication is an individual's most distinctive and significant behavior and the basic building block of literacy. It is through the multisensory process of symbolic interaction that we define both ourselves and our environment, and it is through communication that we are able to link ourselves to that environment. Without communication, it would be impossible to develop the complexity of thought that sets us apart from the other creatures on this planet. In addition to providing the foundation for higher learning, communication is also central to the functioning of political, economic, and social institutions. Thus, in the words of Theodore Gross (1978), Dean of Humanities at New York City College:

> Communication should be a course of study as important to a young person's education as sociology or political science or foreign languages and should be integrated into the liberal arts curriculum. One does not justify the study of literature, history, or philosophy in terms of careers; one should not defend [the study of] communication only on the grounds of popular appeal or the number of jobs available. One must understand its sociology and history and technology and art and literature because it is the subject of our time and of the future. (p. 39)

The second assumption is a belief that continuity of instruction in communication is crucial. The improvement of speaking and listening skills is a lifelong project that must start with the earliest years of life and not stop when basic speech and language skills are in place. Rather, our abilities must be continually modified through learning new vocabulary, developing distinctive patterns of speaking, and—most important—learning means by which talk can be used to achieve goals. As relationships with others come and go and our roles in society change, opportunities for learning and modifying communication strategies are presented. Thus, systematic instruction and supervised practice yield positive returns at any stage in an individual's communication development. For this reason, communication professionals seek to improve individuals' abilities for such communication functions as public speaking, handling informal conversations, interacting with individuals from other cultures, solving problems in groups, coping with an organization's power structure, and becoming more effective producers and consumers of artistic performances and the outpourings of the mass media.

The third assumption is a belief that the improvement of speaking and listening skills is both a concern of the total educational community and an area in which the communication discipline is uniquely qualified to make important contributions. We concur with Ernest Boyer, former President of the Carnegie Foundation for the Advancement of Teaching, when he argued that speaking and listening are so central to education that they deserve both specialized training and emphasis in all classrooms (Scully, 1981). Therefore, in addition to providing course work in communication,

communication professionals are also involved in training parents to enhance the communication development of their preschool children and providing teachers in all disciplines at all academic levels with strategies they can utilize to facilitate the development of communication competence for students in their classrooms. Whatever the level (preschool through graduate school) or content area (art, music, history, science, or math), communication professionals consider it their responsibility to help teachers maximize the communication activities and training of every student.

In addition, however, communication professionals are trained to tailor specialized course work in communication to the social and cognitive development of individual students. Communication professionals are trained not only to diagnose the nature of the communication difficulties, but—more important—to provide an approach to cope with them. Whereas all teachers can, for example, observe that a student's message appears disorganized or that a student is not involved in class discussion, communication professionals have been trained to discover whether this difficulty is caused by (a) a conscious and rational decision to reduce involvement in the situation, (b) fear or anxiety about participation, (c) a physical disability or other skill deficit, or (d) a faulty perception of the requirements of the situation. Then, depending on the cause of the difficulty, communication professionals can identify and implement an instructional approach that is appropriate for the situation (e.g., perhaps a motivational session if the source of the difficulty is conscious choice, systematic desensitization to reduce fear or anxiety, the use of speech models to cope with a skill deficit, or cognitive restructuring to remedy a faulty perception). In addition to helping individuals directly, communication professionals can help other teachers diagnose and solve communication problems. It is important to know, for example, that someone who suffers from shyness or anxiety is likely to be harmed, rather than helped, by being subjected to a regimen restricted solely to additional practice.

Basic communication competency training, as important as it is, is not the sole or even major emphasis of communication professionals. As a discipline concerned broadly with the study of the nature, processes, and effects of human symbolic interaction, the communication discipline is home to individuals who specialize in such diverse areas as the following:

- Code systems (e.g., studying the uses of verbal and nonverbal symbols and signs in human communication).
- Family communication (e.g., studying communication practices among members in a family unit).

- Health communication (e.g., studying doctor–patient and other communication in health care settings).

- Intercultural communication (e.g., studying communication among individuals of different cultural backgrounds).

- Instructional communication (e.g., studying communication in the classroom and other pedagogical contexts).

- Interpersonal communication (e.g., studying interaction occurring in person-to-person and small group situations).

- Mass communication (e.g., studying uses and effects of radio, television, and other communication technologies).

- Organizational communication (e.g., studying interrelated behaviors, technologies, and systems functioning in the workplace).

- Oral interpretation (e.g., studying literature through performance).

- Political communication (e.g., studying communication within local, state, and national political campaigns).

- Pragmatic communication (e.g., studying debate, argumentation, and public speaking as they influence or facilitate decision making).

- Public address (e.g., studying speakers and speeches, including the historical and social context of platforms, campaigns, and movements).

- Theater and drama (e.g., studying dramatic literature through performance).

- Rhetorical and communication theory (e.g., studying the principles that account for human communicative experiences and behavior).

- Speech and hearing science (e.g., studying the physiological and acoustical correlates of speech and hearing behavior).

PROFESSIONAL ASSOCIATIONS

Departments of communication do not operate in isolation. They are influenced both by factors within their local environment (e.g., the institution and the community) and by events at the state, regional, and national levels. With the switch from the perception of being a faculty member at a college to being a faculty member in a department at a college came the growth of professional associations. Faculty members with specific teaching and research interests wanted to meet with faculty members with similar interests. Professional associations followed, producing conventions (a way to meet other teachers/scholars) and publications (a way to learn what was being discovered).

The growth of oral communication in English departments meant an identifiable group of people with strong interests in nonliterature issues. This group of people, belonging to the National Council of Teachers of English (NCTE), felt a need for "autonomy in courses and department organization" (Rarig & Greaves, 1954, p. 501). The feeling that public speaking was different from oral English spawned the National Association of Academic Teachers of Public Speaking (now the National Communication Association; NCA) at the 1914 NCTE convention.

Two major directions defined the field over the next 75 years. One direction, following the origins of the NCA, involved splintering off and forming new associations. The American Theater Association and the American Speech-Hearing-Language Association represent this trend. These groups developed separate questions, publications, and departments. The second trend involved forming subgroups to reflect specific interests within the context of the NCA and the International Communication Association (ICA). Groups such as the American Forensic Association, the Commission on American Parliamentary Practice, the International Society for the History of Rhetoric, and the Religious Speech Communication Association, for example, hold their annual meetings at the same time and same place as the NCA.

The essence of professional associations springs from meetings (conventions, workshops, institutes) and publications (journals, books, monographs, teaching guides, and professional standards). Thus, professional associations create a network that links together people in departments in different parts of the world. Annual national (or state, regional, or international) conventions provide (a) programs for sharing current discoveries and beliefs; (b) meetings for understanding the decisions that the field must make; and (c) the opportunity for individual networking through social events, interviewing for jobs, school alumni gatherings, and so on. In additional to attending the annual meetings, the resources of these professional organizations (and through them those of departments of communication) can be accessed electronically. Both the NCA (http:// www.scassn.org/) and the ICA (http://www.io.com/~icahdq/ica/ica.html/), for example, maintain Web pages. The American Communication Association also has a Web page with important teaching and research resources (http://www.uark.edu/depts/comminfo/www/aca.html), as does the Communication Institute for Online Scholarship, located at Rensselaer Polytechnic Institute (http://www.ciosorg/).

CONCLUSION

As we have discovered, the field of communication is both broad and diverse—and professionals within it have many interests. The theme that ties this diversity of communication professionals together is a common interest in understanding communication as a practical art (Craig, 1989). In the remainder of this book, we explore the research, theory, and methods relevant to communication instruction that allow us to exploit our diversity for practical, pedagogical ends.

REFERENCES

Chaffee, S. H., & Rogers, E. M. (1997). *The beginnings of communication study in America: A personal memoir by Wilbur Schramm.* Thousand Oaks, CA: Sage.

Cohen, H. (1985). The development of research in speech communication: A historical perspective. In T. W. Benson (Ed.), *Speech communication in the 20th century* (pp. 282–298). Carbondale: Southern Illinois University Press.

Cohen, H. (1994). *The history of speech communication: The emergence of a discipline, 1914–1945.* Annandale, VA: Speech Communication Association.

Craig, R. T. (1989). Communication as a practical discipline. In B. Dervin, L. Grossberg, B. O'Keefe, & E. Wartella (Eds.), *Paradigm dialogues in communication. Vol. 1. Issues* (pp. 97–122). Beverly Hills, CA: Sage.

Delia, J. G. (1987). Communication research: A history. In C. R. Berger & S. H. Chaffee (Eds.), *Handbook of communication science* (pp. 20–98). Beverly Hills, CA: Sage.

Gray, G. W. (1949). Research in the history of speech education. *Quarterly Journal of Speech, 35,* 156–193.

Great need for public speaking department. (1912, June). *The University of Oklahoma Magazine,* pp. 17–18.

Gross, T. L. (1978, June–July). The organic teacher. *Change,* p. 39.

Haiman, F. (1951). *Group leadership and democratic action.* Boston: Houghton Mifflin.

Pearce, W. B. (1985). Scientific research methods in communication studies and their implications for theory and research. In T. W. Benson (Ed.), *Speech communication in the 20th century* (pp. 255–281). Carbondale: Southern Illinois University Press.

Potter, D. (1954). The literary society. In K. R. Wallace (Ed.), *History of speech education in America: Background studies* (pp. 238–258). New York: Appleton-Century-Crofts.

Rarig, F. M., & Greaves, H. S. (1954). National speech organizations and speech education. In K. R Wallace (Ed.), *History of speech education in America: Background studies* (pp. 490–517). New York. Appleton Century-Crofts.

Rogers, E. M. (1994). *A history of communication study. A biographical approach.* New York: The Free Press.

Scully, M. G. (1981, April 13). General education called a "disaster area" by Carnegie officials: Need for revival seen. *Chronicle for Higher Education,* p. 1.

Smith, D. K. (1954). Origin and development of departments of speech. In K. R. Wallace (Ed.), *A history of speech education in America: Background studies* (pp. 447–470). New York: Appleton-Century-Crofts.

Wiseman, G., & Barker, L. (1967). *Speech-interpersonal communication.* San Francisco: Chandler.

2

The Goals of Communication Education

Jo Sprague
San Jose State University

There is no need to ask whether a teacher has goals. If, as philosophers tell us, any complex human activity presupposes a telos, some direction or end toward which it strives, then certainly all teaching reflects an underlying purpose. All teachers have goals, but all are not equally aware of their goals or equally able to articulate them.

This chapter is based on the assumption that goal setting is an important prerequisite to every instructional decision that a teacher makes. Whenever you decide to use a certain text, make an assignment, or lecture on a topic, you are choosing these options over other alternatives. Choices imply criteria and criteria imply goals. If a decision is better, then it is better to some end. Despite the compelling logic of this view, teachers tend to rush through goal setting or to skip over this step altogether. New teachers are so worried about finding materials and planning activities they start off on their trip without knowing their destination. Experienced teachers rarely seem to find the time for contemplation and for rethinking their instructional goals. The three sections that follow survey some of the general goals of education, relate these to the unique goals of communication instruction, and then lead you through the steps to follow as you translate your general educational goals into specific objectives for a particular course.

GENERAL GOALS OF EDUCATION

Most college teachers approach the classroom without formal training in educational theory. They lack an introduction to the discussions about the end of education engaged in by philosophers over the ages. You will be richer for exploring the ideas of Plato, St. Thomas Aquinas, Rousseau, Locke, Hutchins, Dewey, and Whitehead. These great thinkers struggled with the same issues that you and I worry about as educators. At the very least, their writings will help you frame your questions. At best, they may even provide some answers. Extending the timeless themes of educational philosophy, each era generates its own lively debate about the purposes of education. The vocabulary changes, but the underlying issue is timeless: Why do we have formal institutions of higher education? Here are four of the most common answers to that question.

The Primary Goal of Higher Education
Is to Transmit Cultural Knowledge

This view presupposes that there are certain important ideas, great works of art and literature, and significant scientific discoveries that a liberally educated person should be familiar with. The purpose of this sort of education is not to create an elite class but simply to ensure entry into mainstream national culture. A person can be technically literate, knowing how to decode words or sentences, yet lack the broader cultural literacy to make sense of a newspaper article or follow the central conversations of cultural leaders (Hirsch, 1987). Beyond the individual benefits of liberal arts education lies a belief that our collective survival demands that the best ideas of the past be kept alive not in a few museums or libraries but in the consciousness of a large segment of society. Many social critics claim that young people lack an understanding of the wisdom and virtues embodied in the finest products of cultural traditions. In embracing change they may repeat mistakes of the past; in celebrating difference, they may lose sight of the shared values that bind a culture together; in opposing dogma and absolutes, they may embrace a form of relativism that is the moral equivalent of "anything goes."

The Primary Goal of Higher Education
Is to Develop Students' Intellectual Skills

The emphasis here is not so much on what students learn as on how they learn; that is, on the processes they perfect through their educational experiences. This approach is sometimes likened to treating the mind as a sort of intellectual muscle that needs to be strengthened and exercised. the most fundamental skills are those of basic literacy. Startling statistics about the inability of many college students to read, write, or compute led to the back-to-basics movement of the 1980s and the standards movement of the 1990s. Teachers of all disciplines are urged to incorporate skills training in reading, writing, speaking, and listening into their instruction. At a less remedial level, the intellectual skills approach centers on critical thinking skills. To survive in a changing world and to participate effectively in a democratic society, students must be prepared to critically analyze and evaluate ideas. The interest in lifelong learning has spawned new interest in the questions of learning how to learn. During their brief years in the formal educational system, students learn techniques of research, inquiry, and problem solving that they can apply to new topics throughout their lives.

The Primary Goal of Higher Education Is to Provide Students With Career Skills

The university can be seen as a provider of specific vocational credentials, a role that has traditionally been assigned to trade schools or to graduate and professional schools. Following the launching of Sputnik, the U.S. educational system was charged to produce more scientists. Universities have been expected to respond to cyclical demands since that time for teachers, computer engineers, business managers, or health care workers. From this perspective, the test of curriculum is its responsiveness to the needs of the workplace. It is a position that has few advocates among educational theorists, but the scarcity of philosophical support for the view of vocationalism as the primary purpose of higher education has not restricted its general popularity. If you ask students why they attend college or ask parents, alumni, and legislators why they fund higher education, the answer will very often have to do with careers.

The Primary Goal of Higher Education Is to Reshape the Values of Society

Not all educational theorists assume that the purpose of the schools is to socialize or enculturate students. If one sees society as flawed at best or evil and repressive at worst, then why should students learn to fit in? They should be taught instead to critique and transform the world. One ongoing strand of educational thought has recapitulated Aristotle's position that *theoria* or scientific knowledge only takes on meaningfulness through praxis or the application of ideas to the problem of living. In this view education finds its telos in the emancipation of the human spirit, an end that is ideally pursued through various techniques of dialectic, consciousness raising, and critical analysis. Dewey's classic works revealed the need to educate reform-minded citizens to keep democracy viable. A contemporary movement known as *critical pedagogy*, based on Freire's *Pedagogy of the Oppressed* (1972), exposes the many ways that traditional education reflects an ideology that preserves existing power relationships. These educators see schools as major vehicles to shape a more just society.

It is evident that these four positions of the goals of higher education are neither exhaustive nor mutually exclusive. Countless other goals have been posited—worthwhile ends, such as the development of character or preparation for citizenship—that cross the boundaries of the four goals discussed here. Most educators see value in several goals. They aim, for example, to provide career training within a liberal arts education or to help students to develop intellectual skills that may lead to a transformation of society. Because time and energy are finite, though, and because the underlying premises of some systems are contradictory, educators cannot stress all of these goals as primary. Having a clear sense of the relative priorities of your own goals for education is essential as you go about making daily decisions as an educator.

UNIQUE GOALS
FOR COMMUNICATION INSTRUCTION

Based on this review of the purposes of all higher education, we can now look at how our own field has approached the problem of determining the purpose of instruction. Identifying our goals is made especially challenging due to the nature of what we teach. Communication is not just another content area for students to master or even just another academic skill. Nor is ours a subject that is new to students. We must recognize that when we say we are going to teach people to communicate we are "teaching" them something they have been doing rather successfully for most of their lives. The ways that they presently communicate are closely tied to their individual attitudes, values, and self-concepts. It is both our strength and our weakness that we change not just what people know, or even what they can do, but who they are.

Setting goals for instruction in communication is further complicated by the fact that we are such a diverse and eclectic discipline. We draw on different intellectual heritages and resonate with the language of different academic orientations ranging from the social sciences to the humanities and arts to applied studies. Without a personal vision of the overarching purpose of our field, those who teach courses across different subareas will tend toward schizophrenia or rigid intellectual compartmentalization.

The Four Goals of Education Applied to Communication

All of the purposes discussed in the previous section justifying education in general have been advanced as reasons for studying communication in particular. Let us revisit these orientations noting how the rationale for each approach takes a form that is distinctive to our discipline.

The Primary Goal of Communication Education Is to Transmit Cultural Knowledge.   The study of communication is often defended in terms of its contribution to a liberal education. In its more modest form, this means keeping alive the great works about communication and the great examples of communication. A large part of the world's literary tradition is found in speeches, debates, and dialogues that are important both because of the timeless issues they address and because of their eloquence of expression.

A stronger statement of our field's role in the liberal arts positions communication as the central process by which a culture develops and survives. One version of the argument goes like this. To understand historical events like wars and revolutions one must grasp the ideas and values that drove people to action. Yet of all the ideas that are written in books and discussed among philosophers, only a few capture the popular imagination and actually change the world. The study of those ideas, how and why they had such impact, is the key to understanding human experience. Thus in a sense, the history of the world is actually the history of rhetoric.

Besides exposing our students to works of rhetorical significance, there is a body of cultural knowledge within our field. Without a grasp of certain terminology and basic content, students cannot proceed to advanced study of small group communication or media studies or intercultural communication. Socializing students to extant communication scholarship is a major goal for some educators.

The Primary Goal of Communication Education Is to Develop Students' Intellectual Skills.   The skills rationale for education takes a special form in our discipline. We go beyond defending the practical importance of speaking, listening, discussing, debating, and relating in our students' lives. We argue that the communication skills we teach are

essential to gaining other knowledge. Students must be able to analyze, organize, refute, and defend ideas if they are to become educated in any field of
study. Indeed, our recent scholarship has gone even further. We now understand that it is only through communication that knowledge is created. Ideas
come into being through social construction; there is no "truth" to be appre-
hended until that truth takes form in language and is processed interpersonally.

The intellectual skills approach to communication study seems to be enjoying renewed popularity. Surveys of the basic course continue to reveal
that many emphasize public speaking skills. The goal of teaching critical
thinking gained importance following World War II with the need for understanding techniques of propaganda analysis. This has taken on new importance as we recognize the tremendous power of the new information
technologies and the electronic media. The Speech Communication Association (1996) has endorsed a set of standards for K–12 students that place media literacy on the same level of importance as speaking and listening.
Traditional methods of dialectic, debate, and discussion long central to communication instruction have been supplemented by a more sophisticated understanding of the cognitive processes involved in critical thinking.

*The Primary Goal of Communication Education Is to Develop
Students' Career Skills.*   Speech and communication educators have
traditionally taken pride in the practical applications of our field of study.
The speech instruction in ancient Greece responded to a need for citizens to
defend themselves in court. Later rhetorical theories were directed to the
needs of statesmen or the clergy. Today we frequently tailor our instruction
to be of the most practical benefit to managers, engineers, attorneys, or
health care professionals. When we apply our theories to various
workplaces we are more likely to stay grounded in reality. Constantly adapting our content helps us remain flexible and avoid taking ourselves too seriously. The danger of this approach, of course, comes when it is seen as
anti-intellectual or as serving the interests of particular institutions outside
the academy. Also, students who are overly specialized in their preparation
may not be as well educated for a changing world as those who have learned
the more universal principles of communication.

*The Primary Goal of Communication Education Is to Reshape the
Values of Society.*   This approach also has a long heritage in our field.
Since Plato's attack on the sophists, scholars have pondered the relation

among rhetoric, truth, and justice. Those who challenge the position that communication can ever be value-free insist that students must be taught to examine the connection of language to social reality. Critical theorists have described language itself as a kind of sedimented ideology that must be critiqued. The study of communication, then, becomes a way to discover the oppressive relations in a culture and to give voice to those who have no power. From these perspectives, communication instruction may have as its goal the identification of sexism in language, the exposure of ideological assumptions in media, or the empowering of individuals to resist subtle intimidation in interpersonal encounters. Students learn to look beyond what is said. They ask also about what is not said and why. Who profits from keeping communication the way it is now? How could changing communication patterns change social reality? Organizational communication students do not just study how to please managers, but also how to be whistle-blowers or boat-rockers when it is ethically mandated. Students of intercultural communication learn not just how to get by when traveling to other countries, but discover the assumptions of their own culture that may hinder their ability to communicate respectfully with some people. Students do not just learn how to work in broadcast media or use the computer as a tool for their research, they examine how their lives are shaped by technology and media in ways they have little control over. Students of persuasion examine how the traditional notion of using argument to defeat an opponent might be supplemented by a feminist vision of invitational rhetoric (Foss & Griffin, 1995).

Tensions in Goal Setting

These four perspectives on the goals of communication instruction reflect the general philosophical orientations identified in the preceding section. When communication educators talk about goals, there are other related themes that emerge in the form of recurring intellectual tensions.

The Tension Between Theory and Skill.   This debate is also cast as a discussion of competence versus performance. In setting goals, teachers have to decide how much stress to place on knowing about communication and how much to place on being able to communicate effectively. The two are not the same. Some students will have a superb grasp of principles but not be able to apply them. Others seem to perform effectively with no idea of what they are doing or why it works. Based on the revered notion that there is nothing as practical as a good theory, some teachers decide that it is best to emphasize the universal principles that students can put to use throughout their lives. It can also be convincingly argued, though, that students need direct practical experiences more than they need abstract principles. The issue is made even more troublesome by the fact that being overly aware of how communication works can sometimes even hinder performance.

The Tension Between Process Goals and Product Goals.   In any instruction, we ask students to create certain products—speeches, papers, answers to test questions—and we hope that those products measure up to our standards. Yet, is our goal really for them to produce a beautiful outline, or rather to learn how to organize ideas? Products are easier to evaluate but processes are what students will reuse after the class is over. Think about the balance of product and process goals you set for your course. Too much emphasis on the former can trivialize instruction; too much emphasis on the latter can leave you with no sound basis for designing instruction or evaluation.

The Tension Between Content Goals and Presentation Goals. Whenever a course involves student presentations we must confront the problem of the relative importance of content or delivery. Deep in the genetic memory of every speech teacher is the sting of Plato's attack on the sophists. In our insistence that we are not engaged in "mere cookery," technique devoid of substance, we seem to need to dissociate ourselves completely from the elocutionists of the 19th century and the Dale Carnegies and Toastmasters of the 20th century. Those who favor a content orientation can justify the centrality of invention in the communication process. Many teachers have privately wondered if we even want to make articulate speakers out of students who have nothing of substance to say, no research to support it, and no sense of responsibility for its impact. Yet people still look to us for advice about delivery and style—advice we are qualified to give with results that can make their lives better.

The Tension Between Goals for Senders and Goals for Receivers of Communication.   Historically our pedagogical concern has been with developing competent speakers, debaters, leaders of discussions, and initiators of interpersonal contact. However, successful communication also requires good listeners, critics, followers, and respondents. People spend more time listening than speaking. Those who are skilled listeners are valued in business. They have successful interpersonal relationships and are discerning citizens. For instruction to most accurately reflect the way communication functions, what ratio of sending goals and receiving goals seems most appropriate?

This brief review of the unique goals of communication education was not designed to have you select any one of the four goals of instruction or to resolve any of the tensions. Throughout your career you will be attracted to these and other goals, frustrated by these and other tensions. More realistic than looking for final resolutions is a commitment to stay involved in the dialogue. You must be conscious of where you currently stand, or at least where you lean, as you begin the process of establishing goals and objectives for any class you will teach.

PREPARING OBJECTIVES FOR A COURSE

If I were to start jotting down at random my goals for a public speaking course I might come up with a list like the following. I want my students to:

- Be ethical in the use of evidence.
- Use Powerpoint to make effective visual aids.
- Know how to adapt an argument to an audience.
- Have good eye contact.
- Feel more confident about speaking.

It is evident that this list is far too random to be of much use in course planning. Some of these objectives are very important, whereas others are trivial. Some deal with what I want students to do, some with what I want them to know, and some with how I want them to feel. Clearly, translating general goals of instruction into specific course objectives demands some system for organizing and prioritizing outcomes. In the domains of learning and the taxonomies of skills we find the basis of such a system.

Classifying the Outcomes of Instruction

Educators usually divide the types of learning into three domains: cognitive, affective, and psychomotor. The cognitive domain concerns knowledge and the development of intellectual skills. The affective domain is made up of attitudes, interests, values, and feelings. The psychomotor domain deals with manipulative or motor-skill activities. Most academic disciplines at the college level emphasize the cognitive domain, and speech communication is no exception. However, instructional goals from the other two domains are evident throughout our curricula.

The psychomotor goals most often encountered have to do with the effective production of speech such as speaking audibly and distinctly and nonverbal skills such as maintaining eye contact and controlling physical movements and gestures. A few mechanical skills may be among minor course goals, such as operating video equipment.

The affective goals of communication instruction are more numerous and challenging. The reduction of communication apprehension is a nearly universal goal in courses requiring oral presentations, one that is usually operationalized by the student's own self-reported feeling of comfort or discomfort. Many classes in rhetoric, public address, oral interpretation, and media studies aim to increase students' appreciation of effective communication. Attempts to instill ethical values in speakers fall into the affective domain as do teachers' efforts to have their students be more rhetorically sensitive, to remain open minded in group discussions, and to respect the freedom of speech of others. (Notice that most of the affective objectives illustrated here are general and noncontroversial. We might consider them metagoals in that they are necessary to preserve dialogue and inquiry so that the study of communication itself can continue. Although professors will profess, they should not indoctrinate. Attempts to force students to accept the instructor's specific attitudes and values are particularly insidious when the goals are not explicitly stated to students, or worse yet, not even consciously acknowledged by the teacher.)

The third domain is best illustrated by introducing Bloom's (1956) taxonomy of educational objectives for the cognitive domain. It will be apparent that most of the instruction in our communication classes can be subsumed under the following categories.

- *Knowledge level.* Remembering, memorizing, recognizing. What terminology, facts, and basic information do you want students to be able to recall?
- *Comprehension level.* Translating, interpreting, extrapolating. What concepts and information should they be able to state in their own words or transform into different formats?
- *Application level.* Making use of previously learned information. What material do you expect students to transfer to new situations to solve new problems?
- *Analysis level.* Breaking an idea or concept down to reveal its component parts and identify its underlying structure. When should students be able

to get beneath the surface to find relations and connections and to make these explicit?

- *Synthesis level.* Arranging and combining elements in such a way as to create a unique product. What complex outcomes do you expect students to produce by putting ideas together in original patterns that clearly did not exist before?
- *Evaluation level.* Making quantitative and qualitative judgments about the value of ideas, objects, or conditions. In what areas do you expect students to establish criteria for appraisal and apply those standards to particular cases?

The usefulness of this taxonomy is in explicating the hierarchical nature of learning. We see the need to organize goals, instruction, and evaluation around intellectual processes rather than around global topics. Use of this taxonomy will help you to avoid three of the most common instructional errors: (a) teaching exclusively at lower levels of cognitive instruction, (b) teaching high-level skills without being sure students have mastered the prerequisite knowledge and skills at lower cognitive levels, and (c) centering instruction at one band of the hierarchy and then evaluating a different level.

Using Behavioral Objectives

Any discussion of educational goal setting must explore the controversy over the specificity of objectives. Though the task analysis models of planning originated earlier in this century, Mager's (1962) brief programmed text *Preparing Instructional Objectives* has most influenced our field. Mager made a case for specifying the goals of instruction as measurable outcomes observable in overt behaviors of learners. He attacked the fuzziness of most educational goals such as "the student will know how meanings are negotiated within speech communities" or "the student will appreciate the style of great orators." What exactly are the students doing when they are knowing? How are they behaving when they are appreciating? To increase the specificity of instructional objectives, Mager recommended that each objective meet these three criteria.

1. The objective must be stated in terms of the student's terminal behavior. Thus behavioral objectives should use concrete verbs. Words like *list*, *identify*, *name*, and *distinguish* replace words like *understand*, *grasp*, and *relate to*.
2. The objective must specify the conditions under which the behavior will be performed. The context in which acts are performed affects how they are

evaluated. Therefore teachers should clearly state which information, tools, equipment, or source material the student may and may not use in demonstrating terminal behavior (Kibler, Cegala, Barker, & Miles, 1974).

3. The objective must specify the criterion level to be attained in order to say that an objective has been achieved. This can take the form of stating a minimum number, a percentage or proportion, the tolerable departure from a fixed standard, or the distinguishing features of successful performance.

The following examples of behavioral objectives illustrate the presence of the three conditions. The behavioral outcome is enclosed in brackets, the conditions of performance are placed in parentheses, and the criterion level is in italics.

(Using the textbook and the supplemental readings listed in the bibliography,) [the student will prepare and present a 10- to 15-minute oral report on a small group communication variable approved in advance by the instructor.] *The report must receive instructor rating of 7 or higher on each of the five criteria—research, analysis, clarity, organization, and delivery—explained in more detail on the attached rating sheet.*

(Without the aid of notes) [the student will list, define, and provide original examples of] *at least five of the eight* [fallacies discussed in lecture.] *The names and definitions must correspond directly with those presented in class and the examples must be valid ones in the instructor's judgment.*

(Following a semester course in oral communication), *at least 80% of the students* [will report significant reductions of communication apprehension from that which they reported at the beginning of the course] *as measured by a drop of at least 5 points on the Personal Report of Communication Apprehension.*

The behavioral objectives movement gained popularity in the late 1960s and early 1970s and was widely advocated as an instructional practice in speech communication. Stating objectives in behavioral terms has distinct advantages. The process of articulating objectives precisely causes instructors to discipline their thinking, to separate the measurable from the unmeasurable, and to isolate the most important aspects of each course. The inclusion of criteria for evaluation makes it more likely that teachers will grade on what they have actually taught. Subjectivity is minimized. When students know exactly what is expected of them, they can put their efforts into achieving the objectives instead of trying to guess what the teacher really wants them to do. Clearly stated objectives help educators to communicate to each other exactly what each class covers so that overall curricular planning can be more coherent.

Not all educators were enthusiastic about the movement to specify all instructional objectives in behavioral terms. The evidence on the effectiveness of objectives was not conclusive. The lower level skills such as knowledge and comprehension lend themselves well to the formula for writing behavioral objectives. When higher level objectives dealing with synthesis or evaluation were written, subjectivity often slipped back into the phrasing with such criterion statements as "in the instructor's opinion." Humanist educators were sometimes uncomfortable with the mechanistic language and flowchart mentality of the behavioral approaches to goal setting. Critics challenged the behaviorist notion that if you cannot measure it, it does not exist. Claiming that often the most important outcomes of instruction are intangible, they cautioned that the preoccupation with terminal behaviors would lead to undue focus on communication products that could be standardized rather than on the processes that are unique to individuals and contexts. It might be asked, if we really want our students to be more alike at the end of a course, or if we hope that they will be more different from each other. The most serious fear was that the behavioral objectives movement might cause educators to set their sights too low. The sincere concern for specifying minimal standards of performance could gradually lead to settling for mere competence instead of hoping for excellence.

How to Write Goals for a Course

1. Begin by Considering the Educational Mission of the Institution and the Department.   You might look at this step as conducting an analysis of the organizational culture that will set the context for your instruction. How does the institution define itself? I have a colleague who sometimes teaches the same class at a community college, a large state university, and a small private church-related college. Even with the same text, the same assignments, and the same personal philosophy, his classes differ somewhat. The differences are not due just to demographics and academic skill levels at the three schools, but largely reflect the philosophy of each campus. Communication instruction is seen to fit into the overall education of students in varying ways.

Academic departments also have diverse missions and emphases. A communication department could have a liberal arts orientation or social science orientation. Programs may exist primarily to provide service courses for other disciplines, to equip students for certain careers, or to prepare majors for graduate school. Some departments have drafted mission statements that reflect a clear vision of what the faculty hopes to achieve. Not all departments have such a clear statement of philosophy, but usually there is a set of guiding assumptions that you can discover.

2. Become Familiar With Any Agreements That Guide the Course Content. Catalogue descriptions are frequently limited to 40 words and provide only the roughest guide of the parameters within which you will plan a course. Often departments have on file more elaborate statements of the minimal requirements for a class. If a course is a prerequisite for others, there are certain areas that must be covered. Service courses must meet the expectations of the client population. In multisection courses, textbooks and materials may be prescribed. Even within the constraints imposed by campus and department, you will still have many choices left to you as an instructor.

3. Establish Course Goals. Select a handful of important outcomes that you value deeply and really wish for your students. State these in terms of their ultimate usefulness. Is it really your goal for students to give an 8-minute persuasive speech using the motivated sequence, or is that a means to the end of being able to arrange persuasive arguments for maximum effectiveness? To keep yourself focused on the essential rather than the merely important, ask yourself questions like these: If the students only learn one thing this term what should it be? What do I hope they remember from this course 10 years from now?

4. Establish Intermediate Goals for Units of Instruction or Key Assignments. For each course goal determine what more specific goals will contribute to the achievement of those outcomes. When in doubt, select the ones that are prerequisite to other important goals, most generalizable to a variety of situations, and most realistic to accomplish in your course.

5. For Each Goal Write a Series of Behavioral Objectives. Follow the preceding guidelines and include the terminal behavior, the conditions of performance, and the criterion level. You will find that there are some objectives that cannot be measured. Obviously these cannot be given substantial weight in evaluation of students. However, do not be too quick to eliminate them from your course if they fall into either of the following categories. First, there may be some affective objectives related to intangible but important values or attitudes. You can keep these goals and try to attain them as long as they do not enter into evaluation. Second, there may be some activities that you are certain will be educational for your students to experience regardless of the outcome. These have been labeled exploratory objectives or experiential objectives. Goals of this sort can enter into evaluation in a minor way, such as giving pass–fail credit for participation in certain exercises or extra credit for selecting enrichment options.

6. Rewrite the Objectives Appropriately for the Various Audiences They Will Serve.   Behavioral objectives are technical tools stripped to minimalist language for analytic purposes. We must remember, though, that objectives serve an important communicative purpose and should be presented for top rhetorical impact. This resembles the task of turning a syllogism into an enthymeme. Only a certain class of academic administrator will respond favorably to the three-part objectives like those illustrated earlier. Students have been shown to respond more favorably to more personal and informal language (Civikly, 1976). Replace the harsh sounding "the student will" with "we will be studying ..." or "each of you will be asked to ..." Objectives written for student syllabi and assignment sheets might well include some clause of motivation as well, such as, "in order to help you critically evaluate the media ..." Objectives written to communicate with your colleagues should stress curricular links such as "in order to prepare students to conduct independent research in advanced courses...." For other teachers of the same class it is helpful to mention the conditions of learning so they can use some of your ideas if they choose. "By having each student bring to class an editorial in which he or she has identified the warrant, claim, and data of an argument ..."

This chapter has invited you to ask a series of important questions: Why should students pursue higher education? Why should they study communication? What should they accomplish in each course? How do you want your students to be different when your class is finished? Realize that these are questions that you will answer over and over throughout your teaching career. An educational philosophy is not static. Postman (1980), in *Teaching as a Conserving Activity*, suggested that schools should serve a thermostatic function, constantly changing and adapting to emphasize whatever society seems to be ignoring at a given time. Educational goals should reflect the needs of society, the nature of students, the content of our discipline, and your own values. Stay alert to all of these factors. As they change and re-configure, your educational goals will necessarily change, too. Enjoy the process of discovering and refining your goals; welcome the challenge of finding new ways to meet them.

REFERENCES

Bloom, B. (Ed.). (1956). *Taxonomy of educational objectives: The classification of educational goals. Handbook I: Cognitive domain.* New York: McKay.
Civikly, J. M. (1976). A case for humanizing behavioral objectives. *Communication Education, 25,* 231–236.
Foss, S. K., & Griffin, C. L. (1995). Beyond persuasion: A proposal for an invitational rhetoric. *Communication Monographs, 62,* 1–18.
Freire, P. (1972). *Pedagogy of the oppressed* (M. B. Ramos, Trans.). New York: Herder & Herder.
Hirsch, E. D., Jr. (1987). *Cultural literacy: What every American needs to know.* Boston: Houghton Mifflin.
Kibler, R. J., Cegala, D. J., Barker, L. L., & Miles, D. T. (1974). *Objectives for instruction and evaluation.* New York: Allyn & Bacon.
Mager, R. F. (1962). *Preparing instructional objectives.* Belmont, CA: Fearon.
Postman, N. (1980). *Teaching as a conserving activity.* New York: Delta.
Speech Communication Association. (1996). *Speaking, listening, and media literacy standards for K through 12 education.* Annandale, VA: Author.

3

An Ecological Perspective on College/University Teaching: The Teaching/ Learning Environment and Socialization

Ann Q. Staton
University of Washington

Higher education in the United States is under scrutiny for how it is preparing students for the complex demands of the 21st century. Ernest Boyer (1990), then President of the Carnegie Foundation for the Advancement of Teaching, noted that "the 1990s may well come to be remembered as the decade of the undergraduate in American higher education" (p. xi). Colleges and universities (whether liberal arts or research oriented) are reemphasizing undergraduate education and reaffirming their missions as institutions that exist to facilitate learning. Barr and Tagg (1995) argued that a paradigm shift is occurring in higher education with the focus shifting from providing instruction to producing learning. Regardless of the semantics of teaching versus learning, there are renewed efforts to "help realize our potential for a more informed, engaged, and self-reflective teaching and learning environment" (Ratcliff, & Associates, 1995, p. 39). Most new faculty are hired because of their expertise in a particular body of academic content, and

31

preparation for the college and university teaching role focuses largely on the subject matter to be taught. Although the environment is considered important in the teaching and learning enterprise, there is too often little or no attention given to it or to the ways in which instructors and students socialize into the environment and into their respective roles. This chapter deals with the teaching and learning environment and socialization.

In order to understand the teaching and learning environment, it is necessary to focus on several dimensions: (a) the classroom context, (b) the institutional context, and (c) the societal context. In addition to the immediate settings, it is essential to have "a sense of the larger context in which teaching and student learning take place" (Hutchings & Wert, 1996, p. ix). As these contexts and their relationships are examined, the interdependence of the academic goals with the environment becomes clear.

The purpose of this chapter is to examine the college and university environment for teaching and learning and the socialization processes of instructors and students that occur within it. The approach taken is ecological; that is, it is based on the relationship among individuals, their immediate settings, and "the larger contexts in which the settings are embedded" (Bronfenbrenner, 1979, p. 21). The chapter is grounded in four assumptions, set forth by Hamilton (1983).

1. Interactions between persons and their environment are important. Both the physical setting of classrooms and the social atmosphere are critical aspects that influence and are influenced by students and instructors.
2. Teaching and learning are continuously interactive processes, rather than causally related. In order to understand life in classrooms, it is important to take a wholistic view of interaction.
3. Person–environment interactions, typically examined within the immediate classroom and school environment, must also be viewed with respect to external forces, such as the family, community, and socioeconomic system. Classrooms are systems nested within larger institutional systems and even larger societal ones.
4. The attitudes and perceptions of the participants—instructors, students, administrators—provide essential data about classrooms and campuses. To gain a depth of understanding, it is necessary to have the perspectives of insiders about events and their meaning to them.

The first section of this chapter discusses the importance of classroom, institutional, and societal environments in understanding college and university teaching. The second section focuses on the socialization process by which instructors and students accomplish the transition into new classroom and campus environments.

ENVIRONMENTS FOR COLLEGE AND UNIVERSITY TEACHING AND LEARNING

The Classroom Context

The college or university classroom generally consists of a group of students and a single instructor, typically a professor or a graduate teaching assistant (GTA). These participants come together in a specific physical setting and interact for a particular duration of time, usually an academic term. The class meets at regular intervals each week for a specified length of time. As the instructor and students interact within the physical environment, a social atmosphere or climate emerges. Norms for appropriate verbal and nonverbal behavior develop, constituting a classroom culture.

Physical Setting. A number of different dimensions constitute the physical environment of the classroom (Cooper, 1995; Knapp & Hall, 1997; Weinstein, 1979). Included are such aspects as the size and configuration of the room, whether the chairs are fixed or movable, the seating arrangement, the level of attractiveness of the room, the location of the chalkboard, the availability of resource equipment (e.g., overhead projector, slide projector, video monitors), the duration of the class, the time of day the class meets, and the number of students enrolled. Each of these factors contributes to the overall environment.

Anyone who has ever sat in a college or university classroom knows that the size and shape of the room make a difference in the communication that occurs and often in the atmosphere that develops. Contrast, for example, a large lecture room with fixed chairs that seat 250 students with a moderate-sized classroom with movable desks that accommodate 35 students. In the large room, the instructor is at the center and must look up to tiers of students. The instructor typically uses a microphone to be heard by all and, unless blessed with extraordinary vision, is unlikely to be able to see clearly the faces of all students. The mode of instruction is almost dictated by the constraints and confines of the room. A highly interactive class session, with students doing most of the talking, is difficult to facilitate because the size of the room makes it impossible for all students to hear one another. Because the desks do not move, it is not easy for an instructor to assign the class to work in small groups. Thus, most instructors of large classes rely on the lecture method. In fact, the room itself is often referred to as a lecture hall (Evensky, 1996). In a moderate-sized classroom with considerably fewer students, an instructor has many more instructional options. The lecture format is possible, but so also are the small group format and the large group discussion.

Just as the size of the room constrains the type of instruction that occurs, the seating arrangement is also influential. A variety of research (Smith, 1979; Sommer, 1969; Totusek & Staton-Spicer, 1982; Woolfolk & Brooks, 1983) indicates that students seated in the first row across the front of the classroom and those seated in a vertical column down the center of the room are the ones most likely to participate. What is not clear is whether it is the seating arrangement that causes students to participate, or whether seating choice by students is a function of their personalities or desire to participate. Whatever the case, it has been demonstrated that teachers maintain eye contact most readily and most often with those students seated in what has come to be termed "the action zone." Similarly, in an alternative seating arrangement such as a circular one, there tends to be increased eye contact and interaction among the classroom participants.

Other important physical dimensions include temporal aspects—the time of day the class is taught and the duration of the session. Students (as well as instructors) know what it is like to attend a class at 8:00 a. m. when neither the body nor the mind is fully awake. Similarly, it is uncomfortable for many students to attend a class immediately after the lunch hour. They find themselves dozing even when genuinely interested in the class; and any instructor who has tried to teach to students who are nodding to sleep knows the difficulty of the task and how disconfirming it can be. It is also a challenge to maintain the attention and focus of students when the class meets for a long period of time. Many students and instructors prefer classes that meet for only 1 hour or even 50 minutes.

Finally, the general attractiveness of the classroom can influence the atmosphere and the interaction that occurs. In the classic study of Maslow and Mintz (1956), researchers found that students in a neutral or unattractive classroom had less energy and were less motivated to complete instructional tasks than were students placed in a room judged to be attractive. Similarly, Franzolino (1977) had college students engage in an instructional-type task in rooms designated as beautiful, average, and ugly. Individual and group scores on the task were higher for students in the beautiful and average rooms than for those in the ugly room. Thus, both of these studies lend support to the importance of the physical environment of the classroom.

Social Atmosphere. "The cultures of teaching are shaped by the contexts of teaching" (Feiman-Nemser & Floden, 1986, p. 515). Both instructors and students bring with them to the classroom certain expectations for the kind of speech that should and should not occur, for the kind of behavior that is and is not appropriate, for the roles that the instructor and students should and should not take, and for the nature of the social atmosphere that should and should not develop. Each person brings in values and assumptions about classroom norms, some that will usually be shared by class members but others that will likely conflict. Within the constraints of the physical setting previously discussed, patterns for communication will develop in the classroom. From the beginning of class, the instructor and students engage in a process of negotiation about classroom norms and patterns, including norms for interrupting, joking, noise level, terms of address, degree of familiarity, and amount and type of classroom interaction. Adaptation by the class members occurs in the process of achieving some degree of harmony. The communication norms and patterns that emerge constitute the social atmosphere and culture of the particular classroom (Condon, 1986). Bowers and Flinders (1990) considered "an understanding of the cultural and language processes that constitute the dynamic environment of the classroom" (p. 22) to be essential knowledge needed by teachers as they are called on continually to make professional judgments.

The Institutional Context

The institutional context refers to the particular type of institution or campus (including the physical facilities as well as structural properties) and the social atmosphere or culture.

Physical Setting. The physical environment of a college or university encompasses such dimensions as the location of the particular department on campus, whether needed resources are housed within the department or must be obtained from outside, the structural arrangement of space within the department, and the allocation of time.

If an academic department is housed in a building that is at the center of campus, for example, the likelihood is increased that students will stop in for unscheduled visits. If most resources for faculty and GTAs are located within the building (e.g., computer terminals, area library, media center), then there is little need for contact with others outside of the department. In these situations, instructors can become isolated from other units on campus.

The structural arrangement of space within the department also influences the interaction that occurs. The placement of faculty and GTA offices, for example, and their proximity to classrooms can have an effect on the frequency of student visits. If students have to check in with a secretary before seeing an instructor, they are less likely to drop in than if they have direct access to instructor offices. If the department has a student–faculty lounge or some other central gathering area, this will increase the interaction between faculty and students. This is in contrast to facilities that are segregated according to rank and serve to decrease interaction. Another spatial dimension has to do with a closed versus open door policy. Instructors who leave their office door open invite students to stop in, whereas it requires more assertiveness on the part of a student to knock on a door that is closed. The placement of a faculty desk is also a spatial factor that can affect interaction. Zweigenhaft (1976) found differences between faculty whose desks served as a barricade between themselves and students and those faculty who were "unbarricaded." Students perceived the "unbarricaded professors" as more willing to give individual attention and more encouraging of different viewpoints.

Finally, just as the temporal dimension is an important one in the classroom environment, it is also important in the institutional environment. The time allotted for office hours by faculty and GTAs is a major factor affecting communication. The sheer numbers of students with whom an instructor can interact, as well as the amount of time given to each one, are often dictated by the number of office hours each week. Instructors who announce to students that they can stop by only during office hours discourage spontaneous visits. This is in contrast to a policy of "come see me whenever I am in the office."

Social Atmosphere. As Geertz (1973) defined cultural patterns, they are "historically created systems of meaning in terms of which we give form, order, point, and direction to our lives" (p. 52). Increasingly, organizations have been viewed as having cultures. From the list of best-sellers (e.g., Deal & Kennedy, *Corporate Cultures*, 1982) to academic books and journals (e.g., Barley, 1983; Frost, Moore, Louis, Lundberg, & Martin, 1985), cultural perspectives of organizations are advocated.

Colleges and universities, as organizations, have their own cultures, or "shared assumptions, priorities, meanings, and values—with patterns of beliefs among people" (Frost et al., 1985, p. 17). A variety of dimensions contribute to the overall culture or social atmosphere: whether the school is primarily a teaching or a research institution, whether the school is public or private, religious or secular, the nature of the student population, whether the particular department is considered a humanities or a social science department, and the political clout of the department.

A school that defines itself as a major research institution sets forth priorities that differ from a college or university whose primary mission is the education of undergraduates. Such differences are likely to be manifested in the allocation of resources and in the reward structure for faculty, for example. Similarly, public and private (religious and secular) institutions differ in the values that are espoused and the atmosphere that permeates the campus. In many Protestant institutions, for example, Christian ideals are proclaimed in public discourse and are made the basis for many of the rules and codes of conduct for faculty and students. The student population generally varies in accord with the culture of the school, as well as serving to constitute the culture.

On a more microscopic organizational level, the department can also be considered as having a culture of its own. As Snow (1959) argued almost four decades ago, a sharp cultural distinction can be made between the humanities and the sciences. These divisions are more prevalent on some campuses than others and have different implications with respect to teaching and research activities as well as to the status, prestige, and influence of a department.

Regardless of the culture that typifies a particular college or university, the pervasive values and norms are critical aspects of the overall environment and, thus, are influential in the teaching and learning environment. Instructors need an understanding of the institutional culture and its social atmosphere as well as the physical context.

Societal Context

The societal context includes both the geographic location of the institution and the cultural values and norms.

Physical Setting. With the founding of Harvard College in 1636, higher education in the United States was launched. Although the curriculum was European in flavor, the setting was New England and the time was colonial (Boyer, 1987). These dimensions influenced the structure and character of the educational system. As the years progressed, American colleges and universities developed in concert with the changing times. Schools located in different regions of the country took on distinct characteristics of the locale. Traditionally, for example, people have spoken of Ivy League schools in the northeastern United States as centers of liberal, political thought, in contrast to more conservative institutions in the south.

Social Atmosphere. Because the values of society are reflected in its colleges and universities, American institutions of higher education are uniquely "American." Although distinctly "American" in their norms and values, this does not mean that there is cultural consistency across colleges and universities. Indeed, as Hirsch (1987) argued, "American national culture is neither coherent nor monolithic, and no convincing attempt fully to define its character has ever appeared" (p. 102). He went on to note that the "politics, customs, technologies, and legends that define and determine our current attitudes and actions and our institutions" are in a state of "constant change, growth, conflict" (p. 103).

Despite continual societal change, there are those who have characterized a culture in American higher education. Bloom (1987) wrote of the values of openness and relativism that permeate American education. Boyer (1987) identified two essential goals of American colleges that are consonant with the long-standing traditional values of individuality and community:

> The individual preferences of each student must be served. But beyond diversity, the college has an obligation to give students a sense of passage toward a more coherent view of knowledge and a more integrated life.... Just as we search culturally to maintain the necessary balance between private and public obligations, in education we seek the same end.... Through an effective college education, students should become personally empowered and also committed to the common good. (pp. 68–69)

More recently, Henry (1994) argued (and lamented) that it is egalitarianism, rather than excellence or elitism, that characterizes the American academy. Regardless of whether one agrees with a particular view of American culture, the colleges and universities in this country are undeniably "American."

SOCIALIZATION INTO COLLEGE AND UNIVERSITY ENVIRONMENTS

When students and instructors come together in new situations and in new environments, they both embark on a socialization experience. Socialization, a process by which "people selectively acquire the values and attitudes, the interests, skills and knowledge—in short the culture—current in groups to which they are, or seek to become a member" (Merton, Reader, & Kendall, 1957, p. 287), is an ongoing and recurrent phenomenon that people experience each time they contemplate and then actually encounter new situations. Berger and Luckmann (1966) referred to this repeated process as *secondary socialization*, a "process that inducts an already socialized individual into new sectors of the objective world of his society" (p. 130).

Types of Socialization

There are two types of secondary socialization: (a) occupational or role socialization, and (b) organizational or cultural socialization. Occupational or role socialization involves individuals learning necessary skills and knowledge to fulfill a particular role (Wanous, 1977). They begin to acquire attitudes and values that resemble those of others in the same role or occupation. Thus, a new college or university student must learn how to act, how to function as a student of higher education, and how being a college student differs from being a high school student. Similarly, a new instructor must learn what it means to be a teacher, must understand how being a teacher differs from being a student, and must take on the trappings of the new role.

In contrast, organizational or cultural socialization is "the process by which a person learns the values, norms and required behaviors which permit him to participate as a member of the organization" (Van Maanen, 1976, p. 67). The emphasis is not on the role, but on the particular organization or institution. A student who transfers from a large, public institution to a small, conservative, religious university will need to adapt to the differences in cultures and to understand that the same behaviors are probably not appropriate in the two contexts. Similarly, an instructor who takes a position at this small, private university must learn what it means to be a faculty member in the culture and must adapt to the different expectations that students, administrators, and the local community have for faculty.

Thus, a new GTA or instructor is undergoing an "ecological transition" that includes changes in role and context as a function of a person's development, maturation, and life cycle (Bronfenbrenner, 1977).

Phases of Socialization

There are three widely discussed phases of organizational socialization (Van Maanen, 1976) that are also applicable to occupational or role socialization. Anticipatory socialization refers to the choice phase or selection process during which an individual makes the decision to join a particular organization or begin a new profession. For students, this may involve a decision to go to college and become a student, followed by a second decision to attend a certain school. As these decisions are made, the student develops expectations about what it will be like to be a student as well as what it will be like to be a student at a specific university. For instructors, an initial decision is made to seek a career as an academic instructor, an institution for graduate education is selected, the appropriate graduate degree(s) is obtained, and a job search is undertaken.

A second phase is that of entry or encounter, during which the newcomer experiences the new situation—either the occupation or the institution—for the first time. A common experience during this entry phase is what is known as "reality shock" (Veenman, 1984). A student confronted with the first week of college classes and the enormous time demands and pressures may realize that the actual experience does not match at all the expectations. The same feeling is also frequently experienced by a new instructor facing job realities for the first time. Differences between the new environment and a previous one may be readily apparent.

The third phase of socialization is that of continuance or adaptation, during which the newcomer makes whatever changes are necessary in order to remain in the role and in the institution. For students, for example, this may involve an altered set of expectations for the time that will be spent studying as course work becomes increasingly difficult. An instructor who initially refused to give students access to her or his e-mail address may begin to use this communication medium after repeated pressure from students.

Dialectical Model of Socialization

Contrasting with a functionalist conception of socialization (Parsons, 1951) is a model of socialization as a dialectical process (Zeichner, 1980). Considered from an ecological perspective, this model is one that focuses on the interaction between people and the environments in which they interact. Unlike the functionalist view, in which the environment dominates the individual, who is merely a passive recipient, the individual in the dialectical model is an initiator who actively influences the environment. The focus is on "the constant interplay between individuals and the institutions into which they are socialized" (Zeichner, 1980, p. 2). The implication of this model for student and instructor socialization into the school environment is that the process is a dynamic one in which individuals must face the constraints of the environment but are not controlled by, and do not necessarily acquiesce to, the environmental demands.

Student Socialization

Research has begun to examine the process of student socialization into schools and campuses, with much of the research focusing on the perspectives of students. It is important for instructors to have an understanding of students' views as they make transitions into new environments.

Two recent studies investigated the socialization experiences of university freshmen. Jorgensen-Earp and Staton (1993) examined perceptions of what it means to be a new freshman by analyzing student-generated metaphors. Data were collected from students on two different campuses, a small private university and a large public university. Five themes emerged across both sets of students: feelings of newness, changes in status (high or low), a sense of control (overwhelmed or in charge), feelings related to engagement (disengaged or belonging), and degree of satisfaction (high or low). There were differences in perspectives only for the theme of status, with twice as many of the students at the small, private university indicating a sense of lowered status as did students at the large, public university. Although additional research is needed to discover reasons for these differences in status perceptions, it is reasonable to speculate that the environment of the private university is a factor.

In a second study, Johnson, Staton, and Jorgensen-Earp (1995) examined the role of communication in the socialization of new university freshmen living in different environments: in fraternity or sorority houses, in campus dormitories, and at home with their parents. Results indicated that the nature of communicative interactions was different for students across residences. Students in Greek houses, for example, "felt that they had a built-in forum for meeting new people, as did dormitory residents to a somewhat lesser extent. Commuting students expressed difficulty making friends because they did not have ready access to a peer group" (p. 348). Although this study did not test empirically the effects of residence on freshmen experience and outcomes, the descriptive accounts provided by students support the importance of communication and the ecological environment in making the transition to a university.

In addition to research on new freshmen, certain of the issues and themes from research on students at other levels may have relevance to higher education (Staton, 1993). In a case study of new kindergarteners, Staton (1990) discovered that part of learning to be a student involves making sense of a new environment that is laced with inconsistencies and contradictions. Similarly, a study (Staton, 1990) of a group of third graders who were new to their grade level and school, found that socialization includes several dimensions: academic, procedural, and social. Students have to adapt to increasingly difficult academic content, adjust to new procedures for classroom work, and learn about and enter into a more complex social environment. Another study (Staton, 1990) found that immigrant high school students socialized readily when their school program was a newcomer orientation center and their classmates were other immigrant students. When they transferred to regular public high schools, however, in environments less friendly to non-native speakers, the socialization experiences were overwhelming for students.

Thus, research has demonstrated that there are differences across campus and school environments and that students face various socialization challenges. Instructors need to be aware of ecological issues that relate to student needs and concerns that affect instruction.

Teacher Socialization

An array of research has examined teacher socialization from both functionalist and dialectical perspectives (Staton & Hunt, 1992; Staton-Spicer & Darling, 1987; Zeichner & Gore, 1990), with most of the studies conducted with preservice or inservice teachers at the K–12 grade levels. Functionalist studies have focused on identifying various outcomes of socialization (e.g., attitude changes and conformity) and agents of socialization (e.g., as cooperating teachers and university supervisors). Dialectical studies, in contrast, have focused more on the process of socialization (Staton-Spicer & Darling, 1986).

What emerges from this literature is the conclusion that neophyte teachers face an array of new situations, ranging from learning the teaching role to interacting with a new set of people to adapting in a new environment. Increasingly, teachers are viewed as active agents who interact with school environments in creative, assertive ways in order to achieve their goals. As is the case with student socialization, the ecology of schooling is an important dimension of teacher socialization.

Graduate Teaching Assistant Socialization

Because GTAs at some universities take responsibility for up to one half of all undergraduate instruction, they are clearly important to the college and university teaching environment (Darling & Dewey, 1990; Smock & Menges, 1985). Their socialization experiences are unique, in that often a GTA must socialize simultaneously to the instructor role and to the graduate student role (Darling & Staton, 1989; Staton & Darling, 1989). According to Darling (1988), most of the research on GTA socialization can be classified into two categories: the training and development of effective teachers and changes in the academic orientation of graduate students. Although informative, such research has not been particularly helpful in illuminating the process of GTA socialization.

In a study of the actual socialization experiences of three first-year GTAs in one department, however, Darling (1986) discovered the importance of the physical environment. In one department, faculty and GTA offices were physically separated, with faculty on the first floor near the mail room, main office, and classrooms, and GTAs on the fourth floor with immediate access only to one another. The physical location of the offices affected interaction and information-seeking behavior, with GTAs talking primarily among themselves and seeking assistance from faculty only rarely.

In a related study, Darling and Staton-Spicer (1986) examined the formal orientation program designed by an academic department to socialize new GTAs. Consistent with the ecological perspective of this chapter, their research was guided by a view of the department as a culture. Analysis of the discourse during the orientation week revealed a culturally meaningful description of teaching assistant, and the conclusion was drawn that "different themes and metaphors would emerge as a product of similar research in other departments/cultures" (p. 24).

Another study by Darling (1988) focused on the socialization of a group of five GTAs in three academic departments during their first term. Their experience was multifaceted, involving socialization into the role of graduate student, the role of teaching assistant, and the particular department at the specific institution. The interplay among the GTA's personal goals, the department's standards, and the role of the university as a research institution lends support to the importance of an ecological perspective.

College and University Faculty Socialization

In addition to studies of GTAs, researchers have also examined the socialization process of new faculty and discovered the impact of the environment on their early experiences. Menges and Brinko (1990) constructed a three-component model of faculty development and socialization: instructional, organizational, and personal. They described the organizational component as a structural one "that focuses on issues such as institutional climate and faculty as members of organizations" (p. 134). Faculty socialization along this dimension ranges "from the individual teacher or class or course through increasingly complex levels within the organization. This continuum extends beyond the institution into the civic community off campus and into groups that define the disciplinary and academic professions" (p. 135). This perspective is consistent with Bronfenbrenner's (1977) notion of the ecological environment as a nested system of structures, moving from the personal level to the larger cultural level.

Several researchers have focused on the importance of the department and institution as new faculty socialize. In an article advocating mentoring, Herr (1994) stated that such a program must be "reflective of the structure and culture of the unit and the institution" (p. 84). She warned that "if there is a clash between the impetus for a mentoring program and the structure and subculture of the institution, the mentoring program is less likely to be accepted and to succeed" (p. 84). In a report of interviews with 100 new faculty, Turner and Boice (1989) concluded that an essential aspect of socialization that can be facilitated by a mentoring program is that of successful entry to the particular environment: "In academe one often hears phrases such as 'the college community' which reflects [sic] the fact that each school is an organic unit with its own mission, character, mores, and expectations of its faculty. Yet traditionally little has been done to speed the successful entry of new faculty into these communities" (p. 71). More recently, in a study of the role of memorable messages in the socialization of new faculty, Dallimore (1997) reported that new assistant professors receive essential information from an array of sources, but that the department is the most valuable source. She concluded: "This finding is consistent with research which contends that individual academic disciplines are distinct and, therefore, will differ in consequential ways" (p. 18).

In addition to an emphasis on the department and the institution as important environmental aspects of socialization, there has been some initial study of the places in which information is exchanged. Dallimore (1997) found that memorable messages are most frequently received in informal settings (e.g., faculty offices; hallways; restrooms; or over lunch, coffee, or beer), in contrast to formal contexts such as orientation programs or faculty meetings. She found this to be the case for vital as well as trivial information: "[B]oth the more significant messages (e.g., like how one balances teaching, research, and service responsibilities in order to get tenure) and the seemingly inconsequential messages (like where to get a stapler or a cup of coffee) are likely to be relayed informally during conversation" (p. 20).

A final environmental dimension that has emerged as important in new faculty socialization is the element of time. In a study of concerns and needs of 66 new faculty at a large state university who kept daily records of their time utilization, new professors reported an average work week of more than 55 hours (Turner & Boice, 1987). Some 50% rated themselves as being "the busiest they had ever been in their lives" (p. 44) and attributed a number of job-related stresses to the time factor. In an expanded study of 100 new faculty, Turner and Boice (1989) found that 83% reported an unacceptable level of "busyness" and approximately one third of the sample indicated they were the busiest they had ever been in their lives. Sorcinelli (1992), drawing from a 5-year study of a cohort of new faculty as well as from research of others, concluded: "The predominant source of stress reported in nearly all studies of new faculty stems primarily from the press of finding enough time to get everything done" (p. 28). Thus, research has indicated that socialization experiences are distinct, even among departments at the same institution, and that where communication occurs (i.e., formal or informal settings) is an environmental dimension that needs to be considered. Finally, balancing time demands appropriately in the new faculty role at the particular institution is an important goal in the socialization of new faculty.

SUMMARY AND CONCLUSIONS

To be prepared for college and university teaching, it is not enough to be an expert in the academic content; one must also have an understanding of the environment for teaching and learning. Three contexts must be considered in order to make sense of the college and university teaching environment: the classroom context, the institutional context, and the societal context. This chapter has presented an ecological perspective in which the focus is on the interaction among people (students and instructors) and their environment (classroom, college or university, societal). A brief discussion has been provided of the physical aspects of each of the three environments, as well as the social atmosphere or culture of each.

In the second part of the chapter, the process of socialization into new school environments has been discussed. New faculty or GTAs are typically involved both in learning a new role and in learning to make sense of a new institution. To be an effective instructor requires more than knowledge of content; it demands successful socialization into the classroom, institution, and perhaps society as well.

Although this chapter has not drawn from research conducted specifically on faculty and GTAs in communication, the applications are relevant. Because the discipline of communication deals with a process-oriented subject matter (i.e., human communication), an understanding of an ecological approach to college and university teaching may be even more critical than for educators in other disciplines.

REFERENCES

Barley, S. R. (1983). Semiotics and the study of occupational and organizational cultures. *Administrative Science Quarterly, 28*, 393–413.

Barr, R. B., & Tagg, J. (1995). From teaching to learning—A new paradigm for undergraduate education. *Change, 27*, 13–25.

Berger, P. L., & Luckmann, T. (1966). *The social construction of reality.* New York: Doubleday.

Bloom, A. (1987). *The closing of the American mind*. New York: Simon & Schuster.

Bowers, C. A., & Flinders, D. J. (1990). *Responsive teaching: An ecological approach to classroom patterns of language, culture, and thought*. New York: Teachers College Press, Columbia University.

Boyer, E. L. (1987). *College: The undergraduate experience in America*. New York: Harper & Row.

Boyer, E. L. (1990). *Scholarship reconsidered: Priorities of the professoriate*. Princeton, NJ: The Carnegie Foundation for the Advancement of Teaching.

Bronfenbrenner, U. (1977). Toward an experimental ecology of human development. *American Psychologist, 32*, 513–531.

Bronfenbrenner, U. (1979). *The ecology of human development*. Cambridge, MA: Harvard University Press.

Condon, J. C. (1986). The ethnocentric classroom. In J. M. Civikly (Ed.), *Communicating in college classrooms* (pp. 11–20). San Francisco: Jossey-Bass.

Cooper, P. J. (1995). *Communication for the classroom teacher* (5th ed.). Scottsdale, AZ: Gorsuch Scarisbrick.

Dallimore, E. J. (1997, February). *The role of memorable messages in the socialization of new university faculty*. Paper presented at the annual meeting of the Western States Communication Association, Monterey, CA.

Darling, A. L. (1986, November). *On becoming a graduate student: An examination of communication in the socialization process*. Paper presented at the annual meeting of the Speech Communication Association, Chicago.

Darling, A. L. (1988, May). *Graduate student socialization: Categories of encounters*. Paper presented at the annual meeting of the International Communication Association, New Orleans, LA.

Darling, A. L., & Dewey, M. L. (1990). Teaching assistant socialization: Communication with peer leaders about teaching and learning. *Teaching and Teacher Education, 6*, 315–326.

Darling, A. L., & Staton, A. Q. (1989). Socialization of graduate teaching assistants: A case study in an American university. *Qualitative Studies in Education, 2*, 221–235.

Darling, A. L., & Staton-Spicer, A. Q. (1986, April). *Communication in the socialization of graduate T.A.'s: An ethnographic study*. Paper presented at the annual meeting of the American Educational Research Association, San Francisco.

Deal, T. E., & Kennedy, A. A. (1982). *Corporate cultures*. Reading, MA: Addison-Wesley.

Evensky, J. (1996). The lecture. In L. M. Lambert, S. L. Tice, & P. H. Featherstone (Eds.), *University teaching: A guide for graduate students* (pp. 9–28). Syracuse, NY: Syracuse University Press.

Feiman-Nemser, S., & Floden, R. E. (1986). The cultures of teaching. In M. C. Wittrock (Ed.), *Handbook of research on teaching* (3rd ed., pp. 505–526). New York: Macmillan.

Franzolino, P. L. (1977). *Effect of aesthetic environment on individual and group task performance*. Unpublished manuscript, Department of Speech Communication, University of Texas, Austin.

Frost, P. J., Moore, L. F., Louis, M. R., Lundberg, C. C., & Martin, J. (1985). *Organizational culture*. Beverly Hills, CA: Sage.

Geertz, C. (1973). *The interpretation of cultures*. New York: Basic Books.

Hamilton, S. F. (1983). The social side of schooling: Ecological studies of classrooms and schools. *The Elementary School Journal, 83*, 313–333.

Henry, W. A., III (1994). *In defense of elitism*. New York: Doubleday.

Herr, K. U. (1994). Mentoring faculty at the departmental level. In M. A. Wunsch (Ed.), *Mentoring revisited: Making an impact on individuals and institutions* (pp. 81–90). San Francisco: Jossey-Bass.

Hirsch, E. D., Jr. (1987). *Cultural literacy: What America needs to know*. Boston: Houghton Mifflin.

Hutchings, P., & Wert, E. (1996). Foreword. In L. M. Lambert, S. L. Tice, & P. H. Featherstone (Eds.), *University teaching: A guide for graduate students* (pp. ix–x). Syracuse, NY: Syracuse University Press.

Johnson, G. M., Staton, A. Q., & Jorgensen-Earp, C. R. (1995). An ecological perspective on the transition of new university freshmen. *Communication Education, 44*, 336–352.

Jorgensen-Earp, C. R., & Staton, A. Q. (1993). Student metaphors for the college freshman experience. *Communication Education, 42*, 123–141.

Knapp, M. L., & Hall, J. A. (1997). *Nonverbal communication in human interaction* (4th ed.). Fort Worth, TX: Harcourt Brace.

Maslow, A. H., & Mintz, N. L. (1956). Effects of esthetic surroundings: I. Initial effects of three esthetic conditions upon perceiving "energy" and "well being" in faces. *Journal of Psychology, 41*, 247–254.

Menges, R. J., & Brinko, K. T. (1990). A three-dimensional model for planning and assessing faculty development efforts. *The Journal of Staff, Programs, and Organization Development, 8*, 133–160.

Merton, R., Reader, G., & Kendall, P. (1957). *The student physician*. Cambridge, MA: Harvard University Press.

Parsons, T. (1951). *The social system*. London: Routledge & Kegan Paul.

Ratcliff, J. L., & Associates. (1995). *Realizing the potential: Improving postsecondary teaching, learning, and assessment*. University Park, PA: The National Center on Postsecondary Teaching, Learning, and Assessment.

Smith, H. A. (1979). Nonverbal communication in teaching. *Review of Educational Research, 49*, 631–672.

Smock, R., & Menges, R. (1985). Programs for TAs in the context of campus policies and priorities. In J. D. W. Andrews (Ed.), *Strengthening the teaching assistant faculty* (pp. 21–33). San Francisco: Jossey-Bass.

Snow, C. P. (1959). *The two cultures: And a second look—An expanded version of the two cultures and the scientific revolution*. Cambridge, UK: Cambridge University Press.

Sommer, R. (1969). *Personal space*. Englewood Cliffs, NJ: Prentice-Hall.

Sorcinelli, M. D. (1992). New and junior faculty stress: Research and responses. In M. D. Sorcinelli & A. A. Austin (Eds.), *Developing new and junior faculty* (pp. 27–37). San Francisco: Jossey-Bass.

Staton, A. Q. (1990). *Communication and student socialization*. Norwood, NJ: Ablex.

Staton, A. Q. (1993). Transitions through the student career. In N. Coupland & J. F. Nussbaum (Eds.), *Discourse and lifespan identity* (pp. 154–172). Newbury Park, CA: Sage.

Staton, A. Q., & Darling, A. L. (1989). Socialization of teaching assistants. In J. D. Nyquist, R. D. Abbott, & D. H. Wulff (Eds.), *Teaching assistant training in the 1990s* (pp. 15–22). San Francisco: Jossey-Bass.

Staton, A. Q., & Hunt, S. L. (1992). Teacher socialization: Review and conceptualization. *Communication Education, 41*, 109–137.

Staton-Spicer, A. Q., & Darling, A. L. (1986). Communication in the socialization of preservice teachers. *Communication Education, 35*, 215–230.

Staton-Spicer, A. Q., & Darling, A. L. (1987). A communication perspective on teacher socialization. *Journal of Thought, 22*, 12–19.

Totusek, P. J., & Staton-Spicer, A. Q. (1982). Classroom seating preference as a function of student personality. *Journal of Experimental Education, 50*, 159–163.

Turner, J. L., & Boice, R. (1987). Starting at the beginning: The concerns and needs of new faculty. *To Improve the Academy, 6*, 41–55.

Turner, J. L., & Boice, R. (1989). Experiences of new faculty. *The Journal of Staff, Program, and Organization Development, 7*, 51–72.

Van Maanen, J. (1976). Breaking in: Socialization to work. In R. Dubin (Ed.), *Handbook of work, organization, and society* (pp. 67–130). Chicago: Rand McNally.

Veenman, S. (1984). Perceived problems of beginning teachers. *Review of Educational Research, 54*, 143–178.

Wanous, J. P. (1977). Organizational entry: Newcomers moving from outside to inside. *Psychological Bulletin, 84*, 601–618.

Weinstein, C. S. (1979). The physical environment of the school: A review of the research. *Review of Educational Research, 49*, 577–610.

Woolfolk, A. E., & Brooks, D. M. (1983). Nonverbal communication in teaching. In E. W. Gordon (Ed.), *Review of research in education* (Vol. 10, pp. 103–150). Washington, DC: American Educational Research Association.

Zeichner, K. M. (1980, April). *Key processes in the socialization of student teachers: Limitations and consequences of over-socialized conceptions of teacher socialization*. Paper presented at the annual meeting of the American Educational Research Association, Boston.

Zeichner, K. M., & Gore, J. M. (1990). Teacher socialization. In W. R. Houston (Ed.), *Handbook of research on teacher education* (pp. 329–348). New York: Macmillan.

Zweigenhaft, R. (1976). Personal space in the faculty office: Desk placement and the student–faculty interaction. *Journal of Applied Psychology, 61*, 529–532.

4

Becoming a Professional

Ann L. Darling
University of Utah

Many of you received a phone call or a letter last spring or early summer and the text of that letter or phone call went something like the following: "Congratulations, you've been admitted to our graduate program AND we will support your graduate work with a teaching assistantship." Hopefully, your immediate reaction was "Yippee!" as well as the appropriate degrees of pride, resolve, and relief. After further thought, and maybe as you began packing and preparing, you may have had a second set of reactions that sounded like, "Oh, no, I don't know if I can do this. What was I thinking?" Both of these reactions are normal and you are encouraged to pay close attention to the first set of reactions, for there is a great deal of accomplishment recognized in the fact that you have been accepted to a graduate program and that you have been granted a teaching assistantship. However, you may have noticed that the second set of responses does not easily go away.

Questions about your ability to handle the new responsibilities and challenges will probably be present for you during much of your first year in the program. During the early days, weeks, and months of your new graduate program and your new teaching assignments, you might find yourself doubting that you will ever "become one of them," or that you will survive to find yourself accepting the title, professor. If it were possible to fast forward to the end of your first year or the beginning of your second year, we would expect to hear you talk about neither how remarkable it was that you were admitted to the program nor about your fears about completing the

49

program. Instead, we would expect you to think, talk, and even feel in ways that reflect your appropriate membership in this new culture, the new role, the new department, and the new university. A look further ahead in your educational experience, to maybe the last year, would probably reveal yet a different picture. At this point we would expect to hear you voice questions about getting a job, of course, but we would also expect to hear you talk about your work as a teacher and a scholar with a certain degree of clarity and confidence that will most likely not be present earlier in our "video-tape" of your life.

A process of socialization will have taken place and through this process you will have changed some of your skills, attitudes, values, and beliefs about teaching and conducting research in the discipline of communication. For many scholars, the graduate teaching assistantship is the best preparation for the future faculty role (e.g., Corcoran & Clark, 1984). In the role of graduate teaching assistant (GTA) and through a process of socialization you will learn many of the skills and acquire some of the dispositions necessary to move smoothly into an academic position. Data suggest that for graduate students in communication, some type of academic position is the most likely postgraduate employment you will experience (Applegate, Darling, Sprague, Nyquist, & Andersen, 1997). Some of you will not enter the academy, but it is very likely that you will teach in some capacity. Therefore, the process of learning to teach and conduct yourself in a scholarly manner is as important to your future after graduate school as is any of the content you will be exploring in your classes and research during graduate school.

Because this experience is so influential in later role performances, this chapter addresses specific dimensions of socialization and role development. Specifically, this chapter begins with a summary of research on the socialization process as it appears to occur for GTAs. A developmental framework describing the process of role development for GTAs is also discussed. Finally, the chapter closes with some ideas about the current context of professional communication scholars, the context in which you are becoming a professional.

SOCIALIZATION DURING GRADUATE SCHOOL

In chapter 3, Staton discussed the socialization process as it appears to occur for both students and teachers. She also described some of the research in the area of graduate student socialization. That research indicates that for all graduate students this process is highly communicative and involves a number of different agents and activities. This chapter provides specific information about some of the agents and activities that appear to play an important role during a GTA socialization process.

Agents of Socialization

Specific agents of socialization vary for each individual. During the GTA experience it is likely that other new and experienced GTAs as well as faculty and sometimes staff will be influential. These individuals will serve a variety of functions for the GTA. Some will provide information, others will offer social and emotional support, and still others will function in some regulatory fashion by displaying or enforcing the rules of the department or profession.

Self. A recent article by Staton and Hunt (1992) summarized a vast amount of research on teacher socialization in order to advance a general model of the teacher socialization process. One dimension of that model is the "self" or individual biography of those engaged in the socialization process. In short, the research summarized by Staton and Hunt demonstrates how an individual's personal biography or history acts as a constant interpretive lens through which the individual constructs an understanding of the new role expectations and the contexts for performing those expectations.

Staton and Hunt (1992) captured much of this research in the following statement: "Education students' prior experiences and beliefs serve as filters for processing program content and for understanding the context of the cooperating classroom"(p. 113). In the context of GTA socialization, we might expect to see a range of individual biographies. For example, an individual who comes from an academic family with a tradition of participating in academic rituals like graduation, convocation, and even a few basketball games brings to the graduate teaching assistantship a set of experiences and beliefs that will influence his or her socialization process. This individual will be likely to interpret the rituals and structure of the new role and department through the lens of his or her past experience. This person might be heard to compare and contrast how things are done "here" with how things were done "there." On the other hand, an individual who enters graduate school as a first-generation college graduate brings an entirely different set of personal experiences and beliefs that will influence the socialization process. This individual might use his or her experiences in the family and community to help understand the structure and expectations of the department. He or she might hold very concrete beliefs about the relation between the university and the community that supports that university.

Peers.   Other new GTAs and experienced GTAs play a significant role in the socialization process. If frequency of contact were a primary indicator of socialization outcome, then these two types of agents would be the most significant predictors of socialization. In a series of examinations (Bullis & Stout, 1996; Darling, 1987; Darling & Dewey, 1995; Darling & Staton-Spicer, 1989), the specific role of fellow graduate students has been explored and described.

Other new GTAs provide a relatively constant source of contact. Typically, new graduate students share offices, take similar classes, and often teach the same classes. Darling and Staton-Spicer (1989) used a qualitative case study approach and reported findings that new GTAs often used other newcomers and experienced GTAs as third-party sources of information. That is, when a supervising faculty member failed to provide promised or needed information, these new GTAs consulted other new and experienced GTAs rather than approach the faculty member. In a similar investigation, Darling (1987) found that new GTAs spoke most frequently with other new GTAs and experienced GTAs about topics related to themselves (their anxieties and frustrations), their jobs, the research they were reading about or beginning to conduct, and social issues or concerns. The functions of these conversations were most frequently reported to be integrative; they served to help the newcomer feel like a part of the culture of the academy and the department. More recently, Bullis and Stout (1996) used a feminist approach to the socialization experience of new GTAs and reported that most of the direct contact and immediate influence in the socialization process comes from other new and experienced GTAs.

Faculty.   Research suggests that faculty do not play a prominent role during the early phases of socialization (Bullis & Stout, 1996; Darling & Staton-Spicer, 1989). In fact, in two separate investigations, the absence of faculty influence during the early phase was distinctly noted (Darling, 1987; Darling & Staton-Spicer, 1989). In both investigations new GTAs held offices near faculty, had weekly meetings with faculty, and took classes from faculty. Still, faculty were not consulted on issues and concerns that were very salient and might have been easily addressed. In both studies new GTAs tended to use passive information-seeking strategies in order to ascertain what faculty might want and expect from them as students and as teachers.

That is, instead of asking faculty directly for information or support, they observed and listened to faculty engaged in other conversations.

During later phases of the socialization process, when attention is directed not at how to be a member in good standing in an individual department but on how to conduct oneself as a credible scholar in the discipline, faculty begin to play a more pronounced role. Studies have demonstrated that the guidance received from a faculty member during the examination and dissertation processes has long-term influence (Weiss, 1981). During the first years of an academic appointment, new faculty report the importance of their graduate advisor and other members of the committee in helping them to acquire the skills, attitudes, and values that guide them in their current positions.

Activities of Socialization

Socialization is a process that engages a number of different activities. Some activities, like a departmental orientation program, are events explicitly directed at socialization goals. Other activities, like informal conversations at the coffee pot, are not structured or planned but serve important socialization functions nonetheless. Models of graduate student socialization (e.g., Rosen & Bates, 1967) have indicated that a wide variety of activities comprise the process. Although not exhaustive, the following discussion includes some of the most prominent activities that characterize GTA socialization.

Orientation.   An orientation event is perhaps the single most powerful socialization event. It is a place where many, and sometimes all, of the members of the "culture" (i.e., the department) come together to display the norms, customs, and values that are held dear. Orientation programs take many different forms and can have a variety of stated goals. New GTAs, however, tend to understand that orientation is primarily a place where the culture of the department is on display and the members of that department begin to demonstrate appropriate role performance and expectations (Bullis & Stout, 1996; Darling & Staton-Spicer, 1989).

Encounters.   Although less clearly defined than the orientation program, qualitative studies of new GTA socialization have demonstrated that encounters (i.e., face-to-face interactions that participants described as notable events in the socialization experience) constitute an important socialization activity (Darling, 1987). As stated earlier, encounters with others about the department, university, and role are numerous and occur primarily with other GTAs. These encounters serve a variety of functions. Most serve to help the newcomer feel like she or he is becoming a member of the department; they serve integrative functions. Other encounters serve more regulative functions, helping the newcomer to be aware of the rules for performance in the department. For the five individuals in Darling's (1987) study, the second most frequently reported function of encounters was regulative. Interestingly, these regulative functions did not appear until after the fourth week of the quarter.

Turning Points.   Bullis and Bach (1989) used turning point analysis to discover and describe important socialization activities from the perspectives of those engaged in the process. Based on interviews with 28 new GTAs from three different communication departments, these authors posited 14 different turning points, plus one miscellaneous category, that appear to characterize the socialization experience for new GTAs. Of those 14, 8 were identified as most indicative of positive and rather immediate identification with the role and with the department: settling in, socializing, sense of community, gaining informal recognition, formal recognition, jumping informal hurdles, approaching formal hurdles, and representing the organization. The turning point gaining informal recognition was especially important in this study. It was characterized by positive comments from peers, but more importantly from faculty, and resulted in the single biggest positive change in identification.

The Later Phases of Socialization

Scholars who study socialization typically refer to it as a cyclical process. Referring again to Staton (chap. 3, this volume), she presented the three phases of teacher socialization most commonly discussed: entry, encounter, and adaptation. Socialization is cyclical and ongoing in that one is constantly moving in and out of environments at work and in the community and this constant movement suggests a never-ending process of socialization.

Schools in general, and graduate schools in particular, are by definition temporary contexts (it is recognized that some graduate students attempt to make this a permanent context, teasing deadlines throughout their graduate career). Furthermore, the purpose of graduate school is to prepare students for a context (i.e., a job) that might, perhaps, become more permanent. Therefore, during the final stages of graduate school an individual might be involved both in the later phase of socialization, adaptation, a phase characterized by comfort with the role and organization and high degrees of role identification, and the anticipatory phase of socialization, that phase associated with high degrees of uncertainty and information seeking.

Unfortunately, no research that examines this particular dimension of the GTA socialization experience has been reviewed. Anecdotal data suggest that the time after course work is complete and exams have been taken but before finishing the dissertation and taking a new job can be very alienating and isolating. At the same time, the energy of anticipatory socialization, getting acquainted with new employment opportunities and possible new colleagues, can be very distracting from the task of writing a dissertation. The literature on phases of relational development, discussing relational disengagement strategies in particular, might be useful in exploring what happens during this time that is critical and can be quite stressful.

ROLE DEVELOPMENT DURING GRADUATE SCHOOL

Sprague and Nyquist (1989) advanced a model of role development that describes changes in teaching assignments, supervision, and relationships with other GTAs specific to the GTA role. The premise of this framework is that through the course of one's graduate program, as both a teacher and a scholar, one evolves through three distinct roles, each containing characteristic performances and needs for support and supervision (Nyquist & Wulff, 1996; Sprague & Nyquist, 1991). A similar framework exploring the communication concerns of teachers has also been proposed (Staton-Spicer, 1983) and explored in the context of GTAs (Book & Eisenberg, 1979; Darling & Dewey, 1995). The Staton-Spicer (1983) framework describes three levels of concern about communicating and thus is proposed here as a framework that provides support for the ideas advanced in the Sprague and Nyquist model. Although empirical investigations of the Sprague and Nyquist model are pending, programmatic research using the communication concerns framework (i.e., the Staton-Spicer model) has been reported and can be used to provide some initial empirical support for the general structure of the Sprague and Nyquist model. Taken together, the two frameworks suggest a three-stage developmental process during which GTAs change in the concerns that they express about teaching, their ability to perform the role, and their need for supervision in the role.

Senior Learner

At the earliest moments of an individual's graduate career, she or he operates most successfully as a senior learner (Sprague & Nyquist, 1989). A new GTA is most familiar with and successful in the student role; success in that role has typically contributed to the decision to enter graduate school and so was part of an anticipatory socialization experience. A new GTA typically has vast experience with being a student but little if any experience with being a teacher. During this stage the new graduate student is likely to feel more confident in her or his performance in the classes she or he is taking than in those she or he is teaching.

As teachers, senior learners are most comfortable in assignments that allow them to operate more as colearners than as full-fledged teachers. Thus, tutoring assignments or responsibilities to provide administrative assistance in a large lecture course are tasks that would be well suited to the senior learner. Using the communication concerns framework, senior learners would be expected to express self level concerns; they would express concerns about their credibility in the classroom and ability to survive the stress of conducting a full hour of classroom instruction (Book & Eisenberg, 1979; Darling & Dewey, 1995). Ideal supervision for a senior learner would include many opportunities to ask questions about the instructional role and concrete guidance about role performance expectations. Sprague and Nyquist (1989) labeled this model of supervision that of "personnel manager" (p. 46).

Colleague in Training

This second phase focuses on the skills or tasks of teaching. The individual has acquired some of the basic perspectives of the teacher's role and can now think both as a student and as a teacher, although typically these remain separate categories for the GTA. During this phase, and perhaps because a certain degree of confidence has been gained, GTAs begin to make attempts to use the newly acquired scholarly language of the discipline in their teaching. Unfortunately, because the student role and the teacher role remain somewhat distinct, some of this linguistic transportation is rough and remains untranslated for the undergraduate students. Teaching assignments that would be most appropriate for the colleague in training include those that provide some freedom to conduct instruction with some support for that instruction. GTAs might be asked to give some lectures in a large lecture course, for example, or run a quiz section or even teach a section of a course that has been designed and is supervised by a faculty member.

According to Sprague and Nyquist (1989), "As TAs settle into the new role, they become more concerned about their lack of teaching skills" (p. 44). After resolving many of their basic concerns about survival, GTAs begin to develop task level concerns (Book & Eisenberg, 1979; Darling & Dewey, 1995). These are concerns expressed about the ability to manage the communicative tasks of teaching, such as running a discussion or preparing a lecture. Because at this stage GTAs appear ready to embrace ideas about teaching, the supervisory relationship described as appropriate for these colleagues in training is that of role model (Sprague & Nyquist, 1989). As role models, supervisors are encouraged to introduce a variety of models and techniques for instruction as well provide personal feedback about the use of those models and techniques.

Junior Colleague

At this final stage of development, the GTA has begun to identify her or his niche in teaching and in conducting research (Nyquist & Wulff, 1996). The individual has been able to integrate the vocabularies and challenges of both teaching and learning so that movement between the two roles is fluid. Furthermore, because the GTA has begun to identify with the role and with the department, she or he is likely to have developed a philosophy of instruction that is useful in guiding pedagogical decisions. Teaching assignments for GTAs at this stage should capitalize on the maturity of the junior colleague. These individuals would benefit from being allowed to design their own course or facilitate the instruction for new GTAs.

Junior colleagues begin to be interested in the outcomes of their instruction. They begin to express concerns at the impact level, indicating an interest in whether or not their students understand and gain from their instruction (Book & Eisenberg, 1979; Darling & Dewey, 1995). It would be tempting to believe that a junior colleague needed no supervision. This is not the case; instead a junior colleague would benefit greatly from a strong mentoring relationship with a faculty member.

THE NEW PROFESSIONAL IN COMMUNICATION

Thus far this chapter has presented information about how socialization and role development appear to occur for GTAs. For the most part the focus has been on the GTA experience itself. However, in a chapter entitled "Becoming a Professional," it is also useful to discuss the contexts that one might enter after graduate school. Many individuals who take a graduate degree in communication enter the academic workforce; they become teachers and professors at institutions of higher education. Others, in increasing numbers, enter the business arena, usually providing some sort of consultation, training, or personal coaching. It is important to note, then, that the context of higher education is changing dramatically and quickly (Andersen, 1997; Kennedy, 1995). The likelihood that the career path for someone currently in graduate school will look something like that of her or his mentor is decreasing.

As Andersen (1997) recently reported, political, economic, and sociological forces are driving the changes currently facing higher education. Today, more individuals are pursuing graduate degrees than ever before. At the same time, there is less political support for funding those degrees with federal or state tax dollars. Institutions of higher education are confronting accountability issues from new fronts and with new force (Kennedy, 1995).

Although each of these trends and all of these issues are relevant to those currently involved in graduate education, several specific trends stand out as especially relevant to an audience preparing to enter the new professional context.

Teaching in a Variety of Contexts

Despite bleak anecdotal data, hard data appear to indicate that people with advanced degrees in communication are being employed in the communication field (Andersen, 1997; Applegate et al., 1997). New PhDs are not, however, taking jobs at research universities in large numbers. Instead, a current hiring trend is that new PhDs and some MAs will take their first teaching position at a community college, a liberal arts university, or a comprehensive college. Furthermore, it appears likely that the new PhD will teach at more than one institution before settling down on a particular campus. Therefore, both graduate programs and students within those programs are advised to prepare for the multiple and different contexts in which one might be employed.

One current project addressing this specific trend is the "Preparing the Future Faculty" program. This program is funded by the Pew Charitable Trust Fund and involves a number of different campuses across the country (e.g., Arizona, Cincinnati, Howard, and Washington). The program seeks to establish training and support for graduate students at research institutions so that they might develop the expectations, skills, and dispositions more characteristic of the kinds of hiring institutions into which they might be placed (Applegate et al., 1997). All universities are being invited to develop similar programs on their campuses and current graduate students are encouraged to explore avenues for developing an understanding of and competence for teaching in a variety of contexts. Furthermore, opportunities to teach in the private sector, for business and industry, are also encouraged (Andersen, 1997). It is expected that the university as the sole provider for higher education will continue to diminish in the coming years.

Teaching With a Variety of Technologies

Although the computer has been around for decades, not until recently has the computer begun to play such a major role in the everyday matters of instruction. Today's teacher in higher education will be expected to be fluent in the use of Web pages and e-mail as well as CD-ROM and interactive networks. Technology will become increasingly taken for granted as an aspect of our instruction. More importantly, technology will continue to change almost as quickly as our ability to purchase and use it. These facts will contribute to a new demand for faculty development on all campuses. There will be an expectation and a need for faculty to continually learn and adapt to the new advances creating a new resource for faculty to build communities of learners among themselves. All campuses, and those currently enrolled in graduate programs, are encouraged to build into their training some expertise in the appropriate and efficient use of technology for educational purposes.

Distance education will also continue to play a large role in the nature and structure of higher education. Those entering the academic workforce may be expected to produce distance education programs. Regardless of whether or not one participates in the production and dissemination of education via distance channels, these programs will play an important role in the curriculum of almost every college and university.

Teaching in a Context of Accountability

Finally, the university is facing increasing demands for accountability and quality control (Kennedy, 1995). This trend is likely to continue as more and more legislatures begin to explore the nature of the faculty work load and the structure of tenure. Where once an individual could presume a certain degree of freedom in the classroom and autonomy in terms of work load, current trends indicate that these presumptions are no longer safe. Graduate programs and graduate students within those programs are therefore encouraged to address issues of accountability and quality management in higher education. Most new faculty members will need to be able to work within and make contributions to this conversation almost immediately. It would be most useful to be apprised of this conversation and have some tools available for immediate deployment.

CONCLUSIONS

Returning to the idea that we might capture the next few years of your life on videotape, this chapter has provided some highlights that we might expect to see on that tape. Given the processes of socialization and role development discussed in this chapter, we would expect to see and hear you move from a level of relative immaturity and dependence on the resources immediately around you to a level of more maturity and independence. Some of the people on that videotape will become your friends for life. Some of the experiences you will draw on well beyond your graduate education.

REFERENCES

Andersen, J. F. (1997). Graduate education trends: Implications for the communication discipline. *Communication Education*, 46, 121–127.

Applegate, J. L., Darling, A., Sprague, J., Nyquist, J., & Andersen, J. F. (1997). An agenda for graduate education in communication: A report from the SCA 1996 summer conference. *Communication Education, 46*, 115–120.

Book, C. L., & Eisenberg, E. M. (1979, November). *Communication concerns of graduate and undergraduate teaching assistants*. Paper presented at the annual meeting of the Speech Communication Association, San Antonio, TX.

Bullis, C., & Bach, B. W. (1989). Socialization turning points: An examination of change in organizational identification. *Western Journal of Speech Communication, 53*, 273–293.

Bullis, C., & Stout, K. (1996, November). *Organizational socialization: A feminist standpoint approach*. Paper presented at the annual meeting of the Speech Communication Association, San Diego, CA.

Corcoran, M., & Clark, S. M. (1984). Professional socialization and contemporary career attitudes of three faculty generations. *Research in Higher Education, 20*, 131–153.

Darling, A. L. (1987, November). *Communication in graduate teaching assistant socialization: Encounters and strategies*. Paper presented at the annual meeting of the Speech Communication Association, Boston.

Darling, A. L., & Dewey, M. L. (1995). Reflection in leadership: An examination of peer leader role development. In M. J. O'Hair & S. J. Odell (Eds.), *Educating teachers for leadership and change* (pp. 203–227). Thousand Oaks, CA: Corwin.

Darling, A. L., & Staton-Spicer, A. Q. (1989). Socialization of graduate teaching assistants: A case study in an American university. *International Journal of Qualitative Studies in Education, 2*, 221–235.

Kennedy, D. (1995, May–June). Another century's end, another revolution for higher education. *Change*, 8–15.

Nyquist, J. D., & Wulff, D. H. (1996). *Working effectively with graduate assistants*. Thousand Oaks, CA: Sage.

Rosen, B. C., & Bates, A. P. (1967). The structure of socialization in graduate school. *Sociological Inquiry, 37*, 4–12.

Sprague, J., & Nyquist, J. D. (1989). TA supervision. In J. D. Nyquist, R. D. Abbott, & D. H. Wulff (Eds.), *Teaching assistant training in the 1990s* (pp. 37–53). San Francisco: Jossey-Bass.

Sprague, J., & Nyquist, J. D. (1991). A developmental perspective on the TA role. In J. D. Nyquist, R. D. Abbott, D. H. Wulff, & J. Sprague (Eds.), *Preparing the professoriate of tomorrow to teach* (pp. 295–312). Dubuque, IA: Kendall/Hunt.

Staton, A. Q., & Hunt, S. L. (1992). Teacher socialization: Review and conceptualization. *Communication Education, 41*, 109–137.

Staton-Spicer, A. Q. (1983). The measurement and further conceptualization of teacher communication concern. *Human Communication Research, 9*, 158–168.

Weiss, C. S. (1981). The development of professional role commitment among graduate students. *Human Relations, 34*, 13–31.

5

Creating a New Course

Jean Civikly-Powell
University of New Mexico

Welcome to a conversation about creating a new course. This conversation, although admittedly singular, invites your engagement and participation through reading, reflecting, and experimenting with the ideas posed. Our conversation takes us to a variety of locations. We start with considering how courses might be "new," and the context and people for the course. We will wrestle with explaining our roles, strengths, and expectations as teachers; teacher and student goals for a course; researching course material; designing a course; and creating a course syllabus. Designing a new course might seem like an incredibly large task that is too often constrained by limited preparation time (Svinicki, 1990–1991). It is also a creative task! The ideas and examples offered in this conversation are designed to help make the development of a new course a manageable, energizing, and even enjoyable task.

THREE PRELIMINARY CONSIDERATIONS

I suggest that the end goal of our work at hand is the development of a new course that will be clearly communicated through a mechanism found in most classes, the course syllabus. Prior to formulating that syllabus, we have some work to do. Three preliminary questions guide us into this process. The first question is, "In what sense is this a new course?" Is it new material that has not been offered previously by a department and for which the department has no record of syllabi, assignments, or tests? It may seem curious to ask if the course is "new" to students, but in our field of communication, it is not uncommon for students to enroll in a class thinking, for example, that they already know pretty much all there is to know about interpersonal communication. How might such entry thinking affect their work in the course and challenge the teacher? A course may also be "new" in the sense that you are teaching the material for the first time. Even if course materials developed by other instructors are available, your approach and handling of the course will have your distinctive signature. What do you want that signature to say about you?

The second preliminary question to pose is, "What is the context for this course and who will likely enroll in the course?" Context can be construed in several ways. It helps to know, for example, how the course fits with other courses in the curriculum. Is the course part of a sequence, and if so, what do you know about the content of the courses that precede and follow this course and how does your course fit in that picture? Context might also conjure up thoughts of where the course will be held and the physical environment of the location (room location and configuration, number of students, seating arrangements, equipment opportunities). The projection about likely students to enroll in the course is also important in designing the course. Freshmen and sophomore level courses and courses for nonmajors often serve to introduce the content of the area of study, whereas upper level courses that are designed for communication majors are likely to be more exacting in theory and research applications. Certainly, if there are estimations of the class demographics (age range, gender/sexual orientation, ethnicities, and abilities), these will provide for a more complete audience analysis around which to design the course material, discussion topics, and assignments.

The third preliminary question is most intriguing: "What do I see as my role as teacher and my teaching goals?" Perhaps my answers to this question will assist you in this introspective exercise. I describe my teacher roles as behaviors. My role is to guide, to provoke thinking and discussion, to prod, to listen, to follow students' leads, to clarify confusions, to critique, to grade, to structure, to mediate, to respect, to challenge, to offer choices, and to assess what is working and not working in the classroom. You may have different ideas about your teaching role. My notion of teaching goals is oriented more toward students and my hope is that they will search out meaningfulness, learn from each other and me, question each other and me, talk about the class topics outside of class (with their friends, family, etc.), and gain confidence in themselves as it pertains to the particular course of study. Whatever your conception of your teaching role and goals, it will form the framework on which you build your course (see Brookfield, 1986, 1990; Grasha, 1996; Sprague, chap. 2, this volume).

COURSE DEVELOPMENT

Researching the Topics

News that you will be teaching a new course may elicit a feeling of exhilaration, a sense of challenge, and a touch of anxiety. In this early stage of planning, it will be helpful to brainstorm and list goals, objectives (Allen & Rueter, 1990), and resources for developing the course. Resources might include course materials previously developed, textbooks and instructor's manuals, journal articles, conference papers, media reports, campus and community experts, newspaper articles and editorials, political cartoons, comic strips, videotapes, excerpts from movies and television programs (news formats, talk shows, situation comedies, soap operas), courtroom proceedings, congressional hearings, literary passages and dialogues, song lyrics, advertisements, speech texts, quotations, and observations of selected interactions (e.g., labor negotiations, mediations, conversations, meetings, interviews). Many resources can be accessed on the Internet information system with the help of an assortment of search engines. Electronic mail and discussion groups are also excellent ways to seek information and ideas. Two examples of helpful listservs are the listserv hosted by the American Association for Higher Education (aahesgit.list.cren.net) and the Teaching Assistant Listserv (t-assist@listserv.arizona.edu). I participate in these discussions as well as more specialized online discussion groups in my areas of study for interpersonal communication and conflict resolution. A more traditional resource is the campus library, which may also offer instruction for online research to such databases as ComIndex (available to academic departments), EducIndex, PsycInfo, SocAbstracts, and ERIC. Other sources of information may be sitting on shelves in faculty offices or in a department library, so assistance for your needs literally may be at your fingertips.

When these resources have been collected and studied, the process begins for selecting and organizing what to use for the course. What information is more relevant and distinctive to the field of communication? Does the reading material match the level of the course and the students' reading and thinking abilities? Will the students be motivated to read the materials? Do you have too much or too little reading and viewing material for the course? Have you considered including optional or suggested materials in your course?

Developing the Course

When you have assembled the resources pertinent to your course, you can then begin to play with what concepts are most central to the course as well as how you see the organization of those concepts and the likely student assignments. Reflect on the concepts and create clusters of study that seem to follow each other. Some common progressions are (a) history, theory, research, applications, implications; (b) levels of communication: cultural, sociological, psychological; and (c) contexts of communication: intrapersonal, interpersonal, small group, mass communication.

Your topic groupings will form the basis for units of instruction in the course; that is, the clusters of topics, each of which is usually covered in 2 to 5 weeks, depending on the topic. Your creativity again is evident as you develop relations among the possible topics. The number of units for a course (usually between two and six) depends on such factors as number of weeks and class sessions, holidays, length of class sessions, coverage within each topic, and projected class activities (individual and group interactions, class reports, reviews for exams, exams, assignment descriptions, feedback about learner performance, course evaluations, guest speakers, films, etc.).

To determine the fit of your topics within the constraints of the course, design a worksheet that lists each class session, the topic for the class, readings to have ready, and any assignments due. Be prepared to rework this sheet several times, for it is likely that new ideas, rescheduling, and different arrangements may come to mind during this process. A sample worksheet is provided in Fig. 5.1 to help you get started.

After you complete your worksheet, see if you can explain the course to a colleague. It is helpful to audiotape these conversations, as it is likely that you will express certain assumptions you are making about the course that may need to be made more explicit in your printed information.

The Five Teaching Plans

At this point, you have now successfully tackled the preparation of the course content. However, effective instruction goes beyond content competence and must address issues of communication competence (Civikly, 1986). In other words, now that you know what you are going to teach, it is time to plan how you are going to teach. The five teaching plans (organization, motivation, interaction, props, and timing) are designed to help you manage and make sense of instructional development. In her application of these five class preparation plans, Richter (1990) envisioned the plans as a tree growing in an educational and world environment, with sun

DAILY CLASS SCHEDULE

Dates	Topic	When readings and assignments are due. Questions are collected at start of class on Thursday.		
		Canary & Cody	Ivy & Backlund	
Jan 16, 18	Course Orientation	pp. 1–17, 21–38	pp. 3–6	
	Definitions & Goals of Interp Comm			
Jan 23, 25	Presenting Self to Others	104–132, 351–353	14–30	Q
Jan 30, Feb 1	Explaining Self	137–165	67–100	W
Feb 6, 8	Disclosing Self	168–190, 365–369	103–139	W
Feb 13, 15	Exam I on Tuesday, Information on Relationship Analysis			Exam I
Feb 20, 22	Gender Conversation		147–175	Q
Feb 27, 29	Comm. as a Relationship Develops	196–219	179–209	Q
Mar 5, 7	Complying with Others	286–309		Q
Mar 19, 21	Responding to Conflicts	314–338		W
Mar 26, 28	Review and Exam (Exam on Thursday)			Exam II
Apr 2, 4	Comm. Challenges in Ongoing Rels.	224–244	213–239	Q
Apr 9, 11	Comm. to Repair/End a Relationship	248–280		Q
Apr 16, 18	Family and Marriage Relationships		303–327	
Apr 23, 25	Friendships and Romantic Relationships		245–271, 275–299 Paper due on 4/25	
Apr 30, May 2	Work and School Relationships		333–363, 367–369	
May 9	Exam III, Thursday, 10 am - noon, C&J 212			Exam III

FIG. 5.1. Class schedule worksheet.

and rain elements representing nurturing, caring, and such things as noise and distractions. The trunk of the tree is the course content with five major limbs as the five plans. The branches from each of the major limbs represent the strategies in that particular plan. For example, the timing plan's branches are labeled as pace, schedule, priorities, and transitions. The presentation plan's branches are labeled as discussion, group work, lecture, games, role play, exercises, demonstrations, reports, and audiovisual. In her graphic design, the roots of this tree of class preparation are teaching resources that include the textbooks, instructor's manuals, workbooks, previous class notes, other teachers, current events, and journal articles. I have a particular liking for the tree representation of the five plans because of the connections of learning to growth and because of the unpredictable nature of how that learning will display itself (often not in the clean simple-structured patterns anticipated by the teacher). A brief description of each plan and its uses for course development and class sessions follows.

The *organizational plan* builds directly on your knowledge of the course content. Common organizational structures are chronological, problem solution, cause–effect, topical, and advantages–disadvantages. At the macrolevel of organizing a course, practice explaining the organization of the units of your course. It is important also to plan and specify the number of sessions needed for introducing the course, covering each unit, and providing closure to the course. Introductions and closures for each unit should also be planned, along with transitions that indicate the connections between units.

At the microlevel of organizing a class session, introductions and conclusions are also part of the plan. Distinctions between covering the day's material and doing so with finesse and polish can be attributed in part to the attention given to three aspects of organization: planned introductions, clear transitions, and crisp conclusions. For each class session, offer an outline of the day's work so that students can see your plan and organization.

The *motivational plan* traditionally has been conceptualized as something teachers should do at the start of the course or the class session, and thereafter motivation becomes the learners' job to maintain. In his book *Enhancing Adult Motivation to Learn,* Wlodkowski (1986) discussed the need for motivational planning at three junctures of instruction: beginning, during, and ending. At each of these junctures, the motivational plan should emphasize different learner qualities. For example, Wlodkowski recommended addressing the learners' attitudes and needs at the beginning, their emotions and stimulation needs in the middle period of instruction, and their competence and reinforcement needs toward the end. For these three time frames, Wlodkowski identified 68 motivational strategies to achieve the specified purposes (e.g., "Provide learners with the opportunity to select topics, projects and assignments that appeal to their curiosity, sense of wonder and need to explore" [p. 256]). The implication of this motivational model is that teachers need to develop a motivational plan for the three junctures of the course and each class session.

The *communication or interaction plan* describes how the teacher anticipates interacting with the class members. How does the course provide for individual, dyadic, group, and presentational interactions? In what ways are learners given opportunities for viewing models of performance, for practice, feedback, group interaction, and class participation? The communication or interaction plan is likely to vary according to the objectives of different units of instruction and class sessions. Instructional strategies that can be used for your communication or interaction plan are extensive: group discussion, brainstorming, case studies for discussion and analysis, simulations, symposia, role playing, individual and group reports, problem-solving tasks, cooperative learning groups, experiments, problem-based learning, question generation by learners, journals, debates, dramatic performances, writing tasks and use of film, videotapes, television programs, print media, computers, and guest speakers. Many of these strategies were discussed by Janes and Hauer (1988), Lowman (1995), McKeachie (1986), Meyers and Jones (1993), Weimer (1990), and in chapters 22 to 30 of this volume.

My use of the term *props plan* is deliberate. The term refers to the assortment of materials, equipment, and arrangements for demonstrating and clarifying the concepts and objectives of instruction. Props include any print materials such as textbooks, readings on library reserve, course syllabi, newsprint pads, visuals, and class handouts (worksheets, inventories, outlines). The board is also a prop and, as such, it helps to plan if and how you will use the board. Props also refer to computers and other audiovisual equipment (videotapes, audiotapes, slides, photographs, films, opaque and overhead projectors). Finally, props include arrangements for visits to libraries, laboratories, museums, community organizations and businesses, and special events and exhibits. Props usually require advance preparation that involves selection, creation, and often some mechanical form of reproduction (photocopying, collating). Arrangement for delivery and operation of equipment also requires planning. Identifying and following your props plan can alleviate last-minute frustrations for both learners and teachers.

The final plan to include in your course and class development is the *timing plan*. At the macrolevel, this plan outlines the number of sessions for each unit of the course. When planning your course, calculate class sessions for course orientation, student presentations, reviews for exams, exams, and course conclusions. At the microlevel, this plan identifies how the time allotted for each class is utilized. The intent of the timing plan is not to strap a teacher to a stopwatch, but rather to provide guidelines on how the class plans can best be managed and covered.

PUTTING IT TOGETHER: THE COURSE SYLLABUS

Perhaps the single best vehicle for representing a course is the course syllabus. The syllabus serves three primary functions: to inform students of the scope of the work, to identify the sequence that the work will follow, and to describe the tasks by which success will be determined (Saunders, 1983). Syllabi also provide a format for communicating specific information about course readings, requirements, evaluation, course policies, and general teaching philosophy (Brinko, 1991; Davis, 1993; Schlesinger, 1987).

Syllabi for my own courses usually run 7 to 10 pages and are presented to the students as a course reference manual designed for use throughout the term. I have found the course syllabus to be extremely useful in helping to establish the tone of the class, share views about learning and teaching, and provide students with straightforward and explicit instructions for course readings, written assignments, and exams. The course syllabus enables students to determine on the first day of class the nature of the class, expectations for participation, written work (including due dates), class procedures and policies, and a sense of the person who is the teacher.

The first page of my syllabus commonly provides course details (title, number, my name and title, time and location of course, my office location and phone, e-mail address, office hours, and course prerequisites), the information on required texts and readings, and a discussion of my teaching style and expectations for the class. Some examples of how I phrase my comments about teaching style and expectations are:

> On a typical day in this class, you will be involved in a conversation with me and other class members about how we communicate in interpersonal relationships. This is not a lecture class. We are likely to spend some time during each class in small groups where your input is critical. We depend on you and look to you for ideas.

> I expect that you want to do well in this class. Here are three keys to doing well: (a) Keeping up with the readings for each week; (b) Participating in the class discussions and work of the day; and (c) Letting me know how you learn best and if you need some help with understanding concepts or assignments.

> My teaching style can be inferred from two of my favorite quotes: "So long as there's a bit of a laugh, things are all right. As soon as this infernal seriousness, like a greasy sea, heaves up, everything is lost." (D. H. Lawrence) and

"Tell me and I'll listen. Show me and I'll understand. Involve me and I'll learn."
(Lakota Indian saying).

I have adopted another variation of expectations for my own behavior
and for student behavior from the work of Arrien (1990). Her life principles, "the four-fold way," apply to many forms of human interaction and are
a good fit to my teaching style: (a) Showing up and choosing to be present,
(b) Paying attention to what has heart and meaning, (c) Telling the truth
without blame or judgment (say what you see), and (d) Being open to outcome, not attached to outcome.

The second page of my syllabus is devoted to evaluation of student work.
I begin with a general statement of the fractionated grading system (A+, A,
A-, etc.) followed by specific descriptions of each course requirement and
its percentage of the course grade. Examples of requirements for a class are:

20% Textbook and questions (paragraph description of weekly assignment to
write five original questions or "I wonder" statements about the readings)

15% Class involvement (paragraph description)

15% Relationship analysis paper (paragraph description)

15% Outside reading, class handout, and group discussion (paragraph description)

10% Test I (paragraph description provides format of tests, review sessions)

15% Test II

10% Test III

Of particular concern to many communication instructors is student participation. I reinforce this in my syllabus several times. The paragraph description for the 15% class involvement grade generally reads as follows:

I cannot stress how important it is to be in class each day. Please arrive on
time (I start and finish on time) and involve yourself in class discussions
and group tasks. Only you can contribute your ideas! Attendance is taken
every day. There are 30 class sessions, so you can calculate attendance by
the percentage of classes you attend (e.g., 27/30 = 90%; 20/30 = 66%). I
evaluate class involvement with the following question: If you were not in
the class, what would others in the class be missing?

The third page of my syllabus is the daily class schedule and it lists the
dates, topics, readings assigned, and assignments due. The topics heading
includes course content and such sessions as "course orientation" and "review and test II" (see Fig. 5.1.).

The fourth page of the syllabus can outline the course policies that you
maintain. I usually title this section "course courtesies and policies" to reinforce the ideas of student respect for each other. The items included in this

section are policies on late work, makeup work, late arrival to class, any extra credit opportunities, academic honesty, and statements of classroom courtesy (e.g., please allow whoever is speaking to complete his or her comments before offering your thoughts, ask for clarification of comments as needed, do not have side conversations when others in class "have the floor").

The remaining pages of the syllabus provide detailed information about the course assignments and several pages of test guidelines designed to help students read the texts and study for the tests. Another helpful feature in a syllabus is a worksheet form so that students can keep a record of their grades for the course along with instructions on how to calculate their course grade.

The course assignment information explains such things as how to prepare the weekly questions, writing a chapter summary, and preparing a research report. When deciding on types of assignments for the course, it would be helpful to review the research on student learning styles that recommends providing variety in the assignments (see Gorham, chap. 19, this volume; Kolb, 1976; Sims & Sims, 1995). By so doing, students with different learning styles can find outlets that reinforce their particular style and encourage exploration of other styles for learning.

The time it takes to develop a thorough syllabus has many payoffs. The most important payoff is the reduction of student uncertainty and anxiety about the course and expectations for successful performance. Another benefit is the all-in-one-place reference manual approach. The inclusion of details on dates, criteria for assignments, and topic suggestions also helps reduce the number of factual questions posed during class about upcoming assignments and allows for discussion of higher level issues pertinent to the objectives of each assignment. I have found that providing details on the syllabus and course manual gives students a full picture of the class and the work entailed, allows students who wish to prepare work early to do so, and conveys a clear sense of teacher organization and commitment to the course and students. As seen from the examples provided, a course syllabus can also combine formal course information with more personal information about your teaching style and goals. Finally, based on the course syllabus, it appears that students develop a positive view of the teacher's credibility and investment of time and energy in the course.

We have talked about many ways to prepare for a course and for class sessions. Another strategy that assists in course planning involves making notes after each class about the effectiveness of the class instruction. You can create a form that works for you. My form has headings such as course number, topic of today's class session, and points in class where students were: most responsive, least responsive, most clear, confused, needed more information, and so forth. When I finish the class session, I take 5 minutes to complete a form. At times, I think I will remember these details and do not need to write down my ideas, but experience tells me that I do not remember the specifics about each class session and what great ideas I had for the next time I taught the class. Now, I have a set of forms that guide me through each session to remind me of questions and activities that were particularly effective and ones that were flat. This process, a form of a teaching journal, has proved useful in keeping me current on my course revisions.

As we near the end of our discussion of creating a new course, please take some time to think about your teaching strengths and ways to maximize these in your teaching experiences. You may, for example, be very good at creating visuals or at telling stories to highlight a concept, or at analyzing interactions, or at describing the nonverbal contexts and dynamics of an interaction. You may excel in computer-generated graphic design and could use these skills to design a more creative course syllabus and class handouts. I have not yet encountered a class that does not appreciate visual enhancements of concepts. These may be in the form computer-generated graphic pic charts that illustrate how pieces of the pie are distributed (I use a pie graphic in my course syllabus to show how the course assignments make up the full course grade). Visuals may also be comic strips on communication styles, photographs, computer animations, or newspaper headlines. Using your imagination is one of the more fun parts of creating a new course.

DEPARTURES

Rather than conclusions, I prefer to think of departures as a fitting description for our conversation because it is a term with multiple meanings. *Departure* is defined as "an act of going away" and as "a starting out" and "a divergence." In your teaching experiences, you will likely have a number of opportunities to create and revise courses. In what ways will you leave the tried and true, start out on a new approach, and diverge from the standard predictable way of teaching that course? Your departures may allow you to see new ways of organizing material, stating objectives, creating teaching strategies, interacting with students, and evaluating student work. Enjoy the journey and enjoy your students and colleagues.

REFERENCES

Allen, R. R., & Rueter, R. (1990). *Teaching assistant strategies: An introduction to college teaching.* Dubuque, IA: Kendall/Hunt.
Arrien, A. (1990). *The four-fold way.* San Francisco: Harper.

Brinko, K. T. (1991). Visioning your course: Questions to ask as you design your course. *The Teaching Professor, 5*(2), 3–4.

Brookfield, S. (1986). *Understanding and facilitating adult learning.* San Francisco: Jossey-Bass.

Brookfield, S. (1990). *The skillful teacher: On technique, trust and responsiveness in the classroom.* San Francisco: Jossey-Bass.

Civikly, J. M. (Ed.). (1986). *Communicating in college classrooms.* San Francisco: Jossey-Bass.

Davis, B. G. (1993). *Tools for teaching.* San Francisco: Jossey-Bass.

Grasha, A. F. (1996). *Teaching with style.* Pittsburgh, PA: Alliance.

Janes, J., & Hauer, D. (1988). *Now what? Readings on surviving (and even enjoying) your first experience at college teaching.* Littleton, MA: Copley.

Kolb, D. (1976). *Learning styles inventory technical manual.* Boston: McBer.

Lowman, J. (1995). *Mastering the techniques of teaching* (2nd ed.). San Francisco: Jossey-Bass.

McKeachie, W. J. (1986). *Teaching tips: A guidebook for the beginning college teacher* (8th ed.). Lexington, MA: Heath.

Meyers, C., & Jones, T. B. (1993). *Promoting active learning: Strategies for the college classroom.* San Francisco: Jossey-Bass.

Richter, D. (1990). Class preparation tree illustration. In J. Civikly-Powell (Ed.), *Classroom teaching skills* (pp. 11–12). Albuquerque: University of New Mexico, Teaching Assistant Resource Center.

Saunders, P. (Ed.). (1983). *Resource manual for teacher training programs in economics.* New York: Joint Council on Economic Education.

Schlesinger, A. B. (1987). One syllabus that encourages thinking, not just learning. *The Teaching Professor, 1*(7), 5.

Sims, R. B., & Sims, S. J. (1995). *The importance of learning styles: Understanding the implications for learning, course design and education.* Westport, CT: Greenwood.

Svinicki, M. D. (1990–1991). So much content, so little time. *Teaching Excellence, 2*(8), 1.

Weimer, M. (1990). *Improving college teaching: Strategies for developing instructional effectiveness.* San Francisco: Jossey-Bass.

Wlodkowski, R. J. (1986). *Enhancing adult motivation to learn.* San Francisco: Jossey-Bass.

II

Preparing Specific Communication Courses

6

Teaching Public Speaking

Stephen E. Lucas
University of Wisconsin

Public speaking is the bedrock of the undergraduate curriculum in most departments of speech and communication. It occupies roughly the same place in relation to historical, critical, and theoretical inquiry in rhetoric and communication research as does written composition in relation to the study of literature in departments of English. It is also a subject of exceedingly rich lineage. Taught more or less continuously in Western civilization since the days of ancient Greece, it has engaged the energies of such thinkers as Aristotle, Plato, Isocrates, Cicero, Quintilian, Saint Augustine, Francis Bacon, Hugh Blair, Richard Whately, James Rush, and Edward Channing.

Although this is not the place to trace the development of rhetorical theory during the past 2,500 years, it is important to view public speaking within the context of its intellectual heritage. Once that is done, we can see that there is no single correct approach to teaching public speaking. Whether it be Plato and Aristotle versus the sophists, neoclassicists versus the disciples of Peter Ramus, or the psychological school of speech education versus proponents of elocution, the teaching of public speaking has long been marked by diverse perspectives, methods, and premises. Moreover, what works splendidly for one teacher or one group of students might fail miserably with another teacher or a different set of students. What follows, then, should be seen as one approach to a subject that has provoked debate among scholars and teachers for the past 25 centuries.

OBJECTIVES AND SIGNIFICANCE OF A COURSE
IN PUBLIC SPEAKING

The first step in teaching public speaking is to have a clear vision of what the course is designed to accomplish. At most schools, public speaking is regarded as a skills course. Its purpose is to teach students how to prepare and present effective public speeches. It also has a certain theoretical component. Most of the principles of effective speechmaking are based on broad theoretical insights derived from centuries of practical experience and confirmed by modern research. In this sense, the materials of a public speaking class are inescapably grounded in theory.

The course, however, is not preeminently concerned with theory. One of the most crucial requirements for teaching any subject effectively is to essentialize—to fasten sharply on what is vital to achieving a given set of educational objectives and to pare down all material that is extraneous to those objectives. Understanding Aristotle's concept of the enthymeme, exploring the dimensions of cognitive dissonance, knowing the major concepts of archetypal metaphor, making fine distinctions among attitudes, values, and beliefs—these are all important to communication study at some level, but they are seldom essential to the introductory course in public speaking. At best, that course can provide an exposure to the basic principles of speechmaking and some opportunity for students to begin to develop their own skills. It cannot turn college freshmen and sophomores into polished orators or sophisticated rhetorical critics any more than it can instill in them a detailed understanding of rhetorical theory or communication research.

This is not to demean the course or to say that it lacks intellectual content—quite the contrary. It is, rather, to recognize the complexity of public speaking and the wide range of cognitive abilities and practical skills involved in creating and presenting effective oral discourse. Think for a moment about what a public speaking class requires of students. It requires that they learn how to choose and narrow a topic; how to determine a central idea and main points; how to analyze and adapt to an audience; how to gather information by conducting library research and personal interviews; how to employ supporting materials soundly, clearly, and persuasively; how to organize ideas strategically for a specific audience and occasion; how to use language accurately, clearly, vividly, and appropriately; and how to control their voice and body so as to deliver a message fluently and convincingly. This is a lot to learn in one academic term without also trying to master a great deal of theory at the same time.

Moreover, with the exception of speech delivery, almost all of the skills taught in a typical public speaking class are integrally connected with critical thinking. The process of speech composition is not much different—and is certainly no less demanding—than that of composing a written essay. We need not apologize for the intellectual content of public speaking courses any more than teachers of English composition apologize for the intellectual content of their courses. Given the inextricable relationship between thought and language, between cognition and expression, there can be no gainsaying the intellectual substance of a well-taught course in public speaking. As we teach students how to choose and develop topics, how to organize their speeches, how to assess evidence and reasoning, and how to employ language clearly and concisely, we are, at the same time, dealing with the invention of discourse, the structure of thought, the validity of claims, and the meaning of ideas. In the process of instructing students how to construct speeches with accuracy, order, and rigor, we are also teaching them how to think with accuracy, order, and rigor.

In short, although introductory public speaking is properly a skills course, it should not be characterized as "just" a skills course. By helping students become capable, responsible speakers, it also helps them become capable, responsible thinkers. In this respect it remains today, as it has been through much of Western civilization, a vital part of humanistic education and democratic citizenship.

PEDAGOGICAL PRINCIPLES: AN INCREMENTAL, EXPERIENCE-BASED APPROACH

In addition to understanding the objectives and significance of a course in public speaking, teachers should have a clear sense of the pedagogical principles underlying a skills course. One of those principles is that people acquire skills incrementally. This is especially true when the subject is as complex and demanding as public speaking. Students have a great deal to learn in a public speaking class, and they cannot learn it all at once. Even if it were feasible to have students read the entire textbook or memorize all the basic principles of effective speechmaking before their first graded speech, it would not enhance their performance appreciably on that speech or accelerate the rate at which they progress on subsequent speeches.

A more fruitful approach is to break the course into several units, each of which takes students through a series of reading, homework, and speaking assignments that build systematically on one another so students can develop their skills cumulatively throughout the quarter or semester. If, for example, the first unit deals with informative speaking, it might concentrate on such matters as choosing a topic, framing a specific purpose and central idea, organizing and outlining the speech, creating introductions and conclusions, and working on basic delivery skills. These constitute the foundation of successful speechmaking at any level. Once they are in place, students are ready to move on to more complex matters such as determining the target audience, building credibility, handling emotional appeals, and using reasoning and evidence. These might be handled in a unit on persuasive speaking, which would follow the unit on informative speaking.

After dealing with speaking to inform and speaking to persuade, students have been exposed to a wide range of conceptual and practical materials. Building on these two units, a third unit might deal with something like commemorative speaking, after-dinner speaking, or speaking to entertain. Because these kinds of speaking depend so much on the resourceful use of language, this would be a good time to focus explicitly on style. Impromptu speaking is another possibility for this unit—or for a fourth unit—because it would allow students to deal with a new aspect of speech delivery while continuing to build on skills introduced earlier in the course.

By this point, students will have taken up all the major skills of speechmaking. A concluding unit, in which students prepare and present their final speech, gives them an opportunity to strengthen their command of those skills. Such a speech might be informative or persuasive, depending on the instructor's preference, or it might be a more specialized speech, such as a rhetorical criticism or a report on a famous speaker, both of which can work nicely as a capstone assignment. In any event, the final speech should require a fairly comprehensive application of the principles of speechmaking dealt with throughout the course.

There are, of course, other ways to structure a course in public speaking, and there are several alternatives to the speeches already discussed. Yet regardless of how the course is organized and what specific speeches are assigned, the principle of teaching skills in incremental units remains the soundest pedagogical approach, for it follows the natural process by which most people internalize knowledge and solidify skills.

It is also consistent with the tenet that learning skills is an experiential process that requires extensive practice and repetition. Although many speech teachers shy away from regular, graded, written homework assignments, such assignments are a valuable way for students to apply the principles discussed in the textbook. Rather than rehashing the reading in lecture, the teacher can use the homework assignment as the basis for class discussion. This has several advantages. The first is that students are more likely to learn the types of reasoning or the methods of organization by working with them rather than merely by reading about them or hearing the instructor talk about them. The second advantage is that students are more likely to complete the reading assignment if they have to turn in a written assignment based on it. The third advantage, which derives from the second, is that the quality of class discussion usually improves dramatically when students have prepared written work in advance. Rather than sitting on their hands with nothing to say about material they have not read carefully (if at all), they often get surprisingly involved in presenting and defending their answers to the homework assignment.

These written assignments can be based on chapter exercises in the textbook or on exercises devised by the instructor or course director. They need not be lengthy or onerous; nor need they require extensive evaluation. In most circumstances, a simple plus or minus, or a check mark for satisfactory completion, is all the grade they require. The purpose is not to make work for either the class or the instructor, but to enhance learning by requiring that students actively deal with the concepts, materials, and techniques of speechmaking on an everyday basis.

If this approach is to be successful, students must be given adequate time between speech assignments to learn the specific principles and skills that are appropriate to each unit of the course. Rather than rushing hastily over the textbook and trying to squeeze in six or seven graded speeches in a single quarter or semester, it often works better to schedule four major speeches and give students more time to prepare each. Not only does this produce better quality speeches, it also gives students greater opportunity to internalize the materials of the course. If students want more work on delivery, it can be provided by an impromptu speech assignment or by a brief one-point speech on a personal topic (my hometown, my most embarrassing moment, my biggest complaint, etc.) that can be prepared overnight without interfering with other work in the class.

Finally, the incremental approach to teaching public speaking requires that instructors have a clear sense of what they hope to accomplish with each daily assignment. Because one-third to one-half of the total class time over a full term is taken up with the presentation of speeches, teachers of public speaking have far fewer class sessions available for instruction than do teachers in most courses. As a result, they need to make sure every daily assignment is clearly formulated to achieve a precise purpose in relation to the overall objectives of the course.

Suppose, for example, that 1 day in the unit on informative speaking is devoted to analyzing sample speeches. The teacher should focus class discussion on those aspects of the speeches—formulating a specific purpose and central idea, developing introductions and conclusions, outlining the speech, and so forth—that are most central to the unit on informative speaking. This may require slighting other aspects—such as style or reasoning—but these can be taken up in later units of the course when students are better prepared to deal with them. Students cannot assimilate all the principles of public speaking simultaneously. In the long run they will learn more if each class session is strategically designed to deal sharply and systematically with particular increments of the public speaking process.

COMMUNICATION APPREHENSION, GRADES, AND OTHER PRACTICAL MATTERS

Questions of pedagogical philosophy and course structure aside, teachers of public speaking face a number of practical concerns such as dealing with communication apprehension, developing standards for grading, preparing speech critiques, encouraging attendance and participation, and maintaining a positive classroom atmosphere. Dealing productively with these matters will go a long way toward ensuring success as a teacher.

There are two types of communication apprehension. The first, and more serious, is known as trait apprehension. People who suffer from trait apprehension experience fear or anxiety in a wide range of communication transactions, from interpersonal exchanges to group discussions to public speeches. Students with high trait apprehension are so fearful about the prospect of speaking before a group that they cannot do so without severe emotional stress. Although as many as 20% of U. S. college students may experience high trait apprehension, most of those will do all they can to avoid taking a public speaking class. Even so, almost everyone who teaches public speaking will periodically confront students with severe trait apprehension.

Although some students are very open about their fear of speaking, others try to disguise it as long as possible—often by concocting a string of excuses for not completing speech assignments on time. Teachers who suspect that a student's poor work may be caused by trait apprehension should raise the issue with the student and, perhaps, may wish to administer one of the diagnostic tests that measure public speaking anxiety. Treatment, however, should not be approached casually. Some departments offer special classes for students who exhibit high trait apprehension, whereas other have individualized programs to help particular students. Because the most extreme cases can require the attention of a professional therapist, the best advice for beginning teachers is to consult the course supervisor or a more experienced instructor whenever they suspect that a student is experiencing severe trait apprehension.

The second type of communication apprehension is known as state apprehension. Corresponding to what is commonly called stage fright, it is the normal anxiety that people experience when called on to communicate orally in a specific setting in which they will be observed and evaluated by other people. Although even the most accomplished orators suffer from this variety of communication apprehension (indeed, many regard it as essential if they are to be properly "psyched up" before taking the floor), it can be devastating for novice speakers if it is not controlled. Fortunately, unlike trait apprehension, which is often aggravated by the required presentations of a public speaking course, state apprehension usually diminishes in severity as students acquire speaking experience. Its negative effects can also be curtailed by following such traditional bromides as being fully prepared for each speech, concentrating on communicating with the audience rather than thinking about being nervous, using a good introduction to build confidence for the rest of the speech, and recognizing that listeners seldom perceive how nervous a speaker really is.

Dealing sensitively and sympathetically with stage fright is especially crucial at the beginning of a public speaking course. Unless students have prior experience in speechmaking, they typically approach the course with a different set of attitudes than they would bring to, say, a course in history, engineering, or accounting. The teacher's task is to ease their initial anxiety by creating an environment in which they can begin to acquire speaking experience with a minimum of perceived risk. Most instructors accomplish this with a brief, nongraded speech assignment. Although there are many approaches to this assignment, one that works particularly well is a 2-minute speech introducing a classmate. In preparation, students should be paired off the first or second day of class so they can interview one another and compose speeches based on the interview. Not only does this speech avoid the awkwardness that affects many students in speeches of self-introduction, it also helps to create bonds among members of the class—especially among those who have interviewed one another—and to promote a healthy psychological climate for the graded speeches to follow.

No matter how healthy that climate may be at the time of the introductory speeches, however, there is no guarantee it will endure once the graded assignments begin. Students take their grades very seriously, and if they believe they are being evaluated unfairly or criticized too harshly, they can quickly develop a deeply negative perception of the teacher and of the course in general. Worse, their self-confidence can be seriously damaged if

the teacher is insensitive to their need for encouragement and positive reinforcement. Yet teachers also have an obligation to assess students objec-
tively on the quality of work they produce. They cannot give students
higher grades than they deserve just to maintain good feelings in the class.
Striking a balance between the psychological needs of the students and the
integrity of the grading system is one of the most difficult challenges facing
a teacher of public speaking.

This challenge can be particularly severe in the case of graduate students
who are teaching the course for the first time. Not only do they lack an established repertoire of instructional methods to guide them, but they often
have less initial credibility than older, more experienced teachers. As a result, students may be more inclined to question their expertise and to challenge their judgment on grades. New instructors should be aware that
everything they say and do in the classroom—their personal appearance,
their command of the material, their tone of voice, their reactions to questions, their handling of speech critiques, and so forth—will affect their
credibility and the respect they receive from students. The ideal, of course,
is to maintain an open, trusting classroom atmosphere in which students
provide psychological support for one another, feel free to take the risks
necessary to develop their speaking skills, and respect the teacher's evaluation with regard to grades.

Although there is no substitute for experience when it comes to grading
speeches, there are some steps you can take if you are a new instructor to enhance your evaluative skills. One, of course, is to talk about grading with an
experienced teacher who is willing to share his or her philosophy, methods,
and criteria. Another is to view a number of student speeches—either on
videotape or in other sections—and see how your assessments of them
stack up against those of veteran teachers. Yet another is to have a more sea-
soned instructor visit your class on a day when students are giving
speeches. By comparing the grades you assigned with those the other instructor would have assigned had it been his or her class, you can get a good
sense of whether you need to make adjustments in either your criteria or
your methods of evaluation.

No matter how grades are assigned, it is extremely important that students receive formal evaluations of their speeches. Because such evaluations are usually the major channel of feedback from the instructor about
the speeches, they need to be handled with great care. Evaluation forms
should indicate clearly the elements of the speech on which the student is
being assessed. They should also allow room for written comments. Such
comments should usually start with discussing positive features of the
speech—even if that means praising something as basic as the choice of

topic (no matter how badly it may have been developed) or the fact that the student has a pleasant speaking voice (regardless of how well the student used her or his voice). It is not necessary, when discussing weaknesses of the speech, to compose a high-powered rhetorical analysis. A better approach is to point out three or four specific items that the student needs to work on in the next speech. Above all, it is crucial that teachers avoid the temptation to come down too hard on students. Evaluations should be realistic in appraising the speech, but they should be written in a kind, optimistic tone that provides hope and encouragement for future speeches.

Another useful practice is to have students prepare evaluations of their peers' speeches. This can be done by assigning particular students as critics for each day's speeches. These students should fill out an evaluation form for every speech delivered that day. By the end of the unit, each student in the class should have served as a critic for 1 day. This can be arranged by assigning students to critique speeches in the class session after they have delivered their own speeches, except, of course, for the last group of speakers, who should be assigned to critique the first group of speeches. Thus if a class contains four speaking groups—Groups A, B, C, and D—Group D will critique the speeches of Group A, Group A will critique Group B, Group B will critique Group C, and Group C will critique Group D. Not only does this arrangement encourage the development of listening skills, it also helps curb the perennial tendency of students to skip class the day after delivering their speeches.

It is particularly important that students attend class on days when they are assigned to speak. Public speaking classes typically run on an extremely tight schedule. If students habitually skip class when they are supposed to speak, the syllabus for the entire course will be quickly thrown off. Perhaps the best way around this is to allow students to choose their own speaking dates. Even that, however, may not solve the problem entirely. Many instructors, therefore, assign an automatic grade penalty to any student who fails to deliver a speech on the specified day because of an unexcused absence. Many also limit students to a maximum of two or three absences for the entire course, with excessive absences resulting in a reduction of the student's final grade. Whatever a teacher's attendance policy, it should be stated clearly on the syllabus so students will be aware of it from the start of the course.

One of the best ways to encourage strong voluntary attendance on a regular basis is to arrange the syllabus so students are required to turn in work, or to complete work in class, on most days. If a homework exercise is due, an advance speech outline is to be handed in, or a chapter quiz is being given, students are more likely to get in the habit of attending class—partly because a portion of their grade is at stake, but also, as we have seen, because class time is usually spent more profitably when students have completed some kind of written work beforehand. Incorrigible as some students may be, most are inclined to attend regularly when they find the class sessions interesting and productive.

In addition to everything we have discussed, there are several basic guidelines for teachers of public speaking to keep in mind:

1. Be thoroughly prepared for every class session.
2. Maintain a professional demeanor at all times in the classroom.
3. Return student work—speech outlines, critiques, written assignments, exams—as quickly as possible, preferably at the next class session.
4. Explain speech assignments clearly and notify students of their speaking dates well in advance.
5. Avoid anything that might be interpreted as favoritism toward individual students or groups of students.
6. Treat students' ideas with respect—no matter how ludicrous they may seem—and do not ridicule or put down a student in class.
7. No matter what your private feelings, do not make negative comments to students about the course, the textbook, the assignments, or other instructors. Such comments undermine your own position, as well as the credibility of the course in general.
8. Seek consistently to accentuate the positive. Remember, much of public speaking is a matter of self-confidence. Do all you can to get your students to believe in themselves.

Finally, it is essential to believe in yourself. Be sure of what you know, but never be afraid to admit that you do not know something. There is no quick and easy formula for being a good teacher any more than there is a surefire set of rules for being an effective public speaker. Both require creativity, commitment, enthusiasm, and lots of hard work. If you bring those qualities to your teaching, you stand a much better chance of instilling the same qualities in your students.

7

Teaching Interpersonal Communication

John Nicholson
Steve Duck
University of Iowa

BECOMING ACQUAINTED WITH THE TASK

Teaching interpersonal communication is somewhat like a romantic rela
tionship on a slow boat to China: The teacher has some hopes about an arrangement that might be pleasant, has some preconceived notions about
the topics and people, meets and gets acquainted with the class (romantic
partner), has a meaning system and ways of thinking about the topic (or
about life) that are quite well developed but not immediately obvious,
tries to make her or his own meaning system relate to the meaning systems
of the students (partner), and progressively reveals deeper and deeper layers of the topic (self) to the students in ways that are related to previously
revealed information (Duck, 1994)—but you cannot easily get off the
boat. Like two strangers becoming acquainted, the class and teacher may
approach each other with some prejudices, may get to know things they
do not like, may form a close bond that lasts beyond the initial task, may
fail to understand one another, can get a lot of personal pleasure out of the
meeting of minds that is represented by the teaching and learning experience, and can experience the teacher–pupil relationship as a bond or a
bind (Wiseman, 1986).

Also like a relationship, specific interactions (classes) can occur within a wider framework of a broader overarching system (the relationship, the course) and are embedded within sets of other structures (the culture as a whole, the teaching culture of the institution, the objectives of the participants in exploration of a romantic relationship or interpersonal communication, or the objectives of the classroom, related as they may be to other courses taught in the department). Just as a personal relationship cannot be entirely eccentric regardless of the cultural context in which it takes place, so, too, a teacher of interpersonal communication must place the subject matter within the experience of the pupils, within the mission of the department, and within the expected norms of pedagogy. The teacher must also confront—and perhaps meet—the expectations held not only by the students, but also by colleagues in the department as a whole.

The teaching of interpersonal communication can be construed as the teaching of the one class on interpersonal communication that the students will ever get—an exclusive relational model—or it can be seen as one of a set of other relevant experiences and information that the student may try out with this new-found teaching partner (interpersonal communication), and that must be compared to other partners (say, a course in nonverbal communication, group communication, gender roles, or relational communication) with which the student is going to become more familiar. Moreover a teacher is faced with planning the whole course on the topic and so may have some view of the development of the teaching to greater depths and levels of challenge, just as relational partners may have notions of expanding and deepening their intimacy or self-disclosure or knowledge of each other. The preparation of a course in interpersonal communication is not, therefore, simply a preparation of the teaching done in front of the class. It is also the development of a relationship over an extended period of time in the context of other materials and experiences to which the students are exposed, and the placing of the whole in the broader life knowledge that the students bring to the class.

There are stages of relationships with subject matter just as there are stages of relationships with partners. Some relational partners come to a new date as experienced seniors in the relational world, others are mere freshmen looking at relationships with new eyes and without the scars of previous encounters with similar romances with the discipline. Depending on the nature of the experience expected by the students, an instructor's early decision making about the class can be guided by the likely depth at which the students can approach the topic. Of course, all students have been previously involved in interpersonal communication just as all would-be romantic relaters have probably been in other relationships at some point.

The challenge that is specific to interpersonal communication is that most people are so familiar with its topics that they do no appreciate either the need to understand, or the difficulty of explaining, those familiar things. Students can easily form the opinion that the topic is commonsensical, banal, and unworthy of careful attention. It is relatively easy to disabuse them of this idea by having them talk through a conflict that they could not solve, but the instructor is ever in need of patience in working through real-life instances that show how everyday life interpersonal communication is more complex to understand than the students initially may realize.

A teacher's first task, as is an early task of relaters themselves, is therefore to clarify which of these features is truly relevant, which is relevant to the teaching of the subject of interpersonal communication, specifically, and which lead to dead ends, intellectually and pedagogically. From such inspection comes the decision about the organization of the class that makes most sense or has the greatest appeal. The instructor, just as the person going on a blind date, needs to reflect on goals, strategies for presentation of self and subject matter, the instrumental endpoint of the relationship, and ways that are best to achieve the disclosure of the material or information. To do such preparation the instructor needs to look into self as well as at the audience or partners and to establish some basic skills of connection with them.

COURSE PREPARATION

Ultimately an instructor must, therefore, have a vision of the destination for the course or a plan for the blind date. It is an uncertain project at best, but, like a relationship, if you know where you want to end up, you are well on your way (Berger, 1993). We encourage instructors to sit down and write out the 3 or 4 or 12 or 17 things they want their students to be able to do, or write thoughtfully about, or explain on an essay exam, or recognize in their own or others' interaction by the time the course is completed. For each item, it helps if the instructor designs or obtains activities, exercises, articles, book chapters, videos, or films that will help students acquire that information or the listed skills.

Course Formats: Lecture versus Skills Options

It is true that every course, like every relationship, will be unique. However, some generalities may be established, just as one can generalize about family and romance. Two general forms in which interpersonal communication and other courses appear are (a) as a lecture course, and (b) as a

skills-oriented course, and of course either of these may be taught at introductory or upper division levels. Although the labels may not be shared
from school to school or class to class and these two forms do not exhaust all
options, they are perhaps the most common forms and they exemplify two
divergent patterns for courses.

Lecture Course.   This is a course pattern in which the instructor or
professor does precisely that—instruct or profess in front of the students by,
as it were, arranging the date, picking the restaurant, and ordering food and
the tickets for the show. In its most driven form, the instructor has a tight
script, a format that restricts options for teacher–student dialogue, and in
such a situation the instructor or professor may assume greater distance
from the students. This pattern may be preferred when the instructor or professor knows what he or she wants the students to hear and know or can best
guide the students to analyze and reflect on things that they would otherwise
not notice. The instructor or professor has great control in such a situation of
the flow of information, but it is the control of a general, not a sergeant. That
is to say, you have enlarged strategic but reduced tactical control.
   Exercising control over the course material in a lecture format can be
exciting. Such a format may allow the instructor or professor to develop a
good example of interpersonal communication—say an instance of a request for a date—clarify some key points about interpersonal communication to get the students thinking, then open the floor to questions or
examples from personal experience that bring the experience to life. This
format can offer the time needed for an instructor or professor to present
and develop ideas in what can otherwise be a one-sided conversation with
students. Any teacher who has been interrupted in order to explain small
details before getting to the meat of a presentation knows the frustration
of that moment. The lecture format can minimize the number of questions
students ask about details you plan to cover later, or details that are insig-
nificant for your purposes.
   The lecture format demands a clear vision on the part of the instructor or
professor about where the course should go and the means that will facilitate that movement. Adaptability may decrease for at least two reasons. The
first reason is to present course material in such a manner requires that the
instructor or professor give the students a relational guide in the form of a
syllabus to help the students understand where they will be going. Once in
the students' hands, the document is often viewed by students and instructor or professor as a prenuptial contract, and amendments to the contract
can be a logistical nightmare. Even minor changes in that prenuptial agreement may be difficult to convey. The second reason is an instructor's or
professor's ethos with students may be largely based on classroom

performance to the exclusion of degrees earned, years of experience, or his or her curriculum vitae. Because this is so, an instructor's or professor's appearance in front of a class can profoundly affect the dynamics of the class, its reputation among students, and future classes as well. Adapting elements of the course on the fly may be understood as incompetence rather than as informed and effective flexibility.

The lecture pattern is often used in courses taught in large auditoriums, with high student enrollments. The geography of the space in which a course is taught and the number of students in the course do not determine the structure of the course, but they may influence the decision to follow one pattern over the other. An instructor may choose to use the lecture pattern in a small class of 20 to 25 students. Although strategic control is a benefit of such a decision, the distance constructed between students and the instructor or professor can be magnified in perception, reality, or both. Depending on how you as a teacher choose to relate with your students, some distance may be welcomed or shunned.

It is not inevitable that lectures be done this way: The daters can negotiate about restaurants and the lecturer can invite questions both directly and indirectly by wondering aloud about a particular problem in a way that can invite students to jump in with answers, with proposals, or (more often) real-life examples. However, in adopting this style of lecturing, the instructor risks losing the clarity of direction that is the major advantage of a lecture format. Some mix of structured lectures and looser lecture style can achieve the benefits of both, however, and especially if the class meets twice a week, a rigid lecture at the start of the week followed by a series of looser formats often serves to control direction but allow maximum student participation, as in the next format.

Skills Course.   This course format is hard to label, but easy to recognize. A skills-based course is one in which the goal of the course is targeted at developing the students' ability to communicate. It is much more "hands on" by design than the lecture course. Although appearing in many forms, this course is probably most effective with high levels of discussion of issues and ideas. Students are encouraged to recognize the relevant communication processes and phenomena in their own relationships and interactions, and are (hopefully) equipped to "do communication" better or to recognize, analyze, and respond to situations in their daily life more effectively. Often a textbook will facilitate this equipping process through skill development exercises and self-evaluation activities.

A course using this structure has some clear advantages over the lecture format. The instructor or professor does not have to carry the class in this format the same way he or she does in the lecture format. Students are encouraged to participate, offer examples from their experience, ask questions along the way, and perhaps most important, to take the lessons from the research, textbook, or lecture and put them into practice. Although such participation is of course not a characteristic to be found only in this type of course, it is this course's defining characteristic and emphasis. This course may have class discussions instead of lectures, and may find a significant amount of class time dedicated to activities and exercises.

Often a less formal tone may dominate the instructor's or professor's classroom interactions. In an atmosphere where trust and self-disclosure are necessities, the distance between student and teacher needs to be diminished. Of course, there is a danger in occupying a position that minimizes distance and in adopting a less formal tone. Students may interpret such posturing as an attempt by the instructor to be their best friend rather than their teacher.

Consequently, an instructor or professor (especially those who may be new or inexperienced) may find his or her authority in more formal situations eroded by their in-class demeanor and the familiar relationship developed through classroom discussion.

In addition to reducing the load the teacher must carry, this format also has some other advantages. Often a skills-based course is easier to justify to students than one focusing on gaining book knowledge. This course offers possibilities of increasing one's communication skills, which can improve ongoing relationships and skill in developing new relationships. As an added bonus, some students see the skills they acquire in these courses as particularly useful in future sales or management careers as well. Students can become excited about understanding what is happening to them, and learning how to manage what they may have previously considered largely uncontrollable processes of relating. Such enthusiasm is difficult to generate in lecture classes.

Introductory Course.   Introductory courses are frequently the courses that a new instructor or professor will be assigned to teach, although we favor the exposure of students to senior instructors and faculty in such classes, where groundwork can often be crucial for later courses. Introductory courses will often have diverse student populations. It is not rare to find communication majors and minors taking a required course seated next to engineering majors taking an elective, next to nontraditional students getting back to school after some years. A typical class may have a mix of new students, sophomores, juniors, and seniors.

Such courses are particularly tough because of their population, the challenge of engaging people with such varying degrees of interest and familiarity with the topic, and the difficulty of helping freshmen and sophomores to think in ways as sophisticated as juniors and seniors— another reason we favor senior teachers taking charge of such classes. Striking the balance between encouraging and facilitating the growth of students yet still reaching all of the students at their particular level of intellectual development is difficult. Often that balance can be reached by using class time to generate and share the information and experiences that establish common ground in the class, and by using individual assignments (discussed later in this chapter) to promote the individual's growth and to foster the application of ideas at the level appropriate for each student and of particular interest to each student.

Upper Division Course.   Upper division courses are those in which students with some foundational understanding must be encouraged to go deeper into topics and processes that compose interpersonal communication. Because these courses may have prerequisites, underclassmen and students who are not communication minors or majors may be excluded from the student pool. Thus, these courses will have more similarity in the degree of experience and understanding students bring to the class. Such similarity may offer the instructor or professor richer opportunities to delve into current thought and research in ways that a more disparate audience would prohibit. Whereas introductory courses may have assignments that encourage students to become familiar with current research and ideas, upper division courses may require students to challenge, extend, or produce new lines of research.

COURSE ORGANIZATION

Given these preliminary considerations, there are clearly a number of principles on which an instructor can base a course in interpersonal communication as in other areas. However, as we noted earlier, interpersonal communication has the mixed advantage of familiarity to the student at some level. The real challenge is to present the familiar aspects of everyday life and make the students reflect on their deeper workings. One can find a book that is appealing and well written and then design the course around that. One can focus on a practical issue of concern to the students themselves (such as roommate interactions) and take the various strands of such an interaction as the clues on which to base the course. One can be driven by the phenomena as experienced in daily life as a whole, for example by the way in which one meets a stranger and comes to know that person, and one can then lay out the various skills, assumptions, presuppositions, and theoretical aspects of the whole experience of coming to know someone. At the most advanced level a fourth option is to take a particular theory and to bind the course structure to an unfolding of the principles of that theory.

These four options are not entirely separable from one another but can be distinguished for the purposes of this chapter. They are also likely to appeal to teachers of different levels of experience. An immediate appeal for the new teacher is to be found in taking a book and working through it, finding out its strengths and weaknesses, and redesigning the course next time around. For the more experienced teacher, who already suffers from hardening of the categories, it may be more enjoyable to take one's own theories about interpersonal communication and transfer them to the student. Indeed it is reasonably likely that a given teacher could enjoy trying different approaches to the same topic of interpersonal communication at different stages of a teaching career, much as relaters may play the field or become exclusively committed to one partner as time goes by.

Book Driven

One way to structure teaching of interpersonal communication is to choose a text and follow that. Of course this is not an approach that is entirely separate from the other approaches described here because the instructor chooses the book on the basis of some predilection. This may be a preference for a particular theory, application, or representations of the unfolding of interpersonal life or for a style of writing, or for a type of approach to subject matter. A course with such a design may be much like the theory-driven or the practical application-driven courses in effect. The instructor is, of course, never prevented from amplifying a book's coverage in more challenging ways that drive a student deeper than the book may go (e. g., by providing extra readings that specifically challenge the position taken by the book). However it also shares some similarities with the cosmopolitan approach to relationships in that there are presumed to be single answers to complex relationship problems and that one book may be equally proficient at answering them all.

This kind of design for a course may be the best option for the beginning instructor because the author of the book has done some of the trying out of the structure of the course and presents the results of that structuring for the new instructor to use. Certainly a well-established book that has run to several editions is a reliable guide to the structuring of the material and even of the discipline itself, and most of these books have done well precisely because they are full of good coverage and good pedagogical ideas.

One must try to choose the text carefully, however, as (to pursue our relational analogy) not all relationships that look promising after you read the personal ad actually turn out to be winners! You must be willing to augment the text where necessary and engage the text in a conversation where you personally may disagree with its conclusions.

An advantage of these texts, like some relational partners, is that they come with accoutrements and goodies (wealth, good looks, good attitudes, resources). Often, for example, these texts come with computerized test banks, lecture notes, activities, or overheads and videos. These resources allow the instructor to put together a more coherent and flashier course with less effort, but at the cost of either buying into the book's general philosophy or else appearing to criticize it too often, which, we have found, often confuses the students and taxes them more than they can usually manage. Students want truth; books give them that. Instructors who frequently challenge the books are often felt to be unnecessarily troublesome firebrands.

The downside is that the instructor commits to a book for 16 weeks, and like any relationship, you may want out after 2 weeks. This option may restrict you once you have built your syllabus around the book and the students have purchased it. Only too soon on your blind date, as the soup arrives for your 10-course banquet, do you find that the soup is roadkill chowder.

Practical Application Driven

In a course drawn from the daily experience of the students themselves, it is also possible to structure the material through consideration of practical applications that can be made of the close analysis of interpersonal communication. Such a class is used to develop the abilities of students in interaction and the students' abilities to recognize that something is going on as we interact. This can often be a "hook" class that can encourage students to take a closer look at relationship processes in higher level communication courses. These days it is refreshing to note that many TV programs such as *Seinfeld* or films such as *When Harry Met Sally* present students with compelling examples of real-life situations to which they could apply their learning of interpersonal communication skills.

Phenomena Driven

Some courses in interpersonal communication can be arranged in a manner that simply reflects the way processes may be understood to unfold in interpersonal life. For example, the subject matter of interpersonal communication can be readily introduced to students by having them think about and use as a structure for the course the unfolding issues that arise in the course of a conversation with a stranger: How does one react to the social group from which one believes the stranger to come and what does that tell us about a variety of substrata of interpersonal communication? How does one greet people, and what does that tell us about cultural prescriptions or norms of behavior and the force of their influence? How does one interpret nonverbal behavior by someone one does not yet know and how do such interpretations change as expectations are set up? How does one frame opening remarks in a conversation on the basis of conversational rules and norms of politeness? How does one get to know a person in greater depth through self-disclosure or good listening skills?

Theory Driven

Some more experienced instructors may prefer to introduce the subject matter of interpersonal communication by way of a specific theory that they apply to the subject matter systematically, defining that as they will. They may have developed a list of theories they consider foundational or primary and they want their students to know, theories that can be well illustrated by application in interpersonal behaviors and communication in social and personal relationships. There are few theories in interpersonal communication that do not at some level attempt to do this or seek to extend themselves beyond specific topics to the broader range of topical concerns of interpersonal communication itself. Instructors may have a theory like dialectical theory or process theories such as life-span theory that help organize the content and sequence of the course.

EVALUATION

Students may be in classes (or relationships) for multiple and various reasons. Some students are there voluntarily, some are required to be there on a blind date. Some are excited about the topic and want to learn, some need the hours to graduate or go on dates to impress friends or rack up notches on some trophy chart. One characteristic that may be shared by all is a concern with grades. For an assistant professor (with PhD in hand) or a graduate student instructor (who remembers how their grades did not really end up being that important years after the fact), it may be easy or tempting to emphasize to students the surpassing value of knowledge and understanding over grades alone. Often such a speech falls on deaf ears. For students, although course content and organization may influence their experience in a class, evaluation is their constant preoccupation. Rather than bemoaning such a state, an instructor is better off accepting it and preparing for it.

After establishing your goals for the course and the skills and proficiencies you hope to develop, you should next think about how you will evaluate proficiency or mastery of course content. Decisions surrounding the means of evaluation of student performance should be based logically on the course format and the instructor or professor goals for the students in the course. Devices and instruments used to evaluate the performance of students are many. Here, however, we discuss a few more popular or useful means specific to interpersonal communication.

Two constant challenges in a course are getting students to read the assigned course material and getting them to engage, think through, and master the course material. We have found that, unsurprisingly, they do this to the extent that they are interested in the topics or materials and that they are reminded of their duties of engagement of it during class. Instruments used to encourage and evaluate the student's success in these areas include quizzes, reflection papers, tests, and research papers. Each can be used in many ways, but here are our favorites.

Quizzes

These are minitests, and they can be usefully integrated in a course to encourage accountability for the readings. A weekly quiz composed of true–false and multiple-choice questions may occupy only 10 to 15 minutes of the class period, yet may do more than reveal who did and who did not read. For example, the quiz can identify for the students the ideas from the chapter that are most significant. Also, the quiz questions can be a starting point for class discussion about the particular readings for that week. One additional advantage of quizzes is the way in which students' grades are compiled using the scores from 10 small quizzes. If students fall behind, and do poorly on one quiz, they have the opportunity to still manage a strong score over the course of the entire semester. The taking of a quiz every week can become a ritual in the class that gives a real sense of coherence, stability, and progression to the course. The obvious drawback to the quiz is that there are so many of them, and someone has to construct them.

Although some textbooks come with question banks, some effort is still required to construct the quizzes, grade them, and record those grades.

Reflection Papers

Another instrument that can be used to encourage accountability for the readings we call reflection papers. These are brief documents (one to two typed pages) in which the students write about the issues in the readings that they found interesting, challenging, or confusing. Students are asked to explore ideas, critique the reading, or ask questions, which means they are building up a progressive record of their thinking or learning. A colleague who uses reflection papers indicated that she could read 25 papers and assign grades (a minus, check, or check plus) in an hour. She also indicated that this gave students the opportunity to have conversations with her about the material, which fostered a more comfortable climate. Further, students had interesting and thoughtful observations and questions to introduce into the class discussion. An alternative is to randomly select people from the class to read out remarks so that students are encouraged to actually do the papers.

Tests

When seeking to determine if a student has learned certain bits of information and can produce them on demand, tests are useful. There are occasions, though, when tests may not distinguish between those students who have memorized all of the information and those who have understood the information. The construction of an exam can also be time consuming. However, tests are an accepted means of student performance evaluation, and students will often feel that they did well on a test or poorly on a test rather than attributing responsibility for the grade on the teacher. ("I got a C," as opposed to, "You gave me a C.")

Papers

Here, the term "papers" refers to major documents that the student produces to satisfy course requirements. There are three types of paper assignments that are particularly useful for interpersonal communication courses. Each varies according to the level of theoretical discussion and the amount of research the student must perform. Also, although using the label "paper," any of these assignments could be presented as a conference-style paper or speech by students instead of or in conjunction with a paper.

Paper Option 1: This sort of assignment asks students to discuss interpersonal communication phenomena they observe in a movie, a television program, their family, their friendships, or their dating relationships. This assignment is well suited for introductory courses. The most significant contribution of this type of paper is that it gets students to identify and discuss interpersonal communication processes in places and contexts with which they are familiar. These assignments may or may not demand that students gather research beyond course readings and usually are intended to sensitize them to interpersonal communication in their own lives, such as the role of nonverbal communication or conflict.

Paper Option 2: This option asks students to engage the course material at a more obviously theoretical level than the first option, such as "How does expectancy violation theory help us understand nonverbal communication?" When using this assignment, students research current interpersonal theories on a given topic and challenge, critique, extend, or test some perspective. For example, students may be asked to obtain and summarize three current articles on interpersonal attraction. After the summary, students are asked to identify the assumptions of the theoretical perspective, critique the theory or theories, and perhaps offer a next step or a new way to think about the phenomena or perspective. This paper works well as the final paper in an introductory course, or as one of the assignments in an upper division course.

Paper Option 3: This option is a hybrid of Options 1 and 2. In this assignment, students are asked to explore an interpersonal communication phenomenon as they encounter it in their lives, and as current theory discusses it. For example, students are asked to identify and describe some event in their interpersonal experience such as a recent argument, a first date, or a party they recently attended. Students are then asked to discuss the event using a theoretical lens from current interpersonal theory. Next, students are asked to explore the overlap and the disparities between their experience and current theory. Finally, students are asked to attempt to explain the reasons for the disparity between their lived experience and theory and to generate a theoretical explanation that can account for their experience. This can be a highly involved and complex assignment, or it can be simplified by eliminating the final theory-building section. This assignment also works well as the final paper of an introductory course or an upper division course.

OTHER USEFUL TOOLS AND STRATEGIES

One instrument is called *fundamentals sheet*, a single sheet of paper that contains the distilled content of the course. Twenty or so single sentences may be designed by the instructor to describe the main point of a given lesson, week, or chapter. For example, "Meaning is not in words, meaning is in people," may be one of the statements. The sheet is given to the students on the first day of the course, and over the weeks that follow, the instructor establishes the first few statements as fundamental to how we would understand interpersonal communication. In subsequent weeks the instructor can build on the statements covered earlier in the semester. The fundamentals sheet serves not only as a road map for the course, but also as a means of understanding of interpersonal communication phenomena. In addition, it creates a shorthand for key ideas in the class and serves to emphasize those items and issues that the instructor considers most significant.

One new option for classes is the use of e-mail for discussions and for information distribution. Some students may desire to continue particularly interesting discussions outside class hours with classmates and the instructor. With the availability of e-mail accounts for many undergraduates, a new forum for discussion has opened up. Students may conduct ongoing chats about course material, problems, questions, or ideas. This tool may only be used by the truly gung-ho, but can be invaluable to those that access it.

CONCLUSION

We have tried to suggest that a useful way to approach the teaching of interpersonal communication is to view it as a relationship being built with the students. Just as other relationships can be facilitated or deadened by certain sorts of activity, so too can teaching interpersonal communication. In some ways the teaching of interpersonal communication becomes a metaphor for itself in that the more two-way interpersonal communication that happens in the course, as in relationships, the better the course is often felt to be. The subject matter of interpersonal communication courses is familiar to students. Thus there is a rich vein of personal experiences and predicaments that can be used not only to stimulate class discussion but also to provide the basis for clarifying the way in which interpersonal communication itself works in real life. In such a manner, its deeper axioms can be clarified through sharing of experiences, the same operative principle, Duck (1994) argued, that occurs in, and provides the basis for, relationships between people.

REFERENCES

Berger, C. R. (1993). Goals, plans and mutual understanding in personal relationships. In S. W. Duck (Ed.), *Understanding relationship processes 1: Individuals in relationships* (pp. 30–59). Newbury Park, CA: Sage.

Duck, S. W. (1994). *Meaningful relationships: Talking, sense, and relating.* Thousand Oaks, CA: Sage.

Wiseman, J. P. (1986). Friendship: Bonds and binds in a voluntary relationship. *Journal of Social and Personal Relationships, 3,* 191–211.

8

Teaching Small Group Communication

Lawrence R. Frey
Loyola University Chicago

I observed previously that "from birth to death, small groups are interwoven into the fabric of our lives" (Frey, 1994a, p. ix), but on reflection, it is more accurate to say that from the day we are born until the day we die, we are woven into the fabric of group life. For we are inherently "group people" whose immersion into familial, educational, recreational, social, occupational, health, spiritual, commercial, political and civic, and many other types of groups over the course of our life span helps define who we are and want to be, how we live and relate to others, how successful we will be, and even how we are put to rest after we die. The small group, therefore, is probably the most important social formation; it is the crucible, the generative site, where individuals and collectives are made and remade. In the words of our Generation-X students, "Groups rule."

Unfortunately, experiences in groups are not always fulfilling. People frequently enter groups hoping to be enriched by working and socializing with others. However, all too often, as time goes on, they find themselves limited in that context, much less happy or productive than they believe they could be. They feel bewildered about why their good intentions went astray; how to go about improving relationships and task work within that group; or what they can do besides avoiding, leaving, or just enduring life with those persons.

Communication educators are in a unique position to make a significant contribution to helping students learn how to create and sustain high-quality group life, for communication is central to group life: "Communication is the lifeblood that flows through the veins of groups. Communication is not just a tool that group members use; groups are best regarded as a phenomenon that emerges from communication" (Frey, 1994a, p. x). Communication is the essential defining feature—the medium—of groups and group life.

Our discipline has long recognized the importance of group communication education; the introductory group course has been an integral component of the undergraduate communication curriculum for over 50 years (Warnemunde, 1986). However, Warnemunde's (1986) national survey revealed a lack of agreement about what should be and wide discrepancy in what was being taught in the introductory course. This chapter responds to the need for unity by offering some pedagogically sound ways to organize the introductory group communication class.

APPREHENDING THE PROVERBIAL ELEPHANT: SETTING SOME BOUNDARIES

One problem in teaching small group communication that Warnemunde's (1986) survey revealed was the sheer amount of material to be covered in a limited amount of time. Although this is a problem for all introductory courses, it is particularly salient in teaching small group communication, which represents a confluence of intrapersonal, interpersonal, organizational, and societal levels of communication. Given the potentially overwhelming amount of material, instructors must put some manageable parameters around the course, recognizing that such boundaries are simultaneously enabling and constraining.

The first parameter is established by the definition of a small group: "A system of three to fifteen individuals who think of themselves as a group, are interdependent, and communicate by managing messages for the purpose of creating meaning" (Socha, 1997a, p. 11). This definition distinguishes small groups from dyads and organizational structures and also differentiates groups from collections of individuals who would not define themselves as a group and are not interdependent with respect to goals, behaviors, and/or context (e.g., 10 people waiting at a bus stop). This definition also makes clear that the course is grounded in a communication approach; although important noncommunication factors privileged in other disciplinary approaches to the study of small groups (e.g., cognitive processes in psychology) are discussed, they are not the primary concern of a small group communication course.

The second boundary concerns the central group activity focused on in the course. The most popular activity is group decision making, which involves "choosing among alternatives in a situation that requires choice" (Gouran, 1997, p. 138). Its pedagogical popularity undoubtedly derives from it being the central focus of research, for pedagogy at the university and college level tends to reflect major research interests. The primary goal of this course, consequently, is to show how communication behavior within small task groups contributes to high-quality decision making.

Those familiar with my work know that I have been a harsh critic of the almost exclusive focus on decision making in group communication scholarship (see Frey, 1994a, 1994c, 1996). However, with some important caveats, I want to endorse the emphasis on communication and decision making within the introductory small group communication class.

First, although decision making is the primary focus, it should not be the exclusive focus, for there are many other important processes that characterize group life, such as how group members create and sustain group identity, socialize new members, develop interpersonal relationships, and make changes in group processes. Decision making, therefore, needs to be infused with other important group communication processes.

Second, most of the empirical research on communication and decision making, and many other group processes, is based on student, zero-history, laboratory groups solving artificial problems created by researchers. Instructors should balance this research with studies of natural groups. (For case studies, see Frey, 1994b, 1995; Hackman, 1990; for using these and other case studies in the classroom, see Lamoureux & Zucco, 1997.) The importance of the group processes mentioned earlier, such as the way high-quality relationships contribute to decision making, becomes even more apparent when one examines real-life decision-making groups (see Gouran, 1994).

Third, in moving from the lab to the field, the organizational work group or team, which is an excellent example of a decision-making task group, should not be the sole exemplar. Families, children's groups, friendship groups, support groups, women's groups, and many other types of groups should not be ignored, for decision making is no less important to these groups. As Seibold (1994) rightly pointed out, "decision making is central to *all* groups' practices" (p. 105). Students, therefore, should be exposed to a wide range of social formations that inhabit the small group landscape.

Finally, probably because of Bales' (1953) argument that getting tasks accomplished often works against maintaining positive interpersonal relationships in groups (see Gouran, Hirokawa, McGee, & Miller, 1994), research and pedagogy have emphasized the contribution of task over socioemotional talk to effective group decision making. Hence, linear, propositional, task-oriented statements characteristic of male talk have been privileged over women's talk, which often takes other forms, such as sharing personal stories (see Meyers & Brashers, 1994; Wyatt, 1993). Deconstructing this dichotomy, instructors should help students appreciate the wide range of communication behaviors that contribute to effective group decision making.

Focusing on communication and decision making in this course is thus appropriate as long as instructors relate it to other important processes, provide examples of decision making in different types of natural groups, and are inclusive about the communication behaviors that contribute to effective group decision making. In line with a multicultural perspective, the goal is to create a multivocalic course that offers students a complex and balanced understanding of small group communication.

THE TIE THAT BINDS:
CONSTRUCTING COHERENT CONTENT

A central concern in teaching small group communication is the need for some coherent framework that helps organize the material. Although there are a number of frameworks, two in particular have traditionally provided such integration, and a relatively recent one offers much promise for doing so.

The first organizing framework is the *systems perspective*. Applying principles from biology to the study of human systems, a small group is viewed as a set of interrelated parts that form a unified social system. The various components of a small group are studied as interdependent, rather than isolated units via their relationships within an input–throughput–output model. Input variables precede the existence of a group, such as the members (e.g., their beliefs and attitudes), available resources (e.g., funds), and the physical and social environments (e.g., the meeting room and the group's place within an organizational hierarchy). Throughput variables, such as communication behavior and decision-making procedures, involve "*how* the group transforms inputs into final products and are characteristics of how the system *functions*, what it actually *does*" (Brilhart & Galanes, 1995, p. 29). Output variables are products of group work, such as the actual decisions made and changes groups enact in their input and/or throughput processes.

The systems perspective offers a compelling framework for organizing the small group communication course. By focusing on the interrelationships among various components, students come to understand how a small group system is, hopefully, more, but if they are not careful less, than the sum of its parts.

A second organizing framework is the *developmental perspective*, which uses a temporal template to understand how a group, its members, and their communication and decision-making processes grow and develop over time. There are four types of developmental models (Poole & Baldwin, 1996):

1. Phase models, which see groups as progressing through a series of stages, such as Tuckman's (1965) linear model of forming, storming, norming, and performing, or the multiple-sequence model, which assumes that groups cycle through any number of different stages in a variety of orders depending on various contingencies (see Poole & Baldwin, 1996).
2. Critical event models, which look at key turning points in group development, and the strategies used to cope with them (e.g., Gersick, 1988).
3. Continuous models, such as Scheidel and Crowell's (1964, 1966) spiral model, which focus on cyclical patterns of group development.
4. Social construction models, such as the structurational model, which explore how decision making becomes structured over time (see Poole & Doelger, 1986).

The developmental perspective is also a compelling model for organizing the small group communication course that resonates with students. They see developmental changes in their own life experiences, and quickly understand the metaphor of a group as having its own life: It is born, it grows and develops, and it eventually ends. This perspective also helps explain how the groups to which people belong and the communication and decision making that characterize those groups change over the course of people's lives.

From an instructor's point of view, the developmental perspective provides a heuristic for synthesizing and integrating course material. Frey and Barge (1997), for example, used a four-phase model—entering the group, encountering others, engaging the task, and ending the group—to organize the course and the chapters of their textbook. The developmental perspective also helps meet the need expressed earlier about relating decision making to other important group processes, for it builds toward decision making, rather than assuming it as the starting point. Group formation and relationship development processes, among others, are examined prior to decision making. Given the complexity of group decision making, this stage can also be divided into meaningful and manageable substages (e.g., conceptual understanding, followed by specific task-group communication, such as leadership, followed by facilitation practices).

A third, relatively new, organizing framework, at least as applied to small group communication, is the *dialectical perspective*. At the heart of a dialectical perspective is the notion of tensions that need to be managed: "A dialectic is a tension between two or more contradictory elements in a system that demands at least temporary resolution" (Littlejohn, 1996, p. 265). A dialectical perspective embraces complexity by recognizing that group life is characterized by deeply conflicting tensions at both the individual and the group level. Although these tensions can never be resolved, they can be managed.

Scholars have demonstrated the richness of a dialectical perspective for understanding interpersonal (see Baxter & Montgomery, 1996) and organizational communication (see Adelman & Frey, 1997), and it is particularly useful for understanding group communication (see Smith & Berg, 1987), especially the central paradox that everyone who joins a group wishes to be both a part of the group and apart from it (Tillich, 1952). The dialectical perspective also helps counterbalance the systems and developmental perspectives, which explain communication and group decision making as characterized by rationality and causal order, which can, in turn, lead to simplistic prescriptions of right and wrong behavior. In contrast, a dialectical perspective helps students recognize that the very same communication behavior (e.g., argumentation) can be simultaneously both facilitative and inhibitive (see Meyers, 1997).

The dialectical perspective can easily be integrated with a developmental perspective (or a systems perspective) to provide a rich organizational structure for examining individual- and group-level tensions over the life span of a task group (see Fig. 8.1). Such integration should, whenever possible, inform the teaching of specific content. For example, there are three major, communication-based, theoretical approaches that explain the relation between communication and group decision making:

1. Functional theory, which asserts that group members must perform certain communication activities, or functions, to arrive at a high-quality decision (see Gouran & Hirokawa, 1996).
2. Symbolic convergence theory, which explores communication practices that promote group consciousness and create consensus around group decisions (see Bormann, 1996).
3. Structuration theory, which examines how structures of rules and resources produced and reproduced in interaction affect group decision making (see Poole, Seibold, & McPhee, 1996).

STAGE/QUESTION	INDIVIDUAL LEVEL	GROUP LEVEL
1. Entering the group: *What am I/we doing here?*	Theme: *Motivating* I want to join the group, but I don't want to join the group. I want the group to do well, but I don't want to put in too much effort. I want the rewards of being a group member, but I don't want to incur the costs of membership.	Theme: *Identifying* We have to agree on the group's goals, but it's also important to respect differences of opinion. We want to encourage discussion about and dissent over the group's mission, but we don't want too much friction. We want people to come into the group committed, but we also want their commitment to grow over time.
2. Encountering others: *How do I/we relate in the group?*	Theme: *Relating* I want to be close to other members, but I also want to maintain my individuality. I want the others to know me, but I don't want to disclose too much information. I want to trust the other members of the group so that I can disclose to them, but I have to disclose to them in order to trust them. I want to be able to criticize the ideas of others, but I don't want to hurt anyone's feelings.	Theme: *Connecting* We want to be a highly cohesive group, but we realize that too much cohesion can hurt our performance. We want to be compatible, but we realize that incompatibility can be effective. We want conflict, but too much conflict can be detrimental.
3. Engaging the task: *How do I/we go about carrying out the task?*	Theme: *Contributing* I want to be a leader in the group, but I also have to be a follower. My personal goals are important, but it's also important for me to help the group meet its goals. I have to behave consistently in the group, but I also have to adapt my behavior to changes in the group situation. I have to achieve my long term goals, but my short-term goals often are just as important.	Theme: *Working* We have to use established procedures to carry out the task, but we also have to develop new procedures as they're needed. We should have clearly defined roles, but we must be able to change roles as the group situation changes. We want group members to be satisfied, but productivity is our bottom line. We want to be satisfied with our work, but we realize that external constituencies also must be satisfied with our product.
4. Ending the group: *How do I/we end the group experience?*	Theme: *Disengaging* I'm ready to leave the group, but I also want to stay. I'm happy with what we've accomplished, but wish we could do more. I want to share my feelings about the group with other members, but I don't want to hurt anyone's feelings.	Theme: *Terminating* We want to say good-bye, but we don't want to say good-bye. We know the group is disbanding, but we also know that we could accomplish even more if we stayed together. We want to discuss our group experience, but some things are better left unsaid.

Fig. 8.1.   Tensions in the life of a task group. From J. Kevin Barge and Lawrence R. Frey, "Life in a Task Group," In Lawrence R. Frey and J. Kevin Barge (Eds.), *Managing Group Life: Communicating in Decision-Making Groups*, p. 41, copyright © 1997 by Houghton Mifflin Company. Reprinted by permission of Houghton Mifflin Company.

Hirokawa and Salazar (1997) recently advanced an integrated model of communication and decision making that combines elements of these theoretical approaches, plus principles from mediational theory, which views communication as the medium by which contextual features (e.g., group structures) influence process criteria of effectiveness (e.g., member effort) and, subsequently, effective decision making (see Hackman, 1990). This integrated model gives a more complete picture of the role communication plays in effective group decision making.

Finally, each perspective just discussed potentially treats a small group as a container with rigid boundaries that is divorced from its surrounding context, leading researchers and educators to focus almost exclusively on internal group processes. All groups, however, are embedded within contexts that affect and, in turn, are affected by groups and their members. *A bona fide group perspective* "challenges the assumption that a group has a fixed location, an existence apart from its environment, and a boundary formed by static borders" (Putnam & Stohl, 1996, p. 149). This perspective calls attention to the fluid, dynamic nature of group membership (stable yet permeable boundaries) and a group's interdependence with its context, thereby relating internal group processes to the broader context and the external activities of group members. For example, Sinclair-James and Stohl (1997) examined group endings (a natural stage of group life that has been woefully neglected) from a bona fide group perspective, showing ways in which a group's ending is affected by stable yet permeable boundaries (e.g., fluctuating membership) and by interdependence with its context (e.g., a group's relative autonomy over timing and procedural control of an ending). Most important, the bona fide group perspective shows how groups, in one sense, never end, for members import expectations and experiences from previous groups to new ones.

In the final analysis, both students and instructors need frameworks to help organize the material discussed in the small group communication course. If this course is to be more than a "variable-analytic" approach to the field, the processes that characterize life in small groups cannot be examined apart from coherent conceptual perspectives.

BECOMING COMPETENT
SMALL GROUP COMMUNICATORS

So far we have focused on theoretical and empirical aspects of small group communication, but attention to practical, skill-based learning is equally important. Communication is an inherently practical discipline that seeks to cultivate communicative *praxis* that yields practical wisdom (see Craig, 1989), and the introductory small group communication course is particularly well-situated for promoting *praxis*, for students need "practical theories" (Cronen, 1995) to manage the many group experiences they will encounter over their lives. Accordingly, students need opportunities to become competent small group communicators. This can best be achieved by structuring the class so that they engage in embodied practices from three orientations or perspectives: participant, observer, and consultant.

First, students should be given classroom opportunities to engage as active participants in decision-making groups. They can be members of a small group that works on a final project throughout the semester (see later comments), or they can participate in various groups during the course. The first offers a sustained, lifelike group experience; the second helps students adjust to the contingencies of particular group experiences.

Some combination of these two procedures probably is most effective; for example, membership in a sustained group project complemented by participation in various groups when experiential activities are employed. There are many experiential instruments and exercises appropriate for the course (see any textbook instructor's manual). As an example, the Thomas–Kilmann MODE instrument (Thomas & Kilmann, 1974) assesses individuals' conflict styles, and the "Win as Much as You Can" exercise, a form of prisoners' dilemma in which teams play an "X" or a "Y" and the payoffs are designed such that competition results in losses for all groups, can be used to illustrate cooperative approaches to group conflict management.[1] The key is using experiential activities to illustrate key theoretical concepts; otherwise, although the exercises may be fun, they are relatively meaningless.

Second, students should be given opportunities to observe, analyze, and evaluate processes that occur within their own and other groups inside and outside the classroom. As participant-observers, students engage in structured observation of groups in which they participate. For example, the System for the Multiple Level Observation of Groups (SYMLOG; Bales & Cohen, 1979) can be used by group members to code their own behavior and the behavior of other members immediately after a group meeting, and the analyses of these data provide detailed feedback about individual and group behavior (see Keyton, 1997a). Students can further increase their participant-observer skills by writing a paper that uses the theories and con-

---

[1]For a copy of, and information about, the Thomas–Kilmann MODE instrument, see Nicotera (1997, pp. 114–120). For a copy of "The Win As Much as You Can" exercise, see Beebe and Masterson (1996, p. 278).

cepts discussed in the course to analyze their own and others' group behavior (see later comments).

As complete observers, students can observe other groups in class using a fishbowl technique where the observed group works in the middle and the observers are stationed around them. The observers can use Bales' (1950) Interaction Process Analysis (IPA), which is a popular methodology for coding the function (as opposed to the content) of communication during group discussion. If students are working on a final project, they can be encouraged to observe and report on a real-life decision-making group (see later comments). There are many college campus groups as well as business and community groups that will welcome observers, especially if giving feedback is part of the observational process.

There are many observational instruments available, and students should receive some experience in actually coding group communication (e.g., using IPA or SYMLOG). After all, it is the analysis of communication behavior that distinguishes this course from a small group course offered in psychology or sociology. Perhaps most important, communication coding schemes provide concrete empirical data about what people actually say in groups that can be used as evidence when making inferential claims about group processes.

Third, by combining participant skills with observational skills, students are in a position to serve as a consultant to small groups, helping members understand, analyze, and enact processes that contribute to effective group decision making. For example, students can serve as consultants to other classroom project groups, or, as mentioned earlier, if they are observing real-life groups, they can offer those groups feedback and recommendations.

The introductory small group communication course should thus be an applied course in the best sense of that term, teaching students how to apply theoretical concepts and empirical research to improve their ability to participate in, observe, and consult with groups. Indeed, one of the unique characteristics of this course is the way theory, research, and practice are interwoven on a daily basis. It is not unusual to start off the class with a lecture, follow with an experiential exercise that illustrates the lecture material, followed by class discussion of the exercise and perhaps some additional lecture, and then conclude with some time provided for project groups to meet. This seamless combination of theory, research, and practice in group interaction increases students' understanding of and ability to enact principles of effective communication and group decision making.

CONCLUDING THOUGHTS: GRADING AND CONFRONTING THE BIAS AGAINST GROUP WORK

The assignment of grades in the introductory small group communication course is a dialectical tension that reflects a delicate balance between individual and group work, theoretical and practical concerns, and written and oral work. Course work in my class is evaluated as follows:

1. Midterm and final examinations (40% of final grade; 20% each).
2. Group project presentation (25%): Students are assigned randomly to a small group and they conduct a project that culminates in an oral presentation to the class at the end of the semester (a written paper can also be required). Relevant group projects include (listed in order of my preference):

    A. An in-depth study of the group communication and decision making of a natural task group, on or off campus. This is a most appropriate project because students apply course concepts to a real-life group.

    B. A small group action enterprise, such as performing community service or attempting to bring about change in a community (especially appropriate for service-learning courses), or making a film, sponsoring a campus program, doing a workshop, and so forth. The presentation focuses on both the enterprise (and because these involve projects outside the classroom, the interdependence of groups with their context articulated by the bona fide group perspective is well illustrated) and how course concepts explain processes associated with action-oriented groups.

    C. A teaching session on some aspect of small group communication. There are topics not discussed in the course or ones that deserve greater attention that can be explored through this type of project.

    D. A survey or a field or laboratory experiment that investigates some aspect of small group communication. This assignment is particularly appropriate for those who have taken a communication research methods course.

3. Analysis paper (20%): This paper, written individually and required midway through the course, asks students to analyze as a reflective participant-observer how their group progressed through the first two phases of group life—entering the group and encountering others (see Frey & Barge, 1997). The paper might include the characteristics of group members, the quality of the interpersonal relationships, the significant symbols that characterize group interactions, and how these affect tensions the group has experienced.

4. Participation (15%): Distributed equally between classroom participation (e.g., completing in-class exercises and assignments and contributing to class discussions) and participation in the group project. The former is evaluated by the professor; the latter by self, peers, and the professor. Given the significant participation this course requires, students should be warned about the importance of class attendance.

Finally, a potentially significant problem in teaching this course concerns students' often negative attitudes toward participating in groups. Keyton (1994) warned:

> At the beginning of every small group communication class I teach, I ask two questions: "How many of you dislike being in groups?" and "How many of you disliked your group experience because you felt that you were the only one making a significant contribution?" Nearly everyone raises his/her hand to both questions. If these adults are representative of most, then it appears that a significant portion of adults have developed negative attitudes toward working in groups, which, in turn, hinders the development of effective group interaction skills. (p. 41)

Negative attitudes toward working in groups, what Sorensen (1981) labeled *grouphate*, is partly a result of growing up in a culture that privileges the individual over the collective (see Poole, 1994), as reflected in students' educational experiences. Although most children belong to many types of groups, these groups focus primarily on individual skill development instead of group communication (see Keyton, 1994; Socha & Socha, 1994). Even the National Communication Association's guidelines do not mention group communication until the seventh grade (Speech Communication Association, 1991)! Although educators are now experimenting with group applications in elementary and secondary schools—from preschool sharing circles, to cooperative learning programs, to peer conflict resolution and mediation groups in high schools—students entering university classes for the next few years have not had such experiences.

A unique challenge in teaching small group communication, therefore, is confronting grouphate. Just as public speaking teachers must deal with the significant influence of communication apprehension (see Lucas, chap. 6, this volume), so too must small group communication teachers potentially deal with the significant influence of grouphate (and its opposite, *grouplove*).

One way is by helping students understand the genesis (see Socha, 1997b), nature (see Keyton, 1997b), and implications (see Frey, 1997) of grouphate. A preliminary grouphate scale has also been developed (see Keyton, Harmon, & Frey, 1996) and may prove helpful in identifying students who are at the extremes (i.e., uncritical hatred or love for group work) and the composition of the class, thereby allowing instructors to make pedagogical adjustments.[2]

---

[2]A copy of the grouphate instrument can be obtained from Joann Keyton (Department of Communication, The University of Memphis, Memphis, TN 38152. e-mail: jkeyton@cc.memphis.edu).

The prevalence of grouphate, however, should not mean foregoing a group project. Just as a public speaking course offers students opportunities to give public speeches, so too should a small group communication course engage students in group work. Although it may be necessary to intervene and, under dire circumstance, disband a dysfunctional project group and offer an alternative, students typically do work through the trials and tribulations of group work and emerge as more competent small group communicators.

Most important, students must come to understand, accept, and appreciate the inevitability of group life. Lumsden and Lumsden (1993) urged instructors to respond to students' oft-heard statement, "I'd really rather work alone," with "Forget it, the twenty-first century works in groups" (p. 3). Although it may be true, as Seibold and Krikorian (1997) claimed, paraphrasing a commercial for a popular reduced-calorie beer, that "the reality for most task-group members seems to be 'more meetings, less fulfilling'" (p. 276), this does not have to be the case. At the most fundamental level, the purpose of the introductory small group communication course is to provide students with theory, research, and practical experiences that help them create and sustain more fulfilling group meetings.

REFERENCES

Adelman, M. B., & Frey, L. R. (1997). *The fragile community: Living together with AIDS.* Mahwah, NJ: Lawrence Erlbaum Associates.

Bales, R. F. (1950). *Interaction process analysis: A method for the study of small groups.* Reading, MA: Addison-Wesley.

Bales, R. F. (1953). The equilibrium problem in small groups. In T. Parsons, R. F. Bales, & E. A. Shils (Eds.), *Working papers in the theory of action* (pp. 111–161). Glencoe, IL: The Free Press.

Bales, R. F., & Cohen, S. P. (1979). *SYMLOG: A system for the multiple level observation of groups.* New York: The Free Press.

Baxter, L. A., & Montgomery, B. M. (1996). *Relating: Dialogues and dialectics.* New York: Guilford.

Beebe, S. A., & Masterson, J. T. (1996). *Communicating in small groups: Principles and practices* (5th ed.). New York: Longman.

Bormann, E. G. (1996). Symbolic convergence theory and communication in group decision making. In R. Y. Hirokawa & M. S. Poole (Eds.), *Communication and group decision making* (2nd ed., pp. 81–113). Thousand Oaks, CA: Sage.

Brilhart, J. K., & Galanes, G. J. (1995). *Effective group discussion* (8th ed.). Madison, WI: Brown & Benchmark.

Craig, R. T. (1989). Communication as a practical discipline. In B. Dervin, L. Grossberg, B. J. O'Keefe, & E. Wartella (Eds.), *Rethinking communication: Vol. 1. Paradigm issues* (pp. 97–122). Newbury Park, CA: Sage.

Cronen, V. (1995). Practical theory and the tasks ahead for social approaches to communication. In W. Leeds-Hurwitz (Ed.), *Social approaches to communication* (pp. 217–242). New York: Guilford.

Frey, L. R. (1994a). The call of the field: Studying communication in natural groups. In L. R. Frey (Ed.), *Group communication in context: Studies of natural groups* (pp. ix–xiv). Hillsdale, NJ: Lawrence Erlbaum Associates.

Frey, L. R. (Ed.). (1994b). *Group communication in context: Studies of natural groups.* Hillsdale, NJ: Lawrence Erlbaum Associates.

Frey, L. R. (1994c). The naturalistic paradigm: Studying small groups in the postmodern era. *Small Group Research, 25,* 551–577.

Frey, L. R. (Ed.). (1995). *Innovations in group facilitation: Applications in natural settings.* Cresskill, NJ: Hampton.

Frey, L. R. (1996). Remembering and "re-membering": A history of theory and research on communication and group decision making. In R. Y. Hirokawa & M. S. Poole (Eds.), *Communication and group decision making* (2nd ed., pp. 19–51). Thousand Oaks, CA: Sage.

Frey, L. R. (1997, November). *Grouphate: Implications for research, facilitation, and pedagogy.* Paper presented at the meeting of the National Communication Association, Chicago.

Frey, L. R., & Barge, J. K. (Eds.). (1997). *Managing group life: Communicating in decision-making groups.* Boston: Houghton Mifflin.

Gersick, C. J. G. (1988). Time and transitions in work teams: Toward a new model of group development. *Academy of Management Journal, 31,* 9–41.

Gouran, D. S. (1994). On the value of case studies of decision-making and problem-solving groups. In L. R. Frey (Ed.), *Group communication in context: Studies of natural groups* (pp. 305–315). Hillsdale, NJ: Lawrence Erlbaum Associates.

Gouran, D. S. (1997). Effective versus ineffective group decision making. In L. R. Frey & J. K. Barge (Eds.), *Managing group life: Communicating in decision-making groups* (pp. 133–155). Boston: Houghton Mifflin.

Gouran, D. S., & Hirokawa, R. Y. (1996). Functional theory and communication in decision-making and problem-solving groups: An expanded view. In R. Y. Hirokawa & M. S. Poole (Eds.), *Communication and group decision making* (2nd ed., pp. 55–80). Thousand Oaks, CA: Sage.

Gouran, D. S., Hirokawa, R. Y., McGee, M. C., & Miller, L. L. (1994). Communication in groups: Research trends and theoretical perspectives. In F. Casmir (Ed.), *Building communication theory: A socio/cultural approach* (pp. 241–268). Hillsdale, NJ: Lawrence Erlbaum Associates.

Hackman, J. R. (Ed.). (1990). *Groups that work (and those that don't): Creating conditions for effective teamwork.* San Francisco: Jossey-Bass.

Hirokawa, R. Y., & Salazar, A. J. (1997). An integrated approach to communication and group decision making. In L. R. Frey & J. K. Barge (Eds.), *Managing group life: Communicating in decision-making groups* (pp. 156–181). Boston: Houghton Mifflin.

Keyton, J. (1994). Going forward in group communication research may mean going back: Studying the groups of children. *Communication Studies, 45,* 40–51.

Keyton, J. (1997a). Coding communication in decision-making groups. In L. R. Frey & J. K. Barge (Eds.), *Managing group life: Communicating in decision-making groups* (pp. 236–269). Boston: Houghton Mifflin.

Keyton, J. (1997b, November). *What happened to trust? Could it be why members hate groups?* Paper presented at the meeting of the National Communication Association, Chicago.

Keyton, J., Harmon, N., & Frey, L. R. (1996, November). *Grouphate: Implications for teaching group communication.* Paper presented at the meeting of the Speech Communication Association, San Diego, CA.

Lamoureux, E. L., & Zucco, M. (1997). *Putting theory into practice* [Instructor resource manual for the book *Managing group life: Communicating in decision-making groups*]. Boston: Houghton Mifflin.

Littlejohn, S. W. (1996). *Theories of human communication* (5th ed.). Belmont, CA: Wadsworth.

Lumsden, G., & Lumsden, D. (1993). *Communicating in groups and teams: Sharing leadership.* Belmont, CA: Wadsworth.

Meyers, R. A. (1997). Social influence and group argumentation. In L. R. Frey & J. K. Barge (Eds.), *Managing group life: Communicating in decision-making groups* (pp. 183–201). Boston: Houghton Mifflin.

Meyers, R. A., & Brashers, D. E. (1994). Expanding the boundaries of small group communication research: Exploring a feminist perspective. *Communication Studies, 45,* 65–85.

Nicotera, A. M. (1997). Managing conflict communication in groups. In L. R. Frey & J. K. Barge (Eds.), *Managing group life: Communicating in decision-making groups* (pp. 104–130). Boston: Houghton Mifflin.

Poole, M. S. (1994). Breaking the isolation of small group communication studies. *Communication Studies, 45,* 20–28.

Poole, M. S., & Baldwin, C. L. (1996). Developmental processes in group decision making. In R. Y. Hirokawa & M. S. Poole (Eds.), *Communication and group decision making* (2nd ed., pp. 215–241). Thousand Oaks, CA: Sage.

Poole, M. S., & Doelger, J. A. (1986). Developmental processes in group decision-making. In R. Y. Hirokawa & M. S. Poole (Eds.), *Communication and group decision-making* (pp. 35–62). Newbury Park, CA: Sage.

Poole, M. S., Seibold, D. R., & McPhee, R. D. (1996). The structuration of group decisions. In R. Y. Hirokawa & M. S. Poole (Eds.), *Communication and group decision making* (2nd ed., pp. 55–80). Thousand Oaks, CA: Sage.

Putnam, L. L., & Stohl, C. (1996). Bona fide groups: An alternative perspective for communication and small group decision making. In R. Y. Hirokawa & M. S. Poole (Eds.), *Communication and group decision making* (2nd ed., pp. 147–178). Thousand Oaks, CA: Sage.

Scheidel, T. M., & Crowell, L. (1964). Idea development in small discussion groups. *Quarterly Journal of Speech, 50,* 140–145.

Scheidel, T. M., & Crowell, L. (1966). Feedback in small group communication. *Quarterly Journal of Speech, 52,* 273–278.

Seibold, D. R. (1994). More reflection or more research? To (re)vitalize small group communication research, let's "just do it." *Communication Studies, 45,* 103–110.

Seibold, D. R., & Krikorian, D. H. (1997). Planning and facilitating group meetings. In L. R. Frey & J. K. Barge (Eds.), *Managing group life: Communicating in decision-making groups* (pp. 270–305). Boston: Houghton Mifflin.

Sinclair-James, L., & Stohl, C. (1997). Group endings and new beginnings. In L. R. Frey & J. K. Barge (Eds.), *Managing group life: Communicating in decision-making groups* (pp. 308–334). Boston: Houghton Mifflin.

Smith, K. K., & Berg, D. N. (1987). *Paradoxes of group life:Understanding conflict, paralysis, and movement in group dynamics.* San Francisco: Jossey-Bass.

Socha, T. J. (1997a). Group communication across the life span. In L. R. Frey & J. K. Barge (Eds.), *Managing group life: Communicating in decision-making groups* (pp. 3–28). Boston: Houghton Mifflin.

Socha, T. J. (1997b, November). *Grouphate: A life-span developmental approach.* Paper presented at the meeting of the National Communication Association, Chicago.

Socha, T. J., & Socha, D. M. (1994). Children's task-group communication: Did we learn it all in kindergarten? In L. R. Frey (Ed.), *Group communication in context: Studies of natural groups* (pp. 227–246). Hillsdale, NJ: Lawrence Erlbaum Associates.

Sorensen, S. M. (1981, May). *Group-hate: A negative reaction to group work.* Paper presented at the meeting of the International Communication Association, Minneapolis, MN.

Speech Communication Association. (1991). *Guidelines for developing oral communication curricula in kindergarten through twelfth grade.* Annandale, VA: Author.

Thomas, K. W., & Kilmann, R. H. (1974). *Thomas–Kilmann conflict MODE instrument.* Tuxedo, NY: Xicom.

Tillich, P. (1952). *The courage to be.* New Haven, CT: Yale University Press.

Tuckman, B. W. (1965). Developmental sequences in small groups. *Psychological Bulletin, 63,* 384–399.

Warnemunde, D. E. (1986). The status of the introductory small group communication class. *Communication Education, 35,* 389–396.

Wyatt, N. (1993). Organizing and relating: Feminist critique of small group communication. In S. P. Brown & N. Wyatt (Eds.), *Transforming visions: Feminist critiques in communication studies* (pp. 51–86). Cresskill, NJ: Hampton.

9

Teaching Rhetorical Studies

Bruce E. Gronbeck
University of Iowa

To be a teacher of rhetorical studies at the turn of the millennium is to be engaged in an exciting yet frustrating pedagogical pursuit. The excitement for many flows from the significance of what has been called the "rhetorical turn" in the human sciences. In all of the social sciences are teacher-scholars who argue that human beings construct their knowledge and their relationships with each other symbolically, and to study those sciences—psychology, sociology, political science, anthropology—as well as society in general, one must be well versed in how people use language and other symbol systems in making for themselves pasts and futures, self identities and social units, literatures and philosophies, secular structures and religious hierarchies. Such construction projects are understood as rhetorical endeavors (Nelson, Megill, & McCloskey, 1987). The frustration comes from the realization that these symbolic activities are patently political activities, as often governed by considerations of power as by thoughts of sociality.

Both the excitement and the frustration that possess students and teachers of rhetorical studies are born of a series of philosophical, social, ethical, and, yes, political propositions:

1. Human beings are symbol-using animals. Among all of the attributes that characterize humans, most determinative of the qualities of their individual and collective lives is their ability to create and manipulate symbols (e.g., Burke, 1962). The power of symbolization is the power to infuse sense-data and experience, that is, the so-called outside world, with *meaning*—with significations, interpretations, evaluations, even transcendent attributes for good or evil. Symbols allow humans to construct personal and public meaning structures, and to control the ways in which "reality" is perceived, ordered, and assessed. Although reality, the "out-there," assuredly has existence independent of human thought, it is meaningless to humanity independent of symbolization.

2. Human beings are social actors. We are purposive creatures who both reflect standards of action given significance and importance by collectivities' symbol systems, and follow prescribed forms of ritual when seeking to express particular ideas and motives in the presence of others. We are actors because, through socialization, we are acculturated to follow social rules in our public behavior in order to be understood and to avoid public sanction or ostracism.

3. As actors, persons are acculturated to play certain roles in certain situations. For most situations we face, there are preoutlined script-like formulas we are expected to follow as we play those roles. To be sure, different persons play those roles differently, for there are gaps or indeterminacies in the role expectations fostered in given situations; and so, a variety of role performances can be counted as "proper" or "competent" when people function as parent, friend, teacher, or President of the United States. Yet, there probably are only a limited number of such formulas available in most situations and only a finite number of performance styles deemed suitable for them (Combs, 1980).

4. By implication, then, the social order is negotiated. As we share meanings with each other via symbols, we negotiate commonly articulated ideas, commonly understood behavior patterns, and commonly agreed-on valuations of those ideas and behaviors. Although there are ideas and behaviors meaningful only to individuals, and although there is an "out-there" that sets some limits to what we can think and do, we work with others to build a "social reality," that is, a way of describing, interpreting, and evaluating aspects of the out-there that we share with others.

5. In such negotiations, some individuals and groups have more influence (power) than others. For much of western history, men have had more influence in defining the world and what can be considered proper behavior in it than have women, Whites than Blacks, rich people than poor, abled than disabled individuals, the middle-aged than either the younger or the older. Those who control meaning making are likely to control other resources of

collectivities as well—money, land, positions of leadership, support from medical and religious institutions, educational processes. An important aspect of the study of rhetoric, thus, is the study of how symbols are used to reflect and enforce power relationships in what might seem to the naive viewer to be negotiations between equals.

6. Such negotiation processes, thus, must be studied rhetorically. Historically, rhetoric has comprised the theoretical and critical-pedagogical examination of power-oriented oral, written, and electronic communication practices. Regardless of whether individual writers about rhetoric have been interested in church or state, philosophy or criticism, education or propaganda, words or visual icons, rhetoric has been centered on affective or pragmatic discourse—on discourse that defines the mutual perceptions of, mediates differences between, and aligns the political and ethical behaviors of collectivities. Rhetoric always has been concerned with processes whereby societies get their work done, with public negotiations taking place between socially and historically situated actors working out their differences.

Rhetorical studies in our time, therefore, is a two-sided academic discipline. Within what can be called the *liberal* or *civic tradition* of rhetorical studies are scholarly efforts to describe, account for, and evaluate public talk about matters of collective importance—political processes, economic influences on policies, social relations, sacred and secular myths and ideologies, inter- and transcultural exchanges (Farrell, 1993; Hariman, 1995). But, within the *critical* or *cultural tradition* of rhetorical studies are efforts to unmask or critique the discourses of power that establish, maintain, and reinforce interinstitutional and interpersonal relationships and hierarchies, the critical-cultural tradition of rhetorical critique of domination, whether done within a French, Foucauldian vocabulary (e.g., Blair & Cooper, 1987; Charland, 1987; McKerrow, 1989) or an English-German, Marxist argot (e.g., Cloud, 1994; Grossberg, 1979; McGee, 1982, 1990; Wander, 1983), provides essays that presume to remake the thoughts and actions of their readers.

The excitement that one derives from teaching rhetorical studies comes from knowing that both the liberal-civic and the critical-cultural traditions engage your students in the central issues of our time: relationships between language use and science (Gross, 1990); the manifestation of politics not only in televised presidential speeches but also in male–female relationships in primetime TV shows (Gronbeck, 1998); 4th of July (Martin, 1958) as well as gay-pride parades and demonstrations (Hayes, 1976). The frustration results from realizing that it is most difficult, perhaps impossible, to teach both simultaneously. Liberal-civic rhetorical studies was born of an Aristotelian, analytical habit of mind, whereas critical-cultural studies was conceived within a Stoic, polemic habit of mind. A rhetorical analysis differs markedly from a rhetorical polemic (Windt, 1972).[1] The liberal-civic rhetorician's work usually ends in some claim to knowledge or reasoned evaluation; the critical-cultural rhetorician's task is more often conceived of as action to change the consciousness and/or behavior of his or her readers.

Whether liberal-civic or critical-cultural in thrust, rhetorical studies is usually divided into subfields: *rhetorical theory*, "the rationale of the informative and the suasory in discourse" (Bryant, 1973, p. 14); *rhetorical criticism*, the interpretive and evaluative examination of practical discourse and discoursing processes (Campbell, 1990; Medhurst, 1989); *rhetorical history*, examination of the rationales for and effects of practical discourse in particular situations (Leff & Sachs, 1990); and *rhetorical pedagogy*, the assumptions guiding attempts to improve individuals' rhetorical performances (Andrews, 1989; Haynes, 1990).[2] The focus of this chapter, therefore, is on ways we can teach rhetorical theory, rhetorical criticism, rhetorical history, and rhetorical pedagogy in undergraduate curricula. It is organized around the instructional goals, strategies, resources, and evaluation processes that, ideally, should accompany undergraduate rhetorical studies.

INSTRUCTIONAL GOALS IN RHETORICAL STUDIES

As may be obvious through everything noted so far, the instructional goals of rhetorical studies are those of critical-liberal arts in general: description, contextualization, and judgment.

Description

A foundational aim of liberal education is the instillation of technical or in other ways precise language that enables its users to talk more accurately and usefully about the world. With the act of naming, as Burke (1962) noted, comes the abilities to assume perspectives on and to express attitudes toward the world. Just as the apprentice carpenter learns to ask for the "mitre box" rather than the "watchamacallit for cutting corners," so students of all disciplines, including rhetoric, must learn technical talk.

---

[1]One must be careful not to draw the line between the liberal-civic and critical-cultural traditions of rhetorical studies too heavily. The liberal rhetorician can be as interested in social reform as his or her critical brethren, and the best critical rhetoricians also are splendid analysts. I am making the distinction sharply here for pedagogical rather than intellectual reasons.

[2]That pedagogy itself is rhetorical is now an argument made regularly by the students of critical pedagogies (e.g., Giroux, Lankshear, McLaren, & Peters, 1996).

The languages of rhetoric are several, depending on the positions from which one examines rhetorical processes—the processes of contextualized meaning making. These languages are the languages of: (a) communication in general (sender/receiver/channels/context or situation/culture/verbal and nonverbal messages/encoding/decoding/feedback); (b) persuasion (audience analysis/targeting/segmentation/fear appeals/credibility/motivational appeals/narrative argument/figure–ground relationships); (c) argument (data/warrant/claim/fallacies/refutation and rebuttal/ syllogisms/enthymemes); (d) dominating political processes (ideology/hegemony/legitimation/power/demographics/race, class, gender/empowerment); and (e) rhetorical theory (Pre-Socratic/Platonic/Aristotelian/ Isocratean/Ramistic/Burkean/Marxist). In these and many other concepts and conceptualizations are found ways of identifying and discussing rhetorical theory, history, criticism, and pedagogy from the 5th century BCE to the present, in both the liberal-civic (especially) and critical-cultural traditions.

A technical vocabulary, of course, is more than simply the mark of an educated person; it is also a tool to discovery, insight, communication, and both individual and shared pleasures, because it allows something to be experienced on a secondary level—not just the mundane but also the critical level of understanding. To discover, say, the "ancient" and "modern" formulas for sermons is to gain insight into the Puritan revolution and to be able to discuss differences between today's homilies (ancient) and sermons proper (modern); that portion of a rhetorical vocabulary, therefore, prepares students for both historical and contemporary talk. A technical vocabulary affects our understanding of the world, guides critical discussions about it, and increases both self-satisfaction and shared experience.

Contextualizations

A second goal of a liberal-critical education is to help people see their world in perspective—to put it into contexts so as to better reflect on its significance. To "put something into context" is to articulate a set of relationships between it and other elements, forces, ideas, or institutions that we think form or account for it. Rhetorical studies seeks to put our public communication habits and processes into such contexts. Consider these seven contexts:

Pragmatic Context.   One can be interested in the pragmatics of rhetoric—its effects on the world. The first logographers (speech writers) of the 6th century BCE were concerned primarily with pragmatics, with constructing speeches for their clients that would win the day in court. "Rhetorical effect" has been a staple study area since then.

Psychological Context.   Two sorts of psychological contexts for rhetorical messages are worth study: (a) The rhetor's state of mind has been studied. For example, what sorts of people construct radically conservative messages (Hart, 1971), and why are their messages so often filled with death-and-illness metaphors (Black, 1970)? (b) The audience's predispositions and tendencies likewise have been studied by scholars. Will a truly hostile audience ever come hear a speaker (Bauer, 1964)? How will different audiences understand and evaluate a message (Condit, 1989)?

Generic Context.   Some types of talk are given often enough that people expect them to possess similar characteristics; a *genre* of discourse is a family of texts with similar features. Aristotle (1954) identified three genres of rhetorical discourses: political, legal, and ceremonial. Such genres also have species; so, in political campaigns we are likely to hear announcement speeches, policy speeches, keynote addresses, nomination speeches, acceptance speeches, debates (joint appearances), *ad hominem* attacks, self-defenses (apologia), victory speeches, and concessions. To learn about genres of rhetoric is to be in touch with important rules of talk, with matters of "rhetorical manners," called *decorum* by the ancients (Burgchardt, 1995; Hariman, 1995).

Sociocultural Context.   Also interesting to examine are the "social rules"—the guides to prudential public behavior—underlying social and political rhetorical processes. For example, what kinds of rhetorical behavior do we expect from presidential candidates? What sorts of things do we expect them to say prior to announcing, during primaries, while giving convention speeches, in the middle of debates, and on the stump during the general election campaign period? Presidential elections are usefully examined dramaturgically, as choreographed acts and counteracts that come together as sociodramas scripted through unwritten social rules—cultural myths and rituals (Gronbeck, 1984, 1995a). Other kinds of rhetorical behavior (e.g., routines for justifying one's conduct when publicly attacked, college commencement addresses, ritualized fights between labor and management) can be examined equally well from a sociocultural perspective.

Ethical Context.   Public talk is powerful enough to make many worry about its morality. Plato (1962) worried that rhetors would pretend to talk about "justice" without knowing what is just and unjust, and that concern has followed rhetoric through its western history. Rhetoricians study, especially, the relationships between rhetorical modes of talking and ethics (Hariman, 1995) and the ways in which public, especially political, rhetoric manufactures or crafts our sense of the moral (Condit, 1987; Condit & Lucaites, 1993).

Institutional Context.   In ancient times, the rhetor—the maker of oral and written rhetorical messages—was conceived of as an individual. Today, many of our rhetors are corporate: the presidential committees, which hire speech writers, that make the messages of the candidates; the production companies that churn out your favorite films; the public relations and lobbying groups that keep products and political positions in the public eye. The National Cattlemen's Association's "lean-'n-healthy" meat-eating campaign, the American Dairy Association ads for cheese, the American Pork Producers's belief that pork is the "other white meat," and the National Fluid Milk Process Promotion Board's "Milk. Where's *Your* Mustache?" campaign are all parts of both lobbying efforts (for governmental price supports) and public relations campaigns (for your continued consumption), waged in the face of nutritional and vegetarian warnings about the consumption of meat and animal products. Rhetorical discourse coming from social, political, economic, and religious institutions needs to be studied as expressions of those institutions' personae.

Political Context.   In today's cultural climate, finally, it is often important for students of rhetoric to ask about the political contexts within which even seemingly nonpolitical messages exist. Sure, a presidential campaign ad must be understood within a political context (the campaign), but so can a Saturday morning cartoon that shows little boys making all of the decisions and little girls just responding to male initiatives (gender and identity politics). Recent studies of controversy over the Vietnam war memorial (Blair, Jeppeson, & Pucci, 1991) and the scientific control over death (Hyde, 1993) are examples of rhetorical critics exploring the political contexts within which seemingly nonpolitical entities operate.

These and other perspectives (e.g., linguistic, psychoanalytical, technical) are available as windows on rhetorical processes. Some of those we have mentioned (especially the ethical, institutional, and political) are presently battlegrounds within the rhetorical community, as the exchange over the politics of mass media representation waged between Celeste Condit (1994, 1996, 1997) and Dana Cloud (1994, 1996, 1997) illustrates. For both the liberal-civic and the critical-cultural rhetorician, however, each perspective is a way of "seeing" rhetoric; with sight comes insight, and with insight comes the knowledge one needs to function as a thoughtful, informed citizen. Contextualization, therefore, is part of the burden of critical-liberal arts education because it helps create fully rounded citizens.

Judgment

If students better understand something from a variety of vantage points, then presumably they ought to be more prepared to assess its beauty or defects, rightness or wrongness, effectiveness or ineffectiveness. Making aesthetic, moral, and pragmatic judgments about people, objects, and processes in informed ways is the mark of a well-educated person. Teaching undergraduates to make informed, subtle, reasoned judgments is a difficult task, generally, and teaching them to make rhetorical judgments seems especially hard, because the object of judgment—a speech, a TV program, a movie—is so ephemeral, yet complex, and because standards of judgment often appear to work at cross purposes.

The problem of ephemerality is especially nasty. Much rhetorical discourse comes at us as an aural-visual montage of sounds, images, and coded symbols in a particular configuration of time and space. Speech, as contrasted with writing, is spoken face-to-face and then lost forever; a television program is experienced in a here-and-now, in some place and at some time, with or without others in the room. Now, speech can be taken down in shorthand or recorded, and the TV program can be videotaped or seen again in reruns, but, technically, once speech or TV is printed or recorded via mechanical reproduction, it is not speech per se nor is it television in its usual flow through our lives. Speech is oral-aural, and television is a situated electronic experience actually quite similar to our experience of speech (Ong, 1982). What all of this means is that the act of judgment we are discussing is based either on individual memory or on some recorded version of the original experience that has been decontextualized, ripped from its originary moment and site of experience, and hence is a different experience. Students must be sensitized to what in most cases are differences in the judgments they make *in situ* and those they make after the fact while contemplating a mechanically produced "text."

Variations in rhetorical standards for judgment, likewise, complicate the assessment process. Six judgmental criteria often are applied to rhetorical processes:

1. Rhetorical effect. Did the speech or televised documentary "work"? Did it accomplish the aims of the rhetor? Such a standard comes right from the

core of rhetoric understood as affective or pragmatic discourse (Hochmuth, 1955).

2. Rhetorical artistry or effectiveness. Was the speech or film strategically sound? Situations may be such that a speaker is doomed from the start by opposing votes, voices, or circumstances, yet it still is possible that the discourse could be adjudged as interesting aesthetically or artistically. It might be "effective" technically even if it did not achieve its primary aims (Parrish, 1968), as some think happened, for example, when Edmund Burke attacked American taxation in 1774 or when Robert Kennedy prophesied America as receiving a cleansing-through-killing in his speech following Martin Luther King Jr.'s assassination in 1968.

3. Ethicality. As already suggested, rhetorical discourses can be assessed on moral grounds: one can use ethical standards derived from democratic principles (Hariman, 1995; Wallace, 1963), pragmatism (or effects; Haiman, 1958), situational ethics (Rogge, 1959; or, more broadly, Condit & Lucaites, 1993), the speaker's own words (K. Campbell, 1972), or understandings of human dignity (Wander, 1984) to assess the moral worth of public talk.

4. Fittingness. Lloyd Bitzer (1968) suggested that we also can judge rhetorical discourse by the degree to which it responds to situational exigencies in a fitting way. Bitzer would ask: Has the rhetorical discourse removed an imperfection from some situation so that people can return to their normal routines and activities? If it does, Bitzer would identify it as fitting.

5. Rhetorical competency. To ask if someone has spoken or performed competently is to inquire whether he or she has observed the social rules that govern talk in a particular situation. This question can be asked about situational expectations (Gronbeck, 1987, on Reagan's first inaugural address) or about the degree to which the message of a speech and way it was presented—its "content" and "form"—work in harmony to produce powerful discourse (Leff & Sachs, 1990, on Edmund Burke's 1780 speech to the sheriffs of Bristol).

6. Empowerment. Particularly among the students of critical-cultural rhetoric there has emerged recently a sixth standard for judgment: empowerment. Insofar as a speech, film, TV program, or piece of writing helps individuals to find themselves as persons or as representatives of a demographic category as well as to present those selves and that group to a larger audience, it is empowering. It defines personhood even in the act of communicating (Palczewski, 1996); such acts show the dominant world as *les voix de l'autre*, the voices of the other (Nakayama, 1997).

These judgments can produce conflict in rhetorical assessment. A speech might "work" pragmatically and yet suppress the personhood of minorities, thus disempowering them; a speaker might tell the truth yet violate situational expectations. In such cases, rhetorical analysts must argue for the relevance of their judgmental criteria. Put another way, students must learn that judgments are more than matters of expressing personal preference or taste. Judgments are propositions demanding not only articulation but also support and even defense through the refutation of countering propositions before others can be expected to accept them. Part of the burden of a critical-liberal arts education is instruction in the art of argumentation in defense of one's positions.

INSTRUCTIONAL STRATEGIES AND RESOURCES IN RHETORICAL STUDIES

So, how and with what can one teach the rudiments of rhetorical studies? In the age of television, VCRs, and digitized computer images and searches, available resources are positively staggering. Teachers must learn to pick and choose resources based on particular instructional strategies.

Published Rhetorical Texts and Textbooks

Given the traditional identification of rhetoric with oratory in speech communication studies departments, teachers commonly do their work with sample speeches in basic public-speaking texts or anthologies of speeches advertised in the National Communication Association or regional speech communication journals. Anthologies containing snippets from the history of rhetorical theory or groups of essays illustrating types of rhetorical criticism also can be found.

Impressive even in this, an early stage of development, are the World Wide Web sites devoted to rhetorical studies. Northwestern University's *douglass.nwu.edu* site allows users to search a vast bank of speech texts and provides links to professional associations, university departments, and other archives holding speech texts. The University of Iowa's *www.uiowa.edu/gw/comm* site opens into visits to film, television, and rhetoric archives, even with an opportunity to directly link to RhetNet, which can be subscribed to for discussion and informational purposes. Also at Iowa is *www.uiowa.edu/~commstud/Fragments*, which can take you to ancient rhetorical resources, women's rhetoric, African-American sites, and technically defined lists of terms.

Once teachers have accessed print and electronic texts, they can take students through them, line by line, paragraph by paragraph, teaching them the important art of close textual analysis. As well, one might be tempted to have undergraduates read from anthologies of rhetorical criticism and rhetorical theory. A problem, though, is that undergraduates are often over-whelmed by theoretically oriented scholarly essays; they will have to be led through them step by step.

Prepared Audiovisual Materials

Available on audiotape (e.g., National Public Radio, 1984) and videotape (e.g., the Educational Video Group's great speeches tapes, 1987) are political orations from Franklin Roosevelt to Bill Clinton. Reels of the *CLIO Award Winning Television Commercials* (e.g., 1973, 1978) and kinescopes of *Television's Classical Commercials 1948-1958* (Diamant, 1971) are in many media libraries, as are films and videotapes showing techniques used in commercial and political ads. Contemporary ads often can be found on a company's web site (e.g., *www.bennetton.com*). A site can be used both as a source for material and as a place to explore particular rhetorical themes; Bennetton's black-and-white ads can be considered in the context of race relations in the United States. Videotaping political events off the air or making use of C-SPAN's educational archives (a library can get teachers access) gives rhetoricians a full array of texts for study.

Working with such materials often forces teachers to open their definitions of rhetoric somewhat. The study of words in the neoAristotelian tradition (Andrews, 1983; Thonssen & Baird, 1948) is a good place to start, but the world of our students is the world of sight and sound; we must also teach them to handle visual and aural codes (Gronbeck, 1993, 1995b). To make students into solid analysts, teachers probably should be doing close, intense, teacher-generated analyses of short scenes, and even single frames from visual materials, using such model criticism to instill in students an appreciation for multimedia rhetoric.

Student-Generated Materials

At the other extreme, teachers can turn over the onus for learning to the students. Students can be sent to the streets to find and analyze the rhetoric of popular culture—billboards, tee shirts, bumperstickers, store logos and shelf arrangements, cafe decor, architecture. They can be asked to videotape a string of ads, a program, an event, or whatever they want to analyze. Especially for teachers working in a critical-cultural framework, students can and even should be made to find their own materials—materials and events they wish to engage critically. To meet what Giroux (1996, p. 72) called the "pedagogical challenge represented by the emergence of a postmodern generation of youth," teachers must learn pedagogies working from the inside out—from inside the life experiences of youth and out into an analytical and political world.

Teachers of rhetorical studies, like the rest, must decide (a) how broadly to define their subject matters when theorizing and exemplifying its progress through society, and only then (b) how to teach that material through a series of pedagogical strategies, from traditional lecture to nontraditional critical pedagogy.

IN CONCLUSION: ASSESSING PEDAGOGY SUCCESS

So, of course, in the end, how can teachers know if they have taught rhetorical studies well? Teachers of mathematics can check outcomes by looking for correct answers; the student's experiment in a chemistry lab comes out well or not. But what about rhetorical studies? In part, teachers can assess their own pedagogical successes by technical examinations of speeches given, films or videotapes produced, computer searches conducted, and prose and poetry selections assembled and orally interpreted. When it comes to the critical-liberal arts portions of our studies, however, the matter of teaching well becomes more difficult to measure. Engaging in rhetorical studies is learning to talk critically about that with which one has been surrounded mundanely all of one's life—informal and formal talk, TV, movies, Web sites. Culture itself is created and maintained through communication processes; the political processes that perpetuate or replace leadership grind away, whether we are attuned to them or not; hegemonic relationships between the powerful and the less powerful are embedded in common sense—in such statements as "Well, that's the way we do things around here."

So, how can we tell if our students have learned to break through the mundaneness of private and public conversation, the "empty rhetoric" of politics that so determinatively affects who we are and how much we have to eat, or the invisibility shields that make gender or race relations so imbalanced yet so easily accepted as natural? Watching students using the vocabulary we have given them, adopting particular perspectives for analysis of a specimen text, or defending their judgment about that text's power to produce states of domination or freedom can give you some answers to that difficult question; but only some. The proof of success in the life of teachers of rhetorical studies comes in the adulthood of those students, when they enter the worlds of work, leisure, and sociality. Only then will you be able to tell whether instruction in the liberal-civic tradition of rhetorical analysis and the critical-cultural tradition of rhetorical critique has made them into active citizens and self-reflexively more open social beings. Only then will teachers of rhetoric discover if they taught their students well.

REFERENCES

Andrews, J. R. (1983). *The practice of rhetorical criticism.* New York: Macmillan.
Andrews, J. R. (1989). "Wise skepticism": On the education of the young critic. *Communication Education, 38,* 178–183.
Aristotle (1954). *Rhetoric; Poetics* (W. R. Roberts & I. Bywater, Trans.). New York: Modern Library.
Bauer, R. A. (1964). The obstinate audience: The influence process from the point of view of social communication. *American Psychologist, 19,* 319–328.
Bitzer, L. (1968). The rhetorical situation. *Philosophy & Rhetoric, 1,* 1–14.
Black, E. (1970). The second persona. *Quarterly Journal of Speech, 56,* 109–119.
Blair, C., & Cooper, M. (1987). The humanist turn in Foucault's rhetoric of inquiry. *Quarterly Journal of Speech, 73,* 151–171.
Blair, C., Jeppeson, M. S., & Pucci, E., Jr. (1991). Public memorializing in postmodernity: The Vietnam veterans memorial as prototype. *Quarterly Journal of Speech, 77,* 289–308.
Bryant, D. C. (1973). *Rhetorical dimensions in criticism.* Baton Rouge: Louisiana State University Press.
Burgchardt, C. R. (Ed.) (1995). *Readings in rhetorical criticism.* State College, PA: Strata.
Burke, K. (1962). *A grammar of motives and a rhetoric of motives.* Cleveland: World Publishing. (Original works published 1945 and 1950)
Campbell, J. A. (1990). Special issue on rhetorical criticism: Introduction. *Western Journal of Communication, 54,* 249–251.
Campbell, K. K. (1972). *Critiques of contemporary rhetoric.* Belmont, CA: Wadsworth.
Charland, M. (1987). Constitutive rhetoric: The case of the peuple Quebecois. *Quarterly Journal of Speech, 73,* 133–150.
CLIO. (1973, 1978). *CLIO award winning television commercials: Educational reels* [Films]. N.p.: ATV-CLIO.
Cloud, D. L. (1994). The materiality of discourse as oxymoron: A challenge to critical rhetoric. *Western Journal of Communication, 58,* 141–163.
Cloud, D. L. (1996). Hegemony or concordance? The rhetoric of tokenism in Oprah Winfrey's rags-to-riches biography. *Critical Studies in Mass Communication, 13,* 115–137.
Cloud, D. L. (1997). Concordance, complexity, and conservatism: Rejoinder to Condit. *Critical Studies in Mass Communication, 14,* 193–197.
Combs, J. E. (1980). *Dimensions of political drama.* Santa Monica: Goodyear.
Condit, C. M. (1987). Crafting virtue: The rhetorical construction of public morality. *Quarterly Journal of Speech, 73,* 79–97.
Condit, C. M. (1989). The rhetorical limits of polysemy. *Critical Studies in Mass Communication, 6,* 103–122.
Condit, C. M. (1994). Hegemony in a mass-mediated society: Concordance about reproductive technologies. *Critical Studies in Mass Communication, 11,* 205–230.
Condit, C. M. (1996). Hegemony, concordance, and capitalism: Reply to Cloud. *Critical Studies in Mass Communication, 13,* 382–384.
Condit, C. M. (1997). Clouding the issues? The ideal and the material in human communication. *Critical Studies in Mass Communication, 14,* 197–200.
Condit, C. M., & Lucaites, J. L. (1993). *Crafting equality: America's Anglo-African word.* Chicago: University of Chicago Press.
Diamant, L. (1971). *Television's classic commercials: The golden years 1948-1958.* New York: Hastings House. (From the Celia Nachatovitz Diamant Memorial Library of Classical Television Commercials, Brooklyn College of CUNY.)
Educational Video Group. (1987). *Great speeches, Vols. 1–4* [Film]. Accompanying textbook: L. Rohler & R. Cook (Eds.), *Great speeches for criticism & analysis.* Greenwood, IN: Allistair Press.
Farrell, T. B. (1993). *Norms of rhetorical culture.* New Haven, CT: Yale University Press.

Giroux, H. (1996). Slacking off: Border youth and postmodern education. In H. Giroux, C. Lankshear, P. McLaren, & M. Peters (Eds.), pp. 59–79.

Giroux, H., Lankshear, C., McLaren, P., & Peters, M. (1996). *Counternarratives: Cultural studies and critical pedagogies in postmodern spaces.* New York: Routledge.

Gronbeck, B. E. (1984). Functional and dramaturgical theories of presidential campaigning. *Presidential Studies Quarterly, 14,* 486–499.

Gronbeck, B. E. (1987). Ronald Reagan's enactment of the presidency in 1981. In H. W. Simons & A. A. Aghazarian (Eds.), *Forms, genres, and the study of political discourse* (pp. 226–245). Columbia: University of South Carolina Press.

Gronbeck, B. E. (1993). The spoken and the seen: The phonocentric and ocularcentric dimensions of rhetorical discourse. In J. F. Reynolds (Ed.), *Rhetorical memory and delivery: Classic concepts for contemporary composition and communication* (pp. 141–157). Hillsdale, NJ: Lawrence Erlbaum Associates.

Gronbeck, B. E. (1995a). Rhetoric, ethics, and tele-spectacle in a post-everything age. In R. H. Brown (Ed.), *Postmodern representations* (pp. 216–238). Chicago: University of Illinois Press.

Gronbeck, B. E. (1995b). Unstated propositions: Relationships among verbal, visual, and acoustic language. In S. Jackson (Ed.), *Argumentation and values: Proceedings of the ninth SCA/AFA conference on argumentation* (pp. 539–542). Annandale, VA: Speech Communication Association.

Gronbeck, B. E. (1998). Text-centered approaches to television criticism. In L. Vande Berg, L. Wenner, & B. E. Gronbeck (Eds.), *Critical approaches to television* (pp. 93–104). New York: Houghton-Mifflin.

Gross, A. G. (1990). Rhetoric of science is epistemic rhetoric. *Quarterly Journal of Speech, 76,* 304–306.

Grossberg, L. (1979). Marxist dialectics and rhetorical criticism. *Quarterly Journal of Speech, 65,* 235–249.

Haiman, F. S. (1958). Democratic ethics and the hidden persuaders. *Quarterly Journal of Speech, 44,* 385–392.

Hariman, R. (1995). *Political style: The artistry of power.* Chicago: University of Chicago Press.

Hart, R. P. (1971). The rhetoric of the true believer. *Communication Monographs, 38,* 249–261.

Hayes, J. J. (1976). Gayspeak. *Quarterly Journal of Speech, 62,* 256–266.

Haynes, W. L. (1990). Public speaking pedagogy in the media age. *Communication Education, 39,* 89–102.

Hochmuth, M. K. (1955). The criticism of rhetoric. In M. K. Hochmuth (Ed.), *A history and criticism of American public address* (pp. 1–23). New York: Longman.

Hyde, M. J. (1993). Medicine, rhetoric, and euthanasia: A case study in the workings of a postmodern discourse. *Quarterly Journal of Speech, 79,* 201–224.

Leff, M., & Sachs, A. (1990). Words the most like things: Iconicity and the rhetorical text. *Western Journal of Communication, 54,* 252–273.

Martin, H. H. (1958). The fourth of July oration. *Quarterly Journal of Speech, 44,* 393–401.

McGee, M. C. (1982). A materialist's conception of rhetoric. In R. McKerrow (Ed.), *Explorations in rhetoric: Studies in honor of Douglas Ehninger* (pp. 23–48). Glenview, IL: Scott, Foresman.

McGee, M. C. (1990). Text, context, and the fragmentation of contemporary culture. *Western Journal of Communication, 54,* 274–289.

McKerrow, R. E. (1989). Critical rhetoric: Theory and praxis. *Communication Monographs, 56,* 91–111.

Medhurst, M. J. (1989). Teaching rhetorical criticism to undergraduates: Special editor's introduction. *Communication Education, 38,* 175–177.

Nakayama, T. K. (1997). Les voix de l'autre. *Western Journal of Communication, 61,* 235–242.

National Public Radio (1984). *Audiotapes of great speeches.* Washington, DC: Author.

Nelson, J. S., Megill, A., & McCloskey, D. N. (Eds.). (1987). *The rhetoric of the human sciences: Language and argument in scholarship and public affairs.* Madison: University of Wisconsin Press.

Ong, W. J. (1982). *Orality and literacy: The technologizing of the word.* London: Methuen.

Palczewski, C. H. (1996). Bodies, borders and letters: Gloria Anzaldúa's 'Speaking in tongues: A letter to 3rd world women writers.' *Southern Communication Journal, 62,* 1–16.

Parrish, W. M. (1968). The study of speeches. In W. A. Lindsey (Ed.), *Speech criticism: Methods and materials* (pp. 76–98). Dubuque, IA: William. C. Brown.

Plato (1962). *Gorgias* (W. C. Helmbold, Trans.). Indianapolis: Bobbs-Merrill.

Rogge, E. (1959). Evaluating the ethics of a speaker in a democracy. *Quarterly Journal of Speech, 45,* 419–425.

Thonssen, L., & Baird, A. C. (1948). *Speech criticism: The development of standards for rhetorical appraisal.* New York: Ronald Press.

Wallace, K. R. (1963). The substance of rhetoric: Good reasons. *Quarterly Journal of Speech, 49,* 239–249.

Wander, P. (1983). The ideological turn in modern criticism. *Communication Studies, 34,* 1–18.

Wander, P. (1984). The third persona: An ideological turn in rhetorical theory. *Communication Studies, 35,* 197–211.

Windt, T. O. (1972). The diatribe: Last resort for protest. *Quarterly Journal of Speech, 58,* 1–14.

10

Teaching Persuasion

Roderick P. Hart
University of Texas at Austin

THE UNDERGRADUATE PERSUASION COURSE: WHY?

I have taught an undergraduate course entitled "Principles of Persuasion" virtually every year since 1970. This course is my passion as an undergraduate teacher. Securing the right to teach it was one of only two demands I made during my first job interview in 1970. A guarantee to teach an eventual graduate course in rhetorical criticism was the second. At the time, it did not occur to me to demand an annual salary as well. Luckily, I was hired by a kindly gentleman who, fearing for my family's welfare, also promised to pay me. Needless to say, I was much more sophisticated by the time of my second job interview in 1979. Then, after securing the right to teach the undergraduate persuasion course and the graduate course in criticism, I immediately initiated a salary discussion. No longer was teaching the persuasion course merely an opiate for me and my people. By 1979 I had learned the essential Marxian couplet: Power is good; pay is better.

Still, there is something empowering about teaching persuasion. It is, I feel, the most fundamentally liberating course in the modern communication curriculum. On the first day of class, I observe to my students that all persuaders ask to borrow just a bit of their minds, just for a little while. Persuaders promise to do no damage when borrowing the values essential to their purposes ("Friends, we all like to save money, so ...") and they also promise, irresistibly, that that which people give most easily—their attention—is a munificence that costs them nothing. Brashly, perhaps, I tell my students that my course will return their minds to them. I tell them that the cupsfull of themselves they willingly loan out to teachers and preachers and cheerleaders in the bleachers can lead to an empty emotional cupboard. I tell them that if they keep giving portions of themselves away that there will be nothing left when they need themselves most—when confused, when frightened, when uninformed, or when pressured for a decision. I tell them that persuasion is a science that moves by increments, that it happens most powerfully when it least seems to happen at all. I tell them that the persuaders from afar—the advertisers, the propagandists, the lawyers, and the politicians—must be understood if one is to lead a self-directed life. However, I also tell them that the persuaders close at hand—the lovers, the parents, the friends, and the neighbors—must also be watched like hawks because persuasion is most effective when it is defined as something else: concern, affection, advice, gossip. I tell them about other exempted persuasions—the "guidance" of the local physician, the "selections" of the corner librarian, the "facts" of the nightly newscaster, the "rules" of the imperious bureaucrat—emphasizing that persuasion by any other name is precisely what persuasion most wishes to be. I try to instill a kind of arrogant humility in my students, a mindset that gives them the courage to disassemble rhetoric but also the wisdom never to underestimate it. A tall order, this.

Middle age is a special time of reckoning in one's life. Perhaps because I now find myself in that exquisitely deplorable condition, I use the occasion of this essay to explore why the undergraduate course in persuasion is important. During my career, I have had many reasons for teaching this course and I explore each of these reasons here. However, at the present time I seem to have only one such purpose, a purpose I find myself phrasing in frighteningly grandiose terms. The great sin of youth—impetuosity—and the great sin of old age—banality—seem rather venial compared to that wondrous excess of middle age—grandiosity—and I earnestly anticipate the day when my grandiosity begins to slide irreversibly into the banal. Until then, I shall tell my students that the persuasion course is the most important course they will take in college. I shall tell them this because it is true. It is true, first, because persuasion deals with human motives and because there is nothing harder to understand, or more important to understand, than human motives. It is true, also, because the persuasion course taps a variety of social scientific traditions and concentrates their insights on a single, central problematic: how symbolic action is transformed into social action. It is true, third, because persuasion always involves choices made by people, which is to say it involves the religion of the humanities—ethics. It is true, fourth, because the persuasion course deals with the socially inevita-

ble; one needs biology to be a physician, thermodynamics to be an engineer, and economics to be an industrialist, but one must only breathe to
need to know something of persuasion. It is true, fifth, because unlike other
communication practices (choral reading, informal conversation, group
conferencing, job interviewing, etc.), persuasion emanates from and results
in policy choices, choices that often become instantiated in highly public,
and hence in massively constraining, ways. It is true, last, because the undergraduate persuasion course does something that many college courses
do not do—it makes a difference in students' lives. In this sense, the persuasion course bears the markings of its parent discipline (communication
studies or rhetoric) and thus represents the essential Deweyan end state:
practical knowledge for the practical business of living.

My sense of things is that there are at least three legitimate motives for
teaching an undergraduate course in persuasion. At various times, I have
been motivated by each. The *practitioner's motive* is perhaps the most
dominant of the three, no doubt because it springs directly from the rhetorical tradition itself. This motive treats the persuasion class as a more
advanced, and more specific, version of the basic course in communication skills. In such a persuasion course, students not only learn the principles of persuasion but also test them out in the laboratory of the college
classroom by preparing and delivering speeches, by assembling audiovisual presentations, by redrafting extant persuasive messages, and so
forth. This version of the persuasion course represents the Isocratean
ideal: Knowledge utilized is knowledge retained. Often, the students attracted to such a course are the sorts of people who will eventually persuade for a living—business majors, prelaw students, would-be
politicians, and those sensing a ministerial vocation. Such students have
long been attracted to speech and communication courses and for good
reason: Rhetorical engagement is an ageless bridge across the chasm of
human misunderstanding. More important, persuasion is a noncoercive
method for securing public cooperation and therefore has ample attrac-
tions from a societal perspective. After all, even when they seek public
cooperation on behalf of making Cheetos the snack food of choice, or
Newt Gingrich a favored legislator, or salvationism a county mandate,
persuaders are doing what they have a right to do and, given the options,
their work simply must be encouraged. A course that increases the number of able persuaders in the world might also add to the world's supply of
eloquence, a not unpleasant eventuality. However, the highest calling of
such a course is to make coercion an increasingly remote possibility in human affairs, a good semester's work indeed for a teacher of persuasion.

The *scientist's motive* for teaching the undergraduate persuasion course best captures the Aristotelian ideal of rhetorical education: studying human influence patterns so that interpersonal psychology can be better understood. This has become a powerful motive since the 1950s in the United States, no doubt paralleling the rise in social scientific studies of human behavior. On many campuses, the persuasion course has become a course in applied social psychology and every persuasion textbook on the market, without exception, borrows heavily from this research tradition. Most often, communication researchers are interested in what social psychologists call the *message variable* in the persuasion process and this message orientation heavily flavors many undergraduate persuasion courses taught today. Instructors inspired by the scientist's motive tend to teach their classes dispassionately, covering such topics as audience behavior, source credibility, models of attitude change, media penetration, and the psychology of language. As social scientific research methods have improved in sophistication, the scientist's motive has become increasingly dominant in certain quarters, even though the third- and fourth-generation laboratory studies produced in support of this model have become increasingly arcane. Moreover, the Brobdignaggian list of qualifications impressed on a persuasion teacher by the partiality of these research findings makes pedagogy increasingly difficult. After patiently explaining to students that recency effects obtain only under certain hard-to-specify, not-invariant, methodologically contaminated conditions, the intellectual bang of an instructor's lecture is all too often reduced to a professorial whimper. "Alas," the persuasion teacher says to the students seated in the lecture hall, "real life is often not a tidy thing." To such remarks, college students often respond with a chorus of noisy, pained silences.

There is a sense in which the practitioner's motive "features" the speaker in the persuasion process and a corresponding sense in which the scientist's motive features the message. In sharp contrast, the *consumerist's motive* features the audience: The teacher inspired by such a motive teases out the strategies used by persuaders on persuadees, thereby equipping students with the intellectual resources needed to ward off unwanted influences. To teach with such a rationale is clearly to play defense. This motive best represents the Platonic approach to rhetoric, an approach that decries the utilitarianism of the Isocratean model and the remoteness of the Aristotelian quest. In many senses, Plato was the ultimate consumerist, decrying the sophists of his day for using cookery to distract citizens from the manifestly true. The modern persuasion teacher is normally less sure what such truth looks like and is often ill equipped to launch a search for it during a 16-week semester. However, the Platonic spirit of critique still remains in many speech and communication departments and still inspires the consumerist's teaching against persuasion (as opposed to the practitioner's teaching of persuasion and the scientist's teaching about persuasion). Typically, the consumerist makes four central arguments in a persuasion class: (a) there is a great deal of rhetoric in the everyday world, more than most people notice and probably more than is good for them; (b) the most fundamental persuasive move made by persuaders is to declare themselves nonpersuaders; (c) a given piece of persuasion achieves its greatest social utility when persuadees accept it knowingly; and (d) the only right more fundamental in a democracy than the freedom to persuade is the freedom not to be persuaded. The consumerist tends to fetishize this latter proposition, often becoming hortatory in class when warning students about the beguiling rhetorics of the day. Normally, students smile pleasantly at such hectoring, tacitly appreciating the storm warnings being signaled but also faintly resenting the avuncular tones in which they are sometimes cast.

The three motives I have sketched out here are not mutually incompatible and many undergraduate persuasion courses are inspired by a mix of them, but most courses tend to emphasize one of these motives and the resulting course profiles differ considerably. Put reductionistically, the practitioner becomes something of a coach, the scientist something of an oracle, and the consumerist something of a crybaby. It is this latter persona that has walked into the lecture hall with me during the last decade or so. I did not summon up it up intentionally. Rather, it emerged as I matured as a teacher and, I suppose, as I aged as a person. But I can fix its onset even more precisely. The scientist's motive waned within me when Jim Jones persuaded more than 900 persons to their deaths in November 1978. Reading the accounts of that incident, I quickly discovered that all too many of these slaughtered innocents had graduated from U. S. colleges and universities. It became apparent to me that having an education or being generally informed provided no necessary antidote to the poison of crazed charismatics. Rather, the Jones incident made me existentially aware that it took a particular kind of knowledge, rhetorical knowledge, to keep such maniacs at bay and that it took certain kinds of instincts, rhetorical instincts, to fight off such maniacs when they could be kept at bay no longer. All of this sounds rather melodramatic, I suppose, and altogether too maudlin for we sophisticates of the academy. However, middle age causes one to cast about for some grand purpose and keeping my students out of the clutches of the next Jim Jones gave me mine. Naturally, it gives me pause to share such personal thoughts in a professional publication and I am not unaware that they could be parodied as some sort of ersatz born-again experience. Still, the Jim Jones incident helped me to learn that source credibility could no longer be treated as a mere variable in some elegant stochastic equation. At least it could not be treated thusly in my clssroom.

My rejection of the practitioner's motive had both practical and political roots. For one thing, it eventually dawned on me that the typical speech or communication department already taught productivity skills in many of its courses and that it only rarely taught receptivity skills. Isocrates was being handsomely accorded his due in the curriculum whereas the critical faculties championed by Plato and Augustine were being given short shrift. Speech and communication students could speak cleverly, it was clear, but what did they listen to, I asked, and did they do so cleverly, I asked further. Little and no, I concluded. I also concluded that any academic discipline teaching an art as powerful as rhetoric also had an obligation to teach techniques for falsifying that art. That is, by analogy, if professors of nuclear engineering can be said to be responsible for the building of nuclear power plants, then so too must they be responsible for inventing safe methods of nuclear waste disposal. The analogy is an imperfect one, as are all analogies, but if speech and communication courses can be said to give aid and comfort and skill to tomorrow's corporate scions or to its established prelates or to the look-alikes in U.S. politics or to those whose advocacy skills protect the affluent in court, then so too must such courses educate the listeners who must sort out the lies and near lies and not lies of these spellbinders. Power tends to collect around rhetoric, after all, and money collects there also. At least in Western democracies, strategic cleverness often belongs to the comfortably walled in rather than to the painfully walled out. Moreover, even the most elementary sort of arithmetic will determine that there are really very few speakers speaking these days and that they are doing so for a limited number of institutionally entrenched reasons. At the same time, there are many, many listeners in the world and their listening is largely untrained; also, these listeners have a panorama of personal, cultural, and economic needs that typically go unmet when they listen. Must the field of communication serve only the few, the speakers? Must it not also educate the many, the audiences? No and yes, I concluded.

For a variety of reasons, then, I found myself becoming a consumerist many years after Ralph Nader did so with Chevrolets. I adopted this posture tentatively, knowing that my students must be given the freedom to become better practitioners (and better informed scientists) and knowing, too, that in my zeal to expose the vagaries of persuasion that I must not become so zealous that I myself become a target for my students' newly developed deconstructive urges. Classroom cant is merely an upscale sort of cant, after all, and thus the persuasion teacher's truest ally in the lecture hall is a healthy sense of self-doubt, and a willingness to question all orthodoxies, even the most personal. More positively stated, the undergraduate persuasion course might best be thought of as a place for showing students that life is a blank canvas for their artistry and not merely a cramped place filled with the etchings of the wise and the powerful. Helping students learn to listen critically is therefore a high calling for the undergraduate teacher of persuasion. To wrest intellectual and emotional power from persuaders and to offer these gifts instead to students is at once a depowering act and an empowering act. Conceivably, on reflection, these same students may choose to return this power to traditional persuaders. However, if they do so on reflection, the teacher of persuasion will have done his or her job well.

Other than idiosyncratic preference, is there one good reason to prefer the consumerist model? Are there two? Yes and yes:

1. There are technological reasons to be a consumerist. The United States is almost single-handedly responsible for having pioneered the most sophisticated methods for creating and delivering persuasive messages known to humankind. Buoyed by such traditions as political rabble-rousing and pamphleteering in the 18th century, religious evangelism and popular lecturing in the 19th century, and mass entrepreneurism and social mobilization in the 20th century, the United States has always been a hotbed for vigorous rhetorical exchange. Many of its institutions—the Congress, the marketplace, the mass media—have become shrines to the persuasive arts. In a free society, of course, all of this is permitted, and indeed encouraged. In a free society, people cannot be made to hear, but in a free society people can be made to listen—if persuaders are clever enough to understand human susceptibilities. For that reason if no other, the persuasion teacher must stand as a bulwark against flackery. Surely any society that has pioneered the 20-second political spot or the computerized telephone solicitation or the personalized mass mailer or the product-centered cartoon show or the socially relevant sitcom or the corporate-cozy theme park or the selling of kitchenware-cum-conviviality also has a responsibility for defending its citizenry against these unseen persuasions. It might even be said that teaching people how to consume persuasion intelligently is something of a patriotic obligation, but perhaps that would sound too much like rhetoric.

2. There are humanistic reasons to be a consumerist. I would like to resurrect an argument here that I made almost two decades ago when asked to comment on new directions in the teaching of human communication. At that time, enrollments in speech and communication classes were beginning to burgeon nationally and students were simultaneously turning away from traditional studies in the humanities. Too loftily, perhaps, I warned that a new Philistinism was stalking the college campus and that that placed special burdens on all teachers in the field:

> If speech communication teachers are to fill the gap created by the New
> Philistinism, they must become more vigorous in teaching the principles
> of human reasoning because their students are not taking sufficient
> course work in logic. Teachers of speech communication must demand
> that their students write, rewrite, and write again because these students
> are not taking advanced courses in English either. Teachers of speech
> communication must expose their students to the world of political con-
> troversy, to the techniques of problem-solving through discussion, and to
> the infinite diversity of human auditors because these students are surely
> not taking extensive work in political science, philosophy, or anthropol-
> ogy.... It is quite possible that my students' inability to understand subtle
> rhetoric when they see it results from their lack of knowledge of the com-
> plex human motivations depicted in that unread Shakespearean play or
> from their unfamiliarity with such historical personages as Joe McCarthy
> and Huey Long. Their untutored critical sensibilities, dulled by a pablum of
> mediated extravaganzas, surely are part of the problem as well. (Hart,
> 1981, pp. 40–41)

At the turn of the century, I see no essential change in these enrollment patterns. Today's students are still woefully uninformed about history and so
they are susceptible to the next Adolf Hitler appearing among them. Today's
students still do not understand the subtleties of human language and so they
can be seduced by the practiced evasions of an O. J. Simpson. Today's students are still ignorant of foreign tongues and international affairs and so they
find appeal in the provincialism of a Jesse Helms. As a college teacher of the
undergraduate course in persuasion, I therefore find myself trying to do in
one semester what the nation's school systems have not been doing for my
students for the last 20 years and what they have not been doing for themselves either. I choose not to bemoan this fate. My students, at least, know
that they do not know and that normally makes teaching them a pleasure.
Imagining what my students would have, however, if they had more of the
humanistic heritage tends to make one wistful in the odd moment.

There are perhaps other good reasons to adopt the consumerist model in
the persuasion classroom but these two reasons are sufficient for me. They
are not sufficient for everyone. Some teachers still feel the weight of tradition
in these matters, arguing that their only legitimate role in the classroom is that
of practitioner's assistant. Having emerged from that same tradition, I have
great respect for this viewpoint even though it is no longer my own—at least
not when I am in the undergraduate persuasion class. I also respect the scientist's pedagogical motives and hope that I have not veered so far to the left
that I have lost sight of a center that holds intellectually. In any event, although I have listened to these alternatives respectfully, I am still resolved to
make unhappy little consumers out of my students.

However, a friend and colleague, Celese Condit of the University of Georgia, has warned me of a subtle, yet grave, danger in the consumerist model and it is a danger that bothers me not a little. Such a model, she argued, could quickly usher in a post-Nietzchean era in which distrust reigns supreme, an era in which no idea is allowed preeminence and hence an era in which any idea—even subhuman ideas—would suffice. She warned me that what I am here calling consumerism undermines trust in trust itself, breeds a kind of dissatisfied quiescence in people, and thereby deenergizes social change. She argued that education should build ideas, not destroy them, and that a teacher who leaves nothing standing at the end of a semester leaves his or her students unprotected against the cold blasts of nihilism. From what I have been able to deduce, Condit herself operates as something of an activist and practitioner in the classroom, teaching students the technique of rhetorical influence so that they, perversely, can turn the tables on those who now control the rhetorical establishment.

I greatly admire Condit's verve, a person who blends scholarly excellence and pedagogical commitment as well as anyone I know. As a result, her critique of consumerism gives me special pause. Finally, however, her model cannot be my model. In many senses, our friendly argument parallels the more acrimonious disputes waged between the deconstructionists and the Marxists. The former have raised semantic suspicion to an art form, asserting that the weight of all messages, all ideologies, and all certainties cannot ultimately be supported by the frail linguistic foundations underpinning them. As critics, their goal is to show the *aporia* in human meaning; to make a reader content with discontentedness; and to demonstrate that no political, religious, or social dialogue can ever be a completed dialogue. The deconstructionist is therefore a searcher.

The Marxists deplore such nonsense and are concerned to show how certain exploitative belief systems work their ways into human affairs (and into human locutions in particular), thereby reestablishing certain establishments and restabilizing what are often completely arbitrary stabilities. As critics (and presumably as teachers), the Marxists' job is to replace such corruptions with more socially enlightened modes of thought and action. Marxists use their insights to undermine both repressive ideas and repressive political systems. The Marxist is therefore a savior.

All of this may seem rather far afield from the humble little undergraduate course in persuasion. My argument, however, is that a dose of deconstruction might not be an altogether inappropriate medicine for what ails today's undergraduates. What ails them is this: excessive respect for formal authorities, insufficient curiosity about language forms, heightened regard for scientized solutions, too much reverence for traditional orthodoxies—in short, too much believing and too little knowing. My students' intellectual health would be especially improved by a helping of the deconstructionists' critical playfulness and an extra helping of their faith that all "isms"—nihilism included—will ultimately betray themselves. Thus, I will continue to pop my students' balloons knowing that, no matter what I say to them, they will work out their own ideologies later in life; as their teacher, I only insist that they do not announce any final versions of these ideologies during their semester with me. For the moment, at least, I will not worry about a post-Nietzchean universe developing on the University of Texas campus because of my persuasion course. Rather, I trust my students' natural inclinations to disagree with one another. I also trust in the stimulative value of a rigorous skepticism—and of the respect for the ironic and the tolerance of the absurd that it entails. I trust, mostly, in the critical mind's wondrous capacity to call a spade a spade and a rhetoric a rhetoric, to depuff puffery and to make mortals out of gods, and to maintain a tenacious resolve that we shall not all fall, lemminglike, into the sea.

REFERENCES

Hart, R. P. (1981). Speech communication as the new humanities. In G. Friedrich (Ed.), *Education in the '80s: Speech communication* (pp. 35–41). Washington, DC: National Education Association.

11

Teaching Organizational Communication

Linda L. Putnam
Charles R. Conrad
Texas A&M University

During the past decade, interest in organizational communication has mushroomed. In 1988, about one half of all communication departments offered one undergraduate course in organizational communication; by 1995, approximately three fourths of all departments offered undergraduate training in this area. Roughly one half of all departments report an increased demand for courses in organizational communication (Treadwell & Applbaum, 1996). The basic course in organizational communication has emerged as "an important vehicle for reflecting the status of our knowledge of the field" (Pace, Michal-Johnson, & Mills, 1990, p. 49).

At the same time, the field has experienced a marked change. Early pedagogy in organizational communication applied extant theories of interpersonal communication, group processes, and information exchange to organizational situations. The development of communication skills was a central part of most courses. Underlying research drew on traditional social scientific perspectives to examine problems in formal, vertical communication or the relations between key variables and superior–subordinate interaction, for example, perceptual congruency, climate, and feedback.

By the mid-1980s, however, organizational communication scholarship shifted to an interpretive and critical turn. The publication of Putnam and

141

Pacanowsky's (1983) *Communication and Organization: An Interpretive Approach* signaled a fundamental change in the way that researchers conceptualized organizations and communicative processes. The dynamic qualities of information processing, symbolic interaction, and meaning creation not only became central elements of research, they were treated as constitutive of organizations themselves. Research and pedagogy moved away from viewing organizations as entities or containers of information to treating them as processes formed by communication and representative of cultures, relationships, images, and texts (Putnam, Phillips & Chapman, 1996).

Recent approaches to organizational communication equate communication and organization with discursive acts that not only constitute but also become the organizing process, for example, treating genres and conversations as organizational texts or examining access to voice as workplace democracy. Critical theories of organizations and organizational–society relationships have gained prominence in the past decade and moved the field into macro-research, increasing the scope of study beyond micro-communication.

Pedagogy in organizational communication has experienced similar changes. By 1995 only 29% of the respondents in Treadwell and Applbaum's (1996) survey listed "basic communication skills" as the central thrust of the course. Rather, the two foci that guided curriculum design in 83% of the departments were "to provide an overview of organizational theories and concepts" and "to help students analyze problems in organizing." In the past decade new topics received increased attention within the course.

Given changes in the scope of the course, it is not surprising that "covering everything" and "students' lack of organizational experience" are two key problems that instructors face (Treadwell & Applbaum, 1996). Covering everything in the course includes the challenges of exposing students not only to literature in the field but to changing demographics in organizational employment, issues in globalization, new organizational forms, and the ramifications of a new social contract with a temporary workforce. Organizational communication instructors must undertake this task with students who have limited work experience.

This chapter examines ways of teaching organizational analysis and critical thinking to students who have limited exposure to organizations. It explores these issues through discussing student assumptions, describing course content and objectives, and reviewing instructional resources and strategies.

MISGUIDED ASSUMPTIONS ABOUT
ORGANIZATIONAL COMMUNICATION

Helping students understand the complexities of organizational communication is difficult because most students have limited organizational experiences. Although a number of students have held part-time jobs in high school and college, they typically have only a modicum of information about the larger repertoires of organizational communication (Jablin, 1987). In fact, many students with part-time jobs have very distant communication relationships with their coworkers and their supervisors (Greenberger, Steinberg, Vaux, & McAuliffe, 1980). Moreover, when students enter the workplace, they often expect their first jobs to be orderly and systematic and are surprised to find the chaos and ambiguity that characterizes much of organizational life (Eisenberg & Goodall, 1997). As organizations have evolved rapidly in the past decade, they are often shocked by changes in competitive environments, the redefinition of careers and employee contracts, and the continuous learning required to succeed. Thus, one of the challenges in teaching organizational communication is finding ways to help students conceptualize the dynamics and complexities of organizations. In effect, students must be trained to bring a communication mindset to bear on organizational components, principles, and theories.

With limited experience as full-time organizational members, students cling to a number of naive assumptions about organizational communication. Students typically seek prescriptions or "five easy steps" to address complex organizational issues. Although instructors can generate guidelines, suggestions, and options for effective communication, variations in organizational cultures and situations make it difficult to prescribe communicative behaviors. For instance, research suggests that the adoption of new communication technology is more successful when members of an employee's social network use this innovation (Fulk, Schmitz, & Steinfield, 1990); however, students need to understand that media skills, task characteristics, and formal training also impact on the sustained use of new technology.

Students also assume that communication is a panacea for solving organizational ills. For example, they might think that the marketing and production departments can reduce their long-standing conflicts of interest through frequent and open communication. More communication, however, typically exacerbates rather than lessens deep-seated conflicts. The panacea of more communication is particularly problematic in organizations because of the sheer volume of information flow, the use of authority and status differences, and the need to understand how and what is communicated at a particular point in time. A similar naive notion is that good ideas will get adopted and disseminated if communication channels are open and frequently used. Good ideas can get lost amidst managerial overload and subsequent inertia, run against the value system or ideology of the organization, or be blocked through political expediency. Although students recognize that power and politics play a key role in organizational decision making, they often minimize the pervasiveness of the political factions that influence daily interactions.

In addition to naive assumptions, students tend to blame individuals for complex problems. Even though individual competencies play key roles in shaping organizational events, complex dilemmas typically penetrate into multiple levels and work units. Many students continue to view organizations as comprised of individuals rather than as systems of coordinated actions in which problems are inevitable. Organizational problem solving, then, entails disentangling message patterns and events rather than simply disciplining or firing a "troublemaker."

Finally, students typically hold an orthodox view of authority in organizations. Issuing legitimate challenges, questioning ethical and moral issues of organizational life, and adopting a proactive rather than submissive attitude toward authority is unconscionable for most students. Students rarely think about resistance as being a part of organizational life. Discussion of issues such as bending the rules, secretarial "bitching," and humor in the workplace introduce micropractices of resistance (Hatch, 1997: Pringle, 1988). Raising issues such as challenging policies, offering alternatives, and providing opportunities for voice get students thinking about resistance on a broader scale. Thus, in addition to helping students understand the organizational communication processes, instructors must challenge these assumptions, heighten organizational analysis, raise issues of power and resistance, and develop maturity in taking action in complex situations.

COURSE CONTENT AND OBJECTIVES

The content of the basic organizational communication course has stabilized during the past decade. Most courses include units on historical traditions, organizational theories, and contemporary topics in the field. Some classes examine these arenas through a specialized lens, such as organizational culture (Bantz, 1993; Kreps, 1990; Pepper, 1995); networks (Stohl, 1995), communication relationships (Albrecht & Bach, 1997), and technological change (Andrews & Herschel, 1996).

Syllabi typically begin with a general introduction to communication, move into a review of organizational theories and theorists, and then cover a wide array of traditional topics, such as organizational structure, leadership, network analysis, conflict management, and decision making. Most courses also include discussions of topics that have become standard during the past decade; namely, organizational culture, power and politics, information technology, and gender and diversity. Instructors add variations to these topics by including such themes as romantic relationships at work, sexual harassment, organizational image and identity, self-organizing systems, management of ambiguity and paradox, workplace democracy, and social support.

Most courses center on two major goals: helping students become better analysts of organizational events and developing students' abilities to think critically about organizational situations. As they become better analysts of organizational events, students learn how communication underlies every domain of organizational life including the operations of teams, leader-member relationships, organizational politics, culture and value systems of organizations, adoption of information technology, customer relations, and organizational crises.

Gaining awareness of the complexity of organizational communication helps students learn how to minimize the ill effects of organizational constraints. For example, if an organization wants to set up a system of self-regulated teams to empower workers, students need to know that communication among team members often evolves into a system of concertive control that exerts undue constraints on members (Barker, 1993, Barker & Cheney, 1994). Developing a system of participation based on the goals and feelings of employees provides an alternative to the concertive process of team-based management (Cheney, 1995).

Once students understand the complexity and possible ill effects of organizational functions, they need to develop skills to think critically about organizational situations. Critical thinking is an ongoing process that occurs while monitoring communication activities as they evolve, following hunches, interpreting events, and taking actions. Training in critical thinking occurs through providing students with exemplars of organizational events and asking them to probe what values and beliefs underlie the situation, what dilemmas or tensions characterize the circumstance, whose interests are represented and how they are represented, who is excluded and why, how the situation is being defined or labeled, what codes or ethical practices apply to the situation, and what options exist for taking action.

From this grounding, three general instructional objectives emerge. The first one is to encourage students to develop multiple perspectives for understanding organizational events (Daniels, Spiker, & Papa, 1997; Miller, 1995; Pace & Faules, 1994). This approach centers on the belief that organizational members operate from implicit, if not explicit, theories of organizational communication. By helping students to understand their own perspectives and exposing them to alternative orientations, the course offers students repertoires for making sense of organizational events. A second general aim is to help students understand the problems, paradoxes, and changes in organizational life (see, e. g., Conrad, 1994; Daniels et al., 1997; Eisenberg & Goodall, 1997). Through the use of a variety of cases and organizational exemplars, students are encouraged to develop flexibility, to balance the tensions of need for control with need for change, and to accept paradox and ambiguity as routine rather than extraordinary occurrences. A third objective focuses on developing communication competencies for appropriate behavior in organizations (Jablin, Cude, House, Lee, & Roth, 1994; Shockley-Zalabak, 1991). Competencies entail both behavioral and cognitive arenas of performance and encompass skills, values, and sensitivities to different situations. For example, training in communication competencies focuses on the knowledge for appropriate rules and norms of behavior as well as on developing perspective-taking abilities to understand when and how to apply these rules.

INSTRUCTIONAL RESOURCES
IN ORGANIZATIONAL COMMUNICATION

To provide students with perspectives for analyzing and interpreting organizational events, instructors draw on a variety of techniques for class discussions and intensive learning. Most instructors rely on faculty lectures and instructor-led discussions as the primary teaching methods in organizational communication (Treadwell & Applbaum, 1996), especially for large classes. Lectures are effective in achieving lower level learning, but they are less effective than are other techniques in teaching analytical and critical thinking skills. They allow the instructor to cover a broad range of topics in a short time and to maintain control of the teaching situation. Because the maximum time frame during which students can absorb new material is approximately 30 minutes, instructors should blend teaching strategies—for example, moving from lecture to discussion to media illustration (Book, chap. 23, this volume).

As class size increases, the number of options for blending teaching strategies narrows. Choosing focused cases, breaking the class into smaller groups to discuss a media clip, having students present position statements at the beginning of class, and developing feedback loops with students provide a blend of teaching strategies and counter the ill effects of large classes. Encouraging students to stay after class to discuss issues, to use e-mail to send messages, and to respond candidly to midterm course evaluations facilitates the development of feedback loops. Instructors also should strive to create learning sets that adapt to the cognitive limits of the teaching situation. For example, a professor might begin with a 20-minute minilecture that introduces new concepts, follow it with a media clip or analysis of a case study, and then conclude with another minilecture that summarizes focal concepts and key issues.

Hence, techniques such as case studies, media clips, novels, and films, can supplement lecturing and class discussions. Intensive learning techniques, in turn, apply theory and course concepts to experiential exercises, such as simulations, role playing, and field investigations.

Strategies for Supplementing Lecture and Class Discussions

One strategy for developing students' skills as organizational analysts is to begin class with a stimulus that encapsulates an organizational situation, for example, a narrative that depicts a sequence of events of key players or a cartoon that embodies key organizational concepts. The stimulus must contain enough information to allow students to make meaningful judgments about the situation. Fortunately, for organizational communication instructors, a wealth of stimuli exists from a variety of sources. Course syllabi and instructor manuals indicate that case studies are one of the most prevalent resources for teaching the course.[1] Approximately three fourths of all departments included in the Treadwell and Applbaum (1996) survey used case studies. These sources are supplemented with newspaper articles and cartoons, novels, television series, educational videos, and films. The key to using these sources effectively is (a) to keep course concepts and theories central to the discussion of the exemplars, using resources to enrich rather than to replace core content material; and (b) to choose them in accordance with the pedagogical format of the class. Some resources are better for instructor-led discussions, whereas others fit small group interactions or written analyses.

Communication scholars typically embrace the practice that organizational texts are open for multiple interpretations to emerge. Some case stud-

[1]The authors express appreciation to the following organizational communication faculty who sent copies of syllabi for teaching the basic organizational communication course: Larry Browning, University of Texas; Patrice M. Buzzanell, Northern Illinois University; Michael W. Kramer, University of Missouri-Columbia; Dan Modall, Ohio University; Craig Scott, University of Texas; Patty Sotirin, Michigan Technological Institute; and Cynthia Stohl, Purdue University.

ies, films, and televised reports are exceptionally open in that they generate a wide variety of interpretations, including ones that contradict each other. Instructors can also open up a text by drawing attention to neglected information, questioning the foundations of interpretations and recommendations, and introducing perspectives that students overlook.

If, however, the goal for a class session is to illustrate a key theoretical construct, then unstructured, lively discussions may obscure more than they illuminate the course content. Using cases to illuminate organizational experiences may require different types of student interactions. Continually focusing the discussion on a key concept or a particular theoretical stance may close off readings of the text. The key is selecting the goals for a class session, choosing resource strategies based on these goals, and adopting one's communication strategies in class discussions to further these goals.[2]

Published Case Studies.   Many organizational communication textbooks include short case examples followed by discussion questions for each chapter (see e.g., Albrecht & Bach, 1997; Conrad & Poole, 1998; Daniels et al., 1997; Eisenberg & Goodall, 1997). A case study is a description or account of a sequence of events that confronts an individual, work unit, or organizational system (Apple, 1986). A typical case summarizes an organizational situation, depicts the actions of the key players, explains their perceptions, describes the sequence of events leading up to the situation, and identifies reactions to the situation (Kreps & Lederman, 1985). Communication-oriented cases capture language, symbols, argument, narratives, and interaction processes of organizational events (Sypher, 1997). Discussions of case studies work most effectively by posing questions prior to the class period in which the case is assigned and pointing to the subtle communication behaviors within the case.

In addition to textbooks, three edited collections focus specifically on organizational communication cases: *Case Studies in Organizational Communication 1 and 2* (Sypher, 1990, 1997) and *Communicating in Organizations: A Casebook* (Peterson, 1994). Other edited volumes draw from organizational behavior (Daft & Dahlen, 1984; Frost, Mitchell, & Nord, 1997; Ritti & Funkhouser, 1994) and organizational sociology (Kanter & Stein, 1979) to address theories and concepts on a wide array of topics, including secrecy, diversity, ethics, joint ventures, and international

---

[2]Perhaps the most important single step in managing the case discussion is to develop a set of "teaching notes" that include the following: (a) a brief synopsis of the stimulus, (b) a statement of pedagogical goals for the class, (c) links to theoretical constructs in the course, (d) a substantive analysis of the stimulus, and (e) a brief bibliography of further readings (Barnes, Christensen, & Hansen, 1994; Christensen, Garvin, & Sweet, 1991; Welty, 1989).

organizational life. Martin and Meyerson (1997) developed an eight-case package, *Link.Com Teaching Cases*, that focuses on the problems of female executives who have broken through the glass ceiling and struggled to change organizational culture. Even though textbooks and edited volumes link cases to particular topics, most cases are multipurpose; that is, instructors can use them to explain an array of topics and to analyze a number of organizational communication concepts.

In addition, popular books, such as Terkel's (1972) *Working* and Garson's (1975) *All the Livelong Day*, can easily be adapted to a case study format. As extended cases, books provide rich material for documenting organizational practices and raising awareness of the likelihood of situations (see, e. g., Freiberg & Freiberg's [1996] story of Southwest Airlines in the book, *Nuts!* and Tompkin's [1993] analysis of the rise, fall, and revival of NASA in *Organizational Communication Imperatives)*. As a resource for teaching analytical and critical thinking skills, case studies serve as alternative ways of knowing about organizational experiences. They teach rhetorical principles about evidence and argument, enhance a student's perspective-taking skills, and show how social knowledge is constructed, not discovered (Sypher, 1997).

Newspaper Articles, Cartoons, Novels, Television, and Film.
Less conventional sources such as newspapers, novels, and television can provide excellent cases and case comparisons that have an added advantage of being current and generally familiar to students. Students can submit case exemplar material from *The Wall Street Journal* or *The New York Times*. Syndicated strips like "Non Sequitur" or "Dilbert" provide quick examples to stimulate thought or discussion. Instructors can display them on projectors to prepare students for course topics as they enter the room and they can be used for examination questions. For instance, the antics of "Ratbert, Evil Director of Human Relations" provides a excellent stimulus for discussing organizational power and politics, and "Dilbert" cartoons on relationships between engineering and marketing departments demonstrate the subtle nuances of intergroup conflict.

Novels and narrative accounts such as *The Soul of a New Machine* (Kidder, 1981), *Something Happened* (Heller, 1975), *Catch-22* (Heller, 1962), and *Death of a Salesman* (Miller, 1976) capture organizational experiences for students to analyze and interpret. Indeed, reading fiction can advance our understanding of organizations by providing tacit knowledge, moral insights, and challenges to the rational-bureaucratic models (Czarniawska-Joerges & de Monthoux, 1994; Phillips, 1995). Episodes of such television series as *L. A. Law*, *Wings*, *Seinfeld*, and *NYPD Blue* drama-tize organizational life, thereby providing exemplars of how the media shape expectations of organizational communication (Vande Berg & Trujillo, 1989). Miller, Mattson, and Stage (1995) recommended ways to use these television shows to depict network roles and patterns of the char-acters. Even unlikely television series treat organizational issues in ways that can be used to stimulate class discussions. For cxamplc, *The Drew Carey Show* and *Dinosaurs* now available on videotape, address issues like downsizing, sexual harassment, and organizational treatment of the envi-ronment in unique ways.

A similar array of case studies is available through television specials and full-length feature movies. The Public Broadcasting System (PBS) fea-tures Tom Peters in at least one special each year—from "In Search of Ex-cellence" to "Coping With Chaos" to "Liberation Management." A catalog of titles and descriptions of PBS programs is available at www.pbs.com. Kanter's (1980) "The Tale of O," uses the notations of "X" and "O" to illus-trate the problem of tokenism in organizational communication. Television news magazines such as *Frontline*, *The Newshour with Jim Lehrer*, *Nightly Business Report*, and *Adam Smith's World* feature provocative exposes on organizational issues. Whenever an organizational story breaks, news mag-azines provide a short professionally produced report and debate within days of the event. Popular movies portray real-life scenarios of organiza-tional communication. Recent examples abound, including the portrayal of the human resources approach in *Modern Times*, studies of leadership in *Nightmare in Christmas Town*, work team communication in *Real Genius*, the documentary of a plant closing in *Roger and Me*, and the impact of downsizing in *Glen Garry, Glen Ross*.

Each of these stimuli can be used to illustrate concepts in conventional ways or they can be deconstructed as texts that trigger alternative meanings. For example, the expose of Disneyland in "In Search of Excellence" offers an extended tribute to the power of communicating organizational values to the workforce. It is also an excellent example of unobtrusive control and the illu-sion of choice. This picture of Disneyland can be contrasted with Van Maanen's (1991) portrayal of "the smile factory" or Smith and Eisenberg's (1987) study of the family metaphor and labor strife at Disneyland. Similarly, *An Evening With Tom Peters,* a PBS program based on Peters' and Austin's (1994) *A Passion for Excellence*, features a number of firms that have experi-enced economic decline or have been implicated in illcgal activity (e. g., Leonard's Dairy or Perdue Farms Chicken). Both published and media cases invite oppositional or resistance readings that provide opportunities to teach students critical analysis of organizational discourse.

Intensive Teaching Strategies

Printed and media cases aid in applying theory to practice without involving extensive time or resources. Other pedagogical techniques immerse students in real or hypothetical organizational experiences, through guest speakers, internships and cooperative learning, role playing, simulations, and field research. Guest speakers provide exciting, firsthand accounts of communication processes in organizations. Organizational leaders, human resource personnel, and employees in the rank and file might serve as speakers. Nontraditional students who are enrolled in the class offer less formal accounts of organizational experiences, as do students who conduct field research projects. Extended internships and co-op experiences immerse students in the day-to-day dilemmas of organizational life. However, these techniques require intensive commitments of institutional time and resources and are typically limited to a small number of students. Simulations, role playing, and field research approximate this type of intense learning experience in the classroom.

Role Playing.   Role-playing exercises require students to enact organizational situations within specific guidelines and persona; hence, students dramatize a specific organizational incident (Falcione, 1977). Even though the roles and circumstances of the incidents are structured, the interaction among the participants emerges spontaneously. Role-playing exercises serve three primary functions. First, they give students an opportunity to practice specific organizational communication skills not typically encountered in classrooms. For example, in enacting performance appraisal interviews, students adapt interviewing techniques to a company's evaluation procedures. Second, role-playing exercises can be used to demonstrate effective or appropriate communicative behaviors in organizations. Finally, role-playing exercises provide concrete exemplars of abstract concepts. Enacting a job assignment conflict between a superior and subordinate helps class members identify messages that exemplify influence strategies.

Approximately 50% of the 285 respondents included in the Treadwell and Applbaum (1996) survey used role-playing techniques to teach this course. Samples of role-playing exercises are available in organizational communication textbooks, in teacher's manuals, and in such supplementary texts as *The Role Play Technique* (Maier, Solem, & Maier, 1975) and *Roleplaying in Business and Industry* (Corsini, Shaw, & Blake, 1961). Supplementary texts also provide guidelines for planing the exercise, orienting participants to their roles, enacting the scenes, and conducting feedback discussions.

The success of a role-playing activity is dependent in part on a student's ability to enact the role effectively. Instructor sensitivity to the interpersonal skills of class members aids in matching participants to role-playing demands, thus promoting a successful performance. Repeated practice also reduces the tendency to overact as well as the anxiety of performing. In evaluating role playing, teachers tend to focus on a student's performance, which often has little relation to the ultimate goal of the exercise. Rather than centering on performance, the instructor might ask students to write reaction papers that apply course concepts to the appropriateness of the interaction. In addition, several students might observe and record communicative behaviors and make presentations on their findings to the class.

Organizational Simulations.   Unlike role playing, students can enact the entire organization in a simulation. Students are assigned to organizational positions and asked to execute routine tasks. They receive job descriptions, but they do not enact a scenario as they do in role playing. Rather, role occupants bring their own personalities and skills to the simulated organization. Compared to role playing, simulations increase the complexity, sophistication, and involvement of students by immersing them in an organizational setting.

Organizational simulations may be highly structured such as HI FLI FIREWORKS (Pacanowsky, Farace, Monge, & Russell, 1977) and SIMCORP (Lederman & Stewart, 1983) or they may rely on participants to create the structure, job functions, job design, rules, regulations, and evaluation process. Simulations require varying amounts of class time, for example, HI FLI FIREWORKS may run for only 90 minutes, whereas SIMCORP is designed for at least 8 weeks or for the entire semester.

Students may find the initial stages of a simulation confusing and anxiety ridden. As they negotiate their roles and learn what other employees expect of them, anxiety is reduced and commitment to the organization increases. Commitment typically reaches its peak when an organizational crisis occurs and a conflict breaks out between work units or departments. Simulations require instructors to commit considerable time and effort before the activity begins, but while the simulation is running, the instructor typically assumes a passive role, allowing events to unfold naturally.

In the debriefing, the instructor must manage emotional reactions triggered by the simulation, must keep discussions of member behaviors at a descriptive rather than an evaluative level, and must analyze the strengths and weaknesses of the organization by applying course concepts. Even though the work involved in conducting an organizational simulation is great, students receive invaluable learning through sharing common experiences, becoming aware of the complexities and subtleties of organizing, wedding organizational communication to practice, and improving critical thinking and communication skills.

Field Research.   In field research, unlike role playing and simulations, students gain first hand insights about organizational situations while assuming the role of a detached observer. Field research is typically conducted as individual or group class projects. Students gain experience in administering, analyzing, interpreting, and reporting data collected to examine specific concepts. Through interviews, questionnaires, and participant observation, students apply theory and course concepts to an analysis of organizational events. The instructor could require a specific research report or use the field projects as an exercise, for example, collecting company logos, interviewing team members, or talking with newcomers in organizations. Students can locate stockholder reports, organizational newsletters, Web pages, and press releases for research projects. They can conduct cultural analyses of their own universities, student organizations, or local churches. The instructor could evaluate written reports, oral presentations to the company or the class, or student evaluations of the research experience.

Although the value of this activity is clear, a teacher must weigh his or her commitment and responsibility to external organizations against the students' knowledge of organizational communication and their research competencies. Practical considerations such as anonymity of participants, confidentiality of results, financial responsibility, and the scope of the project must be negotiated with the participating organizations. Also, the instructor must be prepared to serve as an intermediary, consultant, public relations agent, sounding board, or any other role that is needed to facilitate the research process and to maintain community goodwill for the department and the university.

CONCLUSION

Approximately 80% of our adult lives are spent interfacing with members of organizations. Whether we are in positions of management, are managed by others, or are consumers of products and services, communication is vital to the process of organizing. An organization is not some mysterious entity that acts in a uniform manner. Rather it consists of the messages, information processing, symbols, and interaction patterns of its participants. Communication and discursive practices not only constitute organizations; they become the organizing process.

Teachers of organizational communication aim to help students become better analysts of organizational events, to observe organizational reality through multiple perspectives, and to think critically about organizational situations. Through applying theory and concepts to course activities, instructors create a learning environment in which alternative perspectives of organizational reality emerge. Courses in organizational communication then should help students understand problems and paradoxes of organizational communication, the changing features of organizational life, and the way these features create personal and institutional dilemmas for society.

REFERENCES

Albrecht, T. L., & Bach, B. W. (1997). *Communication in complex organizations: A relational approach.* Fort Worth, TX: Harcourt, Brace.

Andrews, P. H., & Herschel, R. T. (1996). *Organizational communication: Empowerment in a technological society.* Boston: Houghton Mifflin.

Apple, C. (1986, April). *The case study method of instruction: Achieving competency in the organizational communication classroom.* Paper presented at the annual convention of the Central States Speech Association, Cincinnati, OH.

Bantz, C. R. (1993). *Understanding organizations: Interpreting organizational communication cultures.* Columbia: University of South Carolina Press.

Barker, J. R. (1993). Tightening the iron cage: Concertive control in self-managing teams. *Administrative Science Quarterly, 38,* 408–437.

Barker, J. R., & Cheney, G. (1994). The concepts and practices of discipline in contemporary organizational life. *Communication Monographs, 61,* 19–43.

Barnes, L. B., Christensen, C. R., Hansen, A. (Eds.). (1994). *Teaching and the case method* and *Teaching and the case method: Instructor's guide.* Boston: Harvard Business School Press.

Cheney, G. (1995). Democracy in the workplace: Theory and practice from the perspective of communication. *Journal of Applied Communication Research, 23,* 167–200.

Christensen, C. R., Garvin, D. A., & Sweet, A. (Eds.). (1991). *Education for judgment: The artistry of discussion leadership.* Boston: Harvard Business School Press.

Conrad, C. (1994). *Strategic organizational communication: Toward the twenty-first century* (3rd. ed.). Fort Worth, TX: Harcourt Brace.

Conrad, C., & Poole, M. S. (1998). *Strategic organizational communication: Into the 21st century* (4th ed.). Fort Worth, TX: Harcourt Brace.

Corsini, R. J., Shaw, M. E., & Blake, R. R. (1961). *Roleplaying in business and industry.* Glencoe, IL: The Free Press.

Czarniawska-Joerges, B., & de Monthoux, P. G. (1994). *Good novels, better management: Reading organizational realities in fiction.* Reading, MA: Harwood.

Daft, R. L., & Dahlen, K. M. (1984). *Organizational theory: Cases and application.* St. Paul, MN: West.

Daniels, T. D., Spiker, B. K., & Papa, M. J. (1997). *Perspectives on organizational communication* (4th ed.). Madison, WI: Brown & Benchmark.

Eisenberg, E. M., & Goodall, H. L., Jr. (1997). *Organizational communication: Balancing, creativity, and constraint* (2nd ed.). New York: St. Martin's.

Falcione, R. L. (1977). Some instructional strategies in the teaching of organizational communication. *Journal of Business Communication, 14,* 22–34.

Freiberg, K., & Freiberg, J. (1996). *Nuts! Southwest Airlines' crazy recipe for business and personal success.* Austin, TX: Bard.

Frost, P. J., Mitchell, Y. F., Nord, W. R. (Eds.). (1997). *Organizational reality: Reports from the firing line* (4th ed.). Reading, MA: Addison-Wesley.

Fulk, J., Schmitz, J., & Steinfield, C. W. (1990). A social influence model of technology use. In J. Fulk & C. Steinfield (Eds.), *Organizations and communication technology* (pp. 117–140). Newbury Park, CA: Sage.

Garson, B. (1975). *All the livelong day: The meaning and demeaning of routine work.* Garden City, NY: Doubleday.

Greenberger, E., Steinberg, L. D., Vaux, A., & McAuliffe, S. (1980). Adolescents who work: Effects of part-time employment on family and peer relations. *Journal of Youth and Adolescence, 9,* 189–202.

Hatch, M. J. (1997). Irony and the social construction of contradiction in the humor of a management team. *Organizational Science, 8,* 275–288.

Heller, J. (1962). *Catch-22.* New York: Ballantine.

Heller, J. (1975). *Something happened.* New York: Ballantine.

Jablin, F. M. (1987). Organizational entry, assimilation, and exit. In F. M. Jablin, L. L. Putnam, K. H. Roberts, & L. W. Porter (Eds.), *Handbook of organizational communication: An interdisciplinary perspective* (pp. 679–740). Newbury Park, CA: Sage.

Jablin, F. M., Cude, R. L., House, A., Lee, J., & Roth, N. L. (1994). Communication competence in organizations: Conceptualization and comparison across multiple levels of analysis. In L. Thayer & G. Barnett (Eds.), *Organizational communication: Emerging perspectives* (Vol. 4, pp. 114–140). Norwood, NJ: Ablex.

Kanter, R. M. (1980). *A tale of "O": On being different in an organization.* New York, Harper & Row.

Kanter, R. M., & Stein, B. (1979). *Life in organizations.* New York: Basic Books.

Kidder, T. (1981). *The soul of a new machine.* New York: Avon.

Kreps, G. L. (1990). *Organizational communication: Theory and practice* (2nd ed.). New York: Longman.

Kreps, G. L., & Lederman, L. C. (1985). Using the case method in organizational communication education: Developing students' insight, knowledge, and creativity through experience-based learning and systematic debriefing. *Communication Education, 34,* 358–364.

Lederman, L. C., & Stewart, L. P. (1983). *The SIMCORP SIMULATION participant's manual.* Princeton, NJ: Total Research.

Maier, N. R. F., Solem, A. R., & Maier, A. A. (1975). *The role-play technique: A handbook for management and leadership practice.* La Jolla, CA: University Associates.

Martin, J., & Meyerson, D. (1997). *Link.Com teaching cases.* Stanford, CA: Stanford University Graduate School of Business.

Miller, A. (1976). *Death of a salesman.* New York: Penguin.

Miller, K. (1995). *Organizational communication: Approaches and processes.* Belmont, CA: Wadsworth.

Miller, K., Mattson, M., & Stage, C. (1995). *Instructor's manual for organizational communication: Approaches and processes.* Belmont, CA: Wadsworth.

Pacanowsky, M., with Farace, R. V., Monge, P. R., & Russell, H. M. (1977). *Instructor's guide to accompany Communicating and Organizing.* Reading, MA: Addison-Wesley.

Pace, R. W., & Faules, D. F. (1994). *Organizational communication* (3rd ed.). Englewood Cliffs, NJ: Prentice-Hall.

Pace, R. W., Michal-Johnson, P., & Mills, G. E. (1990, December). Trends in the basic course in organizational communication. *The Bulletin* (ABC), 43–49.

Pepper, G. L. (1995). *Communicating in organizations: A cultural approach.* New York: McGraw-Hill.

Peters, T. J., & Austin, N. (1994). *A passion for excellence.* New York: HarperCollins.

Peterson, G. L. (Ed.). (1994). *Communicating in organizations: A casebook.* Scottsdale, AZ: Gorsuch Scarisbrick.

Phillips, N. (1995). Telling organizational tales: On the role of narrative fiction in the study of organizations. *Organizational Studies, 16,* 625–649.

Pringle, R. (1988). *Secretaries talk.* London: Verso.

Putnam, L. L., & Pacanowsky, M. E. (1983). *Communication and organization: An interpretive approach.* Beverly Hills, CA: Sage.

Putnam, L. L., Phillips, N., & Chapman, P. (1996). Metaphors of communication and organization. In S. R. Clegg, C. Hardy, & W. R. Nord (Eds.), *Handbook of organizational studies* (pp. 375–408). London: Sage.

Ritti, R. R., & Funkhouser, G. R. (1994). *The ropes to skip and the ropes to know.* New York: Wiley.
Shockley-Zalabak, P. (1991). *Fundamentals of organizational communication: Knowledge, sensitivity, skills, values* (2nd ed.). New York: Longman.
Smith, R. C., & Eisenberg, E. M. (1987). Conflict at Disneyland: A root-metaphor analysis. *Communication Monographs, 54,* 367–380.
Stohl. C. (1995). *Organizational communication: Connectedness in action.* Thousand Oaks, CA: Sage.
Sypher, B. D. (Ed.). (1990). *Case studies in organizational communication.* New York: Guilford.
Sypher, B. D. (Ed.). (1997). *Case studies in organizational communication 2.* New York: Guilford.
Terkel, S. (1972). *Working.* New York: Avon.
Tompkins, P. K. (1993). *Organizational communication imperatives: Lessons of the space program.* Los Angeles: Roxbury.
Treadwell, D., & Applbaum, R. L. (1996). The basic course in organizational communication: A national survey. *Journal of Administrative Communication Association, 1,* 12–24.
Vande Berg, L., & Trujillo, N. (1989). *Organizational life on television.* Norwood, NJ: Ablex.
Van Maanen, J. (1991). The smile factory: Work at Disneyland. In P. J. Frost, L. F. Moore, M. R. Louis, C. C. Lundberg, & J. Martin (Eds.), *Reframing organizational culture* (pp. 58–76). Newbury Park, CA: Sage.
Welty, W. M. (1989, July–August). Discussion method teaching: How to make it work. *Change,* pp. 41–49.

12

Teaching Nonverbal Communication

Mark L. Knapp
University of Texas at Austin

When Julius Fast's (1970) bestseller *Body Language* hit U. S. bookstores, you could count on one hand the number of college and university courses entirely devoted to the subject of nonverbal communication. Now such courses are commonly found in the curricular offerings of many universities and colleges in departments of communication, anthropology, linguistics, and psychology. In addition, introductory textbooks in the field of communication, especially interpersonal communication, routinely include at least one chapter on nonverbal communication. Thus, students who take a course entirely devoted to nonverbal communication, particularly communication majors, are likely to enter the course with some basic knowledge of the area. Nonverbal communication is so much a part of modern communication education it is hard to imagine that time, not so long ago, when such courses did not exist.

I remember it vividly. I had been teaching a survey course called "Approaches to the Study of Commnication" for several years in the late 1960s. It was an ancestor of what we now call interpersonal communication and was guided by the literature of that time, which focused primarily on psychological constructs and verbal behavior. In response to the research findings I presented in my lectures, students regularly raised questions based on the logic and experience of their everyday living: "Wouldn't the effect of feedback change depending on the speaker's tone of voice?" "Doesn't the way a person dresses have as much influence on credibility as what the person says?" My standard reply to these and other questions was: "Yes, well, you may be right, but I'm not sure anyone has studied that specific question. I'll see if I can find anything." These student inquiries resulted in my accumulating a sufficiently large body of scholarly literature to publish a textbook (Knapp, 1972) that summarized the literature and served as a resource for teachers who wanted to design a separate course in nonverbal communication.

I provide the preceding historical account of the origins of my own professional interest in this area because I believe it serves as an important reminder that it was questions about verbal behavior that eventually led to the development of my separate course focusing on nonverbal communication. Thus, I repeatedly remind my students that a separate course in nonverbal communication should not discourage questions about how verbal behavior interrelates with nonverbal behavior, and I incorporate this perspective into my lectures. There is probably pedagogical value in studying pieces of the process of human interaction separately, but this value is lost if it discourages students from trying to restore the parts of the whole during their development in this course.

GOALS

Like any course, there are many ways to teach nonverbal communication. I try herein to point out options and alternatives, but my biases no doubt predominate. One of the first considerations for an instructor in this course is to carefully identify the nature of the subject matter to be covered in the course. The term *nonverbal* attracts students who have a wide range of expectations for course content. To the speech pathology major, a nonverbal child is one who does not have the ability to use any meaningful oral language. Broadcasting students may be interested in learning about nonverbal messages related to camera angles, whereas marketing and advertising students may be seeking a greater understanding of color and packaging for print media. Some students will be expecting an extended treatment of animal communication. The range of possible student expectations for the course is matched by the literature itself—which ranges from the study of movement in dance to Nazi marching. This makes it all the more important that an instructor of this course clarify his or her goals early.

My own course in nonverbal communication focuses on "normal" human beings (usually adult) and the process of human interaction (usually face to face). There are many goals appropriate to this course, but the following five are especially important for the course as I teach it:

1. Students should leave the course with an understanding of the history of non-verbal study. For many students, this is the only course they will ever take in this area. As such, they should know how the area developed and who are the key figures associated with the major theoretical and research areas.

2. Students should leave the course with an understanding of the major theoret-ical perspectives associated with nonverbal studies, as well as facts derived from research associated with these perspectives.

3. Students should leave the course with an understanding of how nonverbal communication functions with verbal communication. As noted earlier, I try to emphasize these interrelations throughout the course.

4. Students should leave the course with an understanding of how research knowledge can be applied to various spheres of everyday living—for exam-ple, judicial and political processes, management and sales, cross-cultural encounters, classroom transactions, friendships, and romantic relation-ships.

5. Students should leave the course with an understanding of how to analyze their own nonverbal skills and those of others. Because my class is large, en-coding skills receive less attention than decoding skills. Throughout the course, though, in-class experiences and outside assignments are designed to hone observational, interpretive, and performance skills.

SETTING EXPECTATIONS IN OPENING SESSIONS

The opening sessions of any course try to address expected student ques-tions and set the expectations for the course. Topics covered, assignments, grading policy, classroom procedures, time apportioned for lectures and discussion, and various "bookkeeping" matters (such as office hours) are common. There are six additional concerns that are particularly important for instructors of courses in nonverbal communication to address:

1. Normally, the first session of a course is a time when instructors can intro-duce themselves—indicating what kind of teacher they will be. For the non-verbal course, students will be assessing the instructor in ways that are related to the course—for example, does the instructor show a sensitivity to his or her own nonverbal signals? Is the instructor sensitive to student non-verbal messages? Can I learn anything by imitating my instructor? In short, is the instructor a credible source in this area? There are many ways to ad-dress this issue the first day—using your own nonverbal behavior as exam-ples to discuss, talking about the classroom environment as it may affect learning (Woolfolk & Brooks, 1983), and so on. Although the first days are crucial in setting initial expectations for the instructor's abilities in this area, the process continues throughout the duration of the course.

2. The opening sessions of this course should also address the issue of importance (see Friedrich & Cooper, chap. 21, this volume). Although this is a standard issue for many courses, it is especially critical for nonverbal communication, because the importance may not be as obvious for this course as it is for other areas. When describing communication events, it is common for the participants to focus on the verbal transaction. The subtlety and indirect nature of many nonverbal signals often masks their importance. Therefore, I use a modified version of the Two Men Talking exercise first described in Harrison's (1974) *Beyond Words*. In this exercise, students are asked to make attributions about a scene depicting two physically dissimilar men interacting in an office. By uncovering the overhead in predetermined segments, students learn how they use stereotypes and how the revelation of new information may or may not alter previous attributions. This exercise shows students not only how many decisions they make about others based on nonverbal signals, but how important these decisions are. With this exercise, the instructor can elicit student perceptions of honesty, confidence, trust, liking, and status, based wholly on nonverbal signals. These judgments are the substance of interpersonal life, and they help to determine not only how we get along, but also whether we even get together with other people.

3. I also use the Two Men Talking exercise to make another point that represents a crucial perspective for the entire course—the multimeaning capacity of nonverbal signals. Too often students will assume that a particular nonverbal signal means one thing and one thing only. When I ask students to write down the meaning of the word *fast,* many start to write and then look up and ask me which meaning I want; when students are asked to write down what it means when somebody does not look at them, many will not ask for a context to clarify the meaning I am seeking. Instructors have to use particular caution in this area. For example, if you report a study in which liars tended to look away from their questioners more than when telling the truth, some students will interpret this to mean that in conditions where telling the truth is salient, "looking away" can only mean the person is lying. Or, when an instructor tells a student to look at his or her interaction partner because it shows attention, the student may assume that looking at a person means attention—regardless of other contextual and co-occurring signals. Just like verbal behavior, nonverbal behavior has the potential to mean anything, depending on the configuration of behaviors, people, and circumstances. Although it is important to emphasize the multimeaning capacity of nonverbal signals early in the course, it is an issue that will raise its ugly head many times throughout the course.

    Another meaning issue that commonly arises during the course concerns stereotyped meanings versus idiosyncratic meanings. Much research in this area focuses on public settings and people who do not know each other well.

As a result, many of the findings do not account for the specialized meanings that people in close relationships and in private settings may attribute to similar behaviors. For example, students usually point out that the cluster of nonverbal signals associated with liking (Mehrabian, 1972) may or may not appear when communicating "liking" in close relationships (Andersen, 1985; Knapp, 1983).

4. The first days of class are also good times to explain to students the potential problems involved in using nontechnical language to explain the nature of nonverbal signals. At present, we do not have an adequate technical vocabulary for all the behaviors that are discussed in this course, but this should not prevent instructors from using more precise language to distinguish smile[1] from smile[2] (Ekman & Friesen, 1982) and glance[1] from glance[2] (Rutter, 1984), and so on. Although this kind of precision may seem tedious, it helps to ensure a referent that students and instructor share while simultaneously communicating the complexity involved in perceiving and analyzing nonverbal behavior.

5. Good textbooks for this course will caution readers about the generalizability of reported findings—acknowledging that many studies are based on the reactions of White, middle-class U.S. college students who do not have a close relationship. This information is useful, but instructors need to be careful not to overgeneralize and to be open to student input concerning other patterns of behavior. There is plenty of material that examines other age groups (Carmichael & Knapp, 1988; Feldman, 1982), ethnic groups (Halberstadt, 1985), relationships (Halberstadt, 1991; Knapp, 1983; Noller, 1992), and cultures (Ekman & Keltner, 1997) that can help prepare an instructor (if the textbook does not) for issues associated with these areas.

6. There are two student attitudes about the controllability of nonverbal behavior that instructors should try to defuse early in the course. In both cases, students believe that we have very little control over our own nonverbal behavior. In the first instance, students are highly motivated to learn how to "read" another person's nonverbal signals because it will give them power. It is the key to success, because nobody can fool you. Students with this orientation (and there are many) will typically come up after the first day of class and ask how I am able to deal with this ability to know what everyone is thinking. The questioners are understandably nervous and awkward when asking the question, because they believe that I am somehow looking into their very soul as we talk. For these students I point out that in any learning endeavor, the knowledge gained is inevitably incomplete. In the nonverbal area, this occurs for a variety of reasons, including: (a) assuming our senses could pick up all information desired, the nature of human interaction is such that it places constraints on what information is available to us; (b) we probably do not want to process some information so we deliberately shut it

out; and (c) our interaction partners may also not want us to pick up certain information, so they try to hide or mask it.

In response to the "nonverbal behavior tells all" perspective, I point out that in recent years, behavioral scientists have spent a lot of time and energy trying to identify the behaviors exhibited by liars (Ekman, 1992, 1996), but once this information is made public and brought to the awareness of liars, they would have to be crazy not to try to change their behavior. If that is not enough, I point out that we have been studying persuasion for over 2,000 years, but even the best persuaders do not know how to get others to do what they want all the time. Similarly, there are some people who are better communicators because they have developed their skills in sending and receiving nonverbal signals—but even these people are not capable of or interested in reading everything about another person. Finally, to encourage them, I point out that once they have improved their skill level and knowledge, they will not have total power over others but they will have the option of using some skills they do not currently have—skills that can make a significant difference in their lives.

The other student attitude associated with the controllability of nonverbal signals assumes that it is futile to try to learn anything about them because they cannot be changed. This student typically views the course as nothing new or common sense, but his or her common sense is often not sufficient to get a high grade in the course. Unlike the other students who eagerly talk about your prowess in this area, these students do not identify themselves, and, thus, it is difficult to disarm these perceptions. In the absence of individual contact, instructors should make a point of using examples early in the course that are clearly not common sense and examples of people who have, with difficulty, changed nonverbal behavior for their benefit.

INSTRUCTIONAL STRATEGIES

Organization and Sequencing

One of the primary decisions about the organization of this course has to do with whether it will be organized around how nonverbal signals function in achieving several common outcomes sought by communicators (e.g., communicating identity, communicating our relationship to others, achieving accuracy and understanding, managing the interaction, influencing others and ourself, and communicating feelings and emotions) or whether it should be organized around the various signaling systems themselves (e.g., eye gaze behavior, vocal behavior, touching behavior, gestural behavior). Nonverbal textbooks and nonverbal research were originally classified by body parts, but now most textbooks try to combine both orientations.

I try to combine both approaches in my course. The first part of the semester is spent examining the theory and research associated with various individual channels of communication, and the second half of the semester covers the outcomes that have received the most multichannel research attention. Specifically, the course is composed of six units, as shown in Fig. 12.1.

NONVERBAL COMMUNICATION

Professor's Name   Semester
TA's Name   Course Number
                                                          Time & Location

Textbook:

AN INTRODUCTION TO THE STUDY OF NONVERBAL COMMUNICATION:UNIT 1

Week 1 - Orientation; Plan of Course; Assignments; First Day Rituals; Two Men Talking Exercise; Video, "Communication--The Nonverbal Agenda"
Week 2 - Basic Terms/Concepts; History; Phylogenetic Roots of Nonverbal Behavior (video)
Week 3 - Perception & The Process of Observation; Visual Literacy; Videos: Eyewitness Testimony & Interpersonal Perception Test

THE COMMUNICATION ENVIRONMENT: UNIT 2

Week 4 - Environmental Factors; Video: The Goya Nude & Sexual Harrassment
Week 5 - Personal Space & Territory; Video; Film: "Invisible Walls;" Exam #1

THE COMMUNICATORS: UNIT 3

Week 6 - Physical Appearance: What is It? What Difference Does it Make?/Dealing With it. Odor, Hair, Clothes, & Body Adornment, Videos

THE COMMUNICATOR'S BEHAVIOR: UNIT 4

Week 7 - Gestures; Video: "A World Of Gestures"
Week 8 - Touching Behavior; The Face: Identities & Facial Feedback; Video
Week 9 - Facial Expressions of Emotion; Exam #2
Week 10- Eye Behavior; Video; Exercise
Week 11- Vocal Behavior; Video: "The Human Voice"

THE COMMUNICATOR'S BEHAVIOR: MULTI-CHANNEL PERSPECTIVES:UNIT 5

Week 12- Relationship Development & Intimacy; Gender Signals & Identity; Exercise
Week 13- Lying & Deception; Video; "To Tell The Truth" Exercise
Week 14- Status/Power/Dominance; Turn-Taking

NONVERBAL SKILLS: UNIT 6

Week 15- Ability to Effectively Send/Receive Nonverbal Signals; Exercise: "Emotional Charades"

Exam #3 given during final week.

FIG. 12.1   Sample syllabus for a course in nonverbal communicaton.

The first unit addresses a variety of fundamental constructs: (a) the importance of nonverbal signals for accomplishing student goals; (b) an understanding of basic ideas such as meaning, incongruous signals, and the origins of nonverbal behavior; and (c) perceptual and observational processes. The early emphasis on perception, observation, and visual literacy helps prepare students for five outside assignments that ask them to make and interpret observations of nonverbal communication. The second unit addresses environmental factors, including proxemics, that may affect the communication situation. The third unit looks specifically at the communicators per se—emphasizing physical appearance, dress, odor, body adornment, hair, skin color, and the like. The next unit, the longest, examines communicator behavior in various forms: gestures, touching, facial expressions, eye gaze, and vocal signals. The fifth unit focuses on multichannel perspectives. Topics vary, but I commonly focus on the nonverbal signals involved in communicating gender, close relationships, status and power relationships, lying, and turn taking. The last unit of the course deals with the process of developing nonverbal skills.

Size of Class

There is nothing inherent in the subject matter that would determine class size. I regularly teach the course with nearly 300 students, but I have taught it with 30 students as well. The differences are differences associated with any large or small class. With classes over 100, you should have an auditorium with the capacity to effectively show slides, films, videotapes, overheads, and hear audiotapes; a teaching assistant (or two) to grade papers and exams and share the student counseling load; easily graded assignments; primarily "objective" tests; and in-class exercises adapted to large audiences. It is still possible, although more difficult, to obtain quality comments and class interaction in a large class. Instructors with less subject matter knowledge and experience with the course would be well advised to teach the smaller classes at first.

Outside Assignments

I normally have three types of outside assignments: term papers, group reports, and guided observation reports. Term papers and group reports are more likely assignments when the class size is smaller; outside observation assignments can be done with any size class. Each assignment, however, should include some observation. This helps the student blend library research with actual data collection and learn the analytic thinking involved in understanding methods of gathering data and reporting results. Topics for term papers may go beyond the topics discussed in class, but group reports are normally used to give students a chance to learn and present material that would otherwise be presented by the instructor—material central to the course. Even though the assignment is called a report, I emphasize that the presentation of the report is really an assignment in teaching and that student learning should be paramount.

For my large class, I normally have five outside observation exercises that are designed to provide each class member with some data that are pertinent to the theory and research in my lecture for that day. Although each student has done the same assignment, there are many differences in what they observe. These differences in observations provide an excellent foundation for discussing why such differences occurred. These observation assignments are effective in providing active participation in a relevant, real-life learning experience. Assignments I have used in recent years include environmental influences on communication, physical attraction modified by verbal behavior, touching and being touched, looking and not looking at conversational partners, and breaking rules of turn exchange. Because it is impossible to grade these assignments on "correctness," they are instead graded on completeness and whether they are turned in on time. Figure 12.2 provides an example of an outside observation assignment dealing with eye behavior.

Readings

Most readings in my course are from the textbook. With smaller classes, however, extra readings can be assigned if desired. These readings will vary with each instructor's needs, but the main issues regarding selection revolve around technical quality and interest factors. Readings that are interesting as well as technically accurate are, of course, first priority. There is plenty of popular literature in this area that is misleading and inaccurate but easy and fun to read; similarly, there are some exquisitely precise studies of microscopic behavior that do not do a very good job of holding the attention of undergraduate students. Like any course, the readings selected for the course become a part of the course image—for both students and outsiders.

In-Class Exercises

Fortunately, instructor's manuals for the textbooks on nonverbal communication have many exercises to choose from. These exercises are designed to illustrate a point and provide a memorable learning experience, while at the same time keeping the focus on the substance, not the activity itself. Generally, I try not to have too many exercises, because I think it may detract

OUTSIDE ASSIGNMENT #4   Instructor
    Eye Behavior   Course Number

1. Due Date.
2. During a conversation with another person, look directly at them (do not look
   away) for two minutes. If the other person looks away, just continue looking
   at their head so when they return their eyes toward you, your eyes will be
   looking directly at their eyes. Otherwise, try to conduct the conversation as
   you normally would. Describe what happened.
       A. Your reactions and behavior
       B. Your partner's reactions and behavior
3. During a conversation with another person (not the same person you talked to in
   #2 above) avoid looking at the person for two minutes. If the other person tries
   to look at you, continue to look away. Otherwise, try to conduct the conversation
   as you normally would. Describe what happened.
       A. Your reactions and behavior
       B. Your partner's reactions and behavior
4. Watch people's eye behavior in conversation. When you find someone who
   seems to be looking more than you consider normal, try to find out why. You
   may talk to the person if you think it would help clarify things.
5. Watch people's eye behavior in conversation. When you find someone who
   seems to be looking less than you consider normal, try to find out why. You
   may talk to the person if you think it would help clarify things.

Observer's Name: _____

FIG. 12.2.   Example of an outside observation assignment dealing with eye behavior.

from the intellectual focus of the course. There are several in-class exercises
that work for me and can be found in the instructor's manual for the textbook
I co-author with Hall, *Nonverbal Communication in Human Interaction*
(Knapp & Hall, 1996). Three are called: Back Me Up If You Can
(proxemics), The Unusual Interview (eye behavior), and Emotional Charades (sending and receiving ability). For the session on lying behavior, I
have students reenact the old (very old) television show *To Tell The Truth,* in
which four panelists are quizzed about something they all claim to have done,
but that only one has actually done. After questioning, the entire class votes
on who they think is telling the truth and the discussion centers around the
reasons (verbal and nonverbal) for their choices. The gender lecture is pre-
ceded by a panel discussion among four students who are all blindfolded. It
is best if there are differences of opinion on the discussion topic. Prior to the
discussion, however, one male student is asked to engage in nonverbal behavior that is stereotypical of women and one female student is asked to
portray stereotypical male nonverbal behavior. Each of the role players is

seated next to a person who is not aware of anyone else's instructions and are simply told to act naturally. Thus, observers can look for similarities and contrasts between what the students think the other gender does and what at least one member of that gender, on this occasion, actually does. This leads to a sometimes animated discussion of gender stereotypes and provides a worthwhile foundation for a lecture on research and theory in this area. For the session on vocal signals, I play standardized recordings of people ranging in age from 22 to 92 and ask students to guess the person's age; I also have one man and one woman from five different occupations count to 10 and then I ask students to guess their occupation. *The Interpersonal Perception Task* is a videotape I use in order to give students an opportunity to practice what they have learned without any threat of being graded.

Resources

Resources for instructors of this course include published articles and books as well as audiovisual materials. It would be impossible to list all important publications in this area, so the focus is on those resources of most value to new instructors.

Textbooks.   There are many textbooks designed for the undergraduate market. Three recent ones include:

Burgoon, J. K., Buller, D. B., & Woodall, W. G. (1996). *Nonverbal communication: The unspoken dialogue.* New York: McGraw-Hill.
Knapp, M. L., & Hall, J. A. (1996). *Nonverbal communication in human interaction.* Fort Worth, TX: Harcourt Brace.
Leathers, D. G. (1997). *Successful nonverbal communication.* New York: Macmillan.

Reviews, Summaries, and Literature Surveys.   Among the many available, the following publications should be especially useful:

Burgoon, J. K. (1994). Nonverbal signals. In M. L. Knapp & G. R. Miller (Eds.), *Handbook of interpersonal communication* (pp. 229–285). Thousand Oaks, CA: Sage.
Feldman, R. S. (Ed.). (1992). *Applications of nonverbal behavioral theories and research.* Hillsdale, NJ: Lawrence Erlbaum Associates.
Feldman, R. S., & Rimé, B. (Eds.). (1991). *Fundamentals of nonverbal behavior.* New York: Cambridge University Press.
Siegman, A. W., & Feldstein, S. (Eds.). (1987). *Multichannel integrations of nonverbal behavior.* Hillsdale, NJ: Lawrence Erlbaum Associates.

Audiovisual Materials.   In a course so heavily focused on the senses, it is critical that optimum use of audio and visual resources be made. With the availability of video cameras, instructors may wish to make their own visual aids. Instructors can also make audiotapes and develop slides from from book photos—see, for example, Morris' *Manwatching* (1977) and *Bodywatching* (1985). For those who wish to use videotapes, I recommend two approaches: (a) watch for opportunities to videotape relevant programs on news magazine shows (ABC's *PrimeTime*, NBC's *Dateline*, CBS' *48 Hours*) or programs shown on the Learning Channel, the Discovery Channel, and so on; and (b) purchase or rent the following videos:

Communication—The Nonverbal Agenda. 1/2" videocassette. 33 min. Color. (1988). McGraw-Hill, CRM, 110 Fifteenth St., Del Mar, CA 92014.
The Interpersonal Perception Task. 1/2" videocassette.40 min. Color. (1986). University of California Extension Center for Media and Independent Learning, 2000 Center St., Fourth Fl., Berkeley, CA 94704. (See Costanzo & Archer, 1991, for effective ways to use this video.)
The Human Face. 1/2" videocassette. 30 min. Color. (1995). University of California Extension Center for Media and Independent Learning, 2000 Center St., Fourth Fl., Berkeley, CA 94704.
A World of Differences: Understanding Cross-Cultural Communication. 1/2" videocassette. 33 min. Color. (1997). University of California Extension Center for Media and Independent Learning, 2000 Center St., Fourth Fl., Berkeley, CA 94704.
The Human Voice. 1/2" videocassette. 30 min. Color. (1993). University of California Extension Center for Media and Independent Learning, 2000 Center St., Fourth Fl., Berkeley, CA 94704.
A World of Gestures: Culture and Nonverbal Communication. 1/2" videocassette. 28 min. Color. (1991). University of California Extension Center for Media and Independent Learning, 2000 Center St., Fourth Fl., Berkeley, CA 94704.
Language of the Body. 1/2" videocassette. 60 min. Color. (1994). This is one part of a six-part series called *The Human Animal: A Personal View,* narrated by Desmond Morris. Available from Central Missouri State University.

CONCLUSION

I teach a large section of this upper division undergraduate course every semester and each time I eagerly look forward to it. Part of it has to do with the interest that students bring to the course. There is something inherently interesting about the subject matter—these subtleties of human interaction—that makes many students eager to learn. When students are eager to learn, professors are eager to provide learning experiences. Another factor that makes this course a favorite of mine is related to the often hidden or subtle nature of the subject matter. There are many times during the course when these little-noticed actions are identified and discussed and an instructor can actually see the "a-ha" learning experience take place. Seeing that you are having an effect on student learning is the kind of feedback that spurs instructors on. For a variety of reasons, then, this can be a very satisfying course to teach.

The course in nonverbal communication, like some other courses, is also affected by the teaching–learning paradox. The more we learn about nonverbal communication, the more we need a single course to cover the range of complexity of the information accumulating. However, the more we learn about nonverbal communication, the more we realize how misleading it is to talk about nonverbal behavior without discussing other co-occurring stimuli and responses that are critical to understanding the act of human communication. We deal with this paradox in today's curriculum by showing how nonverbal communication fits into the process during introductory courses and providing students the option to explore the subject in greater depth in a more advanced course. My emphasis here has been on the course devoted entirely to nonverbal communication. This information, however, can be used to construct shorter units or to creatively design the course of the future—perhaps a two-semester course that integrates verbal and nonverbal perspectives throughout.

REFERENCES

Andersen, P. A. (1985). Nonverbal immediacy in interpersonal communication. In A. W. Siegman & S. Feldstein (Eds.), *Multichannel integrations of nonverbal behavior* (pp. 1–36). Hillsdale, NJ: Lawrence Erlbaum Associates.

Carmichael, C. W., & Knapp, M. L. (1988). Nonverbal aspects of communication and aging. In C. W. Carmichael, C. H. Botan, & R. Hawkins (Eds.), *Human communication and the aging process* (pp. 111–128). Prospect Heights, IL: Waveland Press.

Costanzo, M., & Archer, D. (1991). A method for teaching about verbal and nonverbal communication. *Teaching of Psychology, 18,* 223–226.

Ekman, P. (1992). *Telling lies.* New York: Norton.

Ekman, P. (1996). Why don't we catch liars? *Social Research, 63,* 801–17.

Ekman, P., & Friesen, W. V. (1982). Felt, false, and miserable smiles. *Journal of Nonverbal Behavior, 6,* 238–252.

Ekman, P., & Keltner, D. (1997). Universal facial expressions of emotion: An old controversy and new findings. In U. Segerstråle & P. Molnár (Eds.), *Nonverbal communication: Where nature meets culture* (pp. 27–46). Mahwah, NJ: Lawrence Erlbaum Associates.

Fast, J., (1970). *Body language.* New York: Evans.

Feldman, R. S. (Ed.). (1982). *Development of nonverbal behavior in children.* New York: Springer-Verlag.

Halberstadt, A. G. (1985). Race, socioeconomic status and nonverbal behavior. In A. W. Siegman & S. Feldstein (Eds.), *Multichannel integrations of nonverbal behavior* (pp. 227–266). Hillsdale, NJ: Lawrence Erlbaum Associates.

Halberstadt, A. G. (1991). Toward an ecology of expressiveness: Family socialization in particular and a model in general. In R. S. Feldman & B. Rimé (Eds.), *Fundamentals of nonverbal behavior* (pp. 106–160). New York: Cambridge University Press.

Harrison, R. P. (1974). *Beyond words.* Englewood Cliffs, NJ: Prentice-Hall.

Knapp, M. L. (1972). *Nonverbal communication in human interaction.* New York: Holt, Rinehart & Winston.

Knapp, M. L. (1983). Dyadic relationship development. In J. M. Wiemann & R. P. Harrison (Eds.), *Nonverbal interaction* (pp. 179–207). Beverly Hills, CA: Sage.

Knapp, M. L., & Hall, J. A. (1996).*Nonverbal communication in human interaction.* Fort Worth, TX: Harcourt Brace.

Mehrabian, A. (1972). *Nonverbal communication.* Chicago: Aldine.

Morris, D. (1977). *Manwatching.* New York: Abrams.

Morris, D. (1985). *Bodywatching.* New York: Crown.

Noller, P. (1992). Nonverbal communication in marriage. In R. S. Feldman (Ed.), *Applications of nonverbal behavioral theories and research* (pp. 31–59). Hillsdale, NJ: Lawrence Erlbaum Associates.

Rutter, D. R. (1984). *Looking and seeing: The role of visual communication in social interaction.* New
    York: Wiley.
Woolfolk, A. E., & Brooks, D. M. (1983). Nonverbal communication in teaching. In E. W. Gordon (Ed.),
    Review of research in education (Vol. 10, pp. 103–149). Washington, DC: American Educational
    Research Association.

13

Teaching Intercultural Communication

Young Yun Kim
University of Oklahoma

William B. Gudykunst
California State University–Fullerton

No two individuals are alike. Differences between people compel us to communicate in the first place and make human communication inherently challenging as well as rewarding. It is challenging because we are always faced with the potential problem of difference in symbols and meanings. Yet communication is the very means by which we express ourselves, acquire new learning, and coordinate our varied social transactions. By and large, communication activities within a given cultural community occur with at least some degree of fidelity. Even though people differ and argue about preferences, they more or less understand each other's messages. Comparatively, communicators of differing cultural backgrounds face more barriers in recognizing and interpreting verbal and nonverbal messages and the implicit assumptions underlying the messages. As Smith (1982) noted, the condition of such significant differences and obstacles in communication presents a special context of communication, commonly referred to as *intercultural communication.*

INTERCULTURAL COMMUNICATION AS AN AREA OF STUDY

The study of intercultural communication reflects the rapid increase in cultural and subcultural interfaces around the world for the past several decades. Intercultural communication has been one of the fastest growing areas in the field of communication since the 1960s and 1970s. Research studies have been conducted to address the various intercultural challenges faced by employees of international governmental and nongovernmental organizations, military personnel, men and women of multinational business organizations, international students, exchange scholars and members of international research teams, Peace Corps volunteers, immigrants, and missionaries, among others. More recently, domestic social concerns for managing cultural diversity and interethnic and interracial relations also have facilitated the study of intercultural communication.

Having begun with largely episodic, atheoretical "fact-finding" studies in the 1960s and 1970s addressing the practical needs of overseas sojourners, the area of intercultural communication has seen an increasing amount of concerted efforts for serious definitional, theoretical, and methodological explorations. These efforts have often taken an interdisciplinary approach, which is exemplified in many of the books authored or edited by intercultural scholars within the field of communication, including *Interethnic Communication* (Kim,1986), *Culture and Interpersonal Communication* (Gudykunst & Ting-Toomey, 1988), *Communication and Cross-Cultural Adaptation* (Kim, 1988), *Theories in Intercultural Communication* (Kim & Gudykunst, 1988), *Handbook of Intercultural and Development Communication* (Asante & Gudykunst, 1989), *Language, Communication, and Culture* (Ting-Toomey & Korzenny, 1989), *Intercultural Communication Competence* (Wiseman & Koester, 1993), *Intercultural Communication Theory* (Wiseman, 1995), and *Becoming Intercultural* (Kim, in press). Individually and collectively, research and publication activities have helped define the area of intercultural communication with increased coherence and rigor, and brought about a closer alignment of the intellectual core of the area with that of the mainstream communication field at large.

ORGANIZING AN INTERCULTURAL COMMUNICATION COURSE: A MODEL

Several college-level textbooks available today offer largely similar conceptual domains of intercultural communication and associated areas (e. g., Condon & Yousef, 1975; Dodd, 1995; Gudykunst, 1994; Gudykunst & Kim, 1997; Klopf, 1995; Martin & Nakayama, 1997; Prosser, 1985; Samovar & Porter, 1995; Singer, 1987). Although commonly sharing a communication focus, these textbooks present differing levels of emphasis on theories and research findings for topic selection and organization, as well as on the degree of practical or applied bent. The textbooks also vary some-what in the identification of the conceptual domain of intercultural commu-nication and its constituent concepts and issues.

Given the variations across textbooks, we present here a model of in-struction presented in our textbook, *Communication With Strangers: An Approach to Intercultural Communication* (Gudykunst & Kim, 1997). This model represents one of the most comprehensive and rigorously re-searched-based treatments of the field available today. It integrates various types of intercultural communication such as interethnic communication, interracial communication, and subcultural communication into a single framework. It is grounded in a view that culture is not only a collective sys-tem of meaning associated with groups of conventionally recognized col-lective distinctiveness such as national, ethnic, and racial groups, but also with all other socially recognized group experiences such as the ones asso-ciated with age, gender, occupation, social class, physical disability, and sexual orientation. This concept of culture is predicated on the notion that shared experiential backgrounds of communicators are relevant to the study of intercultural communication to the extent that they influence indi-viduals' communication behavior and meaning systems. Intercultural com-munication is treated, therefore, as a process of social interaction that is not unique in kind from intracultural communication. All encounters are viewed as intercultural to an extent, and the degree of interculturalness of a given encounter would depend on the degree of heterogeneity between the life experience of communicators. This position is consistent with the theo-retical arguments of Ellingsworth (1977) and Sarbaugh (1979).

Highlighting this broadly based perspective is the concept of the stranger. From Simmel (1922) and Schuetz (1944) to Cohen (1972) and Harman (1987), this concept has been employed in sociology as one of the most powerful tools for analyzing social processes of individuals and groups confronting new social and environmental conditions. As a focal concept for understanding intercultural communication, we conceive strangers as individuals who present a relatively high degree of "strange-ness" and a relatively low degree of familiarity due to differing cultural and subcultural life experiences. Strangerhood is also considered a fig-ure–ground phenomenon. When members of other groups approach our group in our environment, they are the strangers. When we approach other groups in their environment, we are the strangers.

Teaching intercultural communication from an inclusive and integrative perspective, such as the present one, offers several advantages over the frameworks used in some other intercultural texts. As noted previously, our approach treats intercultural communication as a phenomenon that is not unique but one that reflects the same basic underlying process as any inter-personal communication process. In viewing intercultural communication as the general process of communication with strangers, we can overcome one of the conceptual problems of many analyses of intercultural communication; that is, the problem of drawing artificial distinctions between and among intracultural, intercultural, interracial, interethnic, and other types of communication. The integrative perspective requires students to take a wide array of communicator differences beyond the differences rooted in cultural programming (such as basic worldviews, beliefs, and values) to understand differences stemming from various sociological influences (such as situational norms, role relationships, demographic characteristics) and from differences in psychological characteristics of individual com-municators (e.g., stereotype, prejudice, ethnocentrism). As such, the pres-ent approach allows a maximum sensitization of our students to the reality of intercultural communication; that is, no two individuals from the same culture are alike in their behavioral and meaning systems. It also empha-sizes that intercultural communication phenomena are to be understood based on a broad range of interdisciplinary knowledge.

Phase I of the course we are proposing begins by placing communication at the heart of the globalization of human affairs. Against this background, we lay a groundwork for the course by defining culture, communication, and intercultural communication, along with the pivotal concept of stranger. Also presented at this time is a conceptual model of intercultural communication. This model serves as an overview of the multitudes of cul-tural, sociocultural, psychocultural, and environmental forces that influ-ence the verbal and nonverbal communication patterns of two interacting strangers (see Fig, 13.1).

The initial conceptual grounding is followed by Phase II, designed to de-velop a detailed understanding of each of the layers of influences on commu-nication behavior. The influences of culture are examined based on key anthropological and psychological theories about culture and cross-cultural variations such as individualism-collectivism and value orientations. With respect to sociocultural influences, social psychological theories and re-search findings are utilized to link social group membership, social identity, and communication behavior. The psychocultural influences are explained in terms of the cognitive, affective, and behavioral tendencies of individual communicators such as expectations, stereotypes, attitudes, and discrimina-tion. These and related concepts serve as the basis for discussing how each stranger influences the nature and process of intercultural communication. In addition, details of environmental influences are described in terms of the

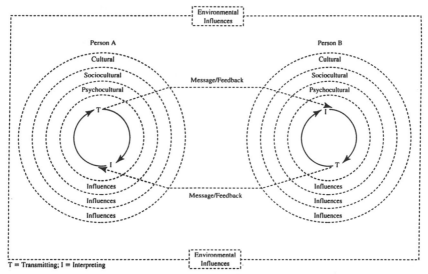

FIG 13.1. An organizing model for studying communication with strangers. From Gudykunst and Kim (1997), p. 43. Reprinted with permission.

characteristics of physical settings, social situation, and psychological experiences of a given environment.

The course then proceeds to Phase III, in which students take a close look at the patterns of interpreting and transmitting communication messages. Informed by various psychological theories and research findings, the students examine human tendencies in perceiving and making attributions about strangers, as well as cross-cultural variations in cognitive styles and patterns of thought. They also learn about the variations in language, verbal behavior, and nonverbal behavior across cultures, as well as the ways in which these behaviors play out when communicating with strangers.

In the final Phase IV, the students explore how the theories and concepts they have acquired can be applied to several important issues of intercultural communication. Issues of personal and social relevance such as what it means to be an effective intercultural communicator, how to manage conflict with strangers, and what challenges need to be overcome to develop interpersonal relationships with strangers are addressed. In addition, the students examine how individuals experience "culture shock" and adapt to a new cultural and subcultural milieu over time. Relatedly, they consider the personal and social meaning of becoming intercultural—a long-term psychic growth beyond the original cultural perimeters as a consequence of extensive intercultural communication and adaptation experiences. The course ends with exploration of some of the ethical issues that frequently confront intercultural communicators, and the challenges and promises of community building across cultural and subcultural boundaries.

The foregoing description of the course contents is summarized in a list of 15 topics organized into four sections, all of which can be adequately covered within an academic semester or quarter.

I. Conceptual Foundations
    1. Introduction
    2. An approach to the study of intercultural communication

II. Influences on the process of communicating with strangers
    3. Cultural influences on the process
    4. Sociocultural influences on the process
    5. Psychocultural influences on the process
    6. Environmental influences on the process

III. Interpreting and transmitting messages
    7. Interpreting messages
    8. Verbal messages
    9. Nonverbal messages

IV. Interaction with strangers
    10. Communicating effectively with strangers
    11. Managing conflict with strangers
    12. Developing relationships with strangers
    13. Adapting to new cultures
    14. Becoming intercultural
    15. Community through diversity

INSTRUCTIONAL METHODS

Like most college-level courses in intercultural communication, this course is aimed primarily at developing in students a level of intellectual knowledge. At the same time, we as instructors find it important to engage our students at the affective and behavioral levels as well. This is because many of the topics and issues of intercultural communication cannot be fully embraced by the students unless they are willing to make some adjustments in their own taken-for-granted cultural habits.

Specifically, the focus of the *cognitive component* is placed on understanding how the intercultural communication process works; what potential psychological barriers need to be addressed; what significant differences exist in worldviews, beliefs, values, norms, and verbal and nonverbal behaviors; what specific factors facilitate or impede the effectiveness in intercultural communication, conflict management, and development of mutually beneficial relationships with strangers; how individuals adapt to a new cultural or subcultural environment; how successful experiences of intercultural communication can aid personal growth; and what it means to strive for building a community out of diversity.

Through lectures and discussions, instructors help students to gain an in-depth understanding of the course contents. Utilizing available audiovisual aids (such as films, videotapes, and slides), group discussions, and personal testimonials of guest speakers, instructors can facilitate active engagements of the students in the learning process and personalize the information presented through lectures and discussions. Brislin, Cushner, Cherrie, and Young's (1986) *Intercultural Interactions: A Practical Guide* contains numerous "cultural assimilator" incidents that deal with issues such as anxiety, disconfirmed expectancies, belonging, ambiguity, confrontation with one's prejudice, work, time, and space, language, roles, importance of group versus individual, rituals and superstitions, hierarchies, values, categorization, differentiation, ingroup–outgroup distinction, learning styles, and attributions. In conjunction with appropriate textbook chapters, these incidents can engage students in analyses and discussions, either individually or in small groups. Also, case studies can be utilized for developing skills to apply concepts and ideas to specific international and domestic issues and events. Newspapers, magazines, television programs, and movies also present real-life cases for classroom use.

The *affective component* stresses the importance of sensitivity, empathy, and motivation to facilitate communication effectiveness. Students are encouraged to suspend their own ethnocentric tendencies and not make hasty and prejudicial judgments about different cultural systems In this learning, students may also participate emotionally in the different experiences of strangers and appreciate their cultural backgrounds as sources of learning and inspiration. One way to guide students' emotional participation is to have them assess aspects of their own perceptual, motivational, attitudinal, and behavioral tendencies. Instructors can use some of the existing self-assessment instruments such as the ones presented by Gudykunst (1994). They may also want to devise new instruments that are more suitable to a particular group of students. In addition, various prepackaged instructional aides such as structured and unstructured exercises, role plays, and simulations are available to enhance the affective involvement of students in the instructional process. Among the more recently published books for experiential learning activities are *Beyond Experience* (Gochenour, 1995), *Cross-Cultural Dialogues* (Storti, 1994), *Developing*

Intercultural Awareness (Kohls & Knight, 1994), *Experiential Activities for Intercultural Learning* (Seelye, 1996), and *Intercultural Sourcebook* (Fowler & Mumford 1995). Further information on various instructional aids is offered by Gudykunst, Ting-Toomey, and Wiseman (1991) and by Wiseman (1997) in his instructor's manual to accompany *Communicating With Strangers* (Gudykunst and Kim, 1997).

Many of these experiential activities help the *behavioral component* of instruction as well. Behavioral learning is designed to increase students' skills in managing their interactions with individuals from different cultures and subcultures. Students learn to adapt their verbal and nonverbal behaviors in such a way that maximizes mutual understanding and development of positive and close relationships. Students' behavioral learning can be enhanced through field experiences in which they actually engage in a task of communicating and building a relationship with someone with a distinctly different cultural or subcultural background. In carrying out such field experiences, students can be guided to keep diaries critically examining their reactions to the intercultural encounters they have had and assessing their communication effectiveness. An additional technique that has been found to be effective in helping students solidify their affirmation of intercultural communication is an essay presentation (or essay contest if students are competitively inclined) at the end of the course. For this task, students are instructed to deliver a persuasive speech based on a thinkpiece on intercultural communication (e.g., "Intercultural communication: A personal point of view"). As they prepare for the speech and see themselves persuade others, students often persuade themselves and deepen their own sense of commitment to effective intercultural communication.

Combinations of these and other creative instructional methods can increase the affective and behavioral learning of students, thereby intensifying their cognitive learning. Such methods are designed to help the students develop necessary knowledge in intercultural communication and an appropriate attitudinal and behavioral foundation for improving their intercultural communication effectiveness. Together, cognitive, affective, and behavioral learning help them manage the potential challenges of intercultural communication and relationship building.

CONCLUSION

The present model of teaching intercultural communication reflects the development of the field of intercultural communication itself over the past several decades. In particular, this approach emphasizes the importance of focusing on an interdisciplinary and comprehensive understanding of the communication process—a focus distinct from a course in cross-cultural psychology or cultural anthropology. It also seeks a balanced integration of theory, research, and practice. Employing a broad and flexible definition of culture and the integrative concept of the stranger, we have proposed a model for organizing a college course on intercultural communication that seeks to increase students' understanding of the nature and process of intercultural communication and many of the associated concepts, theories, and issues. We have also pointed to the importance of coupling the primarily cognitive approach to instruction with affective and behavioral elements, so as to promote students' motivation and affirmative attitude toward cultural and subcultural differences and skills to manage specific intercultural encounters, cultivate interpersonal relationships, and participate in the effort to build intercultural communities on all levels, both within and across national boundaries. Our design further emphasizes the ethical issues that often present profound challenges when individuals of differing ethical and moral systems communicate.

As previously noted, some variations exist among textbooks in terms of the degree of comprehensiveness of topics covered, integration of various intercultural communication situations, and incorporation of theory and research across social science disciplines. Despite such variations, all textbooks reflect a common goal of assisting our students to achieve personal growth beyond the parameters of their own culture by emphasizing the development of a greater willingness to embrace the challenges of intercultural encounters and thoughtfulness with which to "connect" with strangers. This teaching goal is not easily attained, of course. We recognize the difficulty of influencing college students' attitudes and behaviors. This means that, to be effective in teaching intercultural communication, we need to serve as students' role models and a source of inspiration as well as conveyers of relevant scientific knowledge. In this broader capacity, we can guide our students' minds to humanity itself—where differences are not just tolerated but celebrated.

REFERENCES

Asante, M. K., & Gudykunst, W. B. (Eds.). (1989). *Handbook of intercultural and development communication*. Newbury Park, CA: Sage.

Brislin, R. W., Cushner, K. C., Cherrie, C., & Young, M. (1986). *Intercultural interactions: A practical guide*. Newbury Park, CA: Sage.

Cohen, E. (1972). Toward a sociology of international tourism. *Social Research, 39,* 164–182.

Condon, J. C., & Yousef, F. (1975). *An introduction to intercultural communication*. Indianapolis, IN: Bobbs-Merrill.

Dodd, C. H. (1995). *Dynamics of intercultural communication* (4th ed.). Dubuque, IA: Brown.

Ellingsworth, H. (1977). Conceptualizing intercultural communication. In B. Ruben (Ed.), *Communication yearbook 1* (pp. 99–106). New Brunswick, NJ: Transaction.

Fowler, S. M., & Mumford, M. G. (1995). *Intercultural sourcebook: Cross-cultural training methods* (Vol. 1). Yarmouth, ME: Intercultural Press.

Gochenour, T. (Ed.). (1995). *Beyond experience: The experiential approach to cross-cultural education* (2nd ed.). Yarmouth, ME: Intercultural Press.

Gudykunst, W. B. (1994). *Bridging differences.* Newbury Park, CA: Sage.

Gudykunst, W. B., & Kim, Y. Y. (1997). *Communicating with strangers: An approach to intercultural communication.* New York: McGraw-Hill.

Gudykunst, W. B., & Ting-Toomey, S. (1988). *Culture and interpersonal communication.* Newbury Park, CA: Sage.

Gudykunst, W. B., Ting-Toomey, S., & Wiseman, R. L. (1991). Taming the beast: Designing a course in intercultural communication. *Communication Education, 40,* 272–285.

Harman, L. (1987). *The modern stranger.* New York: Mouton de Gruyter.

Kim, Y. Y. (Ed.). (1986). *Interethnic communication: Current research.* Newbury Park, CA: Sage.

Kim, Y. Y. (1988). *Cross-cultural adaptation: An integrative theory.* Avon, UK: Multilingual Matters.

Kim, Y. Y. (in press). *Becoming intercultural: An integrative theory of communication and cross-cultural adaptation.* Thousand Oaks, CA: Sage.

Kim, Y. Y., & Gudykunst, W. B. (Eds.). (1988). *Theories in intercultural communication.* Newbury Park, CA: Sage.

Klopf, D. W. (1995). *Intercultural encounters: The fundamentals of intercultural communications.* (3rd. ed.). Englewood, CO: Morton.

Kohls, L. R., & Knight, J. M. (1994). *Developing intercultural awareness.* Yarmouth, ME: Intercultural Press.

Martin, J. N., & Nakayama, T. K. (1997). *Intercultural communication in contexts.* Mountain View, CA: Mayfield.

Prosser, M. H. (1985). *Cultural dialogue: An introduction to intercultural communication.* Washington, DC: SIETAR International.

Samovar, L. A., & Porter, R. E. (1995). *Communication between cultures* (2nd ed.). Belmont, CA: Wadsworth.

Sarbaugh, L. E. (1979). *Intercultural communication.* Rochelle Park, NJ: Hayden.

Schuetz, A. (1944). The stranger. *American Journal of Sociology, 49,* 499–507.

Seelye, H. N. (1996). *Experiential activities for intercultural learning* (Vol. 1). Yarmouth, ME: Intercultural Press.

Simmel, G. (1922). The social significance of the "stranger." In R. Park & E. Burgess (Eds.), *Introduction to the science of sociology* (pp. 322–327). Chicago: University of Chicago Press.

Singer, M. R. (1987). *Intercultural communication: A perceptual approach.* Englewood, Cliffs, NJ: Prentice-Hall.

Smith, A. G. (1982). Content decisions in intercultural communication. *Southern Speech Communication Journal, 47*(3), 252–262.

Storti, C. (1994). *Cross-cultural dialogues: 74 brief encounters with cultural difference.* Yarmouth, ME: Intercultural Press.

Ting-Toomey, S., & Korzenny, F. (Eds.). (1989). *Language, communication, and culture.* Newbury Park, CA: Sage.

Wiseman, R. L. (1995). *Intercultural communication theory.* Thousand Oaks, CA: Sage.

Wiseman, R. L. (1997). *Instructor's manual to accompany Communicating with Strangers.* New York: McGraw-Hill.

Wiseman, R. L., & Koester, J. (Eds.). (1993). *Intercultural communication competence.* Newbury Park, CA: Sage.

14

Teaching Interviewing

Charles J. Stewart
Purdue University

The interviewing course has become commonplace in the curricula of colleges and universities. Interviewing is a practical course that attracts students and is fun to teach. It is easy to motivate students, most of whom are juniors and seniors with some relevant interviewing experiences, and to generate insightful and lively class discussions. Unfortunately, students often enroll in interviewing courses expecting to be transformed quickly and easily into effective job applicants. Interviewing to them means employment interviewing and "being interviewed." They yearn for simple steps and correct answers to frequently asked questions and are eager to get into interviews with little or no reading and study of theory that is not real world. Students object to written examinations in interviewing courses because they believe firmly that practice makes perfect, even when they do not know what they should be practicing.

Inform students during the first class period, and repeat as often as necessary, that your course will provide them with practical experiences in a variety of interviewing types as well as the principles, theory, and research that will enable them to understand and take part effectively as both interviewer and interviewee. There will be examinations, and interviews will be graded on content as well as execution. Grading standards will be as high as any other advanced college course. A reality check early in the course will significantly reduce complaints that the course was not what they expected.

UNIT 1: INTRODUCTION TO INTERVIEWING

The introductory unit is critical because it introduces students to the principles and practices that are applicable to all types of interviews. Succeeding units will apply and build on these principles and practices and adapt them to specialized interviews. Begin by formulating a working definition that sets the interview apart from other interpersonal forms of communication and identifies its essential ingredients (Barone & Switzer, 1995; Wilson & Goodall, 1991). For example, you may define the interview as "an interactional communication process between two parties, at least one of whom has a predetermined and serious purpose, and usually involves the asking and answering of questions" (Stewart & Cash, 1997, p. 1). *Interactional* identifies an exchanging of roles (interviewer and interviewee), responsibilities, beliefs, and information during interviews. Each party speaks and listens from time to time. *Communication process* emphasizes the interaction of many variables (perceptions, verbal and nonverbal symbols, feedback, situation) with and on one another and a degree of structure not found in mere conversation. *Two parties* denotes that more than two people may take part in an interview (one journalist interviewing two people, two police officers interviewing one suspect, three members of a company interviewing an applicant) but never more than two parties, an interviewer party and an interviewee party. *Predetermined and serious purpose* signifies that, unlike conversations, at least one of the parties has a serious purpose (other than mere enjoyment) and has done some planning and structuring prior to the interview. *Asking and answering of questions* means that most interviews cannot fulfill the goals of the two parties without skillfully asked questions and carefully formulated answers. Discussion of a definition makes students aware, first, that interviewing involves more than appearance, a firm handshake, and a few clever answers and, second, that its forms are many: journalistic, survey, employment, performance review, counseling, problem-solving, persuasive, and informing.

The Ingredients in the Process

Once students understand what is and is not an interview, make them aware of the many ingredients that interact in the complex interview process. This may be the only college course that introduces them to the intricacies of interpersonal communication. They need to understand the nature and importance of relational dimensions between the two parties (similarity, inclusion and involvement, affection and liking, control and dominance, trust); the problems of upward and downward communication inherent in many interviews (employee–supervisor, applicant–recruiter, student–professor); perceptions (of self, other party, and situation); cultural differences; verbal and nonverbal communication; listening; the two fundamental approaches (directive and nondirective); and situational variables such as location, seating, rules, noise, and timing (Littlejohn, 1996).

Place all interpersonal principles into an interviewing context. Provide real-life examples, often from your own or former students' experiences, and encourage students to provide illustrations from their experiences. Examples help students understand and see the relevance of theory and principles and counteract perceptions that interviewing is confined to applicants and recruiters, journalists and politicians, and poll takers and respondents. Make students aware of how often they take part in interviews as interviewer and interviewee. Have students analyze model interviews with built-in strengths and weaknesses. Unlike perfect models that students might emulate, an imperfect model challenges them to distinguish the good from the bad and to offer suggestions for improvements and alternative means that interviewer and interviewee might have employed. When analyzing model interviews, ask questions such as the following to draw out discussion of key interviewing principles: What makes this an interview? How did the relationship between interviewer and interviewee appear to affect the interview? How did perceptions of each party affect the interview? When and why did the parties exchange the roles of interviewer and interviewee? Which approach was dominant: directive, nondirective, or a combination? How did situational variables influence the interview? How effective were the parties as listeners? What problems, if any, resulted from choice of words?

Structuring the Interview

Once students know what an interview is, understand that they are involved in interviews every day, and appreciate the many variables that interact during interviews, emphasize the importance of structuring interviews. A good textbook will discuss the importance of opening, body, and closing and suggest a variety of techniques; do not waste class time merely repeating textbook material (Barone & Switzer, 1995; Stewart & Cash, 1997; Wilson & Goodall, 1991).

The Opening. Emphasize the importance of the opening to the entire interview. Note how the opening sets the tone for the interactions that take place and how it affects disclosure of feelings and information (Krivonos &

Knapp, 1975; Zunin & Zunin, 1986). Have students analyze a variety of interview openings, considering such questions as: How appropriate was the opening for the situation? How appropriate was the opening for the relationship between the parties? How might other opening techniques have affected the interview? Stress the importance of selecting from among a variety of opening techniques the one or ones best suited for the interview type, interviewee, situation, and purpose. Students want simple formulas and rules: Always do X in Y situation and Z will result. Show through sample openings why interviewers must know (a) the techniques and options available, and (b) how to select and adapt these tools to specific situations and interviewees. Divide your class into small groups and provide each with a hypothetical interview situation. Each group must write an opening and then explain to the class why this opening would be appropriate for the situation and the parties involved (Stewart, 1991).

The Body.   Students come to interviewing courses with the belief that interviewers merely think up a few questions or jot down a few ideas in advance and then "wing it." They think they have observed these practices in televised interviews and employment interviews in which they have taken part. Counteract this impression by first introducing them to the *interview guide* (a careful outline of topics and subtopics to be covered in an interview). The traditional guide for journalists (who, what, when, where, how, and why) and samples from insurance claims adjusters, survey takers, performance reviewers, and recruiters show that professionals prepare interview guides. Remind students of simple outline techniques (most of which they have been introduced to in English and communication courses) and how these help in constructing a well-organized interview and minimize the likelihood of failing to cover important topics or issues.

When students understand what a guide is and how it may be used prior to and during interviews, introduce them to *interview schedules* in which the outline of topics and subtopics becomes an outline of primary and secondary (probing) questions. The thoroughness of preparation may range from a nonscheduled interview, merely an interview guide, to a moderately scheduled interview with all primary and possible secondary questions written out, to a highly scheduled interview in which all primary and secondary questions are prepared and asked in the same wording from interview to interview, to a highly scheduled standardized interview that includes all questions and answer options from which an interviewee must select (Stewart & Cash, 1997; Wilson & Goodall, 1991). Interviewers must select the schedule that is most appropriate for their skill levels, amount of preparation time, desired degree of control, the breadth and depth of information needed, the necessity to adapt to particular parties, and the degree of precision, reproducibility, or reliability required. Review sample interviews with students and have them reconstruct the guides or schedules employed. Use hypothetical interview situations to challenge students to select the schedule or combination of schedules most appropriate for each situation.

The Closing.   Emphasize the importance of the closing in maintaining the relationship and trust established during the interview and for future interactions between the interview parties. Discuss common interview closings, including nonverbal signals that "leave-taking" is commencing (Knapp, Hart, Friedrich, & Shulman, 1973; Stewart & Cash, 1997). Have students analyze a variety of interview closings, considering questions such as: How appropriate was the closing for the situation and for the interchanges during the interview? How appropriate was it for the relationship between the parties? Which closing techniques would they have used? Remind students that an interview is not over as long as interviewer and interviewee are within sight or sound of one another.

An ungraded "ice-breaker" interview exercise can provide a reasonably stress-free opportunity both to take part in interviews in the classroom setting for the first time and to discuss the interpersonal communication and structuring principles covered in class and readings (Stewart, 1991, 1997). Divide the class into trios (interviewer, interviewee, and observer) and conduct 5-minute interviews in which interviewers attempt to learn all they can about their interviewees and observers note what is happening and why. Conduct three rounds so each person plays all three roles. When the last round is completed, ask questions such as: How did interviewers open interviews? How did interviewers structure the body of their interviews? Which topics were covered and which were avoided? How did interviewers close interviews? Which interviewing approach (directive or nondirective) did interviewers employ? Did the parties exchange the roles of interviewer and interviewee? How did language help and hinder the interviews? What nonverbal behaviors did you observe, and how did they affect the interviews? Which listening approaches dominated the interviews? How did perceptions of self, other, and situation affect the interviews? How did cultural, gender, racial, ethnic, or age differences between parties affect the interviews?

Types and Uses of Questions

Although questions are the tools of the trade in interviewing, student attitudes are often a variation of "a question is a question, so why are we learning all of these names?" Introduce students to a variety of question types
and how they are essential for successful interviewing (Payne, 1980).
Classroom drills in which students identify types and uses of questions, critique questions, and provide probing or follow-up questions enable them to
learn the art of asking questions

Types of Questions.   Ask students to identify a variety of questions in
four ways: open or closed; primary or secondary; neutral or leading; and a
special tool such as nudging probe, informational probe, silent probe, clearinghouse probe, reflective probe, mirror probe, or loaded question (Barone
& Switzer, 1995; Stewart & Cash, 1997; Wilson & Goodall, 1991). Emphasize, for instance, that interviewers who know and understand question
tools ask bipolar questions only when they want interviewees to answer yes
or no or select between two choices such as agree or disagree. They ask
closed questions only when they want brief answers, they ask leading questions only when they want to influence how a person responds, and they ask
reflective questions when they want to clarify or verify answers.
    As students identify questions, discuss how choices of options might af-
fect answers, degree of self-disclosure, relationships, cooperation, and accurate transmission of information. Explain, for instance, what a mirror
probe, nudging probe, or clearinghouse probe can do for a journalist, job
applicant, counselor, health care provider, or patient. Compare and contrast
question types to show how they are similar and different and perform
unique functions in interviews. Students begin to appreciate how specific
question tools are designed to get information efficiently and effectively
and enhance two-way communication in interviews.

Probing Questions.   Most interviews are nonscheduled or moderately
scheduled, in which probing questions are critical because answers are often vague, suggestible, incorrect, incomplete, superficial, or irrelevant. A
respondent might remain silent. The skilled interview participant must be
able within a second or two to (a) determine if a response is unsatisfactory or
contains clues about feelings, attitudes, disclosure, or potentially important
information; (b) select an appropriate probing or follow-up question; and
(c) phrase the question effectively. Have students supply probing (secondary) questions in sequences such as the following:

Interviewer: What kind of person was your last supervisor?

Interviewee: Demanding.

Interviewer:

Require students to identify the problem with the answer, the possible cause for the problem (including a poorly phrased question), the question tool they would use, and then phrase the probing question. Insist that students ask a probing question and not a primary question that delves into a different area of inquiry. The following is a typical example of a primary instead of a secondary question:

Interviewer: Who do you plan to vote for in the presidential election?

Interviewee: Oh, I don't know.

Interviewer: Which candidate do you think will do the most for college students?

This follow-up question does not get closer to which candidate the respondent is most likely to vote for, the intent of the original question. Discuss a variety of better options such as "Who are you leaning toward at the moment?" or "If the election were being held today, who would you vote for?"

Phrasing Questions.   A great many problems develop in interviews because of poor question phrasing and selection. First, analyze questions that illustrate common phrasing problems. Focus on factors such as language, relevance, information level, complexity, and accessibility (questions that involve social, psychological, or situational constraints). Ask students to identify the phrasing problem and then rephrase the question to make it more effective. Emphasize how a single poorly selected word may lead to a vague, inaccurate, or incomplete answer. Second, analyze questions that commit common pitfalls, such as the bipolar trap, open-to-closed switch, double-barreled inquisition, leading push, guessing game, and yes (no) response (Stewart & Cash, 1997). Have students identify the pitfall each question commits and then rephrase it to make it a better question, avoiding another pitfall.

Question Sequences.   Students think that interviewers merely write down questions that come to mind as they approach an interview. The earlier discussion of interview guides and schedules reduces this perception, but students need to understand that skilled interviewers employ question sequences such as funnel, inverted funnel, tunnel, or quintamensional design (Barone & Switzer, 1995; Stewart & Cash, 1997; Wilson & Goodall, 1991). Ask students to identify the question sequence or sequences apparent in sample interviews to understand the uniqueness of sequences and how they may be used in interviews. Pose hypothetical interview situations and ask students to explain which sequence or sequences they would use in each.

A Skills-Building Exercise

The first graded assignment should challenge students to exhibit and develop the fundamental skills emphasized in Unit 1 that are applicable to most interviews. These include asking well-designed questions, listening carefully to answers to detect clues and problems, probing into answers for valuable information, and being patient and persistent until the necessary information is attained. Many instructors find a case approach in which interviewers are provided with only a brief sketch of an event or happening to be an effective skills-building exercise (Stewart, 1991, 1997). Interviewees should be reticent (answer bipolar questions with a yes or no, closed questions with exactly what is asked for and no more, and open questions with a sentence or two) to force interviewers to listen carefully, be patient and persistent, avoid common question pitfalls, and use a variety of probing questions. They will discover how often they ask bipolar and closed questions and how little information they get when asking them. Instructors may play the role of interviewee because they are more skilled at giving information accurately, maintaining a degree of reticence, and rescuing interviewers who become confused. Because some students see this assignment as "not realistic" and course units as separate rather than cumulative, repeat and illustrate often how the skills being practiced in this exercise are essential for the units that follow and for many real-life situations.

Unit 1 Test

Use a mixture of objective and essay questions. Multiple-choice questions assess knowledge of principles, theories, and research findings. Essay questions (in which students critique openings, closings, and questions; create guides, schedules, and sequences; and discuss uses of interviewing approaches and techniques) assess skills in applying principles, theories, and research. Students complain less about application questions than multiple-choice, true–false, definition, and listing questions.

UNIT 2: INFORMATIONAL INTERVIEWING

The second unit of the interviewing course should delve into both information-giving and information-getting interviews—building on the principles, theory, and research introduced in Unit 1. This unit introduces students to principles and skills necessary for a variety of specialized interviews such as journalistic, employee selection, persuasive, performance review, counseling, and health care.

Information-Giving Interviews

Most of us give information and instructions every day, but we rarely question the nature or success of our techniques. We assume that what we do often we do well, but it is easy to recall major problems caused by ineffective or defective information-giving techniques. Focus on problems encountered when transmitting information orally and the means available to improve accurate transmission and retention of information. Research in health care interactions provides a wealth of examples that illustrate the problems with transmitting apparently simple bits of information to presumably highly motivated interviewees—patients (Parratt, 1994; Rowan & Hoover, 1995).

A simple "parlor" exercise is fun and illustrates dramatically how information is omitted, added, changed, and distorted when passed from person to person (Stewart, 1991, 1997). Send four or five students out of the room; call one in and read a paragraph-length message. Call a second student in and have the first student repeat the message from memory; repeat this procedure until all selected students have heard and repeated the now distorted message. Repeat this exercise two or three times with different messages and added techniques, such as repeating the entire message twice for each student or allowing each student to ask three simple questions before repeating the message from memory. Provide students in the classroom with copies of the messages so they can keep track of what happens as the messages are transmitted from student to student. After trying a number of messages and techniques, discuss why information is lost or distorted and ways to improve information giving, including strategic use of repetitions and questions, structure, elimination of extraneous materials, oral emphasis on key words, visual aids, and control of the setting (particularly noise, interruptions, and other people present).

Survey Interviews

Discuss and illustrate survey principles and techniques because we are in-volved frequently in surveys and polls as interviewers and interviewees. First, act as a person seeking expert advice on how to prepare and conduct a survey on a topic of interest to your students—changes in the school calen-dar, adding pluses and minuses to final course grades, changes in core re-quirements, and bringing different professional entertainment to campus. The students are your experts. Pose questions that require them to consider options influenced by your purpose and limitations such as money and time in which to conduct the survey and report results. Ask, for example: What re-search should you do? Should you conduct a cross-sectional or longitudinal study? What is your population or target group? How many people should you interview and where? How should you select these people? How accu-rate should your results be? How advisable would it be to conduct all or part of your interviews over the telephone? How should you open the interviews and close them? What type of interview schedule should you use?

Second, focus class discussion on survey questions. Discuss question uses, strategies, and scales. Identify amd evaluate survey questions from political, religious, professional, and commercial organizations. Analyze a survey interview to see how it is opened, conducted, and closed. Encourage students to think how questions might be altered to make them more effec-tive and detect information areas left out of the survey.

The Journalistic or Probing Interview

Probing interview principles and skills are essential for many types of inter-views. If you have a significant number of journalism students in your class, adapt this unit to the journalistic interview. Emphasize methods of prepara-tion, selection of interviewees and interviewers, probing questions, common question pitfalls, note taking and tape recording, handling difficult situations and interviewees, and interviewee skills. Be sure to analyze interviewers and interviewees in sample interviews and interview segments.

Information-Getting Exercise

If you have a large number of journalism students in your class, you may design a graded exercise that requires students to act as journalists by as-signing them situations and events to investigate or explore (Benjaminson & Anderson, 1990). If not, then you might use a "career" assignment such as the following (Stewart, 1997). The goal for the interviewer is to learn as much as possible about the interviewee's career preparation, work experiences, employment interviewing experiences, and short- and long-range career goals. This assignment is a summary experience in that it involves all principles and theories students have learned in the first two units of the course. Remind students to review previous readings and notes on openings, schedules, questions, and closings. A central point throughout the course should be the need to adapt to each interviewee because the interviewer rarely knows what information a person will have or reveal or how a person will react to specific questions and the setting. To ensure the need to adapt and to prevent interviewers and interviewees from getting together prior to class to plan their questions and answers, assign interviewees for the day after the class begins. This assignment is more "realistic" and less stressful than the skills-building exercise and it gives students an introduction to the employment selection process they will discuss later in the semester and for which many of them are in the course.

Unit 2 Test

Use a mixture of objective and essay questions. Include application questions in which students create, analyze, and critique. They will learn more by doing than by picking a correct answer out of five choices. Include questions about the roles, strategies, and tactics of interviewees in information getting, survey, and journalistic or probing interviews.

SELECTING ADDITIONAL UNITS OF STUDY

Interviewing courses with students from a wide range of majors tend to introduce them to the major interviewing types encountered in their professional and nonprofessional lives: informational (Benjaminson & Anderson, 1990; Holstein & Gubrium, 1995), persuasive (Larson, 1995; Woodward & Denton, 1996), and employment (Einhorn, Bradley, & Baird, 1981; Gill & Lewis, 1996; Cunningham, 1998). If a course has many students majoring in organizational communication, management, or business, you may include a unit on the performance review (Murphy & Cleveland, 1995). If many students are in the education, psychology, or health care fields, the course may contain units on counseling and health care interviews (Benjamin, 1987; Hansen, 1994; Roter & Hall, 1992). Include units that appear to meet the needs and expectations of your students and school. Do not include so many units that students do not learn the basics essential for interviewing or get a depth of training and experience in the most common forms of interviewing.

CONCLUSION

Regardless of the units covered in your course, focus discussions, analysis, and practice on interviewing principles, theory, and research. Interviewing should be neither an interpersonal communication course nor a management, counseling, or sales course. Introduce students to the approaches, structuring techniques, and question tools available to interviewers and teach them how to select the best ones for each interview. Address instruction and practice to the role of respondent as well as survey taker or journalist, recruiter as well as applicant, counselee as well as counselor, persuadee as well as persuader, and patient as well as health care professional. Make your course practical but insist that students learn principles, theories, and research findings that help them understand and perform effectively.

REFERENCES

Barone, J. T. & Switzer, J. Y. (1995). *Interviewing art & skill.* Boston: Allyn & Bacon.

Benjamin, A. (1987). *The helping interview* (3rd ed.). Boston: Houghton Mifflin.

Benjaminson, P., & Anderson, D. (1990). *Investigative reporting.* Bloomington: Indiana University Press.

Cunningham, J. R. (1998). *The inside scoop; Recruiters tell college students their secrets for success in the job search.* New York: McGraw-Hill.

Einhorn, L. J., Bradley, P. H., & Baird, J. E. (1981). *Effective employment Interviewing: Unlocking human potential.* Glenview, IL: Scott, Foresman.

Gill, A. M., & Lewis, S. M. (1996). *Help wanted: An inexperienced job seeker's complete guide to career success.* Prospect Heights, IL: Waveland Press.

Hansen, J. C. (1994). *Counseling: Theory and practice.* Boston: Allyn & Bacon.

Holstein, J. A., & Gubrium, J. F. (1995). *The active interview.* Newbury Park, CA: Sage.

Knapp, M. L., Hart, R. P., Friedrich, G. W., & Shulman, G. M. (1973). The rhetoric of goodbye: Verbal and nonverbal correlates of human leave-taking, *Speech Monographs, 40,* 182–198.

Krivonos, P. D., & Knapp, M. L. (1975). Initiating communication: What do you say when you say hello? *Central States Speech Journal, 26,* 115–125.

Larson, C. U. (1995). *Persuasion: Reception and responsibility* (7th ed.). Belmont, CA: Wadsworth.

Littlejohn, S. W. (1996). *Theories of human communication* (5th ed.). Belmont, CA: Wadsworth.

Murphy, K. R., & Cleveland, J. (1995). *Understanding performance appraisal.* Thousand Oaks, CA: Sage.

Parratt, R. (1994). Exploring family practitioners' and patients' information exchange about prescribed medications: Implications for practitioners' interviewing and patients' understanding, *Health Communication, 6,* 267–280.

Payne, S. (1980). *The art of asking questions* (2nd ed.). Princeton, NJ: Princeton University Press.

Roter, D., & Hall, J. A. (1992). *Doctors talking with patients, patients talking with doctors: Improving communication in medical visits.* Westport, CT: Auburn House.

Rowan, K. E., & Hoover, D. M. (1995). Communicating risk to patients: Detecting, diagnosing, and overcoming lay theories, *Communicating risk to patients: Proceedings of the conference, September 20–21, 1994* (pp. 74–81). Rockville, MD: U.S. Pharmacopeial Convention.

Stewart, C. J. (1991). *Teaching interviewing for career preparation* (2nd ed.). Bloomington, IN: ERIC Clearinghouse on Reading and Communication Skills.

Stewart, C. J. (1997). *Interviewing principles and practices: Applications & exercises* (8th ed.). Dubuque, IA: Kendall/Hunt.

Stewart, C. J., & Cash, W. B., Jr. (1997). *Interviewing: Principles and practices* (8th ed.). Madison, WI: Brown & Benchmark Publishers.

Wilson, G. L., & Goodall, H. L., Jr. (1991). *Interviewing in context.* New York: McGraw-Hill.

Woodward, G. C., & Denton, R. E., Jr. (1996). *Persuasion and influence in American life* (3rd ed.). Prospect Heights, IL: Waveland Press.

Zunin, L., & Zunin, N. (1986). *The first four minutes* (2nd ed.). Los Angeles: Nash.

15

Teaching Mass Communication and Telecommunication

Thomas A. McCain
Ohio State University

Jeanine Warisse Turner
Georgetown University

The convergence in new media technologies is creating exciting and challenging possibilities for how the mass media and the processes of mediated communication can be taught and understood. The study of the mass media has evolved from an understanding of the press and broadcast media to an exploration of new forms of media that offer many opportunities for innovation and impact. Contemporary students are no longer relegated to the role of audience member, as they now have the opportunity to actively participate in the creation and dissemination of messages. Understanding current events in entertainment, news, the arts, health, and education is related to an understanding of how the media are inextricably woven into the fabric of students' everyday lives. Today students can and will find ways to participate in discussions about these and other topics with others all over the world via the Internet. This transformation of content, transmission, and form of media messages that began in the mid-1980s and continues today is altering conceptions of mass media and audience (Negroponte, 1995). Therefore, the role of learning about the mass media and telecommunications is changing to help students learn about communication technologies and the evolving relationship of audience and message creator.

The traditional media forms of television, radio, newspaper, and films have already expanded to encompass cable television, videotape, multimedia computers, and computer networks. These changes in media form are also transforming the way content is produced and received. For example, an individual is no longer limited to the views of a specific newspaper, but can now create and receive a personalized newspaper comprised of subjects that he or she is interested in from a variety of newspaper sources all over the world (see http://botspot.com for an archive of these "knowbots" that can be used with your students). This changing role of audience can create interesting class discussion as theories created with older media in mind are challenged by new media forms. In addition, there are critical and cultural approaches to interpreting the mass media that can be helpful to students in locating how and why the media are knotted tightly with most aspects of the contemporary world (Douglas, 1994; Fiske, 1987; Grossberg, 1992; Jones, 1995).

TRADITIONAL UNDERSTANDINGS OF MASS COMMUNICATION

Historically, the *mass media* described organizations that engaged in the production or distribution of messages for public consumption by large audiences (television, radio, and newspaper organizations). Telecommunications organizations have been those that traditionally engaged in activities of distribution, transformation, and storage of messages (telephone, satellite, and computer networks). Since the early 1990s many of these relations have changed as new communication technologies have blurred the distinctions between content creators and content distributors (Baldwin, McVoy, & Steinfield, 1996; Dizard, 1997; Straubhaar & LaRose, 1996). However, understanding our traditional conceptions of the mass media can provide a foundation for contrasting how the capabilities offered by many new communication technologies may alter these conceptions.

Encoding and Decoding

Two issues that are central to understanding mass communication phenomenon are the rather separate processes of encoding and decoding. Most courses and curricula need to address: (a) the processes and practices of individuals and organizations that produce, store, distribute, and transform information into mediated communication messages; and (b) the uses, consequences, or effects of this message content and this media form for individuals, groups, societies, and culture. Embedded within these processes is the complex issue of defining what constitutes the message itself. Several theories have been developed that describe the encoding and decoding processes and their relation to one another in a social context (for various summaries and elaboration of these theories, see Becker, 1987; DeFleur & Ball-Rokeach, 1989; McQuail, 1992; McQuail & Windahl, 1993; Severin & Tankard, 1992).

Message Creators and Receivers

Historically, the relationships between source and receiver were seldom interactional because receivers had very limited functional control over the activities of sources (Avery & McCain, 1982). The creators of mass communication messages, or sources, have been involved in exchange processes whereby they sell or trade in audience attention. In the United States, media sources "sell" audiences to advertisers. This practice is becoming more universal, as media are being privatized and supported by advertising the world over (Stevenson, 1994). Mass communication sources have traditionally been groups or organizations and not individuals.

This relationship between source and receiver is changing. With the advent of new communication technologies like the advancement of the World Wide Web, mass media systems that at one time created few opportunities for interaction are now opening up new avenues for message production and exchange. Through the use of electronic bulletin boards, online chat rooms, and the rapid creation and diffusion of personal Web home pages, individuals have the opportunity to create messages to be received by mass audiences. The future promises virtual reality games, demonstrations, and learning environments capable of altering the living and learning of students everywhere.

The convergence of computers and telecommunications technologies are changing at an unbelievable rate. Technologically, computer power of today is 8,000 times less expensive than it was 30 years ago. Telecommunication capability is changing rapidly, too, with local area network speeds increasing 50 to 100 times in the past decade (Ringwall, 1995). Randall Tobias, former Vice Chairman of AT&T, illustrated the rapid advancement in computers and telecommunications technology by noting that similar progress in the automotive technology would produce a Lexus for about $2 that would travel at the speed of sound and travel 600 miles on a thimble of gas (Ringwall, 1995). The rapid pace of technological change in communication technology that at one time was thought of as mass media is also altering how organizations are dealing with their daily practices. In health care, for example, the use of a television-like environment is being used to bring doctors and patients together via telecommunications. These participants bring their expectations about television to an environment that has been traditionally interpersonal (Warisse, 1996). Although technology is changing rapidly, our conceptions and understandings of the mass media and what it means is changing at a "human pace," which is much slower! Therefore, many of our theories and explanations of the mass media, mediated communication, and mass communication are based on more traditional conceptions of media. Dizard (1997) referred to these as "old media."

Theories of "Old Media"

In other communication contexts, transactional and interactional models of communication are prevalent and of high currency. These approaches are of little use in traditional conceptions of the mass media, as the messages created by media industries have a time and space dimension that is quite different from interpersonal or public-speaking situations. Most media messages are not alterable by audiences once they have been encoded by a source. Therefore, for the study of mass communication, channel capacity, technology, and message form become important for understanding mass communication processes. (For further explanations of the changes in telecommunications technologies, their channel capacity, and their influence on message creation and production see Baldwin, et al., 1996; Negroponte, 1995; Straubhaar & LaRose, 1996.)

The focus of most research in mass communication has been on the decoding process—What are the effects? Wanting to understand the audience has resulted from both commercial interests, as well as interest in the media's potential to influence existing values in society. Historically, as the mass media and telecommunications became important sources of value information for individuals and society, the institutions responsible for teaching and monitoring information and values became alarmed. In a relatively short period of historical time, broadcasting and the press became institutions of potential influence similar to the family, church, business, government, and education. The mass media serve a variety of functions as institutions: surveillance of the environment (news reporting), reflections on the news and other phenomenon of importance (editorials), socialization with existing norms and values (education), and entertainment for the non-work-related needs of society (Lasswell, 1948/1960; Wright, 1975). The media can also be viewed as a storytelling machine, communicating the myths and heroes of the culture it reflects (McQuail, 1987). Other conceptions of the media are those of big and powerful institutions, the everyday practices of which shape the knowledge base that society draws from (Turow, 1992).

For individuals, the media are used in a variety of ways that are often unrelated to the content of programs. Broadcast media are used for information, guidance, a source of conversation, and a social avoidance vehicle. They are used for background noise and as a source for parasocial interaction. Some of the uses and gratifications that people derive from the media are related to the salience of their needs, their age group, and the range of options available for need satisfaction (Dimmick, McCain, & Bolton, 1979; Rosengren, Palmgreen, & Wenner, 1985). Individuals are affected by media messages through a host of selectivity filters that govern the reception of messages including selective exposure, attention, perception, and recall (Severin & Tankard, 1992; Zillman & Bryant, 1985).

The issues related to society and the mass media that have received the most attention from parents, politicians, social critics, media personnel, educators, and religious leaders parallel the topics that have been most widely researched by mass communication scholars. The enduring issues for both society at large and media professionals include racism and stereotyping; role models and stereotyping; effects on beliefs, attitudes, and opinions; media portrayals of violence; arousal and pornography; effects on the political process; the electronic church; advertising; cultural imperialism and the flow of information and technology; development and mass communication; freedom of the press; and specific effects on children (Dennis & Merrill, 1996; Jeffries, 1986).

Student research and debate over whether the media influences society or is a reflection of it can create interesting discussion with students and engage them in the important role that mass communication plays in today's society. For example, controversial television shows and the public discussion surrounding them can make the conflicting role of the media in society more explicit for students. A 1997 issue of *Time* magazine presented a chronology of controversial episodes (Handy, 1997). In 1953, the *I Love Lucy* show featured Lucy's expectant son Ricky but use of the word *pregnant* was not permitted on the show. A 1968 episode of *Star Trek* featured television's first interracial kiss. A 1972 episode of *Maude* confronted the abortion issue. A 1997 episode of *Ellen* brought lesbianism to a prominent role in a situation comedy. The producers of these television shows weighed audience support for the issue and advertising sponsor dollars when making program content decisions (Handy, 1997). Discussion of the varying views surrounding controversial programs across the different media types cannot only bring awareness to students, but can also stimulate critical thinking skills. These skills will help students to evaluate the interdependencies between media, content, and social life.

PURPOSES FOR STUDYING MASS COMMUNICATION AND TELECOMMUNICATIONS

The choice of mass communication and telecommunications education within a curriculum needs to be made within the context of the variety of options available. There are several possible general approaches or goals, including (a) preparing students for the world of work and careers; (b) helping students to understand generally the physical, artistic, and social world in which they live; (c) teaching students how to think and solve problems; (d) learning about the accumulation of knowledge in a particular field or specialty; and (e) teaching and learning about values and the valuing processes of societies and individuals. The emphasis that teachers place on these approaches varies within the faculty of any one school and among curricula of different schools. However, it is important that media course objectives be understood in light of the varying possible orientations to instruction and that they be consistent with the general objectives or orientations of other departmental offerings.

Applied Issues

The practical and applied approaches to studying newspaper, radio, television, and the new electronic media are quite popular. Students learn the language of visualization, sound, display, and format across each different type of medium. For all students of communication, some technical skill with communication media seems desirable and with the advent of the World Wide Web and its demand for multimedia content, the need for computer skills and the media has become a necessity. It is ironic that most students spend years studying the form and function of words and books, yet very few with cameras, microphones, computer programs, or television programs. Just as reading skills are taught through writing, viewing skills can be taught by program production courses. This hands-on approach is involving and relevant for the learner, educator, and media industry.

A variety of technical skills and information is required to engage in the production of mediated messages. The practice of making radio programs, music videos, student newspapers, and Web pages allows students to gain these skills in simulated real-world environments. Learning and practicing media skills are essential for all students of media. This is not the same as using the curriculum to prepare students for professional careers in media industries (see Blanchard & Christ, 1993).

What is important to note is that the applied nature of mediated communication, be it the old mass communication paradigm or the emerging personalized media processes, requires that hands-on practice should be part of the curriculum. However, its emphasis should be tempered by other issues regarding resources and department goals. This applied orientation should be understood in the broader context of the importance of mass media and personal media as they operate in contemporary societies.

Theoretical Issues

The theoretical issues that demand attention in studying mass communication involve politics, economics, ethics, and social and psychological impact. Although there are technological imperatives of tremendous importance, much of the structure and content of the media are shaped by accidents and forces of history—such as who owns what, the contemporary hot social issues, and the cost for both consumers and producers. The political, economic, and social pressures that transpired at the time a particular communication technology developed shape for generations the content and the format of a medium within its culture. Although there are similarities in radio and newspapers from country to country, there are profound differences as well. For example, if television is just a technology, then what is broadcast in the United States should be the same as what is broadcast in Nicaragua; but it is not. There should be no difference in the newspapers of the United Kingdom and Sweden, but there are. These issues are playing out in the 1990s between the early users and developers of the Internet and their vision for a new democratic, nonhierarchical media and the commercial interests of companies and service providers who see the Internet as a new form for commerce (Rheingold, 1994). Students need to be able to identify concrete examples of how social, political, and economic factors influence the institutions of telecommunication and the mass media.

In the Persian Gulf war, for example, audiences from London to Tokyo and Oshkosh to Jerusalem witnessed the conduct of bombing raids live and in color in their living rooms as the assault was occurring. Millions around the globe listened and watched as Cable News Network's coverage of this event was instant and unedited. Even the military leaders relied on this coverage to determine what was happening. The smart technology that was used to conduct the war was the same technology reporters were using to send live messages from the front. The Israelis even established a radio station that did not broadcast anything except warning signals that their satellite tracking system used to intercept incoming missiles headed for Israeli towns. Israelis tuned their radio stations to this frequency when they wanted to sleep, but knew that if there was an attack, the radio station would broadcast a message that would awaken them to prepare for the attack. Because of the nature of the terrain, the allied forces were able to string hundreds of miles of fiber optic cable to stay in contact with forces at the front. Those same forces at the front were in contact via e-mail with friends back home who often discussed issues before they made it to the printing presses of the world's newspapers, and often before the chain of command among the military personnel had access to the same information (McCain & Shyles, 1994). New uses of communication technology for both mass communication and personal communication blur old conceptions of the role of the media in contemporary societies.

The rapid diffusion and change in communication technology is part of a change in the structure of modern societies worldwide—simultaneous and seemingly contradictory movements toward localism and globalization. The internationalization of economies (along with cross-national political and social alliances) makes mass communication policy issues incredibly relevant for today's media student. As international interdependence gets nearly daily coverage in the press, another social movement is also occurring across the industrialized world. It is a return to local communities and individuals "cocooning" themselves at home. Both globalization and localism are phenomena that parallel rapid growth in available communication technology and media. The personalized mass media accessible through the Internet allow for groups of persons with similar interests to create *virtual communities* that may not share the same geographical space, but instead share a contextual space. Virtual communities are seen as tremendously involving for the participants, although for some social critics the heavy use of these fora may signal a new form of media addiction (Rheingold, 1994).

Encoding Processes—The Shape of Media Organizations

In order to understand the dynamic processes of mass communication, particularly in relation to new communication technologies, students must be able to identify how particular technologies become a medium of a particular type, serving a particular function and purpose. To understand these issues more clearly, students can study the history of the local ownership of newspapers, radio, television stations, Internet service providers, and cable operators. Who controls what movies are played in town? Who dictates which music is played on local radio stations? How does the local cable operator decide which of the hundreds of cable network offerings that are available will be carried on the local cable network? How do America Online, Compuserve, or Microsoft Network decide which services are free and which require payment for access? Researching answers to these kinds of questions helps students understand the linkages between media institutions and society.

The reason the media and telecommunications are the way they are in each country, as well as in each town and state, has to do with the interaction between (a) what is technologically possible, what it costs, and who is in control; and (b) what constitutes the critical social issues of the day. The possibilities for lively debates should lead to discussions that engage students both inside and outside the classroom.

STUDENT LEARNING ACTIVITIES

Interviewing

One way to discover aspects of both encoding and decoding processes in media and telecommunications is to have students interview a variety of senders and receivers of media. There are professionals who write, produce, engineer, film, distribute, fund, and create media messages everywhere. Telephone personnel, satellite distributors, politicians and newsmakers, and sponsors and cable installers all consider media and telecommunications part of their daily routines. Regular interviewing and discussions with such personnel helps to contextualize the mass media encoding process.

Students might also interview people of different ages, ethnicity, gender, or geographic location regarding their media experiences and dependencies. For example, student interaction with the elderly and children about their television viewing can be a particularly useful way of understanding the variety of meanings and uses that the media have for others. Using international penpals not only helps students and faculty understand other approaches to mass media and telecommunications, but the process of having to explain the U.S. system to others can help to clarify important points about their own existing practices.

Production and Performance

Nothing can make the process of mass communication as vivid as student participation in the production of such things as programs, Web pages, newspapers, magazines, videos, and newsgroups. The organizational experience of collaboration, deadlines, and strict format requirements help students to understand a variety of communication principles.

Critiques and Evaluation

Part of every mass communication course should be a critical evaluation of media messages, websites, or telecommunication services. It is particularly important that programs and content be understood not only for their social meaning, but also in terms of their commercial intent. For example, students can describe advertisements that are shown during a television program and determine the "needed audience" for the show based on the likely purchasers of the products in the spots. Exercises like these help to contextualize the content of both the encoding and decoding processes in U. S. media.

Media Use Exercises

Helping students become aware of their own complicated uses of the media and telecommunication facilitates further understanding of the media and the relations among audience need, audience use, content, and habit. One approach is to have a day where students avoid all media and telecommunication while monitoring and logging their behavior. Another method is to have students log their use of the media and telecommunication over 1 week. This log can be analyzed in a paper and interpreted in light of the audience uses and effects literature. A third approach is to focus on the varying uses and needs of students and to log their media and nonmedia activity in light of these needs. Having students analyze, write about, and discuss their reactions to these activities can stimulate them to think about the role that the media and telecommunications play in their own lives.

Students should also compare the roles various media play in the lives of their community. Have students take a current events story that they are interested in and follow its coverage for a week through a variety of media, such as broadcast television, cable television, radio, film, the Web, and Internet chat groups. The student can then compare and contrast these technologies and the way that they influence one another, as well as the coverage received.

Simulations

There are a variety of mass communication processes for which direct observation or production is impossible given limited resources and time. Simulating media pressures for deadlines may work well. Likewise, creating situations where students must role-play reactions to particular mass communication phenomenon from the viewpoint of different audiences may give them a chance to step into different perspectives and analyze the impact that program variety can bring to different audiences. For example, having students assume the role of first-, second-, or third-world countries can create lively discussions regarding the effects of importation of U. S. television programming and technology. Similarly, the concepts of freedom, censorship, and ownership can be discussed from these perspectives. By incorporating the Internet into simulations, their authenticity can be enhanced. Students can join a variety of newsgroups and gain a sense of the varying values and opinions for different constituencies.

Reading, Writing, and Research

Students should be encouraged to read, analyze, write about, and discuss the media and issues that are influenced by it. Class discussions are greatly improved when students have prepared even a mini-research report prior to class. Writing to telecommunication and media companies with praise or complaints will usually reap a reply, because these companies seldom hear from their users. Sharing these kinds of authentic tasks with one another helps students to understand the ranges of influence they and others can have on the media.

The Internet and the World Wide Web

The Internet and the World Wide Web provide new essential tools and resources for learning about all matters related to mass communication and telecommunications. Every media outlet has a Web page and can be examined, critiqued, and queried. Teachers and students can create websites for their class, for themselves, and for student projects. Students can, for example, be required to use a search engine to discover a relevant site (universal resource locator, or URL) related to the topic for the day's lesson. In this fashion students and teachers are co-creating the relevant content for the course.

It will be essential that contemporary students of communication acquire competencies with the tools of the Internet; tools that facilitate both their participation in encoding and decoding processes of mediated communication. For example, a course called Living in the Information Age that we have developed at Ohio State allows students to learn the necessary skills related to e-mail, browsers, search engines, knowbots, collaborative work tools, and the like by exploring issues of life. There are "living" units on work, education, travel and leisure, health care, news and information, politics, and mass media as they relate to the information age (visit http://

express.sbs.ohio-state.edu for an archive of various versions of this over the years). The University of Texas archives Web-based courses for all disciplines at their site called the World Lecture Hall (http://www. utexas.edu/world/lecture). It is difficult to know at this writing what the tools of networked communication will be when this chapter is read. Suffice it to say, the use and understanding of the Internet and its evolution will be an essential ingredient in understanding the processes and products of mass media and telecommunications.

CONCLUSION

As the world races toward the 21st century, media and telecommunications are playing a more ubiquitous and influential role than ever before. Mixtures of old and new media are part of a changing view of human interdependence. All interested in human communication must deal with this phenomenon in a meaningful way. Among the most challenging and rewarding parts of the new media environment is a role reversal between teacher and student. In the new environment everyone is a learner. The information explosion is so vast and so unprecedented that there is no way that any teacher or student can keep up. In the new media, younger students unburdened with years of learning in a linear fashion are able to create hypertext, multilayered documents with enormous facility and not much apprehension. Video is fast becoming an acceptable form for documenting and presenting ideas and issues available to everyone. Older students and most teachers have more difficulty in writing in parallel and in collaborative modes. Learning with new media and the changing face of the old media require that student expertise as well as teacher expertise be acknowledged and integrated into the classroom and other learning environments. For communication students, the insights and capabilities that can be gained through problem-based learning in a rich and open new media environment promise large payoffs for the future. Because the amount of knowledge that is produced each year on any topic spirals out of control, the ability to find, evaluate, comprehend, and share knowledge with others becomes an increasingly important communicative ability. Knowledge of the resources and tools of the changing mass media and telecommunications services will help our students successfully reach an otherwise precarious jaunt into the future.

REFERENCES

Avery, R., & McCain, T. (1982). Interpersonal and mediated encounters: A reorientation to the mass communication process. In G. Gumpert & R. Cathcart (Eds.), *Intermedia: Interpersonal communication in a media world* (2nd ed., pp. 29–40) New York: Oxford University Press.

Baldwin, T., McVoy, D., & Steinfield, C. (1996). *Convergence: Integrating media, information, and communication.* Thousand Oaks, CA: Sage.

Becker, S. (1987). *Discovering mass communication* (2nd ed.). Glenview, IL: Scott, Foresman.

Blanchard, R., & Christ, W. (1993). *Media education and the liberal arts: A blueprint for the new professionalism.* Hillsdale, NJ: Lawrence Erlbaum Associates

DeFleur, M., & Ball-Rokeach, S. (1989). *Theories of mass communication* (5th ed.). New York: Longman.

Dennis, E., & Merrill, J. (1996). *Media debates: Issues in mass communication* (2nd ed.). New York: Longman.

Dimmick, J., McCain, T., & Bolton, W. (1979). Media use and the lifespan. *American Behavioral Scientist, 23,* 7–31.

Dizard, W. (1997). *Old media new media: Mass communications in the information age* (2nd ed.). New York: Longman.

Douglas, S. (1994). *Where the girls are: Growing up female with the mass media.* New York: Times Books.

Fiske, J. (1987). *Television culture.* New York: Routledge.

Grossberg, L. (1992). *We gotta get out of this place.* New York: Routledge.

Handy, B. (1997, April 14). Roll over, Ward Cleaver. *Time, 149*(15), 78–85.

Jeffries, L. (1986). *Mass media process and effects.* Prospect Heights, IL: Waveland Press.

Jones, S. (Ed.). 1995. *Cybersociety: Computer-mediated communication and community.* Thousand Oaks, CA: Sage.

Lasswell, H. (1960). The structure and function of communication in society. In W. Schramm (Ed.), *Mass communications* (2nd ed., pp. 117–130). Urbana: University of Illinois Press. (Original work published 1948)

McCain, T., & Shyles, L. (Eds.). (1994). *The 1,000 hour war: Communication in the Gulf.* Westport, CT: Greenwood.

McQuail, D. (1987). *Mass communication theory: An introduction* (2nd ed.). London: Sage.

McQuail, D. (1992). *Media performance: Mass communications and the public interest.* Newbury Park, CA: Sage.

McQuail, D., & Windahl, S. (1993). *Communication models for the study of mass communication* (2nd ed.). London: Longman.

Negroponte, N. (1995). *Being digital.* New York: Knopf.

Rheingold, H. (1994). *The virtual community: Homesteading on the electronic frontier.* New York: HarperPerennial.

Ringwall, E. (1995). Telecommunications in healthcare. *The Journal of Information and Management Systems Society, 9,* 49–52.

Rosengren, K., Palmgreen, P., & Wenner, L. (1985). *Media gratification research: Current perspectives.* Beverly Hills, CA: Sage.

Severin, W., & Tankard, J. (1992). *Communication theories: Origins, methods, and uses in the media* (3rd ed.). New York: Longman.

Stevenson, R. (1994). *Global communication in the twenty-first century.* New York: Longman.

Straubhaar, J., & LaRose, R. (1996). *Communications media in the information society.* Belmont, CA: Wadsworth.

Turow, J. (1992). *Media systems in society.* New York: Longman.

Warisse, J. (1996). *Communicative implications of implementing telemedicine technology: A framework of telecompetence* (Doctoral dissertation, The Ohio State University, 1996). Dissertation Abstracts International, 57-10A, p. 4180. (The University Microfilms No. 9710679).

Wright, C. R. (1975). *Mass communication: A sociological perspective (2nd ed.). New York: Random House.*

Zillman, D., & Bryant, J. (Eds.). (1985). *Selective exposure to communication.* Hillsdale, NJ: Lawrence Erlbaum Associates.

16

Teaching Research Methods

Ruth Anne Clark
University of Illinois

One of the first courses I took as a doctoral student was in research methods. Somewhat to my surprise, I found it very exciting. Research reports that had appeared mysterious and complex became comprehensible. By the end of the course, I felt that perhaps I, too, could conduct studies that might yield interesting and useful results. Unfortunately, many students approach their first research methods course with apprehension. They fear that it will require a good background in mathematics, be technical, and seem boring. If well taught, however, students exit their first research methods course with a feeling of exhilaration and sense of accomplishment. They leave being able to understand and evaluate the logic of research reports. With a bit more training, they are able to contribute to a stream of research findings themselves.

The course may be structured in a number of quite different ways, depending on its constituency and students' needs. Beyond the size of the course, the structure will depend on whether the primary objective of the course is to produce intelligent consumers of research (i.e., students who can read, understand, and evaluate research reports) or whether the primary objective is to produce novice researchers (with the choice frequently depending on whether the course serves undergraduate or graduate students). The other fundamental choice affecting the structure of the course is whether it is intended to introduce students to the broad range of methodologies represented in the discipline or at least in a particular department, or whether it is intended to provide more detailed instruction in one or two basic methodologies.

COURSE OBJECTIVES

Objectives common to most introductory research methods courses are that students should:

1. Understand the goal of research and the basic steps in the research enterprise.
2. Realize that designing a research project involves a series of choices and appreciate the consequences of the fundamental choices to be made.
3. Develop a set of criteria for evaluating the value of the research question, the validity of the claims made at the end of the project, the generalizability of the results, and the ethical considerations involved in conducting and reporting research.

Of the goals that vary with the focus of the particular course, two are the most common, although frequently not represented in the same course. Students should:

4. Appreciate the strengths and limitations of alternative research methodologies.
5. Be able to design, execute, and report a simple research project.

The sections that follow correspond roughly to a potential sequence of course topics. Early sections are appropriate for any introductory research methods course. Later sections will vary by the scope of the course and the methodologies emphasized.

ORIENTATION TOWARD RESEARCH DESIGN

Many research methods books, particularly in the social sciences, begin with brief discussions of fundamental issues involved in design, but quickly turn to alternative data analysis models. In other words, these courses focus primarily on models for statistical analysis. Forunately, most research methods books written by communication scholars place primary emphasis on fundamental design choices. In my view, this is the appropriate focus for the introductory research methods course. Graduate students who will be engaging in research will almost certainly take advanced courses in statistics, conversational analysis, rhetorical analysis, survey methods, or whatever serves their interests. The introductory course, therefore, should equip them to make wise choices that precede the analysis of data, as this is probably the only course in the student's career that will have this emphasis.

Consequently, I begin the course by stressing that research is a process of discovery, and that unlike mathematics, there is no formula to dictate a method of answering a particular question. For any research question, an infinite number of approaches is available, and some of these choices will yield more useful results than others. Thus, in this course, we study the kinds of choices the researcher must make as well as their implications.

Because many students are initially apprehensive, I emphasize that most of what we talk about will not be very technical, but actually may seem more like a course in argumentation, focusing primarily on decisions that will yield a strong link between the data that are gathered and the conclusions that are drawn. Unlike debate, however, the researcher should enter the research project with an open mind about the validity of the hypothesis being tested rather than viewing the research project as an effort to prove the hypothesis. Moreover, different terminology will be employed. I try to reassure students that although they will encounter a large number of new terms early in the course, they quickly will become familiar with these terms and research reports will seem less mysterious. In sum, stress that the course focuses on choices available to the researcher and criteria that guide these decisions.

QUESTIONS FOR RESEARCH

One of the first points I underscore is that any research question can be pursued in literally an infinite number of ways. Consider the question, "Do men and women use different strategies to comfort others?" A conversational analyst might elect to videotape a support group and analyze appropriate utterances. An ethnographer might study a group over an extended period of time, noting instances where comforting was appropriate. A more quantitatively oriented researcher might develop some hypothetical situations designed to elicit comforting messages and have a large number of people either write or tape record what they would say in those circumstances so that the researcher could code the messages into general categories. Within each of these broad approaches, still a very large number of different options exist. For example, in the latter instance, the researcher has many options regarding the nature of the situations, the wording of the instructions to the participants, and the categories chosen for analysis. And the decision made regarding each of these options will influence the results obtained.

A second key point regarding research questions is the need for precision, both in defining terms and in specifying the relationship among the concepts or variables of interest. A seemingly simple research question such as "Are speeches better remembered if they contain highly emotional language than if they contain more neutral language?" is open to very different interpretations. *Emotional language* might refer to specific colorful words or to explicit narratives about emotionally charged events. *Better remembered* can be conceived as being able to summarize major themes or being able to recall concrete facts.

SKELETAL DESIGNS

A useful pedagogical principle in approaching any new concept is to begin with the simplest version and later elaborate on options, caveats, pitfalls, special cases, and the like. Certainly this principle should be used in leading novices into the world of research. To illustrate experimental methods, by the second or third class meeting I introduce the basic ingredients. First we talk about independent and dependent variables because a research question or hypothesis will posit a relation about the potential impact of the independent variable on the dependent variable. Sometimes I begin with examples from medical research. Students easily grasp the notion of comparing the impact of two drugs on the survival rate of AIDS patients. Then I talk about simple questions in communication, for instance, "Is offering sympathy or offering assistance more effective in relieving the distress of someone experiencing a problem?" By stressing the notion that the independent variable is the factor expected to produce an effect and the dependent variable is expected to reflect or display an effect, students very quickly are able to identify the two kinds of variables.

Next I note that offering sympathy and assistance are general categories and that the researcher must find ways to instantiate or operationalize these concepts so that their concrete realization is realistic. By the same token, relieving distress cannot be directly observed, so some measure must be found or devised to assess the dependent variable, thereby emphasizing that operational definitions or instantiations of critical variables are essential to the research design.

Moreover, the only way to study the question is in a specific context. Decisions must be made about the type of distressing situations to be studied, by what media they will be presented, and the like, thus stressing the importance of the context in which the variables are embedded as a key element in a design. The researcher cannot investigate distress without specifying distress to whom. In this way, the concept of experimental subjects or participants is advanced as another critical ingredient in the research design. Finally, the concept of potentially contaminating or confounding variables should be discussed. For instance if the offer of assistance were made by a friend going to the home of the distressed individual, whereas sympathy was conveyed by a printed card that arrived through the mail, the degree of personal contact of the two conditions of the independent variable would differ so greatly that it might distort the real relationship between the independent and dependent variables. Within the course of a single class period, I introduce the students to key ingredients in an experimental design: independent and dependent variables, operational definitions or instantiations, embedded context, participants, and confounding or contaminating variables. I would not discuss these concepts in much more detail than I suggested here.

Students need to master these key concepts before moving to any greater level in detail, and a variety of approaches can help them do so. I distribute a list of these key terms, along with definitions and two or three illustrations. I offer research questions for which the class suggests simple designs and identifies the ingredients in these designs. I also supply abstracts of a number of research reports as a basis for students to identify design ingredients. Abstracts are preferable to entire research reports at this stage, because the reports take considerable time for novice readers to digest. I begin the next couple of class periods with some quick exercises to review these ingredients, at least until students appear in control of these concepts.

STEPS IN THE RESEARCH PROCESS

Now the class is ready to read entire research reports and to consider the actual steps involved in the research enterprise. At this early stage in the course, I select readings that are relatively easy to read. Because I concentrate on design features rather than substantive issues, if I were emphasizing primarily quantitative methods, I might choose articles from "brief reports" sections of journals or from a journal such as *Communication Reports* that focuses more on the design than on its theoretical underpinnings. Because most students will not have a background in statistics, I instruct students to read the prose and not be concerned at this point about the statistical findings beyond knowing that a "significant" finding is one that is likely to be stable.

I assign one short research report a day to serve as the basis for a class discussion of the kinds of choices the researcher made. Once the students have been reading these reports for 3 weeks or so, they should be equipped to write an abstract.

The approach to steps in the research process will vary, of course, with the number and depth of research methodologies being introduced in the course; but the key criteria to be invoked should be relatively common regardless of the methodologies discussed. The following are some of the criteria that I stress at each stage of the process.

Clarifying the Question (or Hypothesis)

As already mentioned, a research project cannot begin until the researcher has a clear conceptual definition of the key terms in the question. Consider the question, "Will individuals who are highly ego involved in an issue display less attitude change following a counterattitudinal message than will less involved individuals?" Because ego involvement has been conceived in a variety of ways, such as having vested interest in the outcome of an issue or having had considerable direct experience with the issue, the researcher must determine in precisely what way key terms are being used.

The scope of the question should be clarified. Under what conditions is the question expected to hold true? Is the message a casual comment from an anonymous source or a well-documented presentation made by a highly credible source? Ideally, the researcher will also consider the strength of the claim being advanced. When the question states that one individual will display less attitude change than another, how large a difference is anticipated?

Choosing a Means for Collecting Data

The researcher should select an approach that will maximize useful information. Thus the first decision concerns the basic research paradigm to be used (e. g. experimental, interview, ethnographic). Once that choice has been made, the researcher should be certain that the method of data gathering will provide a straightforward way of answering the central research question. In an experimental design, for instance, the researcher must find or develop a valid measure of the dependent variable. Beyond that, the researcher needs to take account of potentially contaminating variables that might be assessed to make possible an interpretation of the results that rules out the influence of confounding variables. For instance, in the illustration of comparing offers of assistance with expressions of sympathy for their effectiveness in alleviating distress, I might be concerned that the distressed individual would consider the instantiation of one approach more sincere than the other. Thus I might directly assess perceptions of sincerity to assist in the interpretation of results.

The researcher should also consider ways to enhance the explanatory power of the data. For instance, if I were assessing the impact of offers of assistance versus expressions of sympathy by means of some set of scales that would yield numerical data, I would also ask respondents to explain why they felt that way in their own words. Even if I did not systematically analyze these responses, they would provide me with insights that I could use to explain the thinking that was responsible for the results obtained from the scaled data.

Prior to collecting data, the researcher should anticipate potential questions concerning the reliability and/or validity of the data. Suppose, for example, that the researcher were planning to use an observer to code nonverbal behaviors as displayed in a naturally occurring event, such as an exchange between customers and a service representative at an office designed to handle complaints. Critics of the project might question the observer's ability to note a number of nonverbal behaviors at the rapid rate at which they occur. The researcher should anticipate this critique and forestall it, possibly by using multiple observers whose observations could be compared or perhaps by extensive training with methods to assess the reliability of the codings in advance of conducting the actual project.

Collecting Data

Hopefully the act of collecting the data will have been carefully planned and transpire smoothly, but even careful plans can go awry. Consequently, I stress the importance of pilot projects; that is, conducting miniversions of the actual project before launching the major data collection effort. A survey researcher may discover that some questions are unclear. An experimental researcher may find that some instructions are unclear or that the task takes much longer than anticipated. An ethnographer may encounter some unexpected source of hostility or suspicion. Thus the novice researcher should learn the merits of testing the methods to be used before investing a great deal of effort that may be less fruitful than it could have been.

Analyzing the Data

The primary analysis should attempt to provide a straightforward answer to the question that motivated the project. Additional analyses may be performed that discount alternative explanations for the results. Particularly in quasi-experimental designs, where the independent variables have not been manipulated, it may be useful to discount the impact of potentially confounding variables. Suppose, for instance, that I were comparing whether videotapes of the presidential nomination acceptance speeches of the Democratic and Republican candidates were rated as equally effective by an audience composed of individuals of diverse political beliefs. I might need to determine that the videotapes were of equally high fidelity.

Finally, the researcher should consider additional subsidiary analyses that can help explain the primary findings. In the preceding example, if I found that one candidate was perceived as more effective than the other, I could use a variety of techniques to try to explain why. Options include focus groups or codings of a variety of attributes of the message (such as personal illustrations or references to the audience) or of the manner of presentation (animation, poise, eye contact, etc.).

Reporting the Project

The pattern of reporting the project varies widely with the type of methodology. Conversational analyses, ethnographies, and rhetorical analyses read very differently. A number of quantitatively based methodologies, such as experimental, descriptive, and survey, share a common format, and consequently, a description of this format may be useful for all students. The introduction provides a rationale that justifies conducting the study. Rather than reviewing all relevant literature, the introduction offers an argument for the significance of the general area and the unique contribution to be made by the current study and introduces the research questions or hypotheses. The methods section typically describes the participants, materials used (including instantiations of the variables), and a description of procedures that were followed. This section should contain sufficient detail that another researcher could replicate the study. The results section conveys results but does not editorialize about their significance or limitations. By contrast, the discussion section addresses the significance of the study. It may contain a brief, relatively nontechnical overview of the findings, note any limitations in the design, comment on the degree of consistency of the findings with prior relevant research, and attempt to clarify the significance of the findings. From the discussion section the reader should understand what we have learned from this study and why that is (or is not) useful to know.

EVALUATING RESEARCH

Students should be capable of producing a critique of a research report before the midpoint of the course. It is useful, therefore, to identify specific criteria for evaluation.

Significance of the Research Question

Although any project may produce potentially useful results, the time of both the researcher and the consumers is finite. Consequently, the researcher should evaluate the significance of the question before undertaking a project. Caution novice researchers to avoid confusing the significance of a question with its immediate practical applications. Questions that pertain to a broad range of human behavior have potential for considerable significance. Thus a question such as, "What vocal cues identify an individual as being elderly?" may be of greater value than the question, "Do older people use more pronouns than younger people?" Moreover, questions of greater significance frequently focus on issues with explanatory power. Research on gender issues has become more useful as its focus has shifted from straightforward description of men's and women's communicative patterns to seeking understanding of underlying generative mechanisms, such as seeking power or belonging to different cultures. Finally, questions may be more significant when they focus on phenomena that are considered important in their own right, such as general attractiveness, loneliness, success in the workplace, and the like.

Internal Validity

Internal validity refers to the degree of faith that is warranted in the conclusions drawn from the data involved in the investigation. Assessing internal validity is the single most important evaluation that the reader needs to make, for if there are flaws in the design or the conclusions drawn, then the results should not be taken seriously. Procedures for assessing internal validity vary with the methodology. The instructor should provide students with clear guidelines for assessing the internal validity of every methodology studied. For instance, some of the most crucial guidelines that should be emphasized in assessing the internal validity of an experimental design include considerations of whether the operational definitions are realistic and valid instantiations of the independent variable, whether the measures of the dependent variable are reliable and valid, and whether potentially contaminating variables have been adequately dealt with. These guidelines would be more detailed, of course, in the actual classroom presentation.

External Validity

External validity refers to the degree of generalizability of the results beyond the specific context of the investigation. The instructor should encourage students to reason about the generalizability of the results. For example, in an experimental design, such discussions could focus on the typicality of the instantiations of the independent variable, of the context in which the variables are embedded, of the responses of the particular participants, and of the measures of the dependent variables.

Ethical Concerns

The instructor should also sensitize students to ethical issues involved in research. A primary concern is the ethical treatment of participants. Students should consider whether the participants' privacy was violated, for instance, or whether in some way they might have a negative experience, either during the study or following it, as a result of their participation. It will be more difficult for students to assess additional ethical concerns, such as the accuracy of the report of results and fair treatment in terms of authorship and acknowledgment of contributions by those conducting the study, but students should nevertheless be made aware of these issues, particularly if the course is designed to produce novice researchers.

ELABORATING DESIGN CHOICES

If the goal of the course is to produce novice researchers, the instructor may now return to the basic methodology to be stressed and elaborate in ways that will enable students to design projects. In this instance, the instructor may assign students to construct a research design and also to engage in an actual research project, perhaps conducted as a group project. If the goal is to produce informed critics, discussion of design choices is still appropriate, but in a less elaborated manner. More specifically, for critics, discussion of instantiation of the independent variables in an experimental design might focus on the advantages and limitations of actual manipulation versus selecting existing instantiations as well as the merits of conducting pretests. For novice researchers, the discussion would also include topics such as how one determines how many levels of a variable to incorporate and how they should be chosen.

Similarly, for critics, discussions of reliability and validity might focus on what these concepts are and why they are crucial to the internal validity of the study as well as on the signs of reliability and the validity that the reader should look for in a research report, including reliability coefficients and descriptions of techniques used to validate the measures. In courses for novice researchers, these issues would extend to discussions of ways of enhancing the reliability and validity of measures, as well as more detail regarding means for assessing both of these properties.

As techniques for data analysis are discussed, students should now be instructed to read the results sections of research reports in greater detail than they did early in the course.

ALTERNATIVE METHODOLOGIES

The range of methodologies to be introduced can vary widely. Because students will not be able to read a large number of studies from any one methodology, it is crucial to select prototypical and clear representatives and to stress the basic ingredients of each methodology, format for reporting results, and criteria for evaluating it. The assignment for this segment of the course might be to critique studies from three alternative methodologies.

A great many texts and resources exist for teaching research methods. Some introduce a variety of methodologies, whereas others focus on a single methodology. I consulted with colleagues[1] who teach a variety of methodologies. The suggested readings at the end of the chapter represent their recommendations and are separated by methodology.

ASSIGNMENTS

Abstract

Relatively early in the term students should be able to abstract a research report. Consider assigning a specific article, both to ensure that it is clear and straightforward and to make grading easier. A generic format to follow and one or two good models are useful.

Critique a Research Report

In courses introducing a variety of methodologies, you might assign a critique of two or three methodologies, and again, you may want to select the reports, perhaps containing some limitations that have been discussed. For each methodology, consider providing students with a set of guidelines for evaluation along with a good model.

Write a Research Proposal

For this assignment, I relieve students of the responsibility of providing a well-documented case from prior literature for pursuing the question, because I want them to select and justify their design. Students develop a brief introduction, but write the procedures in as much detail as they would for submission to a journal. Again, models are helpful. I assign the research question so that after all proposals have been collected and graded, we can discuss in class the alternative designs proposed and the strengths and limitations of each.

---

[1]For recommending sources, I appreciate advice from Julie Burke, Sally Jackson, Peggy Miller, Daniel J. O'Keefe, David R. Seibold, Carolyn Taylor, Joseph Wenzel, and Shirley Willihnganz.

Group Research Project

If the objective is to produce novice researchers, consider having students participate in a group research project. This provides an opportunity to discuss in detail the kinds of choices that must be made as well as practical experience in the research enterprise. To be sure that the project is manageable in about an 8-week time span, I propose two or three questions and let the students choose one. Design choices should be discussed in detail in class, with the advantages and limitations of each option emphasized. I require students to write individual reports of the project, which provides excellent training in learning to produce reports. It is helpful to provide careful guidelines for the contents of each segment of the report.

SUGGESTED READINGS

Overviews of Multiple Methods

Babbie, E. (1998). *The practice of social research* (8th ed.). Belmont, CA: Wadsworth.
Frey, L. R., Botan, C. H., Friedman, P. G., & Kreps, G. L. (1991). *Investigating communication: An introduction to research methods.* Englewood Cliffs, NJ: Prentice-Hall.
Reinard, J. C. (1994). *Introduction to communication research.* Madison, WI: Brown & Benchmark.
Rubin, R. B., Rubin, A. M., & Piele, L. J. (1993). *Communication research: Strategies and sources.* Belmont, CA: Wadsworth.
Salwen, M. B., & Stacks, D. W. (1996). *An integrated approach to communication theory and research.* Mahwah, NJ: Lawrence Erlbaum Associates.
Smith, M. M. (1988). *Contemporary communication research methods.* Belmont, CA: Wadsworth.

Conversational Analysis

Buttny, R. (1993). *Social accountability in communication.* Newbury Park, CA: Sage.
Nofsinger, R. E. (1991). *Everyday conversation.* Newbury, Park, CA: Sage.
Psathas, G. (1994). *Conversation analysis: The study of talk-in-interaction.* London: Sage.

Ethnography

Denzin, N. K., & Lincoln, Y. S. (Eds.). (1994). *Handbook of qualitative research.* Thousand Oaks, CA: Sage.
Erickson, F. (1986). Qualitative methods in research on teaching. In M. C. Wittrock (Ed.), *Handbook of research on teaching* (3rd ed., pp. 119–161). New York: Macmillan.

Experimental Methods

Campbell, D. T., & Stanley, J. C. (1963). *Experimental and quasi-experimental designs for research.* Chicago: Rand McNally.
Clark, R. A. (1991). *Studying interpersonal communication: The research experience.* Newbury Park, CA: Sage.
Jackson, S. (1992). *Message effects research.* New York: Guilford.

Rhetorical Criticism

Black, E. (1978). *Rhetorical criticism: A study in method.* Madison: University of Wisconsin Press.

Campbell, J. A. (Ed.). (1990, Summer). Special issue on rhetorical criticism. *Western Journal of Speech Communication, 54,* 249–376.

Cooper, M. (1989). *Analyzing public discourse.* Prospect Heights, IL: Waveland Press.

Foss, S. K. (1995). *Rhetorical criticism: Exploration and practice* (2nd ed.). Prospect Heights, IL: Waveland Press.

Scott, R. L., & Brock, B. L. (1980). *Methods of rhetorical criticism.* Detroit, MI: Wayne State University Press.

Survey Methods

Dillman, D. A. (1978). *Mail and telephone surveys: The total design method.* New York: Wiley-Interscience.

Henry, G. T. (1990). *Practical sampling* (Applied Social Research Methods Series, Vol. 21). Newbury Park, CA: Sage.

Salant, P., & Dillman, D. A. (1994). *How to conduct your own survey.* New York: Wiley.

17

Teaching
a Special Topic Course

Lawrence B. Rosenfeld
Michael S. Waltman
University of North Carolina at Chapel Hill

Special topic courses—courses that serve as "wild cards" that allow inter-ested faculty and students to pursue a topic not part of the usual curricu-lum—are on every communication department's list of offerings. Recent special topic courses taught in several departments include:

- Interpersonal Relationships in Contemporary Films
- Interactive Communication Technologies in Organizations
- The Family and Popular Media
- Environmental Advocacy
- Organizational Communication in *Dilbert*
- The Performance of Social Identity
- Ethnographic Study of a Residential Facility for People With AIDS
- Media, Culture, and Public Life
- Cultural History and Rock-and-Roll
- Taking "Like a Family" to Appalachia
- The Construction of Women and Feminism in Popular Discourse
- Communication and Social Cognition
- Superheroes and Communication Competency
- Leadership Lessons Aboard the Starship *Enterprise*

The list of special course topics is limited only by our imagination as a profession.

How is a special topic course different from regular course offerings in a department? What makes the special course topic special? The purpose of this chapter is to provide an introduction to several of the considerations that must be made when contemplating offering a special topic course. Four questions guide our survey: What sources are there for special topic courses? What makes a particular special topic worthy to teach? What are the requirements of a syllabus for a special topic course? What potential problems is an instructor likely to encounter teaching a special topic course?

SOURCES OF SPECIAL TOPIC COURSES

There are three primary sources for special topic courses. First, the courses may reflect the changing nature of our field: Special topic courses may be the best place to try out current interests and areas of study that may not be developed sufficiently enough to warrant a regular place in the curriculum, or that may not be of interest to a large enough group of scholars to persuasively argue for its inclusion in the regular curriculum. Second, the courses may reflect the cross-disciplinary nature of our field: Special topic courses may be a useful vehicle for faculty and students to discuss the adaptation of theories from related disciplines to our own perspective. Finally, special topic courses may reflect the diverse nature of our own discipline: The courses may emerge from an innovative combination of different areas of interest within the profession.

Current Interests and Areas of Study as Sources for Special Topic Courses

What makes an interest or area of study a special topic course in one department and a part of the regular curriculum in another depends on several variables, including faculty research and teaching interests and the availability of faculty to teach courses not part of the usual list of course offerings. For example, although the area of family communication is "expanding rapidly as a specialty area in the communication discipline, as demonstrated by the growing number of family communication textbooks and well-attended family pedagogy panels at … conventions" (Whitchurch, 1993, p. 255), not many departments have faculty whose primary interest is family communication. Many, however, have faculty with enough interest in the area to offer an introductory course on a less-than-regular basis. As interest in family communication increases, and as the number of teachers and scholars trained in the area increases, family communication is likely to go from a special topic course to a regular part of the curriculum.

In contrast to family communication, which is a growing area of interest likely to become a regular course offering in many departments, other current interests and areas of research may be unlikely to make such an easily recognized move to the regular curriculum. For example, "proposals for curricular revision, particularly those calling for culture- and gender-balanced content and pedagogy [to] reflect the reality that institutions of higher education must prepare an increasingly diverse student population for participation in an increasingly diverse society" (Capuzza, 1993, p. 172) are more likely to lead to experimental special topic courses designed to test approaches that may, if successful, be incorporated in a variety of courses. Capuzza (1993) described such a special topic course in which a traditional course in small group communication is modified to consider how race, class, and gender affect communication in this setting (the article is a summary of a 2-year project on curriculum inclusion). If successful, the special topic course may lead to a new approach to teaching small group communication as well as other basic courses.

Finally, there are areas of interest that are likely to stimulate one-shot special topic courses with little chance of being included in a list of regular offerings. For example, analysis of a popular television show may serve as the organizing principle for a course in communication. Winegarden, Fuss-Reineck, and Charron (1993) described how *Star Trek: The Next Generation* may be useful for teaching concepts in a variety of communication courses and, conversely, how a study of the television series may cut across several regular course offerings and, therefore, allow for high-level integration of a department's curriculum. Of course, fading interest in *Star Trek: The Next Generation* limits the number of times that a special topic course can or should be organized around the series, although the idea of using a television series in such a way may be useful for future special topic courses.

Research From Allied Disciplines as Sources of Special Topics

Because of the interdisciplinary nature of our field, it is likely that research from an allied discipline may serve as a stimulus for teaching a special topic course. For example, scholars in the field of communication often have drawn on the work of psychologists in social cognition to inform their own research and to supplement readings in special topic courses such as communication and social cognition. As communication scholars contemplate the ways that communication influences, and is influenced by, human information processing, they have a wealth of information from established research programs in social cognition to supplement their own theorizing and teaching.

Whether or not a course that has its origins in allied disciplines becomes a regular course offering in communication departments depends, in part, on the extent to which research and theories from the allied discipline generate research programs in our own field. If the allied field's research is heuristically valuable and generates questions that are of theoretic interest to communication scholars, then the special topic is likely to flourish. In other words, the state and standing of a special topic area is determined by the state of science of that area in our own discipline.

Courses in interpersonal communication have grown, in part, because communication scholars have drawn on research in fields such as psychology, social psychology, anthropology, and sociology (Knapp & Miller, 1985). Prior to the 1960s, for example, interpersonal communication was a special topic course in many communication departments. The first interpersonal texts generally were based on theories developed by scholars in other disciplines with few references to work by communication researchers. According to Knapp and Miller (1985), it was not until the mid-1970s that original theorizing about interpersonal communication took place. Once interpersonal communication was established as an important area of study in the communication discipline, an introductory course in the area became a usual part of the curriculum. With interpersonal communication a "regular" course, special topic courses could be taught using concepts from other disciplines to expand the study of interpersonal communication; for example, the work of Delia (1977) and his colleagues who initially studied the relation between communication and cognition.

In the mid-1970s, Delia and his colleagues at the University of Illinois drew on the work of psychologists Harold Kelly and Walter Crockett to conceptualize and operationalize cognitive complexity as a core construct in their cognitive theory of communication, constructivism (Delia, 1977). However, constructivists did not rely on psychologists to define the core construct of communication; rather, they relied on their own expertise as communication scholars to define and assess communication. Their research program, like others in communication, possessed a clear heuristic value and asked interesting research questions that benefited from the utilization of research and constructs from other fields. Special topic courses growing out of this research and refining our understanding of interpersonal communication include new perspectives on impression formation, persuasion, message construction, how people choose what to talk about, and the logic underlying how people construct messages.

Special topic courses in the area of health communication also have grown, in part, because communication scholars have drawn on research from fields such as public health, medicine, and marketing (Rogers, 1996). During the 1970s, communication scholars in the International Communication Association established the Division of Health Communication and in 1986 the Health Communication Commission was established in the Speech Communication Association (Ratzan, Payne, & Bishop, 1996). During this time the topic of health communication moved from a unit in courses such as interpersonal communication and organizational communication to a special topic course. At present, membership in the Health Communication Division of the National Communication Association has grown to over 500 members, and the University of South Florida, the University of Maryland, the University of Kentucky, Johns Hopkins University, and Texas A & M University offer master's degrees with an emphasis in health communication (Rogers, 1996). It should not be surprising that this growth corresponds to a proliferation of research and opportunities for funding (Rogers, 1996), and provides the fertile soil for a proliferation of special topic courses that explore health communication both generally (e.g., Communication in Health Organizations) and narrowly (e.g., Public Messages and the Health Risks of Tobacco).

Innovative Combinations of Areas of Interest Within Communication as Sources of Special Topic Courses

Within our own field, special topic courses may emerge from a creative combination of cross-intradiscipline (as opposed to cross-discipline) concerns or interests. For example, Fuoss and Hill (1992) presented a master syllabus for A Performance-Centered Approach for Teaching a Course in Social Movements. Courses in social movements—a part of most communication curricula—are often taught with a rhetorical focus; a performance-centered approach bridges rhetorical and performance studies and supplements the analytical rhetorical approach by providing students with experiential methods of learning. "A performance-centered approach to social movements explores the nature and function of performance within social movements and utilizes performance as its means for studying social movements" (Fuoss & Hill, 1992, p. 77). This approach to examining the 1968 antiwar protests at Columbia University, for example, can combine study of the film *The Strawberry Statement* and an application of Turner's social drama model with "considering the nature and function of cultural performances surrounding the event, such as guerrilla street theater (one genre of cultural performance)" (p. 83).

Lewis (1991) combined the study of new technologies and organizational communication in her master syllabus, Interactive Communication Technologies in Organizations. An organization's adoption of a new communication technology influences "not only organizational procedures, requisite personnel skills, and capabilities in producing, storing, and manipulating information, but also ... the type, frequency and qualities of the human communication" (p. 202). Communication scholars interested in new technologies and organizations combine their different perspectives to study electronic mail, teleconferencing, computer bulletin boards, and other innovations as they are used in the workplace. A special topic course that combines these two concerns can provide students with an understanding "of the complex relationships between human communication, technology, and organizational activity" (Lewis, 1991, p. 203).

TOPIC SELECTION

Students find ways to adapt to less-than-exciting styles of teaching, but compensatory mechanisms are not available for what should have been taught but was not. They listen in good faith to what their teachers have to say, and this trust in their teachers' decisions about course content must not be misplaced. (Ericksen, 1984, p. 13)

What makes a special topic worthy to teach? There are at least four overlapping criteria to consider when answering this question. First, is the course content "cutting-edge" material that provides an indication of new developments in the discipline? Second, is the course organized around a novel application of material studied in other courses? Third, is the course an in-depth study of a narrow content area of interest to a small group of students? Fourth, is the course in response to a unique set of circumstances unlikely to occur again? Ultimately, the special topic course should be taught because there is something at the core of the topic that contributes to departmental curricula and the students' educational needs.

The Cutting Edge Special Topic Course

Much of what is taught in our discipline, except for courses in public speaking, probably started out as special topic courses. As communication departments added film, radio, discussion methods, group communication, television, organizational communication, interpersonal communication, health communication, gender communication, intercultural communication, and other areas of interest, special topic courses played a role in the development of our curricula. New directions may be forged in the discipline with few people at the vanguard: According to the constitution of the National Communication Association, with 100 people signing on, a commission may be created in the organization; 300 people can get together and create a division. The commissions and divisions of our professional organizations define, in a sense, what we as a discipline study: African American Communication and Culture, Applied Communication, Communication Apprehension and Avoidance, International and Intercultural Communication, Interpersonal Communication, Mass Communication, Organizational Communication, Performance Studies, Spiritual Communication, Visual Communication, and the myriad other areas of research and teaching. Each division and commission represents a movement within the field, a stretch in a particular direction, that is heralded with new research programs, new perspectives, and, invariably, new courses. The new courses typically start out as special topic courses and either stay in that category, taught infrequently, or move on to become part of the regular curriculum.

In addition to new directions being pursued by members of a discipline and then institutionalized through the creation of divisions and commissions in a national organization, new directions may be promoted by the national organization itself, or promoted by other agencies that see a need for research and teaching in a particular area. For example, Reiser and Heitman (1993) developed a special topic course in ethics for the biological sciences at the University of Texas–Houston Health Science Center to comply with the "National Institutes of Health mandate that education in the ethical aspects of science be included in the programs that train grant recipients" (p. 876). The course began as an experiment in the teaching of ethics to biology students and remained a regular part of the departmental curriculum because of a perceived social need and a policy imposed by a federal agency.

The Novel Application Special Topic Course

Whereas cutting-edge special topic courses offer content that is new, novel application courses offer students the opportunity to apply material studied in other courses to interesting examples. The application leads the students to an in-depth study of material previously unexamined in such detail. In the end, the special topic course helps students synthesize their ideas into a cumulative knowledge base, and integrate the fundamental and lower level concepts they learned in other courses into broader abstractions and principles.

For example, a course taught at both Northern Kentucky University and the University of North Carolina at Chapel Hill focuses on the analysis of contemporary feature films to explicate interpersonal communication concepts. Recognizing that films are not real life, students complete assigned readings and then compare and contrast what the readings have to offer with what the films present. A unit on communication competence may include comparing and contrasting Cissna and Anderson's (1994) "Communication and the Ground of Dialogue," Daughton's (1996) "The Spiritual Power of Repetitive Form: Steps Toward Transcendence in *Groundhog Day*," and Spitzberg's (1993) "The Dark Side of (In)competence," and then applying the three articles to a discussion of *The Doctor* and *Groundhog Day*.

The In-Depth Study Special Topic Course

Occasions arise when the basis for a special topic course is not the existence of cutting-edge material or the opportunity to apply research and theories to a novel example, but the interest and motivation of a small number of students and a faculty member to pursue a topic in depth. This may be the most common reason for offering a particular special topic course: because several students request the opportunity. For example, although many courses briefly consider the relation between language and communication, Ellis (1993) argued this is an important topic worthy of a special topic course, that is, worthy of (at least) a semester's consideration. Such a course could examine conceptual issues (e.g., the biological predisposition to learn language), as well as topics such as the language features that characterize certain social groups, the relation between language and culture, and language as a social instrument.

The Unique Opportunity Special Topic Course

Unique opportunities—opportunities unlikely to occur again—often provide a good rationale for a special topic course; indeed, either the course is offered or the opportunity is lost. At least four different kinds of unique opportunities lend themselves to the development of a special topic course. First, an opportunity may arise to travel with a group of students, presenting the possibility of special topic courses in intercultural communication, for example, or courses that require cross-cultural comparisons. Second, an individual worthy of study may be on campus or in close proximity, providing the impetus to study her or his communication and the chance to invite her or his participation in the course. Third, a faculty member may have experiences outside the institution that provide a new perspective on how communication operates in a particular context, making it reasonable to offer a special topic course organized around the faculty member's experiences. Fourth, a topic of social relevance may bring together several areas of study not usually associated, lending itself to an interdisciplinary, cross-departmental special topic course involving several faculty.

The first two opportunities—travel and the campus or area visitor—are the most common and, perhaps, institutionalized types of special topic courses in this category. For example, taking a group of students to a film festival may provide the basis for a special topic course on contemporary film, or an ethnographic study of a film festival; and a visit from a former senator, member of congress, or president may provide the stimulus for in-depth study of his or her speeches, writings on political communication, or communication competence.

The other two unique opportunities that may stimulate the development of a special topic course are less common. Faculty members—for example, through consulting work, appointments to political office, and volunteer work—may have experiences that require applying their understanding of communication to circumstances that test their implicit and explicit theories of communication. A special topic course organized around the faculty member's experiences can provide students with an interesting and distinct perspective to study, given the unique interplay among course content, professor expertise, and student interest. For example, a member of the Department of Communication Studies at the University of North Carolina at Chapel Hill served as President of the Sierra Club for 2 years, from 1994 to 1996. Influenced by his experiences, this faculty member teaches an undergraduate course in environmental advocacy that began as a special topic course and, because of its significance and popularity among the students, became a regular part of the curriculum in rhetorical studies. The course explores the rhetorical and persuasive means by which citizens may influence the policies and practices of corporate and governmental organizations that affect our natural and human environments.

The fourth unique opportunity involves a topic of social relevance crossing disciplinary lines and requiring multiple perspectives to understand, which necessitates a special topic course involving several faculty. For example, current research from communication, medicine, social work, psychology, and other areas may be brought together for a special topic course on AIDS. A faculty person from medicine can provide the necessary medical information for understanding the crisis and the medical response to it, and teachers from social work and psychology can discuss the emotional aspects of the disease and methods for helping people with the disease.

Communication scholars can bring an important perspective to understanding AIDS and HIV transmission (Stiff, McCormack, Zook, Stein, & Henry, 1990), the effectiveness of public service announcements (Freimuth, Hammond, Edgar, & Monahan, 1990), and other aspects of the crisis (Norton, 1990). The course also may include study of the performative nature of protests surrounding AIDS as the impetus for social change (Kistenberg, 1995), as well as ethnographic study of communication in a residential facility for people with AIDS (Adelman & Frey, 1994; Frey, Query, Flint, & Adelman, 1998).

DEVELOPING A SYLLABUS
FOR THE SPECIAL TOPIC COURSE

The syllabus for a special topic course is much like the syllabus for any course in that it should provide the students with the following information (Cerny, 1997; Civikly-Powell, chap. 5, this volume; Duffy & Jones, 1995; Matejka & Kurke, 1994): (a) course number, section, and title; (b) instructor's name, office, telephone number, e-mail address, and office hours; (c) prerequisites or corequisites; (d) course description and rationale; (e) goals and objectives; (f) teaching procedures (e.g., class format); (g) required textbooks and other readings; (h) supplementary readings; (i) assignments, and how they will be graded; (j) tests and quizzes, and how they will be graded; (k) rules regarding extra credit, attendance, participation, and plagiarism; (l) available support services; and (m) a course outline and, if possible, a schedule of the specific assignments and topics of each class.

The special topic course syllabus contains all these elements, but several require extraordinary consideration. Because the special topic course is new for both the instructor and the students, there is no history to guide the course or to be used as the basis for expectations. Students who take a course that is a regular part of a department's curriculum have, like the instructors who teach them, a good idea about the general content of the course (including a department-approved catalog description), how the course is typically taught, and so on. Although some expectations may exist for the special topic course—for example, the students "know" that if Professor Jones teaches the course it is likely to require a great deal of class participation and a semester-long project—there is still the anticipation that something new and different is likely. Therefore, the syllabus has to provide more information than usual. Differences between the syllabus for the special topic course and the regular course are not associated with differences in the parts the syllabus contains, but in how detailed those parts are.

Because special topic courses typically have a course number that is high (often it is the last course in the list of offerings, giving it the highest number) prerequisites need to be carefully spelled out. What background should a student in the course have, and how important is it? Can a student without a prerequisite course in her or his background fill in the gap by reading particular articles and books?

The course description, including rationale, goals, and objectives, should be highly detailed. Courses that are a regular part of the curriculum often are accepted as important by both the students and instructors, and therefore need little if any rationale. However, a special topic course needs to be justified, both to the students and to the other faculty in a department. Why is this course being taught? Why should the student take the course? What are the likely benefits to be derived from taking the course? Why does the course merit academic credit and sanctions?

If the special topic course is going to be taught in an unusual way, this needs to be clearly indicated on the syllabus. Courses that require travel (e.g., to a film festival), extraordinary expenses, time away from campus, meeting times that include weekends or evenings in addition to "regular" hours, student-led classes, and so on, need to have these expectations detailed in the syllabus so students can make an informed choice about whether or not to take the course.

Readings for special topic courses, particularly ones that are based on cutting-edge research, may not be usual or particularly easy, and this needs to be explained. For example, required readings may come from unusual sources, such as the World Wide Web, or disciplines unfamiliar to the student (each discipline has its own language, and a student unfamiliar with that language needs to be forewarned that the reading may be difficult). More typically, requiring students to read recent research means assigning journal articles that require a higher level of sophistication than many undergraduate students possess.

Any unusual project assignments (e.g., ones that require a great deal of off-campus work), grading (e.g., using peer review), or rules regarding extra credit, attendance, participation, and so on, must be made explicit. With a clear understanding of what is required and what is expected, students can make the necessary adjustments in their thinking and to their schedules to accommodate the special topic course.

Finally, if the special topic course requires particular skills, it is essential that support services available to the students be indicated on the syllabus. For example, if projects require statistical data analysis, students should be made aware of available help from instructional support services, such as the Institute for Research in the Social Sciences or the office on campus that provides guidance in the use of statistical packages available on both main-frame and personal computers. Similarly, drawing students' attention to help available from your institution's learning center, writing center, and library serves a dual purpose: First, it provides the students with information that may be of use, and second, it highlights the importance of certain skills (e.g., writing) in the completion of course assignments.

In the end, the syllabus should communicate to students that "we are really interested in their understanding the material we offer, that we support their efforts to master it, and that we take their intellectual struggles seriously" (Rubin, 1985). With this message clearly communicated in the syllabus, work can begin on a positive note and help ensure the success of the special topic course.

POTENTIAL PROBLEMS
WITH SPECIAL TOPIC COURSES

Problems associated with teaching a special topic course can affect every stage of course development: getting the course approved by the department, meeting student expectations, putting course material together, and ensuring adequate preparation on the part of the instructor. These are over-lapping potential problems, for example, a course may not be approved because it is not well developed, meeting student expectations may affect how the course is taught, and the instructor's preparation—or lack thereof—may affect all other potential problems.

Course Approval

Generally, permission to teach a special topic course requires little more than approval of a department chair or a subcommittee of faculty in the communication department, and this approval is usually forthcoming so long as a clear rationale is offered that includes the instructor's credentials for teaching the course. However, in those instances in which approval must come from a group outside the communication department, problems are likely to arise, especially if the course content is seen as falling within some other discipline's boundaries. For example, a special topic course in political communication that looks at campaigning in a current election may raise eyebrows in the political science department, and faculty in social work may balk at approving a special topic course in social support not taught by one of their own faculty.

The special topic course is optimally effective if it is integrated into and coherent with the regular curriculum. If faculty see how the special topic course fits with established curricular goals, they may be more inclined to agree that it should be offered, and are more likely to encourage students to consider taking it. From the students' perspective, a special topic course seen as a logical extension of the regular curriculum is likely to have more status and, therefore, appear more attractive. A special topic course that moves too far beyond the parameters of a curriculum's philosophy may not be approved at the outset or, if approved, may not get adequate enrollment.

Student Expectations

Student expectations for a special topic course do not generally differ from student expectations for other courses, except that they are more anxious about the unknown content and teaching format—anxiety alleviated the first day, for the most part, when the syllabus is presented. However, it is often the case that students expect special topic courses to be more fun than regular courses in the curriculum. Expecting a course to be fun is not a bad thing: Student energy and motivation to be in the course (at least at the outset) should be high. The expectation for fun becomes a problem when the students fail to recognize that the course also is substantive. As with the anxiety regarding content and format, expectations for fun may be combined with expectations for high-level work as the syllabus is explained.

Another student expectation that may be problematic is that special topic courses allow for more active participation than other courses. Students in special topic courses often wish to talk about personal experience at the expense of research and theory. A portion of this proclivity may be the belief that active participation is an opportunity a special topic course should provide students. Therefore, in general, instructors teaching a special topic course may well be advised to employ more active learning (Duffy & Jones, 1995; Lowman, 1995; Myers & Jones, 1993) and cooperative learning techniques (Johnson & Johnson, 1994; Johnson, Johnson, & Smith, 1991; Lowman, 1995). These activities will encourage students to work with each other and to become more involved in their own learning. Such learning strategies will capitalize on the students' inclination to contribute their own experiences to special topic courses.

Expectations for active participation are a pronounced problem when a special topic course is based more on interest than on theory and research. Students may be faced with an interesting topic that seems relevant to their lives but is bereft of substantive research. The lack of research to consider elevates personal experience and the experiences of friends and acquaintances to a primary form of proof during class discussions. Unfortunately, when unique, personal experiences clash, the students and the instructor are left with opposing opinions and no clear way to reconcile them. This is not entirely bad: The students and the instructor may learn from one another by engaging each other in this way. However, at some point, students and teacher should be able to move beyond anecdotal evidence and speak a language that generalizes beyond individual experience.

Student Preparation

Because a special topic course is not a usual part of the curriculum and may not have specific courses with which it relates that could serve as prerequisites, some enrolled students may not have adequate background. As a result, the schemas that they possess for understanding the course material may be unelaborated and simple, making it necessary to spend more time than desired or originally planned discussing background material. On the other hand, because individual departmental curricula tend to be fairly coherent and organized around shared faculty perspectives, the same special topic course may have advanced and experienced students enrolled—some who have taken three or four related courses from the regular curriculum—with fairly complicated schemas for understanding the course material. The end result of the typical enrollment in a special topic course is students with widely varying degrees of preparation and background (e.g., students may be in the course who are majoring in other departments). Although this may be a problem in many upper-level courses, it seems to occur more frequently in special topic courses.

Few satisfactory solutions to this problem are available, and the students may naturally divide into two groups based on background, with advantages in class discussion and assignment completion going to those more prepared. Requesting students with little background to read material on their own, or providing a few quick "catch-up" lectures are not practical solutions: The students may not read suggested material, and the catch-up lectures may be either too dense and complex or not dense enough to be useful. There are a variety of ways, however, that the problem of a wide disparity in backgrounds may be managed through the syllabus. First, the syllabus should make it clear what background is expected and offer specific readings that all students in the class should be familiar with from the beginning of the course. Also, the readings should be listed in the order in which the less prepared students should read them, and the purpose of the ordering should be made clear when discussing the syllabus. Second, the syllabus should offer a detailed framework for the course around which new information may be organized, helping those with less background see connections that may not be obvious to them. Third, the instructor might pose, in the syllabus, a central question for each class meeting—a question that,

again, provides a framework for organizing the information read and discussed in class. Each of these solutions is designed to help the students develop organizing principles for the course, both in its entirety and class by
class—organizing principles that those with more background are likely to
possess prior to the course.

Instructor Preparation

Instructor under- and overpreparation may lead to two different problems,
neither of which is unique to special topic courses. Regarding
overpreparation, when faculty teach a special topic course stemming from
their current research, there may be a tendency to require readings that are
methodologically too sophisticated for the students, or that assume more
background than the students possess. Similarly, assignments may push the
students to understand and apply material too quickly. The instructor, excited about the work, may be attempting to thrust the students into the role
of colleague, for which they are unprepared.

Two suggestions for course preparation may help avoid these problems.
First, the instructor should set aside some time before writing the syllabus
to reflect on the extent to which he or she has established realistic goals for
the course. One of our colleagues noted (A. McCarthy, Personal Communication, March, 17, 1997) that it was difficult to distance herself from the
material: "deciding what was a 'must' read, and what was optional, was difficult because things in the latter category were really great and important
articles." Second, the instructor should avoid looking as if she or he is in-
dulging herself or himself rather than offering course work that is central to
the student's major or plan of study. One of our colleagues had to contend
with this perception at the beginning of the semester; however, the students
eventually became excited about the class after she sold them on the ideas
being addressed.

Why would a department approve a special topic course for which the instructor was underprepared? Although underpreparation is less of a problem than overpreparation, it is likely to occur when the special topic course
is organized around research that is very new or quickly evolving. For example, a course focusing on new information technologies may focus on
ones that are so new that they become obsolete or common by the time the
articles and textbooks are published. Preparing a syllabus for such a course
requires developing an attitude of "we are all in this together," so that gaps
in understanding are not perceived by the students or the instructor as a
problem with the instructor's preparation.

CONCLUSION

Special topic courses come from a variety of sources: They may reflect the changing nature of our discipline, our status as an interdisciplinary field, and how the different areas of communication may be integrated and combined to inform each other. A particular special topic course may be worthy to teach because it presents cutting edge material about new developments in our discipline; provides students with a novel application of familiar material; encourages in-depth study of a narrow content area; or takes advantage of a unique set of circumstances, including an opportunity to travel, interact with a visiting scholar or public figure, share a faculty member's relevant experiences outside the institution, or study a topic of social relevance that requires a cross-departmental course to be successful.

The syllabus for a special topic course, although much like the syllabus for any course, has several distinct characteristics, including an explicit discussion of the background students need and a highly detailed course description, including a rationale, goals, and objectives. Novel teaching approaches also should be clearly indicated on the syllabus, including any unusual project assignments or grading criteria. A special topic course, unlike a regular course in a curriculum, is an unknown for the students, and it is the job of the syllabus to provide enough information to allay fears and to set the parameters within which the students and instructor will work.

Finally, special topic courses often come with special problems: getting the course approved (How does the course fit with the regular curriculum? Is anyone likely to object to the course?); meeting student expectations (What expectations do the students have? Do their expectations mean that a certain teaching style is necessary?); putting course material together (Do the students have sufficient background?); and ensuring adequate preparation on the part of the instructor (Is the instructor too excited or too prepared, such that the goals of the course and the expectations for assignments are unreasonable? Is the course content so new or changing so rapidly that it is impossible to be fully prepared?).

Given their many sources of inspiration, reasons for being offered, special considerations, and potential problems, it is clear that the concept of the special topic course is not a homogeneous one. Therefore, the contributions of various special topic courses to departmental curricula, to student interests and needs, and to the development of the discipline, may be diverse. Today's special topic course may become a regular part of the curriculum tomorrow or it may fall into the category of "interesting idea." Predicting the future of our discipline is as onerous a task as predicting what next year's special topic courses are likely to be. Will special topic courses with titles such as Communication and Information Technology, Social Theory and Cultural Diversity, and Environmental Advocacy shape the discipline sufficiently so that the next edition of *Teaching Communication: Theory, Research, and Methods* will have to contain chapters on each in the section titled "Preparing Specific Communication Courses"? Or, will they go the way of previous special topic courses that were interesting at the moment but of no lasting impact?

Whether a one-shot course, a course offered sporadically as requested, or a course that moves to its own niche in the regular curriculum, a special topic course fulfills an important function for students, faculty, departments, and our field. Special topic courses serve as the workshops in which the future of the discipline is forged.

REFERENCES

Adelman, M. B., & Frey, L. R. (1994). The pilgrim must embark: Creating and sustaining community in a residential facility for people with AIDS. In L. R. Frey (Ed.), *Group communication in context: Studies of natural groups* (pp. 3–22). Hillsdale, NJ: Lawrence Erlbaum Associates.

Capuzza, J. C. (1993). Curriculum inclusion and the small group communication course. *Communication Education, 42*, 172–178.

Cerny, J. (1997). Developing a course syllabus. http://www.hcc.hawaii.edu/ education/ hcc/facdev/DevelSyllabus.htm/.

Cissna, K. N., & Anderson, R. (1994). Communication and the ground of dialogue. In R. Anderson, K. N. Cissna, & R. C. Arnett (Eds.), *The reach of dialogue: Confirmation, voice, and community* (pp. 9–30). Cresskill, NJ: Hampton.

Daughton, S. M. (1996). The spiritual power of repetitive form. Steps toward transcendence in *Groundhog Day. Critical Studies in Mass Communication, 13*, 138–154.

Delia, J. (1977). Constructivism and the study of human communication. *Quarterly Journal of Speech, 63*, 66–83.

Duffy, D. K., & Jones, J. W. (1995). *Teaching within the rhythms of the semester.* San Francisco: Jossey-Bass.

Ellis, D. G. (1993). Language and communication. *Communication Education, 42*, 79–92.

Ericksen, S. C. (1984). *The essence of good teaching.* San Francisco: Jossey-Bass.

Frey, L. R., Query, J. L., Jr., Flint, L. J., & Adelman, M. B. (1998). Living together with AIDS: Social support processes in a residential facility. In V. J. Derlega & A. P. Barbee (Eds.), *HIV infection and social interactions* (pp. 129–146).. Thousand Oaks, CA: Sage.

Freimuth, V. S., Hammond, S. L., Edgar, T., & Monahan, J. L. (1990). Reaching those at risk: A content-analytic study of AIDS PSAs. *Communication Research, 17*, 775–791.

Fuoss, K. W., & Hill, R. T. (1992). A performance-centered approach for teaching a course in social movements. *Communication Education, 41*, 77–88.

Johnson, D. W., & Johnson, R. T. (1994). *Learning together and alone: Cooperative, competitive, and individualistic learning* (4th ed.). Needham Heights, MA: Allyn & Bacon.

Johnson, D. W., Johnson, R. T., & Smith, K. A. (1991). *Active learning: Cooperation in the college classroom.* Edina, MN: Interaction.

Kistenberg, C. J. (1995). *AIDS, social change, and theater: Performance as protest.* New York: Garland.

Knapp, M. L., & Miller, G. R. (1985). Introduction: Background and current trends in the study of interpersonal communication. In M. L. Knapp & G. R. Miller (Eds.), *Handbook of interpersonal communication* (pp. 7–24). Beverly Hills, CA: Sage.

Lewis, L. K. (1991). Interaction communication technologies in organizations. *Communication Education, 40*, 202–212.

Lowman, J. (1995). *Mastering the techniques of teaching* (2nd ed.). San Francisco: Jossey-Bass.

Matejka, K., & Kurke, L. B. (1994). Designing a great syllabus. *College Teaching, 42*(3), 115–117.

Myers, C., & Jones, T. B. (1993). *Promoting active learning: Strategies for the college classroom.* San Francisco: Jossey-Bass.

Norton, R. (1990). The communication scholar in the AIDS crisis. *Communication Research, 17,* 733–742.

Ratzan, S. C., Payne, J. G., & Bishop, C. (1996). The status and scope of health communication. *Journal of Health Communication, 1,* 25–41.

Reiser, S. J., & Heitman, E. (1993). Creating a course on ethics in the biological sciences. *Academic Medicine, 68,* 876–879.

Rogers, E. M. (1996). The field of health communication today: An up-to-date report. *Journal of Health Communication, 1,* 15–23.

Rubin, S. (1985, August 7). Professors, students, and the syllabus. *Chronicle of Higher Education,* p. 56.

Spitzberg, B. H. (1993). The dark side of (in)competence. In W. R. Cupach & B. H. Spitzberg (Eds.), *The dark side of interpersonal communication* (pp. 25–49). Hillsdale, NJ: Lawrence Erlbaum Associates.

Stiff, J., McCormack, M., Zook, E., Stein, T., & Henry, R. (1990). Learning about AIDS and HIV transmission in college-age students. *Communication Research, 17,* 743–758.

Whitchurch, G. G. (1993). Designing a course in family communication. *Communication Education, 42,* 255–267.

Winegarden, A. D., Fuss-Reineck, M., & Charron, L. J. (1993). Using *Star Trek: The Next Generation* to teach concepts in persuasion, family communication, and communication ethics. *Communication Education, 42,* 179–188.

III

Organizing
the Instructional Context

18

Classroom Roles of the Teacher

Kathleen M. Galvin
Northwestern University

Teaching implies a multifaceted and changing relationship. The noun *teacher* seems to indicate a singular entity—a teacher is a person who performs the act of teaching—yet, the more time you spend in classrooms, the more you recognize the complexity of the teaching–learning process. Rather than a one-dimensional, linear process, teaching is a multidimensional, interactive process. Reflective teachers continually ask themselves "Who am I for these students in this classroom?", "How are they impacting my life?", and "By what means do students make sense of the knowledge and skills developed in this discipline?" Classroom roles provide one lens for examining the intricacies of the teaching–learning process.

Historically, roles have been conceived of as positions—a static view describing a series of expectations for an occupant of a given position, such as, teacher or student. Such expectations convey beliefs about how a role should be enacted no matter what the circumstances (Linton, 1945). According to this traditional view, the role teacher implies the performance of a list of behaviors, such as: (a) teachers come to class prepared, (b) teachers treat all students equally, and (c) teachers evaluate student performance.

Some role theorists (Homan, 1985; Timpson & Tobin, 1982) view the college classroom from a dramatist perspective, drawing parallels between acting and teaching, maintaining both exercise one's capacity to learn, problem solve, and communicate. The dramatist metaphor represents teachers as performers playing a part. Classic instructional literature describes teachers as managing multiple roles including supporter, evaluator, disciplinarian, expert, facilitator, socializing agent, formal authority, ego ideal, or person (Mann et al., 1970). These one-dimensional approaches overlook the effects that other parts of the instructional setting have on teacher performance.

More recently, roles have been viewed from an interactive perspective, emphasizing their emerging aspects and the behavioral regularities that develop out of social interaction (Millar, 1996). In this interpretation, roles serve to reduce anxiety that would arise from constantly choosing between alternative behaviors; they create an organizing structure for one's self and for social interactions, thereby reducing the need for constant negotiation. Classroom roles are viewed as repetitive patterns of behavior by which classroom members (teachers and students) fulfill classroom functions. This approach is congruent with the transactional nature of encounters experienced by teachers or students, a position that describes each party in an interaction as mutually involved. Such a view of classroom interaction implies that teachers and students are engaged in a constant mutual influence process with each simultaneously affecting how the other communicates. Millar (1996) argued this should be viewed as a dialogical process as "the teacher as well as the student must attend to the intentions and understandings of the other to sustain a teaching–learning interaction" (p. 161). Hart (1986) captured the essence of this process: "Teachers act. They act on people. And they are acted upon in return. This is the physics of educating" (p. 5).

In this chapter, I maintain that classroom roles of the teacher are dynamic, evolving, and unpredictable because they are intrinsically linked to, and dependent on, student roles within a defined context. In the following pages I explore this position through an examination of contextual issues, role development, role functions, and role conflict.

CONTEXTUAL ISSUES

With each passing decade, the college or university instructor faces exponential change. Management educator Vaill (1996) used the term "permanent white water" to describe today's complex, turbulent, changing environment, arguing that we live in a world of conditions that are "regularly taking us all out of our comfort zones and asking things of us that we never imagined would be required" (p. 14). Therefore no universal consensus exists on normative expectations or enactments. Roles are no longer taken for granted or prescribed; rather they are negotiated and renegotiated within a particular context such as the institution in which you find yourself. In addition, your institution may be in flux because colleges and universities are reinventing themselves to meet the demands of external forces.

Institutional mission will impact on your classroom experience. In a school with a strong commitment to teaching, your efforts will be monitored carefully, a faculty development program will provide support, and the reward structure will privilege excellent instruction. Students will expect individual attention. At other institutions you will keep your teaching concerns to yourself because the research mission overshadows the classroom commitment. Students regretfully expect to be kept at some distance.

Specific departmental expectations directly affect your teaching. If you are expected to administer a departmental exam at the end of the term, you cannot ask students to design their own learning evaluation measures. If you receive feedback from your department chair that your persuasion course is too difficult for freshman, you may change your materials for the next term. You may maintain required office hours and teach required classes.

Some institutions are calling on communication faculty to work as consultants to the communication across the curriculum initiative, or to participate in newly designed programs, such as in an engineering applied design program that integrates communication. Such faculty function as coaches or facilitators responding to student needs. As these examples demonstrate, roles are enacted within a context that frames the interaction process. Teacher and student roles are developed and maintained thorough communication congruent with institutional expectations.

ROLE DEVELOPMENT

Classroom roles emerge through a complex twofold process that involves (a) role expectation, and (b) role performance. In both cases, personal background, relationships with significant others, system expectations, and feedback affect teacher role development.

Role Expectation

Much of your life has been spent in classrooms—evaluating teachers and developing implicit expectations about teaching. Your former instructors serve as instructional models impacting your expectations. As you considered a teaching career, you may have resolved to nurture fine writers, as your creative writing teacher did, or you may have decided never to ridicule poor speakers, as your basic speech course instructor did. You may have found intercultural communication or oral history to be so fascinating that you planned to incorporate such issues in many of your classes.

On a personal level, if you attended schools with a homogeneous religious, ethnic, or socioeconomic student body, you may base your instructional expectations on this experience. If your undergraduate school emphasized an experiential approach to interpersonal communication, you will bring different expectations about what class time should include than a colleague who heard only theoretical lectures on the subject. You may have studied with one professor for three or four classes, resolving to "teach like Professor Griffin someday." If you enjoyed small group work, you are likely to use small groups in your teaching.

Significant others, such as your college peers, establish expectations about how good teachers behave. Their criticism or praise influences how you view "good" or "bad" classroom behavior. The hours spent drinking coffee and comparing teachers set strong expectations for future behavior.

Finally, messages from the educational system influence expectations. While job hunting, faculty may tell you their students are brilliant and highly self-motivated, information that establishes very specific expectations for classroom behavior. It is in these ways that beliefs and background, significant others, and the general system expectations influence role expectations.

Role Performance

New instructors immediately encounter the difference between expectations and reality. No matter how carefully you have planned, there will always be some, if not many surprises that alter your classroom behavior. Thus role performance implies how you enact the role.

Personal characteristics affect teacher behavior. Your own learning style will impact how you construct and respond to actual learning situations (see Gorham, chap. 19, this volume). You may exhibit a field-dependent learning style, responding best in collaborative and affective situations, or you may be field independent, preferring to focus on tasks, objectives, and analysis (Whitkin & Moore, 1975). If you are highly analytical, you may critique points of organization or reasoning in a speech that someone else might miss; if you are collaborative and reflective you may engage in extensive dialogue with the presenter regarding underlying beliefs. Your learning preference may be abstract or concrete, active or reflective (Kolb, 1984). Such factors will impact your actual performance.

In addition, your classroom responses are influenced by characteristics such as your gender, age, cultural heritage, and value system (Nussbaum, 1992), and similar characteristics of students affect your role enactment.

Significant evidence suggests that men may learn differently from women, older students may learn differently from the traditional college-age student, and persons from varied cultures may learn differently (Upcraft, 1996). If you are teaching primarily returning female adult students, your instructional practices will be different than if you have a mixed-gender class of traditional-age learners.

Sometimes you will surprise yourself by your inability to act according to your expectations. For example, although you may wish to hold discussions, your personal anxiety may surface whenever students raise unpredictable ideas and, in order to keep control, you may return to lecturing. Although you wish to use simulations, you may find your lack of experience keeps you from being comfortable with this approach. Positive surprises also may occur when expectations do not meet reality. A teacher who expects to lecture regularly may feel drawn to a collaborative learning approach.

A major report on life in college classrooms indicates a frequent mismatch between faculty and student expectations, a gap that leaves both parties unfulfilled (Boyer, 1987). The faculty want to explore scholarly ideas with appreciative students. "'Intellectually meek' students wanted everything spelled out and were willing to conform for the sake of grades" (Boyer, 1987, pp. 140–141).

Other faculty also influence how you enact a role. A colleague may say, "I refuse to support your move to develop a competency test for the basic course" or "Here are my outlines for the language unit, which might help you." In his study of new faculty, Boice (1992) indicated that few reported colleague support.

Finally, as noted earlier, the institutional system influences performance. The curriculum committee may mandate a specific number of writing assignments within the speech course. The basic course committee may decide to drop the rhetorical analysis assignment and replace it with an interviewing experience. You may wait for years to teach your favorite subject because another professor or department "controls" the course.

Whatever your current state of role development, be assured it will be different in 5 years and in 25 years. Personal changes will be reflected in your classroom expectations and performance. Societal and institutional changes will be reflected in the students and systems you encounter.

ROLE FUNCTIONS

Role functions provide a more specific means for examining classroom life. The image of a system as a mobile can be used to visualize the various role functions within a classroom that affect the balance of the institutional system.

Figure 18.1 pictures a mobile containing the various role functions needed to keep the system operating and balanced. From a transactional perspective, teachers, students, and significant others may perform as part of each role function. The primary role functions are: (a) providing content expertise, (b) providing learning management, (c) providing evaluative feedback, (d) providing socialization, and (e) providing personal models.

Providing Content Expertise

The finest teachers care passionately about their subjects, finding joy in talking about the field of study that pervades their lives. Such instructors are committed to creating changes in their students through thoughtful structuring of content that connects to their students' lives. Communication instructors experience countless opportunities to excite students. The most memorable teachers use the previous night's presidential address as an example of a rhetorical device or describe family systems theory at work in a new film. Communication becomes part of one's intellectual life, rather than an isolated academic responsibility. Students contribute to this process through questions, challenges, individual knowledge, and personal research. Such classrooms reflect a sense of intellectual heritage as well as recognition of current thought.

Although content expertise may result partly from graduate school training, over time it depends on a teacher's willingness to keep abreast of his or her chosen area and explore the complexities of the communication field

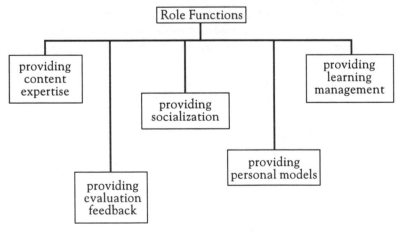

FIG. 18.1.   The various role functions within the classroom.

and its related areas. Today's courses in political communication, telecommunications, or the performance of culture were originally exploratory offerings taught by persons exploring interconnections of theories and research perspectives.

Managing Learning

Not only must teachers know their subjects; they must communicate them effectively to learners. When Boice (1992) asked new faculty about the kind of help they needed most as teachers, he received universal perceptions that the "hardest tasks are learning what level of lecture difficulty was appropriate for students and managing reasonable preparation time for classes" (pp. 57–58). By their third and fourth semesters, nearly half of the experienced new faculty had relaxed their styles to encourage more student participation. In his study of master college teachers, Epstein (1981) concluded:

> There is many a tried, but no true method for doing this: Socratic teaching, sonorous lecturing, sympathetic discussion, passionate argument, witty exposition, dramatics and other parts of derring-do; plain power of personal example, main force of intellect, and sometimes even bullying. (p. xii)

Each instructor creates, alone or with student input, the specific learning process, including diagnosis, objective setting, selection of strategies, and evaluation. Effective teachers demonstrate an ability to use a wide range of methods or strategies (such as discussion, lecture, higher order questioning, or role playing), selecting the appropriate one based on perception of student needs. Throughout the term, the teacher uses learner feedback to modify original goals and plans.

Management includes the creation of a classroom climate designed to support a particular type of learning. For example, teachers of performance or discussion-oriented classes work to establish a safe and supportive climate for taking risks and the sharing of personal opinions. Rules and disciplinary policies are developed as an intrinsic means of supporting the desired learning climate.

Currently, communication professors are involved in educational efforts such as collaborative learning, communication across the curriculum, or learning communities, all of which have implications for managing learning. In his discussion of learning communities, Angelo (1996) described them as places where faculty, students, and other members of the educational community work collaboratively toward shared goals:

> In learning communities everyone has both the opportunity and responsibility to learn from and help teach everyone else. Faculty become less purveyors of information and more designers of learning environments and experiences, expert guides, and practicing master learners themselves. (p. 1)

In practice, learning communities typically feature purposive groupings of students, shared scheduling, significant use of collective and collaborative learning approaches, and an emphasis on connecting learning across course and disciplinary boundaries. Therefore, faculty need teamwork skills and an ability to recognize communication opportunities and implement them.

Providing Evaluation and Feedback

Most educational institutions require a formal evaluation on the completion of a specified unit of study. Often the function of evaluation serves to demonstrate a separation of teachers and students on the basis of power. It could, however, serve to engage them in a cooperative development of evaluation measures. According to Fuhrmann and Grasha (1983), assigning grades may be perceived as negative if grades allow faculty to exercise superiority and unnecessary control over students, who view the grade solely as an academic end. Grades may be perceived as valuable if they are used to motivate, reward student accomplishment, or provide feedback. The use of the evaluation function interacts significantly with the management of learning.

The nature of the communication field necessitates that classroom members develop skills in critiquing or delivering feedback on oral performance. Students must receive carefully created critiques designed to foster continued improvement. Such feedback may be given by the teacher, other students, or both. A review of research on providing feedback suggests that teachers need to be knowledgeable about the effects of various types of feedback and should consciously provide appropriate criticism to student speakers. In addition, the research indicates that students can be trained to give helpful feedback to peers (Book, 1985).

Faculty must also evaluate themselves using methods such as self-reflection, student feedback, and peer and chair evaluation (see Vangelisti, chap. 29, this volume). The current emphasis on peer review for formative purposes has the potential to provide faculty with valuable feedback because the "emphasis is on development, where efforts toward improvement can be directed toward any or all professional roles" (Keig & Waggoner, 1994, p. 12).

Providing Socialization

Classrooms are the settings for academic socialization to an entire field and to models of thinking. Teachers serve as gatekeepers to a world that represents their field as well as the values, assumptions, and types of intellectual life that characterize their discipline. A representative of an academic field and way of life, a teacher discusses his or her intellectual positions, research interests, and the process of intellectual growth. Students question, react, and contribute positions learned elsewhere.

A teacher's classroom behavior may include lectures and anecdotes describing positions taken by members of the field and reasons for these positions. In addition, a teacher may describe his or her academic background, past professional positions, current research interests, and intellectual struggles. Out-of-class behaviors may include personal conversations on choices of graduate schools and future careers.

Classrooms are also the scene of more personal socialization as teachers exert influence regarding social values. In Hart's (1986) words, teachers are revolutionaries, insurgents, and liberators as "they make people better than they thought they could be" (p. 4). Communication courses speak directly to values that support democratic citizenship, interpersonal growth, or political awareness.

In specific cases, faculty become mentors for one or more students, serving as a guide to life in the academic world of communication. Issues of sensitivity to students, a scholar's curiosity, academic ethics and values, publication directions, and personal boundaries may be explored over time between mentor and student, a relationship that enhances both parties.

Providing Personal Models

Teachers teach who they are as well as what they believe intellectually. From the first moments in a classroom, students construct a persona for their instructor. Although some instructors deliberately cloak themselves in distance or mystery, most portray many sides of their nature, engaging students in mutually rewarding relationships. Teachers share personal anecdotes, family stories, or feelings about certain significant moments in the class. Students refer to family and work experiences, as well as to their developing values and intellectual position. Kirp (1997) captured this interaction in the following way:

> Professors deliver lectures, hold office hours, supervise theses. Meanwhile, students fabricate character studies, hang on to the inadvertent

asides, the jokes that slip out, the impromptu examples, because this is the raw material from which they can convert presentations of ideas into presentations of self. In doing so, students invite themselves not just to their professors' lectures but also into their lives. (p. 12)

This relationship may continue outside of disciplinary boundaries as students seek personal guidance about family, romantic, or personal growth issues.

Sometimes a teacher serves as a role model—an adult who appears to have reached a desired level of intellectual and personal development. This person demonstrates ways to manage prejudicial classroom comments or use technology creatively. Bonwell (1996) suggested faculty should serve as a role models because "students are more likely to take risks if they see the instructor is more willing to take risks as well" (p. 5). Within the communication field, students expect to view a teacher as a model of personal communication competence as well as a communication scholar.

The preceding five role functions could be expanded to include additional categories. Whatever the categories, they will reflect the interactive nature of the functions. As you already know, this interaction may not occur smoothly or predictably. The final section of this chapter addresses some of the conflicts that may occur as teachers and students together attempt to create a learning environment.

ROLE CONFLICT

Teaching has been described ideally as two persons sitting on either end of a log and talking. At key moments, teaching resembles that image—an intense interlocking of two minds. A thoughtful teacher struggles to confront and understand concerns that surface as one's being (background, beliefs, experience, values) comes into contact with that of another person or system. Conflicts may occur over differences in the priority of role functions or the choices within role functions. These interpersonal and intrapersonal conflicts are related to role development and role functions.

Interpersonal Conflicts

When role expectations or role exactments of significant others collide, role conflicts develop. For example, you may wish to present your content knowledge in stimulating large group lectures, but students or administrators may pressure you to use some collaborative learning groups. You may plan to manage classroom learning as a facilitator, forcing students to take responsibility for extensive independent work. The class, however, may resist this approach by consistently arriving unprepared or remaining silent, forcing you to confront the issues directly or alter your methods.

Your position within the college system may contribute to role conflict. If you are a graduate teaching assistant, you may find yourself constantly negotiating the boundaries of a system. You struggle with questions such as, "To what extent am I a full-fledged teacher and to what extent am I still a student?" and "Will undergraduates treat me differently than they would a full-time faculty member?" The ambiguous "in between" status may leave you open to more conflictual experiences than those faced by full-time faculty.

Background experiences provide you with role expectations for managing classroom differences or disagreements. Hocker (1986) described this well: "If one had as models professors who were imperious and demanding but rigorous and fair, one might try to emulate that style in class" (p. 75). On the other hand, she suggested if one learned from professors who were empathetic and concerned about the personal growth of their students, a different style of conflict resolution would be adopted.

In today's classrooms professors can expect to encounter student resistance and behavior problems (Lee, Levine, & Cambra, 1997) as well as highly charged or offensive comments directed to other students. The conflict management style you develop will reflect your expectations and experiences in the performance of classroom confrontation (see Plax & Kearney, chap. 20, this volume).

Intrapersonal Conflicts

When teachers experience incongruity between role expectations and performance, internal conflict arises. On occasion, such conflict serves the productive function of driving you to meet a desired expectation. In other situations, you may realistically or reluctantly revise your expectations and rely on the feedback of students or colleagues to inform your perception of teaching effectiveness. Students experience similar types of internal conflict when their expectations do not match the feedback given to their performance.

Finally, faculty members face a special type of internal conflict when confronting interface issues. An educational myth suggests that teachers can and should treaty everyone equally. Yet reality tells you that you connect easily or positively with one student, whereas your contact with another is negative or distant. In some cases, this linkage or lack of linkage is so powerful that it can interfere with fairness in the classroom. Interface issues arise when a strong internal psychological concern is triggered by another classroom member. A brash, confrontive student may remind you of your immature teenage self and evoke feelings of discomfort; a shy student may remind you of your own reticence and lead you to be overprotective. These powerful, emotional reactions to a student signal an internal conflict and you need to consider whether the problem lies in the student or in yourself.

Conflicts are less likely to arise when all parties believe they are engaged in meaningful work. The effective functioning of a classroom depends on the cooperative attitude and intellectual curiosity of all members. If faculty and students do not see themselves as having important business to do together, prospects for effective learning are diminished (Boyer, 1987).

The teaching–learning process is enhanced when members of the classroom community can make explicit and negotiate, if necessary, their role expectations and performance of role functions. When all persons involved in learning enrich each other, sparks fly. If learning is to be constructed as inherently dialogical, the teacher as well as the student must attend to the intentions and understandings of the other to sustain a valued teaching–learning interaction.

REFERENCES

Angelo, T. (1996). Seven shifts and seven levers: Developing more productive learning communities. *The National Teaching & Learning Forum, 6,* 1–4.

Boice, R. (1992). *The new faculty member.* San Francisco: Jossey-Bass.

Bonwell, C. (1996). Building a supportive climate for active learning. *The National Teaching & Learning Forum, 6,* 4–7.

Book, C. (1985). Providing feedback: The research on effective oral and written feedback strategies. *Central States Speech Journal, 36,* 14–23.

Boyer, E. (1987). *College: The undergraduate experience in America.* New York: Harper & Row.

Epstein, J. (Ed.). (1981). *Masters: Portraits of great teachers.* New York: Basic Books.

Fuhrmann, B., & Grasha, A. (1983). *A practical handbook for college teachers.* Boston: Little/Brown.

Hart, R. (1986, February). *Sex, drugs, rock 'n roll and speech: Why we're in Tucson.* Speech delivered at the meeting of the Western Speech Communication Association, Tucson, AZ.

Hocker, J. (1986). Teacher–student confrontations. In J. Civikly (Ed.), *Communicating in college classrooms: New directions for teaching and learning* (pp. 69–78). San Francisco: Jossey-Bass.

Homan, S. (1985). The classroom as theatre. In J. Katz (Ed.), *Teaching as though students mattered: New directions for teaching and learning* (pp. 69–78). San Francisco: Jossey-Bass.

Keig, L., & Waggoner, M. D. (1994). *Collaborative peer review: The role of faculty in improving college teaching* (ASHE-ERIC Higher Education Report No. 2). Washington, DC: The George Washington University.

Kirp, D. E. (1997, May–June). Twenty-seven ways of looking at a classroom. *Change 29,* 10–18.

Kolb, D. (1984). *Experimental learning: Experience as the source of learning and development.* Englewood Cliffs, NJ: Prentice-Hall.

Lee, C., Levine, T., & Cambra, R. (1997). Resisting compliance in the multicultural classroom. *Communication Education, 46,* 29–43.

Linton, R. (1945). *The cultural background of personality.* New York: Appleton-Century-Crofts.

Mann, R., Arnold, S., Binder, J., Cytrynbaum, S., Newman, B., Ringwald, B., Ringwald, J., & Rosenwein, R. (1970). *The college classroom: Conflict, change and learning.* New York: Wiley.

Millar, S. B. (1996). New roles for teachers in today's classrooms. In R. Menges, M. Weimer, & Associates (Eds.), *Teaching on solid ground* (pp. 155–178). San Francisco: Jossey-Bass.

Nussbaum, J. F. (1992). Effective teacher behaviors. *Communication Education, 41*, 167–180.

Timpson, W., & Tobin, D. (1982). *Teaching as performing*. Englewood Cliffs, NJ: Prentice-Hall.

Upcraft, M. L. (1996). Teaching and today's college student. In R. Menges, M. Weimer, & Associates (Eds.), *Teaching on solid ground* (pp. 21–42). San Francisco: Jossey-Bass.

Vaill, P. (1996). *Learning as a way of being*. San Francisco: Jossey-Bass.

Whitkin, H. A., & Moore, C. A. (1975). *Field-dependent and field-independent cognitive styles and their educational implications*. Princeton, NJ: Educational Testing Service.

19

Diversity in Classroom Dynamics

Joan Gorham
West Virginia University

Teachers frequently bring to the classroom habits shaped by modeling and experience. We tend to teach as we were taught, to assume that all of the people we teach are like we were (or how we think we were) as students, to develop syllabi, objectives, and lesson plans from the perspective of "covering" material we have personally found interesting or important. Students, however, come to us with differing expectations and needs, differing orientations toward education, differing baseline skills on which to build, and differing ways of processing information. This chapter examines those differences.

WHAT IS IT WE WISH TO ACCOMPLISH?

In his *Basic Principles of Curriculum and Instruction,* (1949), Ralph Tyler, the father of the instructional objective, identified four fundamental questions that must be answered in developing any curriculum or plan of instruction: (a) What outcomes should the school (course, unit, lesson) seek to attain? (b) What experiences can be provided that are likely to attain these outcomes? (c) How can these experiences be effectively organized? and (d) How can we determine whether these outcomes are being attained? A clear and precise answer to the first question is necessary before approaching the others: What do I want students to do or know or think or feel as a result of this learning experience?

Answering this question deserves more introspection than it is usually given. In communication courses, desired learning outcomes might include knowledge of the field: theories, rules, research, and principles that will ground students' understanding of the communication process. They might include abilities to demonstrate self-presentation or public communication skills. They might further include goals of building self-confidence, of guiding students toward greater knowledge of self, of internalizing the value of communicative competence, or of transferring knowledge and skills to applications outside the classroom. They might encompass broader goals of the educational experience, such as learning how to learn, developing writing and critical thinking skills, contributing to the celebration of diversity, and valuing education. They might include practical goals such as reinforcing habits of punctuality, responsibility, organization, and effort (see Sprague, chap. 2, this volume).

Prioritizing and addressing these goals requires an understanding of what students bring with them to our classes. Where are these particular students in relation to where we would like them to be? What do the students want? What do we know about differences in how students learn? What impediments to learning must be acknowledged? How can I accommodate diversity in evaluating student performance?

WHERE ARE THESE PARTICULAR STUDENTS IN RELATION TO WHERE WE WOULD LIKE THEM TO BE?

What we need to accomplish in the classroom differs depending on whom we are teaching. When we are teaching a basic communication course that is part of the freshman core, the objective of reinforcing practical "studenting skills" should be more central than if we are teaching an upper division elective for communication majors. We may carry with us nostalgic notions that students are supposed to come to us knowing how to read a syllabus, how to organize an essay, when and how to contact an instructor for help, or why attending class is important. The reality in contemporary institutions with student-centered philosophies and heightened interest in student retention is that all lower level courses are expected to include goals of helping students learn how to succeed in school. Such objectives are part of the courses' place in the students' overall educational experience.

When we are teaching students with limited proficiency in speaking English, expectations for their achievement in a public speaking course must be appropriate. When we are teaching students who have elected to take our course because they value the importance of becoming effective communicators, our task is different than when we are teaching students who question the value of our subject matter. We cannot ignore the fact that many students who take communication courses to meet graduation requirements do not expect to like them, do not initially believe that the concepts or skills addressed are useful, and do not expect any value beyond the credit hours earned. If we believe that the study of communication is a meaningful endeavor, we cannot ignore the importance of affective objectives.

WHAT DO STUDENTS WANT?

Students want to be respected. They are increasingly pragmatic, approaching courses as consumers who expect to get what they pay for. They want to believe that teachers care about them and understand their needs.

What students want from a course, what they see themselves as paying for, may be different from what a teacher wants them to want. Some students are motivated primarily by grades, some by learning, some by both, and some by neither (Milton, Pollio, & Eison, 1986). This mix of values among students creates a challenge for teachers as they address Tyler's (1949) essential questions: How will I organize this course? What will I ask students to do? How will I evaluate how students are doing in achieving the desired outcomes?

Students with high learning orientation and low grade orientation (High LO/Low GO) often resent taking required courses that are not perceived as related to things they want to know, but become involved and challenging participants when a personal "hook" between subject matter and individual interest has been established. They will often seek personal contact with their instructors, take risks in choosing difficult topics for assignments, and impress us as intellectually and emotionally able. They may also fail to comply with requirements that do not meet their personal goals. They may turn in thought-provoking 5-page or 25-page papers when the assignment requested 10; they may present captivating speeches that cannot be evaluated by the criteria presented for a particular assignment; they may choose not to edit and resubmit a paper if they think they met their own objectives the first time. As teachers, we hope they do not bend the rules too far to "make" the grade we feel they "earned."

High LO/Low GO students challenge us to look carefully at our instructional objectives and means of evaluation. If we believe they are bypassing objectives that are truly important to their learning, we need to communicate clearly why mastering those objectives is of value to them. If we find it difficult to do so, we need to reevaluate our assessment measures, particularly the relative emphasis placed on demonstration of lower level versus higher level cognitive learning outcomes.

Students who are primarily grade oriented (Low LO/High GO) tend to view all aspects of the classroom in terms of effects on the course grade. Instructional procedures and policies that make getting a good grade easy are valued; activities viewed as not related to grades are seen as a waste of time. Grade-oriented students appreciate teachers who very explicitly specify criteria on which performance evaluations will be based. They resent teachers who are perceived as subjective in their grading. They can be very selective in their attention to descriptive feedback, ignoring any suggestions not related to evaluation.

Low LO/High GO students are the most likely type to drop courses in which they are not doing well, and to cheat; however, they will be motivated to do things we consider important, such as attending class or providing feedback to their peers, if they can earn points toward their final grade by doing so. Sometimes teachers are annoyed by this orientation; Low LO/High GO students are the most likely to be those whose grades we want to "curve down." Their presence challenges us to closely examine grading schema so we are comfortable that assessment of competence has not been overridden by assessment of compliance. If our instructional objectives and evaluative measures are solid, Low LO/High GO students will learn in spite of themselves.

Students who are both grade and learning oriented (High LO/High GO) would seem to present the ideal profile: students who want to make learning personally relevant but also conscientiously comply with whatever the instructor asks of them. They are, however, the students who experience the most stress in the educational environment and who score the highest on measures of performance or test anxiety. Diminishing counterproductive levels of concern over evaluation through clear objectives, detailed information on assignments, and opportunities to obtain formative feedback helps to keep their anxiety over grades from getting in the way of their desire to learn.

Students who are older than the traditional student or who are juggling student, spouse, parent, and employee roles often fall into the High LO/High GO category. Their decision to be in our classroom is usually intentional and goal directed. Their investment of time and money is tangible, and they see both learning and grades as tangible rewards for that investment. They are likely to bring with them their own objectives for applying what they learn, particularly in the case of practical communication concepts and skills, to their personal experience base. Some adult students have a good deal of sophisticated, firsthand experience, the kind that can be intimidating to an instructor who is considerably younger and not particularly confident in his or her expert power base. Most of these students have a strong desire for some sense of control over both grade and learning outcomes. Setting objectives with rather than for these students often fosters a sense of "joint ownership" that is comfortable for both instructor and student.

Students who are neither grade or learning oriented (Low LO/Low GO) are frequently disinterested, absent, and unresponsive to feedback. They may be in school because their parents sent them, to have a good time, or to avoid getting a job. They may also be immature students who need help in defining priorities and developing their identity as a student. Teachers, who were rarely this type of student themselves, often have difficulty understanding students who seem to place no value in either the intrinsic or extrinsic reward structures of educational institutions. We can turn some of them around by demonstrating that we offer something they value; we will lose others.

WHAT DO WE KNOW ABOUT DIFFERENCES IN HOW STUDENTS LEARN?

Learning styles have been defined as the "cognitive, affective, and physiological traits that serve as relatively stable indicators of how learners perceive, interact with, and respond to learning environments" (Keefe, 1982, p. 43). Style elements may be conditions under which an individual is most comfortable and prefers to learn or factors that must be considered for information to be processed and stored. They include distinctions in how individuals perceive and process information; distinctions among visual, auditory, and kinesthetic orientations; differences in affective or motivational needs; and differences in preferred learning environments. Regardless of the focus of assessment, recommendations throughout the learning style literature reflect several common themes: Different people learn in different ways; individual learning styles are measurable; teachers and institutions should consider learning style in instructional delivery; students' understanding of their own learning styles can help them make useful adaptive decisions; and matching and mismatching learning style and instructional technique has significant implications for both cognitive and affective learning (Gorham, 1986).

Curry's (1983) analysis of various learning style models led her to suggest that style elements can be likened to the layers of an onion, with the inner layers more stable than the outer layers. *Cognitive personality* elements are at the core of the onion. Probably the most extensively researched conceptualization of cognitive personality is Witkin's field dependence–independence continuum (Witkin, Dyk, Oltman, Raskin, & Karp, 1971). Field-independent (FI) persons use predominantly internal cues when making judgments; they are "splitters" who have little difficulty learning separate parts of a whole out of context. Field-dependent (FD) persons are "lumpers" who use predominantly external cues and learn best once they have "the big picture." In any classroom, we are likely to find students who range from highly FD to highly FI. In some classrooms, such as those in programs serving educationally disadvantaged students from lower socioeconomic backgrounds, the majority of students may tend toward field dependence (Gorham & Self, 1987). Field dependence is also a likely characteristic of students from high-context cultural backgrounds.

FIs learn well when concepts and skills are divided into small units that eventually pull together into a larger frame of understanding. They are comfortable learning information and then being tested on recall of that information, without knowing up front where individual bits of knowledge will ultimately fit within an overall schema. They respond positively to course designs that are "logical" and "ordered" in their approach to developing the topic being studied. North American teachers, whether applying what has traditionally been taught about writing lesson plans in teacher preparation classes or simply modeling their own teachers, tend to approach course design from an FI perspective. FD students are at a disadvantage in such classes.

FDs learn best with models and practice. They appear to depend more on impression than on expression; they are better able to "feel" their way through various public speaking opportunities (developing a gestalt sense of what works and what does not work along the way) than they are able to pull together the lessons of separate units for demonstration in one or two final performances. FDs' learning is enhanced when performance can be compared to examples rather than to an abstract ideal; if they experience only poor models they have difficulty analyzing problems in what they observe, despite discussion of effective communication strategies. FDs tend to be less competitive, to desire frequent feedback, and to be responsive to cooperative learning and mastery learning models. They are particularly attentive to nonverbal cues and they are strongly influenced by their emotional responses to both class material and the individual teaching that material.

The middle layers of Curry's "onion" represent *information-processing style*, an individual's intellectual approach to assimilating information. The outer layers represent *instructional preferences*, such as lecture versus group discussion. Information-processing differences among individuals represent an interaction between cognitive personality traits and instructional preferences. For example, McCarthy (1987) classified learners into four information processing types based on combined preferences for concrete versus abstract and active versus reflective learning (see fig. 19.1).

Type One learners perceive information concretely and process it reflectively. They are innovative, imaginative, and concerned with personal relevance; they need to clarify how a new concept or area of study links with previous experiences before they are receptive to learning it. They learn best through methods that encourage brainstorming, peer interaction, and empathy.

Type Two learners perceive information abstractly and process it reflectively. Schools are traditionally designed for these learners, who value sequential thinking, details, and expert opinion. They are data collectors, more interested in ideas than applications, and they learn best in structured environments with teachers who assume the role of information giver.

Type Three learners perceive information abstractly and process it actively. They seek utility and enjoy solving problems that test theories against common sense. They resent being given answers, and they have a limited tolerance for "fuzzy" ideas that cannot be applied practically. They learn best with teachers who act as coaches and facilitate hands-on experience.

Type Four learners perceive information concretely and process it actively. They learn well by trial and error, with teachers who serve as evalua-

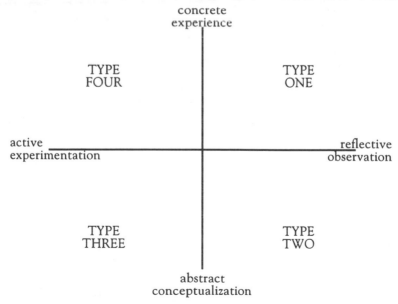

FIG. 19.1.   Information-processing styles.

tors and remediators but who encourage self-discovery. They are dynamic learners with a very practical orientation; they prefer to teach themselves and then to share what they have learned with others.

McCarthy's study of 17- and 18-year-old high school students categorized 35% as Type One, 22% as Type Two, 18% as Type Three, and 25% as Type Four learners. She subsequently suggested that teachers develop instructional units that move through the four quadrants, addressing each student's information-processing style in the process (McCarthy & Morris, 1995a, 1995b). A unit on speech introductions, for example, might begin with students reading or listening to speeches with and without effective introductions and discussing their reactions, followed by small group discussions analyzing students' impressions of the purpose of a speech introduction (Type One). The instructor would then teach the concept, explaining the objectives and techniques of gaining attention (Type Two). Students could then, on their own or in groups, formulate three or four introductions for the same speech, decide which they like best, and explain why (Type Three). They would be asked to prepare an outline for a speech they would give and to write several possible introductions on a separate page. Students would later exchange outlines, clarify content as needed, write two or three possible introductions for their partner's topic, evaluate the options, and discuss similarities and differences between speaker- and partner-generated ideas (Type Four). A unit on nonverbal communication might begin with the instructor asking students to participate in several illustrative activities (e.g., "Pick a partner. Look him or her in the eyes. Now slowly move forward, maintaining eye contact, until your noses touch."), proceed through a lecture on theory and related research, continue with students trying and reporting on responses to some nonverbal norm-breaking attempts outside of class, and end with groups designing simple studies that address questions of interest.

Instructional planning of this type is likely to accommodate visual, auditory, and manipulative learners at various points. The redundancy is instructionally sound and students learn to "style flex" through exercising less preferred abilities. The instructor may cover fewer concepts in a course, but a greater percentage of students will understand those concepts that are presented.

WHAT IMPEDIMENTS TO LEARNING MUST BE ACKNOWLEDGED?

Anxiety is a major impediment to learning. In highly stressful situations, individuals undergo physiological changes and adaptive responses that hinder their ability to manage the situation; they respond so strongly to the stress that they cannot respond appropriately to the task at hand. The more public or more evaluative the context, the greater the stress is likely to be. Thus, people who are confident and competent drivers may find themselves unable to parallel park when attempting to demonstrate that ability when taking the test that will determine whether or not their driver's license will be renewed. Different people find different situations a source of anxiety. Some are particularly anxious about the prospect of self-disclosure. Some cannot sing in public. Some experience disabling writer's block when faced with a blank computer screen and the task of producing a manuscript that will be submitted for critical review. Among every 25 students in our classes, on average 5 will test high on measures of communication apprehension. For these students, actual or anticipated communication with another person or persons produces a level of fear or anxiety that impedes their ability to perform.

High communication apprehensives (CAs) are likely to favor larger, lecture-type classes with few opportunities for student–student or student–teacher interaction. They will often drop a class with high communication requirements. One study (Richmond & McCroskey, 1989) found that over 50% of high CAs dropped a required public speaking course during the first 3 weeks, just before the first speech was due. Other studies have shown that high CAs are likely to be absent on days when they are scheduled for presentations, that they sit at the back and sides of classrooms to avoid recognition, and that they almost never volunteer to participate, even when they know the right answer. In some instances, high CAs will knowingly give wrong answers to reduce their chances of being called on again. High CAs told that they would be asked to explain information given in class to another student were found to recall 20% less than those not anticipating a requirement of engaging in communication with a peer (Richmond & McCroskey, 1989).

Communication classes are likely to place value on communicative behavior, even when they are not strictly performance classes. When teachers expect class participation, particularly in required performance classes, they must be aware that approximately one in five students will experience anxiety that goes beyond manageable stage fright. Treatments such as cognitive restructuring and systematic desensitization can reduce communication apprehension. They require training to administer and are most appropriately used in situations where high CAs have been identified and offered specialized help. Skills training itself may improve communication behavior and result in modest reductions in communication apprehension.

Students who become confident in their knowledge of how to give an effective speech may perform better and feel less anxious as a result; however, such effects are usually related to the degree to which high CAs recognize skill deficiencies and voluntarily commit themselves to improving them, and to the degree to which the goals of the skill training are narrowly and specifically defined.

Knowledge of communication apprehension has obvious administrative and curricular implications. If the development of basic oral communication skills is perceived as a desired goal for an educational program, and if requiring a performance course is perceived as a fitting means to that end, then the existence of a single, generic "Comm 100" is clearly insufficient. Many instructors, however, find themselves teaching in precisely that situation. For them, communication apprehension must be recognized as a salient difference among individual students. Skill objectives must be narrowed and targeted to students' needs, affective objectives explicitly recognized, "stake" in a given instance of evaluation minimized, and achievement evaluated against an attainable standard.

HOW CAN I ACCOMMODATE DIVERSITY IN EVALUATING STUDENT PERFORMANCE?

The process of assigning grades in a course should be relatively dispassionate. Evaluation should be a means of assessing learning outcomes and grades a shorthand for communicating success in achieving those outcomes. If students are told what is expected of them and assessed in terms of something else, their affect for the teacher, and probably the subject, will be diminished. Students in the same course should be evaluated based on their achievement of the same course objectives; however, measures of achievement should acknowledge diversity in the classroom.

Measuring cognitive learning via only midterm and final examinations may, for students with high test anxiety, assess their anxiety more than what they know. Introducing a more frequent schedule of quizzes, with less evaluative weight assigned to each, and providing clear study guides to increase students' sense of control as they prepare for evaluation, will provide a better indication of what test-anxious students have learned without handicapping nonanxious classmates. Competitive grading in a speech performance class is likely to reward students who liked speaking to begin with and cause students who feared speaking at the outset to dislike or fear it more. Introducing a cooperative learning environment, narrowing objectives for each assignment, and focusing on formative feedback will help some students manage their anxiety without compromising the learning of others. Preassessing communication apprehension and providing alternative classes designed to help high CAs disarm the anxiety they experience at the prospect of speaking to others is more likely to accomplish the objective of improving oral communication skills than is the requirement that all students learn the same things in the same basic course.

A common approach to assessing achievement of higher order cognitive objectives (e.g., synthesis, evaluation, application) is asking students to write papers. Teachers need to recognize that evaluations of such assignments may, intentionally or not, assess writing skill as much as subject area understanding. The logical development of ideas is frequently central to evaluation of written assignments. European Americans value a quasilogical style that links physical evidence, statistics, and expert testimony to drawing conclusions that must therefore be true. However, what constitutes logic is culture bound, as are standards for what constitutes evidence. International students who have mastered English vocabulary are likely to continue to organize their ideas following patterns associated with their native languages.

English is a speaker-responsible language. Asian, Middle Eastern, Latin American, Native American, and African cultures are listener responsible, characterized by indirect indication of the speaker's or writer's intent and assumptions of implicit shared knowledge rather than the need to convey facts. These are high-context cultures. Social roles are important, bonds between people are nurtured, and much meaning is taken from nonverbal cues.

Students from high-context cultures are comfortable with more ritualized forms of interaction and less so with spontaneous interaction. They are accustomed to more formal teacher–student roles and less classroom involvement than that desired by many European American communication teachers. Teachers can either choose to recognize these differences in evaluating student participation or work specifically toward teaching the skills of and providing practice in "active studenting." In either case, the objectives should be clear to both teacher and students.

Simply put, it is not fair to evaluate students on skills and abilities we are not willing to teach them. This does not mean that we should not have standards for evaluation; rather, it means that we need to build courses around instructional models and means of assessment that give students a fair shake at achieving, and demonstrating their achievement of, those standards. If we are going to grade students on their ability to write logical papers, we need to include teaching them how to do so among our instructional objectives. If we are going to grade students on their ability to express their ideas using standard English grammar and dialect, we need to teach those who don't already do that why and how to do so.

CONCLUSION

Just as physicians and pharmacists have learned that the same dose of a drug has different effects on different individuals, and that alternative prescriptions are often indicated, teachers must recognize that there are alternative approaches to achieving instructional objectives. If our goal in communication classes is to have a meaningful impact on each student's communicative ability, we must acknowledge and respond to individual needs, orientations, learning styles, and abilities that might otherwise compromise success.

REFERENCES

Curry, L. (1983, April). *An organization of learning styles theory and constructs*. Paper presented at the Annual Meeting of the American Educational Research Association, Montreal. (ERIC Document Reproduction Service No. ED 235 185)

Gorham, J. (1986). Assessment, classification, and implications of learning styles in instructional interactions. *Communication Education, 35,* 411–417.

Gorham, J., & Self, L. (1987). Developing communication skills: Learning styles and the educationally disadvantaged student. *Communication Research Reports, 4,* 38–46.

Keefe, J. W. (1982). Assessing student learning styles. In *Student learning styles and brain behavior* (pp. 43–53). Reston, VA: National Association of Secondary School Principals.

McCarthy, B. (1987). *The 4MAT system: Teaching to learning styles with right/left mode techniques.* Barrington, IL: Excel.

McCarthy, B., & Morris, S. (1995a). *4MAT in action: Sample units K–6.* Barrington, IL: Excel.

McCarthy, B, & Morris, S. (1995b). *4MAT in action: Sample units 7–12.* Barrington, IL: Excel.

Milton, O., Pollio, H. R., & Eison, J. A. (1986). *Making sense of college grades.* San Francisco: Jossey-Bass.

Richmond, V. P., & McCroskey, J.C. (1989). *Communication apprehension, avoidance, and effectiveness* (2nd. ed.). Scottsdale, AZ: Gorsuch Scarisbrick.

Tyler, R. W. (1949). *Basic principles of curriculum and instruction.* Chicago: University of Chicago Press.

Witkin, H. A., Dyk, R., Oltman, P. K., Raskin, E., & Karp, S. A. (1971). *A manual for the embedded figures test.* Palo Alto, CA: Consulting Psychologists Press.

20

Classroom Management: Contending With College Student Discipline

---

Timothy G. Plax
Patricia Kearney
California State University, Long Beach

In a typical college classroom of 30 students, we can expect about 6 or 7 students to refuse to go along with something the teacher wants them to do (Burroughs, 1990). At first glance, a resistance rate of only 16% to 20% may not seem particularly alarming; it may not even seem all that problematic. A closer look, however, reminds us that it only takes one or two students to ruin an entire class. When a student interrupts constantly, challenges our authority, incites other students, or insists that she or he knows more than we do, we eagerly anticipate the end of the school year. These kinds of student disruptions are endemic to the college classroom (Burroughs, 1990; Burroughs, Kearney, & Plax, 1989; Kearney & Plax, 1992; Kearney, Plax, & Burroughs, 1991).

Virtually all teachers are frustrated by the fact that some students are reluctant to assume conciliatory, cooperative student roles. This reality is meaningful especially for beginning teachers. Anxious to please, stimulate, and educate like no teacher before them, new teachers can become confused, angry, and disenchanted when students fail to appreciate their efforts (Kearney, 1987). Attempting to adjust to the realities of the classroom, beginning teachers become socialized into a "we–they" culture. The resulting teacher–student alienation is expressed in teachers' complaints as they sigh among themselves and worry about the future of education: "Students have some nerve questioning my authority!" "Students have changed; they don't care about learning. Students just want to be entertained!" (c.f., Sacks, 1997). Importantly, none of these charges suggest a proactive approach to structuring the learning environment in a way that teachers will want to teach and students will want to learn.

This chapter examines issues that are pertinent to classroom control and focuses on techniques that can make your task of teaching easier. While reading this chapter, keep one important fact in mind: Knowing the content you are supposed to teach is not a sufficient condition for teaching. Even so, new teachers often spend an inordinate amount of time preparing to teach by learning and relearning the content. Comparatively little time is spent on those activities that set up a climate that is conducive for disseminating that content. To be effective teachers, we must go beyond the subject matter and ask ourselves what we should do to ensure that students will be open and responsive to learning.

The most common response to this question has focused on discipline. Discipline is often construed as a panacea for all learning-related problems. Proponents argue that all the formal training in a content area is useless without a well-disciplined classroom. No matter how well you, as the teacher, know the subject matter, students may still challenge your credibility, dislike your personality, or prefer to engage in what they believe to be more meaningful activities. Contemporary educators can ill afford to demand student submission as a function of teacher authority. Students will not do what you want them to simply because you are the teacher.

Even so, the public continues to clamor for more classroom discipline. Educators are evaluated, retained, and tenured on their abilities to make students learn. For many instructors, good teaching is equated with student control. Administrators are quick to reprimand beginning teachers for their tendency to be too permissive.

Ironically, too much discipline actually works against learning. Highly disciplined classrooms fail to stimulate greater learning and are often associated with increased disruption. No research evidence exists to suggest that more discipline, in and of itself, leads to greater teacher effectiveness. On the contrary, teachers who employ frequent discipline find their classrooms even harder to manage. More rules, harsher penalties, and "get tough" policies fail to gain student compliance (Wlodkowski, 1982).

HOW DO COLLEGE STUDENTS MISBEHAVE?

Research shows that college students engage in both active and passive forms of misbehavior and resistance (Burroughs, 1990; Burroughs et al., 1989; Kearney, Plax, & Burroughs, 1991). Active misbehaviors (i. e., overt attempts to disrupt learning), include cheating, asking counterproductive questions, challenging the teacher's authority, diverting classroom talk from the lesson, interrupting, leaving class early (or walking in late), and talking with friends. On the other hand, passive, or covert, misbehaviors include inattention to teacher, lack of attendance, turning in assignments late (or not at all), sleeping through class, and reading the newspaper or doing other "more important" homework in class.

For teachers who are unprepared for such misbehavior, two primary reactions result. Many beginning teachers too quickly give in to student resistance. Although it might seem reasonable to allow Sally extra time to type a paper, others in the class may resent this exception. Other new teachers are guilty of being too heavy handed. Having been told "not to smile before Christmas," these teachers wind up taking themselves and their rules far too seriously. Consider the possibility that Sally may be going through a very real crisis and, as a result, should be given the opportunity to turn in her paper late. After all, these are adult students who suffer from adult problems. A loss of a parent, divorce in the family, pregnancy, car accidents, and rape all constitute adult problems that are not infrequent.

It turns out that when students misbehave, teachers prefer them to use passive, as opposed to active, resistance (Kearney et al., 1991). After all, passive resistance is less likely to disrupt the entire class, to result in contagion effects, and to engage the teacher and student in some sort of power struggle. Students report that they prefer to use passive forms of resistance as well. They may comply only partially or reluctantly by skimming the reading assignment or failing to complete all the homework. Although both teachers and students may prefer contentious or defiant students to act like willing compliers or just sit quietly in the back of the room, the subsequent problems associated with that stance are likely to be even more troublesome and demanding in the long term. Whereas passive misbehaviors may be ignored or overlooked, active resistance is likely to expose the problem and clarify the reasons for teacher concern.

WHY DO STUDENTS MISBEHAVE?

Recognizing that adult students can and do misbehave is the first step in dealing with misbehavior. Understanding why students misbehave is crucial for coping with or managing students when they engage in resistance. Although it is a natural tendency to attribute blame to students for problems in the classroom, ownership often must be shared. When students fail to respond favorably to us as teachers, we need to begin by looking at students' attributions about what we do or fail to do.

In fact, evidence shows that students misbehave largely because their teachers do (Kearney, Plax, Hays, & Ivey, 1991). Based on a sample of 250 college students, over 1,700 teacher misbehaviors were reported and coded into 28 different types. The five most frequently cited categories of misbehaviors included teachers who engaged in sarcasm or put-downs, canceled class, strayed from the subject, tested unfairly, and delivered boring lectures. Further analyses revealed that all 28 categories could be reduced to three dimensions: teacher incompetence, offensiveness, and indolence (Table 20.1 lists all 28 misbehavior categories with sample descriptions of each.)

Misbehaviors reflecting *incompetence* suggest a lack of basic teaching skills. Incompetent teachers do not seem to care about either the course or students, do not bother to learn students' names, make their tests too difficult, and, at the same time, are unable or unwilling to help students succeed. The profile of *offensive* teachers suggests that they are mean, cruel, and ugly. Offensive teachers humiliate students, play favorites, intimidate, and are condescending, rude, and self-centered. *Indolent* teachers are reminiscent of the absent-minded college professor. Such teachers fail to show up for class and arrive late when they do, forget test dates, neglect to grade homework, constantly readjust the syllabus, and "underwhelm" students by making their classes and tests too easy.

On the surface, of course, some teacher misbehaviors may not appear to be misbehaviors at all. We have all known a professor who took great delight in boasting that students rarely receive As from him or her: Students have to "work in my class," and if they cannot master the material, then they obviously "aren't working hard enough." At times students may not work hard enough, but an alternative explanation resides with the teacher. Perhaps the content is too hard and prerequisite material is needed, or perhaps the standards for mastery are unrealistically high. Although we have no problem with standards, a continually skewed distribution of low grades does not say much for this professor's effectiveness as a teacher.

Students expect to do well when they work hard at learning. When their efforts to learn the content are continually punished by low grades, students are likely to fault the teacher. Teachers who take pride in punishing students by systematically overloading them with content or imposing unattainable objectives are teachers who want their students to fail. The term *professor-*

TABLE 20.1

Teacher Misbehavior Categories With Sample Descriptions

Absent

Does not show up for class, cancels class without notification, and/or offers poor excuses for being absent.

Tardy

Is late for class or tardy.

Keeps Students Overtime

Keeps class overtime, talks too long or starts class early before all the students are there.

Early Dismissal

Lets class out early, rushes through the material to get done early.

Strays From Subject

Uses the class as a forum for her or his personal opinions, goes off on tangents, talks about family and personal life and/or generally wastes class time.

Confusing/Unclear Lectures

Unclear about what is expected, lectures are confusing and vague, contradicts him or herself, jumps from one subject to another and/or lectures are inconsistent with assigned readings.

Unprepared/Disorganized

Is not prepared for class, unorganized, forgets test dates, and/or makes assignments but does not collect them.

Deviates From Syllabus

Changes due dates for assignments, behind schedule, does not follow the syllabus, changes assignments, and/or assigns books but does not use them.

Late Returning Work

Late in returning papers, late in grading and turning back exams, and/or forgets to bring graded papers to class.

Sarcasm and Putdowns

Is sarcastic and rude, makes fun of and humiliates students, picks on students, and/or insults and embarrasses students.

Verbally Abusive

Uses profanity, is angry and mean, yells and screams, interrupts and/or intimidates students.

Unreasonable and Arbitrary Rules

Refuses to accept late work, gives no breaks in 3-hour classes, punishes entire class for one student's misbehavior, and/or is rigid, inflexible, and authoritarian.

Sexual Harassment

Makes sexual remarks to students, flirts with them, makes sexual innuendos, and/or is chauvinistic.

Unresponsive to Students' Questions

Does not encourage students to ask questions, does not answer questions or recognize raised hands, and/or seems "put out" to have to explain or repeat him or herself.

Apathetic to Students

Does not seem to care about the course or show concern for students, does not know the students' names, rejects students' opinions, and/or does not allow for class discussion.

Inaccessible to Students Outside of Class

Does not show up for appointments or scheduled office hours, is hard to contact, will not meet with students outside of office time, and/or does not make time for students when they need help.

Unfair Testing

Asks trick questions on tests, exams do not relate to the lectures, tests are too difficult, questions are too ambiguous, and/or teacher does not review for exams.

Unfair Grading

Grades unfairly, changes grading policy during the semester, does not believe in giving As, makes mistakes when grading, and/or does not have a predetermined grading scale.

Boring Lectures

Is not an enthusiastic lecturer, speaks in monotone and rambles, is boring, too much repetition, and/or employs no variety in lectures.

Information Overload

Talks too fast and rushes through the material, talks over the students' heads, uses obscure terms and/or assigns excessive work.

Information Underload

The class is too easy, students feel they have not learned anything, and/or tests are too easy.

Negative Personality

Teacher is impatient, self-centered, complains, acts superior, and/or is moody.

Negative Physical Appearance

Teacher dresses sloppy, smells bad, clothes are out of style, and cares little about his or her overall appearances.

Does Not Know Subject Matter

Does not know the material, unable to answer questions, provides incorrect information, and/or is not current.

Shows Favoritism or Prejudice

Plays favorites with students or acts prejudiced against others, is narrow-minded or close-minded, and/or makes prejudicial remarks.

Foreign or Regional Accents

Teacher is hard to understand, enunciates poorly, and has a strong accent that makes it difficult to understand.

Inappropriate Volume

Does not speak loudly enough or speaks too loud.

Bad Grammar/Spelling

Uses bad grammar, writes illegibly, misspells words on the exam (or on the board) and/or generally uses poor English.

itis often used to label teachers who engage in misbehaviors of content overload and unrealistic learning expectations.

Not all students' misbehaviors, of course, are a direct result of teacher misbehaviors. Students bring with them a history of classroom experiences that impact their current behaviors. Check first to determine if you might be the source of their misbehavior. Only as a last resort should you consider other student-related factors. A number of simple strategies can be employed to solve the student's problem. Often, a student's communication anxieties can be eased, for instance, by omitting student participation during class as a major requirement for the final course grade. We do not suggest, however, that all student problems become your problems. Sometimes, there just are not solutions you can or should enact. Sometimes, students must learn to adapt or cope by themselves.

Generally, then, college teaching is not without its share of discipline problems. Not unlike elementary and secondary students, college students engage in both active and passive forms of resistance to teacher authority. Understanding the source of student misbehavior is helpful, particularly when we recognize that teacher misbehaviors are a major cause of student disruptions in the classroom. An examination of those behaviors that we can change (our own!) is the first and sometimes final step in altering others' behaviors.

WHAT TEACHER BEHAVIORS INVITE STUDENT RESISTANCE?

Recognizing the sources of student disruptions and noncompliance gives us some indication of teacher characteristics that encourage or discourage student resistance. Research on student motivation points to teacher behaviors as primary factors in students' interest or motivation in a course. Assuming that students who are enthused about a class are more likely to behave in ways that contribute to learning, we can expect demotivated students to resist teacher attempts to keep them on task.

When college students were asked to identify those things that motivate or demotivate them to do their best in a class, a number of teacher characteristics were derived (Christophel & Gorham, 1995). Importantly then, there are things teachers do to motivate students and there are things teachers do that demotivate. Interestingly, the researchers investigating this issue found that the things teachers do to demotivate influence students more than what teachers do to motivate (Christophel & Gorham, 1995). Apparently, for students to remain motivated to work, it matters more what teachers do wrong than what they do right.

An examination of those teacher behaviors that students define as demotivators, suggests a list of misbehaviors not unlike our own categories of teacher indolence, offensiveness, and incompetence (see Table 1; Kearney, Plax, Hays, & Ivey, 1991). Prescriptively, then, teachers should be sensitive to behaving in ways that students could construe as misbehaviors that have the potential to demotivate.

A second, and perhaps an even more important, teacher characteristic that impacts student compliance is immediacy. No teacher variable has been shown to contribute more consistently to students' motivation and learning than nonverbal immediacy. Defined as perceptions of physical and psychological closeness, immediacy behaviors of approach typically include smiling, eye contact, forward body lean, vocal expressiveness, open gestures, and body movement (Mehrabian, 1967, 1968, 1969). Immediate teachers influence positive perceptions of interpersonal closeness, sensory stimulation, liking, warmth, and friendliness.

Research shows that teacher immediacy is associated with a number of other positive outcomes as well. For instance, with immediate teachers, students report greater affect toward the course, subject matter, and the teacher (Kearney, Plax, & Wendt-Wasco, 1985; Plax, Kearney, McCroskey, & Richmond, 1986). Students are also more motivated to remain on task and to learn when they have immediate instructors (Christophel, 1990; Frymier, 1994). Students report greater compliance (or less resistance) with immediate teachers (Kearney, Plax, Smith, & Sorensen, 1988). Taken together then, it comes as no surprise that the following causal relation was supported in research: Immediate teachers cause students to appreciate or value the learning task at hand. In turn, such affectively based motivation causes students to learn the material (Rodriguez, Plax, & Kearney, 1996).

Conversely, nonimmediate teachers are perceived as less motivating, less affect gaining, and less approachable. They are also more likely to face student resistance in the classroom. More recently, Thweatt and McCroskey (1996) concluded that nonimmediate teacher behaviors should be classified as another type of teacher misbehavior. These researchers found that teachers who engage in nonimmediate behaviors of avoidance or withdrawal were perceived by their students as actually misbehaving (Thweatt & McCroskey, 1996). Other research reveals that students were able to predict that contact with their more nonimmediate teachers would be less rewarding (and more punishing) than contact with their more immediate teachers (Shepard, Kearney, & Plax, 1996). Not surprisingly, students further indicated a greater reluctance to meet with and talk to their nonimmediate teachers. Nonimmediate teachers, then, are more likely to be associated with student problems. In order to minimize student resistance and learning problems, then, teachers should communicate an openness and a willingness to interact with their students by being nonverbally immediate.

WHAT TEACHER BEHAVIORS PREVENT STUDENT RESISTANCE?

Teachers who choose to "own" the problem of student misbehavior or resistance will find support for their position in a contemporary approach to discipline. Within this newer tradition of classroom management, discipline loses its name, meaning, and pervasive emphasis. Rather than forcing students to learn, the teacher creates and manages a classroom where techniques are employed to influence students to want to learn. Specifically, classroom management refers to teacher behaviors that "produce high levels of student involvement in classroom activities, minimal amounts of student behaviors that interfere with the teacher's or students' work, and efficient use of instructional time" (Emmer & Evertson, 1981, p. 342). Rather than focusing attention on student misbehavior, this alternative implies a preventative stance toward discipline. Do not wait for problems to occur; prevent them from happening in the first place!

The appeal of classroom management has its roots in a line of research in educational psychology that demonstrates that the single best predictor of learning is academic engagement time (Woolfolk, 1987). Although a variety of teacher and student behaviors are also associated with student achievement, the amount of active time spent on specific academic tasks consistently results in higher achievement gains. The strongest link between teacher instruction and student achievement is student task engagement. Teachers who keep their students motivated and involved in mastering objectives are more likely to be effective in helping students learn (Woolfolk, 1987). This fundamental principle has led educational researchers to identify those teacher behaviors that influence students' academic engagement time—positively or negatively. Several important conclusions and recommendations can be drawn from this literature:

1. Teachers who are "with it" are those who are keenly aware of what is going on in their classroom at all times (Kounin, 1970). "With-it-ness" skills allow teachers to notice discrepancies in the classroom early and put a stop to them before they spread throughout the class. Such ripple effects suggest that misbehaviors are highly contagious and have a way of infecting other students unless they are checked early. With-it teachers notice when a student in the back yawns and another student on the sideline initiates talk with a peer.

Without-it teachers overlook or ignore instances of cheating, socializing in class, and sleeping during lectures. Recognizing that not much is missed by with-it teachers, these classroom managers are less likely to commit either timing errors (waiting too long to intervene) or target errors (accusing the wrong student for a particular misbehavior; Kounin, 1970; Woolfolk, 1987). Teachers who seek to minimize student misbehaviors, then, had better be with it!

2. Being able to deal with more than one task at a time or what Kounin (1970) called *overlapping,* is another characteristic of effective classroom managers. For example, in the middle of a lecture, the teacher may notice that someone looks confused. At the same time, another student walks in late. While finishing her or his thought aloud to the class, the teacher makes a mental note to anticipate questions about an earlier point and hands the attendance sheet to the tardy student. All five activities are completed without missing a beat. Without the ability to overlap, teachers are likely to interrupt the lesson frequently and attend to peripheral activities. When that happens, momentum is disrupted and students become inspired to stray from the task.

3. Momentum is measured by the presence or absence of down times or slowdowns (Kounin, 1970). The point here is that the teacher is in charge of pacing. At no time during instruction should lengthy pause time be evident. Students should have no reason for abandoning their attention toward the teacher (or the instructional activity). When down times or slowdowns occur, students are likely to find other, more entertaining activities to engage their attention. We often observe lack of momentum when an inexperienced teacher assigns students to small group activities and then requires that all the students wait patiently until every small group is finished with the task. Students who must wait are likely to become impatient, frustrated, and bored.

Changing or maintaining a given activity in the classroom is determined by two factors: work completion rates and estimates of students' attention span (Doyle, 1986). *Completion rates* refers to a criterion group. That is, students between the 10th and 25th percentiles in class ability should be the referent for maintaining momentum. Although this estimate may be more suitable for elementary or secondary classrooms, the issue to keep in mind is that changing pace or establishing momentum requires the class to move ahead even when some students may not be finished with the task. Students' *attention span* should be considered as well. An exercise or film that the teacher thought was interesting may not be perceived similarly by the class. If that is the case, then it is wise to quickly abandon the plan and move on to something else.

4. Effective classroom managers establish explicit, reasonable rules early in the term (Biehler & Snowman, 1986). Unfortunately, many of us are guilty of imposing a rule only after we see an instance of the violation. Be sure your rules are communicated clearly and frequently until all students have learned them. Reasonableness is a key to rule planning. An "unreasonable" rule of one of the authors was pointed out to her while she taught a unit on Rules. She no longer uses the arbitrary rule of "stapling your papers together." Instead, she brings a stapler with her to class and passes it around before student papers are turned in. We recognize that all rules are potentially reasonable; however, classroom rules should be educationally based. Stapled papers may keep you more organized and reduce the possibility of losing pages, but stapled papers do not enhance learning in the classroom. Other examples of arbitrary rules include not allowing chewing gum, the use of pencil versus a pen, lined versus unlined paper, assigned seating, and participation requirements.

5. Interestingly enough, effective classroom managers typically have fewer rules than ineffective ones. At the same time, good managers regularly enforce the rules they do have (Emmer, Evertson, Sanford, Clements, & Worsham, 1984; Evertson, Emmer, Clements, Sanford, & Worsham, 1984). It is wise, therefore, to keep the list of rules brief. The more rules a teacher has, the harder it is to scrutinize and apply consequences to every rule violation. Consistency is essential to rule imposition simply because teacher consistency provides students with reliable expectations of teacher behavior. As a result, students learn to depend on predictable teacher responses to regulate their own behavior. When a rule is explicitly stated, students learn what behaviors are expected and what consequences will be applied should they fail to deliver. When a teacher imposes a rule irregularly, then students become confused about what the teacher really wants or expects from them. Without consistent rule application, some students will follow the rule, but others will not.

    Other classroom management techniques are discussed in detail by Emmer et al. (1984) and Evertson et al. (1984). Differentiating effective from ineffective classroom managers, these researchers reported that positive questioning techniques, use of motivational messages (cues and prompts), attending more often to positive than negative student behaviors, providing students with good role models, giving frequent feedback, holding students accountable, and planning success-oriented learning experiences are all strategies that good teachers employ regularly. The end result is that effective managers increase students' time spent on task. Students become more engaged and achieve at higher levels when taught by teachers who are competent classroom managers, nonverbally immediate, and motivating.

AND IF THAT DOES NOT WORK,
WHAT ELSE CAN TEACHERS DO?

Even the most well-managed classroom is likely to be disrupted occasionally. Instructional communication researchers argue that classroom management sometimes demands that we persuade our students that learning is important, enjoyable, and beneficial to their overall well-being (Kearney, 1987). Early studies on this type of classroom influence were framed within French and Raven's (1959) concept of power. Power in the classroom refers to the teacher's ability to influence students to do something they would not have done had they not been influenced. Thus, the teacher's ability to strategically employ different types of power can impact the potential success of his or her classroom management.

Within this research tradition, the first two studies (McCroskey & Richmond, 1983; Richmond & McCroskey, 1984) relied on general descriptions of five power bases: reward, coercive, referent, legitimate, and expert. The results of that research provide indirect support for more contemporary beliefs about discipline in the classroom. Teacher authority and discipline in the traditional sense have little or no meaning in today's classroom. That is, legitimate or assigned power ("Do it because I'm the teacher!") as well as coercive or punishment power ("If you don't, you'll get an F!") were both negatively associated with cognitive and affective learning. Both types of power closely resemble notions of teacher authority and discipline.

Recognizing the limitations of relying on general descriptions of power, subsequent studies derived an extended typology of power-based teacher influence strategies (Kearney, Plax, Richmond, & McCroskey, 1984, 1985). Based on responses from teachers themselves, 22 behavior alteration techniques (BATs) resulted. Unlike the bases of power explicated in the early studies, these BATs demonstrate that teacher power is often indirect. In other words, power need not be restricted to direct appeals. BATs that teachers report frequently using are student centered, referencing inherent student benefits through compliance ("Try it, you'll like it!"). Teachers also rely on student audience effects, or those strategies that appeal to students' peers and reference groups for compliance ("The rest of the class is doing it."). Asked which of the techniques were most and least effective for influencing student behavior, teachers consistently identified the more prosocial, reward-type strategies as effective, whereas antisocial or punishment-based BATs were perceived as ineffective.

Similarly, students' perceptions of BATs used in the classroom showed that prosocial-type BATs were positively associated with cognitive or affective learning, whereas antisocial BATs were negatively related to both learning outcomes (McCroskey, Richmond, Plax, & Kearney, 1985; Plax, Kearney, McCroskey, & Richmond, 1986; Richmond, McCroskey, Kearney, & Plax, 1987). If we equate learning with effectiveness, then we can conclude that teachers and students agree on the preferred use of prosocial compliance-gaining techniques.

Knowing that prosocial strategies are the method of choice for optimizing classroom managerial skills, why is it that some teachers continue to use antisocial means of control? Unfortunately, many teachers initially try to employ a prosocial management approach, but are unsuccessful and give up. Moreover, training teachers to adopt and tactically employ prosocial verbal messages of control overlooks the essential contributions of nonverbal messages that underscore meaning; how teachers communicate may be more critical than what is actually said to obtain student compliance.

Accordingly, the interaction between teachers' nonverbal immediacy behaviors and the use of either prosocial or antisocial BATs on students' resistance was tested (Kearney, Plax, Smith, & Sorensen, 1988). Four groups of college students were presented with descriptions of four types of teachers. The first group was presented with the image of a friendly, nonverbally immediate teacher (smiling, positive head nods, vocally expressive, purposeful gestures, relaxed and open body position) who requests that the student come to class more prepared from now on. This immediate teacher was described as using a prosocial BAT ("Because it will help you later on in life" or "You'll find it a rewarding and meaningful experience"). For the second sample of students, the same immediate teacher description was used, except that instead of a prosocial technique, antisocial BATs were inserted in the scenario ("Because I told you to" or "I'll lower your grade if you don't"). The third and fourth sets of students received descriptions of a nonimmediate, aloof instructor (tense, reserved, vocally unexpressive, seldom smiles, avoids looking at students) who used either the prosocial or the antisocial techniques, respectively.

Students who were presented with the immediate teacher scenarios, regardless of the BAT employed, reported greater likelihood of compliance than did those students who imagined themselves with the nonimmediate teachers. The overwhelming contributor to student compliance, then, was nonverbal behaviors of the teacher as opposed to the relative pro- or antisocialness of the technique type. Given the two immediacy conditions, however, students reported greater compliance tendencies with the immediate teacher who used prosocial rather than antisocial techniques.

Additional analysis revealed that students distorted or selectively perceived the strategy type employed in the immediacy–nonimmediacy scenarios. When students were asked to indicate the relative prosocial or antisocialness of the BATs employed, students in both of the immediate teacher conditions perceived the teacher to be using prosocial techniques, even when the antisocial BATs were used. Similarly, for the nonimmediacy conditions, students believed both teachers to use antisocial strategies. These findings offer additional support for one of the recommendations we made earlier: By engaging in nonverbal immediacy behaviors of approach, teachers will find their students to be more willing to comply and less willing to resist.

Correspondingly, new teachers should be exposed to the variety of available prosocial techniques that can assist them in their influence attempts. After examining preteachers' and experienced teachers' perceptions of the techniques they would use to gain the compliance of particular types of misbehaving students, it is imminently clear that preteachers limit their alternatives to primarily one or two techniques. In contrast, experienced teachers are much more likely to avail themselves of a diversity of prosocial BAT types (Kearney & Plax, 1987; Kearney, Plax, Sorensen, & Smith, 1988; Plax, Kearney, & Downs, 1986; Plax, Kearney, & Tucker, 1986). Similarly, Roach (1991) found that both graduate teaching assistants (GTAs) and professors rely more on prosocial than antisocial BATs to gain student compliance. However, when compared to experienced professors, GTAs were perceived to use BATs with greater frequency overall and they were more likely to employ antisocial BATs. Roach argued that because GTAs may be perceived to be less powerful than professors, GTAs may actually encounter more classroom discipline problems, thus necessitating more interventions. Alternatively, GTAs may not be practicing those classroom management techniques that prevent misbehaviors from happening in the first place.

SUMMARY

Removing the expectation that students will occupy roles of submission as a function of teacher authority is prerequisite to successfully managing the classroom. Alternatively, preparing and maintaining a learning environment that encourages student compliance and enhances on-task behaviors can minimize the need to impose discipline. Assuming this preventative stance requires attention to who we are and what we do as teachers. We can begin by becoming sensitive to our own misbehaviors that prompt student resistance and demotivate students in their efforts to learn. We can also practice nonverbal immediacy behaviors of approach that motivate students, increase positive affect toward learning, and minimize students' resistance.

Moreover, we can employ classroom management strategies that prompt and maintain student on-task behaviors. For instance, we can better monitor student behaviors by engaging in both "with-it-ness" and overlapping skills. We can pace our instruction so as to maintain a high level of momentum that continually alerts students to the task. The consistent application of reasonable, as opposed to arbitrary, rules will define for students our expectations (and consequences) for their behavior.

Communicating persuasively is also an important supplement to what we can do to contend with student misbehaviors. Recognizing the need to convince students that task engagement is essential for learning, effective, more experienced teachers are likely to draw on a variety of BATs. Even in well-managed classrooms, a student may be reluctant to participate; another may choose not to attend regularly. Eliciting cooperation from these students may require more than proper pacing or establishing a rule. Such students may need further motivation. The use of prosocial messages can provide students with positive incentives for task engagement. However, prosocial messages must be communicated within the framework of positive nonverbal behaviors. Establishing an immediate, approachable relationship with students will help them perceive that our influence attempts are in their best interest.

As this chapter reveals, structuring the classroom for work need not rely on trial and error. Instead, the research on teacher misbehaviors, nonverbal immediacy, classroom management, and compliance gaining provides us with a systematic approach to maximizing students' academic engagement time. Hopefully, this chapter provides you with some useful suggestions for preventing and contending with student discipline problems in the college classroom.

REFERENCES

Biehler, R. F., & Snowman, J. (1986). *Psychology applied to teaching* (5th ed.). Boston: Houghton Mifflin.

Burroughs, N. F. (1990). *The relationship of teacher immediacy and student compliance-resistance with learning.* Unpublished doctoral dissertation, West Virginia University, Morgantown.

Burroughs, N. F., Kearney, P., & Plax, T. G. (1989). Compliance resistance in the college classroom. *Communication Education, 38,* 214–229.

Christophel, D. (1990). The relationship among teacher immediacy behaviors, student motivation, and learning. *Communication Education, 39,* 323–340.

Christophel, D., & Gorham, J. (1995). A test-retest analysis of student motivation, teacher immediacy, and perceived sources of motivation and demotivation in college classes. *Communication Education, 44,* 292–306.

Doyle, W. (1986). Classroom organization and management. In M. C. Wittrock (Ed.), *Handbook of research on teaching* (3rd ed., pp. 392–431). New York: Macmillan.

Emmer, E. T., & Evertson, C. M. (1981). Synthesis of research on classroom management. *Educational Leadership, 38,* 342–347.

Emmer, E. T., Evertson, C. M., Sanford, J. P., Clements, B. S., & Worsham, M. E. (1984). *Classroom management for secondary teachers.* Englewood Cliffs, NJ: Prentice-Hall.

Evertson, C. M., Emmer, E. T., Clements, B. S., Sanford, J. P., & Worsham, M. E. (1984). *Classroom management for elementary teachers.* Englewood Cliffs, NJ: Prentice-Hall.

French, J. R. P., Jr., & Raven, B. H. (1959). The bases of social power. In D. Cartwright (Ed.), *Studies in social power* (pp. 150–167). Ann Arbor: University of Michigan Press.

Frymier, A. B. (1994). A model of immediacy in the classroom. *Communication Quarterly, 42,* 133–144.

Kearney, P. (1987). Power in the classroom. *Journal of Thought, 22,* 45–50.

Kearney, P., & Plax, T. G. (1987). Situational and individual determinants of teachers' reported use of behavior alteration techniques. *Human Communication Research, 14,* 145–166.

Kearney, P., & Plax, T. G. (1992). Student resistance to teacher control. In V. P. Richmond & J. C. McCroskey (Eds.), *Power in the classroom: Communication, control, and concern* (pp. 85–100). Hillsdale, NJ: Lawrence Erlbaum Associates.

Kearney, P., Plax, T. G., & Burroughs, N. F. (1991). An attributional analysis of college students' resistance decisions. *Communication Education, 40,* 325–342.

Kearney, P., Plax, T. G., Hays, E. R., & Ivey, M. J. (1991). College teacher misbehaviors: What students don't like about what their teachers say and do. *Communication Quarterly, 39,* 309–324.

Kearney, P., Plax, T. G., Richmond, V. P., & McCroskey, J. C. (1984). Power in the classroom IV: Teacher communication techniques as alternatives to discipline. *Communication Yearbook, 8,* 724–746.

Kearney, P., Plax, T. G., Richmond, V. P., & McCroskey, J. C. (1985). Power in the classroom III: Teacher communication techniques and messages. *Communication Education, 34,* 19–28.

Kearney, P., Plax, T. G., Smith, V. R., & Sorensen, G. (1988). Effects of teacher immediacy and strategy type on college student resistance to on-task demands. *Communication Education, 37,* 54–67.

Kearney, P., Plax, T. G., Sorensen, G., & Smith. V. R. (1988). Experienced and prospective teachers' selections of compliance-gaining messages for "common" student misbehaviors. *Communication Education, 37,* 150–161.

Kearney, P., Plax, T. G., & Wendt-Wasco, N. J. (1985). Teacher immediacy for affective learning in divergent college courses. *Communication Quarterly, 33,* 61–74.

Kounin. J. S. (1970). *Discipline and group management in classrooms.* New York: Holt, Rinehart, & Winston.

McCroskey, J. C., & Richmond, V. P. (1983). Power in the classroom I: Teacher and student perceptions. *Communication Education, 34,* 176–184.

McCroskey, J. C., Richmond, V. P., Plax, T. C., & Kearney, P. (1985). Power in the classroom V: Behavior alteration techniques, communication training, and learning. *Communication Education, 34,* 214–226.

Mehrabian, A. (1967). Orientation behaviors and nonverbal attitude communication. *Journal of Communication, 17,* 324–332.

Mehrabian, A. (1968). Influence of attitude from the posture, orientation, and distance of a communicator. *Journal of Consulting and Clinical Psychology, 32,* 296–308.

Mehrabian, A. (1969). Some referents and measures of nonverbal behavior. *Behavioral Research Methods and Instrumentation, 1,* 213–217.

Plax, T. G., Kearney, P., & Downs, T. M. (1986). Communicating control in the classroom and satisfaction with teaching and students. *Communication Education, 35,* 379–388.

Plax, T. G., Kearney, P., McCroskey, J. C., & Richmond, V. P. (1986). Power in the classroom VI: Verbal control strategies, nonverbal immediacy and affective learning. *Communication Education, 35,* 43–55.

Plax, T. G., Kearney, P., & Tucker. L. (1986). Prospective teachers' use of behavior alteration techniques: Reactions to common student misbehaviors. *Communication Education, 35,* 32–42.

Richmond, V. P., & McCroskey. J. C. (1984). Power in the classroom II: Power and learning. *Communication Education, 33,* 125–136.

Richmond, V. P., McCroskey, J. C., Kearney P., & Plax, T. G. (1987). Power in the classroom VII: Linking behavior alteration techniques to cognitive learning. *Communication Education, 36,* 1–12.

Roach, K. D. (1991). Graduate teaching assistants' use of behavior alteration techniques in the university classroom. *Communication Quarterly, 39,* 178–188.

Rodriguez, J. I., Plax, T. G., & Kearney, P. (1996). Clarifying the relationship between teacher nonverbal immediacy and student cognitive learning: Affective learning as the central causal mediator. *Communication Education, 45,* 293–305.

Sacks, P. (1997). Higher education at the end of the millennium. *Thought and Action, 13,* 69–80.

Shepard, C. A., Kearney, P., & Plax, T. G. (1996). *The relationship among teacher immediacy, student predicted outcome value, and extra-class communication.* Unpublished manuscript, California State University, Long Beach.

Thweatt, K. S., & McCroskey, J. C. (1996). Teacher nonimmediacy and misbehavior: Unintentional negative communication. *Communication Research Reports, 13,* 198–204.

Wlodkowski, R. J. (1982). *Discipline: The great false hope.* (ERIC Document Reproduction Service No. ED 224 782)

Woolfolk, A. E. (1987). *Educational psychology* (3rd ed.). Englewood Cliffs, NJ: Prentice-Hall.

21

The First Day

Gustav W. Friedrich
Rutgers University

Pamela Cooper
Northwestern University

I can always tell on the first day of class whether it'll be a winner or a dud. If the teacher makes a good impression, it'll be great. If not, well ... if it ain't good, then it ain't gonna get better. For me to know the class will be good, the teacher has to let me know that she is available for questions of any caliber concerning her topic. She also has to let me know that she is approachable.

The first meeting of a class is much too important to be treated as something to be gotten over with as quickly as possible. Teachers who simply put in an appearance, see if all the students are there, make an assignment for the next time, and dismiss class early are missing an important opportunity. Not only does this approach send students away frustrated because they do not get their basic questions answered, the instructor misses an important opportunity to demonstrate his or her commitment to the course, to the students, and to the communication discipline. This chapter, therefore, describes strategies that can help teachers use the first session of a class productively.

Although both students and teacher, through their communication, jointly create the class, the task of this chapter is to describe teacher choices and activities that are potentially useful for the successful launching of a class. Although the chapter is, therefore, by choice teacher centered, the most logical beginning point is the student perspective: What is it that students attempt to learn from the opening session of a class? The framework for answering this question is provided by the socialization literature as it has been utilized and interpreted by Staton (1990) and her colleagues.

Socialization, according to Merton, Reader, and Kendall (1957), is "the process by which people selectively acquire the values and attitudes, the interests, skills and knowledge—in short, the culture—current in groups in which they are, or seek to become a member" (p. 287). Socialization is either primary (the process by which children become part of society) or secondary (the process by which already socialized individuals acquire new roles). The focus here is on the process of secondary socialization, whereby students acquire the knowledge and skills that are necessary to perform the role of student in a particular classroom. Van Maanen and Schein (1979) suggested that this process can be viewed as occurring in three phases: *anticipatory* (based on the catalog, other students, and campus folklore, students anticipate what the course will be like), *entry* (during the first days of the class, students judge the course based on first impressions), and *continuance* (as the course unfolds, students may modify their initial perceptions). This chapter focuses on the first two phases of the secondary socialization of students into a classroom.

As students take their seats for the first day of a class (entry phase of secondary socialization), there are a number of things that they want to know about the class. Although partial answers to their questions may have been obtained haphazardly from, for example, campus folklore, the questions still remain—and a major purpose of the first session of a course is to answer them. To summarize what our students told us when, over the past several semesters, we asked them what they hope to learn during the first class period, there are three categories of information that students wish to acquire:

1. Course coverage: What will the course cover? How will it relate to other work?
2. Course rules: How will the course be conducted? What will be the work load? What type of exams are given? How will grades be determined?
3. Teacher personality: What kind of person is the teacher going to be? Will the teacher be easily accessible? Easy to talk with?

How do students acquire this information? Staton borrowed from Berger and Calabrese's (1975) uncertainty reduction theory (URT) a description of information-seeking strategies that are used in the process of secondary socialization. Within URT, Berger and Calabrese (1975) argued that "when strangers meet, their primary concern is one of uncertainty reduction or increasing predictability about the behavior of both themselves and others in the interaction" (p. 100). This analysis appears equally applicable to the process of secondary socialization of students as they enter a class for the first time. URT describes the communication strategies aimed at reducing uncertainty as passive, active, or interactive. With passive strategies, information is acquired by means of unobtrusive observation—the individual observes his or her environment and the individuals in it, and attempts to make sense of the situation without the help of others. Active strategies require the individual to interact with "third parties" to obtain information. Thus, rather than asking the teacher directly about the number of tests in the course, a student might ask another student. Interactive strategies are those employed when individuals directly interact with a primary source of information in order to reduce uncertainty (e.g., they ask the teacher, rather than a fellow student, about the teacher's policy concerning class absences).

In short, then, as students enter a class on the first day, their task is to begin the process of acquiring their new role as student by reducing uncertainty about (a) the nature of the course, (b) the course mechanics, and (c) the personality of the teacher. The strategies available to them for doing so are passive (e.g., sitting back and observing), active (e.g., asking questions of fellow students), or interactive (e.g., interacting directly with the teacher). The strategies an individual student will actually use, of course, depend on a variety of factors, including the personalities of both student and teacher.

Having identified three categories of information that students hope to glean from the activities of the opening session of a class, this chapter turns now to teacher choices and strategies that are potentially relevant and useful for coping with student expectations within each category.

COURSE COVERAGE

As suggested earlier, there are at least two issues related to course coverage that students would like to see addressed during the opening session of a class: What will the course cover? How will it relate to other work?

Tackling the second issue first, it is perhaps best addressed orally at the beginning of the period. In doing so, the teacher has an opportunity to function in the role of socializing agent—familiarizing students with the language and viewpoints of the communication discipline. This can be accomplished by describing how the course fits within the curriculum of the department. For example: Why does the department offer this course?

How long has it done so? Is the course an elective or a required one? What is the rationale for this status? How does the course relate to other courses offered by the department? Is the course theory oriented, skill oriented, or a blend of both? The discussion of these issues can productively incorporate highlights of both the history of the department and the history of the communication discipline.

The specific course content is ideally presented in the form of a printed course syllabus that can be handed out to the students at the first session of the class. At a minimum, this syllabus should spell out both the objectives for the course and the topics to be covered. In addition to obvious advantages for the students, preparing such a syllabus forces the teacher to carefully think through what he or she wishes to accomplish with the students during the term. It also serves as an aid to pacing the course so that all areas get covered. Without it, because some areas of a course are of greater interest to the teacher (and students) than others, it is easy to focus on interesting topics and suddenly discover that the course is far behind schedule.

Some teachers include on their syllabus the dates on which specific topics will be discussed. Others, because they wish flexibility should they get slightly behind or ahead, merely list the topics and their order of discussion. The advantage of this approach is that the student is not in a position to judge whether the teacher is "behind" or "ahead." In addition to listing topics, the syllabus can also list assignments and their due dates—a practice that minimizes the misunderstood assignment, the forgotten assignment, or the assignment that had to be given after the bell has rung. (For additional suggestions about the creation of a syllabus, see Civikly-Powell, chap. 4, this volume.)

COURSE MECHANICS

A syllabus can also be used to address many of the issues that relate to students' second area of concern, course mechanics—how the course will be conducted. The syllabus can, for example, specify the number of assignments, the number of quizzes, tests, and so on that will be given during the term—and, perhaps more importantly, the weights that will be assigned to each in calculating the final grade. In developing these weights, Kohls (n.d.) advised teachers to allow themselves 5% to 10% leeway in the total—telling their students that this percentage is allocated to the teacher for personal evaluation above and beyond the specific grades and is used to reward, for example, excellent participation, a positive trend in grades, or other circumstances that may develop concerning a specific student.

In addition to listing grade-related policies on the syllabus, a frank discussion about what it will take to receive a given final grade is warranted: What will it take to get an A? What will it take to flunk? Although such issues are awkward to discuss, our whole educational system makes students "grade oriented." It is, therefore, necessary to accept the fact that most students are going to be concerned about grades and then work hard to make the grading rules for the course as clear, public, and fair as it is possible to make them. Students can also be told to ask for clarification whenever they are in doubt about their standing in the class.

In addition to grading-related issues, the rules of the game for classroom and course behaviors should also be clearly specified. For example: What are the teacher's attitudes toward attendance, make-ups, and excuses? Is classroom participation important? Should students raise their hand and be called on before speaking? Will there be specific seating assignments? What are the expectations concerning cheating, plagiarism, and outside help on assignments? How should students address the teacher (Mr. or Ms.? Professor? Doctor?) and how will the teacher address them (first name? Mr. or Ms.?)? Obviously, some instructors prefer to say many of the later things aloud, perhaps when they introduce themselves to their classes.

More important than the specific choice a teacher makes on such issues is the fact that the teacher makes and consistently enforces a choice. In his review of the research on classroom organization and management, Brophy (1983) pointed out that the key to a well-functioning classroom is to maintain a continuous academic focus for student attention and engagement. This is best accomplished by:

1. Carefully thinking through, well in advance of starting the class, the procedures and routines that possess the potential to work best.
2. Teaching and implementing the key classroom procedures and rules both early in the class and consistently.
3. Engaging in the following three major clusters of behaviors as the term progresses: (a) behaviors that convey purposefulness (e.g., strategies that show concern about maximizing the time available for instruction and about seeing that students learn the content—not just that they are well behaved), (b) behaviors that teach students how to behave appropriately (e.g., being clear about what teachers expect of students and teaching students how to do things when necessary), and (c) skills in diagnosing students' focus of attention (e.g., being sensitive to student concerns and continuously monitoring students for signs of confusion or inattention).

In short, as stated by Brophy (1983):

It is clear from this research that the key to effective management is prevention; effective managers are distinguished by their success in preventing problems from arising in the first place rather than by special skills for dealing with problems once they occur. Their success is not achieved through a few isolated techniques or gimmicks. Rather, it is the result of a systematic approach, which starts with preparation and planning before the school year begins, is implemented initially through systematic communication of expectations and establishment of procedures and routines at the beginning of the year, and is maintained throughout the year. The approach is maintained not only by consistency in following up on stated expectations, but by continually presenting students with well-chosen and well-prepared academic activities that focus their attention during lessons and engage their concentrated efforts during independent work times. (p. 271)

Although Brophy's (1983) review summarizes classroom organization and management issues that arise over the course of a term, a substantial number of studies have directly addressed the issue of how teachers establish themselves with their students during the first few days or weeks of school. Most of these studies have focused on the elementary classroom, producing consistent findings: The effective teacher begins the year by setting up an efficient and smoothly running classroom where instruction, not management, is the major thrust. The first few days involve explicit statements of the teacher's expectations and rehearsals of the teacher's chosen routines. As these expectations and routines become internalized, the teacher is able to call up these routines with minimal cues to the students—thus minimizing time on management concerns and maximizing time for instruction.

Illustrative of this research is a study by Brooks (1985). He investigated the first day of school at the junior high school level by videotaping and comparing first-year "brand new" teachers with veteran "superstar" teachers during their lst, 2nd, 10th, and 28th days of school. He found the following behaviors to be most conducive to success:

1. Routinization: Similar tasks were accomplished daily in a similar manner—routinely and swiftly.
2. Visual scanning: "Superstars" maintained direct eye contact with the entire class in order to gauge the collective attitude of the group.
3. Businesslike tone of voice: A no-nonsense, "let's get to work" tone was used to create a businesslike attitude toward learning.
4. Behavioral and academic expectations: Effective junior high teachers stated daily reminders of behavioral and academic expectations. On the first day, the method of presenting rules consisted of (a) stating the rule, (b) providing

a student-centered rationale for the rule, (c) explaining the consequences of breaking the rule, and (d) giving a good example of what the infraction looked like.

5. Anticipation of confusion: Effective junior high teachers anticipated areas of student confusion. For example, if most students made a similar error on homework assignments, effective teachers addressed this obvious confusion. Effective teachers also anticipated confusion by calling for questions before initiating the day's lesson.

Brooks (1985) concluded:

Good school years begin with well-planned and executed first days that permit the teacher to establish a cooperative learning environment and permit the students to find out what is expected in the classroom. Effective first day procedures meet teacher and student needs and increase the likelihood of an effective second day. (p. 78) The effective lesson opening on second and subsequent days, according to Brooks, will typically include a quick call to order in a businesslike tone of voice, fast-paced roll taking, an opening remark that includes behavioral and academic expectations for the students, an apparent anticipation of areas of confusion in the explanations given, and a call for questions.

TEACHER PERSONALITY

Perhaps the most important of the three categories of questions that students sitting in the classroom on the first day of class have on their minds is "What kind of person is this teacher going to be?" In many cases, teachers do not start the first day with a clean slate. Assuming that the teacher has taught before, campus folklore has already contributed to the students' database. Teacher reputations start building with the first class taught on campus and continue to shape student perceptions over an individual's teaching career. How one builds on (or repairs) these initial impressions is the topic of an area of theory and research known as *impression management.*

One of the major theorists who has discussed self-presentation is Goffman (1959, 1963). Goffman analyzed human behavior via a theatrical metaphor. According to him, people are actors, structuring their performances to make impressions on audiences. People in focused interaction take turns presenting dramas to one another. For example, when we teach, we take on that role (however we define it) and present that character—the teacher. We want students to form that impression of us. How we dress, arrange the learning environment, the language we use, and so on, all help students form an impression of us as a teacher.

These impressions are formed quickly. Ask students the question "What will this class be like?" after the first class meeting and they can tell you. The quote at the beginning of this chapter is from one of our students after the first class period. This student makes a decision about a class and the instructor after only 50 minutes.

In his discussion of teaching as relational development, DeVito (1986) indicated the importance of first impressions for the teaching–learning process:

> First, the impressions are inevitable and form despite attempts to avoid prejudging anyone. Second, they have a powerful effect on how the relationship progresses. Third, and perhaps most important, these impressions are resistant to change. The primacy effect (the tendency to give disproportionate weight to what is perceived first) operates like a filter through which later impressions pass. Confirmatory information, we know, is received more easily and retained longer than contradictory information. First impressions, then, are crucial for the student, the teacher, and the teacher–student relationship. (p. 54)

What type of impression, then, should a teacher want to create? The answer to this question, of course, varies greatly with such factors as teacher resources, teacher definition of role, course objectives, and student personalities. Whatever the nature of the answer, however, it is wise to recall that the goal of teaching is student learning. Thus, teachers not only want to create the impression of being warm and likable, they also need to be perceived as knowledgeable, confident, and in control. How do teachers do this?

Burgoon, Buller, and Woodall (1996) provided a general analysis of what happens the first time individuals meet, which they summarized as "principles" of first impressions:

1. People develop evaluations of others from limited information. Because talk is frequently limited to social amenities and topics such as the weather, we rely heavily on nonverbal cues.
2. First impressions are based on stereotypes. Because of the bombardment of nonverbal information on our senses, we need some way to classify this abundance of information.
3. Initial impressions are formed by treating others as objects, judging them on the basis of outward appearances.
4. Many stereotypical judgments are relatively accurate. Intuition is nothing more than tuning in to all available information, and that information frequently steers us in the right direction.

A variety of individuals have explored the communication variables that impact on perceptions of teacher competency. Programs of research include those on teacher immediacy and nonverbal expressiveness, educational humor, teacher communicator style, teacher clarity and instructional explicitness, and strategies for coping with student misbehavior. Much of this research has been summarized by Cooper (1995), Kougl (1997), and Nussbaum (1992). These variables, plus others such as self-concept, self-disclosure, descriptiveness, owning feelings, empathy, listening, response styles, and behavioral flexibility are all important to the successful management of first impressions. The communication instructor who is familiar with this literature is able to make informed decisions about how best to manage impressions during the opening session of a class.

It must be remembered, of course, that an individual plays the teacher role within the constraints of his or her resources. Luckily, there is not a single script for the successful performance of the teacher role. Thus, for example, if you are not good at telling jokes, do not tell them; if you tell them well, use them to capture interest and make a point.

CONCLUSION

As we began this chapter, we suggested that the first session of a class is much too important to waste. As teachers and students first meet, both attempt to discover a comfortable mode of existence. For students, this means learning as much as possible about the teacher and the class, establishing their own identity, and gaining as much control over the situation as possible. Hopefully, this chapter has provided useful suggestions for productively coping with these first-day expectations of students.

ACKNOWLEDGMENT

Many of the ideas in this chapter owe a debt to the unpublished notes of R. L. Kohls, a professor of agricultural economics who for many years taught a seminar on college teaching at Purdue University.

REFERENCES

Berger, C. R., & Calabrese, R. J. (1975). Some explorations in initial interaction and beyond: Toward a developmental theory of interpersonal communication. *Human Communication Research, 1,* 99–112.
Brooks, D. (1985). The first day of school. *Educational Leadership, 43,* 76–78.
Brophy, J. E. (1983). Classroom organization and management. *The Elementary School Journal, 83,* 265–285.
Burgoon, J. K., Buller, D. B., & Woodall, W. G. (1996). *Nonverbal communication: The unspoken dialogue* (2nd ed.). New York: McGraw-Hill.

Cooper, P. (1995). *Speech communication for the classroom teacher* (5th ed.). Scottsdale, AZ: Gorsuch-Scarisbrick.

DeVito, J. (1986). Teaching as relational development. In J. Civikly (Ed.), *Communicating in college classrooms* (pp. 51–60). San Francisco: Jossey-Bass.

Goffman, E. (1959). *The presentation of self in everyday life*. Garden City, NY: Doubleday.

Goffman, E. (1963). *Behavior in public places*. New York: The Free Press.

Kohls, R. L. (n.d.). *Do as I say; not as I do*. Unpublished manuscript, Purdue University.

Kougl, K. (1997). *Communicating in the classroom*. Prospect Heights, IL: Waveland Press.

Merton, R., Reader, G., & Kendall, P. (1957). *The student physician*. Cambridge, MA: Harvard University Press.

Nussbaum, J. F. (1992). Effective teacher behaviors. *Communication Education, 41,* 167–180.

Staton, A. Q. (1990). *Communication and student socialization*. Norwood, NJ: Ablex.

Van Maanen, J., & Schein, E. H. (1979). Toward a theory of organizational socialization. *Research in Organizational Behavior, 1*, 209–264.

IV

Selecting and Evaluating Instructional Strategies and Tools

22

Selected Tools and Methods to Engage Students in Learning

Donald H. Wulff
Jody D. Nyquist
University of Washington

In an article that has received widespread attention since its publication, Barr and Tagg (1995) suggested that there is a paradigm shift taking place in undergraduate education—from an emphasis on teaching to an emphasis on learning. They explained:

> In the learning paradigm ... a college's purpose is not to transfer knowledge but to create environments and experiences that bring students to discover and construct knowledge for themselves, to make students members of communities of learners that make discoveries and solve problems. (p. 15)

Consistent with such a perspective, we have focused this chapter on selected instructional methods that can actively engage students in course content. In addition to the initial discussion of syllabi, we have included five basic instructional strategies that require active student participation: writing, oral presentations, small groups, case study methods, and field study methods.

How technology will soon affect each of these strategies is an ongoing question. We already know, for example, that instructors are placing syllabi on the World Wide Web, that students turn to the Web for supplemental reading and resources, that students participate in discussion groups using computers, that faculty and students interact using e-mail, and that some instructors teach public speaking via the computer. For the present, however, we recognize that there are basic tools and methods that instructors can use to engage students in the learning process, regardless of whether instructional technology is involved.

SYLLABI

Although we do not usually think of a syllabus as a way to engage students in our courses, syllabi do provide significant opportunities to focus students on the learning of course content (see Civikly-Powell, chap. 5, this volume). Grunert (1997) suggested that a learning-centered syllabus can be an important tool to "reinforce the intentions, roles, attitudes, and strategies that you will use to promote active, purposeful, effective learning" (p. 3).

Meyers and Jones (1993) suggested that "a syllabus that will stand up to the demands of active learning needs to be more comprehensive" (p. 37). Other professionals point out that a comprehensive syllabus sends important messages about the instructor's investment in the course and provides an opportunity for the instructor to engage students in course content, expectations, and course readings (Brookfield, 1995; Grunert, 1997).

Addressing Course Content

Most syllabi contain an overview of the content of a course, major course goals, and topics to be addressed. A comprehensive syllabus, however, provides additional ways to engage students in the course content. For example, in some cases, instructors can create interest by using the syllabus to present the content as "problematic," identifying questions to be addressed, showing new directions in or frameworks for thinking about the content, briefly explaining how students will engage in thinking about important issues, and showing how the content of the course fits into the larger overall scheme of the discipline. Additionally, the syllabus provides a way for the instructor to take the important step of explaining how the content reflects the perspectives and experiences of a pluralistic society (Musil, 1997; Olguin & Schmitz, 1997; Schmitz, 1992). Especially when students are expected to consider a variety of perspectives in the discovery and construction of knowledge, the instructor can point out that major readings for the course "reflect new scholarship and research about previously under-represented groups" in such a way that no one perspective is held up as the norm or simply "tagged on" rather than integrated as a basic part of the content (Davis, 1993, pp. 43–44). Grunert (1997) proposed that, as one possibility, the instructor can use the syllabus to "encourage students to approach the field actively as ethnographic field-workers who want to understand the social and intellectual practices of the field" (p. 17).

Addressing Students' Expectations for the Instructor's Role

An explanation of the instructor's role is particularly important in courses where students are actively involved because the instructor role often changes in ways that can be atypical from the students' perspective. Brookfield (1995) recommended that the instructor include in every syllabus a section entitled something like "My Core Beliefs About Teaching and Learning," "What You Should Know About Me as a Teacher," or "Assumptions That Guide This Course" (pp. 109–110). Such a section can provide not only a sound rationale for a course, but also a way to clarify expectations for contributions that the instructor will be making to the course.

Clarifying the Instructor's Expectations for Students

A carefully planned syllabus, in addition to clarifying the instructor's role, also can provide students with a sense of their own responsibility for achieving the course objectives (McKeachie, 1994). If, for example, the instructor expects students to come to class having completed reading assignments and prepared to think collectively in small groups, the syllabus provides an opportunity to establish that expectation explicitly. As Grunert (1997) suggested:

> If critical thinking, problem solving, and inquiry are part of your course, it is helpful to tell students that they will be asked to consider multiple viewpoints and conflicting values and to imagine, analyze, and evaluate alternate positions on issues or solutions to problems. (p. 16)

Because an important part of participation in any active learning approach is self-monitoring, the syllabus is also a place to help students understand what their role will be in monitoring and assessing their own progress during use of strategies designed to get them more actively involved. Meyers and Jones (1993) suggested that a cover letter on the syllabus provides one way to address expectations for students, simultaneously personalizing the classroom atmosphere from the outset.

Preparing Students to Use Course Readings

Too often, the use of a reading in a course is never discussed explicitly. Students sometimes figure out the function of the reading by themselves through trial and error, but often not without confusion and frustration. When a textbook provides frameworks or perspectives that are inconsistent with those presented in lectures, for example, students can become confused. Similarly, students can be dissatisfied if they are required to read and take tests on supplemental material that is not carefully integrated into a course. Therefore, the instructor should view the comprehensive syllabus as a chance to explain the function that reading materials will fulfill in the course and to suggest how students might use the readings. In the process, it is helpful for the instructor to remember that experienced scholars have particular frameworks and perspectives that assist them in gleaning key ideas from scholarly readings and that students are unlikely to have such refined reading skills.

Regardless of how comprehensive the syllabus is in addressing course content, expectations, and readings, it can still be flexible. Flexibility in syllabus design is particularly important if the instructor is teaching a course for the first time. At a minimum for any syllabus, leaving an "open" day at midpoint or the end of the term allows the instructor to address potential student overload as well as unexpected challenges. With a student-centered syllabus, however, flexibility means adapting to a particular group of students. In some cases, then, the instructor may want to distribute the syllabus for discussion on the first day of class and make revisions based on student input and needs before preparing it as a final document (McKeachie, 1994). Some instructors prefer such an approach as a way to preassess students' needs and preferred styles and to engage students in the learning process. In addition to reflecting sensitivity to students' needs, such flexibility decreases the adjustments that have to be made during the term and sets expectations for students taking some responsibility for their own learning.

However instructors proceed in preparing the syllabus, they should consider its use as an instructional tool to engage students. Particularly in courses in which students play an increasingly active role in their learning, instructors can use comprehensive syllabi to draw students into course content and set the tone, structure, and expectations. To do so, however, an instructor must refer to the syllabus frequently as a course proceeds. The more an instructor can use the syllabus to clarify expectations for a course, the better the chance that the students can engage in fulfilling those expectations successfully.

WRITING

Communication instructors have long used writing assignments in their courses. Depending on the instructors' goals, the writing assignments range from the writing of speeches, critiquing of speeches, and keeping of journals about communication behavior to the analyzing of field study notes and writing of reports. Typically, however, the primary use of writing has been evaluative. Communication instructors use essays or term papers, essay tests, or critiques of books and articles to see how close the writer can come to capturing what the instructor has been presenting or requiring in the class readings. Although this is a valuable use of writing for assessment purposes (White, 1994), writing can be used in broader ways to stimulate "conceptual involvement and investigation in order to encourage the growth of students' intellectual capacities" (Knoblauch & Brannon, 1983, p. 471). This intellectual growth can best be fostered by promoting instructor–student dialogues as an instructor comments during a revision process or responds to ungraded student writing.

Promoting Instructor-Student Dialogue During Writing

Composition theorists have consistently advocated a view of writing as process rather than finished text (Sorcinelli & Elbow, 1997). At a minimum, this kind of writing requires four stages: (a) student drafting of an initial document, (b) instructor response, (c) student revision, and (d) instructor response and evaluation of a finished product. This writing-as-process view has been advocated as a means of enabling students to "write to learn." As Knoblauch and Brannon (1983) pointed out:

> The concern is to create intellectual dialogue as a way of stimulating more learning, to use writing as a means of personal discovery but also as a means of communicating the honest extent of the writer's understanding, including difficulties, inadequacies of insight, imperfect or unproductive connections among ideas and information so that a more experienced learner can provide through reinforcing commentary some new directions for exploration. (p. 471)

Using the draft–response–revision–response process as a way of clarifying ideas and guiding student learning provides an opportunity to interact with the student early in his or her thinking. The instructor can respond to analytical errors and lack of student understanding of basic concepts or philosophies, as well as omissions of essential information. More importantly, this instructor–student dialogue can encourage the pursuit of specific lines of inquiry, provide missing information, challenge and expand on students' tentative thinking, and encourage the revision process. The quality of the instructor's comments on student papers, therefore, becomes critical. To promote instructor–student dialogue, the instructor must take the role of a reader trying to understand the writer rather than the role of a judge measuring against an imaginary ideal product. This process allows the instructor and the student to work together to develop a better finished product based on the feedback and revision effort, and it enables the student to value rewriting as a way to enhance thinking rather than as a punishment for an inferior product.

Promoting Instructor–Student Dialogue Without Emphasis on Assessment

Although all writing should promote personal growth, communication instructors can employ specific writing assignments to enable students to explore various concepts without concern for assessment; in other words, to write with personal discovery as the primary goal. Writing assignments that are not evaluated for a grade offer a view of how students are processing information so that an instructor can identify snarls in students' thinking and make necessary adjustments in sequencing, repetition of instruction, reteaching, and encouragement.

This point can be illustrated with an example of a journal assignment given to a student in a course on rhetorical theory. The assignment was to compare and contrast Ramus' view of rhetoric in his reformed curriculum with Bacon's view of rhetoric in his *Advancement of Learning*. One student wrote:

> I'm really not sure about this "stuff." Seemingly, Ramus' purpose is to classify all knowledge into some neat and complete category system. But can we divide all knowledge into these neat little boxes? Was there just simply less to know in Ramus' time? Or does his classical model of knowledge allow one to feel like the truth is knowable and can be completely classified? But then Bacon's point is important. The illusion of completeness may be the price you pay. *Partitio*—the false allure of dividing things neatly? Bacon seems to argue for "ideas in progress." Clearly, his thinking reflects more closely that of today's, but what about the core of knowledge that everyone says college students are lacking?

Such a journal entry provides an opportunity for the instructor to respond to uncertainties, misconceptions, and confusion at an early stage in the student's thinking. Equally important, however, the response can include suggestions that enable the student to think more deeply about the subject matter. One professor provided such a response to the student:

> You are on the right track in underscoring that Ramus' principal interest was in classification. Keep in mind those overlapping charts about the procedures of rhetoric and dialectic we passed out and discussed in class and how the students in those days were expected to know all the details of both rhetoric and dialectic by heart! Think how much easier it would be to memorize Ramus' system. But also consider the price of this simplification. What is substantively lost in one's understanding of rhetoric if, on Ramus' system, "invention" is given to dialectic and rhetoric is left with only "style" and "delivery?" On Bacon I think you are onto something important, and you could profit by carrying your thought further. How does Bacon provide a keen sense of order—but without creating the illusion of completeness?

Not only is this type of writing assignment useful in teaching rhetorical theory, but it is a powerful strategy for teaching all communication concepts.

Ungraded writing assignments can be used in various ways to teach important information (Fulwiler, 1997; Young, 1997). For example, an instructor for a basic introductory communication class with 250 students in it might begin with a 1-minute essay in which students analyze or respond in some way to a previous day's homework assignment with a focus on identifying areas needing clarification or questions the reading material may have raised. Following this opening exercise, students could exchange papers and respond to each other's writing, enabling students on a daily basis to be writers, readers, and respondents to peer thinking and writing about the intellectual substance of the class. The students could then orally ask questions that the instructor would answer before the day's lecture begins. Or, students might work in small groups to respond in writing to part of a day's lecture either during the middle or near the end of the class session. Group papers, another approach to creating dialogue about writing, require students to draft arguments, positions, or explanations; read others' writing and respond; and then come to consensus about how the group can best represent the ideas in final written form.

Such activities, in addition to providing guided experiences in writing, can establish dialogues between instructors and students and among students. Also, the writing activities can lead students to increased awareness of substantive issues in the course, personal coherence or disagreement with the ideas presented, and improved levels of intellectual commitment and penetration. The instructor, in turn, can gain access to students' reasoning, the connections students make when dealing with the course material, and areas that remain confusing and puzzling for students. (See Sargent, 1997, for additional ideas for establishing dialogues among and between students and instructors.)

Becoming adept at using writing as an instructional strategy to accomplish specific goals requires thought and planning that cannot be addressed sufficiently in this short treatment. Nevertheless, it is important for communication instructors to realize that writing, when used as a tool for learning content, provides a powerful method for engaging students in the assimilation of information and the application of communication concepts.

STUDENT ORAL PRESENTATIONS

As would be expected, student oral presentations represent one of the instructional strategies most often used by communication instructors. Clearly, classes in public speaking, interpersonal communication, oral interpretation, and debate are primarily student performance courses. To practice and exhibit mastery of the course content, the student must have ample opportunity to "try on" effective behaviors under supervision and receive systematic feedback from the course instructor and members of the class.

However, student oral performances are in themselves a powerful strategy for teaching knowledge of all kinds (Berkeley Staff, 1986). Like writing, oral performance assignments are too often used solely for evaluation of a student's proficiency, in this case competency in speaking. A broader conception of student oral performances would enable communication instructors to recognize the opportunity for establishing an oral dialogical relationship with students as a vehicle for teaching any set of truths, concepts, or understandings. Such presentations enable instructors to view students' thought processes, cognitive connections, frameworks, or schema used for processing information when students must tell others, in an orderly, coherent, audience-adapted way, about new insights or knowledge.

Student individual or panel presentations, debates, readings, and role plays provide effective ways of covering curricula (Students can lecture too!) in courses at all levels. In fact, it seems puzzling that so often upper division and graduate communication courses only require students to write when all in the discipline agree on the power and influence of the oral communication act.

In a rhetoric course focused on speeches of historical figures, for example, students can conduct research that enables them to sketch the periods in which the people lived, including strong influences and societal values that

provided the contexts in which the individuals wrote and spoke. Oral presentations that attempt to explain to classmates how the historical figures
thought about specific issues of the periods in which they lived can clearly
demonstrate students' grasp of course material. Class member responses to
the presentations can further inform the instructor about students' mastery
of the subject matter.

Another example might be an upper division course in children's communication development. The instructor can teach the course powerfully
by assigning students to work together in groups to research, synthesize,
and report to the class on topics such as the effects of media on thinking
skills of children, the effects of friendship groups on children's communication development, and communication strategies that facilitate children's language development. Such presentations gain valuable student
time on task outside class sessions in terms of research and preparation time
required from individuals or groups of students. In addition, the desire of
students to perform well in front of their peers provides a motivational
force that is not always present for a written assignment that typically only
the instructor sees.

Debate offers another effective approach for teaching course content.
For example, in a rhetoric class, the instructor might ask students to debate
the idea of the "classical bias" and its influence on our interpretation of the
medieval period. Students in an oral interpretation course could debate the
interpretation of Antigone in the context of being a woman during the classical period, or, in an interpersonal course, students might argue the differences between Stewart and D'Angelo's (1988) and Miller and Steinberg's
(1975) definitions of interpersonal communication, an early distinction in
the field. In other instances, informal debates between pairs of students
who hold opposing points of view gained from the reading of course materials can motivate classmates to become informed, analyze the perspectives, and form their own opinions. With any of the debate formats, though,
the instructor must specify the rules to ensure that the instructional content
of the debates becomes the primary goal of all speakers.

Again, as with writing, the instructor must attend carefully to providing
both explicit instructions for the oral assignment and content-specific oral
or written feedback in response to the student presentations. When used as
an instructional strategy, oral performance may or may not be evaluated for
a grade. The importance of establishing an instructor–student dialogue
should be a major concern. Student oral presentations provide access to the
ways in which students are processing course material long before midterm
or final examinations provide a formal evaluation. The instructor then has

the opportunity to clarify misunderstandings and offer new ways of thinking at a formative stage of the students' mastery of the course content.

Some communication instructors routinely use student speeches, panel discussions, debates, lectures, interviews, student readings, and role plays to teach communication content. The Sonnenschein and Whitehurst (1984) studies on the importance that critiquing has in the mastery of information, however, suggest that students need more opportunities to listen to and critique others' presentations. Student presentations are not an abdication of the instructor's responsibilities, but rather class time well spent for both speakers and listeners.

SMALL GROUPS

Although *small group* has been defined in a variety of ways, using small groups for instructional purposes typically involves having four to six students work together to enhance their understanding of the course content. Groups in a variety of forms can be established on an informal, temporary basis or on a more permanent basis for long-term, cooperative course projects. Although students can share and explain factual information in groups, small groups are more commonly used in communication as a way to engage students in thinking critically about basic content.

When instructors plan and structure activities carefully, small groups can provide a number of advantages. For example, when a class becomes too teacher-centered or too focused on the instructor talking, small groups can provide a way for a greater number of students to be simultaneously involved in the class and to take more responsibility for their learning. In addition, working in small groups tends to increase students' motivation, partly because students enjoy the opportunity to interact with their peers, but also because students care about how their peers perceive them. Small group discussions also provide ways for students to compare their ideas with the ideas of their peers, simultaneously providing students with opportunities to improve competency in expressing, supporting, and evaluating ideas orally. If students use specific frameworks from the discipline as they talk about content in their small groups, they can learn a way of thinking about content or a way of approaching problem solving. Finally, evidence supports interaction in small groups as a way to enhance student learning. Some results, for example, suggest that students retain information longer when they have a chance to verbalize it, particularly when they verbalize it to their peers (Webb, 1982). Garside (1996) reported that small groups have significant effects on students' learning of higher order critical thinking skills. Bargh and Schul (1980) explained such findings by suggesting that sometimes students in small groups assume teaching roles that provide them with new perspectives and enable them "to see previously unthought of new relationships between the elements. It may be this building of new relationships that facilitates a better fundamental grasp of the material" (p. 595).

To realize these potential advantages, instructors must plan carefully for the use of small groups. They can do so by thoughtfully determining appropriate objectives, defining small group tasks clearly, thinking about the best ways of clarifying the instructor's role, establishing expectations for students, and helping students think about various roles that emerge in small group interaction.

Determining Objectives for Use with Small Groups

Instructors should select small group activities because of the specific objectives that need to be accomplished (Bonwell & Sutherland, 1996). Specifying the outcomes of group activities is particularly important because of the potential incongruity between the goals and the way learning is measured in small group activities. If, for example, the goal is to have students use the group process so that each student can develop individual understanding, a set of skills, or a way of thinking, then it is appropriate to evaluate learning in the class by measuring the progress of individual students. If, on the other hand, a major goal for group work is to solve problems or generate ideas as a group, then evaluation of the effects of group processes should be based on the group's progress toward designated goals.

Defining Small Group Tasks

A key prerequisite to students' successful participation in groups is a clearly defined task to achieve designated goals. It is inadequate to tell students to "get together and discuss" or to "solve the problem." At the very minimum, instructors need to take time to create a rationale for the task, describe what students will do in their groups, clarify expectations for the final product from each group, and monitor progress.

Clarifying the Instructor's Role

The use of small groups does not relinquish the instructor's responsibility. It does require, however, that the instructor function more as a facilitator of learning than a source of knowledge. In addition to providing thorough planning and thoughtful description of the task, the facilitative role requires determining how much experience with small groups students have in order to decide how much structure and support to provide (Bonwell & Sutherland, 1996). The role also requires that the instructor answer questions for specific groups and, occasionally, meet with groups to monitor progress and provide feedback about learning and group functioning (Smith, 1996). An important part of the role is summarizing and synthesizing in ways that help students make connections. Because students need to see direct links between outcomes of the group activity and the content for which they feel responsible, the instructor must schedule adequate time for debriefing group activity, either at the end of a single class period or at the beginning of a subsequent class.

Establishing Expectations for Students' Preparation

It is also helpful to clarify for students what the use of small groups requires from them in terms of preparation, participation, and debriefing. Presumably, in order to use small groups to achieve objectives related to understanding, application, analysis, synthesis, or evaluation, students must have prior knowledge of topics to be discussed. When students bear major responsibility for obtaining that information, the instructor must state those expectations explicitly and assign activities that encourage student responsibility (Bonwell, 1996). For example, the instructor who wants students in an oral interpretation class to generate alternative interpretations of the poem "Daddy" by Sylvia Plath (1993) can make sure students read the poem in advance by requiring that they bring to class a one-page summary of their individual interpretations. Additionally, when groups are to function outside the boundaries of the in-class time, the instructor can help students prepare by suggesting ways to obtain useful background information and resources, structure the discussion, and debrief (Kuh, Douglas, Lund, & Ramin-Gyurnek, 1994). Preparing students for their involvement in small group activities decreases chances that they will have difficulty understanding the task, waste valuable time, or digress to "pooling of ignorance." Such preparation is particularly important because once groups start the task, the instructor often does not have access to the progression of students' thinking.

Helping Students Think About Various Roles in Small Groups

Active participation in small groups requires interpersonal skills that some students may not possess. Each person brings to the group task a variety of personality variables that create interpersonal relationships and affect the levels of participation, the satisfaction, and, ultimately, the outcomes of the group. It is important, then, for instructors to talk to students about the various task, maintenance, and personal roles that group members might assume and about the kinds of skills that are helpful when the different roles emerge in the group process. In addition, instructors should establish a classroom atmosphere of trust and respect where students know that they can express ideas openly, that their individual ideas will be valued, and that they can receive specific reinforcement and feedback. Instructors can also take steps to ensure that members of a group know each other and that they are able to arrange themselves so they can see and hear everyone else in the group with minimal distractions.

As with other strategies, a particular approach to the use of small groups can succeed only if it has been carefully selected, implemented, and debriefed. Getting students to work effectively in small groups is not an easy task, and initially failure is a real possibility. However, instructors can begin to address the challenges of this particular instructional method by recognizing that engaging students in their learning through the use of small groups requires just as much planning and preparation as formal presentations.

CASE STUDY METHOD

Case study, or what is referred to as the case method of instruction, has emerged as a dynamic instructional strategy offering great potential as a learning approach for university students. Closely identified with the Harvard Business School, the case study method was described by Christensen and Hansen (1987) as an "active, discussion-oriented learning mode, disciplined by case problems drawn from the complexity of real life" (p 16). The method requires active oral participation by students led by instructors utilizing broad repertoires of facilitative behaviors. Problem-based learning (PBL), a similar method that has emerged from a number of medical schools, "derives from the theory that learning is a process in which the learner actively constructs knowledge" (Gijselaers, 1996, p. 13). Although space prohibits explication of this teaching method, communication instructors should investigate its potential for instruction (Wilkerson & Gijselaers, 1996).

Case study methods have evolved from the initial use of narrative snapshots designed to trigger discussion about a company's problems at a given point in time to what has been described more recently as "complex educational instruments, based on carefully designed research plans and intensive field research" (Christensen & Hansen, 1987, p. 26). Christensen and Hansen (1987) suggested the following definition:

> A case is a partial historical, clinical study of a situation which has confronted a practicing administrator or managerial group. Presented in nar-

rative form to encourage student involvement, it provides
data—substantive and process—essential to an analysis of a specific situation, for the framing of alternative action programs, and for their implementation recognizing the complexity and ambiguity of the practical
world. (p. 27)

In communication, the case study method appears to be used most often in
courses in interpersonal, organizational, small group, and instructional communication. Relevant examples include incidents of blocked or ineffectual
communication within a firm or organization, teacher–student confrontations in a classroom setting, interpersonal conflicts between a supervisor and
a subordinate, or the difficult deliberations of a community group attempting
to prevent the construction of a high-rise apartment house.

The most effective cases require application of particular course content
and cannot be adequately solved unless the course material has been mastered. Usually they require students to do extensive research on the problem,
including determining the severity and consequences of the incident described in the case, precedents used in similar cases, possible solutions, ramifications of the adoption of various plans, and implementation implications.

Case studies must reflect an appropriate sequencing of levels of difficulty from simple to complex. Instructors need to provide students with explicit instruction about the case study method including how they should
prepare for the discussion, what is expected of them during the discussion,
and how they will be evaluated. As McKeachie (1994) pointed out:

Typically, one of the goals of the case method is to teach students to select
important factors from a tangle of less important ones that may, nevertheless, form a context to be considered. One does not learn such skills by being in perpetual confusion, but rather by success in solving more and
more difficult problems. (p. 160)

In addition, the instructor has to prepare carefully by analyzing the case
in detail and creating questions that will elicit student responses that can be
built on to provide opportunity for the collective solving of the problem.
Use of the method also requires that an instructor concentrate very carefully on contributions of students and how they are advancing the thought
line toward an eventual resolution of the problem based on adequate theory
and proven communication principles.

Generally, instructors should begin by using a few cases in their classes
and then assess student reception and conceptual achievement to guide subsequent applications. Too often, instructors announce an entire course as
being a case study course and then struggle to find or develop cases no matter what they are attempting to teach. The case study method, like any other

instructional strategy, should be used, however, only when it provides the best vehicle for attaining the goals of the unit or course.

Professors using the case study method report heightened student engagement, more effective application of problem-solving skills, and increased instructor satisfaction with the quality of the resulting classroom interaction. The drawbacks of the method include the lack of available high-quality cases that demonstrate the communication principles being taught and the time investment required to write cases and to work through the case study process.

FIELD STUDY METHODS

Researchers often use field methods for collecting data for research, but instructors rarely think of field study methods as learning tools for students' use in mastering course content. In the discipline of communication, the use of field methods is typically reserved for classes focusing on methodology in qualitative, interpretive, or ethnographic research. Nevertheless, field methods can be, and have been, successfully used as a major instructional tool in other communication classes.

This use entails getting students into a setting where they can observe, interview, and study environments to collect information about a phenomenon of interest to the class. Instructors use some variation of these methods when they ask students to conduct information-gathering interviews and synthesize the information for in-class presentation. However, when field methods are used as a more developed learning tool, instructors usually prepare the students to be novice researchers who will learn while making contributions to the development of course content.

The approach is particularly potent in communication courses because there are so many contexts in which human interaction can be observed. For example, in teaching a course in adolescent communication in which a goal is to have students identify what adolescents talk about with their peers, some class members might observe adolescents on junior high school playgrounds or in classrooms. Others might ride school buses or arrange to attend adolescent extracurricular activities. In an organizational communication class in which a major goal is to have students explain how subordinates react to innovations instigated by their supervisors, students might become involved in organizational settings to observe interactions and to interview supervisors and subordinates.

There are a number of reasons instructors might consider using field methods to achieve the objectives for communication courses. First, such a teaching strategy gets students actively involved in the learning process.

Instead of being passive receptacles for knowledge dispensed in the classroom, students are in the field generating knowledge; and they learn to compare and contrast the content from the field with what they obtain in the controlled environment of the classroom. In many instances, the learning has the potential of becoming a collaborative process in which students compare and contrast their findings to understand more fully the phenomena of interest. Second, such methods provide students with a richer sense of the phenomena being studied. In the previously mentioned adolescent communication course, for instance, college students may read a book, listen to the instructor, or even try to generate a list of topics that they think adolescents might talk about in everyday life. However, when these students study adolescents in natural settings, on the playground, in the classroom, or on the school bus, for example, the students obtain an enhanced sense of adolescent communication; and they can assess whether the material presented in class does represent the world outside the classroom. Finally, using basic field methods assists students in learning a rudimentary research process including data collection, data analysis, testing and validating hypotheses, presenting findings, and exploring implications.

Because of the complexity of preparing students to use field methods, instructors need to plan carefully when using the approach. Some of the major considerations in implementing field methods to enhance student learning in communication courses include setting objectives, arranging the logistics, preparing students for their roles, and assuming different instructor roles.

Setting Objectives

It is important, of course, to identify the major student outcomes desired and then determine if they warrant the time spent in traveling to the field, collecting data, and conducting analyses. If major course goals include having students compare and contrast information from different sources or learn to analyze, synthesize and categorize, then instructors might want to consider the ways that field methods could be added to their repertoires of teaching methods.

Arranging Logistics

A major logistical problem in using field methods is one of matching students and field settings. Depending on the level of the students, instructors may be able to make the assignments and let students decide issues of entry and access. However, if students need assistance finding and arranging to visit appropriate field sites, instructors may have to use their knowledge and credibility to identify potential field settings and make initial contacts. Either way, once instructors have resolved issues of matching students and settings, they will need to provide students with specific information on responsibilities, policies, and guidelines for interacting with site contacts and for conducting the studies.

Preparing Students

Many undergraduates will not have prior experiences with field methods. Even though some students may have conducted interviews or more formal observations, most students will not have utilized systematic ways of collecting and analyzing data and reaching conclusions. Therefore, the instructor will want to schedule time at the beginning of the course or before a specific exercise to talk to the students about such basic topics as identifying a research question, gaining access to the field as a participant or nonparticipant observer, taking field notes during interviews and observations, collecting documents, moving from field notes to tentative hypotheses, analyzing the data, and reporting the results of their work. Furthermore, because most students will have had little previous experience as researchers, they may come to class expecting the instructor to be the major source of information for the subject. Consequently, the instructor will need to spend time discussing with them not only the appropriate protocol for getting into and working in the field as researchers but also the changes in the instructor and student contributions to the class as a result of the research.

Assuming Different Instructor Roles

When instructors use field methods as an instructional strategy, they should be prepared to assume a variety of roles, including field methods practition-er, content expert, individual consultant, and facilitator. In the roles of field methods practitioners, instructors will assist students in deciding how to obtain and make sense of data from a particular context, set ethical standards, and make sure such projects are within research parameters set by the institution. As content experts, instructors will be responsible for providing content to which students may compare and contrast the data they generate in the field. Instructors may assume consultant roles as they work with individual students who have particular problems analyzing their data or who have generated particularly interesting or puzzling insights about the phenomenon being studied. Finally, as facilitators, instructors will have to provide ongoing summary, analysis, and synthesis to help the students connect the information generated in the field to the instructional objectives of the course.

SUMMARY

The intent of this chapter has been to provide an overview and introduction to selected instructional methods that instructors can use to engage students in learning in communication courses. Although the approaches discussed represent a diverse set of strategies, some consistent themes about the use of such methods have emerged. First, it is important to remember that course objectives determine which methods are most appropriate for working with a particular body of content. Therefore, to begin thinking about how to convey the content of courses, instructors should specify the learning outcomes they wish to achieve. A second theme is that the various strategies are ways for helping students learn. The strategies have been discussed not as methods for evaluating students' mastery of the content, but rather as ways of helping students master the content. Another theme has been that instructor thought and preplanning are essential before implementation in the classroom, including thinking about the special issues related to the procedures, the roles and responsibilities of instructors and students, the kinds of interactions involved, and the special logistical problems. Therefore, long before any one of these issues appears as a difficulty in the classroom, the instructor will have given special attention to it and begun to devise appropriate ways to address it. A final issue that has emerged consistently throughout the chapter is related to the importance of integration and evaluation. In order to continue to use such instructional strategies successfully, the instructor must help students integrate them by showing direct links between the activities and the content being studied. Finally, the instructor and the students must be continually monitoring and evaluating the strategies used in terms of overall usefulness for achieving course objectives.

This chapter cannot address more than a limited number of instructional tools and methods or the many issues related to their use. Nevertheless, it does provide basic ideas, guidelines, and themes that can serve as a starting point for serious thought about ways to engage students in learning in communication classrooms.

REFERENCES

Bargh, J. A., & Schul, Y. (1980). On the cognitive benefits of teaching. *Journal of Educational Psychology*, *72*, 593–604.

Barr, R. B., & Tagg, J. (1995). From teaching to learning—A new paradigm for undergraduate education. *Change*, *27*(6), 13–25.

Berkeley Staff. (1986, Fall). Berkeley launches writing and speech program. *Teaching at Berkeley*, p. 1.

Bonwell, C. C. (1996). Enhancing the lecture: Revitalizing a traditional format. In T. E. Sutherland & C. C. Bonwell (Eds.), *Using active learning in college classes: A range of options for faculty* (New Directions for Teaching and Learning, No. 67, pp. 31–44). San Francisco: Jossey-Bass.

Bonwell, C. C., & Sutherland, T. E. (1996). The active learning continuum: Choosing activities to engage students in the classroom. In T. E. Sutherland & C. C. Bonwell (Eds.), *Using active learning in college classes: A range of options for faculty* (New Directions for Teaching and Learning, No. 67, pp. 3–16). San Francisco: Jossey-Bass.

Brookfield, S. D. (1995). *Becoming a critically reflective teacher.* San Francisco: Jossey-Bass.

Christensen, C. R., & Hansen, A. J. (1987). *Teaching and the case method.* Boston: Harvard Business School.

Davis, B. G. (1993). *Tools for teaching.* San Francisco: Jossey-Bass.

Fulwiler, T. (1997). Writing back and forth: Class letters. In M. D. Sorcinelli & P. Elbow (Eds.), *Writing to learn: Strategies for assigning and responding to writing across the disciplines* (New Directions for Teaching and Learning, No. 69, pp. 15–25). San Francisco: Jossey-Bass.

Garside, C. (1996). Look who's talking: A comparison of lecture and group discussion teaching strategies in developing critical thinking skills. *Communication Education, 45,* 212–227.

Gijselaers, W. H. (1996). Connecting problem-based practices with educational theory. In L. Wilkerson & W. H. Gijselaers (Eds.), *Bringing problem-based learning to higher education: Theory and practice* (New Directions for Teaching and Learning, No. 68, pp. 13–21). San Francisco: Jossey-Bass.

Grunert, J. (1997). *The course syllabus: A learning-centered approach.* Bolton, MA: Anker.

Knoblauch, C. H., & Brannon, L. (1983). Writing as learning through the curriculum. *College English, 45,* 465–474.

Kuh, G. D., Douglas, K. B., Lund, J. P., & Ramin-Gyurnek, J. (1994). *Student learning outside the classroom: Transcending artificial boundaries* (ASHE–ERIC Higher Education Rep. No. 8). Washington, DC: The George Washington University, School of Education and Human Development.

McKeachie, W. J. (1994). *Teaching tips: Strategies, research, and theory for college and university teachers* (9th ed.). Lexington, MA: Heath.

Meyers, C., & Jones, T. B. (1993). *Promoting active learning: Strategies for the college classroom.* San Francisco: Jossey-Bass.

Miller, G. R., & Steinberg, M. (1975). *Between people: A new analysis of interpersonal communication.* Chicago: Science Research Associates.

Musil, C. M. (1997). Diversity and educational integrity. In J. G. Gaff, J. L. Ratcliff, & Associates (Eds.), *Handbook of the undergraduate curriculum: A comprehensive guide to purposes, structures, practices, and change* (pp. 190–211). San Francisco: Jossey-Bass.

Olguin, E., & Schmitz, B. (1997). Transforming the curriculum through diversity. In J. G. Gaff, J. L. Ratcliff, & Associates (Eds.), *Handbook of the undergraduate curriculum: A comprehensive guide to purposes, structures, practices, and change* (pp. 436–456). San Francisco: Jossey-Bass.

Plath, S. (1993). Daddy. In S. Barnet, M. Berman, & W. Burto (Eds.), *An introduction to literature* (10th ed., pp. 615–617). New York: HarperCollins.

Sargent, M. E. (1997). Peer response to low stakes writing in a WAC literature classroom. In M. D. Sorcinelli & P. Elbow (Eds.), *Writing to learn: Strategies for assigning and responding to writing across the disciplines* (New Directions for Teaching and Learning, No. 69, pp. 41–52). San Francisco: Jossey-Bass.

Schmitz, B. (1992). Cultural pluralism and core curricula. In M. Adams (Ed.), *Promoting diversity in college classrooms: Innovative responses for the curriculum, faculty, and institutions* (New Directions for Teaching and Learning, No. 52, pp. 61–69). San Francisco: Jossey-Bass.

Smith, K. A. (1996). Cooperative learning: Making "groupwork" work. In T. E. Sutherland & C. E. Bonwell (Eds.), *Using active learning in college classes: A range of options for faculty* (New Directions for Teaching and Learning, No. 67, pp. 71–82). San Francisco: Jossey-Bass.

Sonnenschein, S., & Whitehurst, G. (1984). Developing referential communication: A hierarchy of skills. *Child Development, 55,* 1936–1945.

Sorcinelli, M. D., & Elbow, P. (Eds.). (1997). *Writing to learn: Strategies for assigning and responding to writing across the disciplines* (New Directions for Teaching and Learning, No. 69). San Francisco: Jossey-Bass.

Stewart, J., & D'Angelo, G. (1988). *Together: Communicating interpersonally, instructor's resource guide* (rev. ed.). Reading, MA: Addison-Wesley.

Webb, N. M. (1982). Student interaction and learning in small groups. *Review of Educational Research,* *52*, 421–445.

White, E. M. (1994). *Teaching and assessing writing: Recent advances in understanding, evaluating, and improving student performance* (2nd ed.). San Francisco: Jossey-Bass.

Wilkerson, L., & Gijselaers, W. H. (Eds.). (1996). *Bringing problem-based learning to higher education: Theory and practice* (New Directions for Teaching and Learning, No. 68). San Francisco: Jossey-Bass.

Young, A. (1997). Mentoring, modeling, monitoring, motivating: Response to students' ungraded writing as academic conversation. In M. D. Sorcinelli & P. Elbow (Eds.), *Writing to learn: Strategies for assigning and responding to writing across the disciplines* (New Directions for Teaching and Learning, No. 69, pp. 27–39). San Francisco: Jossey-Bass.

23

Explanatory Skills

Katherine E. Rowan
Purdue University

When Professor A reaches a complex idea in his lectures, he scratches his head, grimaces, and then talks. He seems to understand his material, and everyone says he is brilliant. But few understand his explanations.

Down the hall, Professor B is explaining the same material. He uses many of the same esoteric words Professor A does, but somehow he makes sense. Further, what he says seems refreshingly nonobvious and, occasionally, profound. He can be demanding, and his tests are hard, but his lectures are interesting, his explanations understandable, and his responses to questions clear.

There are many factors that may account for the differences between Professor A and Professor B, but one important one is explanatory skill. The arts of lecturing and explanation-as-teaching are discussed extensively in many works (e.g., Davis, 1993; Dinham, 1996; Lowman, 1984; Martin, 1970; Satterfield, 1978). However, for the most part, these materials analyze explanatory skills in terms of effective preparation, mastery of subject matter, organization, style, and delivery. Frequently omitted is discussion of strategy for explaining. That is, there may be differences between Professor A and Professor B in their comprehension of course material, preparation for class, organization, and delivery skills, but these differences may not fully reveal why Professor B is clearer than Professor A. The key difference may lie in these teachers' implicit theories of students' likely confusions and the teachers' ideas about overcoming these confusions.

Extensive research in instructional design, educational psychology, communication, applied linguistics, and science education shows that there are classic obstacles to comprehension of complex subject matter and tested methods for addressing these difficulties (e.g., Mayer, 1983; Mayer & Sims, 1994; Merrill & Tennyson, 1977; Rowan, 1988, 1990, 1995; Rukavina & Daneman, 1996; Shuy & Larkin, 1978; Shymansky & Kyle, 1988; Woloshyn, Paivio, & Pressley, 1994). Good explainers probably know these confusion sources intuitively and have thoughtful notions about addressing them. The purpose of this chapter is to extend good explainers' intuitions by presenting research-supported approaches to anticipating and overcoming confusion. Additionally, the chapter reviews recent work on ways instructors can help students explain complex material to themselves.

A CONCEPTUAL FRAMEWORK
FOR DIAGNOSING AND OVERCOMING
LIKELY CONFUSIONS ABOUT IDEAS

Although there is no substitute for directly testing students' understanding of a topic, there are ways of formally identifying aspects that are likely to be confusing. That is, just as physicians are aided in diagnosis by knowledge of the major sources of pain (e.g., infection, bacterial or viral; injury, cut or burn; etc.) so too are explainers aided if they have a conceptual model of the likely sources of difficulty people may have in understanding an idea.

Explanatory Discourse Defined

In this chapter, *explanatory discourse* is defined as messages promoting understanding about subject matter. This discourse type is different from "explanation as proof" (Martin, 1970). As Kinneavy (1971) argued, scholarly discourse presents explanations designed to prove some representation of reality. These explanations are produced by experts and judged by fellow experts on several criteria such as the adequacy of their evidentiary base. In contrast, teachers, textbook authors, and some popular nonfiction writers are concerned with explanation as teaching. This second type of explanation can be explored by determining the principal causes of confusion likely to beset students and tested methods for overcoming these difficulties.

THREE KEY SOURCES OF CONCEPTUAL CONFUSION

Research suggests that the difficulties students have in understanding complex ideas may be usefully categorized as one of three types. An idea may be chiefly confusing because it involves (a) unfamiliar concepts or familiar words used in unfamiliar ways (e.g., rhetoric as a field of study, the concept *heat* in physics), (b) difficult-to-picture structures or processes (e.g., taxonomies of human languages, accounts of how persuasion occurs, or how the Mars land rover works), or (c) notions difficult to understand because they are counterintuitive (e.g., the idea that words do not have inherent meanings or that the Earth is weightless). Scholars in a variety of fields have explored each of these obstacles to understanding, identifying message features effective at overcoming each. I refer to people's efforts to address each of these difficulties as a certain type of explanation. There are *elucidating explanations,* which are efforts to clarify the meaning of terms; *quasi-scientific explanations,* which help audiences mentally model complex phenomena; and *transformative explanations,* which help audiences understand counterintuitive or implausible ideas (Rowan, 1988, 1995). Each of these explanation types and the message features most likely to make them effective are discussed in turn.

Elucidating Explanations

Elucidating explanations are designed to help people understand the meaning and use of a term. Instructors use elucidating explanations when they help students distinguish validity and reliability or indicate the range of phenomena that "count" as communication according to particular definitions. The name *elucidating* is used because this sort of discourse attempts to clarify distinctions in meaning.

Research shows that when people are struggling to understand the meaning or use of a term, they are in fact struggling to distinguish a concept's essential (always present) from its variable (frequent but not necessary) meanings. Thus, good elucidating explanations focus students' attention on this distinction. Specifically, researchers have found that good elucidating explanations contain: (a) each of a concept's critical features, (b) an array of varied examples, and (c) opportunities to practice distinguishing examples from nonexamples by looking for critical features (e.g., Merrill & Tennyson, 1977; Tennyson & Cocchiarella, 1986).

Because elucidating explanations help students distinguish essential from unessential meanings, the first feature of good elucidating explanations is a statement of this essential meaning. Such a statement can take the form of a definition, or it can be a discussion of reasons why common inferences about a concept's meaning are incorrect. In communication classes, instructors present elucidating explanations when they discuss the core term "communication." For instance, they may define communication as processes that create shared meaning (Swanson & Delia, 1976), and then ask whether communication necessarily involves two people. Such a discussion focuses students' attention on the intended interpretation of the phrase, "shared meaning." Similarly, news stories sometimes alert readers to essential meanings of words by offering brief definitions and noting what a term does not mean. Articles about food irradiation may explain that irradiation is a process of exposing food to gamma rays to destroy microorganisms. Additionally, they may note that being irradiated means "exposed to radiation" not "becoming radioactive." Research shows that when confusion about essential versus associated meanings is likely, comprehension can be aided by explaining both what a term means and what it does not (Merrill & Tennyson, 1977).

A second feature of good elucidating explanations is a range of varied examples. That is, intuition tells explainers that when a concept is unfamiliar, one should clarify its meaning by offering an example of its use. However, research in instructional design says that students are most likely to distinguish essential from associated meanings of concepts when they consider a range of varied examples (Merrill & Tennyson, 1977). Seeing a range of applications decreases the likelihood that students will think a single feature of one example is essential in all uses of a term. If students have always heard the word *grammar* used in a prescriptive sense, they may assume that all grammars are prescriptive, rather than descriptive. Good explainers avoid leading students to inaccurate inferences such as this by illustrating a concept's application in a varied set of examples. Trenholm and Jensen (1992) offered an effective elucidating explanation of the concept *speech act* by defining this term and then offering several varied instances of its use:

> People don't generally talk just for the fun of it. When we use language, we use it to accomplish specific goals. The things we intend language to do for us are called *speech acts*. Examples of speech acts are promising, questioning, threatening, praising, declaring, warning, requesting, and so on. (p. 217)

This passage lists a range of speech act types. Some are positive (praising) and some negative (threatening); some are frequent in language use (questioning, requesting) and others are less frequent (warning). Students reading this explanation have a better chance of understanding what counts as a speech act than they would if Trenholm and Jensen (1992) had offered only one example or only positive examples.

The third feature of effective elucidating explanations is a discussion of nonexamples (Merrill & Tennyson, 1977). Nonexamples are instances someone might think are examples but are not. In my science journalism classes, I ask students to suggest fields that are "definitely science" and fields that are "definitely not science" as a way of generating a definition of science. The examples students offer of science are typically biology, chemistry, and physics. The definite nonexamples are fields such as religion or art. Once the definite instances are established, we consider the less clear-cut cases and ask ourselves whether we want them to be examples or nonexamples. So, for instance, we discuss fields such as psychology, history, communication, and anthropology. Some students will argue one of these fields is definitely a science, and others will argue it definitely is not. The point of such discussions is to determine the features of meaning we want to say are truly essential. For instance, many students initially say that experiments are essential in all instances of science. However, trouble arises when we consider fields such as astronomy where experimentation may be less frequent than observation. Frequently, it is hard to define familiar notions such as science or art or religion using these steps, but the effort to do so helps clarify thought about critical meanings.

Enhancing the Benefit of Elucidating Explanations. According to instructional design research, simply hearing or reading a good elucidating explanation of a complex concept such as validity or communication or science does not, in itself, ensure that students will master the meaning and use of such concepts. Mastery occurs when students have opportunities for "inquisitory practice" (Merrill & Tennyson, 1977, p. x). That is, students need repeated chances in class discussion, workbooks, homework, or other contexts to practice distinguishing examples from nonexamples by noting the presence or absence of a concept's essential features. Elementary school students obtain such practice in workbook exercises asking them to classify types of clouds, sentences, and so forth. College students can use this type of workbook or computer-aided practice as well to master basic notions such as the sentence–fragment distinction. Additionally, college students benefit from reflective exercises where they develop their own definitions for abstract terms. For instance, college students trying to decide if telemarketing counts as an instance of mass communication, should be able to ask themselves about the essential features of mass communication and whether telemarketing includes each feature.

Quasi-Scientific Explanations

The second type of explanation is the quasi-scientific. This type assists students in envisioning complex structures or processes. An instructor uses quasi-scientific explanations when helping students picture communication models, the workings of the human respiratory system, or a typology for Indo-European languages. I use the term *quasi-scientific* because this form of explanation helps people understand scientific or scholarly representations of reality. Scientists attempt to prove the adequacy of some representation of reality (Kinneavy, 1971); quasi-scientific explanations render such representations envisionable.

Because the key difficulty in envisioning complex structures and processes lies with sorting out main from minor features, good quasi-scientific explanations assist this process by highlighting the main points, key structures, or critical connections. An extensive body of research shows that certain message features are effective in guiding students to recognize main points and key structures (e.g., Gentner, 1988; Gilbert & Osborne, 1980; Loman & Mayer, 1983; Mayer, 1983; Mayer & Anderson, 1992; Rukavina & Daneman, 1996; Woloshyn et al., 1994). These features include *signaling devices* (e.g., titles, previews, headings, topic sentences, and transitions), *figurative language* such as organizing analogies (e.g., "Wetlands are nature's kidneys: They filter impurities") and *graphic aids* (e.g., drawings, models, animation).

Some research has explored teachers' use of quasi-scientific explanation. For instance, Dagher (1995) observed 40 science teachers in their classrooms. This researcher found teachers using analogies in several ways. One biology teacher compared the activities of the AIDS virus to that of an "alien taking slaves." Her seventh graders were probably able to picture the activities of the AIDS virus because of the way she used dramatic, familiar notions (i.e., motion-picture depictions of aliens invading Earth) to help them understand this new material. In one part of her lesson, the teacher said:

> You can think of a virus kind of like an alien that comes to Earth, and enslaves all the people on the Earth and makes them do exactly what he wants them to do. That's what a virus does. And this AIDS virus just happens to pick as its target the T-cells. Those white blood cells. It gets into the body, it gets into those T-cells, and it turns the T-cells into its slave, so to speak. Doesn't let the—shhh—doesn't let the T-cells do the jobs that they're supposed to do [of attacking disease agents]. (p. 264)

This explanation lacks precision, but its vividness and "picture-ability" probably helps students scaffold rough mental models of how the AIDS virus disables the human immune system.

Importantly, message features that assist envisionment of complex material not only improve recall and comprehension, they also help students use their newfound knowledge creatively to solve problems (e.g., Loman & Mayer, 1983; Mayer, 1983; Mayer, Bove, Bryman, Mars, & Tapangco,

1996). In two decades of work, Mayer and his associates have tested the impact of envisionment aids such as signaling devices, figurative language, and graphic aids on students' understanding of explanatory messages. For example, in some studies, randomly selected students were exposed to texts with headings, previews, and transitions, while others read the same texts without such textual highlighting (Loman & Mayer, 1983; Mayer, et al., 1996); in other experiments, some students saw diagrams with captions and explanatory text, whereas others saw only the text (Mayer, 1989; Mayer & Anderson, 1992; Mayer & Sims, 1994). Mayer and his colleagues found that students with access to enhanced quasi-scientific explanations (i.e., those with signaling or organizing analogies) could understand more of the messages' main points, and apply their knowledge creatively. For instance, Mayer and Sims (1994) found that students exposed to concurrent animation and narration on how bicycle pumps work were better at explaining why the pumps might fail than students who received the same information but in successive order (i.e., first narration, then animation). Mayer et al. (1996) found that students exposed to captioned diagrams explaining the conditions under which lightning will strike were better at suggesting factors that could reduce the intensity of a lightning strike than were students who received an unillustrated account of the same information.

Enhancing the Benefit of Quasi-Scientific Explanations. An instructional technique known as *elaborative interrogation* assists students in building connections between their own distinctive prior knowledge and new, difficult-to-envision material (McDaniel & Donnelly, 1996; Pressley, McDaniel, Turnure, Wood, & Ahmad, 1987; Seifert, 1993). Elaborative interrogation requires students to read an explanatory passage and then ask themselves why the phenomenon in question occurs. McDaniel and Donnelly (1996) showed that university students who tried to explain some just-learned material to themselves were better able to answer fact questions and make correct inferences about the information than were their counterparts who did not participate in the elaborative interrogation activity. Students in this study read 12 science passages explaining phenomena such as collapsing stars and the Earth's rotation. For instance, the "star" passage read: "Collapsing stars spin faster as their size shrinks. Stars are thus like ice skaters who pirouette as they pull in their arms. Both stars and skaters operate by the principle called 'conservation of angular momentum'" (p. 518). Those in the elaborative interrogation condition also received a follow-up question, such as "Why does an object speed up as its radius gets smaller (as in conservation of angular momentum)?" (p. 518).

McDaniel and Donnelly (1996) argued that explaining why requires students to construct their own mental models of difficult-to-envision phenomena. This finding suggests that communication faculty should routinely ask students to produce "why" accounts or diagrams to help them understand important phenomena that are difficult to envision. For instance, elaborative interrogation may help students envision sampling distributions (e.g., Quilici & Mayer, 1996), attributional patterns (e.g., Kelley, 1971), message features associated with behavioral change (e.g., Witte, 1992), and so forth.

Transformative Explanations

Transformative explanations help students understand ideas that are difficult to comprehend because they are implausible. Some ideas seem counterintuitive because people have their own tacit but powerful "alternative theories" that conflict with orthodox scholarly conceptions. Frequently, transformative explanations are needed to help students understand counterintuitive ideas in physics. For instance, people struggle to understand the reflective property of light (i.e., the notion that we never see opaque objects directly; instead we see light waves reflected from them). Similarly, in communication classes, students have difficulty understanding that meanings are in people, not words, or that the human mind partly creates the reality it perceives. Transformative explanations are so named because they help students "transform" lay notions into orthodox scholarly ones.

Because students' chief difficulties in understanding counterintuitive notions lie in seeing why their own, implicit theories may be inadequate, good transformative explanations begin by discussing the implicit theory and demonstrating its limitations, rather than simply explaining the expert view.

Specifically, researchers have found that the best transformative explanations are those that (a) state the "implicit" or "lay" theory about the phenomenon, (b) acknowledge the apparent plausibility of this lay theory, (c) demonstrate its inadequacy, (d) state the more accepted account, and (e) demonstrate its greater adequacy (Hashweh, 1988; M. G. Hewson & P. W. Hewson, 1983; P. W. Hewson & M. G. Hewson, 1984; Hynd & Alvermann, 1986; Kuhn, 1989; Rowan, 1991; Shymansky & Kyle, 1988). Although many explanatory efforts omit the first three of these steps, research shows that if the implausibility of a notion is the basis for students' difficulty with it, then failing to address the lay notion frequently means that students retain and use it to guide thought and action. Some research has shown that even physics majors and science teachers who can manipulate equations associated with counterintuitive notions or describe accepted notions accurately still retain some of their lay theories if they have not actively confronted and overcome these ideas (Anderson & Smith, 1984; diSessa, 1982). Said differently, people are intuitive scientists. Like scientists, they do not give up their deeply accepted notions until presented with excellent reasons to do so.

Although transformative explanations are not easy to produce, they frequently are fascinating because they directly confront powerful intuitive notions about the familiar. Interestingly, a journalist used a transformative explanation in a story about research on communication and marriage (O'Connell, 1997). The story began:

> [*State the lay theory.*] "What we have here is a failure to communicate."
>
> [*Acknowledge its apparent plausibility.*] That cliche, from the movie *Cool Hand Luke*, has been quoted for years as a testament to the importance of good communication skills. If only we all knew how to talk with and listen to each other, the world would be brimming with brotherhood and amity.
>
> [*Reject the lay theory.*] Not so, say more and more researchers.... Nowhere has the value of communication been more oversold than in marital relationships, says Brant Burleson, a professor of communication at Purdue University.
>
> [*Demonstrate its inadequacy using examples familiar to the audience.*] Studies show that when one or both spouses are dissatisfied, the better the communication skills, the less satisfied they are. Why? They are using their nifty skills to stick it to each other.
>
> Skilled communicators take the perspective of the other person, Burleson says. They know not only what will help the other person but "exactly where to put the knife and twist it as well."
>
> But what about all those "mirroring" exercises we've been drilled in? The one in which we listen nondefensively while our partner says stuff like, "I feel embarrassed when you wear your leopard-print leggings to church."
>
> "Mirroring can be useful if the problem is lack of clarity or people not understanding each other," Burleson says.
>
> [*State the alternative, expert view and demonstrate its greater adequacy using familiar examples.*] "But not all problems in marriages are communication-related. People have affairs, spend too much money, disagree over how the kids ought to be raised. Bad communication can exacerbate those problems, but there's no guarantee that good communication is going to solve those problems." (p. E1)

Instead of beginning her story with the finding that communication training can sometimes harm a marriage, reporter Loraine O'Connell intrigued *Orlando Sentinel* readers by presenting their own theory first—that improved communication solves all marital problems—acknowledging its widespread acceptance in the next paragraph, and then questioning it. Like scientists, people do not give up their theories easily, so the reporter did not simply reject the lay view. Rather, she identified cases that call the lay view into question, such as the idea that people who really understand one another can "stick it to" each other. Cases that a lay theory cannot explain motivate people to reconsider a lay view; without such motivation, people typically do not reject their lay theories (Rowan, 1991). O'Connell (1997) then presented the alternative view, that some problems in marriage are communication related and others are not, and offered Burleson's examples of problems that stem from dissimilar values or some other source rather than inability to understand one another. This transformative explanation is effective because the reporter intuitively recognizes that the story will be more interesting for readers if they can question their implicit theory using examples it does not seem to explain, rather than simply learning about some expert's idea.

Enhancing the Benefit of Transformative Explanations.
Research suggests that elaborative interrogation (i.e., asking students to explain, in their own words, why a just-explained notion may be the case) is helpful in facilitating understanding of counter-intuitive ideas, just as it is in mastering difficult-to-picture information. A study by Woloshyn et al. (1994) explored learning in contexts where students studied notions that were inconsistent with their prior knowledge; (for example "Although some people think the light of the sun is only red and yellow, it is made of every different color including blue and violet" (p. 79). Those students who engaged in elaborative interrogation were more likely to remember such statements than those who did not.

Lay theories develop about familiar phenomena for which people have expectations (e.g., heat, light, weight, disease, communication, gender, race, language). Understandably, people feel that everyday experience corroborates their lay theories. Consequently, deeply held lay theories tell students that they get colds from going outside without coats or that incorrect grammar is a sign of intellectual inferiority in others. Instructors should not expect to be able to debunk lay theories easily. Instead, perhaps it is more appropriate to expect students to recognize contexts in which lay theorizing is likely to develop (i.e., contexts involving very familiar phenomena) and to learn ways of questioning these ideas.

CONCLUSION

Sometimes people object to my argument that the three types of explanation discussed here are discrete. They rightly note that transformative explanation involves quasi-scientific explanation, and that elucidating explanations may be embedded in both. Certainly, there is merit to this objection. In my teaching, however, I find it useful to think about the main reason a set of ideas is likely to be confusing for students and then organize a class segment to overcome that principal difficulty.

To explain, teachers need more than thorough mastery of course material, good lesson plans, and smooth delivery. They need to understand the reasons why students are likely to find some subject matter difficult to understand. We would have very little faith in doctors who simply tried every cure instead of first diagnosing their patients' ailments and selecting treatments that fit their diagnoses. Similarly, explaining is an art that should proceed with careful analysis and informed strategy selection.

Just as there are physicians who vary in diagnostic skill, there will always be teachers whose explanations are more illuminating and more entertaining than those that others produce. But with conceptual tools for determining why some notion is likely to be confusing and empirically tested strategies for addressing that confusion, good explainers have additional resources for refining their intuitions and making their explanations of complex subject matter effective.

REFERENCES

Anderson, C. W., & Smith, E. L. (1984). Children's preconceptions and content-area textbooks. In G. Duffy, L. Roehler, & J. Mason (Eds.), *Comprehension instruction* (pp. 187–201). New York: Longman.

Dagher, Z. R. (1995). Analysis of analogies used by science teachers. *Journal of Research in Science Teaching, 32,* 259–270.

Davis, B. G. (1993). *Tools for teaching.* San Francisco: Jossey-Bass.

Dinham, S. M. (1996). What college teachers need to know. In R. J. Menges, M. Weimer, & Associates (Eds.), *Teaching on solid ground: Using scholarship to improve practice* (pp. 297–313). San Francisco: Jossey-Bass.

diSessa, A. A. (1982). Unlearning Aristotelian physics: A study of knowledge based learning. *Cognitive Science, 6,* 37–75.

Gentner, D. (1988). Are scientific analogies metaphors? In D. S. Miall (Ed.), *Metaphor: Problems and perspectives* (pp. 106–132). Atlantic Highlands, NJ: Humanities Press.

Gilbert, J. K., & Osborne, R. J. (1980). The use of models in science teaching. *European Journal of Science Education, 2,* 3–13.

Hashweh, M. (1988). Descriptive studies of students' conceptions in science. *Journal of Research in Science Teaching, 25,* 121–134.

Hewson, M. G., & Hewson, P. W. (1983). Effect of instruction using students' prior knowledge and conceptual change strategies on science learning. *Journal of Research in Science Teaching, 20,* 731–743.

Hewson, P. W., & Hewson, M. G. (1984). The role of conceptual conflict in conceptual change and the design of science instruction. *Instructional Science, 13,* 1–13.

Hynd, C., & Alvermann, D. W. (1986). The role of refutation text in overcoming difficulties with science concepts. *Journal of Reading, 29,* 440–446.

Kelley, H. H. (1971). *Attribution in social interaction.* Morristown, NJ: General Learning Press.

Kinneavy, J. L. (1971). *A theory of discourse.* New York: Norton.

Kuhn, D. (1989). Children and adults as intuitive scientists. *Psychological Review, 96,* 674–689.

Loman, N. L., & Mayer, R. E. (1983). Signalling techniques that increase the understandability of expository prose. *Journal of Educational Psychology, 75,* 402–412.

Lowman, J. (1984). *Mastering the techniques of teaching.* San Francisco: Jossey-Bass.

Martin, J. R. (1970). *Explaining, understanding, and teaching.* New York: McGraw-Hill.

Mayer, R. E. (1983). What have we learned about increasing the meaningfulness of science prose? *Science Education, 67,* 223–237.

Mayer, R. E. (1989). Systematic thinking fostered by illustrations in scientific text. *Journal of Educational Psychology, 81,* 240–246.

Mayer, R. E., & Anderson, R. B. (1992). The instructive animation: Helping students build connections between words and pictures in multimedia learning. *Journal of Educational Psychology, 84,* 444–452.

Mayer, R. E., Bove, W., Bryman, A., Mars, R., & Tapangco, L. (1996). When less is more: Meaningful learning from visual and verbal summaries of science textbook lessons. *Journal of Educational Psychology, 88,* 64–73.

Mayer, R. E., & Sims, V. K. (1994). For whom is a picture worth a thousand words? Extensions of a dual-coding theory of multimedia learning. *Journal of Educational Psychology, 86,* 389–401.

McDaniel, M. A., & Donnelly, C. M. (1996). Learning with analogy and elaborative interrogation. *Journal of Educational Psychology, 88,* 508–519.

Merrill, M. D., & Tennyson, R. D. (1977). *Teaching concepts: An instructional design guide.* Englewood Cliffs, NJ: Educational Technology Publications.

O'Connell, L. (1997, May 2). Bad communication may not be problem. *The Orlando* (Florida) *Sentinel,* p. E1.

Pressley, M., McDaniel, M. A., Turnure, J. E., Wood, E., & Ahmad, M. (1987). Generation and precision of elaboration: Effects on intentional and incidental learning. *Journal of Experimental Psychology: Learning, Memory, and Cognition, 13,* 291–300.

Quilici, J. L., & Mayer, R. E. (1996). Role of examples in how students learn to categorize statistics word problems. *Journal of Educational Psychology, 88,* 144–161.

Rowan, K. E. (1988). A contemporary theory of explanatory writing. *Written Communication, 5,* 23–56.

Rowan, K. E. (1990). The speech to explain difficult ideas. *The Speech Communication Teacher, 4,* 2–3.

Rowan, K. E. (1991). When simple language fails: Presenting difficult science to the public. *Journal of Technical Writing and Communication, 21,* 369–382.

Rowan, K. E. (1995). A new pedagogy for explanatory public speaking: Why arrangement should not substitute for invention. *Communication Education, 44,* 236–250.

Rukavina, I., & Daneman, M. (1996). Integration and its effect on acquiring knowledge about competing scientific theories from text. *Journal of Educational Psychology, 88,* 272–287.

Satterfield, J. (1978). Lecturing. In O. Milton & Associates (Eds.), *On college teaching* (pp. 34–61). San Francisco: Jossey-Bass.

Seifert, T. L. (1993). Effects of elaborative interrogation with prose passages. *Journal of Educational Psychology, 85,* 642–651.

Shuy, R. W., & Larkin, D. L. (1978). Linguistic considerations in the simplification/clarification of insurance policy language. *Discourse Processes, 1,* 305–321.

Shymansky, J. A., & Kyle, W. C. (1988). A summary of research in science education—1986 [Special issue]. *Science Education, 72*(3).

Swanson, D. L., & Delia, J. G. (1976). *The nature of human communication.* Chicago: Science Research Associates.

Tennyson, R. D., & Cocchiarella, M. J. (1986). An empirically based instructional design theory for teaching concepts. *Review of Educational Psychology, 56,* 40–71.

Trenholm, S., & Jensen, A. (1992). *Interpersonal communication* (2nd ed.). Belmont, CA: Wadsworth.

Witte, K. (1992). Putting the fear back into fear appeals: The extended parallel process model. *Communication Monographs, 59,* 329–349.

Woloshyn, V. E., Paivio, A., & Pressley, M. (1994). Use of elaborative interrogation to help students acquire information consistent with prior knowledge and information inconsistent with prior knowledge. *Journal of Educational Psychology, 86,* 79–89.

24

Lecturing

Cassandra L. Book
Michigan State University

Instructional strategies may be considered on various continua from teacher controlled to student controlled, from much to little student input, from expository to indirect, or from deductive to inductive. Lecturing tends to be on one end of the continuum with most teacher control, least student input, most expository form, and most deductive mode of instruction. Although these characteristics are neither negative nor positive, they do help to define the lecture. Sistek (1986) cited Simpson as saying: "Sir Barcroft used to define a lecture as a process by which information is transferred from the notes of the lecturer to the notes of the student without going through the minds of either" (p. 1). Such a definition raises concern about the value of the lecture method. Chaudron and Richards (1985) stated that "the function of lectures is to instruct, by presenting information in such a way that a coherent body of information is presented, readily understood, and remembered" (p. 3). However, they recognized that not all lectures inherently function in these ways.

One purpose of teaching is for students to gain and retain new knowledge and to be able to transfer it to other contexts. Use of the principles of learning enhances teachers' effectiveness and students' achievement. These principles of learning suggest that people learn best when they (a) actively participate in the learning, (b) have knowledge (or specified feedback) of the results of the learning, (c) know what they are expected to learn, (d) know the purpose of what they are learning, and (e) find the learning to be meaningful to them. These principles of learning provide guide-

333

lines for the development of effective instructional practice, including how one prepares, delivers, and follows up a lecture.

People learn better when they are using as many senses as are appropriate. Lewis (1980) noted that "people retain about 10% of what they hear, 30% of what they read, 50% of what they see and 90% of what they do" (p. 27). The more actively involved people are in the learning process, the better they learn. Given the limited involvement of the senses in the lecture, the teacher who chooses to lecture needs to recognize the frailty of the mode that relies solely on talking and should attempt to enhance or reinforce the message with visual aids or other methods of instruction.

In the modern classroom, chalkboards and overhead projectors are being replaced by computers with projection screens. Presentation software such as Microsoft PowerPoint (Microsoft, 1992) or Claris Works (Claris Corporation, 1997) are being used to create visual outlines of lectures complete with graphics and even motion to draw attention to key points. Lectures are enhanced by visuals that draw from the World Wide Web or CDs. Videotapes or Quicktime movies augment lecture materials. In addition, a video scanner can allow a teacher to project print materials onto a screen and magnify sections of it. Elmo, a document camera, can be used to project an opaque, slide transparency, or actual artifacts onto a screen. In essence, the use of the technology (hardware and software) that currently exists can bring to life the words of a lecture. In addition, many faculty are now putting outlines of lectures on the Web so students can access the notes from sites beyond the classroom at any point in time. The virtual classroom is up and running!

Cashin (1985) summarized the strengths of the lecture approach as follows:

(1) Lectures can communicate the intrinsic interest of the subject matter; (2) Lectures can cover material not otherwise available; (3) Lectures can organize material in a special way; (4) Lectures can convey large amounts of information; (5) Lectures can communicate to many listeners at the same time; (6) Lectures can model how professionals in a particular discipline approach a question or problem; (7) Lectures permit maximum teacher control; (8) Lectures permit minimum threat to the student; (9) Lectures emphasize learning by listening. (p. 2)

Cashin (1985) described the weaknesses of the lecture approach as follows:

(1) Lectures lack feedback to the instructor about the students' learning; (2) In lectures, the students are passive, at least they are more passive than the lecturer; (3) Students' attention wanes quickly in 15 or 25 minutes ac-

cording to studies; (4) Information learned in lectures tends to be forgotten quickly; (5) Lectures presume that all students are learning at the same
pace and level of understanding; (6) Lectures are not well suited to higher
levels of learning—application, analysis, synthesis, influencing attitudes
or values, developing motor skills. Lecturing is best suited to the lower levels of knowledge and understanding; (7) Lectures are not well suited to
complex, detailed, or abstract material; (8) Lectures require an effective
speaker; (9) Lectures emphasize learning by listening. (pp. 2–3)

In addition to the preceding strengths of lecturing, there are practical reasons to lecture. A lecture requires few materials or equipment (e.g., audiovisual equipment), thus making it a teaching strategy that can be adapted to
a variety of settings on short notice or used by the itinerant teacher who
moves from classroom to classroom. The lecture provides flexibility in
content that can be altered spontaneously for different audiences and is not
dependent on a particular size of audience to be successful. A good instructor will understand and weigh these characteristics of the lecture method
when determining which instructional method to use in teaching for a particular goal.

In light of these characteristics, the effectiveness of the lecture method
can be compared with other methods of instruction. The conclusions
reached about the effectiveness of one teaching method over another must,
of course, always be considered in terms of the objectives of instruction.
McKeachie (1986) summarized a series of studies comparing lecture and
discussion methods. When achievement was measured by factual tests, no
significant differences between students' achievements in a discussion or a
lecture class were found. However, when measures of delayed recall were
taken, the discussion method was superior. McKeachie also reported a
study in which the lecture resulted in higher scores on tests of specific information, in contrast to discussion yielding higher scores on measures of
problem solving. Other studies reported by McKeachie demonstrated that
students are more interested in courses taught via discussion or have more
positive attitudinal outcomes in discussion courses as compared to lecture
courses. As McKeachie (1986) recommended, "In a course in which the instructor must not only give information but also develop concepts, the use
of both lectures and discussion would thus seem to be a logical and popular
choice" (p. 84).

Tatum and Lenel (1985) reported a comparison of self-paced and lecture
and discussion teaching methods for a general psychology course:

The results revealed little difference in course performance for the two
teaching methods, except that the self-paced students performed better
on the unit (chapter) tests. No differences were found between the two

methods with respect to performance on the final exam, retention one year later, or average course grade. The results further revealed that the students were more satisfied with the self-paced courses than with the lecture/discussion courses. (p. 2)

These authors noted that their "findings are consistent with other studies that have shown that self-pacing results in positive attitudes toward the course, despite the fact that there was little evidence for improved course performance" (p. 19), and reasoned that the students' greater sense of autonomy, greater opportunity to retake tests and achieve mastery of the material, and greater personal contact with the instructor during the self-paced course may help to explain their preference for the self-paced course.

According to Davis and Alexander (1977), the comparison of lecture with other methods of instruction indicates that "the lecture is generally as effective as other techniques when the objective is the transmission of information" (p. 15). However, they added, "Lectures are most appropriate for the transmission of information and less appropriate than discussion when the instructional objectives involve the application of information, the development of problem solving skills, or the long-term modification of attitudes" (p. 15). Brock (1977) asserted that the lecture method is less effective than other methods "when students are average or below average in academic preparation or intelligence" (p. 2). Thus, the lecture method is a useful instructional strategy, but is limited in reaching some goals and some students.

CHARACTERISTICS OF A GOOD LECTURE

A good lecture is more than telling, for it involves arousing the students' interest and thinking about the content, it organizes and summarizes key ideas, and it provides a basis for students to remember the new information and generate their own examples or applications of the content. The good lecture must have solid content, a logical structure, and ample and accurate examples. It should involve the principles of learning for maximum pedagogical effect. It should be delivered in an engaging and audible manner with effective use of eye contact, sincerity, movement, facial and vocal variety, and use of audiovisual aids.

At the center of a good lecture is the lecturer's coherent, thorough, and accurate knowledge of the content. The teacher of communication must know the facts, concepts, and principles of, for example, public speaking, interpersonal communication, and group discussion and must be able to present that subject matter in a meaningful way to the learners. Supplementary material, teachers' resource guides, and textbooks help to organize the content and the pedagogical content knowledge for the teacher, but they provide only one aspect of the curricular understanding needed by a teacher. A teacher cannot teach what is not known, and the limitations of knowledge become apparent in the ability to elaborate, define, and explain concepts, principles, and their relationships.

How much the teacher includes in the lecture and how the material is organized can aid students' understanding and retention of the content. To begin with, the good lecturer should not attempt to cover too much within one lecture. The need for limiting lecture content has been reinforced by medical educators (Russell, Hendricson, & Herbert, 1984), who cautioned:

> The amount of information a student can learn within the span of a lecture is limited and the lecturer actually defeats the purpose by exceeding that limit. The data suggest that an instructor speaking at a rate of about four sentences per minute should introduce new material in only about 100 sentences during a 50-minute lecture. That would amount to approximately 50% of the total lecture time for an instructor speaking at an average rate. An equal period of time should then be devoted to reinforcement. (p. 887)

Thus, the good lecturer will develop two or three key points with sufficient elaboration to make them meaningful, interesting, and memorable. McKeachie (1986) pointed out that although the structure of the subject matter should guide the organization of the lecture, it is also important to fit the content to the knowledge base of the students. Brock (1977) advocated "adopt[ing] some organizational scheme for each lecture (e.g., topical, problem-solution, chronological), mak[ing] the organization of the lecture explicit," and "providing students with a lecture outline" (pp. 9–10). Brock's recommendations are consistent with the principle that students learn better if they know what they are to learn. Apparently, students are aided when the structure of the content of the lecture is made evident to them and when connections among ideas are clarified. With nonnative English-speaking students, Chaudron and Richards (1985) also found that phrases that signal "major transitions and emphasis in the lectures [e.g., what I'm going to talk about today ...] are more conducive to successful recall of the lecture than micro markers [e.g. because, then, well ...]" (p. 16). Davis and Alexander (1977) recommended that the lecturer "summarize a lesson or part of a lesson so that students get a sense of completeness and structure" (p. 12). A summary may restate main points, review the lecture objective, and show how the parts of the lecture are related. Providing the overall structure, using language to show relationships, and emphasizing ideas all help students to understand and retain the lecture content.

In addition to solid content and meaningful structure, the good lecturer should incorporate as many principles of learning into the lecture as possible. Specifically, after ensuring that students have the necessary prerequisite knowledge (e.g., through readings, study guides, previous lectures), the good lecturer will establish a "learning set." Davis and Alexander (1977) stated that a "learning set means attracting and focusing students' attention on materials to be covered, arousing their interest, and helping them direct their efforts toward achieving desired learning goals" (p. 5). Similar to the methods a speaker uses to introduce a speech, the good lecturer may ask provocative questions, pose a problem, tell a story, present a powerful quotation, give a demonstration, or use some activity that focuses attention on both the speaker and the subject. The good lecturer provides an advanced organizer or a guideline of what students expect to learn. An advanced organizer previews the topics to be covered either orally or in writing. The lecturer may tell the students why the material is important to learn and how it is related to previously learned material. If the students are learning a skill or receiving instructions for an assignment, the specific procedures to be followed and the salient points to look for or include should be highlighted. Ensuring that the students have the prerequisite knowledge, are attending to the topic and the lecturer, and know what is to be learned and why it is worth learning are essential components of establishing the learning set.

The next principle of learning that a good lecturer uses is to engage the students actively in the learning of the material. The caution is that teachers must be sure the content has been taught before asking students questions about it or asking them to practice using unlearned knowledge. Asking "guess what's in my head" questions or making assignments before teaching content does not give students correct or relevant knowledge and often gets in the way of the desired learning. Teachers should engage students in asking and answering questions about new content or have students summarize in their own words the new information as a means of reinforcing the content. When asking the students questions, teachers should give them time to respond; wait time is a pedagogical technique that is underused. Most teachers wait only a few seconds for a student response before asking another question, turning to another student, or giving the answers themselves. Giving students ample opportunity to reflect on the new knowledge or to incorporate the new knowledge with prior knowledge is necessary for students to enhance their learning and their motivation to learn.

It is important for students to know if their answers are correct for more learning to occur. Thus, teachers should correct incorrect responses and recognize correct responses. This check on student comprehension provides feedback to the lecturer on how well his or her lecture was received and provides a reinforcement for students' learning. In addition, knowing that they will be held accountable for responding in class motivates students to attend to the lecture.

Finally, the effective lecture will be delivered in a stimulating manner. Generally, lectures that are delivered extemporaneously (using notes, but not read from a manuscript) are received best in the typical classroom. (Formal lectures may be read from prepared manuscripts when the occasion dictates it.) This extemporaneous style allows the lecturer to insert examples, adopt language that is appropriate to the specific class, reinforce points that are seemingly unclear, respond to questions from the students, and generally remain flexible. In this mode the teacher can maintain eye contact with students and more effectively manage the classroom. In addition to speaking in an audible tone and using clear articulation and correct pronunciation, the lecturer is advised to use a friendly, lively delivery style.

Although not specifically related to the lecture, Norton (1983) reported three studies on educators' communicative styles. Among the conclusions he reached are "The effective teacher is very animated and lively ... the ineffective teacher is also significantly less friendly, dramatic, precise, and attentive" (p. 235). "In addition, the ineffective teacher is not very relaxed and does not use a dramatic style" (pp. 236, 238). He concluded that "getting others to fantasize, catching people up in stories, and being entertaining are strongly, positively associated with teacher effectiveness in an overall linear fashion" (p. 245). Norton (1986) recommended the development of a dramatic style for the teacher who wishes to be perceived by students as effective. Similarly, Brock (1977) listed factors (e.g., activity, novelty, humor, realism) that "influence a listener's attention, [but said] intensity or enthusiasm may be the central ingredient in motivating listeners" (p. 12). He noted "that a positive relationship exists between the enthusiasm which students perceive that their lecturer exudes and their learning of the course material" (p. 12).

MAKING THE LECTURE CLEAR

The importance of developing the concepts or ideas presented in a lecture cannot be overestimated. Such expansion of the lecture material is the heart of lecturing, for it makes the key points meaningful and memorable. As stated by Davis and Alexander (1977), explaining is "the skill of elaborating on a subject matter point (i.e., an idea, concept, or principle) so as to increase the student achievement of the relevant learning objectives. The process of explaining involves both the instructor and the student; it should not be limited to teacher talk" (p. 10). Research on teacher clarity, although not derived solely from lecture situations, can inform the lecturer concerning what can be done to increase the clarity of a lecture. The research on teacher clarity has consistently identified the importance of (a) defining the concept or idea, (b) supplying both accurate and sufficient numbers of both positive and negative examples highlighting the critical attributes, (c) explicating or elaborating on why the example is a positive or negative example of the concept, (d) checking on students' understanding, (e) using specific language (free of vagueness terms), and (f) using connected discourse (free of mazes).

Several researchers (Cruickshank, Kennedy, Bush, & Myers, 1979; Gage, et al., 1968; McCaleb & White, 1980; Tennyson & Park, 1980) found support for teachers explaining the critical attributes of a concept and giving appropriate examples and nonexamples of the concepts. Hines, Cruickshank, and Kennedy (1985) found that the use of relevant examples during explanation is one of the teacher behaviors most strongly related to learner achievement and satisfaction. Gage et al. (1968) and Cruickshank et al. (1979) also found that students value teachers who provide examples and then explain them. Explication occurs when the teacher explains why the example illustrates the concept or definition and explicitly identifies the attributes in the examples that correspond with the general or abstract terms in the definitions. The value of teachers checking on student understanding (by use of questions or by having the students repeat back what has been taught) is discussed in research by Cruickshank et al. (1979), McCaleb and Rosenthal (1983), and Hines et al. (1985). Hines et al. found that asking questions to determine if students understand the information is strongly related to both learner achievement and satisfaction.

The effect of vagueness terms (e.g., some, a little, perhaps, and actually) on student achievement has been studied by Hiller, Fisher, and Kaess (1969), Smith (1977, 1985), and Smith and Land (1981). Both correlational and experimental data indicate that student learning is impeded by teacher language that features excessive use of vagueness terms. However, Book, McCaleb, and Meloth (1987) reported that vagueness terms expressed by teachers in a naturalistic classroom setting are not as excessive as those contrived in research and, thus, are not related to student awareness of the concepts taught. Another language variable studied by Hiller et al. (1969), Smith (1977), and Smith and Land (1981) is mazes, or "false starts or halts in speech, redundantly spoken words, and tangles of words" (Smith & Land, 1981, p. 38). Although negative relationships between mazes and achievement were found, lessons were scripted to include an excessive amount of mazes.

Book et al. (1987) did not find mazes to be significantly related to student awareness of what was taught, and they proposed that instances of mazes found in the naturalistic classroom setting are not excessive in number or overly intrusive for the flow of thought. In addition, these authors proposed that problems with vagueness terms and mazes may be more related to the teacher content knowledge (or lack thereof) than to pedagogical knowledge or skill. They concluded that a focus on the positive aspects of clarity (e.g., inclusion of definition of terms, sufficient and accurate examples, explication of how the examples relate to the concepts taught, and confirmation or check on student learning) may enhance instruction more than mazes or vagueness terms detract from instruction. Thus, it is imperative for the lecturer to be knowledgeable of content, provide a variety of illustrations or examples that clearly illustrate the critical attributes of the definition or concept presented, and check on students' understanding of those concepts. Although excessive use of mazes and vagueness terms should be avoided, the lecturer should be less concerned with the "ahs" and "ums" that may interrupt the flow of speech and should be more concerned with the content and explication of that content.

Powell and Harville (1990) examined the relationship between clarity and student evaluation of the class, willingness to engage in behaviors taught in the course, willingness to enroll in a course of similar content, and evaluation of the instructor. Clarity was significantly positively correlated with each of the four outcomes for white students, Latino students, and Asian American students and accounted for the greatest proportion of variance in evaluations of the class and evaluations of the instructor. In addition, nonverbal and verbal immediacy were significantly related to teacher clarity for each of the ethnic groups. Thus, this research added to the literature about the value of clarity, its relationship to teacher immediacy, and the perception of clarity by multicultural students.

Civikly (1992) made a valuable contribution to the study of clarity by reviewing pertinent research on the topic and expanding the consideration to include message clarity and student clarification behavior. She focused on the relational nature of instruction and indicated that an examination of clarity should include teachers' and students' thinking as well as information encoding and processing. Her review also highlighted various instruments for assessing clarity in the classroom, although few of them get at the interactive characteristic of assessing clarity that Civikly called for.

USING HUMOR IN THE LECTURE

A descriptive study by Bryant, Comisky, and Zillman (1979) of 70 college class presentations noted that, on average, teachers made an attempt at humor about every 15 minutes and that "in general, most of the humor was conveyed through stories and brief comments" (p. 115). Similarly, Civikly (1985), focusing on teacher self-reports of uses of humor when teaching, concluded that "three humor types were consistently ranked high: (1) stories and anecdotes, (2) exaggeration, and (3) jokes on oneself.... The lowest ranked humor types included ethnic jokes, dirty jokes, putdowns, sexual jokes, and religious jokes" (p. 7). Although a wide variety of types of humor may be used, college teachers tend to use just a few. As Gorham and Christophel (1990) indicated, students evaluated both the quantity and type of humor and concluded that an overuse of self-deprecating and tendentious (biased) comments generally was negatively perceived.

More recently Neuliep (1991) compared the use of humor by high school teachers with that of college teachers and concluded that high school teachers use humor less frequently. He did however develop a scheme of 20 types of teacher humor that is divided into five broad categories: teacher-targeted humor, student-targeted humor, untargeted humor (focused on issue or topic), external source humor (e.g., historical incident, cartoons, photo, article, or demonstration), and nonverbal humor. This taxonomy of humor provides a useful approach to talking about types of humor and studying the impact of various types of humor.

Civikly (1985) reported that "five reasons were consistently reported as the reasons for using humor: (1) to make students feel comfortable, (2) relieve tension in the class, (3) create interest and maintain student attention, (4) relieve boredom in class, and (5) have a good time" (p. 7). In addition, Civikly (1986) cited earlier research with Darling to conclude that "the development of a relationship between teacher and student is critical to the student's accurate interpretation of teacher humor. Without some relational base, students are unsure of the teachers' motives" (p. 62). Although the reasons for using humor may seem appropriate to the instructor, it is important that students also share in the interpretation of humor as appropriate.

The relationship of students and teacher is, in part, affected by the teacher's perceived immediacy (use of communicative behaviors to enhance physical and psychological closeness). The study by Gorham and Christophel (1990) revealed that more immediate teachers use more humor and enhance more student learning. They also noted differences in the types of humor used by low and high immediate teachers as well as the fact that certain types of humor had more positive effects.

Student perceptions of teacher use of humor may affect their perception of the classroom climate and their evaluation of the teacher. Berlin (1978) found significant positive correlations between (a) teachers' intentional use of humor and students' perceptions of a positive classroom climate and

(b) students' perception of the humor as appropriate and positive ratings of the classroom climate. However, neither intentional nor appropriate humor used by the instructor was significantly related to student success in the class as measured by an overall grade. Tamborini and Zillman (1981) examined the comparative effect of no humor, sexual humor, other-disparaging humor, and self-disparaging humor on student perceptions of a lecturer's intelligence and appeal. They reported that "a speaker using self-disparaging humor is more appealing to members of the speakers' own sex than to members of the opposite sex" but "a speaker using [sexual] humor is likely to be more appealing to members of the opposite sex than to members of the same sex" (p. 431). They concluded that variations in humor have no effect on student perceptions of lecturers' intelligence.

In a further analysis of data on the relationship between college teachers' use of humor and students' evaluations of teachers, Bryant, Comisky, Crane, and Zillman (1980) found that "male teachers who used funny stories frequently received more positive overall teaching evaluations ... [and] ... were perceived as more appealing and as having superior delivery" (p. 516) and that "females that frequently used humor generally received lower evaluation scores on competence and delivery factors as well as on the measure of overall teaching effectiveness" (p. 518). These authors concluded that lecturers' usage of humor is recommended, but only for male teachers. On the other hand, Gorham and Christophel's (1990) research found that female teachers' use of humor did not have a negative effect. Thus, the findings about male and female teachers' use of humor are inconclusive to date.

Although the results of studies that examine the effect of humorous lecturers and humorous examples on comprehension and retention are varied, in general they do not indicate that humor aids retention. Kaplan and Pascoe (1977) concluded that "the benefits of humor in the classroom are most clearly demonstrable for recall of humorous examples" and that "general comprehension and retention of a classroom message is not significantly improved by the use of humor" (pp. 64–65). Gruner and Freshley (1979) also found no difference in recall for either immediate or delayed testing of materials presented with humorous or nonhumorous exemplary materials. Finally, Desberg, Henschel, Marshall, and McGhee (1981) found that learning and memory are not facilitated by the use of related humor in a lecture. Although participants find humorous presentations more enjoyable, they do not retain more of the information presented in a humor-related condition than in a repetition-controlled condition. In effect, the authors found that "repetition whether or not through the use of humor enhances recall" (p. 4). Thus, although research supports the use of some forms of humor when it relates to the content taught (as a means of reinforcing concepts), caution is recommended in the use of humor.

As indicated in recent research summaries (Edwards & Gibboney, 1992; Gorham & Christophel, 1990), the relationship of the type and frequency of humor, particularly its relevance to content and tendentious nature, vary in students' perceptions across male and female teachers. It appears that the quality of humor used in conjunction with other immediacy behaviors may lead to the most desirable learning outcomes. Humor can contribute to building a positive learning classroom climate.

CLASSROOM ENVIRONMENT

The physical arrangement of the room also requires the attention of the lecturer. Arranging the seats in a manner that either focuses students' attention on the speaker or an overhead screen, or that prepares the class to engage in discussion (e.g., horseshoe or circle) can enhance the ease with which the purpose of the day's activities is fulfilled. In addition, the lecturer may need to close window blinds to shade the room from an outside glare, increase or decrease the heat in the room, or remove other physical distractions (e.g., writing on the chalkboard left from the previous class). In essence, the lecturer should attempt to make sure the environment does not distract and is as conducive to good listening or participation as possible.

SUMMARY

This chapter has emphasized the need to select the lecture method when it is most suitable for the objectives to be accomplished and the mix of student, teacher, and environmental characteristics. Once selected as the strategy, the lecturer needs to overcome weaknesses that are inherent in the method by incorporating content, structure, and style that utilize the principles of learning. Informing students why the information in the lecture is important and useful and how it is related to other material that has been taught previously or will be taught subsequently is important. Students also need to know in advance what is being covered in the lecture, and they need verbal cues that show the relationship among, and provide appropriate emphasis of, key points. The lecture should be limited in information density to a few key points that are elaborated on with multiple examples and reinforced visually or verbally and through students' illustrations.

The teacher needs to check on student understanding of the content by asking for summaries of key points, responding to questions, or giving students practice in using the concepts during the lecture period. Feedback regarding the accuracy of student understanding is also essential to enhance learning. Finally, a variety of stimuli, including, for example, use of humor, visual aids, or activities, is important to maintain students' attention and motivation to learn. There are many ways in which a lecturer can vary the lecture method (see Frederick, 1986, for examples). Regardless of the form, the lecturer must be certain that that content is accurate, thorough, and elaborated on in a way that assists the learner in understanding, retaining, and transferring the information.

REFERENCES

Berlin, E. (1978). *The relationship of instructor humor to classroom climate and student success in the course*. Unpublished master's thesis, Michigan State University, East Lansing.

Book, C. L., McCaleb, J. L., & Meloth, M. (1987). *Refining a teacher training program: Complementing content knowledge with pedagogical knowledge in clarity*. Unpublished manuscript, Michigan State University, College of Education, East Lansing.

Brock, S. C. (1977). *Aspects of lecturing: A practical guide for IDEA users*. Manhattan: University of Kansas, Center for Faculty Evaluation and Development in Higher Education.

Bryant, J., Comisky, P. W., Crane, J. S., & Zillman, D. (1980). Relationship between college teachers' use of humor in the classroom and students' evaluations of their teachers. *Journal of Educational Psychology, 72*, 511–519.

Bryant, J., Comisky, P., & Zillman, D. (1979). Teachers' humor in the college classroom. *Communication Education, 28*, 110–118.

Cashin, W. E. (1985). *Improving lectures* (Idea Paper No. 14). Manhattan: Kansas State University, Center for Faculty Evaluation and Development.

Chaudron, C., & Richards, J. C. (1985, April). *The effect of discourse markers on the comprehension of lectures*. Paper presented at the annual meeting of the Teachers of English to Speakers of Other Languages, New York.

Civikly, J. M. (1985, November). *Teachers' reports on their uses of humor when teaching*. Paper presented at the annual meeting of the Speech Communication Association, Denver, CO.

Civikly, J. M. (1986). Humor and the enjoyment of college teaching. In J. M. Civikly (Ed.), *Communicating in college classrooms* (New Directions for Teaching and Learning, No. 26, pp. 61–69). San Francisco: Jossey-Bass.

Civikly, J. M. (1992). Clarity: Teachers and students making sense of instruction. *Communication Education, 41*, 138–152.

Claris Corporation. (1997). Claris Works (Version 4.0) [Computer software]. Cupertino, CA: Author.

Cruickshank, D. R., Kennedy, J. J., Bush, A. J., & Myers, B. (1979). Clear teaching: What is it? *British Journal of Teacher Education, 5*, 27–33.

Davis, R. H., & Alexander, L. T. (1977). *The lecture method: Guides for the improvement of instruction in higher education* (No. 5). East Lansing: Michigan State University, Instructional Media Center.

Desberg, P., Henschel, D., Marshall, C., & McGhee, P. (1981, August). *The effect of humor on retention of lecture material*. Paper presented at the annual meeting of the American Psychological Association, Los Angeles. (ERIC Document Reproduction Service No. ED 223 118)

Edwards, C. M., & Gibboney, E. R. (1992, February). *The power of humor in the college classroom*. Paper presented at the annual meeting of the Western States Communication Association, Boise, ID.

Frederick, P. J. (1986). The lively lecture—8 variations. *College Teaching, 34*(2), 43–50.

Gage, N. L., Belgard, M., Dell, D., Hiller, J. E., Rosenshine, B., & Unruh, W. R. (1968). *Explorations of teacher's effectiveness in explaining* (Tech. Rep. No. 4). Stanford, CA: Stanford University, School of Education.

Gorham, J., & Christophel, D. M. (1990). The relationship of teachers' use of humor in the classroom to immediacy and student learning. *Communication Education, 39*, 46–62.

Gruner, C. R., & Freshley, D. L. (1979, November). *Retention of lecture items reinforced with humorous and non-humorous exemplary material.* Paper presented at the Speech Communication Association Convention, New York.

Hiller, J. E., Fisher, G. A., & Kaess, W. (1969). A computer investigation of verbal characteristics of effective classroom lecturing. *American Educational Research Journal, 6,* 661–675.

Hines, C. V., Cruickshank, D. R., & Kennedy, J. J. (1985). Teacher clarity and its relationship to student achievement and satisfaction. *American Educational Research Journal, 22, 87–100.*

Kaplan, R. M., & Pascoe, G. C. (1977). Humorous lectures and humorous examples: Some effects upon comprehension and retention. *Journal of Educational Psychology, 69,* 61–65.

Lewis, W. J. (1980). *Interpreting for park visitors.* Philadelphia: Eastern Acorn Press.

McCaleb, J. L., & Rosenthal, B. (1983). Relationships in teacher clarity between students' perceptions and observers' ratings. *Journal of Classroom Interaction, 19*(1), 15–21.

McCaleb, J. L., & White, J. A. (1980). Critical dimensions in evaluating teacher clarity. *Journal of Classroom Interaction, 15*(2), 27–30.

McKeachie, W. J. (1986). *Teaching tips: A guidebook for the beginning college teacher* (8th ed.). Lexington, MA: Heath.

Microsoft. (1992). Microsoft PowerPoint (Version 3.0) [Computer software]. Redmond, WA: Author.

Neuliep, J. W. (1991). An examination of the content of high school teachers' humor in the classroom and the development of an inductively derived taxonomy of classroom humor. *Communication Education, 40,* 343–355.

Norton, R. (1983). Communicator style: Theory, applications and measures. Beverly Hills, CA: Sage.

Norton, R. W. (1986). Communicator style in teaching: Giving good form to content. In J. M. Civikly (Ed.), *Communicating in college classrooms* (New Directions for Teaching and Learning No. 26, pp. 33–40). San Francisco: Jossey-Bass.

Powell, R. G., & Harville, B. (1990). The effects of teacher immediacy and clarity on instructional outcomes: An intercultural assessment. *Communication Education, 39,* 369–379.

Russell, I. J., Hendricson, W. D., & Herbert, R. J. (1984). Effects of lecture information density on medical student achievement. *Journal of Medical Education, 59,* 881–889.

Sistek, V. (1986, June). *How much do our students learn by attending lectures?* Paper presented at the annual conference of the Society for Teaching and Learning in Higher Education, Guelph, Ontario, Canada.

Smith, L. R. (1977). Aspects of teacher discourse and student achievement in mathematics. *Journal for Research in Mathematics Education, 8,* 195–204.

Smith, L. R. (1985). Teacher clarifying behaviors effect on student achievement and perceptions. *Journal of Experimental Education, 53,* 162–169.

Smith, L. R., & Land, M. L. (1981). Low inference verbal behaviors related to teacher clarity. *Journal of Classroom Interaction, 17*(1), 37–41.

Tamborini, R., & Zillman, D. (1981). College students' perception of lecturers using humor. *Perceptual and Motor Skills, 52,* 427–432.

Tatum, B. C., & Lenel, J. C. (1985, August). *A comparison of self-paced and lecture/discussion teaching methods.* Paper presented at the annual meeting of the American Psychological Association, Los Angeles.

Tennyson, R. D., & Park, O. (1980). The teaching of concepts: A review of instructional design research literature. *Review of Educational Research, 50,* 55–70.

25

Large Lecture Classes

Paul E. Nelson
Ohio University

Judy C. Pearson
Virginia Tech

One of the authors could hardly believe his eyes when, as a second-year student at the University of Minnesota, he stepped into Northrup Auditorium for a Psychology 1 class with 5,000 other students. After one quarter of excellent instruction from two internationally known professors, instant help from an army of aisle-roving graduate teaching assistants, and two humbling machine-scored exams, he emerged with new respect and even a measure of awe and admiration for the large class.

Since that experience long ago, he taught 1,200 public speaking students in Jesse Auditorium at the University of Missouri and taught sections of 400 students in a basic hybrid course at Ohio University. Both authors are former basic course directors who spent many years teaching large sections of the basic courses; composing electronically scored exams; and solving problems of attendance, grade inflation, low-and high-tech equipment, and training teaching assistants. This chapter shares our collective experience and some research findings about the large class.

DOES CLASS SIZE MATTER?

Educators have always had a love–hate relationship with large classes. The president, provost, or dean who loves that head count, the low cost of instruction, and the marvelous efficiencies of teaching hundreds or thousands at once is, in the next breath, telling prospective students and their parents that small classes and a low student–teacher ratio are the institution's measure of commitment to undergraduate education. Myths about large classes include, but are not limited to, the following: the larger the class, the lower the teaching evaluations; the large class bottom feeds on the cognitive learning levels (Bloom, 1976) never rising much above recall and recollection and practically never reaching analysis and synthesis; large classes mean passive learning; and students prefer small classes. If these are myths, then what is true?

Boyer (1987) had the right idea when he said in his book, *College: The Undergraduate Experience in America:*

> The central qualities that make for successful teaching can be simply stated: command of the material to be taught, a contagious enthusiasm for the play of ideas, optimism about human potential, the involvement of one's students, and—not least—sensitivity, integrity, and warmth as a human being. When this combination is present in the classroom, the impact of a teacher can be powerful and enduring. (p. 154)

Size is not the important variable. Instead, what matters most in teaching evaluations, student perceptions of the course, and even the amount and quality of learning is not the size of the class, but who teaches the class and how it is taught.

McKeachie (1980) noted in an article about class size, large classes, and multiple sections that "large classes are not generally inferior to smaller lecture classes when traditional achievement tests are used as a criterion.... Probably of more significance than class size per se is its relation to the teaching method used" (pp. 26–27).

Gilbert (1995) expressed it succinctly: "Small classes are neither necessary nor sufficient to ensure high quality student learning, growth, and development. What matters most is not the size of the class, but what goes on in the class" (p. 7). If size matters less than other factors, then what can the teacher of a large class do to make a large class effective?

A LACONIC REVIEW OF THE LITERATURE

Large classes are used to teach communication courses in fundamentals, public speaking, interpersonal, intercultural, mass, persuasion, argumentation, public relations and even small groups (Beebe & Biggers, 1986; Hazelton, 1986; Larson, 1986; Pearson, 1986; Semlak, 1986; Warnemunde, 1986; Weaver, 1986). Alternatives to large classes have spawned approaches such as personalized systems of instruction (Gray, Buerkel-Rothfuss & Yerby, 1986; Seiler, 1983; Seiler & Fuss-Reineck,

1986), computer-assisted instruction (Dabbagh, 1996; DeLoughry, 1995), videotapes (Rosenkoeter, 1984), and problem-based learning (PBL). But the large class remains, and the newest classroom buildings are incomplete without a large "smart classroom" with all of the latest in high technology educational equipment (Roberts & Dunn, 1996).

That first-year students prefer small classes, whereas juniors and seniors prefer large classes (Feigenbaum & Friend, 1992) is mildly surprising because the myth is that nobody prefers large classes. The researchers concluded that positive experience with large classes can possibly build a preference for them. Another possibility is that upper division students generally experience far fewer large classes and may desire more of them in the last 2 years.

A study of 4,000 courses on 16 U.S. campuses revealed that student evaluations went down as the class size approached 250 but went up as class size grew even larger (Wood, Linsky, & Straus, 1974). Therefore the myth about evaluations going down may be true up to a certain point, but in the largest of classes it may be untrue. In addition, a Canadian researcher concluded that "teaching evaluations are found to be negatively related to class size only if the instructor is inexperienced" (Gilbert, 1995, p. 3).

The current trend is to move from " the sage on the stage," the role played by professors who lecture, to "the guide on the side," the role played by professors who facilitate learning by encouraging active learning. An outstanding and highly readable book on learning strategies is Davis' (1993) *Better Teaching, More Learning*. That book details five teaching strategies: training and coaching, lecturing and explaining, inquiry and discovery, groups and teams, and experience and reflection. People who profess in large classes need to know the wide array of learning strategies that can be adapted to the large class. Davis' book is particularly good at defining, explaining, and illustrating instructional concepts, many of which could be applied to large classes.

What are some means of making big classes a palatable prospect for the receiver of our teaching and learning strategies? The following are some methods of providing shared ownership between teacher and students in the big lecture hall. Inexperienced teachers should select carefully among the strategies because some—like managing a midclass "sound off"—require skill and credibility.

SHARED OWNERSHIP

In small classes students are said to feel a sense of inclusion and ownership because they make up a visible and audible portion of the group. In a large auditorium, the feeling of isolation, separation, and anonymity loom large and invite passivity, silence, and absence. How the professor creates a sense of ownership is one key to success in the large lecture. Gleason (1986) said, to the extent possible, the large course should be treated as you would treat a small one. Here are some ideas for helping students feel companionship and esprit de corps with hundreds of classmates in the same cavernous auditorium.

- Create a class greeting. Reduce the anonymity by giving everyone a way to greet the professor and each other on the street. The greeting can be the number of the course, an abbreviated course title or something created by the professor. We had hundreds of students who would "101" us on the street, but they could just as easily have said "Fundies," "Comm," or "Aristotle." The private language made the students feel special.
- Give students the minutes before class. Just as the mindlessly bored students from the previous class barreled out of the auditorium, our "Mr. Music," a self-confessed music lover from the class chosen by the students, rushed to the front of the room to play 10 minutes of music provided by students who brought the tapes and CDs every day. To any mature adult the sounds might be awful, but to the students the 8-foot speakers were awesome—and the daily music in largest classroom on campus gave them some ownership that they valued.
- Give students a few minutes in class to demonstrate their communication skills. The students in one 2-hour class with 400 students received a 10-minute break during which nobody could leave the auditorium. That break was their time to "sound off," an opportunity for students in the class to speak for a minute or two about anything they wished to a large audience. Most spoke—about campus elections; a classmate's birthday; or campus, state, and national issues—but some chose to perform—aerobics, baton twirling, marching, singing, dancing, and playing musical instruments. The performers became known, and their popularity pleased them. Students did have to tell the professor before the class that they wanted to "sound off." Students were competing for the opportunity to perform in front of a large audience.

FEEDBACK

If ownership can be a problem in a big class, so can feedback for the professor. Generally the larger the audience the less likely the professor is to receive specific feedback. On the other hand, if the teacher makes a mistake or says something upsetting, the groan from a large group can deliver an unmistakable message. Here are some ideas for engendering in the large class the same kind of immediate, specific, and useful feedback that professors ordinarily receive in small classes.

- Create a feedback group in the auditorium. Every professor in a large lecture needs more overt feedback than he or she is likely to receive, so assign feedback. Have Row 10 respond overtly to the class on Tuesday and Row 17 respond on Thursday. Create an arbitrarily assigned group of "101 Cheerleaders" (preferably seated in close proximity) and call them something like "the cheerleaders," "the wildcats," or "the feedbackers." They are supposed to let you know if they did not hear, if they did not understand, or if they have a question. A University of Maryland zoology professor distributes four sets of signs that say: "Slow Down," "Repeat That," "Point?," or "So What?" By the end of the third week, students no longer use the signs because they feel comfortable telling him what they think (Greenberg, 1996).

- Give 60-second assignments that take only minutes to write. These nongraded assignments provide class participation, involvement, and feedback (Harwood, 1996). In 5 minutes or less, have students write down an experience in the last week when something that was happening in their life positively impacted their communication with someone else. Have students provide an example of a communication problem of their own that is bothering them. Have them write briefly of an instance when something they said to a group made a difference. These brief written messages provide a rich supply of examples that can be used in this and other classes. The best ones are brought up in class and discussed. For an instructional model on writing exercises in small classes see de Caprariis' (1996) article in the *Journal of General Education*.

- Have a few students provide you with a copy of their notes. If you can still find carbon paper, give out five sheets before class to students from whom you request a copy of their notes. Or photocopy the notes of "volunteers" after class. Students seem to cooperate fully, and the teacher finds out how the lessons look when filtered through the student mind. Usually, you will spot some misunderstandings that can be cleared up at the next class meeting. Mostly you will be surprised how little of what you said and did is recorded in some student notebooks.

- Be available before and after class. In a class of 1,000 very few students will seek out the professor in the office, but students will approach the professor before and after class. Plan on hanging around with the students waiting for the previous class to evacuate the auditorium and plan on staying after class to answer any student questions. While the students are playing their music before class begins, you are asking and answering questions in the hallway. Telling students that you have "an open door" or office hours will simply mean that few students will ask you anything.

- Recognition and reward. Who wrote some of the best explanations of why people should take communication courses? Have those writers stand in class and give them a round of applause. Who earned the highest grade in the examination? Ask (due to privacy law) the student with the highest grade if he or she minds if you present a departmental ballpoint or t-shirt in front of class. Have 20 students do a message distortion exercise in front of class and start by having them say who they are. In any given quarter approximately 100 of our students—one fourth of the class—have been in front of class for recognition and reward or for participating in some exercise. Feedback and active participation conspire to encourage learning.

LEARNING IS NOT A SPECTATOR SPORT

Active involvement—both mental and physical—can enhance learning (Bloom, 1976; Zayas-Baya, 1977–1978), but most large classrooms are a study in passivity. Here are some suggestions for how to involve students in a mass class.

- Classroom exercises invite mental and physical activity. To shatter student stereotypes about what is possible in a very large class, have everyone do the same exercises that you might use in your small class. In 10 to 15 minutes, 400 students can find 9 other students in the auditorium who share unseen characteristics with themselves. Who is a democrat, which fellow student is a Baptist, and is anyone else pregnant? It is a very noisy and rambunctious exercise, but the debriefing demonstrates a very high level of commonality among human beings, reveals the basis of interpersonal interaction, relates to audience analysis in public speaking, and invites students in an anonymous lecture hall to initiate purposefully with dozens of other students on the first day of class. Most exercises work in settings large and small.

- Exercises can be entertaining, but they can also be highly instructional. Students submit their most painful communication situations on paper, the professor selects one that is particularly well written and instructive, and the class approaches this "problem" as a case study in communication by analyzing, evaluating, and synthesizing. As Gilbert (1995) said, "Students indicate greater learning and greater enjoyment in courses in which instructors examine for higher-order thinking and reasoning" (p. 3).

- Questions and answers. An informal study at Ohio University showed that on average students asked two questions in each hour of class—in communication courses. In a class with 400 students, the number of questions asked and answered ranged from 10 to 15. Active interplay between teacher and students in the large class is an important aspect of learning, and in this case it happened more often in the large class than in the small class. Students ought to be the voices heard when debriefing exercises, revealing the point of a demonstration, or analyzing a case study.

- Games, problems, cases, simulations, and demonstrations. At Harvard one of the authors watched professors present and process a case study per day for weeks to a class of 100 upper level administrators. Communication professors can do the same thing with first-year students. Nelson (1986) recommended that professors use stimulus words or phrases, such as *think about, consider, remember, recall, picture in your mind, visualize, mentally list, what if,* and *summarize to yourself* to encourage thinking. Mentally engage students in a solving a problem, demonstrating perceptual distortion with a staged event in the class, demonstrating roles in the small group, witnessing and criticizing a few of the best student speakers from the public speaking course, showing the power of language on behavior. Erickson and Erickson (1979) demonstrated that most students prefer simulation and game exercises within the large section, and Frederick (1987) suggested that small groups in large classes provide "energy and interaction" (p. 50). The large communication classroom practically invites town hall discussion on an issue or a formal debate about some problem. The class can cheer, boo, and argue with the participants. All of these actively engaging activities tend to encourage learning better than a professor's best lecture on the concept. An old Teton Lakota Native American saying should be inscribed on the syllabus of every professor: "Tell me, and I'll listen. Show me, and I'll understand. Involve me, and I'll learn" (Frederick, 1987, p. 45).
- Provide tutors, proctors, mentors, and helpers. The 10% of the students who earn an A or A minus in our big class are invited to serve as helpers in the big course with independent study credit the next quarter. Volunteers are interviewed, and those selected earn the opportunity to meet 2 hours per week with any student who seeks help in a scheduled group session, help proctor exams, work one-on-one with students who are at risk, and read exams to the learning disabled. Most volunteers earn one credit for 2 hours of work per week. The best students feel very special when they are junior teaching assistants for a course, when they can prepare students to beat the exam, and when they teach a group of students. The student assistants can provide the professor with helpful feedback about what students do and do not understand.
- The incomplete outline. After first providing complete outlines of the class session, we learned that students just walked off with them and left for the student union. The incomplete outline encourages active learning by leaving out the names of concepts, the main points of an exercise, and the key ideas for solving a case study. As the class session proceeds, the students fill in
missing information which keeps their minds active.
- Vary your script. Frederick (1987) suggested that students' diverse learning styles require different strategies for teaching not only on different days, but within each class (see Gorham, chap. 19, this volume). He encouraged "en-

ergy shifts within a class about every twenty minutes by changing both the activity and the voice or voices that speak" (p. 46). We started every class session with student music, opened the class with a written (on the overhead) statement of the learning objectives for the day, placed a break for "sound off" in the middle of the class period, and always saved some piece of very important information for the end: an answer to the problem posed in the first part of the class, the answers to the quiz questions, the parameters of the impending exam, or the way the case study was handled by another group. Use technology to enrich your course with big sound, colorful imagery, and attractive ancillaries to your instruction. Team teaching (Krayer, 1986; Magnan, 1987) helps bring in different voices and so does inviting graduate students, colleagues, debate and individual events students to participate as guests in the course. Vary the script, alter the mode of instruction, introduce different voices and increase the learning.

NUTS AND BOLTS

Fundamental to managing a large class are questions of control, organization, and process.

- The Ten Commandments. Our syllabus looks like a rule book, introduced on the first day of class with all of the solemnity of Dante's *Inferno*. Control is the most basic problem in a large class. Instruction is impossible if a few hundred students are reading the paper, sipping cola, or throwing spit wads. Similarly, you cannot have people popping up to go to the bathroom during your class nor can you have students showing up anytime in the first 20 minutes and leaving after "halftime." Therefore the syllabus includes the usual points plus the official university policy on plagiarism; an attendance policy; the rule that nobody comes late or leaves early; the rule about no newspapers, drinking, or eating in class; and the dates and points on exams, quizzes, and assignments. To underline the serious tone of the class, a nongraded paper is assigned (an example from their own life that illustrates why people need to know more about communication). However, to break the solemnity and the stereotype of large classes, we do an exercise that will have everyone romping around the room for 10 minutes in the middle of the class hour. The bottom line in large classes is that the professor controls the class or little learning will occur.
- Attendance policy. After teaching classes ranging from 400 to 1,200 students, we have concluded that having no attendance policy invites nonparticipation that affects grades. Some students think that the professor's lessons can be more easily learned by simply reading the book and taking the exams. They think the teacher does not care. We care so much that students are required to attend every class. Students' presence is invaluable because they are active

participants in the course; exercises, cases, and demonstrations cannot be done without them. They cannot be absent without a valid excuse (most of the valid ones are listed in the syllabus) in which case they fill out a form (also appended to the syllabus) that they submit to the professor. That means every student who misses class sees the professor, which provides an opportunity to help the student with his or her plight. Every student chooses a seat for the quarter on the second class meeting, and every student receives a few points for being in class. Attendance takes the student helper only 5 minutes, and the math is easy because few students miss the class. Attendance cards can be used in almost any size class, but the paperwork is heavier than using a seating chart and assigned seats.

• Process quizzes, exams, and papers quickly. Professors who delay the return of tests and papers dissipate instructional effects. After a few weeks, students care less about their work and more about their grade. In all classes rapid feedback is essential. We give five unscheduled quizzes of 10 questions each. Students receive immediate feedback on the quiz because instantly after the quiz all questions and answers are read to the class. The answers are binary (all true or false) so that they are easy to grade. One person can check them all in an hour. On graded papers, due dates should be staggered so the teacher can return the paper at the next class meeting. Electronically scored exams are easy to return by the next class period, even in a very large class.

WHO TEACHES THE COURSE?

One of us was profoundly surprised to be told by the chair in his first few days as an assistant professor that "next week you will begin taping the ten 1-hour videos for the 1,200 students in the basic course." Often the large lecture is assigned to some hapless assistant professor who is only dimly aware of the awesome task ahead. That is not an intelligent way to handle the large section.

As has already been mentioned, inexperienced professors can give mass instruction a bad name and the professor a negative evaluation (Gilbert, 1995). Furthermore, many students take only one course in a discipline, and they draw many of their conclusions about the discipline from the professor in that course. Much better that the course be a magnet that attracts majors than a theater of the absurd that invites a lifetime negative impression of an entire field. After going to school for 20 years, how many of the many teachers and courses do any of us actually remember? Do you best remember the course or the teacher? Wasn't the teacher instrumental in developing the disposition toward the subject matter?

The best, not the newest, of teachers should be placed in large courses. Not everyone who is effective in a graduate seminar is good in the auditorium with undergraduates. After many years of basic course conferences, we have noticed that certain characteristics emerge among the successful mass class teachers: They truly love the stage, enjoy translating concepts for the uninitiated, exhibit a very positive outlook, seem unusually immediate and homophilous (Hurt, Scott, & McCroskey, 1978), and are enamored with their field of study. They are part actor/actress, part disciplinarian, and part teacher/scholar, but always they create an aura of energized excitement about their subject matter.

Department chairs should carefully ponder what the discipline knows about source credibility and instructional prowess before assigning someone to teach the single largest number of students who are ever exposed to our field of study.

CONCLUSION

Class size matters, but it matters a lot less than who teaches the course and how it is taught. Although the large lecture does not invite intense, interpersonal immersion between teacher and student, it may produce unintended positive outcomes. As one researcher puts it, "the independence fostered by large classes may help produce the independent, self-directed, lifetime learners everyone seeks" (Gilbert, 1995, p. 4). Some students prefer large classes, especially upper division students, and student evaluations of course and instructor actually seem to elevate when the class is truly large (over 250 students). Negative evaluations of large classes can be attributed largely to inexperienced teachers; otherwise the evaluations compare favorably with the best of the small classes.

Professors in large classes do need to seek active learning by adopting a wide repertoire of teaching strategies such as those suggested by Davis (1993) and in Weimer's (1987) *Teaching Large Classes Well*. We suggest multiple methods of establishing shared ownership, feedback, and active learning in the large class. We also recommend some ideas for managing, organizing, and processing students, activities, and assignments. Finally, we recommend that the best, not the newest, professors be assigned to the large classes both to attract majors and to give the largest number of students the most positive impression possible about our discipline.

REFERENCES

Beebe, S. A., & Biggers, T. (1986). The status of the introductory intercultural communication course. *Communication Education, 35*, 56–60.

Bloom, B. S. (1976). *Human characteristics and school learning*. New York: McGraw-Hill.
Boyer, E. (1987). *College: The undergraduate experience in America*. New York: Harper & Row.
Dabbagh, N. (1996). *Creating personal relevance through adapting an educational task, situationally, to a learner's individual interests*. Paper presented at the proceedings of selected research and development presentations at the 1996 eighteenth national convention of the Association for Educational Communications and Technology, Indianapolis, IN. (ERIC Document Reproduction Service No. ED 397787, on WWW)
Davis, J. (1993). *Better teaching, more learning: Strategies for success in postsecondary settings*. Phoenix, AZ: Oryx.
de Caprariis, P. (1996). Writing exercises and teaching roles in large-enrollment courses. *Journal of General Education, 45*(1), 39–52.
DeLoughry, T. J. (1995, March 31). Studio classrooms. *Chronicle of Higher Education, 41*, 19–20.
Erickson, K. V., & Erickson, M. T. (1979). Simulation and game exercises in large lecture classes. *Communication Education, 28*, 224–229.
Feigenbaum, E., & Friend, R. (1992). A comparison of freshmen and upper division students' preferences for small and large psychology classes. *Teaching of Psychology, 19*(2), 12–16.
Frederick, P. (1987). Student involvement: Active learning in large classes. In M. Weimer (Ed.), *Teaching large classes well* (pp. 45–46). San Francisco: Jossey-Bass.
Gilbert, S. (1995, April). Quality education: Does class size matter? *Research File, Association of Universities and Colleges of Canada, 1*, 1–8.
Gleason, M. (1986). Better communication in large courses. *College Teaching, 34*, 20–24.
Gray, P. L., Buerkel-Rothfuss, N. L. & Yerby, J. (1986). A comparison between PSI-based and lecture-recitation formats of instruction in the introductory speech communication course. *Communication Education, 35*, 111–125.
Greenberg, J. (1996, February). The editor's corner. *Teaching and Learning News, 5*(3), 2.
Harwood, W. S. (1996). The one-minute paper: A communication tool for large lecture classes. *Journal of Chemical Education, 73*(3), 229–230.
Hazelton, V. (1986, November). *Teaching a large lecture public relations course*. Paper presented at the meeting of the Speech Communication Association, Chicago.
Hurt, H. T., Scott, M. D., & McCroskey, J. C. (1978). *Communication in the classroom*. Reading, MA: Addison-Wesley.
Krayer, K. J. (1986). Implementing team learning through participative methods in the classroom. *College Student Journal, 20*, 157–161.
Larson, C. U. (1986, November). *Teaching a large lecture persuasion course*. Paper presented at the meeting of the Speech Communication Association, Chicago.
Magnan, S. S. (1987). Teaming teachers and modifying class size: An experiment in first-year French. *The French Review, 60*, 454–465.
McKeachie, W. J. (1980, February). Class size, large classes and multiple sections. *Academe*, pp. 26–27.
Nelson, J. (1986). Improving the lecture through active participation. *College Student Journal, 20*, 315–320.
Pearson, J. C. (1986, November). *Teaching a large lecture interpersonal course*. Paper presented to the Speech Communication Association, Chicago.
Roberts, G. A., & Dunn, P. M. (1996, July). *Electronic classrooms and lecture theatres: Design and use*. Paper presented at EdTech '96 Biennial Conference of the Australian Society for Educational Technology, Melbourne, Australia.
Rosenkoetter, J. S. (1984). Teaching psychology to large classes: Videotapes, PSI and lecturing. *Teaching of Psychology, 11*, 85–87.
Seiler, W. J. (1983). PSI: An attractive alternative for the basic speech communication course. *Communication Education, 32*, 15–25.
Seiler, W. J., & Fuss-Reineck, M. (1986). Developing the personalized system of instruction for the basic speech communication course. *Communication Education, 35*, 126–133.
Semlak, W. D. (1986, November). *Teaching a large lecture mass communication course*. Paper presented to the Speech Communication Association, Chicago.
Warnemunde, D. E. (1986). The status of the introductory small group communication course. *Communication Education, 35*, 389–396.
Weaver, R. L., II. (1986, November). *Teaching a large lecture introductory speech course*. Paper presented at the meeting of the Speech Communication Association, Chicago.

Weimer, M. (1987). *Teaching large classes well.* San Francisco: Jossey-Bass.

Wood, K., Linsky, A., & Straus, M. (1974). Class size and student evaluations of faculty. *Journal of Higher Education, 45*(7), 524–534.

Zayas-Baya, E. P. (1977–1978). Instructional media in the total language picture. *International Journal of Instructional Media, 5,* 145–150.

26

Interaction Skills in Instructional Settings

Janis Andersen
San Diego State University

Jon Nussbaum
Loretta Pecchioni
University of Oklahoma

Jo Anna Grant
University of Nebraska–Lincoln

Excellent classroom instructors are skilled at stimulating and sustaining relevant classroom discussion. Questions, opinions, shared contemplations, uttered insights, and lively exchanges are important components of well-functioning classrooms. Even a technical dissection of teaching skills highlights the importance of teacher ability to create interaction. For example, the microteaching clinic at Stanford University initially identified nine technical skills essential to effective teaching (Dunkin, 1987). Seven of those are directly related to classroom interaction: fluency in asking questions, reinforcing student participation, utilizing probing questions, utilizing higher order questions, facility with divergent questions, appropriate utilizing of nonverbal cues to reduce reliance on teacher talk, and utilizing interaction techniques to alleviate boredom and inattentiveness. In short, effective teaching is largely characterized by instructors who are competent interactants, skilled in interactional discourse. In addition, the focus on the use of discussion formats and peer learning techniques increases the need for the teacher to be able to not only exhibit, but also teach and reinforce appropriate interaction skills among the students (Cooper, 1995). This chapter discusses intcractional teaching techniques, particularly discussion management, with a somewhat prescriptive orientation in the hope that exposure to verbal and nonverbal strategies for promoting classroom interaction will improve classroom experiences.

THE APPROPRIATE REALM

Instructional Goals

Interactive teaching is both an attitude and a set of skills. The first important attitudinal component of successful interactive teaching is a desire to limit the use of interactional techniques to those instructional goals that are best met through classroom discussion. Many individuals within the communication discipline hold an often subconscious bias regarding the importance and necessity of human interaction. Rather than assign interaction to its proper place in the universe, many hold misconceptions about its value, believing interaction to be a complete panacea. Instructional research documents interactive teaching as best suited for accomplishing some, but not all, instructional goals. The skilled instructor views interactional discourse as an essential instructional tool, choosing it when the instructional goals are compatible with the tool.

More specifically, the lecture method is preferred for promoting direct acquisition of information, particularly new information (McKeachie & Kulik, 1975), whereas a personalized systems approach is best for producing mastery learning of essential course material (Kulik, 1987). In contrast, classroom discussion is a preferred method of instruction for promoting critical thinking, problem-solving ability, higher level cognitive learning, attitude change, moral development, and communication skill development (Gall, 1987). Additionally, discussion strategies assist students' acceptance and belonging and they create higher levels of classroom cohesion (Stanford & Stanford, 1969), as well as increasing student motivation (Michaelsen, 1994).

In his book on teaching tips for the beginning college teacher, McKeachie (1994) outlined eight specific instructional outcomes that are particularly appropriate for the discussion technique. The use of discussion is warranted when the instructor wants to:

1. Help students learn to think in terms of the subject matter by giving them practice in thinking.
2. Help students learn to evaluate the logic of, and evidence for, their own and others' positions.
3. Give students opportunities to formulate applications of principles.
4. Help students become aware of and formulate problems using information gained from readings or lectures.
5. Use the resources of members of the group.
6. Gain acceptance for information or theories counter to folklore or previous beliefs of students.
7. Develop motivation for further learning.
8. Get prompt feedback on how well objectives are being obtained (pp. 31–32).

In summary, in terms of instructional objectives, the discussion method is superior for achieving many higher level cognitive objectives (see Bloom, Englehart, Furst, Hill, & Krathwohl, 1956) and many affective objectives (see Krathwohl, Bloom, & Masia, 1956). Because classroom discussion is time consuming, it is highly inefficient for information transference goals. Thus, low-level cognitive objectives are best met through alternative instructional strategies.

Interactional Skill

In addition to instructional objectives, a second limiting factor mitigating against the use of classroom discussion is the interactional skill of classroom members. A successful discussion requires interactional skill by both the instructor and the students (Cooper, 1995). Interactional skills are perhaps more developed in communication instructors—and certainly the development of student interactional skills is a more central instructional outcome for students of communication. Nevertheless, interactional skills are both a necessary prerequisite for successful discussions and an important by-product of the process. With less skilled teachers and students, other teaching strategies will better facilitate immediate instructional objectives. Often, developing instructors must choose between a long-term goal of further enhancing instructional skills and a short-term goal of doing the best teaching possible at this point in time. Teachers who strive for excellence choose both alternatives some of the time.

Student Characteristics

The final issue that we address concerning the limits of classroom discussion involves characteristics of individual students and their optimal learning situations. A wide variety of student personality factors, psychological predispositions, cognitive styles and abilities, and cultural and gender differences have been examined for their impact on classroom outcomes (for brief overviews of these areas, see Bank, 1987; Debus, 1987; Dunkin & Doenau, 1987; Kahl, 1987; Sinclair, 1987). Because an excellent classroom teacher creates a classroom situation that is most effective for resident students, student characteristics should be considered when deciding to use a discussion teaching strategy. The student characteristic most likely to predict a negative outcome with discussion techniques is high anxiety. Sinclair (1987) explained that high anxiety is not always debilitating in learning situations but is dependent on the features of the learning environment. For example, generally highly anxious students, as well as students with high levels of communication apprehension, outperform low-anxiety students when task difficulty and ego involvement are low. Research suggests that from first grade to college, highly anxious students prefer and perform best in teacher-directed classrooms (Sinclair, 1987). High-anxiety students are superior achievers in lecture-oriented classrooms, whereas low-anxiety students perform best in classrooms with student-centered teaching methods, such as class discussion. Although interaction is facilitative of many instructional goals for most students, it appears to be generally detrimental to highly communication-apprehensive students. Thus, Brophy and Good's (1986) general advice to "call on nonvolunteers frequently" (p. 363) sharply contrasts with McCroskey's (1977) specific admonition to wait for signs of volunteering before calling on the quiet, communicatively apprehensive students. An unusual classroom with only high communication-apprehensive individuals would be taught best if discussion strategies were minimal or nonexistent. More usual classrooms with a mixture of students are taught most effectively with a mix of teaching strategies.

Research on the favorableness of discussion strategies for a particular sex or ethnic group is indirect. Discussion is a recommended strategy for changing attitudes and enhancing moral development, two relevant concerns with gender and ethnic prejudice. However, research suggests that teachers have differential interaction patterns with minority students (Dunkin & Doenau, 1987). Teachers tend to have fewer positive and more negative interactions with minority students. Minority students are called on less, respond less, and initiate teacher interaction less frequently. Teachers also have been found to direct different types of questions to minority students. Similarly, research suggests that teachers respond differently, particularly in terms of nonverbal cues (Bossert, 1981), to students of differing sexes. For instance, teachers give more feedback, better quality feedback, and more chances to get the correct answer to male students than to female students (Barbieri, 1995). In terms of responding with an appropriate instructional strategy (based on ethnicity and gender), the admonition to classroom teachers is a challenge to use discussion methods within communication patterns that deny prejudicial bias. Discussion necessitates more frequent classroom interactions, with this greater frequency creating the possibility of either diminishing or enhancing prejudicial messages.

RESPECTFUL ENVIRONMENTS

Moral Dispositions

Beyond consideration of the appropriate realm for classroom interaction, interactive teaching involves an overall approach to the classroom setting. The most effective class discussions are enacted in an environment where participants share mutual respect and instructional responsibility. Bridges (cited in Gall, 1987) delineated group norms, which he labeled *moral dispositions* and deemed necessary for good discussion:

> Participants should evidence: willingness to be reasonable and be influenced by others' evidence; peaceableness and conformance to such rules as "only one person talks at a time;" truthfulness in what one says; giving each person the freedom to speak his or her mind; the belief that participants are equal and that each one of them potentially has knowledge of relevance to the discussion; respect for all members of the discussion group. (p. 235)

Instructors who use discussion techniques should evidence these attitudes in their interactional styles and reinforce consistent student behaviors. Cooper (1984) suggested that the success of the discussion method requires a vow to let questions "live." Quoting from Frost (1974), she warned against killing a question: "It is a fragile thing. A good question deserves to live. One doesn't so much answer it as converse with it, or better yet, one lives with it" (Cooper, 1984, p. 117).

Supportive Climates

A supportive classroom climate indicates that a mutual respect attitude is being promoted. Gibb (1961) suggested that defensive climates are created by evaluation, control, superiority, and a certainty orientation. On the other hand, supportive climates are fostered by description, spontaneity, equality, and provisionalism. Supportive climates encourage greater interaction, trust, participation, and involvement. Using Gibb's notion, Cooper (1995) outlined 13 pragmatic suggestions to help teachers create participative, supportive classroom climates:

1. Accept and develop students' ideas.
2. Accept and develop students' feelings.
3. Praise rather than criticize.
4. Encourage.
5. Insure a level of success for all students.
6. Listen.
7. Allow for pupil talk.
8. Abide by the rules for effective feedback.
9. Communicate about your communication.
10. Accept pupil mistakes.
11. Don't seek instant closure.
12. Be authentic.
13. Use a variety of responses. (pp. 145–146)

Student-Centered Teaching

This attitudinal profile of an effective classroom discussion leader was characterized by McKeachie (1994) as *student centered* rather than *instructor centered*. Although other names can be used to label this approach, they identify a classroom orientation that encourages greater student participation and breaks away from a traditional instructor-dominated approach.

Cooperative Learning. This technique requires permanent classroom work groups (Michaelsen & Black, 1994). Here, instructors are seen as course designers and managers of the instructional processes. Classroom management is accomplished through a six-step sequence (Michaelsen, Fink, & Watson, 1994):

1. Individual study assures that students are prepared by studying assigned class materials.
2. Individual testing consisting of 15 to 20 short answer or multiple-choice questions taken from the assigned readings or homework.
3. Group testing provides for group accountability and peer teaching. The test is identical to the individual test and is taken and scored immediately following it.
4. Written group appeals "galvanize a group's negative energy from having missed questions into a focused review of potentially troublesome concepts" (Michaelsen & Black, 1994, p. 6).

5. Instructor feedback provides additional explanations before the application of concepts.
6. Application-oriented activities promote the learning of essential concepts or skills, build group cohesiveness, and ensure individual accountability.

Classroom Discussion. Another type of student-centered teaching uses classroom discussion. What many incorrectly label classroom discussion is really recitation. In recitation, the predominant classroom discourse pattern is teacher question–student response–teacher feedback–new teacher question. In contrast, true class discussions involve mutual influence among all group members with members directing remarks to the entire group. True classroom discussion will have many interactional sequences with student remark following student remark (Gall, 1987).

In a discussion mode, the instructor is not the sole information provider or organizational determiner; group members share in these functions. Instructor dependence is reduced, and group norms guide the interactional process. Incidentally, this can raise or lower achievement standards, depending on group expectations. In short, classroom discussion is optimized when an instructor relinquishes the instructor control and authority that are characteristic of a more teacher-dominated classroom.

In summary, interactive teaching begins with a set of attitudes. Effective instructors are cognizant of the instructional goals, interactional skills, and student characteristics that suggest reliance on discussion techniques. Furthermore, teachers who are effective classroom discussion leaders are student centered. They create mutually supportive classroom climates and model and reinforce appropriate discussion orientations. Interactive teachers willingly relinquish some teacher domination and control, trusting mutual influence processes to appropriately direct and sanction discussion behaviors.

Obviously, effective interactive teaching involves more than attitude or desire. Its successful accomplishment necessitates the competent enactment of discussion skills. In the next section, some of these skills are delineated, and practical suggestions for their classroom use are provided.

DISCUSSION SKILLS

For successful learning to occur through discussion, both the teacher and the students must be well equipped with the necessary skills. This may require the instructor to not only model appropriate skills, but to explicitly teach the elements required (Supon & Wolf, 1993). For example, the classroom environment constrains student question asking because of a student's perception of limits due to class size and time, fear of negative re-actions from peers and the instructor, and uncertainty about what it is he or she does not understand or how to express that lack of understanding (Dillon, 1981). Therefore, when students do ask questions, they tend to be procedural or clarifying in nature, or a question in response to the teacher's questions (West & Pearson, 1994). The teacher may need to make time to incorporate learning about thinking and questioning strategies for the class to have successful discussion. In addition, instructors should be aware that minority students may have different strategies for managing classroom interaction, particularly question asking (Cunconan, 1996). With this in mind, the remainder of this section focuses on specific teacher-oriented behaviors.

Questions

Well over 70% of the average school day (across all classrooms) is taken up with questions (Hoetker & Ahlbrand, 1979), with the vast majority (between 75% and 90%, depending on the classroom) of those questions being initiated by the teacher (Gliessman, 1985). Teachers pose questions because they believe that questions "assist students with comprehension and retention, as well as the application of presented material ... [in addition] they ... attract and maintain students' attention, encourage participation, and facilitate classroom discussion" (Cunconan, 1996, p. 10).

The field of education has taken the lead with regard to research about the use of questions within the classroom. Good and Brophy (1987) indicated that research investigating classroom questions remains one of the most popular areas of educational research. Countless studies have been conducted investigating every imaginable aspect of classroom questions. Many of these studies have used verbal coding schemes based on either Flanders' (1970) count of teacher use of questions or on the more sophisticated schemes originating with Bloom et al.'s (1956) taxonomy of educational objectives.

The research generated within the field of education has not produced consistent findings. The usefulness of classroom questions appears to be dependent on such factors as course content, student knowledge level, and teachers' ability to manage the classroom discussion from which the questions emerge. Most educational researchers find no evidence that type or level of question predicts positive learning by students (Brophy & Good, 1986; Good & Brophy, 1987).

Good and Brophy (1987) suggested that the only data that support a correlation between question use and academic achievement are investigations that study the frequency of question usage in the classroom. Frequent questions by the teacher are not only an indicant of active teaching (which has been linked to effective teaching within the communication literature; Norton & Nussbaum, 1980); they also present students with an opportunity to express themselves orally within the classroom. Thus, questions help to keep students on task.

Difficulty Level of Questions

When a teacher asks a question for the class to answer, how many students within the class should know the answer to that question? Research suggests that most questions asked by the teacher should elicit correct responses from the majority of students. At times, when the course content is complex, it may be useful for the teacher to pose questions that only a few students can answer correctly. Teachers should realize that higher level questions may raise the cognitive functioning ability of the students or they may turn the student off to the classroom discussion. Because a large portion of the content of basic communication courses centers on basic skill development, it may be wise for teachers to structure the level of questioning so that most students can answer the majority of questions. This reinforces student participation and maintains a high level of activity within the classroom.

Cognitive Level of Questions

Just because a question is difficult to answer does not mean that the question is asked at a high cognitive level. The research that reports on the benefits of asking students questions at higher cognitive levels is inconsistent. No consistent positive correlation exists between higher level cognitive questions and student learning gains. In fact, several research reports suggest that lower level questions actually increase student achievement, even on higher level objectives (Brophy & Good, 1986). Brophy and Good (1986) believed that "we should expect teachers to ask more lower-level than higher-level questions, even when dealing with higher-level content and seeking to promote higher-level objectives" (p. 363).

An important issue that has been ignored by researchers is question sequencing. It seems obvious that when a teacher is asking a series of questions, those questions need to move from lower level to higher level. This is easier said than done, however. Cooper (1984) provided a good example of question sequencing utilizing Bloom's taxonomy of cognitive learning.

Clarity of Questions

Grossier (1964) wrote that all good questions are clear, and research supports this claim (Rosenshine, 1968; Wright & Nuthall, 1970). An unclear question will cause confusion and anxiety on the part of the student. Thus, teachers should formulate and communicate clear questions to classrooms.

Postquestion Wait Time

Brophy and Good (1986) believed that after a question has been asked, the teacher should pause, allowing students to think before the teacher calls on them for answers. Cooper (1984) warned teachers not to answer their own questions.

Although it may seem quite strange, teachers have a difficult time waiting for students to respond (Rowe, 1974a, 1974b). In a series of studies, longer wait times by teachers positively correlated with more active participation in the class and with higher quality participation (Rowe, 1986; Swift & Gooding, 1983; Tobin & Capie, 1982). Wait time becomes more important as the function of the question changes. As stated by Good and Brophy (1987), "If questions are intended to stimulate students to think about material and formulate original responses rather than merely to retrieve information from memory, it is important to allow time for these effects to occur" (p. 494).

Selecting the Respondent

Each teacher is faced with the problem of who to call on once a question is asked. The research on this issue is quite complex, depending on grade level, socioeconomic status, and the use of small group assignments within the classroom. For the communication teacher, it may involve control of the assertive student to provide all students with an opportunity to participate. Overt participation correlates positively with achievement for older students. Thus, the teacher must organize the class to permit a wide range of student participation, encouraging volunteering and inviting nonvolunteers in appropriate nonthreatening ways.

Misused Questions

Because question research indicates an overall positive correlation between the frequent use of questions and positive classroom outcomes, a discussion of question types that can lead to unproductive student responses is warranted. Grossier (1964) pointed to four types of questions that teachers should generally avoid: (a) yes–no questions, (b) tugging questions, (c) guessing questions, and (d) leading questions.

Yes–No Questions.   Grossier (1964) and Good and Brophy (1987) noted several dangers in yes–no questions. First, the yes–no question usually serves only as warm-up for another question. For example, the teacher may ask, "Does Mark Knapp write about relationship stages?" After the student responds, the teacher says, "What are they?" Grossier (1964) asserted that the first question was a waste of time.

A second danger of the yes–no question is that it encourages guessing. Because either answer has a 50% chance of being correct, students do not need to concentrate on learning but need only offer either answer to respond in some way. The third danger is that yes–no questions have low diagnostic power, in that responses to them do not permit evaluation by the teacher on how to proceed.

Tugging Questions.   Good and Brophy (1987) wrote that "tugging questions or statements often follow a halting or incomplete student response ("well, come on," "Yes … ?")" (p. 488). The major difficulty with these questions is that the teacher provides no additional information to the student. It would be better for the teacher to give the student the answer rather than nagging or drawing the student out needlessly. This kind of nagging lowers student self-esteem and lowers classroom affect.

Guessing Questions.   The field of communication has the perfect guessing question and every communication teacher asks it. The question is asked in many different ways but goes something like this: "How is communication defined?" The question requires students to reason and then to guess, because students often lack the required information to formulate a correct response (if, indeed, there is a correct response). According to Good and Brophy (1987),"Guessing questions are useful if they are related to teaching strategies that help students think rationally and systematically and if they are designed ultimately to elicit a thoughtful response" (p. 488). The major difficulty with guessing questions is that they may encourage impulsive or irrational thought, which can be self-defeating. To ask a student to define communication when there is no answer can lead to a useful discussion or it can turn students into very cynical consumers of communication content.

Leading Questions.   Questions such as, "Don't you agree that self-disclosure is an important component of communication?" should not be used in the classroom. These leading questions reinforce student dependence on the teacher and nullify independent thought (Good & Brophy, 1987).

Teacher Responses

The interactive nature of the classroom depends as much on student answers to teacher questions and how the teacher responds to the answers as it does on questions asked by the teacher. Several scholars have offered suggestions concerning proper teacher reaction to student responses (Cooper, 1984; Good & Brophy, 1987).

Reacting to Correct Responses.   When a student responds to a teacher's question correctly, the teacher should acknowledge the correct response in an overt fashion (anything from a head nod to direct praise). The teacher must be careful not to praise in an inappropriate manner. Black (1992) found that praise is most effective when it is personal, sincere, and focused on improvement.

Reacting to Partly Correct Responses.   A common occurrence within the classroom is student answers that are only partly correct. It is important for the teacher to acknowledge the correct part of the response and then attempt to secure more information from the student. If the student cannot give additional correct information, the teacher should move on to another student or give the correct response.

Reacting to Incorrect Responses.   An incorrect response from a student should be followed by a teacher statement that the response was not correct to prevent student confusion. Often the teacher can follow with an explanation of why the answer was incorrect and how the student can give a correct answer the next time he or she is called on. Teachers should subtly praise student attempts, however, if they wish to encourage future interaction.

Reacting to No Response.   Perhaps the most frightening experience encountered by a teacher is to ask a student or class a question and receive no response. When this occurs, it is best to wait an appropriate amount of time, attempt to rephrase the question, and then simply give the answer. Brophy and Good (1986) wrote that a teacher should train students to give an "I don't know" reply rather than respond with silence.

In summary, the effective use of questions is a major skill in interactive teaching. Good questions are moderately difficult or easy, are well sequenced, are at the appropriate cognitive level, and are clear. Good questioners allow ample response time and appropriately spread interaction opportunities among many students. Effective questioners generally avoid yes–no questions, tugging questions, guessing questions, and leading questions.

Nonverbal Interaction

Interactive teaching involves more than verbal interaction. Through nonverbal cues, the instructor creates the relational messages that encourage or discourage interaction. In this section, we describe the workings of some of these nonverbal cues.

Seating Arrangement.   Relatively consistent research suggests a correspondence between student participation and classroom location. Students closer to the teacher (or those facing the teacher more directly) participate more. One question arising from classroom participation research is whether high verbalizers choose interactive seats or whether interactive locations create high verbalizers. Smith (1987) reported empirical support for a mutual influence. Thus, a u-shaped or a circular classroom arrangement is recommended for facilitating classroom discussion among the greatest number of students (Patterson, Kelley, Kondracki, & Wulf, 1979; Todd-Mancillas, 1982).

Teacher Immediacy.   One cluster of teacher nonverbal behaviors that has been studied by communication researchers is teacher immediacy. Immediacy behaviors include eye contact, head nods, smiles, gestural activity, vocal animation, open body posture, forward leaning posture, and other approach-oriented behaviors. They signal accessibility, involvement, arousal, and interest. Empirically, immediacy behaviors have been directly related to affective learning. Theoretical supposition and indirect evidence support a link to increased student classroom participation. Andersen and Andersen (1982) identified numerous experimental studies that found greater amounts of verbal interaction in more immediate laboratory conditions. Thus, higher levels of teacher immediacy are likely to result in greater student involvement and more overall classroom interaction. This has been found to be true whether the student's culture has expectations of high or low teacher immediacy (McCroskey, Sallinen, Fayer, Richmond, & Barraclough, 1996).

Turn Taking.   Classroom procedures often ritualize interaction and turn taking by having students raise hands to acquire the floor. Students are then recognized by the teacher for their speaking turn. Friedrich (1982) summarized this language game and its rules, suggesting that the rules have remained stable over time. Friedrich pointed out that although 80% of classroom talk typically involves asking, answering, or reacting to questions, only 20% of the questions require student thinking. Sixty percent ask for recall of fact, and 20% are procedural (Gall, 1970).

This classroom ritual is antithetical to classroom discussion. Imagine how dinner conversation would change if all participants had to be recognized by the head of the family for their speaking turn. Even very large families have not typically resorted to a ritual this stifling. In group interaction, participants regulate conversation through eye contact, body leans, head nods, mouth opening, and gestural starts. These turn preparation cues signal an interest in and desire for interaction. More spontaneous systems like these can be adopted for classroom settings. If you feel that the classroom group is too large to be totally controlled by the nonverbal cues, a more spontaneous discussion would occur if the rules allowed the person speaking to call on the next person with a hand raised. (The teacher, as well as the students, would vie for the floor.) Additionally, a second turn-taking rule might dictate that the next comment must have relevance to the previous one. This ensures discussion continuity and progression without direct teacher interference, and it improves student interactional skill.

Teacher Reinforcements.   Although verbal praise is an appropriate reinforcer for student participation, many nonverbal cues are more powerful, less disruptive, and judged more genuine. Teacher attention, eye contact, facial expression, and body orientation are powerful cues of acceptance and appreciation. In fact, it is possible to be verbally correcting of the content while being nonverbally appreciative of the interaction attempt. A reinforcing nonverbal demeanor will improve student participation and student affect.

In summary, attention to classroom arrangement and a greater reliance on nonverbal immediacy behaviors will enhance student involvement. Altered turn-taking rules can enhance spontaneous discussion. An appropriate use of nonverbal reinforcement messages will improve classroom interaction.

CONCLUSION

This chapter discusses the issue of interactive teaching. We have attempted to convince the reader(s) that interactive teaching is a powerful instructional strategy that, when used appropriately, can result in positive instructional outcomes. This strategy, like others, works best when used within an instructional arena that is best suited for it. Excellent classroom instructors remain flexible and choose instructional strategies to best accomplish instructional goals, but will incorporate a variety of instructional strategies in their classroom in order to increase the likelihood that each student's particular optimal learning style will be utilized from time to time. Thus, interactive teaching is an essential but not sufficient instructional skill.

REFERENCES

Andersen, P. A., & Andersen, J. F. (1982). Nonverbal immediacy in instruction. In L. L. Barker (Ed.), *Communication in the classroom: Original essays* (pp. 98–120). Englewood Cliffs, NJ: Prentice-Hall.

Bank, B. J. (1987). Students sex. In M. J. Dunkin (Ed.), *The international encyclopedia of teaching and teacher education* (pp. 571–574). Oxford, UK: Pergamon.

Barbieri, M. (1995). *Sounds from the heart: Learning to listen to girls.* Portsmouth, NH: Heinemann.

Black, S. (1992). In praise of judicious praise. *Executive Educator, 14*(10), 24–27.

Bloom, B. S., Englehart, M. D., Furst, E. J., Hill, W. H, & Krathwohl, D. R. (1956). *Taxonomy of educational objectives. Handbook 1: Cognitive domain.* New York: McKay.

Bossert, S. T. (1981). Understanding sex differences in children's classroom experiences. *Elementary School Journal, 81*, 255–266.

Brophy, J., & Good, T. L. (1986). Teacher behavior and student achievement. In M. C. Wittrock (Ed.), *Handbook of research on teaching* (3rd ed., pp. 328–375). New York: Macmillan.

Cooper, P. J. (1984). *Speech communication for the classroom teacher.* Scottsdale, AZ: Gorsuch Scarisbrick.

Cooper, P. J. (1995). *Communication for the classroom teacher* (5th ed.) Scottsdale, AZ: Gorsuch Scarisbrick.

Cunconan, T. M. (1996). *The conceptualization, measurement, and validation of a student's propensity to ask questions in the college classroom.* Unpublished doctoral dissertation, University of Oklahoma, Norman.

Debus, R. L. (1987). Students' cognitive characteristics. In M. J. Dunkin (Ed.), *The international encyclopedia of teaching and teacher education* (pp. 564–568). Oxford, UK: Pergamon.

Dillon, J. T. (1981). A norm against student questions. *Clearing House, 55*, 136–139.

Dunkin, M. J. (1987). Technical skills of teaching. In M. J. Dunkin (Ed.), *The international encyclopedia of teaching and teacher education* (pp. 703–706). Oxford, UK: Pergamon.

Dunkin, M. J., & Doenau, S. J. (1987). Students' ethnicity. In M. J. Dunkin (Ed.), *The international encyclopedia of teaching and teacher education* (pp. 568–571). Oxford, UK: Pergamon.

Flanders, N. (1970). *Analyzing teacher behavior.* Reading, MA: Addison-Wesley.

Friedrich, G. W. (1982). Classroom interaction. In L. L. Barker (Ed.), *Communication in the classroom: Original essays* (pp. 55–56). Englewood Cliffs, NJ: Prentice-Hall.

Frost, G. E. (1974). *Bless my growing.* Minneapolis, MN: Augsburg.

Gall, M. D. (1970). The use of questions in teaching. *Review of Educational Research, 40*, 707–721.

Gall, M. D. (1987). Discussion methods. In M. J. Dunkin (Ed.), *The international encyclopedia of teaching and teacher education* (pp. 232–237). Oxford, UK: Pergamon.

Gibb, J. (1961). Defensive communication. *Journal of Communication, 11*, 142–148.

Gliessman, D. (1985). *Questioning in classrooms.* (ERIC Document Reproduction Service No. ED 303 840), Indiana University, Bloomington, IN.

Good, T. L., & Brophy, J. (1987). *Looking in classrooms* (4th ed.). New York: Harper & Row.

Grossier, P. (1964). *How to use the fine art of questioning.* New York: Teachers' Practical Press.

Hoetker, J., & Ahlbrand, W. P. (1979). The persistence of recitation. *American Educational Research Journal, 6*, 145–167.

Kahl, T. N. (1987). Students' social backgrounds. In M. J. Dunkin (Ed.), *The international encyclopedia of teaching and teacher education* (pp. 574–584). Oxford, UK: Pergamon.

Krathwohl, D. R., Bloom, B. S., & Masia, B. B (1956). *Taxonomy of educational objectives: Handbook 11. Affective domain.* New York: McKay.

Kulik, J. A. (1987). Keller plan: A personalized system of instruction. In M. J. Dunkin (Ed.), *The international encyclopedia of teaching and teacher education* (pp. 306–311). Oxford, UK: Pergamon.

McCroskey, J. C. (1977). *Quiet children and the classroom teacher.* Urbana, IL: Eric Clearinghouse on Reading and Communication Skills.

McCroskey, J. C., Sallinen, A., Fayer, J. M., Richmond, V. P., & Barraclough, R. A. (1996). Nonverbal immediacy and cognitive learning: A cross cultural investigation. *Communication Education, 45,* 200–211.

McKeachie, W. J. (1994). *Teaching tips: Strategies, research, and theory for college and university teachers* (9th ed.). Lexington, MA: Heath.

McKeachie, W. J., & Kulik, J. A. (1975). *Effective college teaching.* In F. N. Kerlinger (Ed.), *Review of research in education* (Vol. 3, pp. 165–209). Itasca, IL: Peacock.

Michaelsen, L. K. (1994). Classroom organization and management: Making a case for the small-group option. In K. W. Prichard & R. M. Sawyer (Eds.), *Handbook of college teaching: Theory and application.* Westport, CT: Greenwood.

Michaelsen, L. K., & Black, R. H. (1994). Building learning teams: The key to harnessing the power of small groups in higher education. In S. Kadel & J. Keehner (Eds.), *Collaborative learning: A sourcebook for higher education* (Vol. 2, pp. 65–81). State College, PA: National Center for Teaching, Learning & Assessment.

Michaelsen, L. K., Fink, L. D., & Watson, W. E. (1994). Pre-instructional minitests: An efficient solution to covering content. *Journal of Management Education, 18,* 32–44.

Norton, R., & Nussbaum, J. (1980). Dramatic behaviors of the effective teacher. In D. Nimmo (Ed.), *Communication yearbook 4* (pp. 565–579). New Brunswick, NJ: Transaction.

Patterson, M. L., Kelley, C. E., Kondracki, B. A., & Wulf, L. J. (1979). Effects of seating on small group behavior. *Social Psychology Quarterly, 42,* 180–185.

Rosenshine, B. (1968). To explain: A review of research. *Educational Leadership, 26,* 275–280.

Rowe, M. (1974a). Science, silence, and sanctions. *Science and Children, 6,* 11–13.

Rowe, M. (1974b). Wait-time and rewards as instructional variables, their influence on language, logic, and fate control: Part I—Wait time. *Journal of Research in Science Teaching, 11,* 81–84.

Rowe, M. (1986). Wait time: Slowing down may be a way of speeding up! *Journal of Teacher Education, 37,* 43–50.

Sinclair, K. E. (1987). Students' affective characteristics. In M. J. Dunkin (Ed.), *The international encyclopedia of teaching and teacher education* (pp. 559–564). Oxford, UK: Pergamon.

Smith, H. A. (1987). Nonverbal communication. In M. J. Dunkin (Ed.), *The international encyclopedia of teaching and teacher education* (pp. 466–476). Oxford, UK: Pergamon.

Stanford, G., & Stanford, B. D. (1969). *Learning discussion skills through games.* New York: Citation.

Supon, V., & Wolf, P. (1993). *Tearing down the walls to promote student-generated questions.* ERIC Document Reproduction Service No. ED 361 336, Bloomsburg University, Bloomsburg, PA.

Swift, J., & Gooding, C. (1983). Interaction of wait time feedback and questioning instruction middle school science teaching. *Journal of Research in Science Teaching, 20,* 721–730.

Tobin, K., & Capie, W. (1982). Relationships between classroom process variables and middle school science achievement. *Journal of Educational Psychology, 74,* 441–454.

Todd-Mancillas, W. R. (1982). Classroom environments and nonverbal behavior. In L. L. Barker (Ed.), *Communications in the classroom: Original essays* (pp. 77–97). Englewood Cliffs, NJ: Prentice-Hall.

West, R. L., & Pearson, J. C. (1994). Antecedent and consequent conditions of student questioning: An analysis of classroom discourse across the university. *Communication Education, 45,* 299–311.

Wright, C., & Nuthall, G. (1970). The relationships between teacher behaviors and pupil achievement in three experimental elementary science lessons. *American Education Research Journal, 7,* 477–492.

27

Individualized
Approaches to Instruction

William J. Seiler
B. Scott Titsworth
University of Nebraska–Lincoln

Gage and Berliner (1992) wrote, "*individualized instruction* involves both one-on-one teaching and independent study. It allows, but does not ensure, individualized instruction. That is, individualized instruction—its goals, materials, subject matter, and methods—may or may not be adapted to a single student" (p. 448). Gage and Berliner suggested that individualized learning is at times better described as adaptive because it may be carried out with one individual or groups of students at one time. There are many different techniques for implementing individualized instruction; thus, it is our purpose to discuss its rationale, its theoretical base, and several of its most predominant formats.

RATIONALE FOR INDIVIDUALIZED INSTRUCTION

Individualized approaches to instruction began their rise to popularity during the 1960s, and 1970s, and still continue to gain in popularity. Dissatisfaction with the conventional classroom, its basic assumptions, and, most importantly, its lack of effectiveness as well as the introduction of technologies into the classroom has prompted many educators to reexamine their use of traditional instructional methods.

During the 1950s, Skinner (1954) and other behavioral psychologists questioned the usefulness of traditional teaching methods (e.g., lecture and discussion) because they were inadequate for providing the proper individual reinforcement and motivation for students to learn. Many educators concluded that any approach that assumes every student is the same is bound to miss the mark for some students.

THEORETICAL FOUNDATION
FOR INDIVIDUALIZED INSTRUCTION

Since the work of Skinner, our view concerning learning and the conditions of its occurrence has changed dramatically. This change is the result of a system that arose from the experimental analysis of animal and human behavior—a system known as reinforcement theory. We know that reinforcement plays a significant role in teacher and student interaction, and that much of student satisfaction is derived from reinforcement.

The general principles that underpin most individualized instruction are summarized by reinforcement theory. Some of these principles are:

1. Positive and negative human behaviors are learned by means of reinforcement.
2. A reduction in reinforcement can weaken previously or currently learned behavior.
3. Punishing a behavior will decrease the amount of times a behavior will occur.
4. Humans learn to generalize concepts to new and different situations.
5. Learning should occur in small continuous steps.
6. When learning has occurred it should receive immediate positive reinforcement.
7. A learned behavior can be weakened or eliminated by removing the reinforcer that created it.
8. There are secondary or generalized reinforcers (e.g., attention, approval, or affection) that can be meaningful even if a person has not been deprived of them (Scott & Young, 1976; Skinner, 1969).

These principles do not include all that is necessary for the learning of behavior, but they are important to the foundation and psychology of most individualized learning. An underlying goal of individual learning is to teach students to work and learn on their own. Individualized learning allows students to take responsibility for their own learning as well as teaches them how to learn.

METHODS OF INDIVIDUALIZED INSTRUCTION

The most widely used methods of individualized instruction include tutoring, independent and self-directed study, mastery learning, personalized system of instruction (PSI), and computer-assisted instruction (CAI).

Tutoring

Tutoring is one of the purest forms of individualized instruction. When education was available only to the elite and wealthy, tutoring was the main method of instruction. Today, however, tutoring is usually associated with corrective instruction or help for students who are having difficulty learning. It is not unusual for the tutor to have little or no special training in education. In fact, tutoring that is done today is often done by peers or paraprofessionals with little or no training.

According to Gage and Berliner (1992), "although the specific content of tutoring determines the particulars of the process, certain general components are widely recognized. The tutor should *diagnose* and then *remedy*, all the while providing *encouragement and support*" (p. 466). In other words, the goal is to find the student's difficulty, help the student overcome the difficulty, and provide feedback along with lots of reinforcement.

Advantages of Tutoring. Tutoring is one of the most personable forms of individualized instruction. It is geared to meet the needs or specific difficulties of individual students. The attention given to students is generally unmatched by any other method of instruction.

The effects of tutoring, when peers are involved in the process, have been desirable for both the tutor and the student. Gage and Berliner (1992) indicated that the effects are positive in terms of cognitive objectives (e.g., scores on achievement tests) and affective objectives (e.g., self-esteem).

Cohen, Kulik, and Kulik (1982), in a meta-analysis of 52 studies examining tutoring in elementary or secondary school classrooms, found:

1. The examination performance of students who were tutored was better than the performance of those who were not tutored.
2. Tutored students express more positive attitudes toward the subject matter being taught.
3. Programs using peer tutors also had positive effects on those children who serve as tutors.
4. In addition, the peer tutors gained a better understanding of the subject they were tutoring.

In summary, Cohen et al. (1982) concluded, "This meta-analysis confirms some things that have been suspected about tutoring. It shows, as many commentators have suggested, that tutoring benefits both tutors and tutees on both cognitive and affective levels" (p. 247).

Disadvantages of Tutoring. There are few, if any, disadvantages to tutoring in terms of learning. There are some disadvantages in terms of the time and cost. Bloom (1984a) indicated that tutoring, in spite of all of its advantages, could lead to more favorable treatment of some students over others. Thus, he cautioned teachers to provide favorable conditions for learning for all students by increasing the emphasis on higher mental process learning. The lack of training of some volunteer tutors could also create more harm than good. If untrained volunteers are used, monitoring of tutoring activities may be necessary.

Independent and Self-Directed Study

The purpose of individualized instruction is to promote independence. Individualized instruction techniques that allow for student autonomy from the formalized classroom are independent and self-directed study. In both of these forms of instruction, the teacher usually assigns students to projects that may last from a few days to an entire semester. The purpose of such assignments or courses is to free students from the formalized classroom setting. At the college level, independent studies often take the form of research projects or a specialized content area that is not offered via scheduled classes.

The independent or self-directed study often uses a written contract, negotiated between the student and teacher, that specifies (a) what the student is to learn, (b) how the student will demonstrate what he or she has learned, (c) the resources to be used in accomplishing the goals of the contract, (d) the procedures or tasks that are to be done, (e) stages of appraisal leading to completion of the task, (f) a schedule, and (g) the how the project or assignment will be evaluated on completion (Gage & Berliner, 1992).

Teachers should consider how much independence to give the student. The degree of independence given to the student should take into account the student's background, experience, maturity, and academic abilities. The right amount of independence to give each individual student is a decision that must be made by the teacher in collaboration with the student. According to Ward (1973), there are three levels of independence: guided study, cooperative planning, and individual pursuit. The levels emphasize the degree of instructor involvement that is needed. For instance, with students who show little self-discipline or ability to be on their own, a guided study approach might be best. Other students may just need occasional monitoring with the cooperative planning approach, and those students who need little or no direction may use individual pursuit.

Advantages of Independent and Self-Directed Study. The opportunity for students to grow intellectually and be under the supervision of an instructor is one of the best advantages of the independent or self-directed methods. These techniques provide an opportunity for students to do work that ordinarily might not be covered in a specific course or to apply research methods on their own outside of a class structure. The student can be given as much independence as deemed appropriate by the instructor.

Disadvantages of Independent and Self-Directed Study. Confer- ences with students need to be planned and often come at inopportune times for the instructor. Independent studies often require more resources than more traditional courses. It is difficult to do more than a few independent studies at one time, and not all teachers are disciplined enough to organize and carry out independent studies. Thus, it is important that teachers find what works best for them before agreeing to do independent or self-directed work outside of their more formalized classroom assignments.

Mastery

The term *mastery learning* refers to a large and very diverse category of instructional methods. The principal defining characteristic of mastery learning is the establishment of criterion levels of performance that represent mastery of a given concept (Guskey, 1994). After mastery criteria are established, there are frequent assessments of student progress toward meeting the criteria. Students who fail to initially meet the criteria are provided corrective instruction that enables them to meet the criteria on later assessments (see Block & Anderson, 1975; Bloom, 1976). Although mastery learning is centered on the outcome of students meeting established criteria, it is conceptually distinct from outcome-based education (Guskey, 1994). Mastery learning is a method of instruction, whereas outcome-based education is a curriculum reform initiative.

The idea of mastery learning was developed by Bloom (1968) and later elaborated by Block (1971). Bloom (1976) included a strong emphasis on the use of instructional variables such as cues, participation, feedback, and reinforcement. Although these variables are not unique to mastery learning (Slavin, 1987a, 1987b), the way in which they are used helps ensure that most students are able to achieve mastery. Thus, mastery learning is distinct from other instructional models in that it promotes the success of all students through individualized pacing (Pressley & McCormick, 1995).

The theoretical foundation established by Bloom has manifested itself in a variety of specific instructional approaches to mastery learning. Slavin (1987a) described three primary forms of mastery learning:

1. The PSI or the Keller Plan, which we discuss later. This form of mastery learning is used primarily at the postsecondary level.
2. The continuous progress form of mastery learning involves students working on individual units of instruction at their own rate. Criteria for unit tests are established and corrective instruction is provided for students who do not master the information initially.
3. Group-based mastery learning or learning for mastery (LFM) involves a teacher presenting information to the entire class and then administering a "formative test" to all students. A criterion, usually between 80% and 90%, is established for passing the test. Students who do not meet the criterion are given corrective instruction. Corrective instruction may include tutoring (by the teacher or another student), small group instruction (where the teacher goes over skills and concepts missed by the students), or student work on alternate activities. Block and Anderson (1975) suggested that the corrective instruction should be different from the original instruction. After corrective instruction, students are then administered a "summative test" to determine whether mastery has been achieved. Students achieving mastery usually receive an A for the unit regardless of the number of tries necessary.

In addition to the techniques of mastery learning described by Slavin (1987a), newer variations of mastery learning are emerging. For instance, Bloom (1984b) suggested a combination of mastery learning and cooperative group learning. Similar to LFM, cooperative mastery learning uses small groups for corrective intervention. Instead of using direct instruction like LFM, cooperative mastery learning allows members of cooperative learning groups to discuss material prior to the summative test. The advantage of cooperative mastery approaches is that students can use cooperative learning groups to discuss concepts that "are 'at the edge' rather than 'at the center' of their abilities" (Mcvarech & Susak, 1993, p. 198).

In summary, mastery learning is an approach to individualized instruction that emphasizes the optimal combination of objectives, instruction, materials, and time to allow most students to be successful at most tasks. There is less emphasis placed on making quantitative and qualitative distinctions among students and more emphasis on ensuring that all students achieve predetermined objectives. The critical steps necessary in mastery learning include:

1. The establishment of clear criteria and behavioral objectives;
2. The use of criterion referenced tests to track student progress; and
3. The use of corrective instruction to aid students who fail to meet the criteria.

Advantages of Mastery Learning. Bloom claimed that mastery learning can result in higher achievement and equal learning outcomes for students. When comparing mastery and nonmastery conditions, Bloom (1976) found that mastery learning conditions resulted in 90% of students achieving high learning outcomes whereas only 10% of the students achieved those same outcomes in nonmastery conditions. Meta-analyses of mastery learning studies have found that mastery learning has a significant effect on student achievement. The conclusions of these reviews indicate that mastery students almost always outperform nonmastery students (Block & Burns, 1976; Burns, 1979; Kulik, Kulik, & Bangert-Drowns, 1990). In concrete terms, the average mastery student performed at the 70th percentile, whereas the average nonmastery student performed at the 50th percentile on summative tests (Kulik et al., 1990).

Although achievement gains are perhaps the most substantial advantage of mastery learning, empirical research has revealed additional advantages. These other advantages include:

1. Better recognition and adaptation to student individual differences and learning styles (Biemiller, 1993).
2. Increased levels of student motivation toward learning content material (Bergin, 1995; Lai & Biggs, 1994).
3. An improvement in higher order thinking skills provided that criteria are constructed to tap those skills (Mevarech & Susak, 1993).

Disadvantages of Mastery Learning. Much of the criticism of mastery learning centers on the basic assumption that there are trade-offs between time and achievement. This is the basis for what Arlin (1984a, 1984b) referred to as the "time–achievement–equality" dilemma. He argued,

Given individual differences among students and a relationship between these differences and time needed to learn, one can reasonably argue that

the more we provide equality of time to students, the more we obtain inequality of achievement; and the more we obtain equality of achievement,
the more we will have to provide inequality of time to students. (Arlin,
1984a, p. 66)

Muller (1973, 1976) and Cox and Dunn (1979) criticized mastery learning for these reasons:

1. Students may develop a false sense of security because there is no fixed
   amount of time for learning.
2. It holds back faster students unless they are given additional objectives
   while slower students receive corrective instruction.
3. It commits a large portion of instructional resources to slower learners.
4. It assumes that learning must be equal among students and this assumption
   is difficult to defend in nonskilled areas.

Additionally, Lai and Biggs (1994) argued that the typical application of
mastery learning promotes lower order rather than higher order processing
of information.

PSI

In March 1963, Keller wrote in his diary that the PSI is "one of the most exciting and most radical (courses) ever given in a university setting" (Keller
& Sherman, 1974, p. 7). A month later, Keller wrote:

> The education program ... represents a distillation of many things: the
> method of laboratory teaching at Columbia ... the use of programmed in-
> struction where possible; the treatment of textbooks, lectures, confer-
> ences, etc., as rewards for passing through various stages of individual
> study and experimentation; the use of lectures as inspirational rather than
> truly instructional; the measurement of progress by compilations of things
> that the student has successfully done, rather than by grades on examina-
> tions. (p. 7)

Little did Keller know that the plan he described would bring about a re-
naissance of individualized instruction in thousands of colleges and universities. It has been estimated that over 6,000 courses (in almost every
discipline) have been organized around the Keller plan.

Using the theoretical principles of reinforcement theory, PSI is based on
five defining features: (a) mastery learning, (b) self-pacing, (c) a stress on
the written word, (d) proctors, and (e) the use of lectures to motivate rather
than to supply essential information (Sherman, 1974).

The *mastery* feature requires that students in the PSI method be called on to respond frequently and with responses that have consequences. The course's content is broken down into small units of instruction and, unless a student demonstrates mastery of a unit, he or she may not be allowed to move on to the next unit. The theoretical base of PSI suggests that if activities are to produce positive consequences for the learner, repeated testing must take place, with errors resulting in a program of remediation rather than in penalties.

It is important that success be rewarded (Scott & Young, 1976). Therefore, grades must reflect accomplishments, not the number of mistakes made along the way; and grading must be determined on absolute rather than on normative standards, which are competitive or comparative. A criterion is often set to determine success or when acceptable work has been done. This criterion can be set at any level, but most often is set at 80% to 90% correct.

The theory behind PSI suggests that if activities are to produce positive outcomes, learners must be allowed to learn at their own rate; learning should occur in small, sequential segments; and several trials should be allowed in order for students to obtain success. The traditional approach (and the instructors who use it) generally adheres to the notion of either success or failure, thereby allowing students only one opportunity to succeed. For example, in most traditional communication courses, students are given one opportunity to present an informative speech, with evaluation almost always based on that one trial. If students succeed, that is great, but if they fail, that is too bad—the course must go on. This approach to instruction, according to Scott and Young (1976), is at odds with the process by which humans learn. They suggested that most learning requires several trials and is often characterized by a high rate of failure.

The mastery requirement (whether in part or in full) leads to the second feature, *self-pacing*. Given that PSI methods require mastery, they must allow students to go at their own pace. Mastery cannot always be commanded on schedule, because individual differences must be taken into account. Some deadlines, however, are mandatory; for example, whatever are set as the minimum level criterion tasks must be completed within the time limits of the course—a semester, quarter, or whatever.

Given that not all learning can occur with one trial or at the same rate, the PSI approach allows for repeated trials. Students can repeat activities or assignments several times with no penalties. Student are encouraged and often required to repeat activities until they are successful—that is, to learn from their mistakes rather than to be punished. Therefore, the goal of PSI is for the student to master content and skills in order to complete the course as well as to receive a grade according to ability and not according to others' successes or failures.

Units of information in the PSI method are deliberately small. Thus, students are not pressured to learn more than is practical at one time. Tests are used not only to evaluate students' progress, but also to provide feedback on what students have learned and what they need to learn. Moreover, students are frequently tested over shorter units of instruction, and are given immediate feedback.

The last three features follow directly from the first two. Because some self-pacing is required, a lockstep approach of disseminating information is impossible. *Written materials,* therefore, become the major informational source. Audiovisuals, videotapes, computer-assisted learning, and other innovations to aid students in their learning may supplement the written materials. A study guide is almost always required stating the objectives, offering suggestions concerning how to study, indicating relevant resources, containing assignments, and providing sample test items. The heavy reliance on the written word requires that the materials are written clearly and the objectives are specified.

Because the PSI method allows students to use repetitive testing, to work at different speeds, and to involve themselves in a wide range of materials, there must be a means to supplement and amplify the student–teacher contacts made by the instructor. This leads to the fourth feature—the use of *proctors* or tutors. Proctors are usually students who have previously taken the course. They are often selected on the basis of their academic success, personality, and interest in participating in the course. Proctors provide almost all of the individual attention to students. The proctor, according to Keller (1968), is not only an essential feature but may be the most valuable aspect of the PSI approach. As mentioned earlier, part of reinforcement is attention, approval, and personal concern for the well-being of the student. The proctor is able to provide all three. The proctor-to-student ratio (generally 1:10) allows for a good deal of interaction and provides an effective vehicle for student learning. Students find the proctors capable of answering most of their questions and often more willing to interact than a full-time faculty member. With training, proctors can learn to correct and grade tests, tutor, evaluate assignments, and record grades.

The use of *lectures*, the fifth feature, differs from that in the traditional classroom. Lecturing is not a major teacher commitment in the PSI method and is used to supplement and motivate. Thus, the teacher becomes a creator of classroom materials and a manager of a learning system.

PSI has many different variations. Boylan (1980) found that approximately 95% of existing PSI courses use some mastery learning and self-pacing, that 88% stress the written word, and that 78% use proctors. Of those responding to Boylan's survey, only 51% use lectures for motivating students. Further, Boylan found that of 303 respondents, 33% (99) use all five of the PSI features within their courses.

Advantages of the PSI. The major advantage of the PSI method is that it allows learning to occur in an atmosphere that emphasizes positive outcomes. The emphasis is on making students feel good about what they have learned. Students are allowed to make mistakes and correct them, with multiple opportunities for improvement.

The PSI method is well suited for most disciplines and is particularly well suited for teaching communication. Learning how to be an effective oral communicator requires a combination of complex cognitive and psychomotor skills. The acquisition of the cognitive information necessary to be an effective communicator requires mastery of various principles and concepts. In addition, an effective communicator needs psychomotor skills that require practice, feedback, and repetition to be successful. The PSI approach provides students with immediate feedback, allows the flexibility of self-pacing, and provides students with individual help. Although it can be argued that other models of instruction include some of these features, there is empirical support showing the PSI model to be less costly and more enjoyable, efficient, and effective than traditional approaches.

Assuming all things are equal, according to Seiler (1983), the PSI method of instruction costs approximately one fourth that of a traditional method. Students rate the PSI method to be more enjoyable, more demanding, and higher in overall quality and contribution to learning than traditional approaches. On similar exams, the achievement by students in PSI versus traditional courses is higher by about 8%. Students in PSI-taught courses retain about 14% more information than those in traditionally taught courses. Students rate PSI-taught courses higher in interaction and in the personal attention they receive compared to most other methods of instruction. According to Kulik, Kulik, and Cohen (1979a), "PSI generally produces superior student achievement, less variations in achievement, and higher student ratings on college courses, but does not affect course withdrawal or student study time in these courses" (p. 307).

Heun, Heun, and Ratcliff (1976) stated that "Individualized instruction is, by definition and long experience of the authors, a more personalized learning system. Each learner is recognized as a unique person" (p. 188). In a comparison study between PSI-based and lecture–recitation approaches, Gray, Buerkel-Rothfuss, and Yerby (1986) found that students in the

PSI-based model tend to equal or do better than students in the lecture–recitation format in the following four areas: (a) attitudes toward and satisfaction with the course, (b) academic achievement, (c) reduction of communication apprehension, and (d) growth in communication skills.

Disadvantages of the PSI. No method of instruction is perfect, and PSI, despite its many advantages, does have a number of disadvantages and limitations. Developing an effective PSI course is extremely time consuming, often requiring from 1 to 4 years. This may be prohibitive in some cases.

Also, there is a tremendous time commitment required of the teacher in maintaining the PSI format—that is, the teacher must be constantly updating the course to make it better (Seiler, Schuelke, & Lieb-Brilhart, 1984).

The PSI method reduces the number and type of student activities that can be effectively dealt with in performance courses. For example, in many traditionally taught communication classes, students are involved in roleplaying and other similar activities. In the PSI format, these activities must be limited because of the testing that must take place.

There is a slight tendency for students who enroll in PSI-taught courses to withdraw more frequently than from other methods of instruction. In 17 of the 27 comparisons, the PSI withdrawal rate was higher than other methods. Although this is a concern, it is not a major disadvantage because the difference in withdrawals between PSI and other methods is not statistically significant (Kulik, Kulik, & Cohen, 1979a).

CAI

CAI is an approach to individualized instruction that utilizes computer technology to implement many of the principles discussed previously in this chapter. Because of rapid advancement in computer hardware and software over the past 15 years, CAI has become increasingly prevalent in classrooms at all education levels (Kettinger, 1991; Skinner, 1988). The impact of computerized instruction on education was underscored by Secretary of Education Richard Riley (1994) when he commented that it "has changed forever the ways in which we can communicate, teach, and learn" (p. 1).

At the heart of CAI lies an instructional technique called *programmed instruction.* Programmed instruction was first identified by Skinner (1954) in a paper titled "The Science of Learning and the Art of Teaching." Skinner claimed that education was not providing adequate opportunities for students to learn. The philosophy behind Skinner's alternative is that students can learn complex ideas if they are taught in small, progressive steps and are reinforced immediately for each response or answer. Such immediate feedback, in Skinner's view, is a powerful and motivating reward for students.

Although the term *program* implies a connection to computer technology, programmed instruction is an instructional technique that has a much broader application. Programmed instruction may be found in textbooks, course packets, workbooks, and computers (Fernald & Jordan, 1991). According to Skinner (1954, 1986), the basic tenets of programmed instruction include:

1. Clearly articulated learning objectives that may include criteria based on recognition, recall, synthesis, and application.
2. Content material that is broken down into small steps (called *frames*) so that the student does not have to learn too much at once.
3. Content material organized into a logical sequence so that material learned initially prepares students to learn more difficult material later.
4. Students must actively learn and respond to the program so that they construct rather than simply recognize a response.
5. The program should provide students with immediate feedback about their responses.
6. The student should be provided with multiple opportunities to drill and practice using a variety of examples and contexts.
7. The program should follow the principle of scaffolding where stimulus information is given to the student initially and then gradually removed as the student internalizes the information.

Programmed instruction is used for courses in a variety of disciplines, is well suited for learning more "basic" material, and, when compared to standard texts, results in higher student achievement (Fernald & Jordan, 1991; Tudor & Bostow, 1991).

CAI provides a new dimension to programmed instruction—the use of computers instead of printed texts. The computer can provide immediate as well as individualized feedback and can adapt instruction to meet the individual needs of each student (Brothen & Schneider, 1993; Kettinger, 1991). It is clear that computer technology, through the use of multimedia, can individualize instruction in ways that traditional textbooks cannot.

Advantages of CAI.   The combination of CAI and programmed instruction has distinct advantages in the instructional setting. Gage and Berliner (1992) suggested that a major advantage of CAI is its ability to individualize instruction. Computers can easily store, process, and retrieve responses generated by individual students or groups of students. Additionally, computers can analyze the time lapse between the presentation of a stimulus question or problem and the student response. Other advantages of CAI include:

1. CAI saves time that may be spent on drills and is very effective for teaching basic skills and concepts (Barnes, Swenhosky, & Laguna-Castillo, 1988; Fernald & Jordan, 1991).
2. CAI results in higher feelings of self-efficacy and motivation on the part of students (Isaacs & Harnish, 1989; Lepper & Malone, 1987; Skinner, 1988).
3. CAI also results in a small, yet significant, gain in student achievement (Kulik, Kulik, & Cohen, 1979b; Tudor, 1995).
4. CAI has been successfully combined with learning strategy instruction (e.g., teaching students to "question" or "elaborate" on the text) to enhance learning and achievement (Hannafin & Carney, 1991).

Disadvantages of CAI.   Developing effective and efficient programs is difficult, very time consuming, and in some cases quite costly. In addition, a study by Hoffman and Waters (1982) found that only students who were able to quietly concentrate, pay attention to details, memorize facts, and stay on a single task until completion benefit from CAI. Pritchard (1981) suggested that students who use computers must have a specific learning style that includes: (a) manual dexterity, (b) attention to details and accuracy, (c) an aptitude for learning visually, (d) willingness to sit still, (e) preference to work alone, and (f) strong intuitive and diagnostic ability. In short, CAI is a powerful learning tool, but it may not be well suited for all learning styles.

The key to effective utilization of CAI and programmed instruction is the preparation stage. Kumar (1995) suggested 21 guidelines for using this technique. We have condensed those guidelines to the following:

1. Design the learning tasks with clear learning objectives in mind. Those objectives should tap into all three domains of learning (cognitive, affective, and behavioral).
2. Design the material with the learner in mind. Presentation of material should be varied so those students with varied learning styles will benefit.
3. Keep information organized. Advance organizers, small units of instruction, and logical sequencing will aid students in information processing.

4. Scaffold instruction. Scaffolding assumes that as students begin to internalize information, direct instruction of that information is eliminated; the information becomes an ingrained part of the student's repertoire of knowledge.

5. Allow for frequent assessment and reinforcement. Students must be aware of gaps in understanding before moving on to new information. Correct responses should be reinforced so those students are motivated to continue.

ACKNOWLEDGMENTS

We wish to acknowledge Chas D. Koermer (McAliley) for his work on the first edition of this chapter. The first edition of the chapter was funded in part by a George Holmes Research Fellowship from the University of Nebraska, Lincoln.

REFERENCES

Arlin, M. (1984a). Time, equality, and mastery learning. *Review of Educational Research, 54,* 65–86.

Arlin, M. (1984b). Time variability in mastery learning. *American Education Research Journal, 21,* 103–120.

Barnes, J. W., Swenhosky, F. J., & Laguna-Castillo, M. (1988). Using an instructional LAN to teach a statistics course. *Technological Horizons in Education, 16,* 80–84.

Bergin, D. A. (1995). Effects of a mastery versus competitive motivation situation on learning. *Jounral of Experimental Education, 63,* 303–314

Biomillor, A. (1993, December). Lake Wobegon revisited: On diversity in education. *Educational Researcher, 22,* 7–12.

Block, J. II. (Ed.). (1971). *Mastery learning.* New York: Holt, Rinehart & Winston.

Block, I. H., & Anderson, I. W. (1975). *Mastery learning in classroom instruction.* New York: Macmillan.

Block, J. H., & Burns, R. B. (1976). Mastery learning. In L. S. Schulman (Ed.), *Review of research in education* (Vol. 4, pp. 3–49). Itasca, IL: Peacock.

Bloom, B. S. (1968). Learning for mastery. *Evaluation Comment, 1,2.*

Bloom, B. S. (1976). *Human characteristics and school learning.* New York: McGraw-Hill.

Bloom, B. S. (1984a). The search for methods of group instruction as effective as one-to-one tutoring. *Educational Leadership, 41,* 4–17.

Bloom, B. S. (1984b). The 2 sigma problem: The search for methods of group instruction that are as effective as one-to-one tutoring. *Educational Researcher, 13,* 4–16.

Boylan, H. R. (1980). PSI: A survey of users and their implementation practices. *Journal of Personalized Instruction, 4,* 40–43.

Brothen, T., & Schneider, J. (1993). A computerized application of psychology's top 100. *Teaching of Psychology, 20,* 186–187.

Burns, R. B. (1979). Mastery learning—Does it work? *Educational Leadership, 37,* 110–113.

Cohen, P. A., Kulik, J. A., & Kulik, C. C. (1982). Educational outcomes of tutoring: A meta-analysis of findings. *American Education Research Journal, 19,* 237–248.

Cox, W. F., Jr., & Dunn, T. G. (1979). Mastery learning: A psychological trap? *Educational Psychologist, 14,* 24–29.

Fernald, P. S., & Jordan, E. A. (1991). Programmed instruction versus standard text in introductory psychology. *Teaching of Psychology, 18,* 205–211.

Gage, N. L., & Berliner, D. C. (1992). *Educational psychology* (5th ed.). Boston: Houghton Mifflin.

Gray, P. L., Buerkel-Rothfuss, N., & Yerby, J. (1986). A comparison between PSI-based and lecture-recitation formats of instruction in the introductory speech communication course. *Communication Education, 35,* 111–125.

Guskey, T. R. (1994, September). Outcome based education and mastery learning. *The School Administrator, 51*(8), 34–37.

Hannafin, M. J., & Carney, B. W. (1991). Effects of elaboration strategies on learning and depth of processing during computer based instruction. *Journal of Computer-Based Instruction, 18*, 77–82.

Heun, L. R., Heun, R. E., & Ratcliff, L. L. (1976). Individualizing speech communication instruction. *Communication Education, 25*, 185–190.

Hoffman, J. L., & Waters, K. (1982). Some effects of student personality on success with computer-assisted instruction. *Educational Technology, 22*, 20–21.

Isaacs, M., & Harnish, R. (1989). Microcomputer demonstrations in a mastery-based personalized system of instruction course. *Collegiate Microcomputer, 8*(1), 27–39.

Keller, F. S. (1968). Good-bye teacher. *Journal of Applied Behavior Analysis, 1*, 79-89.

Keller, F. S., & Sherman, J. G. (Eds.). (1974). *Keller plan handbook.* Menlo Park, CA: Benjamin.

Kettinger, W. J. (1991, August). Computer classrooms in higher education: An innovation in teaching. *Educational Technology, 31*, 36–43.

Kulik, C. L., Kulik, J. A., & Bangert-Drowns, J. (1990). Effectiveness of mastery learning programs: A meta-analysis. *Review of Educational Research, 60*, 265–299.

Kulik, J. A., Kulik, C. C., & Cohen, P. A. (1979a). A meta-analysis of outcome studies of Keller's Personalized System of Instruction. *American Psychologist, 34*, 307–318.

Kulik, J. A., Kulik, C. C., & Cohen, P. A. (1979b) Research on audiotutorial instruction: A meta-analysis of comparative studies. *Research in Higher Education, 1*, 321–341.

Kumar, M. (1995, May–June). Twenty-one guidelines for effective design. *Educational Technology, 35*, 58–61.

Lai, P., & Biggs, J. (1994). Who benefits from mastery learning? *Contemporary Educational Psychology, 19*, 13–23.

Lepper, M. R., & Malone, T. W. (1987). Intrinsic motivation and instructional effectiveness in computer-based education. In R. E. Snow & M. J. Farr (Eds.), *Aptitude, learning and instruction: III. Conative and affective process analyses* (pp. 255–286). Hillsdale, NJ: Lawrence Erlbaum Associates.

Mevarech, Z. R., & Susak, Z. (1993). Effects of learning with cooperative-mastery method on elementary students. *Journal of Educational Research, 86*, 197–205.

Muller, D. J. (1973). The mastery model and some alternative models of classroom instruction and evaluation: An analysis *Educational Technology, 13*, 5–10.

Muller, D. J. (1976). Mastery learning: Partly boon, partly boondoggle. *Teachers College Record, 78*, 41–52.

Pressley, M., & McCormick, C. B. (1995). *Cognition, teaching, and assessment.* New York: HarperCollins.

Pritchard, W. J., Jr. (1981). Instructional computing in 2001: A scenario. *Phi Delta Kappan, 62*, 322–325

Riley, R. W. (1994, May 25). [Testimony before the Senate Committee on Commerce, Science, and Transportation, United States Senate]. Washington, DC: U. S. Government Printing Office.

Scott, M. D., & Young, T. J. (1976). Personalizing communication instruction. *Communication Education, 25*, 211–221.

Seiler, W. J. (1983). PSI: An attractive alternative for the basic speech communication course. *Communication Education, 32*, 15–28.

Seiler, W. J., Schuelke, L. D., & Lieb-Brilhart, B. (1984). *Communication for the contemporary classroom.* New York: Holt, Rinehart & Winston.

Sherman, J. G. (1974). *Personalized System of Instruction: Forty-one germinal papers.* Menlo Park, CA: Benjamin.

Skinner, B. F. (1954). The science of learning and the art of teaching. *Harvard Education Review, 24*, 86–97.

Skinner, B.F. (1969). *Contingencies of reinforcement: A theoretical analysis.* New York: Appleton-Century-Crofts.

Skinner, B. F. (1986, October). Programmed instruction revisited. *Phi Delta Kappan, 68*, 103–110.

Skinner, M. E. (1988, February). Attitudes of college students toward computer-assisted instruction: An essential variable for successful implementation. *Educational Technology, 28*, 7–15.

Slavin, R. E. (1987a). Mastery learning reconsidered. *Review of Educational Research, 57*, 175–214.

Slavin, R. E. (1987b). Taking the mystery out of mastery: A response to Guskey, Anderson, and Burns. *Review of Education Research, 57*, 231–235.

Tudor, R. W. (1995). Isolating the effects of active responding in computer based instruction. *Journal of Applied Behavior Analysis, 28,* 343–344.

Tudor, R. W., & Bostow, D. E. (1991). Computer programmed instruction: The relation of required interaction to practical application. *Journal of Applied Behavior Analysis, 24,* 361–368.

Ward, B. A. (1973). *Minicourse 15: Organizing independent learning, intermediate level.* (Teachers handbook). New York: Macmillan.

28

Instruction by Design: Technology in the Discourse of Teaching and Learning

Sally A. Jackson
University of Arizona

Curt Madison
Yukon-Kuskokwim Health Corporation

The incorporation of communication technology into instruction presents communication educators with issues and opportunities different in kind from those faced by instructors in other fields. Communication educators share with other educators a wish to use new technology appropriately and well. But in consequence of the special disciplinary significance of communication technology, we also often have the opportunity to make it do double duty in our classes, first as a solution to a teaching dilemma and then, beyond that, as an opportunity to stimulate reflection on the malleability of the communication process.

We see this happening as a natural intellectual progression that starts with the workaday task of getting some teaching done and ends in enormously creative acts by teachers and students. Most of us approach technology at first as a means of improving standard teaching practices, either through literal automation of those practices (such as automated testing and grading) or through refinement of practices (such as substitution of electronic "slide shows" for projection of handmade transparencies).

This initial problem-focused step often has a side benefit: Improvements in practice often open unexpected new directions by making the design features of discourse more visible to us and more malleable. Technology solutions to one problem suggest new possibilities that lead us to experiment even with practices not previously regarded as problematic. For example, the invention of automated grading opens not only the possibility of immediate feedback (a beneficial side effect of automation) but also the possibility of learning protocols that are tailored (automatically) to the information needs of the student. A feature of paper-and-pencil testing, the delay between answering and feedback, becomes visible because the automation of grading introduces a contrasting feature as a side effect. The side effect also spins off other side effects, because any mechanism that can give feedback to a test can also deliver other content, drawing attention to another taken-for-granted feature of teaching, its tendency to adapt to group rather than to individual needs. At these moments of invention and discovery, technology enhancements do not merely substitute for other ways of getting things done but offer opportunities for redesigning our practices.

From an interest in new designs, a natural next progression is to a more abstract interest in designability itself. Reflection on designability leads to reflection on why we choose one design or another, to comparison among alternative processes and alternative outcomes. When communication educators incorporate technology into teaching, their decisions about how to teach a body of content serve also, intendedly or unintendedly, as models for students in how to deploy their own expertise in the management of discourse. The design process, the significant features of the resulting design, and the intended and unintended consequences of these features for the discourse should all be made as accessible as possible to analytic consideration by students of communication.

In this chapter, we mention a wide variety of tools that might be used in teaching communication. However, introducing or explaining the state of the art is not our primary purpose. Instead, we want to make a single major point, which is that technology gives us the opportunity both to redesign the discourse of teaching and learning and to display to our students the fact that discourse is designable. We develop this point through examination of several cases in which technology deployed to solve a specific problem served also to cultivate insight into communication design. Each case covers a specific teaching problem, the significant design features of a proposed solution, the contribution of the technology to solving the problem, the contribution of the technology to students' insight into discourse design, and the generalizable lessons from the experience reported. Two of our three cases involve courses taught in disciplines other than communication; however, their topics (race relations and cultural difference) are closely allied to topics typically taught in communication, and the technology decisions in each case were based partly on advice from communication scholars. Each case shows how instruction by design can be instruction in design.

CASE 1: FROZEN CACTUS BULLETIN BOARD FOR RACE AND ETHNICITY COURSE

Sociology 160 is an introductory-level elective at the University of Arizona on the topic of race and ethnic relations. Taught as a large lecture, this course presents a range of standard communication dilemmas, such as finite talk time, competition for the floor, and teacher topic control. Because of its sensitive subject matter, it also presents dilemmas related to topical and personal inhibition. Any comments made by the students in class would be sure to be offensive to someone as they grappled with attitudes about race and ethnic identity. The professor noted that typically in the lectures, students only spoke in comments that burst out with a vehemence. The performance aspects of speaking before such a large number of fellow students inhibited commentary other than short statements within politically correct positions. Most students were reluctant to express thoughts that might be offensive to others in some unknown way and reluctant to open themselves to ridicule. The need to get opinions opened to inspection in an active, engaging way for a class of more than 300 students was a pressing requirement.

In the spring of 1994, the Communication Collaboratory entered into an arrangement with the course professor to try to meet this requirement and to evaluate the outcomes. An electronic bulletin board (BBS) devoted to discussion of the course content was created as a collaborative effort by Alfonso Morales (from sociology) and Curt Madison (from the Collaboratory). "Frozen Cactus" (so named because users in Alaska were encouraged to join the discussion with the students in Tucson) operated entirely from a simple 486 PC sitting on a desktop. The BBS worked in conjunction with the twice-weekly lecture, so it was an enhancement rather than a substitute for in-class discussion. Students accessed the bulletin board from on-campus computer labs or through their own dial-up e-mail accounts from home.

Significant Discourse Design Features

Two features of the BBS stand out as significant for this large lecture class: asynchrony and anonymity. These features do not replicate face-to-face teaching but seek to improve on it (Turoff, 1995).

Asynchrony is the capacity of the system to accept contributions to a discussion without regard to the time they are made. There is no difference to the look and feel of a comment if it is made 2 minutes or 2 days after a previous comment. For purposes of course-related conversation, asynchrony had several specifiable advantages. First, the BBS was always available for use. Students could ruminate over in-class discussions as long as they liked and then post a comment. Second, the BBS kept archives of the conversations. Students could read old comments and continue a thread over the course of several weeks without loss of freshness. Finally, the BBS eliminated pressure to respond in the next turn position. Free from the need to position contributions in a synchronous stream of talk whose relevance recedes inexorably into the past, students could take as long as they liked to compose a comment without risking the loss of a conversational hook to hang it on. They might even find other discussion threads relevant to the elaboration of their points. Issues tended to get examined and reexamined from many perspectives. Topic control dominance based on speech style and facility with English diminished.

Anonymity was designed into the system through use of pseudonyms chosen by the students and knowable only to the instructor and system operator. When a student is identified as the author of a comment, the comment has implications for social identity, some of which are outside the student's control. Some such implications are intended and desired (e.g., solidarity with a social group). Others are imposed as speakers are cast into undesirable stereotypes by listeners. Because social identities are vulnerable and hard-won, they cannot be risked without concern. Multiple and potentially conflicting goals of creating positive social identity while expressing poignant insights create difficulties inhibiting to candid contributions. Especially for this class, the identity risks inherent in discussion of the course topics posed threats to the very purpose of the course by suppressing the externalization of views that needed to be aired and critiqued. Anonymity greatly reduced these risks.

Frozen Cactus as a Solution to Dilemmas of Practice

Recall that the dilemmas of practice motivating Frozen Cactus had to do mainly with constraints on amount and kind of talk by students. Considered simply as a response to these dilemmas, Frozen Cactus was an unqualified success. During the 6 weeks of operation in conjunction with the course, 16,282 messages were posted to 23 separate discussion rooms by more than 450 users. To give a point of reference, 16,000 oral comments taking 1 minute each would exhaust six semester-long courses. Frozen Cactus expanded talk time by a very large multiple of what would be possible in the confines of 3 contact hours weekly. Much of this talk was voluntary. Students were encouraged to post messages to the message rooms by the chance to earn extra credit toward a better grade. However, nearly all students soon passed the maximum number of postings for credit and continued in the interaction just for the sake of the talk. More important, the bulletin board changed the quality of interaction.

First, the freedoms associated with anonymity allowed and encouraged explorations into risky areas that would have been more inhibited in public discussion. For discussion of race and ethnicity, getting negative stereotypes and other unsympathetic opinions expressed is an important step toward more positive viewpoints, but from a communication perspective, it is preferable to get this done in a fashion that does not commit individuals to sustained defense of initial positions. Anonymous posting allowed very controversial views to be expressed and discussed.

Second, the asynchronous format allowed for very extended elaboration of topics. Frozen Cactus was divided into "rooms," each devoted to a different topic, and within these rooms topical threads could be introduced and discussed over long periods of time. One such thread concerned a demonstration done in class by the professor. Claiming that the departmental copier had broken, the professor passed out his limited supply of midterm study guides to groups defined in terms of history of oppression, with the most oppressed groups (brown-skinned women) served first and the most privileged groups (White men) served last.

Over an 8-day period this incident was discussed exhaustively. The earliest comments recorded emotional reactions to the demonstration, which led to reframings of the demonstration as a representation of much more consequential real-world processes, which led in turn to discussion of the real-world processes the demonstration called into question. The advantage of the asynchronous discussion was evident in sustained involvement and depth.

Frozen Cactus as Instructive About Design

At the end of the 6-week period in which the bulletin board was active in Sociology 160, the students were given 2 days to register their comments about using the system. All of the 135 comments were favorable. Despite the awkward interface of the BBS that prevented online editing and spell checking, the students became very involved in the content dialogue. They appreciated being able to speak their piece and find responses from people they would not otherwise interact with. They also learned lessons about the way discourse design affects the content of what is discussed, as is clear from a sample of their postings on the last days. Students commented not only on their own feelings about participation, but also on the ways the design of the system allowed for a change in the quality of discussion. Access to others' attitudes and ability to express opinions freely were advantages mentioned over and over. One student expressed hope that the system would be used more widely because "it can help a lot of people who can't have open, objective, adult discussions with other strangers." Another described it as "one of the coolest things I've ever done" and gave as a reason that "it gives us a chance to respond to each other without all of that annoying yelling."

Lessons for Other Courses in Other Subjects

Most large lecture classes do not exploit the resource of student-to-student discourse, with the consequence that participation is uneven and limited and students have little chance to compare themselves with a group norm. Asynchronous discussion provides practical means to encourage student dialogue about course content. The BBS used in Sociology 160 offered anonymity and topical threading, and these are just two of many features that could be manipulated to adapt the discussion format to the special needs of the course.

Other resources available to serve this same function are electronic mailing lists for classes (listservs), conferencing systems, and chat environments. Electronic mailing lists allow the instructor and the students in a class to send mail to every other participant; however, any organization of class-related mail is left in the hands of each individual student. A conferencing system typically offers archiving and threading of messages posted, and students visit the conference for planful participation rather than receiving messages one at a time in mail. Chat environments allow synchronous conversation online and may also keep archives of conversations.

Almost every college computer center will support some form of asynchronous online communication. Where this is not the case, the most natural champions of such resources are communication faculty. At Arizona, we felt strongly enough about this to support a BBS directly through the Communication Collaboratory and to participate in the selection of a centrally supported commercial conferencing system for the campus.

CASE 2: ONLINE LABS IN STATISTICS
AND RESEARCH DESIGN

Communication 280 and 281 are undergraduate courses in research methods (Laboratory Methods and Field Methods) required of all communication majors at the University of Arizona. Each enrolls over 200 students at each offering, structured as 2 hours of lecture and 1 hour of discussion (in groups of 25) weekly. The purpose of these two courses is to prepare students to reason about social science data, partly to support other courses in the curriculum that are heavily dependent on empirical research (such as social influence) and partly to equip students to speak as experts in real-world situations requiring confrontation with empirical reports or with quantitative data (such as interpretation of poll data and design of opinion surveys).

Preparing students for what they will actually be expected to do with methodological concepts is very challenging in courses organized as large lectures. What is desired is very active and very extensive practice in social scientific reasoning, most ideally a dialogue designed to advance toward disciplined reasoning practices through examination and refinement of commonsense reasoning practices. For example, most people do not naturally reason well about randomness, but their reasoning about random events and random fluctuations can be improved both through dialogue and through direct experience.

However, a large lecture format offers limited opportunities for students to engage in active discussion of data and argument over interpretations, and it offers even more limited opportunities for the lecturer to assess the current understandings of the students and leverage those understandings into steps toward disciplined thought. Discussion sections with smaller groups multiply the talk time available to each individual student, although not enough, and although this improves the students' opportunities to speak, it does not improve the lecturer's access to the students' understandings.

Significant Discourse Design Features

We pointed out earlier that asynchronous discussion tools like bulletin boards can help to turn a finite amount of talk time into an indefinitely expandable discussion space. For the purposes of Communication 280 and 281, more was needed than a mere increase in opportunities to talk. Helping students learn to reason as experts within a discipline requires discourse specifically structured to draw attention to the ways in which disciplined reasoning practices contrast with personal opinion and common sense.

Bulletin boards and other open discussion formats are not designed to do this. One of the most useful features of a bulletin board or other open discussion is that it lets students see many different equally reasonable opinions expressed. However, where the objective is to try to advance toward disciplined thought and expression, open discussion formats run the risk of teaching an unintended lesson that most social science questions can be answered intuitively and that different intuitions on these questions are merely matters of opinion.

For the communication research sequence, we wanted a more structured dialogue type, designed for progression toward disciplined reasoning. Interactive lesson protocols were developed for delivery over the World Wide Web, within a Web course construction kit (POLIS) developed in the Communication Collaboratory. POLIS lesson protocols are replicable structures that allow for standard dialogue types in which students write short open-ended responses to prompts arranged in some strategically determined order. For example, one common protocol (fashioned as a kind of online recitation) asks a question, takes the student's answer, returns the student's answer juxtaposed with an expert model, and asks for the student's observations about the differences between the contributed answer and the model answer. Unlike bulletin boards or other conferencing systems, POLIS protocols allow every student to respond to every prompt as if they are the first to answer, but then to have the benefit of others' answers after giving their own.

For Communication 280 and 281 as presently taught, students complete one or more POLIS lessons weekly as a substitute for discussion in small sections. Lab space is reserved for students who wish to do lessons with a teaching assistant present, but students are allowed to work online from any Internet connection.

POLIS Lesson Protocols as a Solution to Dilemmas of Practice

The main objectives were to engage students actively in analysis and application and to make their current understandings available to the lecturer. Having students write open-ended responses to several distinct questions each week provided a very high level of activity, as compared with earlier teaching strategies dependent on discussion during the 3 hours of class meetings weekly. Archiving student responses and making these accessible on the World Wide Web returns information to the instructor day to day, at a level rarely possible in large lecture classes. Sampling through lists of student responses to the weekly questions, and especially through the students' comments on how their own responses compared to the expert models, provides a very rich picture of how the class understands the course concepts.

As compared with guided discussion in class, online POLIS protocols have several distinct advantages associated with built-in or optional design features. First, every student is active; they cannot simply listen as other students respond to the lecturer's questions. Second, every student can have immediate feedback if the instructor chooses to provide a model answer. Third, students can have the benefit of seeing a very diverse range of other students' answers to the same prompt whenever the instructor chooses for student responses to be displayed to the Web. Fourth, the instructor can see how all of the students are doing, not just how a few volunteers in class are thinking about the material. With the pervasive use of POLIS lessons in these two courses, we have been able to guarantee against passive processing and to assure that students will at least attempt the active application of concepts often treated simply as vocabulary.

POLIS Lesson Protocols as Instructive About Design

Communication 280 and 281 are designed to teach students about research methods, not to teach them about communication technology or its role in discourse design. However, the technology solutions created for these courses are quite striking in their effects on students, and many students have considered the use of the POLIS lesson protocols to be the most important feature of the classes. Students frequently comment on how unusual it is to have course work that requires personal use of class concepts and on the importance of active engagement both to learning and to a sense of relevance. Consistent with our general philosophy that communication instructors should use their technology solutions to draw attention to design features and their interactional consequences, we take every opportunity to draw attention to the design decisions we have made and to encourage reflection on the designs themselves. For example, in the methods courses, we often build lessons around such questions as whether online instruction improves learning outcomes. These "incidental" mentions of design do not appear as formal discussion of design, but they nevertheless help students to begin thinking of design as something chosen strategically, as something for which they personally have expertise to contribute.

Web-based instruction is presently undergoing rapid evolution (Harasim, Calvert, & Groencbocr, 1997; Khan, 1997; Reeves & Reeves,

1997; Relan & Gillani, 1997). POLIS itself has evolved from a set of protocols built for daily use in these courses into a campuswide support system
managed by the university computer center. During the 1996–1997 academic year, over 80 courses used the system. The generalized use of POLIS
is another resource we can employ to help our students to build a sense of
disciplinary expertise: Knowing that a system designed within their own
circle of acquaintance is the principal instructional support tool offered to
other disciplines can help our students envision themselves as innovators,
and as potential discourse designers.

Lessons for Other Courses on Other Subjects

The use of online lesson protocols in these courses points to the possibility
of making large lecture classes highly interactive. Methods courses are
only one common course type that can profit from this solution. At Arizona,
online protocols of this type have also been used extensively in argumentation class (to support practice in analysis of argument and identification of
fallacies), in public speaking (to support anonymous student-to-student
feedback on speeches), in organizational communication (to substitute for
recitation-style in-class discussion of readings), and in many other classes.

What has made such pervasive use of online protocols possible is POLIS
(http://www.u.arizona.edu/ic/polis). POLIS supplies scripting and programming so instructors need only contribute content. Other similar systems such as TopClass (http://www.wbtsystems.com) can be used to do
some of the same things. To find up-to-date information on availability or
comparative quality of different Web course kits, search the world wide
web using such resources as Altavista (http://altavista.digital.com). Print
resources on instructional technology age very quickly, and even electronic
lists change location often enough that it is best to simply get used to making frequent searches for the material needed at the time of need.

Where no Web authoring tool comparable to POLIS is available, it is
possible to return the insights learned through invention of online protocols back to the classroom and achieve some advantages with no technology support at all. For example, the recitation-style lesson we have found
so useful can be emulated in the classroom by having students work in
pairs, taking turns answering questions for which the partner holds a suggested standard answer. A series of application dialogues of this kind, incorporated into daily class meetings, loses only one feature of the online
version, the capacity to archive the student responses, maintaining active
engagement, immediate feedback, and internalization of expert standards
for performance.

CASE 3: DISTRIBUTED CLASSROOM
FOR EXAMINATION OF CULTURE

A combination of budget reductions, drops in student enrollment, and the desire to improve the quality of instruction in Alaska led to an audacious experiment in distributed learning during the fall of 1995. A partnership of education and telecommunication organizations delivered a university class via two-way video and two-way audio. The project broke new ground in Alaska by combining the Public Broadcasting System (PBS) open broadcast system with a closed-circuit compressed video network. Success depended on close cooperation among the administrations of all three major campuses of the university system, commercial telecommunication providers, and the university licensed PBS station. One concern in the design of the first protoype was to show how distributed learning could do more than just deliver information from the university to the rural villages and to show how collaborative learning structures could be implemented in distributed classrooms. Collaborative learning has as distinctive elements (a) elicitation of students' tacit knowledge about a subject; (b) acknowledgment of personal perspectives as valid beginnings for the construction of new knowledge; and (c) opportunities for alternation among such roles as learner, leader, researcher, skeptic, advocate, and so on (Bensusan, 1997; Ryder & Hughes, 1997).

The course chosen for the Alaska partnership demonstration was Alaska Native Studies 461 (Native Ways of Knowing). Taught by philosophy professor Oscar Kawagley, the course sought to cultivate empathic understanding of Native American epistemology. The course attracted 36 enrolled students taking part from Fairbanks, Anchorage, Barrow, Bethel, and Juneau. Hundreds of nonenrolled viewers throughout the state watched the course on the PBS network.

In addition to administration and faculty concerns for providing learning opportunities, bringing technology to bear on this problem required solving broad physical and cultural barriers. Fifteen hundred roadless miles separated students in the demonstration course, precluding even an initial class meeting for getting acquainted. The absence of comprehensive fiber-optic or microwave relay network across the state forced reliance on satellite-based delivery, a newly developing infrastructure. To these inhibiting physical and technical challenges, distance instruction in Alaska adds a distinct cross-cultural challenge: Rural students include many Inupiaq and Yup'ik Eskimos; Aleuts; and Athabaskan, Tlingit, Haida, and Tsimshian Indians.

Because the available bandwidth in the compressed video network was not sufficient to provide acceptable picture quality for preproduced video interview segments, project planners decided to use the normal television broadcast mode to deliver the class. This choice had enormous impact on the learning environment. Open broadcast resulted in the unanticipated consequence of an unenrolled audience throughout Alaska. Nielson ratings pegged this audience at over 1,000 viewers in Anchorage and Fairbanks alone.

Given the controversial nature of some of the course topics related to religion and ethnic relations, the instructor was especially committed to stimulating students' interest in each other's ideas by creating an attitude of respect and trust among them. At the same time, however, the instructor and students were on live public television attracting a large audience who vicariously and voyeuristically witnessed their struggles.

Significant Discourse Design Features

The distributed classroom constructed of two-way audio and video communication and open broadcast had two significant design features: first, the ability of students to participate from a local context, and second, the partial inclusion of an unenrolled audience.

Participation From Within a Local Context. An essential feature of this project was the distributed nature of the "classroom." Students, most of whom were older than the typical college student and already had families and jobs, could remain in their physical and cultural contexts whenever they stepped outside the virtual room. Although the project was meant to provide integration of the system and greater accessibility for the students, it also allowed students to avoid the disruption caused by having to relocate to a somewhat foreign environment. Further, it removed the stigma often associated with students returning to their villages as half-assimilated urban dwellers.

Rather than seek homogenization of the student cohort through placement in a common context, the distributed classroom drew on the resources of the local context to embed concepts in lived experience and to give authentic contrasts between localities. The expectation in collaborative learning is that each student contributes uniquely to the process. Students in this course were encouraged to view the multiple sites as an expansion of the resources available to the group. Instead of the usual difficulties diverse learners face in relating course content to their personal circumstances, the students' contextual interpretations of all the ideas were explicitly discussed. Students were encouraged to talk over course materials with other members of the community as well as to interview local elders and attend local events to report back to the class.

Partially Included Public.   Although open broadcast was an incidental rather than an essential feature of the course design, the decision to broadcast the class was an important one. All communities in the state were able to view the class live on Saturday afternoon and by tape delay Sunday afternoon as a part of normal PBS offerings. Those people who tuned into the show were typically casual viewers who saw a few episodes or parts of episodes. They probably did not follow all the discussions, nor did they build the semester-long context for understanding the subtle interpretations of epistemology. Their partial involvement in the discourse provided a strong design element.

The enrolled students faced a unique challenge of orientation to their role as students. They were both learners with performance requirements and TV actors without scripts. The public exposure settled on them an unforeseen responsibility regarding their learning. Every enrolled student reported being approached on the street with comments about the course content, so each of them became a de facto interpreter of intriguing or controversial issues. In at least one case, a student was called by someone from another village several hundred miles away (but still within the cultural region) who had a question. The small population in Alaska assured that every student was likely to be seen by personal acquaintances.

In addition, the members of the general audience gave further elaboration to some of the issues discussed in class. Students then became representatives of their local community by voicing concerns or interpretations to the statewide audience.

Distributed Classroom as Solution
to Dilemmas of Practice

The three pedagogical concerns noted earlier were all addressed by the combination of a distributed classroom and a general partially included audience. The project was very successful in eliciting students' tacit knowledge by noting the special circumstances that were associated with each student. The student in the state capital reported on legal issues, subsistence hunters on the Bering Sea traded perspectives with fisheries enforcement officials in Anchorage, and a student with a 40-year history working in rural Alaska gave a historical framework to medical practice. Without the accessibility afforded by the multiple student sites, this heterogeneous student cohort could not have convened.

Personal perspectives gained greater stature as valid beginning points because each student's perspective was bolstered by input from the unenrolled audience in the five different localities. Opinions did not need to be seen as simply idiosyncratic when they represented, and were validated by, a larger group of general viewers. The various religious and ethnic epistemologies were pressed to present an inherent logical coherence, but no one perspective could show a complete picture. Students were forced to grapple with the dilemma of accepting one perspective and losing some explanatory power versus accepting all the perspectives and losing coherence.

The partially included general audience prodded the students to adopt a full range of roles. They had to explain issues to people by drawing on their more complete exposure to the course content as well as interpret comments back to the class.

Distributed Classroom as Instructive About Design

The purpose of the course was to increase appreciation for diverse cultural understandings, but like the other two cases, the use of innovative technology also taught lessons about the way discourse design affects discourse content. The fact that the class meetings were broadcast statewide obviously affected the students' sense of the seriousness of the discourse as well as their willingness to speak. However, it was the exploitation of local circumstances and community perspectives that gave rise to sophisticated reflections on discourse design. Among other things, the course design had the capacity to stimulate reflection on the degree to which individual belief gains justification from consensus within a community and on the importance of immersion in a culture to understanding its practices. One student commented in a final paper for the course:

> If I had not been living in a Native community and trying to involve myself in traditional Native activities, the class would have been [only] an interesting detour into different societal philosophies ... [because] it explored general ideas that applied to many Native groups.... My experiences in Barrow were what taught me about the Inupiaq way of knowing. What the course taught me about generalized Native concepts helped me to better appreciate my more specific experiences in Barrow.

Lessons for Other Courses on Other Subjects

The Native Ways of Knowing demonstration project involves a use of technology that is both highly specialized to its circumstances and extremely expensive. Although many communication educators will involve themselves in distributed learning, few will face the environmental constraints faced in this case. What broader lessons does it offer?

First, the demonstration showed how distance and heterogeneity could be transformed from problems into resources. Distance was exploited to introduce a sense of immediacy in the content of the material. As one student commented, "When we talked of snow or whaling, our counterparts in Barrow were there with first-hand experience." Heterogeneity was exploited to put each student in the position of making unique contributions, imbuing all contributions with value and importance. As another student said, "People told what they knew," basing what they knew not on common literature but on highly differentiated individual experience. The success of these exploitations was so compelling as to create an independent justification for distance education. Any communication course dealing with culture could profit from the model of this course by recruiting diverse students to participate on a distance basis or by teaming with similar courses taught at other institutions. It should not be assumed that this participation would have to involve two-way video; with the objective of assembling diverse participants, any number of technology solutions are possible, especially those relying on the Internet to create a common discussion space.

Second, the demonstration pointed to a resource we have rarely used in education, the power of public or community participation. The unexpected presence of the unenrolled audience had a profound impact on this course. The casual viewers became sources for more information as well as interlocutors for the students. Students gained a greater depth of understanding of their course material as they took on the roles of interpreter and advocate. Moreover, they took on public responsibilities that made it all but impossible to treat the classroom discourse simply as a set of assignments to be completed and requirements to be met. Most of us will never participate in live broadcast of our classes, but some of the same profound effects on course participation might be obtained with functional substitutes for broadcast. The same alternation of roles and the same sense of significance might be achieved, for example, by having students build and maintain public information Web sites or by having students share responsibility for a "communication hotline" offered as a public service. Encountering the community as representatives of a discipline in this way allows students to see the relevance of their own discipline to broader concerns and to get accustomed to speaking from a discipline-based expertise.

CONCLUSION

We have suggested that in solving mundane teaching problems (which we can do at the simplest level of encounter with technology), we acquire capabilities that commonly extend beyond the solution of the current problem to open new possibilities. Exploration of these new possibilities involves us in manipulating discovered features of discourse design, sometimes resulting in the invention of new practices. Reflecting on when and how and why to manipulate design features leads us in turn to consideration of the design process itself and the values expressed in any design for teaching and learning.

In the three cases discussed, technology did more than simply solve a problem. In each case it defined a set of practices, the properties of which were available to students as materials for reasoning about such issues as the relation between identity and interpretation and the relation between process and product. What start as tools to teach with become objects to think with (Turkle, 1995), for ourselves and for our students.

REFERENCES

Bensusan, G. (1997). *The escalator* [Paper posted on the World Wide Web]. Flagstaff, AZ: Author. Available http://jan.ucc.nau.edu/~hgb/esc.html.

Harasim, L., Calvert, T., & Groeneboer, C. (1997). Virtual u: A web-based system to support collaborative learning. In B. Khan (Ed.), *Web-based instruction* (pp. 149–158). Englewood Cliffs, NJ: Educational Technology Publications.

Khan, B. H. (1997). Web-based instruction (WBI): What is it and why is it? In B. Khan (Ed.), *Web-based instruction* (pp. 5–18). Englewood Cliffs, NJ: Educational Technology Publications.

Reeves, T. C., & Reeves, P. M. (1997). Effective dimensions of interactive learning on the world wide web. In B. Khan (Ed.), *Web-based instruction* (pp. 59–66). Englewood Cliffs, NJ: Educational Technology Publications.

Relan, A., & Gillani, B. (1997). Web-based information and the traditional classroom: Similarities and differences. In B. Khan (Ed.), *Web-based instruction* (pp. 41–46). Englewood Cliffs, NJ: Educational Technology Publications.

Ryder, R. J., & Hughes, T. (1997). *Internet for educators*. Upper Saddle River, NJ: Prentice-Hall.

Turkle, S. (1995). *Life on the screen: Identity in the age of the internet*. New York: Simon & Schuster.

Turoff, M. (1995). *Designing a virtual classroom* [Paper delivered to the International Conference on Computer Assisted Instruction (ICCAI'95), National Chiao Tung University Hsinchu, Taiwan]. Available http://www.njit.edu/njIT/Department/CCCC/VC/Papers/Design.html.

29

Evaluating the Process

Anita L. Vangelisti
University of Texas at Austin

> *The evaluation of faculty is not a new phenomenon, yet it continues to elicit reactions in faculty ranging from cold apathy to heated anger.*
> —Arreola (1984, p. 79)

For most people involved with academics, the activities, decisions, and issues associated with teacher evaluation invoke less than positive images. Teachers often link the prospect of being evaluated to anxiety about measuring up to a nebulous set of standards, obtaining an important promotion, or avoiding embarrassment in front of peers. Administrators must deal with the design and implementation of evaluation programs, as well as with people who are particularly concerned with setting those programs into action: distressed teachers, worried parents, dissatisfied students, and, more recently, zealous attorneys (e.g., Bailey, 1986; Deneen, 1980; Eble, 1984; Zirkel, 1996). Students have to take the time to respond to questions that, from their perspective, may have little immediate impact on their education.

Despite such difficulties, the process of teacher evaluation is an important one. It represents not only a complex set of problems, but a powerful influence for, and on, contemporary education. This chapter addresses issues that are central to the instructional evaluation process, providing a framework with which to describe, weigh, and improve current evaluation practices. More specifically, the chapter focuses on four questions: (a) Why should teachers be evaluated? (b) What are the available means or methods for evaluation? (c) What teaching activities should be the focus of evaluation? and (d) Who should do the evaluating? Finally, criteria for assessing

409

the representativeness of teacher appraisals are examined, and guidelines for evaluation are suggested.

WHY EVALUATE?

Why should educators design, implement, and act on instructional evaluations? What purposes do evaluations serve? Some early discussions, in fact, suggested that teacher evaluation is a futile, if not impossible exercise (e.g., Highet, 1954, as cited in Dunkin & Biddle, 1974). Today, although educators continue to ask questions regarding the effectiveness and importance of teacher evaluation (e.g., Brandt, 1996; Huddle, 1985), most now see the process as useful, necessary, and even essential to good teaching.

On a global level, teacher evaluation can be defined as a description of how an instructor compares to a given set of implicit or explicit standards. It provides a record of what happens, instructionally, in and out of the classroom—a record that can be used publicly, by groups such as administrators and students, as well as personally, by teachers themselves. The basic reason, then, for conducting teacher evaluations is to generate public and personal information concerning instructional practices.

Public Information

From a public standpoint, the accountability provided by teacher evaluations is a necessary precursor to the legitimization of instructional practices (e.g., Lessinger, 1980; Ornstein, 1981). In the absence of accountability, educators leave not only their efforts, but also the fruits of those efforts open to criticism. Of particular concern is a group that Seldin (1980) and others referred to as outsiders—individuals such as parents, government leaders, and advocacy groups who, although not directly involved in the process of education, have strong influence on the direction it takes. The views these people hold about teachers and instructional practices often affect decisions that are made concerning education (Gerstner, 1994). If, as many claim, education policies and practices require the moral and financial support of outsiders, educators are obligated to supply evidence demonstrating that such support is warranted.

In addition to a general public accountability, teacher evaluations can provide valid, reliable information for personnel decisions. Although few teachers look forward to the process of being evaluated, most, if not all, would prefer promotion and tenure decisions to be based on relatively objective, systematic information. In this regard, when conducted and interpreted carefully, teacher evaluations can function to limit the subjectivity and the biases that may influence such decisions.

The public information generated by teacher evaluations also may help students choose courses and programs of study that best accommodate their educational goals. Although the data provided by evaluations typically are tied to teacher effectiveness, they can include material describing course content, grading procedures, or even instructional techniques. Students who have particular preferences or learning styles can use this information to select courses that meet their needs (see Gorham, chap. 19, this volume).

Finally, as public accounts, teacher evaluations help to define criteria for research on teaching (Gage, 1972); they provide researchers with guidelines and suggest variables, processes, and events that are relevant to the study of effective instruction. Contrary to the fears of some, the explanatory goals of educational research are not undermined by using information generated by teacher evaluations (see, e.g., Wragg, Wikely, Wragg, & Haynes, 1996). Indeed, when researchers utilize data from both the people doing the evaluations and the individuals being evaluated, they gain a great deal of information concerning the variables and processes that influence effective teaching. Furthermore, teachers who take an active role in the evaluative process gain the opportunity to become more effective researchers and problem solvers in their own classrooms (Friedrich, 1982), thereby bolstering their abilities to develop and test new instructional strategies.

Personal Information

In addition to providing public information to various constituencies, teacher evaluations generate personal information for instructors concerning the way they teach. Because this type of personal data encourages many teachers to set goals and improve their instructional techniques, evaluations focused on providing feedback to teachers for the purpose of professional development have become more popular in recent years (Duke, 1995).

Without some sort of evaluation, teachers are left in an informational vacuum concerning their performance; the degree to which they meet criteria set for them by administrators and others remains questionable (Poster & Poster, 1993). In this sense, teacher evaluations represent a salient form of socialization—whether explicit or implicit—providing newcomers and veterans with information about what it means to be a "successful" teacher as well as what they need to do to become successful.

The first and perhaps most common type of information provided to teachers involves the diagnosis of in-class instructional problems. Using a clinical metaphor, McDonald (1980) suggested four steps for such a diagnosis: (a) identify whether there is a problem, (b) identify the causes of the problem, (c) prescribe ways to improve the problem, and (d) assess subsequent moves toward improvement. By taking steps such as these, teachers not only receive feedback with regard to behaviors or instructional techniques that need improvement, but they also are given a means by which to change. This latter issue is particularly important because if instructors lack the knowledge necessary to make a change or do not receive feedback as to improvements resulting from their efforts, little (if any) lasting change is likely.

Another type of personal information provided to teachers is an assessment of the nonteaching aspects of their performance. These might include professional activities, selection of textbooks or readings, course syllabi, classroom activities, methods of presentation, assignments, or tests (Dressel, 1978; Peterson, 1995). Feedback concerning these facets of teachers' work can be used both to enhance individual instructors' courses and to contribute to the development and modification of more widely applied curricula (Braskamp, Brandenburg, & Ory, 1984; Doyle, 1975).

Teacher evaluations, in short, function as an important source of information. Publicly, they provide accountability to outsiders, data on which to base personnel decisions, information to help students make appropriate academic choices, and criteria for research. Personally, they provide teachers with information about their in- and out-of-class instructional practices; they furnish instructors with a relevant comparison base for the assessment of their own behavior.

HOW DO WE EVALUATE?

At the university level, teacher evaluations usually involve some sort of written appraisal, whether in the form of rating scales or more open-ended recommendations (Peterson, 1995). In some cases, evaluations will also include informal classroom visits from peers or supervisors or interviews with students. Whatever the form of the evaluative tool, its specificity and structure depend, to a great extent, on the type of appraisal being conducted. Most teacher evaluations fall into one of two basic category types. The first type is diagnostic or *formative*. Formative evaluations are conducted to define teachers' strengths and weaknesses—usually with the goal of improving instructional skills. When used to get a general picture of teachers' skills, open-ended or free-response items are often appropriate, because they allow for a broad range of responses. Limiting evaluators' feedback to a predetermined set of behavioral or attitudinal categories prior to obtaining more descriptive information may unduly constrain the appraisal.

The second type of evaluation is *summative*. Summative evaluations are conducted to provide information to administrators, students, or other parties, and they most often assess teachers' performance with regard to a standard set of instructional practices. When evaluators are looking for strengths or weaknesses in particular areas of teaching (e.g., delivery of material, textbook selection, course organization), open-ended questions may generate information that is too broad or too general. In such cases, rating scales, designed to target behaviors and techniques of particular interest, are an appropriate choice.

Whether formative or summative, teacher evaluations usually utilize one of three methods: written appraisals, interviews, or observations.

Written Appraisals

Compared to interviews and observations, written appraisals probably vary the most in terms of specificity. On one end of the continuum, written appraisals may take the form of rating scales, which require evaluators to rate the extent to which instructors conform to a particular set of qualities. On the other end are questionnaires composed of open-ended items, which require evaluators to generate their own response and sometimes even choose the focus and subject of the evaluation.

Written appraisals offer the advantage of being easily obtained from a large number of respondents in a short period of time and, partly for that reason, "have enjoyed unrivaled status" (Dunkin & Biddle, 1974, p. 59; see also McGreal, 1988; Peterson, 1995) as an evaluation tool. Although the same type of information often can be obtained through personal conferences or interviews, written appraisals, in most cases, are more expedient. Also, the form of written appraisals is such that respondent anonymity is easily preserved. Particularly in the case of student or peer evaluations, more candid responses may be obtained in this nameless context.

Despite these advantages, rating scales and less structured written appraisals are relatively limited in what they assess and the detail with which they assess it. Questions are often selected without any pretesting as to relevance and, as a result, may not detect some of the more subtle differences between effective and ineffective teaching (McGreal, 1990).

Interviews

Although more costly than written data, interview-based assessments give the evaluator the advantage of being able to follow up on information of particular interest. Inclusion of secondary or probing questions may be important in some cases when the nature or quality of teacher practices is being explored. For instance, diagnosing instructional difficulties may require more than a single, straightforward question (e.g., "If given the opportunity, what changes would you make in the way your instructor delivers, organizes, or selects class material?"). Similarly, whether for diagnostic or research purposes, describing factors that affect teacher–student interaction or students' attitudes toward learning might call for the added detail provided by interviews.

Interviews, however, are extremely expensive in terms of both time and effort. To obtain reliable, systematic data, interviewers must first be trained in data collection and recording techniques (Poster & Poster, 1993). Given that conducting a single interview usually takes the same amount of time as collecting written questionnaires from a large group of respondents, for many, the cost of interviews may be excessive.

Observation

Like interviewing, collecting observational data allows for a great deal of flexibility on the part of the evaluator. If, midway through the observation period, some behavior or technique of particular interest is noted, the observer can include that element in the database. On-site or field research is also particularly effective for describing less obvious or more complex elements of behavior and attitudes that might go unreported by rating scales (Babbie, 1997). Further, observational methods provide an account of what happens as it happens, rather than relying on retrospective data.

Observation, however, is quite expensive and, unless tested extensively for both validity and reliability, may be less appropriate for administrative or personnel decisions than other methods, such as written appraisals. In an often-quoted statement, Gage (1972) noted:

> Observation by expert judges of teaching probably cannot be used for administrative appraisals. Observers are hard enough to ignore when they are friends or researchers, whose impressions will not affect one's standing. But when the teacher knows he is being looked over by someone whose opinion will determine his promotion or salary, his performance may depend more on his nerve than on his teaching skill. (p. 172)

Others further note that the results of observation may be influenced as much by how the data are recorded and later presented as by the data themselves (Doyle, 1983; Wragg et al., 1996). This suggests that teachers who happen to be assigned to an observer with poor note-taking or presentation skills could receive less positive evaluations than they deserve. Although such biases may not pose major problems for diagnostic or formative evaluations, their role in summative evaluations used for personnel decisions could be professionally devastating.

WHO SHOULD EVALUATE?

Whereas choosing an evaluative method depends in part on the type of evaluation being conducted, selecting an evaluator has the added complexity of a relationship—an association between the evaluator and the teacher that can affect the results of any assessment. In some situations, this association is short-lived. The evaluator may have little if any interaction with the teacher before or after the appraisal is conducted (e.g., someone who works at the school's center for teaching effectiveness). When this is the case, relational issues (e.g., the degree of liking or animosity the evaluator feels toward the teacher) play a relatively small role in the appraisal process. By contrast, when the association between the evaluator and the teacher is ongoing (e.g., when the evaluator is a colleague or a student), the influence of relational factors likely is more salient. Many times, evaluators who are well acquainted with the teachers they are judging bring added richness and texture to the appraisal. Knowledge of historical information, changes in teachers' instructional practices, and the results of prior evaluations all can offer valuable contextual information to any assessment. If, however, the relationship between the evaluator and the teacher is strained, these same factors, as well as others, can profoundly and perhaps unfairly affect the evaluator's judgments.

One way to both capitalize on the benefits and minimize the biases that various evaluators bring to teacher appraisals is to include data from multiple sources in any evaluation. Most experts suggest that instructors who are being evaluated develop a *dossier*—a collection of data that serve as evidence of teacher quality (Peterson, 1995). Typically, four groups of people provide evaluations that are included in the dossier. They are students, colleagues, alumni, and the teachers themselves.

Students

Due, in part, to the amount of exposure they have to teachers, students, in many cases, serve as the best sources of information concerning teachers' instructional styles and course content. The status differences that are inherent in student–teacher relationships (as well as the sophistication with which many students approach the task) usually make students inappropriate observers. However, written appraisals and interviews with students are more effective and are often utilized.

Regardless of the method implemented, interpretation of evaluative information collected from students should be made with some caution. Although most research suggests that student survey reports are reliable and useful for teacher evaluations (e.g., Peterson & Stevens, 1988; Scriven, 1994), some studies have demonstrated that factors such as students' expected course grade (Centra, 1980), class size (Marsh, Overall, & Kesler, 1979), and teachers' rank (Marsh, 1980) may affect the ways students judge their instructors. Even if the likelihood of these variables consistently influencing teacher evaluations over time is minimal, such factors should be considered when student-based assessments are interpreted.

Colleagues

Although they lack the day-to-day exposure that students have to individual instructors, colleagues such as principals, department chairs, deans, and other teachers are often used to judge a variety of in- and out-of-class instructional activities. Given time to develop observation skills and to conduct observations, for example, colleagues can make repeated classroom visits to gather information for diagnostic purposes. For more formal, personnel-related assessments, colleagues often employ rating scales and open-ended written appraisals to evaluate teaching skills; course materials; and activities such as advising, service, and curriculum development.

While collegial evaluations may not be affected by the same type of relational contingencies that influence student assessments, relationships between teachers and colleagues placed in an evaluative role deserve equal consideration. On one hand, collegial relationships may affect evaluations. In the case of observation-based assessments, for example, generalizations are often made from a small number of observations and, as a result, may be based more on relational factors or first impressions than on instructors' actual classroom behaviors. On the other hand, regardless of their validity, evaluations may affect collegial relationships. If taken personally, a negative evaluation might not only result in strained interaction between a teacher and an evaluator, but could generate legal action by the teacher (e.g., Bailey, 1986; Centra, 1979).

Alumni

Because their accounts are retrospective, instructors' former students usually are not able to provide detailed descriptions of course structure, materials, or even teachers' behavior. They can, however, give global assessments of instructors and comparisons of instructors' qualities to other teachers. As a consequence, although alumni evaluations typically are not used for diagnostic purposes, they can serve as one of several sources of information for personnel decisions.

Data from previous students can be collected in the form of written appraisals, telephone interviews, mail surveys, or exit interviews with graduating seniors. Written assessments, although more easily administered than interviews, often do not have as high a response rate (Babbie, 1997). However, the standardization of interviewing skills required to ensure reliability across interviewers may make written responses more feasible. Regardless of the method, collecting evaluative data from alumni is an expensive process and, as a result, is usually done for small-scale rather than large-scale evaluations.

Self

Even though instructors' views of teaching and their own role as a teacher can affect the way they judge themselves (Kremer-Hayon, 1993), self-assessments serve a useful, and often necessary, purpose for many types of evaluation (Peterson & Chenoweth, 1992). Teachers, for instance, are probably the best reporters of the content and organization of their courses. In fact, detailed descriptions of materials such as course assignments, syllabi, class activities, and student achievement may not be obtainable from any other source. For the purposes of diagnosing problems related to class preparation (or even making personnel decisions with reference to out-of-class practices), some sort of self-evaluation, therefore, often is essential. In addition, because instructor and student ratings of global classroom variables (e.g., student involvement or teacher support) are relatively consistent (Braskamp, Caulley, & Costin, 1979), self-evaluations can be used to supplement appraisals made by others.

Including teachers as participants in their own evaluation provides most teachers with a sense of control and efficacy. Being told by a peer or superior that a particular area needs improvement is one often effective form of motivation—participating in the identification of the problem and diagnosis of its cause is another. For example, when encouraged to watch and evaluate videotapes of their teaching, instructors can note for themselves any difficulties they might have and, if the videotaping is conducted periodically, can observe improvements over time. Similarly, setting and accomplishing goals for out-of-classroom change provides teachers with a sense of accomplishment that might otherwise be difficult to attain.

WHAT SHOULD BE EVALUATED?

Unfortunately, limited time and financial resources often prohibit many of the individuals who conduct teacher evaluations from focusing specifically on the improvement of teachers' instructional skills. Teacher evaluations instead are done primarily for summative purposes, to distinguish the "good" teachers from the "bad" (Duke, 1995; Searfoss, 1996). Indeed, Doyle (1978) noted that "the practitioner's task requires knowing which criteria differentiate 'good' from 'poor' teachers. It is of little additional utility, in an immediate sense, to know why" (p. 143). Using statements such as this one as guidelines for what to assess, those who conduct teacher evaluations often employ very global indexes of teacher quality to determine overall effectiveness. Although pragmatically, there may be a great deal to be said for what Doyle termed the "practitioner's" approach to evaluation, limiting appraisals to the identification of "good" and "bad" teacher qualities has two fairly serious implications.

The first may be best illustrated by drawing a distinction between evaluation and description. Many appraisals provide information that is evaluative; that is, teacher qualities are noted in terms of how well or how poorly they fit a given set of criteria. What is often lacking in these appraisals, however, is descriptive information. Data identifying specific teaching activities such as preparation, ability to convey knowledge of the course material, and textbook selection are not detailed. This leaves whoever is using the evaluation in a dilemma when it comes to interpreting the results. If, for example, an instructor is rated poorly, and little descriptive information is available, we have no idea whether the low ratings are because of the way the teacher lectures, because he or she is a tough grader, or because he or she selected an inappropriate textbook. In short, the evaluation provides little that is of use for those interested in improving instruction. Regardless of whether teacher appraisals are employed for faculty development or for decisions involving promotion, some description of what is being evaluated is important.

The second implication of limiting teacher appraisals to the identification of "good" and "bad" teacher qualities involves a lack of focus on the students as active coparticipants in the learning process. The failure to evaluate how and why teachers are effective, rather than only whether they are effective, insinuates that students are passive information receptacles (Wilson, 1995). Obviously, from a communication perspective, the instructional process involves a great deal more than the emission and absorption of information. Given that teacher evaluations, in part, are accounts of classroom happenings, failing to include some components of teacher–student interaction is a flaw.

Admittedly, incorporating a measure of teacher–student interaction into current teacher evaluations is a major undertaking. Although studies of classroom interaction are on the increase and the centrality of communication to instructional processes is more frequently acknowledged than it used to be (see Andersen, Nussbaum, Pecchioni & Grant, chap. 26, this volume; Plax & Kearney, chap. 20, this volume), researchers and practitioners continue to debate what constitutes effective teaching (Cruickshank & Haefele, 1990). If, as such debate suggests, efforts to develop and implement a tool for assessing teacher–student interaction are somewhat premature, those administering teacher evaluations, at the very least, should include an appraisal of students' outcomes (i.e., student affect toward the teacher) rather than focusing only on "good" and "bad" teacher qualities (e.g., Greer, 1994). Assessing student outcomes may not capture the complexity of teacher–student interaction, but it does include the student as an important part of the teaching process.

EVALUATING THE EVALUATION

Validity

Regardless of which aspects of instruction are incorporated into teacher evaluations, addressing questions related to validity is vital when interpreting any appraisal. Is the evaluation an accurate representation of teacher practices and behaviors?

Responses to questions such as this one can be framed in terms of three types of validity: predictive, content, and construct validity. *Predictive validity* deals with the degree to which the measure accurately estimates some external variable (Nunnally, 1978). In the case of teacher evaluation, predictive validity typically involves the accuracy with which a particular evaluative technique can predict or distinguish the "product" of teaching: student learning, achievement, or affect. *Content validity* is the extent to which a measure representatively samples the substance of the area being assessed. It could be, for example, that the items included on a student rating scale are irrelevant in determining teacher quality—or that one or two important components are not tapped (Dunkin & Biddle, 1974). Finally, *construct validity* involves the degree to which the measure permits inferences about underlying traits (Anderson, Ball, Murphy, & Associates, 1975). If an effort is being made to measure a teacher's "enthusiasm," for example, in-class observers might note variations in the teacher's voice, the number of times he or she smiles at students, and the variety of techniques he or she uses to present class material. The evaluator concerned with construct validity would ask questions concerning the extent to which these behaviors represent the more general construct of enthusiasm. Could it be, for instance, that an instructor might smile quite a bit and not be enthusiastic? Do a variety of presentation techniques have to be implemented, or is there some other aspect of presenting course material that better represents a teacher's enthusiasm?

Reliability

In addition to assessing validity, evaluators need to be concerned with issues of reliability—that is, the extent to which the measures being used in the evaluation yield similar results if implemented repeatedly. Reliability can be assessed in at least three ways. The first, *internal consistency,* is based on the degree to which ratings for similar items correspond to one another. For instance, an evaluator would expect to find high correlations between items measuring instructor competence, knowledge of material, and expertise in course content. If the ratings on each of these items were substantially different for the same teacher, the evaluation would not be a reliable one. The second type, *interrater* reliability, involves the extent to which different raters' assessments agree with one another. For teacher evaluations, this type of reliability is particularly relevant when observational methods are used. If observers are not able to agree on the definition of behavioral categories and whether an instructor displays these behaviors, their ratings lack interrater reliability. The third and final type of reliability, *test–retest*, focuses on the degree to which measurements agree with one another across time or, for most teacher evaluations, at two different times during the term. This method increases the generalizability of the evaluation, because more than one assessment is made. However, when the time interval between assessments is in excess of a few days, it is important to recognize that any changes in the evaluation may be attributable to intervening variables rather than actual changes in instruction.

Cost

Although few would argue with the importance of establishing the validity and reliability of teacher evaluations, on a very pragmatic level those conducting evaluations have limited funds (see Norris, 1993). School administrators and educational researchers, as a result, are restricted in their abilities to design and implement evaluation programs. It would be optimal, for example, to conduct some form of evaluation at regular intervals throughout the school year, as it would be to have a large number and variety of evaluators. The costs of achieving these two elements alone, however, are prohibitive for many programs. Multiple assessments conducted by different evaluators not only require people who are willing to do the evaluations, they also demand individuals to design the program, train the evaluators, process the data collected, and put those data to use.

GUIDELINES FOR EVALUATION

Valentine (1992) noted that "Implementing an evaluation system that improves personnel performance and removes incompetent teachers without creating a climate of mistrust and malcontent is one of the most elusive tasks in education" (p. 1). Indeed, after outlining some of the requirements for obtaining a valid, reliable account of what happens in the classroom, the appraisal of teacher performance appears to be very elusive. Those in the positions of designing and implementing teacher appraisals face the constant dilemma of balancing evaluation goals with practical constraints tied to time, effort, and finances. Those interpreting teacher appraisals must keep in mind potential biases and limitations of the evaluator and of the evaluative method. Those who are evaluated must deal with being assessed with what are often imperfect tools.

Centra (1983) summarized a number of suggestions, however, that may make the development and implementation of teacher evaluations less elusive for all parties involved. He recommended that: (a) multiple sources be used, (b) multiple sets of student ratings be used, (c) a sufficient number of student raters be obtained, (d) course characteristics be taken into account, (e) global ratings be stressed more than other ratings for personnel decisions, (f) diagnostic information for teaching improvement be supplemented, (g) procedures for administering the forms for student ratings be standardized, and (h) rating forms not be overused.

Although addressing each of these suggestions is probably not a feasible goal for every evaluation program, the tenor of Centra's (1983) recommendations can be captured in three general, and perhaps more easily applicable, guidelines. First, consider the purpose of the evaluation. What are the goals of the appraisal and what, more specifically, is the object of the evaluation? Answering these questions should provide some direction as to the type of measure that would be most effectively implemented as well as who should perform the evaluation. Second, regardless of the purpose, use multiple indicators. A variety of measures will not only provide different types of information, but will serve as a means to assess the validity and reliability of that information. Finally, consider the specific characteristics of the course and the instructor being evaluated. Which types of evaluative techniques will most adequately assess the goals of the course and the instructor's ability to achieve those goals? Are there circumstances or previously established relationships that might mandate for or against the use of a particular evaluator?

Obviously, these and other suggestions will not eliminate all of the concerns associated with teacher evaluation. Like most forms of assessment, the appraisal of teacher performance will always be subject to criticism and, thus, always subject to suggestions for improvement.

REFERENCES

Anderson, S. B., Ball, S., Murphy, R. T., & Associates. (1975). *Encyclopedia of educational evaluation: Concepts and techniques for evaluating education and training programs.* San Francisco: Jossey-Bass.
Arreola, R. A. (1984). Evaluation of faculty performance: Key issues. In P. Seldin (Ed.), *Changing practices in faculty evaluation* (pp. 79–85). San Francisco: Jossey-Bass.
Babbie, E. (1997). *The practice of social research* (7th ed.). Belmont, CA: Wadsworth.
Bailey, G. W. (1986). Firing a teacher? Be sure your case will hold up in court. *Executive Education, 8,* 29–31.
Brandt, R. (1996). On a new direction for teacher evaluation: A conversation with Tom McGreal. *Educational Leadership, 53,* 30.
Braskamp, L. A., Brandenburg, D. C., & Ory, J. C. (1984). *Evaluating teaching effectiveness: A practical guide.* Beverly Hills, CA: Sage.
Braskamp, L. A., Caulley, D. N., & Costin, F. (1979). Student ratings and instructor self ratings and their relationship to student achievement. *American Educational Research Journal, 16,* 295–306.
Centra, J. A. (1979). *Determining faculty effectiveness.* San Francisco: Jossey-Bass.
Centra, J. A. (1980). *Determining faculty performance.* San Francisco: Jossey-Bass.
Centra, J. A. (1983, February). The fair use of student ratings. *Postsecondary Education Newsletter,* pp. 1–2.
Cruickshank, D. R., & Haefele, D. L. (1990). Research-based indicators: Is the glass half-full or half-empty? *Journal of Personnel Evaluation in Education, 4,* 33–39.
Deneen, J. R. (1980). Legal dimensions of teacher evaluations. In D. Peterson & A. Ward (Eds.), *Due processes in teacher evaluation* (pp. 15–43). Washington, DC: University Press of America.
Doyle, K. O., Jr. (1975). *Student evaluation of instruction.* Lexington, MA: Lexington.
Doyle, K. O., Jr. (1978). Interpreting teaching effectiveness research. *Viewpoints in Teaching and Learning, 54,* 141–153.
Doyle, K. O., Jr. (1983). *Evaluating teaching.* Lexington, MA: Lexington.
Dressel, P. (1978). *Handbook of academic evaluation.* San Francisco: Jossey-Bass.
Dunkin, M. J., & Biddle, B. J. (1974). *The study of teaching.* Washington, DC: University Press of America.
Duke, D. L. (1995). The move to reform teacher evaluation. In D. L. Duke (Ed.), *Teacher evaluation policy* (pp. 1–11). Albany: State University of New York Press.
Eble, K. E. (1984). New directions in faculty evaluation. In P. Seldin (Ed.), *Changing practices in faculty evaluation* (pp. 96–100). San Francisco: Jossey-Bass.
Friedrich, G. W. (1982). Classroom interaction. In L. L. Barker (Ed.), *Communication in the classroom* (pp. 55–76). Englewood Cliffs, NJ: Prentice-Hall.
Gage, N. L. (1972). *Teacher effectiveness and teacher education: The search for a scientific basis.* Palo Alto, CA: Pacific Books.
Gerstner, L. V. (1994). *Reinventing education.* New York: Dutton.
Greer, R. D. (1994). The measure of a teacher. In R. Gardner, D. M. Sainato, J. O. Cooper, T. E. Heron, W. L. Heward, J. Eshleman, & T. A. Grossi (Eds.), *Behavior analysis in education: Focus on measurably superior instruction* (pp. 161–171). Pacific Grove, CA: Brooks/Cole.

Highet, G. (1954). *The art of teaching*. New York: Vintage.

Huddle, G. (1985). Teacher evaluation—How important for effective schools? Eight messages from research. *National Association of Secondary School Principals Bulletin, 69*, 58–63.

Kremer-Hayon, L. (1993). *Teacher self-evaluation: Teachers in their own mirror*. Boston: Kluwer Academic.

Lessinger, L. N. (1980). Accountability ensures improvement. In J. W. Nolls (Ed.), *Taking sides: Clashing views of controversial issues* (pp. 151–172). Guilford, CT: Duskin.

Marsh, H. W. (1980). The influence of student, course, and instructor characteristics in the evaluation of teaching. *American Educational Research Journal, 17*, 219–237.

Marsh, H. W., Overall, J., & Kesler, S. P. (1979). Class size, students' evaluations, and instructional effectiveness. *American Educational Research Journal, 16*, 57–70.

McDonald, F. (1980). Principles and procedures in observing classroom instruction. In D. Peterson & A. Ward (Eds.), *Due process in teacher evaluation* (pp. 89–113). Washington, DC: University Press of America.

McGreal, T. L. (1988). Evaluation for enhancing instruction: Linking teacher evaluation with staff development. In S. Stanley & J. Popham (Eds.), *Teacher evaluation: Six prescriptions for success* (pp. 1–29). Alexandria, VA: Association for Supervision and Curriculum Development.

McGreal, T. L. (1990). The use of rating scales in teacher evaluation: Concerns and recommendations. *Journal of Personnel Evaluation in Education, 4*, 41–58.

Norris, N. (1993). Evaluation, economics, and performance indicators. In J. Elliot (Ed.), *Reconstructing teacher education: Teacher development* (pp. 31–38). London: Falmer.

Nunnally, J. C. (1978). *Psychometric theory* (2nd ed.). New York: McGraw-Hill.

Ornstein, A. C. (1981). Accountability: Prospects for the 1980s. *School and Community, 57*, 24–25.

Peterson, K. D. (1995). *Teacher evaluation: A comprehensive guide to new directions and practices*. Thousand Oaks, CA: Corwin.

Peterson, K. D., & Chenoweth, T. (1992). School teachers' control and involvement in their own evaluation. *Journal of Personnel Evaluation in Education, 6*, 177–189.

Peterson, K. D., & Stevens, D. (1988). Student reports for schoolteacher evaluations. *Journal of Personnel Evaluation in Education, 1*, 259–267.

Poster, C., & Poster, D. (1993). *Teacher appraisal: Training and implementation* (2nd ed.). London: Routledge.

Scriven, M. (1994). Using student ratings in teacher evaluation. *Evaluation Perspective, 4*(1), 1–6.

Scarfoss, L. W. (1996). Can teacher evaluation reflect holistic instruction? *Educational Leadership, 53*, 38–41.

Seldin, P. (1980). *Successful faculty evaluation programs*. Crugers, NY: Coventry.

Valentine, J. W. (1992). *Principles and practices for effective teacher evaluation*. Boston: Allyn & Bacon.

Wilson, S. M. (1995). Performance-based assessment of teachers. In S. W. Soled (Ed.), *Assessment, testing, and evaluation in teacher education* (pp. 189–219). Norwood, NJ: Ablex.

Wragg, E. C., Wikely, F. J., Wragg, C. M., & Haynes, G. S. (1996). *Teacher appraisal observed*. London: Routledge.

Zirkel, P. A. (1996). The law of the lore? (laws that govern teacher evaluation). *Phi Delta Kappan, 77*, 597.

30

Evaluating the Product

Rebecca B. Rubin
Kent State University

What is the end product of instruction? Traditionally, we view an increase in skill or knowledge as learning products in communication classes. Communication skills are typically evaluated through assessment of behavior or performance, whereas knowledge is evaluated via a written mode, usually by examination or term paper. In both cases, evaluation serves as feedback to students on how they are progressing.

The course objectives determine whether skills or knowledge or a combination of the two is the appropriate target for evaluation. For example, public speaking classes usually focus on both knowledge and skill in public speaking. Therefore, both knowledge and performance must be evaluated. However, theory classes focus, instead, on knowledge about communication. Sometimes the availability of a reliable and valid evaluation technique will determine the course objectives; some instructors of interpersonal communication classes measure knowledge because they perceive a lack of a valid and reliable skill measure.

This chapter examines ways of evaluating communication products in the classroom. First, I examine basic principles that guide evaluation; second, I explore common methods of evaluation of classroom performance—the use of criticism; third, I discuss the ways in which we evaluate knowledge in communication classrooms; and fourth, I consider the difficult process of computing course grades.

BASIC PRINCIPLES OF EVALUATION

There are two basic approaches to evaluation used in classrooms today. *Norm-referenced measurement* compares one student's progress with that of his or her peers. With norm-referenced measurement, all students are rank ordered, and grade cutoffs are based on how well the class does. Norm-referenced methods can unduly punish moderate-ability students in a class of high-ability or high-achievement students and unduly reward moderate- or high-ability students in a class with low-ability or low-achievement students.

Criterion-referenced measurement, the preferred method, is based on absolute, objective performance standards or criteria. Evaluation closely adheres to behavioral objectives and focuses students on mastering content rather than on outperforming their peers. All students have the opportunity of doing well (or failing to do so). Criterion-referenced procedures reduce test or evaluation anxiety, in that students know what criteria are used to decide their grades, which reduces competition. Smythe, Kibler, and Hutchings (1973) compared norm-referenced to criterion-referenced measurement in communication classes and argued that predetermined criteria are necessary in classroom teaching and evaluation. If students are to receive grades on their communication, there must be preset standards or evaluative criteria that relate closely to the content, focus, and objectives of the course. Whatever the approach, two further criteria of evaluation are important: validity and reliability.

Validity refers to how accurate and comprehensive an evaluation is. Is the critique, exam, or paper really measuring learning or skill development? Content validity, one type of validity, refers to how broad based the evaluation is. For example, does the exam cover all aspects of the text and lecture material? Does the critique sheet used in evaluation have all the categories present on which the evaluation is based?

Reliability deals with consistency and dependability. Is an instructor consistent in his or her ratings for all students? Are all speeches, papers, and essay exam answers rated using the same criteria? With objective exams, are all questions working in the same way for all students? Validity and reliability are essential in measuring communication performance or knowledge.

EVALUATION OF PERFORMANCE

Instructors are both critics and evaluators of the communication skills they teach. In fact, evaluations that take place in the classroom are based on criticism, so whatever is said in class should be aligned with the criteria used for the evaluation. Cathcart (1981) suggested that students learn about speaking by engaging in criticism of their own communication or that of their peers. Thus, valid criteria must be developed to guide the criticism and ultimately serve as a basis for evaluation. Postcommunication criticism stimulates creative thinking and interest in the communication process, calls attention to student strengths and weaknesses, gives instructions for improvement, and motivates students to do better in the future (Smith, 1961). Opinions vary, however, on the who, what, how, and when of speech criticism.

Who Should Give the Criticism?

Criticism can come from the instructor, the student, or the student's peers. Instructors are probably the most valid and reliable critics because of their training and experience in observation. Students, however, can be asked to provide criticism of their own communication, either orally in class or in writing. This is especially effective if the student has a videotape to review. Typically, self-evaluation helps students identify their goals and critical judgment skills, and it provides a means of reinforcement when they do well (Harris, 1963).

Peers can also provide helpful criticism in the classroom. Although most students focus their comments on content and delivery, speakers consider negative comments to be especially helpful (Book & Simmons, 1980). In any evaluation process, the course goals and standards must be clear to student raters. Balcer (1958) argued that teachers must know where the class is going and communicate this to students. Students should evaluate each other only when they understand and accept the standards, and they should comment on content before delivery when evaluations are given in class. Sometimes, peer evaluators are graded on their critiques (by comparing them to the instructor's) to make sure they apply criteria accurately instead of participating in a popularity contest.

Errors can occur with peer raters, however, and peer raters can be highly unreliable. They can disagree with each other and with the instructor (this would produce low interrater reliability). Student ratings are consistently higher than instructors' ratings (Carlson & Smith-Howell, 1995; Wiseman & Barker, 1965) except when profanity is used in speeches, and then the ratings are lower (Bock, Butler, & Bock, 1984). Student critics who cannot adjust to the message and fear being a critic tend to give higher grades (Bock & Bock, 1984). Student critics who are next up to speak are also more lenient in their grading. After they are finished speaking, raters become more negative. Thus, it is not clear that peer evaluations are valid and reliable. Criticism peers give in class is helpful, but the grades may not be accurate.

What Should Be Critiqued?

The communication literature is replete with criteria and rating scales for evaluating public speaking performance. Knower (1929) once proposed that rating scales increase open-mindedness in teachers and make them more accurate. In essence, rating scales force the instructor to specify the criteria before beginning the evaluation process. This basic principle has guided the discipline for the last 70 years.

Several published instruments contain standard criteria for judging public speaking performance. Most textbooks have their own set of criteria and include similar qualities. The important point is that the qualities identified in the criticism should be those that are emphasized and taught in the class. For example, speech speed should not be critiqued or evaluated if it is not taught in the class. *Evaluating Classroom Speaking* (Bock & Bock, 1981) is a handy guide to the rating process. One new, valid, and reliable evaluation method has been developed by Morreale, Moore, Taylor, Surges-Tatum, and Hulbert-Johnson (1993), called *The Competent Speaker*; it is available from the National Communication Association and described fully by Morreale (1994).

How Should It Be Given?

Oral or Written?   Criticism and evaluation can be oral or written in nature. For example, the instructor can provide: (a) oral criticism, using concrete ideas that focus on the next step to be mastered; (b) written criticism (either a checklist, rating scale, or open-ended written critique); (c) a question–answer period, which can reveal weaknesses in a speech; or (d) written evaluation, a grade based on criteria (Holtzman, 1960).

Instructors must determine which methods are most appropriate and feasible. Oral criticism should focus on growth and improvement, and it should also motivate the student to do better next time, yet it should be kept short and to the point. In general, criticism should be offered by giving clear examples of the points made, and instructors should avoid lengthy discussion of moot or controversial questions. When students provide criticism of their peers, instructors should acknowledge all student criticism contributions. Brooks and Friedrich (1973) provided additional suggestions.

The criticism need not always be oral, however. Written criticism is often more useful than oral criticism in that it is more tangible and students can save it for later reflection. Written evaluations are sometimes created by students for their peers in public speaking classes, and these are later discussed with the instructor (Hildebrandt & Stevens, 1960). Written criticism reinforces the oral criticism given in class.

Behnke and King (1984) computerized the speech criticism process. Their *Communication Education* article details how to code criticism and comments and how to construct individualized critiques for students. They reported that students like this system because it frees the instructor from writing during the speech (more eye contact) and the instructor can give lengthy comments and suggestions.

Positive or Negative, General or Specific?   Research suggests that positive comments should be given during oral critiques in class (Bostrom, 1963). Criticism that focuses on one main idea designed to improve a student's ability, step by step, is more effective than providing a long list of behaviors that need to be changed (Holtzman, 1960). Positive comments enhance student attitudes about speaking, whereas negative ones diminish these attitudes. Positive comments are also appreciated more by students than negative ones. When criticism is negative, it should be atomistic and impersonal (Young, 1974).

Atomistic comments, detailed remarks that focus on specific aspects of the speech, are more helpful than holistic, general, and vague ones (Young, 1974). Impersonal comments, ones that focus on aspects of the speech rather than on the speaker, are more helpful than personal ones, especially when they are directed at aspects of delivery. This is because student speakers become defensive when they feel they are being attacked personally. Because rating reliability is higher for specific traits than for a general impression (Clevenger, 1964), an atomistic, detailed form might also be more reliable.

Using Rating Scales.   A variety of scales exist for turning criticism into evaluation. Simple numerical scales list the criteria for speech performance and assign numbers representing grading criteria to each. Most researchers advocate using between four and six steps. It appears that a 5-point scale is ideal, especially because it conforms to the A through F grading system used in most colleges. For example, assume that content is one category for criticism and evaluation. Under content, there might be five or six specific aspects of content that are taught in the class, one of which might be organization of ideas. Using a 5-point scale to critique organization of ideas, we would most likely create steps related to possible levels of achievement: excellent, good, satisfactory, poor, and unacceptable. These five steps must be clearly defined in the critic's mind so that he or she can clearly distinguish between them. Excellent might mean that the ideas presented were clearly organized in a distinguishable pattern (chronological, problem–cause–solution, etc.). *Good* might refer to an organization pattern that was clearly constructed but the student strayed from the pattern at one point, and so on. These five steps could be converted into a numerical system (5–1 points) or letter (A–F) system when the total grade is computed for the performance.

When to Give Criticism

Opinions are mixed about when to give criticism in the classroom. Braden (1948) argued that feedback is important immediately after each speech. Dedmon (1967), however, suggested that criticism should be given at the end of the period (not after every speech), perhaps because of the possibility of overlapping.

Overlapping results when an evaluator writes a critique and rates a speaker during the speech or while the next speech is in progress. This affects immediate and delayed comprehension of information presented in speeches (lower for overlap condition) and evaluation of speeches (grade on second speech is higher when overlapped; Barker, Kibler, & Hunter, 1968). This says that a failure to listen critically inflates ratings. Therefore, an oral critique or some other form of lapse time between speeches (perhaps peer criticism) will allow instructors time to complete their evaluations, or scores will be inflated for the overlapped speaker. A computerized system of compiling criticism might be used to save time (Behnke & King, 1984).

Evaluating Nonspeech Communication Skills

Although speeches are the primary focus of rating in the communication classroom, small group, interview, and interpersonal communication are also evaluated. Gouran and Whitehead (1971) studied group discussions and found that participants do not differ greatly from observers in their ratings. They suggested that, to increase reliability, several observers or participants be used. Beebe and Barge (1994) developed a new rating scale for group communication that can be used by observers or participants (via videotape).

Several interpersonal scales exist (Hay, 1994). Rubin and Martin (1994) developed a simple, self-report 10-dimension measure, and Spitzberg and

Hurt (1987) identified four molar clusters (interaction management, altercentrism, expressiveness, composure), each consisting of 10 molecular behaviors. These scales can be used to evaluate interpersonal skills.

Objectivity and Bias in Rating

Because of the oral nature of student presentations, rating objectivity and reliability are particularly important. In this section, I examine basic elements of objectivity, characteristics of raters that lead to biased ratings, normal judgmental tendencies of raters, the importance of reliability, and ways to improve reliability through rater training.

Objective Rating lessens fear in communication classes, increases respect for the art of communication and the teacher, provides greater substance to knowledge and understanding by students, and enhances students' abilities and skill. According to Kelley (1965), important elements for objective evaluation include: (a) a set of standards used for all students, (b) options in choosing speech techniques (e.g., students can choose either an illustrative story, a humorous anecdote, or a profound quote to begin a speech), (c) instructions on what not to do, (d) criticism aimed at the next step for maximum improvement, and (e) an understanding that some principles and techniques contribute more to success than others. Kelley concluded that instructors should standardize their requirements (yet allow for individual style and personality), criticize on issues of bad choice and effect, and use an incremental system for evaluation (not just A, B, C).

Stiggins, Backlund, and Bridgeford (1985) outlined several *biasing tendencies* in assessing communication skills. They pointed out that teachers are often not trained adequately in assessment; cultural biases sometimes exist, certain characteristics of tests (ambiguous items, environment, scoring procedures) can lead to increased bias, and student evaluation anxiety can influence ratings. Other forms of bias also exist: leniency, trait error, central tendency, halo effect, logical error, rating two consecutive items alike, and comparison of a peer's performance with one's own skills. Stiggins et al. argued that, although all these problems exist with rating oral performance, it is still a better alternative than a written test when assessing oral communication skills.

Research measurement literature consistently points to *natural tendencies* of raters or judges that lead to biased ratings (see Stiggins et al., 1985). One researcher, for instance, found that easy-to-persuade raters were more lenient (Bock, 1970). Leniency errors are those made when the rater gives speakers the benefit of the doubt in all close calls; halo effects are when raters view certain speakers as able to do no wrong; and trait errors are overall biases toward the speech based on some trait of the speech, such as its organization or theme. Of course, raters can be too severe or prone to making "horned effect" evaluations also. Bock and Bock (1977) found that female raters were too hard on all speakers when a male experimenter was present, and male raters were too hard on all speakers when a female experimenter was present. These results suggest that teachers can set up expectancies and confound student raters (male or female) when they evaluate speeches in class. If students give critiques before the instructor gives his or her comments, this type of bias might be eliminated.

Training improves the validity and reliability of the rating process in classrooms. In one study, graduate students who were trained with videotape and instruction were more consistent raters (less variation among raters) than those without training (Bowers, 1964). Through videotape, rater training can be made consistent for all raters; Gundersen (1978) provided a detailed example of how a training program can be established using videotapes of speakers.

Training students to give criticism on speeches is important because of the great probability of judgmental errors during the criticism process. Trained raters commit fewer leniency and halo errors (Bohn & Bohn, 1985). Leniency and halo errors are common when raters know that the speaker will see the results. Bohn and Bohn (1985) concluded that if you are going to use students' peers as raters, they should be trained. They provided a good bibliography on rating scales and raters.

Using a panel of trained student critics also helps increase the reliability of the evaluation. Without training, raters use different criteria when they evaluate a speech (Tiemens, 1965). Clevenger (1963) found that raters with more years of training and experience in teaching speech also had higher test–retest reliability.

Tips for Criticism and Evaluation

1.   Determine behavioral objectives for instruction.
2.   Identify and delineate criteria to be used in evaluation; these should reflect what you teach in class.
3.   Use oral criticism in addition to written after each speech; student and peer comments should come first, for they provide you with time to complete your own thoughts.
4.   All students should understand the standards and scales used in the evaluation; they should be trained to make their ratings consistent.
5.   Criticism should be positive and specific; focus on elements for future improvement.

6. Use a rating scale with four to six steps representing levels of achievement; students can track their own progress easily with this system.

7. Do not prejudge students based on their socioeconomic status, race, gender, level of anxiety, level of academic achievement, degree to which you know them, how much you like them, or your attitude about the topic; also, do not let how rigidly you hold your beliefs or your own level of persuasibility influence your ratings.

EVALUATION OF COMMUNICATION KNOWLEDGE

Purposes of Testing

New instructors find it difficult to create communication exams because not only are they unsure about what questions to ask, they are unaware of the various purposes of testing. Measurements are used for diagnosis (to assess learning ability or determine initial instructional level for the class), for estimating achievement or progress (the purpose of most exams), for guiding and motivating learning (sometimes ungraded pop quizzes serve this purpose), and for research. In most classes, the purpose of testing is to measure achievement or knowledge.

We must measure what we teach. If factual knowledge is taught, use an objective test. If understanding is taught, use essay tests or papers. If self-diagnosis or awareness is what is taught, then a self-report instrument can be used. Douglas (1958) provided some helpful hints for improving measurement for various purposes.

Nunnally (1972) also provided some helpful hints on test construction. He suggested that students should be given a schedule of testing at the beginning of the course. Because college students must plan their work around a testing schedule, no pop quizzes should be given. Although unannounced tests can be used to spot-check student progress (as a result of unexpected problems in a class), they should not be used for grading purposes.

Planning the Exam

Goyer (1962), Newcombe and Robinson (1975), Nunnally (1972), Milton and Edgerly (1976), and Tinkelman (1971) provided the following 10 suggestions and instructions for planning exams. First-time teachers should read more about test construction and the sources just named are good places to start.

1. Consider the test or course objectives and the content or subject matter of the test. A valid test is one that serves its intended function. In the classroom, an exam assesses level of performance at a particular point in time rather than measuring a particular personality trait or predicting future achievement in an area. Tests are used as teaching devices, as well. They show what information is understood and what needs further clarification.

2. Develop a blueprint or test outline of the material to be covered. This plan should guide question construction.

3. Use a representative sample of questions from all assigned material, not questions from just one chapter or subsection of the material. The more items on the exam, the more representative the sample of questions will be (content validity). Longer tests, then, better discriminate mastery of information in the testing area.

4. Create test items matched to the objectives. If knowledge of a subject is being assessed, then a written format (multiple choice, essay, matching, true–false, completion, problems, or interpretation questions) should be used. If skill is assessed, a behavioral method is most appropriate. Also, decide on the specific objectives of the exam: Are you concerned about memory of facts, or ability to understand simple or complex principles, to use principles to evaluate proposed solutions to problems or to solve problems, or to extend old principles to new ones? Tests can measure understanding, recall, memory, comprehension, and critical judgment; the questions created must be matched with the purpose.

5. Consider that there will be sources of error in the exam. Student performance can fluctuate because of mood, physical health, lack of sleep, and so on. Also, there will be errors due to guessing (a fill-in-the blank question is more reliable than a multiple-guess or true–false question). Scoring errors can also occur (even with machine scoring). Alternative forms of an exam (for large lecture classes) can be used to prevent cheating and to test for reliability. Be sure to give more than one or two exams during the semester or quarter so that characteristics of the student or exam will not be a major source of error in the student's overall grade.

6. Allow enough time for the questions during the exam. A time limit should be set up so that 90% of the students will feel that they have ample time for the test (the other 10% will never feel that they have enough time). You will need to put a limit on the number of items you use. With multiple-choice questions, allow one to two questions per minute. Ten minutes should be sufficient for essay questions requiring a one-half page answer.

7. Any exam, whether objective or essay, should be constructed with clear instructions. These can be clarified in class if necessary, but students who arrive late will not benefit from in-class clarification, and some students will not be listening. It is always best, therefore, to use detailed written instructions on

the exam and corrections on the chalkboard. Also, pay careful attention to the physical features of the exam: spelling, punctuation, wording, clarity, and general appearance.

8. Keep the test results on file during the semester. It is difficult to discuss a student's answers when the test has been lost. Give the answer sheets to the students at the end of the semester, or store them for a year in the event that a student questions a grade after the class is over. Also, security must be tight around exam time or copies will disappear, sometimes without your realization that they are gone.

9. During the test, move quietly around the room to answer questions and prevent cheating. Write the time on the chalkboard occasionally if no clock exists in the room so students can budget their time. Also, the physical setting should be quiet, well-lit, and not overly crowded.

10. Once you create good questions, you might want to keep your exam questions for use in the future. Using separate answer sheets with test booklets solves this problem. Information about the responses to each question should be given to the student on the answer sheet, but the questions can be turned back in to the teacher. Spend time going over answers and questions in class or during office hours, but hold onto those questions. Also, when booklets are used, they can be reused for other sections of the class, saving on copying expenses. If you use test booklets and separate answer sheets, a grading key can be constructed that eases grading. On the answer sheets, have students write the words *true* and *false* when true–false questions are used or have them circle a T or F (a, b, c, d, and e for multiple choice) instead of trying to decipher their handwriting.

Types of Questions

There are two basic types of questions. Recognition questions—multiple choice, true–false, and matching—give students the various answers and ask only that they recognize which one is correct. Recall questions—supply or completion, short answer, essay—require students to remember and provide the answers. In part, as a consequence, recall questions demonstrate higher competence than recognition items alone (Wesman, 1971). Objective (nonessay) tests are more reliable than subjective essay exams, because with essays, evaluation is often based on writing ability, vocabulary, spelling, and other grammatical bases. In this section, a variety of objective and subjective questions are explained and examples of each are given.

Multiple-choice (guess) items are versatile and can be used to test for facts, evaluation, application of principles, skills, and definitions. In everyday usage, however, many multiple-choice questions are ambiguous and emphasize trivial points. Multiple-choice questions consist of two main parts: the problem and the set of alternatives. The problem should point to the theme of the correct or best alternative answer, yet incorrect alternatives should be plausibly related to the problem (do not use joke answers), and the correct alternative should resemble in appearance the incorrect ones. With multiple choice, one alternative need not be absolutely correct, just better than the others. The correct (or best) alternatives should be randomly ordered to avoid guessing, and correct responses should be evenly distributed among the letters (we tend to put the correct answer as *c* too often).

The multiple-choice problem and alternatives should be clearly written. Avoid rote memory problems (e.g., specific numbers of things or percentages), negatively stated or double-negative items, grammatical cues that give the answer away (e.g., *a*, *an*), and superfluous detail in the problem. Each problem should be independent of every other problem. With the alternatives, do not use clues to the correct alternative (signaled by words such as *all*, *always*, and *never*) or alternatives that overlap or include each other (a, b, a & b, all of the above); instead, have four to five clear choices. Do not ask questions containing controversial issues. All in all, make sure something worthwhile is measured. An example of a good multiple-choice question is:

EX1: Multiple-choice questions should include:

 a. Clues to the correct alternative.

 b. Alternatives that overlap each other.

 c. Negatively stated responses.

 d. Rote memory material.

*e. Four or five choices.

Haladyna and Downing (1989, p. 46) identified the following qualities for good multiple-choice questions: (a) use plausible distractors, (b) question/completion format, (c) emphasize higher level thinking, (d) keep option lengths similar, (e) balance the key, (f) avoid grammatical clues, (g) avoid clues to the right answer, (h) avoid negative stems, (i) use only one correct option, (j) give clear directions, (k) include main idea in stem, (l) avoid "all of the above," and (m) avoid "none of the above."

True–false items are easy to compose, yet it is difficult to create statements that are absolutely true, because not much is always true or false. Students have a 50% chance of guessing correctly with these, so this form of question is unreliable. Teachers and students, in their asking and answering, tend to lean toward either true or false answers, making this form of assessment even more unreliable. Many experts (e.g., Nunnally, 1972) advise against using true–false questions. However, if they must be used, limit the statement to a single idea, avoid specific determiners or qualifiers (*all, sometimes, usually, never, always*), be sure each statement is unequivocally true or false, avoid negative and double-negative statements, and use an equal number of true and false statements. Also, be sure all sentences are of about equal length (there is a tendency for longer ones to be true). An example of a good true–false question is:

> EX2: True–false items are reliable forms of assessing student knowledge. (F)

Matching questions are used to cover a lot of material in a relatively small space. There is usually a list of items (which should be no longer than eight) and a list of options (which should be 50% longer than the list of items). All items and options should relate to the same central theme. The instructions should clearly indicate how the matching is to be performed. An example of a good set of matching items is:

> EX3: On the left you will find five different types of exam questions and on the right are some definitions. Choose one correct definition from the right-hand column for each of the exam questions on the left, and write the letter in the space provided. Each definition will be used no more than once.

__ (d) 1. True-false	a. one or two words that students supply
__ (a) 2. Fill-in-the-blank	b. a group of answers to a question from which one correct alternative is chosen
— (b) 3. Multiple choice	c. a puzzle solved through clues consisting of word definitions
— (e) 4. Matching	d. a statement that is judged for its veracity
— (g) 5. Essay	e. a list of definitions that are related to a list of terms
	f. identification of or definitions of terms given
	g. a lengthy statement consisting of an answer to a question
	h. a problem that is solved through computation

Supply or completion items (fill in the blank) eliminate the possibility of guessing and focus on naming and labeling. These items are useful when testing knowledge of simple names, dates, and facts. Authorities suggest that only one or two blank spaces be used per sentence, making sure that only one term will complete the blank. Leave only important terms blank, and place the blank space near the end of the sentence. Avoid repeating the textbook phrasing word for word (or students will attempt to memorize the text), and avoid grammatical cues to the correct word (e.g., *a* or *an* will give clues to the first letter of the word). An example of a good fill-in question is:

> EX4: The type of test question that leaves a blank at the end of the sentence for students to complete is called _____.

Essay questions require recall and phrasing of ideas in one's own words. Be sure to limit the scope of the questions to get the size answer you expect, and ask for answers that can be given in the time you allow for each. Provide enough detail in the question to lead to a correct response, phrase the question so it reflects a high level of understanding, and avoid asking for students' personal feelings (no way to grade these).

The type of question must match the cognitive objectives of the exam, and the type of question is reflected in the explicit instructions. For example, if you want to test knowledge, you might ask students to "name and describe" or if you want to test comprehension, you might ask students to "compare and contrast" or "give an example of." A question that seeks to test ability to synthesize ideas might begin with "develop a theory" or "create a model." If you want to test ability to analyze, you might ask "what reasons are given," and if you want to test students' evaluation skills, the question might begin with "what reasons can you see" or "evaluate the reasoning given."

To increase content validity, use a larger number of short-answer items instead of a smaller number of long-answer items. Be careful, however, not to require too much writing for the time allotted for the exam. To combat the time problem, some instructors give students a choice of answering a certain number of questions, but this is poor practice. All students should be required to answer the same questions to obtain a comprehensive view of students' knowledge as opposed to how well they do on those questions they know. Open-book tests should also be avoided if you want to measure learning. An example of a good essay question is:

> EX5: Name and explain three reasons why essay questions are valid indicators of achievement.

Grading Exams

An answer key makes grading of objective exams simple and quick;

however, there is more to do than just grading these exams. We need to analyze objective exams to see if the exam discriminates between good and poor students (as it should), which items are too easy or too hard (examine the chance factor [e.g., 50% in true–false], the range of difficulty, and then omit or rescore easy items in future use of the test), and which test items best discriminate between those who did well and those who did not (those who do well should not get the easy items wrong). Campus testing or computing centers can compute these statistics for you if you use the mark-sensitive forms they provide.

Grading essay exams (and papers) is more difficult. To eliminate possible bias, remove students' names from their papers or have them provide a code that is translated at a later date. There are two main ways of grading the essays: through *holistic* (general impression) or through *analytical* criteria. The analytical method is more valid and is explained here.

First, write an ideal answer or outline the major points for use in scoring the essays; to make certain your answer is complete, get a colleague to do the same. Use reasonable expectations for grading criteria (no one will recall all the information). Second, use a numerical point scale for each question and determine (before reading the essays) the meaning of the points. Certain items might be weighted in relation to the page-length limit for the answers. Third, total all the points and assign grades after all the individual questions are graded.

When reading the essays, do not let factors other than knowledge (spelling, handwriting, grammar) influence the score unless you are also teaching these; if so, create a separate grade for writing style. Score all answers to one question before going on to the next so that your standards do not shift. Fatigue can affect your use of your grading standards, so take breaks during grading. The breaks should come between questions. If possible, have a fellow instructor read your set of exams to be sure you are using your criteria consistently.

Tips for Grading

1. Consider the course objectives and functions of the test.
2. Make sure the test covers all the material covered in class and in the textbook.
3. Choose the question format most appropriate for your purpose.
4. Consider how much error is in the test and adjust for it.
5. Check the test length.
6. Provide clear instructions to the questions in the test booklet.
7. Have students answer questions on separate answer sheets; discuss the

answers to the exam but return the answer sheets only at the end of the semester.

8. Grade essays and papers using an analytical method of evaluation.

COMPUTING COURSE GRADES

Students deserve a sensible method for combining grades from the various assignments into a grade for the course. If only objective exams are used in a class, for example, the raw scores could be combined and standards developed for final letter grades (e.g., 90% for an A, below 60% for an F). Or, if all exams are created to total 100%, they could be averaged or weighted by importance (some weight the final exam heavier than a regular exam, especially if it is comprehensive). If only essay exams are used in a class, these grades could be averaged, and more weight could be given to longer tests (e.g., the final exam). If there is a mixture of exams or of exams and performances, a 5-point scale could be used to reduce all grades to this system (4.5–5.0 = A; 4.0–4.4 = B; 3.0–3.9 = C; 2.0–2.9 = D; 1.9 or less = F). These could then be averaged, weighted, or both. Your numerical grade equivalency system must be devised before the class begins and then adhered to throughout.

Again, one must keep in mind the objectives for the course in deciding how to compute these grades, and the system that will be used should be presented clearly to students in the syllabus at the beginning of the class. Students can then see what is considered most important in the class. When devising a weighting system for assignments, certain ones clearly should carry more weight. In the basic communication class, speeches to inform, persuade, and stimulate are usually given more weight than speeches of introduction, parliamentary procedure, impromptus, and debate. Perhaps one half of the course grade would be based on speeches, one fourth on exams, and one fourth on outlines and other written assignments.

How Not to Grade

In general, students should be graded on achievement or learning, not on their class attendance, a curve, effort, work habits, personal preferences, character traits, or attitudes toward you or the class. Your evaluation of a student's attitude and personality is subjective and should not receive a grade.

Assigning grades to students and computing course averages should not be done with guilt or feelings that the grade represents the student as a person; rather, grading should be based only on what the student has done in the class during that particular semester. Instructors should keep in mind that a C is an average or normal grade, and guilt about the effect of a grade on a student's future should not inflate the instructor's grades.

Class Attendance.   Is showing up for class a course requirement? Is that all you want, or do you want active participation, thorough and on-time work, and improvement of knowledge or skill? Grades should reward that which is most important, and class attendance should be significantly less important than other objectives. It is better to deduct points for lack of attendance than to give points for attending (check your university's policy on class attendance and approved absences). If you must grade class participation, set standards and a variety of levels, and keep detailed records for each student. Students who feel they deserve higher course grades will surely confront you about the most subjective grade in the class, and that will be the participation grade. You will need to account for all your grades.

Grading on a Curve.   Students who believe that grading on a curve will improve their grades do not understand the basic principle behind the practice. These students want all their grades raised, but grading on a curve is different. A curve assumes a normal curve with a mean of 50 and a standard deviation of 10; this rarely occurs. The normal curve then determines the percentage of students in each letter grade, so there are about equal numbers of A and F students, a larger number of B and D students, and an even larger number of C students. Most classes have too few students to use this accurately, so Terwilliger (1971) advised against it.

There are two major problems with "grading on the curve." If you have a class of highly capable students (in that all students would receive an A or B on an absolute scale), a student could fail an exam or speech with a B grade. This could have major ramifications for students' futures in that talented students would find it hard to get into graduate schools because they happened to be rank ordered in a particular class. Obviously, classes with students who are all low in capability request grading on the curve so that students who have only partially met the course objectives will have a chance to receive an A in the class. With this system, a student's grades might be inflated, and future failure in graduate school could be easily understood. Absolute standards for evaluation will help dispel claims of unfair grading practices.

Grading on Improvement.   Grades should not be based on improvement or progress. It is common and easy for students at low ability levels to improve, making significant gains, whereas it is hard for those at high levels to improve as much. A better system would be to weigh more heavily later assignments; in this way, the lower skilled students would have an opportunity to improve before the more important assignments.

Grading on Effort.   Students should not think that you grade on effort or input (Sussman, 1975). If they do, quality will be disregarded. Students will spend hours working on projects, as though they are punching a time clock, yet may never achieve the quality standards that you set up. Disappointment results because of this. Perceptions of equity are based on investments or inputs and on rewards or outcomes. Teachers need to justify to students their grading systems so students see achievement of assignments, rather than investment of time, as the relevant outcome.

The system advocated in this chapter, then, focuses on the necessity of having equitable standards (ones that are related to the course being taught), communicating these standards to students at the beginning of the course, and using these standards consistently for all students. This is important for evaluating all products in communication classes, whether they be speeches, group discussions, term papers, or exams. Final grades in the class should reflect the knowledge and skill called for in the course's design, and students should be given equal opportunity to demonstrate knowledge and skills in the class.

REFERENCES

Balcer, C. (1958). Evaluation in the speech class—Growth in desirable attitudes. *Central States Speech Journal, 9,* 13–14.

Barker, L. L., Kibler, R. J., & Hunter, E. C. (1968). An empirical study of overlap rating effects. *Speech Teacher, 17,* 160–166.

Beebe, S. A., & Barge, J. K. (1994). Small group communication. In W. G. Christ (Ed.), *Assessing communication education: A handbook for media, speech, and theatre educators* (pp. 257–290). Hillsdale, NJ: Lawrence Erlbaum Associates.

Behnke, R. R., & King, P. E. (1984). Computerized speech criticism. *Communication Education, 33,* 173–177.

Bock, D. G. (1970). The effects of persuasibility on leniency, halo and trait errors in the use of speech rating scales. *Speech Teacher, 19,* 296–300.

Bock, D. G., & Bock, E. H. (1977). The effects of sex on the experimenter, expectancy inductions, and sex of the rater on leniency, halo, and trait errors in speech rating behavior. *Communication Education, 26,* 298–306.

Bock, D. G., & Bock, E. H. (1981). *Evaluating classroom speaking.* Urbana, IL: ERIC Clearinghouse on Reading and Communication Skills.

Bock, D. G., & Bock, E. H. (1984). The effects of positional stress and receiver apprehension on leniency errors in speech evaluation: A test of the rating error paradigm. *Communication Education, 33,* 337–341.

Bock, D. G., Butler, J. L. P., & Bock, E. H. (1984). The impact of sex of the speaker, sex of the rater and profanity type on language trait errors in speech evaluation: A test of the rating error paradigm. *Southern Speech Communication Journal, 49,* 177–186.

Bohn, C. A., & Bohn, E. (1985). Reliability of raters: The effects of rating errors on the speech rating process. *Communication Education, 34,* 343–351.

Book, C., & Simmons, K. W. (1980). Dimensions and perceived helpfulness of student speech criticism. *Communication Education, 29,* 135–145.

Bostrom, R. N. (1963). Classroom criticism and speech attitudes. *Central States Speech Journal, 14,* 27–32.

Bowers, J. W. (1964). Training speech raters with films. *Speech Teacher, 13,* 228–231.

Braden, W. W. (1948). Making speech criticism acceptable to the student. *Southern Speech Journal, 13*, 91–93.

Brooks, W. D., & Friedrich, G. W. (1973). *Teaching speech communication in the secondary school.* Boston: Houghton Mifflin.

Carlson, R. E., & Smith-Howell, D. (1995). Classroom public speaking assessment: Reliability and validity of selected evaluation instruments. *Communication Education, 44*, 87–97.

Cathcart, R. S. (1981). *Post-communication: Critical analysis and evaluation* (2nd ed.). Indianapolis, IN: Bobbs-Merrill.

Clevenger, T. (1963). Retest reliabilities of ten scales of public speaking performances. *Central States Speech Journal, 14*, 285–291.

Clevenger, T. (1964). Influence of scale complexity on the reliability of ratings of general effectiveness in public speaking. *Speech Monographs, 31*, 153–156.

Dedmon, D. N. (1967). Criticizing student speeches: Philosophy and principles. *Central States Speech Journal, 18*, 276–284.

Douglas, J. (1958). The measurement of speech in the classroom. *Speech Teacher, 7*, 309–319.

Gouran, D. S., & Whitehead, J. L. (1971). An investigation of ratings of discussion statements by participants and observers. *Central States Speech Journal, 22*, 263–268.

Goyer, R. S. (1962). The construction of the objective examination in speech. *Southern Speech Journal, 28,* 27–35.

Gundersen, D. F. (1978). Video-tape modules as a device for training speech raters. *Southern Speech Communication Journal, 43*, 395–406.

Haladyna, T. M., & Downing, S. M. (1989). A taxonomy of multiple-choice item-writing rules. *Applied Measurement in Education, 2*(1), 37–50.

Harris, C. W. (1963). Some issues in evaluation. *Speech Teacher, 12*, 191–199.

Hay, E. A. (1994). Interpersonal communication. In W. G. Christ (Ed.), *Assessing communication education: A handbook for media, speech, and theatre educators* (pp. 237–256). Hillsdale, NJ: Lawrence Erlbaum Associates.

Hildebrandt, H. W., & Stevens, W. W. (1960). Blue book criticisms at Michigan. *Speech Teacher, 8*, 20–22.

Holtzman, P. D. (1960). Speech criticism and evaluation as communication. *Speech Teacher, 8*, 1–7.

Kelley, W. D. (1965). Objectivity in the grading and evaluation of speeches. *Speech Teacher, 14*, 54–58.

Knower, F. (1929). A suggestive study of public-speaking rating scale values. *Quarterly Journal of Speech, 15*, 30–41.

Milton, O., & Edgerly, J. W. (1976). *The testing and grading of students.* New Rochelle, NY: Change.

Morreale, S. P. (1994). Public speaking. In W. G. Christ (Ed.), *Assessing communication education: A handbook for media, speech, and theatre educators* (pp. 219–236). Hillsdale, NJ: Lawrence Erlbaum Associates.

Morreale, S. P., Moore, M., Taylor, P., Surges-Tatum, D., & Hulbert-Johnson, R. (1993). *The competent speaker.* Annandale, VA: Speech Communication Association.

Newcombe, P. J., & Robinson, K. F. (1975). *Teaching speech communication: Methods and materials.* New York: McKay.

Nunnally, J. C. (1972). *Educational measurement and evaluation* (2nd ed.). New York: McGraw-Hill.

Rubin, R. B., & Martin, M. M. (1994). Development of a measure of interpersonal communication competence. *Communication Research Reports, 11*, 33–44.

Smith, R. G. (1961). The criticism of speeches: A dialectical approach. *Speech Teacher, 10*, 59-62.

Smythe, M. J., Kibler, R. J., & Hutchings, P. W. (1973). A comparison of norm-referenced and criterion-referenced measurement with implications for communication instruction. *Speech Teacher, 22*, 1–17.

Spitzberg, B. H., & Hurt, H. T. (1987). The measurement of interpersonal skills in instructional contexts. *Communication Education, 36*, 28–45.

Stiggins, R. J., Backlund, P. M., & Bridgeford, N. J. (1985). Avoiding bias in the assessment of communication skills. *Communication Education, 34*, 135–141.

Sussman, L. (1975). A theoretical analysis of equity and its relationship to student evaluation. *Southern Speech Communication Journal, 40*, 321–334.

Terwilliger, J. S. (1971). *Assigning grades to students.* Glenview, IL: Scott, Foresman.

Tiemens, R. K. (1965). Validation of informative speech ratings by retention tests. *Speech Teacher, 14*, 211–215.

Tinkelman, S. N. (1971). Planning the objective test. In R. L. Thorndike (Ed.), *Educational measurement* (2nd ed., pp. 46–80). Washington, DC: American Council on Education.

Wesman, A. G. (1971). Writing the test item. In R. L. Thorndike (Ed.), *Educational measurement* (2nd ed., pp. 81–129). Washington, DC: American Council on Education.

Wiseman, G., & Barker, L. (1965). A study of peer group evaluation. *Southern Speech Journal, 31,* 132–138.

Young, S. (1974). Student perceptions of helpfulness in classroom speech criticism. *Speech Teacher, 23,* 222–234.

V

Tackling Some Unique Teaching Assignments

31

Directing Multiple Sections of the Basic Course

Douglas M. Trank
University of Iowa

The basic communication course is the only course within our discipline that is required by a significant number of other departments and colleges for graduation. Surveys over the past 2 decades have indicated that the basic communication course is required of noncommunication majors in a majority of the institutions across the country. This unique characteristic provides healthy departmental enrollments and excellent visibility across campus, but it also places burdens on teachers and directors of the basic course. Although teachers in the basic course share responsibility for delivering a quality product, the ultimate responsibility for the quality of a course with several sections inevitably belongs to the director of the course.

That responsibility is often complicated by the director's status within the department. The basic course director is frequently a newly graduated and recently hired assistant professor. That person is expected to meet the normal expectations for tenure and promotion; that is, to contribute to the service and teaching needs of the department and to publish an acceptable quantity of research of sufficient quality to gain tenure and promotion within the specified time allowed. In institutions with a relatively large number of sections of the basic course, these additional responsibilities for the director can complicate what is already a demanding professional commitment. Although this chapter does not explore all of the duties and responsibilities of a basic course director, the major issues and those that frequently cause serious problems are examined. The issues discussed are focused around the educational justification for the basic course, typical approaches to the course, problems unique to programs with multiple sections, and administrative concerns for the basic course director.

EDUCATIONAL JUSTIFICATION FOR THE BASIC COURSE: A DUALITY OF PURPOSE

Basic course directors, if they are to be effective with all the audiences that have a vested interest, must operate from a philosophy that allows the basic course to function both as a service course and as an essential part of a student's liberal education. Unfortunately, some individuals view the term *service course* with negative connotations, as something less important than other courses within the department. It is far more productive and accurate to realize that fulfilling a duality of purpose—providing a curriculum that is a primary service to other disciplines and providing instruction that is at the core of a liberal arts education—is a unique and rewarding opportunity.

Basic course directors must be concerned with the nature and purpose of instruction in the basic course. Should it focus on theory or application or some integration of the two? Should it attempt to teach the history of the discipline, the nature of human interaction, critical thinking and decision making, interpersonal or group theory, or should it fulfill functions more directly related to other missions of the department? Regardless of the size or the nature of the institution or the inclination of the faculty, most basic courses in communication share two fundamental goals: to introduce students to the discipline of communication and to meet basic communication proficiency needs. It is obviously possible to design a basic course that fulfills many functions, including one that meets the expectations of faculty outside the department and satisfies the specific requirements of the communication faculty. What is critical for the effectiveness of the basic course director, however, is that the faculty within the department and the administration agree and support the position of the basic course director.

TYPICAL APPROACHES TO THE BASIC COURSE

In some institutions, the nature of the basic course is decided by colleagues and administrators outside the communication department. If, for example, the college of business and the college of education want their students to have experience and instruction in public speaking, the faculty of the department will provide a public speaking orientation if they want the course to continue as a requirement for those colleges. Other colleges or departments may want a different orientation. Although others may well have a degree of input into the nature of the basic course, the course director and the faculty in the communication department must assume the ultimate control over the course. After all, they possess the expertise in communication instruction and have a responsibility to ensure that what is being taught reflects the best theory and research available.

Communication departments typically continue to teach the basic course through one of three standard approaches. As Hugenberg (1994) argued, the basic course has been extraordinarily resistant to change over the past several decades and most programs and courses exist essentially as they were years ago. Although it is difficult to generalize too far in describing these courses, the interpersonal course generally emphasizes a theoretical approach to understanding human interaction. The competent communicator in this approach is one who understands the nature and process of human communication. In a public speaking course, the competent communicator is one who can prepare and present a variety of types of messages for different purposes to different audiences. The emphasis here is on the "public" performance of students. The combination or blend course shares many theoretical and experiential approaches and the emphasis is broader than in either of the other courses. Other adaptations of these approaches and combinations are provided by a number of institutions.

Information on orientations toward the basic course, instructional methods used by various programs, and issues related to administrative concerns can be found in the results of regional and national surveys. They document, for example, a continued shift in the orientation of the basic course toward a public speaking approach at the expense of the interpersonal and multiple or combination approaches. Over half of the basic course programs have reported a public speaking approach, a third a combination or blend approach, and the remaining programs were split between communication theory, interpersonal, and small group approaches (Gibson, Hanna, & Huddleston, 1985; Trank, Becker, & Hall, 1986).

The Basic Course Committee of the National Communication Association and the Midwest Basic Course Directors' Conference offer annual meetings and conferences where basic course directors share information and research results specifically related to the basic course. The Central States Communication Association, Eastern Communication Association, Southern States Communication Association, and Western States Communication Association also sponsor such conferences and meetings on a regular basis. Information about all of these organizations and conferences can be obtained from the National Communication Association. Basic course directors can discover the nature of the basic course at other institutions by attending such conferences and seeking out the results of regional and national surveys.

PROBLEMS UNIQUE TO BASIC COURSE PROGRAMS WITH MULTIPLE SECTIONS

The basic course director must serve as the educational leader for the most critical program within most undergraduate communication departments. A survey of a representative sample of the more than 2,000 institutions on the National Communication Association's mailing list reported a mean basic course enrollment of nearly 900 students each year. A liberal interpretation of these data would place the total national enrollment close to 2 million students each year (Trank et al., 1986). This population will continue to be critical to the success of many departments, our colleagues, and our discipline.

Consistency Across Sections

Most institutions have enrollments that necessitate multiple sections of the basic course. Because of the content and performance nature of many of our approaches to basic course instruction, small sections are frequently desirable and necessary. In addition, as McKeachie (1994) argued, smaller classes provide superior learning outcomes in terms of retention, critical thinking, and attitude differentiation—all typically central issues in the basic communication course. Multiple sections present problems not necessarily found in other instructional situations. The degree of consistency of instructional practices and content across sections is a critical issue for the basic course director. Students in Section 10, for example, have the right to expect that the instruction they receive (their assignments and classroom activities, the goals and objectives, and the content) is very similar to that which the students in Section 167 receive. Equally important, at least in their minds, the students want to be assured that grades are distributed fairly and equitably across sections, regardless of the instructor. Students frequently complain that their roommate or friend in another section did only half the work they did, or that they received a lower grade than those in other sections because they had "tough" instructor compared to all the "easy" instructors their friends talk about. This problem is not restricted to only very large programs, but is likely to appear for any course that has more than one section.

Even though most faculty and students realize that absolute equality of instruction and evaluation across a large number of sections is impossible, the basic course director has the responsibility to ensure some degree of consistency across sections and across semesters. Although this is accomplished to a certain extent by decisions that the director and the faculty make about the educational justification and the purpose and the approach for the basic course discussed earlier, the decisions made regarding the specificity of the syllabus or course guidelines and the training of instructors are equally critical. In large institutions, the basic course is typically staffed and taught almost entirely by graduate teaching assistants (GTAs) or part-time faculty. A majority of basic course instruction, however, takes place in community colleges and smaller colleges where GTAs are not available. Although it is no less important, it is sometimes more difficult to achieve uniformity with different faculty teaching the same course than it is with GTAs or part-time faculty.

A basic course director may have difficulty forcing a particular content, textbook, or approach on colleagues who have been teaching this course for several years or who may not want to teach at the basic level. It may also be difficult for them to become enthused about the innovative ideas and novel approaches developed by a basic course director who might have considerably less teaching and administrative experience than many of the instructors for the course. In these situations, the basic course director obviously needs to secure the input of colleagues before making all decisions about the course. At the opposite extreme, a basic course director may be faced with a situation where half or more of the GTAs assigned to teach the course have no experience and are coming to campus for the first time shortly before they are expected to begin teaching. Many of them may have never taught before. In this case, the director needs to provide detailed and specific materials for the instructors and, in fact, cannot wait until these instructors have opportunities for input into the development of the course.

Many basic course directors advocate a prescriptive approach for organizing the course that calls for minimal involvement from the instructors in the planning stage. This approach requires the basic course director to develop a syllabus to be used by all instructors, complete with content, activities, and exercises. The basic course director selects the textbook that will be used in the course, determines which instructional strategies are appropriate for achieving the various goals and objectives of the course, and devises strategies for achieving consistency of evaluation of student performance across sections and situations. A far less prescriptive approach requires the basic course director to determine, either alone or with the faculty, the goals and approach for the course. These goals, along with the general content and perhaps major units of instruction, are presented in a set of general guidelines for instructors to follow. Instructors are frequently allowed a choice from a list of appropriate textbooks and are asked to make decisions about teaching strategies that work best for them in particular situations within the general guidelines. This approach works most effectively where the department has sufficient staff and resources to provide a continual advisor and supervisor function for the GTAs who are assigned to teach the basic course. It is also used in situations where the basic course is staffed primarily or entirely by regular full-time faculty.

It is more common, however, to find the basic course director somewhere between these extremes. Regardless of the degree of control, consistency across sections of a large basic communication course can only be accomplished with the cooperation of all those involved in the delivery of that course. In situations where a significant number of sections of the basic course are staffed by faculty with limited teaching experience, the director must establish an ongoing instructional program in order to ensure the continuous quality and consistency of instruction. The following section examines some of the elements of such programs for professional development of the instructional staff.

Professional Development Programs

Directors must make some important decisions, including what leadership style they plan to adopt with their teaching staff. Although the pressure for consistency of instruction is strong, and seems to recommend a highly directive style, recent research on leader effectiveness suggests that a very different leadership style may be appropriate. House and Podsakoff (1994) asserted that "outstanding leaders transform organizations by infusing into them ideological values and moral purpose, thus inducing strong commitment, rather than by affecting the cognitions or the task environment of followers, or by offering material incentives and the threat of punishment" (p. 55). Basic course directors may do well to examine the research on transformational leadership as they form their approach to professional development programs. To the extent that professional development is linked to internalization of important disciplinary and instructional values rather than simple compliance with standards and expectations, professional development programs may actually reduce the amount of monitoring required and at the same time engender considerable professional growth.

Although the primary responsibility of the director is to provide quality instruction for the undergraduates enrolled in all sections of the course, there is a concomitant responsibility to help the basic course staff develop their abilities as instructors. The director needs to establish an atmosphere where the graduate student instructors and part-time faculty know that they are viewed as valuable members of the faculty and are given a certain degree of freedom and responsibility for what they do in the classroom. An obvious way for basic course directors to begin establishing such an atmosphere is to view themselves as advisors and teachers rather than as supervisors and trainers.

If a relationship is established in which the role of the director is to supervise, correct, and punish inappropriate behavior, it is likely that instructors will avoid the director whenever possible. If the director adopts this overseer role, instructors will likely withhold information about their classes for fear that their teaching will be criticized or that they will be reprimanded. Reducing opportunities for communication between director and instructors decreases consistency of instruction across sections and decreases the morale of the basic course staff. Such a relationship is clearly counterproductive to the goals of improving both the teaching competencies of the staff and the outcomes of instruction in the basic course.

Most large basic course programs have a preservice workshop lasting from 2 to 5 days before the beginning of the semester. Creating a supportive climate at this point provides positive benefits throughout the term (Andrews, 1983; Hugenberg, 1994; Trank, 1986). In addition to providing an early opportunity for developing positive interpersonal relationships among the teaching staff, the workshop is an important time to establish the goals for the course, convey the general guidelines and day-to-day chores that must be completed throughout the term, and see to the immediate and personal needs of the teaching staff.

An increasing number of departments also conduct weekly seminars for the instructional staff throughout the term. Some continue the seminars for the entire year, and a few give graduate credit for completing the course. Topics for such seminars include the range of subjects found in this book—from establishing objectives to final evaluation and assigning grades. These seminars give the director the time and opportunity to talk about teaching strategies, classroom management, responding to and evaluating student presentations, leading discussions, attendance policies, registration, schedules, and final grade sheets. Examples of such professional development programs and considerable advice regarding the teaching and training of GTAs and part-time staff is readily available (e.g., Andrews, 1983; Chism & Warner, 1987; Dixson, 1994; Moore, 1984; Trank, 1985, 1986; Yingling, 1984).

ADMINISTRATIVE CONCERNS FOR THE BASIC COURSE DIRECTOR

The final section of this chapter deals briefly with administrative details that are critical to the effective operation of the basic course program. The problems that frequently hinder the effectiveness of the director of the basic course—budgets for new equipment, the size of the general expense budget, not enough faculty, not enough clerical help, too many students for faculty size, quality of undergraduate students—are the same problems that are perceived as the most serious for department chairs (Becker & Trank, 1988). The severity and extent of these problems within any department directly affect the decisions the director makes about the instructional staff, resources, and delivery and support systems for the basic course.

Delivery and Support Systems for the Basic Course

An increasing number of departments moved to a large lecture approach to teaching the basic course in the past, primarily to reduce the cost per credit hour of instruction. As budgets within departments held steady or declined as enrollments rose, the basic course became a logical and necessary target for exploring possible alternative instructional strategies that would save or revert a substantial portion of the departmental budget. Although the large lecture format no longer enjoys widespread popularity across the country, it remains one of a number of alternative delivery systems.

Other alternatives also appear to be driven, at least in part, by financial imperatives. Gray, Buerkel-Rothfuss, and Yerby (1986) claimed that the mandate to reduce costs has forced directors and administrators to search for educational models that provide the highest number of student credit hours for the lowest investment of faculty time. The personalized system of instruction, originally defined by Keller (1968), is one of the better known alternative delivery systems (see Seiler & Titsworth, chap. 27, this volume). This is a complex system that involves student self-paced learning and the extensive use of proctors, who are usually undergraduates who have taken the course. It also necessitates a facility that can manage the ongoing multiple activities of test taking, tutoring, presenting speeches, and studying. It requires strong, organized leadership from the director of the basic course and substantial support from the administration and faculty.

The majority of basic course programs across the country continue to deliver the basic course in the traditional small-section format. An increasing number of these programs, however, are using undergraduate assistants or undergraduate facilitators in a variety of ways to reduce the cost of instruction. Although using undergraduates to assist in the instruction of the basic course may provide financial benefits to the department and the college, it presents additional problems for the director in terms of supervision and evaluation of instruction and ensuring consistency across the program.

The director may also be responsible for a speaking lab, where students can get individualized help for problems ranging from speech organization to communication apprehension. More recently, scholars and instructors have become increasingly interested in problems associated with nonnative speakers of English in the basic course classrooms and labs. As the number of international students in our institutions continues to increase, this issue will command additional attention from basic course directors.

Instructional Concerns in the Basic Course

Many directors have become painfully aware that, although they have the responsibility for the quality of instruction in the basic course, they have little actual authority over the instructors who teach that course. In large research institutions where the basic course is taught primarily by graduate students, the director typically has little control over the selection process. Graduate students are recruited for their academic ability; unfortunately, impressive Graduate Record Examination scores and outstanding undergraduate grade point averages do not guarantee a high level of competence as an instructor in the classroom. Rapid turnover of GTAs, especially in programs that hire large numbers of master's degree students, is another concern for the basic course director. It is difficult to maintain continuity in a program when a significant percentage of the teaching staff is new each year.

Even though basic course directors may have little control over who teaches the course, they are generally responsible for coordinating the evaluation of that instruction—usually through some form of written student evaluations of the course and instructors at midterm or at the end of the term. If a cafeteria type of evaluation system is used, it is advisable to have a common core of questions for all instructors in order to make comparisons across sections and over several semesters. The director can make more informed judgments about instructional effectiveness by visiting the instructors' classrooms, examining their class handouts and syllabi, and examining student folders containing the work completed during the term. Some of these evaluations, if they are to be immediately helpful for instructors, should occur well before the end of the term while there is still an opportunity to alter approaches to the class. Such evaluation ought to have two primary purposes: to reward and praise excellent instruction and to identify situations where instructors need additional help to improve classroom performance. The director must place evaluation in a positive context in order to minimize the anxiety and confusion that it creates for the instructional staff.

The director must also be concerned about the distribution of grades across the course. Because the basic course is frequently taught in small sections with considerable student–instructor interaction, grade inflation is a common concern. Grades need to convey a realistic assessment of the students' work for the semester, but they also convey a message about communicative abilities to a wider audience across and beyond the academic community. The procedure is unfair if some instructors' grades are considerably higher or lower than those given by colleagues teaching the same course. The course director can provide guidance by giving the instructors the profile of grades for the course from past semesters and by providing the profile of grades for students at midterm. Those who seem unreasonably high or low can be encouraged to share a set of papers with other instructors or visit other instructors' classes and evaluate student speeches together. The role of the director here is to advise and teach.

The director also has a major responsibility regarding decisions about which instructional resources will be used in the basic course. The publishing and marketing of textbooks is a major financial enterprise, and the director ought to enlist the assistance of a committee of experienced basic course instructors to select the textbooks for the course. Publishing companies are providing increasingly attractive packages of ancillary instructional materials for basic communication textbooks. For some programs, the need for videotaped examples of student speeches, instructor's manuals, computerized banks of examination questions, and student workbooks are central issues in the selection of a textbook.

Procedural Concerns in the Basic Course

Finally, there are a number of concerns that affect the entire department but that are essentially the responsibility of the basic course director. Decisions about the course that need to be published in college or university catalogs, schedules of courses, and related materials are often needed 6 to 18 months ahead of time. If the basic course is required, provisions and procedures for exemption examinations need to be made. The basic course director is usually responsible for writing and administering the exemption examinations and, if students are required to give speeches, training and scheduling instructors to evaluate those presentations. If the department does not have a policy regarding plagiarism, the director ought to establish one for the basic course. The same is necessary for issues like responsible use of language, human rights, required attendance, and student appeals.

The director is also responsible for scheduling instructors into the respective sections of the basic course. In institutions where regular and part-time faculty teach the course, other teaching responsibilities may take precedence over the basic course assignment. When dealing with graduate students, the director may need to wait until their schedules of courses are complete before attempting to schedule their teaching assignments. Policies concerning absences from teaching, cooperation with research studies, and extra teaching assignments need to be clearly stated for all instructors. The director must also plan a budget and procedure for allocating additional materials such as videotapes, duplicating materials, paper, and other instructional aids.

CONCLUSION

There are obviously many responsibilities and duties for a basic course director that vary depending on the nature of the course and the department. The issues discussed in this chapter focused around the educational justification for the basic course, typical approaches to the course, problems unique to programs with multiple sections, and administrative concerns for the basic course director. This discussion provides a starting point for those who may want to learn more about the basic course or for those who suddenly discover that they are about to become a director of the basic course.

REFERENCES

Andrews, P. H. (1983). Creating a supportive climate for teacher growth: Developing graduate students as teachers. *Communication Quarterly, 31*, 259–265.

Becker, S. L., & Trank, D. M. (1988). Why are you so happy? Predictors of communication chairpersons' satisfaction. *Association for Communication Administration Bulletin, 63*, 36–43.

Chism, N. V. N., & Warner, S. B. (Eds.). (1987). *Institutional responsibilities and responses in the employment and education of teaching assistants*. Columbus: The Ohio State University Center for Teaching Excellence.

Dixson, M. D. (1994, November). *Directing associate faculty: A rich resource for the basic course*. Paper presented at the Speech Communication Association Convention, New Orleans, LA.

Gibson, J. W., Hanna, M. S., & Huddleston, B. M. (1985). The basic speech course at U.S. colleges and universities; IV. *Communication Education, 34*, 281–191.

Gray, P. L., Buerkel-Rothfuss, N. L., & Yerby, J. (1986). A comparison between PSI-based and lecture-recitation formats of instruction in the introductory speech communication course. *Communication Education, 35*, 111–125.

House, R. J., & Podsakoff, P. M. (1994). Leadership effectiveness: Past perspectives and future directions for research. In J. Greenberg, (Ed.), *Organizational behavior* (pp. 45–82). Hillsdale, NJ: Lawrence Erlbaum Associates.

Hugenberg, L. W. (1994, November). *Preserving the integrity of the basic speech course: An examination of current practices.* Paper presented at the Speech Communication Association Convention, New Orleans, LA.

Keller, F. S. (1968). Good-bye teacher. *Journal of Applied Behavior Analysis, 1*, 79–89.

McKeachie, W. J. (1994). *Teaching tips.* Lexington, MA: Heath.

Moore, L. L. (1984, February). *Orientation for first time teaching assistants: A course approach.* Paper presented at the Midwest Basic Course Director's Conference, Youngstown, OH.

Trank, D. M. (1985). An overview of present approaches to the basic speech communication course. *Association for Communication Administration Bulletin, 52*, 86–89.

Trank, D. M. (1986). A professional development program for graduate instructors in communication and composition. *Resources in Education*, ED 277 052. ERIC document.

Trank, D. M., Becker, S. L., & Hall, B. (1986). Communication arts and sciences in transition. *Association for Communication Administration Bulletin, 58*, 8–20.

Yingling, J. M. (1984, February). *Training the first-time teaching assistant: An adaptation of the Friedrich/Powell program.* Paper presented at the annual Midwest Basic Course Director's Conference, Youngstown, OH.

32

Directing
Debate and Forensics

Thomas A. Hollihan
University of Southern California

For more than 200 years, U. S. college students have learned the principles of argumentation and have developed their public speaking abilities through participation in academic debate. The first debating society was established at Harvard in 1722, and by the time of the Revolutionary War, Princeton, Columbia, William and Mary, and Rutgers (Queens College) all had debating societies in place (Potter, 1954). The first intercollegiate contest occurred when Yale met Harvard at Cambridge in 1892, to debate the topic "Resolved: that a young man casting his first ballot in 1892 should vote for the nominees of the Democratic Party."

Intercollegiate debates became so popular that by 1897, colleges and universities throughout the country participated. The debates often attracted large audiences and provided entertainment for students and the local citizenry. These public debates provided opportunities for people to learn about and discuss the complex social and political issues of the day. The debates were often fiercely competitive, and matches between rival campuses often attracted substantial press attention (Potter, 1954). College administrators, who then, as now, sought to promote the achievements of their students and faculty, came to appreciate the positive press coverage their debate victories garnered. To help assure debate successes, in 1910, the first faculty debate coaches were hired to help students improve their preparation and delivery skills (Cowperthwaite & Baird, 1954).

The drama and excitement of intercollegiate debates proved, however, no match for college football. With the advent of intercollegiate sports competitions, it became more difficult to attract large public audiences for debates. Yet students still sought training and competition in debate, and debate coaches searched for ways to create opportunities for competition. Beginning in the 1920s, tournament debating became popular. In tournaments students could compete in as many as 6 to 10 (and eventually as many as a dozen) debates over the course of a weekend. Although students got to debate more often, they lost the opportunity to develop their skills in speaking to large public audiences. Tournament debates frequently occurred only in the presence of a single judge, and whereas before debaters sought to convince ordinary citizens, now they debated primarily for expert judges. Soon tournaments also offered students opportunities to compete in oratory, extemporaneous speaking, and oral interpretation.

With the hiring of the first debate coaches, one of the most demanding yet rewarding careers in communication was created. In addition to the ordinary professorial tasks of teaching classes, serving on committees, and conducting research, the college debate and forensics coach works closely with students to prepare them for competition, accompanies them to intercollegiate tournaments, serves as a critic and judge at those tournaments, and, in many cases, drives all night through inclement weather to get home in time to teach the next morning. Despite the extraordinary demands, however, the rewards in coaching are also great. Forensics training challenges students to learn by stimulating their competitive instincts and, because forensics activities are so time consuming, the students who are drawn into the activity tend to be among the brightest and most motivated students on campus. It is a pleasure to teach students who want to learn and who genuinely aspire to do their best. The long hours working with students and accompanying them to tournaments also permits coaches to develop close personal mentoring relationships with students that are far more rewarding and enduring than most student–faculty contacts.

Today forensics programs may offer students training and experience in several different types of debate, oratory, extemporaneous speaking, oral interpretation of literature, or a whole range of other "individual" speaking events. Some college programs specialize in only one type of forensics training, whereas others may compete in all of these activities.

This chapter offers recommendations for new forensics coaches, or for those who might someday become coaches. It provides a rationale for forensics education, suggests how a new director might define the scope of his or her program, provides a few tips on administering a program (recruiting, budgeting, publicity, etc.), and finally, suggests how forensics coaches should prepare for and be evaluated for promotion and tenure.

A RATIONALE FOR A FORENSICS PROGRAM

Despite the long history of forensics activities, and the fact that hundreds of colleges and universities, thousands of high schools, and tens of thousands of students annually participate in forensics, "selling" a forensics program to one's departmental colleagues and college administrators can nonetheless be a difficult task. Building and maintaining support for your program is an important part of the job of any forensics director.

The benefits of forensics training are easy to document. As I have already mentioned, forensics attracts bright and motivated students to your department and your campus. Forensics students tend to get good grades (despite the demands of competition—perhaps because of them), score well on standardized tests, and gain admission to good graduate and law schools. They also tend to be outgoing and highly verbal students who will impress your colleagues and your administrators. A successful and visible forensics program attracts favorable press attention and helps recruit new students to your campus.

Despite all these benefits, however, forensics programs are costly, and thus they are often vulnerable, especially during times of budget tightening. Forensics directors are thus continually appealing for additional funds to support their programs and always arguing that their programs deserve support. The strongest argument in support of a forensics program is that forensics competition provides a unique learning laboratory for gifted students. Viewed from this perspective, forensics is akin to an honors program, and the educational opportunities for gifted students are often more costly than those for average students. The forensics-as-laboratory argument also permits you to compare the costs of forensics to the cost of providing laboratory education in the sciences, engineering, or broadcasting. By comparison, forensics is a bargain. Forensics also provides educational opportunities that cannot be duplicated in the classroom. If your department offers graduate degrees, you can also argue that assigning graduate students as assistant coaches enriches their education and helps prepare them for careers in forensics. I never described my forensics program as an "extracurricular" activity; when budgets are under close scrutiny the "extras" always get cut first. Instead, I always characterized forensics as "cocurricular" and as vital to the integrity and appeal of the undergraduate offerings in communication.

Many administrators calculate the costs for a program by determining the cost per student served. Forensics programs seem very expensive when their costs are figured this way. They seem less expensive if one calculates cost by determining the cost per round of competition. It is important to keep records of the number of tournaments your students attended, how many rounds they competed in, and how many hours they spent in preparation. Emphasizing the intensity of the learning laboratory makes your arguments on costs more compelling.

A common argument about the cost of forensics programs is that they serve too few students given the faculty and departmental resources they consume. I caution you against responding to this argument by greatly expanding the size of your program. As programs grow they consume even more resources. In order to prepare students adequately for competition you will need to have other faculty or graduate students assigned to assist you. You will need to provide more judges to accompany your students to tournaments. You will need more money for transportation, lodging, meals, and entry fees. Increasing the size of the squad seldom produces greater efficiencies; it typically ends up requiring more money. A very large forensics squad might also diminish the credibility of your argument that forensics is an honors program for gifted students. Finally, the greater the number of students in the program, the less time you as forensics director will have to work closely with them. The director of a very large program may ultimately become more of an administrator (concerned with managing the budget and warding off entropy) than a teacher. The most effective forensics programs are those that are small enough for students to develop real feelings of closeness and cohesion with their peers and their instructors.

How large should your squad be? That depends on your goals, the size of your budget, your proximity to tournaments, the number of other faculty or graduate student assistant coaches who offer to help you out, your teaching load, and the unique situation on your campus. The average squad is from 8 to 25 students and, if you are alone, I caution you against trying to teach more than 15 or 20 students.

Many forensics directors justify the worth of their program, and indirectly its cost, by arguing that they win a lot of trophies. Everyone likes winners, and a winning squad is a tremendous asset in your appeal for funds. Do not, however, make tournament victories the primary rationale for your program. Forensics is not football. The dangers in celebrating your successes too loudly should be apparent: First, not all years will be equally successful. Second, administrators come to expect successes and take them for granted, thus they may take away support after a mediocre season but not reward you after a great one. Third, a program justified primarily on the basis of tournament victories trivializes forensics by sending a message to your students that you value wins more than you value the solid academic achievements that they make. Certainly your successes should be savored, and you should make certain that you promote your squad's achievements so that people on campus and in the community are aware of them, but remember that competition is the means by which you achieve your goal, not the goal itself.

Another important strategy for building a strong forensics program is to contact alumni from your college or university who competed in forensics. If your college had a forensics program in past years, you will likely find that you have a ready group of advocates for your program among its alumni. If you are teaching in a college that has never before had a forensics program, do not despair. Look around campus and in the community for people who may have competed in high school forensics, or for other colleges. Often they will step forward to testify to the benefits of their forensics experiences. Undoubtedly, you will find forensics alumni in positions of leadership and responsibility in your community—forensics attracts and helps such people develop their talents. Often these alumni are willing to dig into their own pockets to help support your program, but even if they are not in a position to contribute money, they may offer their services as assistant coaches or tournament judges, and they may use their contacts in the community or on campus to support your efforts.

DEFINING THE SCOPE OF YOUR PROGRAM

The size and scope of your program will depend on the resources available to you, the amount of time you have to invest, and the skill and experience levels of your students. Obviously an intercollegiate program—where students travel to tournaments and compete against students from other colleges and universities—is more costly and time consuming than an on-campus program. Intercollegiate programs are more common than on-campus programs, however, because students are motivated by the opportunity to travel for competitions.

As the director, you should have the primary control of your program, but it is important that you define the scope for the program in consultation with your departmental colleagues, chairperson, and dean. It is much easier to maintain an effective program in an environment where your colleagues and superiors understand and share your goals. Remember also that your program should be designed to be a part of the department's curriculum in communication. As such, it is important that the faculty be involved in discussions over its focus and orientation.

Define your goals by considering your own skills and resources, those of your students, the size of your budget, and the extent of any help you can expect to receive. Your squad can choose to compete in debate, individual events, or both, depending on your goals. The choice of which activities you will compete in is the first means by which you begin to establish the objectives for your program.

If you are new to forensics coaching, and especially if you do not have prior experience as a competitor, I encourage you to attend some local tournaments to observe the different types of forensics activities before deciding which events to coach during your first season. Although all forensics activities provide students opportunitities to improve their communication skills, there are important differences in the objectives of the activities. As they have developed in recent years, Cross Examination Debate Association (CEDA) and National Debate Tournament (NDT) teams debate emphasize research, argumentation, and refutation skills a bit more than they do public speaking skills. Students get their topics during the summer and debate the same topic over and over at several different tournaments. In order to compete successfully, they will need to spend many hours in the library doing research, and many more hours developing their affirmative and negative case positions. Parliamentary debate, on the other hand, focuses much more on students' public speaking abilities, use of humor, and extemporaneous speaking skills. Students typically get their topics only a short time before they actually debate, and may never be asked to debate on that topic again. If you find yourself coaching a squad populated with students with no prior debate experience it may be a bit easier to field competitive teams in parliamentary debate than in NDT or CEDA. I would also encourage you to contact other coaches in your area to learn what kind of debate they compete in and what predominates in your area. It will be much easier to find competitions for your students if you compete in the same type of debate as the other schools in your region.

You might also decide to limit your squad's participation to individual events. Competition in individual events emphasizes the development of students' speaking skills rather than research or argumentation skills, but also offers students insights into the aesthetic and interpretive dimensions of communication. If you do not have debate experience yourself, you might find it very difficult to begin coaching students in debate, and in that case, individual events might be a more appropriate avenue for developing your program. My own biases are such that I prefer to see programs compete in both debate and individual events, because I believe that both activities uniquely develop students' abilities, but I think that directors must develop programs that are appropriate for their particular situation.

SUGGESTIONS FOR THE ADMINISTRATION
OF YOUR PROGRAM

Before you begin your first season as a forensics director, you need to do some planning. First, you must determine what resources you have available to you for the year: How much money do you have to spend? What limitations do you face in how to spend it? Does the college supply you with transportation? What insurance or liability problems do you face? And so on. Second, you need to determine how many students will compete on the squad. If you are taking over an established program, you need to find out how many students are returning. If you are developing a new squad, you need to do some recruiting. You should decide what you take to be an optimal size for your program before you begin recruiting. You do not want to attract more students to your program than you have the resources to serve. Third, once you know how much money you will have available to you and the number of students, you can begin to project your season. This means figuring out what tournaments you will attend and how much they will cost. This is a difficult task, because you must also predict how quickly your students' talent will develop.

To learn about the tournaments in your area, you will need to consult a forensics calendar. The American Forensic Association (AFA) publishes a comprehensive calendar that lists tournaments in both debate and individual events. To get a copy of the calendar, you should contact the Executive Secretary of the AFA.[1] In fact, you should join the AFA. Your membership will include a subscription to the journal *Argumentation and Advocacy*, which offers very helpful essays on argumentation and forensics. In addition, the AFA will also send you a packet of materials to help you get your program established, as well as information about how you can contact other forensics coaches and organizations in your area.

Once you get the calendar, you will need to plan your tentative schedule for the season. Try to determine what tournaments you will attend, how many students you will send to each, and what the costs will be. You must plan for transportation costs, entry fees, lodging, meals (or a meal allowance for each student), judging fees, and so on. Always budget at least 10% more for each tournament than the minimum amount you think you will need; your expenses on a forensics trip, like those on a vacation, are almost always more than you anticipate. There are no hard and fast rules on the number of tournaments you should plan to attend in a given season. My

---

[1]Currently, the Executive Secretary of the AFA is James W. Pratt, Box 256, River Falls, WI 54022–0256; E-mail: James.W.Pratt@uwrf.edu.

goal was usually to have each student compete in three to five tournaments each semester. Experienced students will typically desire and need to attend more tournaments than will beginners. I also tried to mix the schedule so that all students attended both local tournaments and tournaments that were a bit more prestigious and farther from home. These "reward" trips helped motivate students and gave them something to shoot for as the season and their skills progressed.

I tried to schedule at least one or two tournaments each season that virtually the entire squad attended. This helped build team unity and communicated to the squad that everyone contributed to the squad results. As your squad grows in size and quality, you can also compete for tournament sweepstakes awards, which are given for overall squad excellence.

Squad unity and good relations among forensics competitors are important to the quality of life—yours and theirs. Forensics students are competitive; they are drawn to the activity because it affords them the opportunity to compete. Challenging them to direct their competitive urges against students from other schools rather than their teammates can be a real problem and can frustrate even the most experienced coach. I always told my students that forensics was a meritocracy that rewarded excellence, but excellence did not simply mean tournament successes. It also meant work effort, improvement, contribution to the squad, and a positive attitude. As a coach you should always try to be consistent and fair in your dealings with students. As you come to know your students, you will find that you enjoy some of them more than others. However, you need to communicate to all the criteria that you will use to decide who will compete at what tournaments, who will be paired together, and so forth. If you stick to those criteria, you will have fewer problems. I recommend that you avoid running a "star program" in which only your most gifted students get resources and your attention. Running this kind of program can sometimes seem very tempting. You have only a limited amount of money to spend and a limited amount of your own time. The natural tendency is to lavish both on your most successful and committed students. I think this undermines squad morale and denies the benefits of forensics to some of the students who may ultimately profit most from their participation in the activity. I am not advocating that all students should get the same amount of money spent on them, or even the same amount of your time, but I do believe all students should be made to feel that they belong and that they are part of the team.

Recruiting students is one of the most important elements in maintaining a successful program. Concentrate on recruiting students in your own classes and in other classes in your department. Make announcements at the start of each term to make sure that students are aware of the program. Go out of your way to encourage particularly bright or communicative students to become involved. Do not wait for students to find you; go out and find them. Many students are either unaware of forensics or are apprehensive about their ability to compete while also doing their classwork. You need to overcome these barriers to participation. Contact faculty in other departments. Students in political science are often interested in debate. Students in English or theater arts are often interested in individual events. Work hard to cultivate relationships with faculty in these other departments so that they will recommend their best students to you. These relationships will also prove useful when it is time for you to get your students excused from classes so they can attend tournaments! Take out an advertisement or try to get a story in the school newspaper on forensics. You might also host a campuswide demonstration debate. For example, the National Communication Association's Committee on International Discussion and Debate sponsors tours of international debate teams from Great Britain, Russia, and Japan. Hosting one of these international teams for an audience debate against your students can be an excellent way to attract attention for your squad. You might also schedule an individual events reading hour so that students and other faculty see your students present their best speeches and thereby learn about your program.

You should also recruit students from local high schools. Attend one or two local tournaments, observe rounds, and visit with the students. Be upbeat, friendly, and positive in describing the merits of your college and your program. Do not focus only on the superstars. Often the competitors who are not the high school stars do better in college competition; they may also be easier to coach! You should also consider hosting a high school tournament on your campus—nothing is more effective in recruiting students to a college than visits to the campus. Consult with the officers of the National Forensic League in your area before selecting a date for your tournament, however, so you do not conflict with other already established tournaments. If you do decide to host a tournament, there are some very useful books that you should consult to help you prepare. I especially recommend works by Zarefsky and Goodnight (1980) and Klopf and Lahman (1973).

Many forensics coaches neglect to publicize the achievements of their squad. In order to gain recognition for the program, it is important to keep your campus and community informed. Send press releases on the forensics squad to the campus and community newspapers, and perhaps even to your campus administrators. Display the awards that your squad wins in the office of the communication department. Mail a newsletter to your alumni. Remember my earlier cautions, however, and do not emphasize the number of trophies that you win to the point that they become the primary justification for your program. At the same time, keep people on your campus aware of the fact that you field a competitive and successful team. It will be more difficult for some future administrator to kill your program (or starve it of needed resources) if you have made it visible on your campus and if it is clearly identified as a source of institutional identity and pride.

EVALUATING FORENSICS COACHES

The college forensics coach has an unusual job description. He or she must do all the things expected of his or her departmental colleagues, also spending many hours coaching students and traveling to tournaments. The issue of how this coaching time should be evaluated for merit reviews and promotion and tenure decisions is a source of some disagreement. I believe that all forensics coaches need to discuss how they will be evaluated with their chairperson and dean early in their careers so there is no ambiguity about the criteria that will be employed.

Most colleges and universities evaluate faculty in terms of teaching, research, and service. Forensics coaches should be evaluated by the same general criteria as are the other faculty members in their department. Thus, if the institution values research in considerations of merit, promotion, and tenure, then the forensics coach should be expected to conduct research. The amount of research expected should, however, reflect the difference in time available to the forensics coach, and research in argumentation and forensics pedagogy should be regarded favorably. Forensics coaching activities should be valued as part of the coaches' teaching performance, and he or she should be evaluated in such a way as to recognize that a forensics coach has far more contact hours with students than do most other professors. Finally, because forensics coaches typically do things like host tournaments that are very time intensive, they should receive credit for them under service.

Different departments and institutions should be expected to establish unique criteria for evaluating their faculty. My concern is that forensics coaches understand the challenges they face in such evaluations and that they become proactively involved in working out the general criteria with which they will be evaluated in advance. There is one final argument with regard to promotion and tenure that deserves discussion. Forensics coaching is so demanding that very few professors elect to make it the focus of their entire career. Consequently, it is important that coaches keep reading and writing in other areas as well so that when they decide to leave the ranks of active forensics coaches they are able to make other contributions to their department and their discipline.

CONCLUSIONS

A career in forensics coaching is unique because it gives you an opportunity to work closely with gifted students, participate in a worthwhile and challenging activity, and see the results of your teaching weekly throughout the season as your students compete in tournaments. Although forensics coaches are often as competitive as their students, the forensics community is almost always a friendly and open group. Most established coaches will go out of their way to help a new or less experienced coach develop a program. The entire forensics community is committed to increasing the number of programs and students involved. Consequently, you should always feel free to call on other coaches in your area for assistance. Hopefully, this brief chapter has provided some useful hints that will help you get started. Good luck to you should your choose to work in forensics.

REFERENCES

Cowperthwaite, L. L., & Baird, A. C. (1954). Intercollegiate debating. In K. Wallace (Ed.), *History of speech education in America* (pp. 259–276). New York: Appleton-Century-Crofts.

Klopf, D. W., & Lahman, C. P. (1973). *Coaching and directing forensics*. Skokie, IL: National Textbook.

Potter, D. (1954). The literary society. In K. Wallace (Ed.), *History of speech education in America* (pp. 238–258). New York: Appleton-Century-Crofts.

Zarefsky, D., & Goodnight, G. T. (1980). *Forensics tournaments: Planning and administration.* Skokie, IL: National Textbook.

33

Communication
in the 2-Year College

Darlyn R. Wolvin
Prince George's Community College

Andrew D. Wolvin
University of Maryland, College Park

President Clinton's vision of K–14 education for all Americans has moved the community college to center stage in higher education. Indeed, under the President's plan, "the role of this unique institution will change ... and may make the difference as to whether we get from here—to there" (Adelman, 1997, p. A19).

Already, 2-year campuses are at center stage. Approximately 49% of all undergraduate students enrolled in U. S. higher education are enrolled in 2-year institutions, institutions known variously as junior colleges, community colleges, technical colleges, and even some proprietary independent colleges. They can be identified essentially as institutions that offer an Associate of Arts or Associate of Science degree to students who complete a 2-year curriculum of, typically, 60 credit hours.

The American Association of Community and Junior Colleges estimates that in the Fall 1994 semester, 5,529,710 students were enrolled in credit courses on 2-year campuses (*Digest of Education Statistics*, 1996). It is significant to note, also, that although roughly 49% of all undergraduates are enrolled in these institutions, approximately 45% of all first-time enrollees in U. S. higher education are enrolled in 2-year programs (Y. Li, personal communication, January 13, 1997). The average college tuition figure for these 2-year students in 1995–1996 was $7,039 a year (*Digest of Education Statistics*, 1996).

Two-year colleges were begun in the early 20th century to serve an important "junior" college purpose—to provide greater access to higher education for local populations. Some of these schools emerged directly from the public schools systems as extensions of (and usually governed by) the secondary schools in the jurisdiction. Other junior colleges were developed by private groups, typically religious organizations desiring a Bible-based college. Still other junior colleges were established by universities to provide feeder institutions permitting students to fulfill the first 2 years of a curriculum at a satellite campus.

The notion of the junior college has given way in contemporary times, however, to a broader, more comprehensive view of most 2-year institutions as community colleges. As community colleges, these campuses have evolved to fulfill four important functions: collegiate, career, developmental, and community (see Travis, 1996). These functions offer an important framework for distinguishing the institutions and for shaping the work of a communication faculty on such a campus.

The collegiate function of a 2-year institution is to provide the foundation of a student's general education, permitting the student to take the required courses that facilitate transfer to a 4-year institution. On completion of a curriculum at a 2-year school, the transfer student is able to move to the intended campus with most or all of the credits on his or her transcript intact. The primary focus on these freshman and sophomore years at the 2-year college is to get the general education requirements completed so that the junior and senior years can be centered in a major department at the 4-year school. It should be noted, however, that many 2-year schools offer a full array of courses in a curriculum, providing a substantial base in a major program, as well as the general education courses.

Much of the collegiate transfer curriculum in the 2-year institution has been shaped by 4-year requirements. In most states, 2-year offerings are directly parallel to the 4-year curriculum so that students will be able to make direct transfer of credits. The collegiate function of the 2-year institution has undergone some revision—particularly as enrollments in 2-year transfer programs has declined (a decline that coincides with disenchantment with liberal arts and an intense focus on vocational goals on the part of many students in higher education).

A second function is the career program of the 2-year institution. This segment of the school is designed to provide students with solid vocational skills and certification of those skills through an Associate of Arts or Associate of Science diploma. Students enroll in any of a number of vocationally oriented programs on these campuses, including technical fields such as electronics technology and computer technology and specialized fields such as criminal justice, nursing, and office management.

Career programs are strong on 2-year campuses. Burgeoning enrollments and support from business and industry have encouraged administrators to put vast resources into these programs. Faculty positions offer excellent opportunities for individuals who are specialists in a career field to share their experience and expertise with those aspiring to enter the field. The consistent interest in vocational goals on the part of today's students suggests that career programs will remain a strong part of the 2-year college mission.

An important third function of the 2-year institution is developmental education. The perceived decline in U. S. literacy has led to the establishment of programs and courses to enable high school graduates to gain basic academic skills that they missed in their prior education. Indeed, in 1995, 17% of all community college students were enrolled in remedial course work (*National Postsecondary Student Aid Study*, 1996). Developmental education programs are designed to offer remedial studies in such areas as writing, math, study skills, and reading. Many of the courses do not carry academic credit or are identified as developmental in nature on a transcript. Frequently, these courses are staffed by faculty hired especially for their background in developmental education, and the administration of these programs usually is separate from the collegiate departments on the campus. Careful articulation of the objectives and the curriculum is essential to integrating the developmental mission with the other functions of the 2-year school.

A fourth function of 2-year institutions is community education. This mission has evolved from the continuing education role assumed by colleges and universities after World War II. The community education function has played a major role in redefining many 2-year schools as community colleges—offering educational opportunities directly to a local, community-based population.

The community education program usually takes the form of special classes, workshops, and seminars offered without academic credit. A wide array of offerings may be made available to a community, including professional skills (e.g., resumé writing, time management), personal skills (e.g., family dynamics, memory development), and special interests (e.g., flower arranging, wine tasting).

These four functions of the 2-year institution contribute to the uniqueness of the community or junior college and offer interesting career opportunities for the communication educator. It is helpful to consider how these functions shape the student body that one is likely to encounter on the 2-year campus.

In an earlier work (Wolvin & Wolvin, 1972), we drew a profile of the diversity of community college students from research. Our general conclusion was that, although community college students can be of any level of academic ability, they are likely to come from a family whose parents are of lower socioeconomic backgrounds with little education beyond high school. Further, the community college student is more likely to be from an ethnic minority and be older in age than the typical 4-year college student.

A survey of public community colleges in the spring of 1986 offers additional insight into the student population. The results reveal that 36% were enrolled with the intent of transferring to 4-year institutions (the collegiate function). At the career level, 34% of the students were enrolled in order to prepare for a new occupation, and 16% were in classes to gain skills for their current occupation. Another 15% of the students were enrolled in classes to fulfill a personal interest (tapping the community function of the colleges), and 4% of the students were enrolled for the purpose (the compensatory role) of improving their English, math, or reading skills (Center for the Study of Community Colleges, 1986).

This profile illustrates the heavy emphasis on the collegiate and career functions of the 2-year schools and illustrates the need for having both types of programs in a comprehensive institution. Likewise, it is important to consider that the average age of students enrolled in any of these credit courses is 29 years old (Integrated Postsecondary Education Data Systems 1995 Fall Enrollment Survey, 1996). Between 1975 and 1994, 2-year schools experienced a phenomenal enrollment growth of 39% (*Digest of Educational Statistics*, 1994). It should be recognized that many of these institutions have open enrollments and are charged with providing equal access to all persons in a particular community. As a result, students tend to come to the campuses with varying levels of academic ability. Many of them are not enrolled on a full-time basis because they work at full-time jobs while taking courses part time. As Cohen and Brawer (1982) noted, "Two words sum up the students: number and variety" (p. 29).

Thus, the communication educator on the 2-year campus is likely to find a very diverse, older student population, often enrolled part time, with varying purposes for being there. The challenge, then, is to provide a program that can meet the needs of this diverse population.

To meet the objectives of the collegiate function, the community college program ought to, minimally, provide the basic communication course traditional in our discipline. Although the concept of "the" basic course has altered somewhat, evidence (Gibson, Hanna, & Huddleston, 1985) suggests that such a course typically takes a public speaking approach. Leininger (1987), however, discovered that the "hybrid" fundamentals course is most often the one required of students. Such a course, designed to be consistent with the communication requirements of students in 4-year institutions, is an important foundation on which to build the rest of the collegiate curriculum.

Additional courses (similar to those at the freshman and sophomore levels in 4-year institutions) might include Introduction to Interpersonal Communication, Introduction to Small Group Communication and Leadership, Debate, Intercultural Communication, and Listening. Many of these basic-level courses are designed to provide students with a solid foundation in theory along with communication skills in the content areas.

Institutions approach these courses in different ways. At Prince George's Community College in Largo, Maryland, for instance, students are required to take a basic communication course that is designed to transfer to 4-year Maryland institutions. The course, offering units in intrapersonal, interpersonal, and public communication, is a hybrid course with a careful balance of theory and skills. Lane Community College in Oregon offers a required Listening course of its students—a course that can transfer to other Oregon and Northwest schools that offer work in this area of communication. The transferability of courses usually is articulated carefully with faculty and administrators at the 4-year schools to ensure that students will indeed receive transfer credit for the course (Hegstrom, 1981).

Some 2-year schools also offer what is essentially a 2-year major in the field. Designed as a preprofessional degree program, for instance, Lorain County Community College offers a sequence of courses for students in theatre, media performance, media production, and speech communication and rhetoric. The communication preprofessional program at Lorain highlights career opportunities for its students. As described in the Lorain County Community College Brochure (1987):

> People trained in speech communication/rhetoric can enter into the business field in such areas as public relations, personnel, labor relations, customer service, human resources, training and development, and sales; or they can pursue a career in public service as a speech writer, foreign service officer, campaign director, or fund raiser. (p. 1)

The career curriculum in 2-year schools parallels the transfer-focused, collegiate curriculum in the sense that course offerings provide a basic foundation in theory and skills. The career curriculum usually is not aimed specifically at communication majors but is designed for students in any of a wide range of other career fields. Students in career curricula may be required to take a communication course that might be, again, a hybrid course offering work in intrapersonal, interpersonal, and public communication applied to career settings (see Wolvin & Corley, 1984; Wolvin & Wolvin, 1977, 1981). Other course offerings might include classes tailored to specific majors: Interpersonal Communication for Nurses, Business and Professional Speaking, Speech for the Engineer, and so on (see Doyle & Engleberg, 1981).

In a survey of state instructional offices and community college career advisory committee members in various occupational areas, Muchmore and Galvin (1983) identified those communication skills viewed as absolutely essential (or very necessary) for the immediate entry of 2-year college students into career fields. The most important speaking skills were (a) use words understood by others; (b) use words, pronunciation, and grammar that do not alienate others; (c) phrase questions properly in order to get accurate information; (d) explain specific requirements to others; and (e) organize messages so that others can understand them. The most important listening skills were (a) understand directions, (b) obtain necessary factual information, (c) identify important points when given oral instructions, (d) understand accurately questions and suggestions of others, and (e) distinguish between fact and opinion. Community colleges have been urged to develop career curricula that meet these perceived communication needs of the workplace.

The developmental curriculum can (and should) be structured to parallel skill acquisition and development for students in the English, math, and reading areas. Many schools find that offerings in basic oral English for nonnative speakers of English are important, particularly for schools in areas with a heavy influx of international students. Voice and articulation courses may be useful to provide remedial students with work on pronunciation and vocal clarity. Some schools couple this with listening work in the developmental curriculum in order to enable students to build skills in both reading and listening comprehension (see Miller & Young, 1981; Strain & Wyson, 1981). The developmental program at Jefferson Community College in Louisville, Kentucky, for instance, offers a developmental speech course (entitled Individual Growth and Human Relations) for students who are (a) unsure of themselves in speaking situations, (b) hesitant to take a traditional speech course, (c) returning to school after some time and unsure of their academic skills, or (d) below the eighth-grade level in reading or writing skills (Course Syllabus, 1987). To meet the individual needs of developmental students (many of whom are nonnative speakers of English), Golden West College in Huntington Beach, California, has created courses based on skill assessments and competency-based laboratory components utilizing peer and volunteer tutoring techniques (Ratliffe & Hudson, 1986).

Although many educators decry the need for colleges to provide remedial work in basic skills, the reality is, in the words of Boyer (1987), that "far too many of today's students lack a solid academic foundation ... and these deficiencies prove to be a serious barrier to academic progress" (p. 76). The Carnegie Foundation study on the undergraduate curriculum revealed that over 80% of institutions of higher education offer remedial courses in basic skills (Boyer, 1987).

The community curriculum also is an area that offers considerable potential for development. Special workshops and seminars in organizational communication, male–female communication, family communication, and business and professional speaking are attractive offerings in community-based programs. These offerings function both as campus-based courses and as offerings taken into corporate settings as part of contracted training and development work for organizations in the community (see Strom, 1981). One well-developed community education program is that offered by Oakland Community College in Orchard Ridge, Michigan. Communication training and development in such areas as conflict resolution and management communication has been offered for such corporations as Chrysler, Michigan Bell Telephone, Mercy Health Corporation, and General Motors (Leininger, 1986).

The community curriculum tends to be the least integrated, for these programs frequently contract for the seminars and workshops with people other than the overworked faculty of the campus departments. Indeed, many of these programs operate with a director and staff who handle the programs for the entire campus, so there is little if any discipline base for the offerings. Research on the community college as a center for continuing education (Nespoli & Martorana, 1983–1984), however, supports the conclusion that "it seems clear that life-long learning and community-based activities in general are more and more becoming an accepted part of the American community college philosophy" (p. 5).

In addition to a strong curriculum aimed at meeting student needs in the four areas of collegiate, career, developmental, and community education, many community colleges have found it productive to develop a dynamic cocurricular program that complements the curricular offerings. Most typical is the debate or forensics program, which at many schools rivals 4-year school programs in terms of both activity and funding. The national organizational Phi Rho Pi provides leadership for 2-year schools in the debate and forensics area, and the annual national tournament is always well attended.

Fielding such a comprehensive program in a 2-year college requires faculty prepared to address the diverse needs of students. The 2-year school is, first and foremost, a teaching institution, so the demands and the priorities arc on effective teaching. As a result, individuals who are preparing for careers in community college communication education should consider carefully how to prepare for the teaching and professional responsibilities the 2-year school requires (Wolvin & Engleberg, 1989). Further, rewards through salary increments and honors are based heavily on student, peer, and administrator evaluations of one's teaching performance. Although faculty at these institutions are encouraged to participate in professional activities (professional associations, research and publications, campus and community service), the rewarded focus is on one's work as a teacher.

Many of these schools offer considerable support to faculty as teachers. Because the typical semester teaching load may be 12 to 15 credit hours (with two or three or even more different course preparations), 2-year institutions offer support for the teaching function. Miami–Dade Community College in Florida, for example, has implemented a plan to hire, evaluate, and reward new faculty who are devoted primarily to the college's teaching and learning mission (Jenrette & Napoli, 1994).

To support the teaching mission, many 2-year schools have well-equipped, well-staffed learning resource centers with up-to-date audiovisual materials and print holdings. Golden West College has the Speech Communication Center for peer tutoring and competency-based testing. Oakland Community College in Michigan and Prince George's Community College have elaborate videotape laboratories. Lorain County Community College has a state-of-the-art professional television studio. Likewise, faculty in many 2-year schools are presented with opportunities for faculty development in any of a number of instructional areas such as curriculum writing, teaching styles, and evaluation techniques. In addition, many are offered travel support to attend professional meetings and conferences such as the annual National Communication Association convention (which has a very active community college section).

Thus, the 2-year institution offers opportunities and challenges to those who wish to be faculty members in comprehensive programs devoted to teaching diverse groups of students. As a nontraditional institution of postsecondary education, the 2-year school often is in a state of change and development, providing a dynamic atmosphere for faculty and students alike. The communication educator committed to effective teaching and creative work at the undergraduate level will find this to be a rewarding career avenue.

ACKNOWLEDGMENTS

We appreciate the assistance of Kent A. Phillippe, Research Associate, American Association of Community Colleges, Washington, DC.

REFERENCES

Adelman, C. (1997, April 15). Community colleges: Drop-in centers no more. *The Washington Post*, p. A19.

Boyer, E. L. (1987). *College: The undergraduate experience in America*. New York: Harper & Row.

Center for the Study of Community Colleges. (1986, Spring). *National survey of students enrolled in credit classes*. Unpublished report, University of California, Los Angeles.

Cohen, A. M., & Brawer, F. B. (1982). The American community college. San Francisco: Jossey-Bass.

Course syllabus. (1987). *Individual growth and human relations*. Louisville, KY: Jefferson Community College.

Digest of Education Statistics. (1994). Washington, DC: U. S. Department of Education, Office of Educational Research and Improvement.

Doyle, S. L., & Engleberg, I. N. (1981). Integrating nursing majors into the group discussion and interpersonal communication courses in the community college. *Association for Communication Administration Bulletin, 35*, 68–71.

Gibson, J. W., Hanna, M. S., & Huddleston, B. M. (1985). The basic speech course at U. S. colleges and universities: IV. *Communication Education, 34*, 281–291.

Hegstrom, T. G. (1981). The Denver Conference recommendations: A status report. *Association for Communication Administration Bulletin, 35*, 62–71.

Integrated Postsecondary Education Data Systems 1995 Fall Enrollment Survey. (1996). Washington, DC: U. S. Department of Education, National Center for Education Statistics.

Jenrette, M., & Napoli, V. (1994). *The teaching learning enterprise: Miami Dade Community College's blueprint for change*. Bolton, MA: Anker.

Leininger, J. E. (1986, April). *Speech communication education in business and industry*. Paper presented at the meeting of the Central States Speech Association, Cincinnati, OH.

Leininger, J. E. (1987, November). *Choosing between basic courses to meet students' needs in the community college*. Paper presented at the meeting of the Speech Communication Association, Boston.

Lorain County Community College. (1987). *Theatre, media, performance, media production, and speech communication/rhetoric* [Brochure]. Lorain, Ohio: Author.

Miller, M. B., & Young, B. (1981). A comprehensive developmental studies program which includes reading, oral and written communication, arithmetic, counseling, and tutoring. *Association for Communication Administration Bulletin, 35*, 72–75.

Muchmore, J., & Galvin, K. (1983). A report of the Task Force on Career Competencies in Oral Communication Skills for community college students seeking immediate entry into the work force. *Communication Education, 32*, 207–220.

National Postsecondary Student Aid Study: 1992–1993 Undergraduate Table Generation System. (1996). Washington, DC: U. S. Department of Education, Office of Educational Research and Improvement.

Nespoli, L. A., & Martorana, S. V. (1983–1984). Tensions in defining community college missions: Problem or opportunity? *Community College Review, 11*, 3–11.

Ratliffe, S. A., & Hudson, D. D. (1986). *A description of a student-staffed, competency-based laboratory for the assessment of interpersonal communication skills*. Unpublished manuscript, Golden West College, Huntington Beach, CA.

Strain, B., & Wyson, P. (1981). A report of developmental speech courses in selected community colleges. *Association for Communication Administration Bulletin, 35*, 76–77.

Strom, J. C. (1981). Organizational communication in the community college. *Association for Commu-*
   nication Administration Bulletin, 35, 78–80.
Travis, J. E. (1996). Rebuilding the community: The future for the community college. *Community Col-*
   lege Review, 23, 57–72.
Wolvin, A. D., & Corley, D. (1984). The technical speech communication course: A view from the field.
   Association for Communication Administration Bulletin, 49, 83–86.
Wolvin, A. D., & Wolvin, D. R. (1977). Developing the speech communication course for the techni-
   cal/career student. *Association for Communication Administration Bulletin, 19*, 37–42.
Wolvin, A. D., & Wolvin, D. R. (1981). The status of the technical speech communication course in
   community and junior colleges. *Association for Communication Administration Bulletin, 38*,
   29–31.
Wolvin, D. R., & Engleberg, I. N. (1989). Community colleges and communication education. *Commu-*
   nication Education, 38, 322–326.
Wolvin, D. R., & Wolvin, A. D. (1972). The speech communication curriculum in the community college. *Today's Speech, 29*, 9–14.

34

Distance Education

John A. Daly
University of Texas at Austin

Thirty years from now the big university campuses will be relics. Universities won't survive. It's as large a change as when we first got the printed book.... It took more than 200 years (1440 to the late 1600s) for the printed book to create the modern school. It won't take nearly that long for the big change. Already we are beginning to deliver more lectures and classes off-campus via satellite or two-way video at a fraction of the cost. The college won't survive as a residential institution. Today's buildings are hopelessly unsuited and totally unneeded.

—Drucker (1997, p. 127)

Scary? Exciting? It depends. But certainly, more real than many of us imagine. For the single biggest challenge facing educators in the next 20 years may be distance education. Throughout the world people are starting to take courses and even complete entire degrees without often, if ever, stepping on a traditional campus. This change away from ivied halls to virtual campuses will profoundly affect every communication educator.

WHAT IS DISTANCE EDUCATION?

At its core, distance education is instruction conducted via technologies that significantly or completely eliminate the traditional face-to-face exchanges of teachers and students. Today, many programs falling under the rubric of distance education combine mediated and face-to-face encounters

481

with instructors. In the future even limited face-to-face interactions will fade, replaced by technologies such as desktop interactive video conferencing. According to many forecasts, the notion of any sort of immediate teacher–student interaction, whatever the media, may disappear in favor of facilitated, self-paced instructions through the computer.

Today, distance education incorporates many media. Video (e.g., "passive" methods such as videotapes and one-way television or "interactive" video conferencing), audio (e.g., tapes, telephony), written materials (e.g., correspondence courses), computer-based CDs and other forms of computer-assisted instruction, as well as computer-mediated instruction (e.g., the Internet and the World Wide Web) are some ways information (aka education) is delivered to students. Most people, knowledgeable about distance education, see a strong and ongoing migration toward the Internet and similar technologies. Video, voice, and print materials can be offered over the Internet in cheap, fast, and effective ways. Immense resources are already available on the Web. In addition, the Internet offers a degree of "instant" interactivity unavailable in other media. For these reasons (and because of space limitations) I predominantly use the Internet (and the World Wide Web) as an example of distance education throughout this chapter.

WHY DISTANCE EDUCATION?

Many faculty members are skeptical about distance education. Remembering the hoopla about other technological innovations in education (e.g., instructional television) that came to little, they dismiss distance education as just another educational fad that will fade. Ignore it and it will go away. Trust me—distance education is different. Why? Partly because distance education is the culmination of many important and enduring trends—the idea of lifelong learning, the notion of personalized instruction, the concept that time and space matter less today, the need for very practical "just in time" education, the increasing time demands placed on people that make traditional educational arrangements impossible, the growing belief that learners are personally responsible for their education, the belief that education ought to be more "learnercentric," and the burgeoning role of technology in our lives. All of these trends point toward distance education. Until recently, books and professors could only be in one place at one time. Consequently, a campus was needed that could serve as a repository of knowledge and a "home" to teachers. Technology makes this essentially unnecessary today.[1] Proponents of distance education argue that there are three main advantages to this new form of education: increased access, better learning, and lower expenses.

Access

If you live in Austin, New York City, Paris, Singapore, Denver, or any other large city you have a wealth of educational opportunities. You can take college and postgraduate courses at any number of schools, large libraries are easily accessible, and expertise on almost any topic is just a relatively short jog away. This is not so if you live 200 miles north of Boise or 300 miles south of Mexico City. Distance education offers people, especially those in relatively isolated areas of the world, incredible new opportunities for learning. Students living anywhere can tap into courses offered by some of the best professors. Done well, distance education can expose participants to intellectual leaders that most students would never meet, much less learn from in classes. If a world-renowned scholar in family communication is based in eastern Australia, today few individuals outside of the south Pacific would ever be able to study with her on a regular basis. On the other hand, via distance education, students from throughout the world have the opportunity to learn from this individual. Moreover, students can take courses through distance education that are unavailable on their own campuses. For instance, few schools today offer courses on Chinese rhetoric, parliamentary procedure, or environmental communication. If you want exposure to such topics and they are not offered on your campus, you either have to move to take the course or you do not take it. With distance education, students avail themselves of courses worldwide. However, it is more than access to teachers and classes. Distance education also offers learners access to an incredible wealth of information. Students can use library resources that were, until only very recently, available to few people; they can see sights, experience sounds, and interact with others throughout the world almost effortlessly on the Web. Not only are physical distances transcended, but time is as well. Many people, for either personal or professional reasons, have difficulty adapting their calendars to the mostly fixed schedules of traditional education. Distance education, in its best manifestations, allows people to work at their own rates and on their own schedules.

---

[1]Some forms of distance education have a long history. Correspondence courses have been available for over 100 hundred years. The first educational radio license was granted to the Latter Day Saints' University in Salt Lake City in 1921. Soon after, in 1922, the University of Wisconsin and the University of Minnesota received similar licenses from the federal government. In 1950, Iowa State University began broadcasting televised educational programming. In various guises, the Open University has been popular in Britain (and other nations outside of the United States) for many years.

You may complete the class over three or four weekends. I might take 9 months. You may finish the course at home after putting the children to bed. I might find it easier to do on long airplane trips.

Learning

The biggest question faced when reviewing the literature on distance education is whether it is an effective method for teaching. The evidence is surprisingly strong: For many topics students seem to learn as much, and sometimes more, via distance education as they do in traditional classrooms.[2] This is especially true in lecture classes where the primary role of students is as note takers. What is the difference between sitting in a classroom of 350 students listening to an instructor who is standing in front of the class and listening to him or her through some mediated technology? In fact, distance education can add dimensions unavailable in the traditional classroom. One is something akin to the rewind button. In a traditional classroom if I fail to grasp what the instructor is saying, I either raise my hand and ask the instructor to repeat what was uttered or I remain in a quandary. Distance education allows me to "rewind" what has been said to hear or see it again. The advantages of distance education for learning go far beyond "rewind." Many students find the methods of instruction available via distance education preferable. For some, it is because they can set their own pace. For others, the nature of the interface is preferable—different learners have different learning styles and newer technologies for distance learning maximize the choices students have about how they want to learn.

One special learning opportunity provided by distance education is the diverse group of "classmates" often enrolled in a course. In traditional classrooms, there is a great deal of classroom homogeneity; in distance education settings, heterogeneity is more common. A distance-based class may include typical undergraduates (e.g., 18- to 24-year-olds, going to school full time), part-time students perhaps a little older, individuals working full time and taking the course because of job needs, and senior citizens enrolled out of interest. Everyone learns from everyone else.

Expense

Have no doubt: The reason policymakers are so intrigued by distance education is the potential for incredible economic returns. Distance education

---

[2]It should be noted that in many of the studies comparing distance education to more traditional forms of instruction there has been a selection bias—people who enroll in distance education courses are often more mature and more motivated than the comparison samples.

can be much cheaper than traditional education. Certainly there are sizable costs at the start (e.g., technology, transmission, maintenance, infrastructure, production, support), but after these investments are made, costs decrease quickly. For instance, once a Web page is "up" and well received by the community, it can be used by many, many students over and over again. The per-student cost of delivering the course is small compared to the traditional classroom. How so? First, students throughout the world can enroll in the course. They all pay tuition and fees. Where once 30 students, all on one campus, would register for the course, now thousands may. Second, your instructional budget plummets. Certainly, at start-up you need course designers, content experts, and technical gurus, but after the course is established, all you need are people (not necessarily faculty members) to regularly update the course and facilitate student learning. Third, there are virtually no real estate costs. Because most students can take the course from home or from other computer sites, the expenses associated with constructing and maintaining classrooms disappears. Fourth, only a few schools need to devise a course on a particular topic. If the University of Oklahoma offers an excellent course on communication theory, why should we, at the University of Texas, offer one as well—especially if ours is not as good as the one at Oklahoma (certainly, a most unlikely scenario)? Consequently, it becomes unnecessary for every campus to offer every course.

WHAT SKILLS DO STUDENTS NEED TO PARTICIPATE EFFECTIVELY IN DISTANCE EDUCATION?

Distance education introduces an entire new set of skill requirements for learning. One is an ability to easily use appropriate media. For instance, students embarking on a distance education course over the Web must be comfortable and familiar with computers in order to discover high-quality content in an environment littered with information of varying quality.

As important as media skills are independent study skills such as time management, personal class involvement, and peer group support. Traditional education essentially forces students to manage their time: Classes happen on a strict timetable, tests are scheduled, and semesters or terms begin and end in predictable ways. None of this is necessarily so in distance education. Consequently, students who succeed in distance education environments must be masterful time managers. They also need to work hard at staying involved in their courses. At some institutions today, a class is simultaneously taught on campus and broadcast off campus via television. Off-campus students often feel less involved in the class than their more immediate, on-campus peers. To be successful, off-campus students must force themselves to create a sense of class involvement. In distance education, students also often lack an immediate peer group or easy access to instructors. They need to proactively find ways of creating relationships with others in the course and with their instructor through electronic mail, telephone, faxes, and personal meetings.

Distance education is not for everyone because the locus of responsibility shifts to the pupil from the teacher. Students who work independently, who are excellent time managers, who are comfortable with the technology, and who do not feel a strong need for face-to-face interaction with instructors or fellow students can prosper in distance education. Students who find themselves needing those sorts of things are well advised to move to distance education with caution.

WHAT SHOULD A TEACHER DO IN DISTANCE EDUCATION?

Suppose you decide to create and deliver a course via distance education. What are some tasks you will face? First and foremost, determine what your goals are for the course. What do you want students to know, understand, and perhaps do when they finish the course? Second, determine the constraints you are working under. What sort of budget do you have? How much time do you have to learn new technologies? How much effort can you expend creating the course? What sorts of constraints do your students face? Only after identifying your goals and the constraints you must work within should you embark on creating a distance education unit. When you begin this foray, consider the following.

Materials

Many of the materials (e.g., lectures, exercises) you use in traditional classrooms may not be appropriate for distance education courses. In the typical college classroom, there is a great deal of homogeneity among students in both experience and demography. That makes it easy to prepare instructional materials. In distance education you need to prepare materials for an audience far more heterogeneous in every way. Some of your pupils will come from nontraditional educational backgrounds, others from very traditional ones; some will be from the United States, others potentially from outside the United States; some will be young, others far older; some will be interested in your topic for immediate practical applications on the job, others will enroll for sheer personal interest. Your examples will need to be encompassing and your content broad.

Just as important, your materials must match the media you use. Media significantly affect, and even constrain, content. For instance, were your distance education course video based (e.g., interactive video conferencing, a television series, or tapes that might be sent to students), you would face numerous requirements because of that medium: Airtime is expensive; people do not want "talking heads"; your viewers, accustomed to the major networks, expect a level of visual quality that may be hard to offer. Even ignoring legal concerns of copyright, many materials you use in a traditional classroom are unsuitable or inappropriate for your distance education audience. Video, because of its expense, is also difficult to "update" quickly.

Were you to devise a Web-based course, a first step would be to look at other courses offered over the Web. For college teachers a good starting point is the "World Wide Lecture Hall" (www.utexas.edu/world/lecture) which has links to hundreds of course home pages devised by people in a variety of academic fields. There are numerous ground rules for developing a home page (there are sites on the Web that help you understand what to do[3]). For instance, page lengths should be short, links should be relevant, the format should be consistent, and "fill time" (the length of time it takes for a screen to fill up) needs to be fast because many students will access the page over modems that are quite slow. At the current time, incorporating video into a Web page is not generally advisable. In most cases, it takes too much time for students to upload and the quality is not high enough. In the future, though, video will be a critical part of any instructional Web course.

Remember, the goal of any distance education program, in the end, is to be technologically transparent. That means that after students become familiar with the process and media, they stop thinking of what they are receiving in terms of any technology and instead think of the learning. To accomplish this requires a great deal of work.

Consider, as well, the rigors of constantly updating and improving the course. The initial excitement of creating a distance education course often wanes as it becomes clear that constant revisions are necessary. Nothing is more embarrassing than dated material and for any number of reasons, technology wears thin much sooner and much more obviously than yellowed lecture notes.

Delivery Matters

Just as in the traditional classroom, the quality of the teacher's delivery matters. Many techniques used to clearly communicate lessons in tradi-

---

[3]Many excellent resources (as of August 12, 1997) can be found at www.dcn.davis.ca.us/lacarrol/webspin.html. Other excellent resources include a manual put together by Sun (www.sun.com/styleguide) and one by Yale (info.med.yale.edu/caim/manual).

tional classrooms can also be used in distance education (e.g., chunking key ideas; maintaining a clear focus; and using methods and tools such as "preview-present-review," vibrant examples, and interesting case studies). However, distance learning limits the use of other techniques. For instance, what about those nonverbal behaviors that lead some teachers to be seen as dynamic, enthusiastic, and interested? In Web-based courses, printed words and animation replace body movements. In video-based programs, too much enthusiasm can backfire. Humor may not work as well because of time delays in some media (e.g., video conferencing over ISDN lines). Asking questions, probing responses, and interacting with students are skills that many teachers do not find completely natural in traditional classrooms. Add the distance and all that comes with it, and you can imagine how difficult it is to create an environment of active learning.

Create Opportunities for Interaction

In most better distance education programs, interaction among students is considered vital. Some of that interaction is done face to face at regular meetings. Much of it is done electronically: Some courses require active participation on a listserv or discussion group; some mandate group work among students for course projects.

Just as important as peer interaction is interaction between student and teacher. In traditional classrooms, teachers monitor what is happening as instruction progresses. Teachers see faces, nodding or looking quizzical; they quickly determine who is participating and who is bored; they see, at a glance, who is engaged in classwork and who is not. These nonverbal cues disappear in many forms of distance education. Further, the cues that do exist are affected by the technologies.

In sophisticated distance education programs, instructors (or facilitators) overcome this limitation by arranging opportunities for students to directly and more "immediately" interact with them. They use toll-free telephone numbers, evening office hours, and even personal visits. Some programs have annual or semiannual gatherings where students meet other students and instructors. Some instructors "personalize" their courses by making biographical information and photographs of themselves readily available.

At the same time, understand that the whole structure of the educational experience changes. In the traditional classroom, the instructor is the center of attention. Whether it is through lecturing, leading group work, managing discussions, or answering questions, the teacher is dominant. This changes in distance education. Often, the teacher is simply one more person in the interaction.

Logistic Issues

In creating distance education courses, you face logistic challenges even beyond the design of the course and the acquisition of the technology to support the course. For instance, how do students from different institutions register and pay for the course? How are materials distributed (and how are their costs recovered)? How is the course scheduled (e.g., does it match a regular semester, offer opportunities for accelerated completion)? How do students get credit for the course (i.e., will the course be transferable)? If the course is televised, what about scheduling room time? What about designing the room (studio) for the course?[4] If there are tests in the course, how are they proctored?[5] How do students get reading materials unavailable at local libraries or via the Web? In some programs, students e-mail a major regional library that then forwards copies of requested materials, but who pays for this service? Suffice to say that a journey into distance education is not an easy one. But with proper preparation it can be an exhilarating learning experience for both you and your students.

SOME BIG ISSUES

Although many people rush pell-mell toward distance education, there are some issues that need careful consideration by both teachers and policymakers.

The Campus Experience

Students come to campus not only to learn academic subjects, but to grow as people. They come to experience a world often unfamiliar to them. While on campus, they encounter all sorts of nonacademic activities that enrich their experience—parties, intramurals, and weird campus movements. They run into an instructor in the Union and share a cup of coffee; they spy a classmate at the gym and begin to chat about life; they build, maintain, and end romantic relationships. At graduation, they leave different people not only because of the classes they took, but because of a rich variety of unplanned and yet memorable campus experiences they had over the years. Will these

---

[4]In many television-based courses (either one-way or through video conferencing) teachers will have some students in the room (studio) with them and others at a distance. This approach of having dual audiences, although quite popular, is also not often optimal. Certainly, most teachers prefer this approach because it provides some "live" bodies for immediate feedback, but students may not. Students at a distance feel excluded from the interactions and students in the room get annoyed by the demands of the equipment used to produce the distance portion of the course.

[5]For some courses, students go to testing centers established at different schools in the area. Tests are administered by individuals who are paid to proctor.

experiences happen in distance education environments? Probably not. And, if they do, they will certainly be in very different forms.

The Centrality of Face-to-Face Communication

There is something very special about face-to-face communication. A letter or even a phone call cannot replace the very special nature of talking to someone one-on-one—seeing his or her face, hearing the voice, experiencing the almost tactile sense a good discussion between student and teacher offers when it is unmediated by any technology. Many of us believe that students ought to meet and talk with their professors on a daily basis whether in class, offices, or incidental meetings. Those encounters create the very special motivation so essential to learning. Distance education cannot provide this. At best, there is minimal face-to-face contact. Advocates of distance education suggest that even today face-to-face communication is available through means such as video conferencing. Moreover, as technology makes the Web more video friendly, mediated face-to-face exchanges will be easily obtained. Be that as it may, those conversations are not, and will not be, as vital as what is found in today's classroom.

Student Access

Today, access to many forms of distance education is determined by wealth: Poor individuals, unable to afford the technologies that form the foundation of distance education, are limited in their participation. If you cannot afford access to a computer, you cannot experience the Internet. Wealthier people, on the other hand, have vast opportunities to explore the Internet, buy videos, and enroll in all sorts of technologically advanced courses. In the future, as the costs of technology decrease, the access issue may reverse—most people will receive the bulk of their education via distance technologies and the wealthy few will be able to afford the richer, more varied on-campus experience. The potential societal implications of this pattern are disturbing.

Content Versus Methods

As technology plays more and more of a role in education the difference between *what* is being taught and *how* it is taught wanes in magnitude. Indeed, in very sophisticated distance education programs, what is taught is already being determined, to a great extent, by the media. The text becomes the course. Technology and pedagogy become inseparable. Television requires certain sorts of content (highly visual, fast-paced); Web-based instruction requires certain sorts of displays. This integration will require fundamental changes in the ways teachers think about their subject matter, their courses, and their teaching styles.

The Teacher as "Star"

Distance education may make certain individuals, gifted in either the technology or in their personal delivery style via a certain technology, the "stars" of education in ways that may not please all of us. Students, given the choice of a number of courses on an identical topic, offered by different schools via distance education, may opt for the most attractive, most charismatic instructor over perhaps the content. By itself, this is not necessarily bad. The same thing happens on campus today: A few faculty are well known for their teaching and their courses are always oversubscribed. However, the charismatic power of these individuals is restricted to a particular campus. If traditional campuses fade in favor of virtual ones, these few gifted faculty could hold sway over far more students.

More broadly, the teaching styles of many instructors may not transfer well to distance education. Like many actors of the silent film generation, who were unable to make the transition to "talkies," many teachers used to the classroom, the chalkboard, and one-on-one conversations may experience great difficulty in teaching with new methods such as video conferencing.

The Changing Professorate

Distance education may well be the "professor unemployment act" of the next century. Why? Because to the extent that distance education takes hold, we will not need many faculty members in the roles they hold today. If a world-famous scholar-teacher is offering a course in classical rhetoric via distance learning, why would students contemplate taking it from anyone else? Only that one gifted professor is needed. What about the many instructors at different campuses who had been teaching that topic? Do they still have jobs? Many experts in distance education suggest a radically new conception of teaching in which faculty no longer serve as instructors in the traditional sense. Instead, they are facilitators, answering questions from students, monitoring pupils' progress through the course, managing evaluation procedures, and generally serving as learning coaches. As Dennis Jones, President of The National Center for Higher Education Management Systems pointed out, the changes we are discussing "imply important shifts in teaching behavior. Most significantly, they require a quite different kind of instructor—one able to 'coach' rather than 'teach' and one who is most comfortable providing individualized guidance" (Jones, 1996, p. 4).

Although attractive for some, for others this is a distasteful waste of intellectual talent. Parenthetically, in many current cases, the remuneration for "coaches" is far less than that of the traditional teacher. The process of moving to distance education, however, will also create new opportunities: Many new positions will arise for instructional designers and instructional technicians who will create and maintain courses.

The rewards associated with education will also change. Currently, the rewards, in many schools, for developing and delivering distance education are minimal, but this will change as distance education becomes more a part of the educational environment. It will also bring with it new questions. For instance, how will teaching loads be arranged? What counts as a class? How do we evaluate faculty efforts in distance learning? Colleges and universities will have to devise reward structures for the work involved in distance education. Otherwise, private providers (e.g., University of Phoenix, International University College) and consortia of educational units (e.g., the Western Governors) will take the leadership role. In the increasingly competitive world of higher education, this may not be optimal.

There is one other observation about the potential impact distance education will have on the professorate. It is possible that the ascent of distance education will trigger an entirely new concept of the university. What is an academic department when proximity is unimportant? Might it be that instead we will have worldwide communities of scholars and teachers sharing common intellectual interests?

Determining Course Content

Who controls what you teach over distance education? Were you to develop your own course and offer it from your office computer you might maintain some effective control over what students experience. Yet, as the "business" of distance education grows, this control may be lost. For instance, many of the better distance education programs emerging in the United States are being produced by private or semipublic organizations that legally control the "rights" to program materials. Course designers and instructors sign over their rights as part of their contract. Consequently, they lose academic control of the course. Their content may be modified without their knowledge; the course may continue to be offered long after its material is considered dated; portions of one course can be added to other courses without the knowledge of the academics who created either course. Perhaps, in the end, this is inevitable, but it raises all sorts of intellectual issues that need careful consideration.

Just as important, who determines the content of distance education courses? In the traditional classroom, teachers take responsibility for selecting the materials to be taught. Optimally, the same will be true in distance education. Experienced instructors will select course materials, unify them into distance education courses, and students will profit from both the material and the ready accessibility of teachers. In many cases, though, this may not turn out to be the case. Instead, the market may determine what content is included and experienced teachers may disappear in favor of content providers and facilitators.

Communication instructors face special concerns with their content in distance education. Some of our courses require a level of interactivity not found in many other disciplines. How can you teach a public speaking class when there is no classroom for students to give speeches? What can a teacher of performance of literature do without a room full of vocalizing participants? The first response of many communication teachers is "Well, then, distance education is not for us. Our stuff needs to stay in the traditional classroom."

There are three problems with this response. First, this is denying the future. Like it or not, distance education is on its way. It is a train that will not be stopped. Communication educators have a choice: We get on or we get left behind. Today, being left behind makes us irrelevant. In fact, some schools today mandate that any course required as part of a degree program must be available both in the traditional classroom and via distance education. Opting out of distance education means our courses will simply not be included in the degree requirements of many majors.

Second, many courses we teach, beyond the basic ones, require relatively little oral performance. As the discipline of communication has matured, there has been a proliferation of course work that summarizes research and theory with few, if any, required oral activities. These courses are quite suitable for distance education. But what about classroom participation? Evidence generally suggests that distance education via computers can have as much, if not more, interaction, than the traditional classroom. Students interact, for example, via e-mail, in chat rooms, and through video conferencing. Although certainly not identical to face-to-face exchanges, the modality still permits many learning interactions. In fact, some students are more comfortable interacting over computers than they are in classrooms.

Third, what about those courses that by their nature demand oral performances? There are innovative ways to accomplish the performance via distance. For example, some schools and organizations already offer presentation skills over the Internet. How is this done? Some have students make presentations to local community groups (audiences much more heterogeneous than the typical student groups we normally use as classroom audiences). Students have their speeches videotaped and send them to their instructor or facilitator for evaluation. In the future, even mailing videotapes may become unnecessary. Technically oriented experts in distance education tell us that soon we will be able to submit videos through the Internet just as today you scan a photograph into a computer and electronically forward it. At that point, it will be possible to have a presentation class composed of students who view one another making speeches through the Internet.

CONCLUSION

Clearly, distance education brings with it innumerable opportunities for all of us. It will force faculty to learn new skills and will significantly increase educational opportunities for students. It will add to our definition of communicative performance. For instance, we will need to teach people how to effectively use video conferencing, work with group-decision support systems, and design Web pages. Distance education will also refresh our discipline. In marketing there is an old but very important principle: You never fall in love with your product—instead, you fall in love with what people do with your product. Adaptive organizations understand this principle. Nonadaptive ones fade because they forget it—note the slide rule business or the typewriter industry. Distance education reminds us that our business is not real estate (the classroom), but learning.

With some notable exceptions, history tells us that most media do not replace older ones. Instead new media add to our arsenal of communication. The printed word early on created a fear that learned conversation would be replaced by the technology of the book. Many decried the invention of the radio because of a fear that people's reading ability would wane. Television was seen as replacing both the book and the radio. Yet today, bookstores are full and radio stations proliferate. Certainly with distance education some things will be lost, but others will be gained.

SELECTED READINGS

Beare, P. (1989). The comparative effectiveness of videotape, audiotape, and telelecture in delivering continuing teacher education. *American Journal of Distance Education, 3*, 57–66.

Berge, Z., & Collins, M. (1995). *Computer mediated communication and the online classroom.* Cresskill, NJ: Hampton.

Bernt, F., & Bugbee, A. (1993). Study practices and attitudes related to academic success in a distance learning program. *Distance Education, 14*, 97–112.

Khan, B. (Ed.). (1997). *Web-based instruction*. Englewood Cliffs, NJ: Educational Technology Publications.

Keegan, D. (1990). *Foundations of distance education*. London: Routledge.

Lenzer, R., & Johnson, S. (1997, March 10). Seeing things as they really are. *Forbes, 159*, pp. 122–128.

Misanchuk, E. (1994). Print tools in distance education. In B. Willis (Ed.), *Distance education: Strategies and tools* (pp. 109–129). Englewood Cliffs, NJ: Educational Technology Publications.

Moore, M., & Kearsley, G. (1996). *Distance education: A systems view*. Belmont, CA: Wadsworth.

Schlosser, C., & Anderson, M. (1994). *Distance education: A review of the literature*. Ames: Iowa Distance Education Alliance, Iowa State University. (Eric Document Reproduction Service No. ED 382 159).

Verduin, J., & Clark, T. (1991). *Distance education: The foundations of effective practice*. San Francisco: Jossey-Bass.

Willis, B. (1993). *Distance education: A practical guide*. Englewood Cliffs, NJ: Educational Technology Publications.

SOME RELEVANT WEB SITES

- http://www.uidaho.edu/evo/dist10
  A wonderful manual on issues facing people thinking of creating a distance education course. Broken into 15 units, the manual covers many of the issues discussed in this chapter.

- http://www.lucent.com/cedl/ace.html
  This is a summary of the "Guiding Principles for Distance Learning in a Learning Society" produced by a broad collection of scholars and professional associations including the American Council on Education.

- http://www.caso.com
  A database of courses and programs offered through distance education.

- http://www.uwex.edu/disted/home.html
  This is the home page for the University of Wisconsin's distance learning group. It is quite informative, with a number of useful links.

- http://www.nchems.com/news0396.htm#promise
  This is the newsletter of a major educational organization. The particular issue referenced here is a summary of some of the rationale behind the Western Governors University initiative. The Governors of most of the Western states of the United States have agreed to creative a virtual university open to students from throughout the region.

- http://www.nki.no/~morten/
  An online report on pedagogical techniques for computer-mediated communication.

- http://www.acacis.open.ac.uk
  A clearinghouse of information with an impressive list of references and summaries of research on distance learning. (Also see http://www.open.ac.uk/info/other/ICDL/ICDL-Facts.html.)

- http://www.kn.pacbell.com/wired/vidconf/descripion,html#what.
  A brief description of video conferencing in the classroom and library.

REFERENCES

Drucker, P. (1997, March 10). Interview by R. Lenzner & S. Johnson, "Seeing things as they really are." *Forbes, 159,* 127.

Jones, D. (1996, March). The promise of technology-based instruction: What we are learning. *National Center for Higher Education Management Systems News,* 2–6. (http.//www.nchems.com /news0396.htm#promise).

35

Extended Learning

Virginia P. Richmond
West Virginia University

I have had the opportunity to participate in non-campus based graduate programs offered by the Communication Studies Department at West Virginia University (WVU) continuously since 1974. For most of that period I have served as coordinator of those programs, and for 3 years I served as director of all off-campus programs for WVU. I currently coordinate two graduate degree programs in communication (Communication in Instruction and Corporate and Organizational Communication) as well as service courses in health communication for graduate programs in health promotion. These experiences have enabled me to observe the potential for extended learning programs in the field of communication on a first-hand basis.

Extended learning is the contemporary term used to identify instructional programs that are offered by a college or university at a site or sites other than the home campus of that institution. Such programs have their roots in programs developed by land-grant universities, which have attempted to extend educational opportunities to individuals in communities throughout the state or region served by the given university since 1863. WVU, which was founded as a land-grant university in 1863, has been one of the leaders in such programming since its inception. Today, extended learning programs have expanded far beyond the relatively few land-grant institutions. Many institutions now offer programs throughout the state or region they serve, and some offer programs in many other parts of the United States and even in other countries. The basic concept of such programs is to take the university to the students instead of making the students come to the university. Such programs have made educational opportunities much more available to individuals living in areas at some distance from educational institutions and literally made educational advancement possible for millions who would not have had such opportunities otherwise.

It is safc to say that virtually every institution today has some form of extended learning program, even if it only involves occasional noncredit training classes. Hence, if you teach at an institution of higher learning, it is highly likely that you will have an opportunity to become involved in an extended learning program if you seek it. Usually teaching in such programs provides an opportunity for supplementing a faculty member's income, so that may provide sufficient motivation for you to explore this opportunity. I believe, however, that the potential value to the faculty member of the experience in working in extended learning is an even more powerful reason to do so.

Immediately after World War II our department began offering graduate classes through what was then called the "off-campus credit program" of the university. For the next quarter-century, these classes were offered on an occasional basis. In 1973 the department experimented with two graduate classes in instructional communication. Within 4 years this offering evolved into a comprehensive graduate degree program in instructional communication offered throughout the state. The students, not one of whom was required to take any communication class, have made it clear that communication is definitely worth studying and can be useful to those in the teaching profession who want to continue their education.

On the basis of the success of the WVU program, Richmond and Daly (1975) suggested that the field of communication might strengthen its future prospects if "we are willing to adapt our programs to the needs of our society" (p. 6). The authors' goal, seeking to establish communication curricula for the older, nontraditional student who is attempting to continue or extend his or her education, is equally relevant today.

This perspective has been popular for decades in fields such as education, business, and agriculture. Although in the past many professionals in the field of communication were unsure of the benefits to be accrued through working with extended learning programs, today most leading programs in the field have an extended learning component. Thus, young scholars planning careers in communication can be virtually certain that they will someday have the opportunity to be involved in an extended learning program of some type.

This chapter reviews characteristics of the extended learning student, examines the adult learner as a consumer, and considers what our field has to offer to extended learning students. In addition, this chapter reviews what one should know before working with extended learning students and explores the outcomes of extended learning programs.

CHARACTERISTICS OF THE EXTENDED LEARNING STUDENT

The most obvious characteristic that distinguishes between the extended learning student and the typical college student is the age difference: Extended learning students are usually older than the typical college student. They are often beginning to pursue an education or extend their educational background after being out of school for a number of years. This age difference may or may not be an advantage for learning. The one fact that is indisputable is that the older student is just as capable of cognitive, affective, and psychomotor learning as the younger student. No matter what the conventional wisdom might be, one can indeed teach old dogs new tricks.

A second characteristic of the extended learning student is that he or she is typically employed, usually full time. Most adult learners have already chosen a career track (and are actively pursuing it) while seeking to continue their education. As a result, they attempt to adapt their school curriculum and schedule to their work schedule. For most adult learners, employment is their first priority. If the extended learning program gets in the way of the job, the extended learning program is discontinued.

A third characteristic of the extended learning student is the high probability of marriage and children. Although the trend of married couples not having children is increasing, the traditional marital model is still the norm for most of these students. There may be a few dual-income, no-children couples in an extended learning class, but you can expect the vast majority of students to be married with children. This, of course, places both a financial strain and, in many cases, a time strain on the student. It also impacts the amount of time students are willing or able to spend on a learning task outside class and their perceptions of the usefulness of such tasks.

A fourth characteristic of the extended learning student is her or his commitment to a given profession or occupation. For example, in any particular adult education class, there might be students from legal, secretarial, health, financial, business, and educational professions. Although some individuals in extended learning classes are seeking to change fields of employment, most are not.

A fifth characteristic of the extended learning student is an interest in knowledge for immediate use. Such students need to see meaningful application for the content the instructor is teaching now. Extended learning students generally are not interested in content that might not be useful to them in the immediate work or home environment.

Most teachers have either said or heard, "You may not be able to use this content now, but in the future it will be useful to you." Although this might work with younger, more inexperienced students, it usually does not work well with older, employed students. Such students are primarily interested in subject matter that will be helpful either for improving their interpersonal lives or for improving their work lives. If an instructor cannot demonstrate how the curricula is applicable now or in the very near future, then the extended learning student may conclude that the course is useless.

Adult learners ask questions such as: "How will this work in my job? What is the usefulness of this? Why are we doing this? How will this benefit me, my organization? Will I see any immediate results if I try this idea? Do you think my spouse might benefit from this course?" If an instructor of adult learners cannot answer questions like these, he or she will have to revise the curricula to adapt to the needs of the students—or there will be no students left to adapt to.

A sixth characteristic of extended learning students is limited time to devote to studying for class. The instructor of adult learners must remember that members of this unique audience are already committed to meeting the demands of a job. This restricts the instructor's ability to require extensive study time. Most students need to have the majority of the course content covered in class. If the instructor insists on extensive homework between classes, he or she can count on some students not returning and others simply not doing the work. This is not because these students are lazy. The overwhelming majority are not. However, life places more nonacademic demands on these students than it does on traditional full-time students.

A seventh characteristic of the extended learning student extends the sixth characteristic. In addition to having limited time for studying, the older student also has limited time for completing projects and activities outside of class. This also results from a temporal commitment to the job and family. Hence, the instructor must be sensitive to an adult learner's schedule and focus on activities and projects that are of prime benefit to the student, primarily activities that the student can complete in his or her job or home environment.

A final characteristic of extended learning students is that they are among the most highly motivated students an instructor can have in class—if the content is perceived as relevant. On the other hand, if the content is not perceived as relevant, the extended learning student often simply disappears from the course. As suggested previously, most extended learning students need to see the usefulness of the content and obvious, positive results of employing the content at work or at home. If these criteria are met, the students will continue in the course.

The most critical period for the retention of extended learning students is the first class meeting. The instructor must be able to demonstrate that the course will be of benefit to the different people in the class. The instructor should not suggest that the course will involve "an in-depth look at several theories related to.... " This introduction will turn off many adult learners, and they will leave thinking "another typical abstract college theory course with very little application for me." The instructor should begin the course with an interesting exercise, presentation, or activity that illustrates the relevance of the course to each student's profession or lifestyle. As adult educators and researchers have suggested, the adult learner is a unique individual, and the program of instruction has to be personalized in a way that fits individual needs (Andrews, Houston, & Bryant, 1981; Warnat, 1979).

THE ADULT LEARNER—OFTEN A NAIVE CONSUMER

When older, nontraditional students search for classes to improve their home or work environment, they often overlook speech communication classes. Most of them do not want to give speeches, and they do not know that speech and communication classes are not necessarily the same. When informed that speech courses are available, they often think of classes such as public speaking, parliamentary procedure, and group leadership or group dynamics. The perception that public speaking is what the field of speech communication is about is still a common misconception of many extended learning students. The only referent many people have for the field is a speech class they had in high school or were required to take in college, extremely unpleasant memories for many adults.

The general public tends to be uninformed about changes in the field of communication. Many adult learners took a public speaking class in their early college career and still think the field is primarily concerned with giving speeches. The field of communication has not yet succeeded in enlightening most potential adult learners about the content areas available in the field. In fact, in many cases we have continued to offer traditional content areas in extended learning programs long after they have been replaced in regular campus programs.

The weakness of traditional speech classes for many adult learners is that they seldom or never confront situations in which the content given in the class can be employed—and the potential students know this. For example, when adult learners are asked, "How often do you think you will be required to give a public speech in your occupation?" the majority of them usually respond with "Never." When adult learners are asked if they would like to be better at public speaking, many indicate they would, but not at the price of having to take a public speaking class. Their rationale is that they have secured positions in which they will not be asked to give public presentations. When they were younger, they may have shaped their lives and careers around not being required to give a public speech (Richmond, 1984; Richmond & McCroskey, 1995).

The preceding paragraph is not meant to demean basic public speaking courses or to suggest that they are not useful for the right group of adult learners. Rather, the point to be made is that many adult learners are naive about what the field has to offer and think only in terms of the basic speech classes offered in their high school and college experiences.

WHAT WE CAN OFFER THE ADULT LEARNER

Many academic disciplines are not faced with the question of what they have to offer the adult learner through extended learning programs. They have already addressed the issue and have provided an extended education for the older student for many years. Our field has just recently begun to pursue expansion in this realm. Richmond and Daly (1975) suggested an "almost inexhaustible need" (p. 8) for interpersonal communication specialists to assist in adult education. They also argued that "both the society and our field will benefit" (p. 8) from providing services to adult learners such as teachers, nurses, civil service employees, police, or business and labor organizations. The expansion of extended learning programs in the field of communication has progressed rapidly at some institutions, but not at all at others. Perhaps this is because professionals in the field do not realize what the field can offer. Because people in this field are specialists in one area or another, it is perhaps difficult to see the full range of the field's potential.

Although almost every area taught in regular academic programs can potentially find a place in extended learning, those mentioned here have been found to receive very positive responses from extended learning students with varied backgrounds. After students become familiar with what the field of communication has to offer, the following areas are frequently seen as the most interesting and helpful: nonverbal communication, organizational communication (primarily supervisor–subordinate interaction), the effects of TV and other media (particularly on children), interpersonal communication, communication and gender, male–female communication, family communication, overcoming shyness, and intercultural communication. In addition, adult learners typically respond very well to a course focusing on basic communication theories—although if given a "theory" title, many may shy away from it.

The field of communication has no shortage of content areas that are interesting and applicable to the extended learning student. Although the general communication principles remain the same, the application may vary from teacher to banker to nurse. As communication professionals we have the knowledge, but we must take the time and make the effort to adapt that knowledge to the needs of a very diverse population of potential adult learners.

WORKING WITH THE EXTENDED LEARNING STUDENT

The instructor must understand that adults participate in extended learning programs for a variety of reasons. They continue their education because they enjoy taking classes, to get away from home, to improve their interpersonal or home life, to change things at home or work, to obtain a better job, to feel good about themselves, because they simply enjoy learning, or because they have nothing better to do. Whatever the reason, the critical element that must be present in the course is application. The adult student must see value and usefulness for the content or he or she will simply drop out.

If an instructor is to be successful in adult education, he or she must personalize the class content for the individual student. Although much instructional time should be spent directly providing students with content, some time must be spent discussing how the concepts can be tailored to the students' concerns, problems, and environments. For example, if teaching about nonverbal communication in the workplace, instructors should demonstrate how use of space, seating, color, lighting, and so on can impact the teacher–student relationship, the banker–client relationship, the nurse–patient relationship, or whatever relationship is relevant to the students in the class.

The teacher of extended learning students must also know more than communication. The extended learning instructor must have a working knowledge of the world of the audience. He or she must be able to understand and "speak the language" of the students in order to allow the students to understand and grasp the usefulness of the concepts.

Last, the instructor of adult learners must, on many occasions, be capable of and willing to present a "dog and pony show" that captures and keeps the students' attention. In this respect, traditional and adult learners are very similar. Both want their instructor to be animated, dynamic, interesting, and responsive to their feedback and questioning. If the instructor does not meet these expectations, traditional students may continue to attend the class—because they are required to do so. Adult learners are much more likely to "take a hike." Being a teacher of adult learners may be more demanding than teaching younger students. However, the outcomes of a successful extended learning experience can be well worth the extra effort.

OUTCOMES OF EXTENDED LEARNING PROGRAMS

When one successfully implements an extended learning program or teaches a successful extended learning class, the positive outcomes are numerous. Among the more obvious outcomes include the personal satisfaction of the teacher as a result of having the opportunity to teach highly motivated students, and the feeling that one is contributing to society in a very positive way. Three outcomes are not as obvious, but are extremely important:

1. The students will have high levels of cognitive, affective, and behavioral learning. They are motivated to achieve, and they will achieve at high levels. They will also take the content and apply it within their organizational and personal environments.

2. The instructor will have a learning experience. Teachers learn from their students what communication concepts work in the real world and what concepts do not. The effective extended learning instructor can use this student feedback to develop instructional content that will work outside the basic undergraduate classroom.

3. As a program becomes strong and produces good students, the program itself will be strengthened and expand. Students will promote the usefulness and applicability of the program to others in their organization and community. Other professional people will learn from the extended learning students that the field of communication has much to offer.

Working with extended learning students can make the learning environment more challenging for the teacher, as well as more rewarding. As communication teachers, we are capable of providing useful content to the extended learning student, which will help make the student a more effective and useful member of our society.

REFERENCES

Andrews, T. E., Houston, W. R., & Bryant, B. L. (1981). *Adult learners: A research study*. Washington, DC: Association of Teacher Educators.

Richmond, V. P. (1984). Implications of quietness: Some facts and speculations. In J. A. Daly & J. C. McCroskey (Eds.), *Avoiding communication: Shyness, reticence, and communication apprehension* (pp. 145–155). Beverly Hills, CA: Sage.

Richmond, V. P., & Daly, J. A. (1975, January). Extension education: An almost inexhaustible job market for communication grades. *ACA Bulletin, 11*, 6–8.

Richmond, V. P., & McCroskey, J. C. (1995). *Communication: Apprehension, avoidance, and effectiveness* (4th ed.). Scottsdale, AZ: Gorsuch Scarisbrick.

Warnat, W. I. (1979). *A new dimension of adult learning: Inservice education*. Syracuse, NY: National Council of States on Inservice Education.

36

Consulting

John A. Daly
University of Texas at Austin

As I started planning this chapter, I polled a number of colleagues at different schools across the country about consulting. This informal and decidedly unsystematic poll yielded some interesting reactions. One respondent, with a look of disdain on his face and clear distaste in his voice, said:

> Why would any scholar want to sell his soul? The moment you start consulting is the moment you give up hope of a real academic career. If people want to consult, they should leave this place and get jobs in business. It's not scholarship. You're paid to do scholarship. Having people on a faculty consult sullies all of us.

A second individual's response was markedly at odds with the first:

> Consulting, huh? Boy, those guys really make money. I wish I could do more of it. I've given a few talks, but I'd like to do more. The money is great and it's easy work if you can get it. All you do is entertain, and they pay you a lot. What we need to do is find a way to get more consulting deals for everyone. We could all get rich!

A third person reflected back on her years of consulting by saying:

> It's the toughest work I do, but it's also the most rewarding. You deal with real people coping with real issues in the real world. You've always got to be prepared. The people you work with are paying serious money for everything you offer and they want bottom-line answers. They aren't paying for gloss. They know when you don't know your stuff. The way I judge how

helpful I am is by whether I get invited back again. If I do, it isn't because
I'm entertaining or fun, it's because people can see I've worked hard. I've
offered my expertise and it counted in their lives.

Administrators of communication programs had the same reaction. One
told me she did not understand how anyone could afford to remain in the academic world without consulting—schools do not pay enough. A second
brusquely said that people in his department who spend time consulting do
not deserve merit raises—they have given up their academic integrity, and
more importantly, they were making enough "on the outside" not to worry
about the paltry amounts the department distributed for merit. Another one
said that the only people in her college who were capable of successful consulting were those who were highly competent in their academic jobs.
Good teachers and good researchers, she said, are also good consultants.
Why? Because in the end, people hire consultants for both their acknowledged topic expertise and their palpable ability to teach that material in interesting, informative ways.

You will hear many, or all, of these comments if you ask people in a communication department about consulting. Some people think you should do
it and others disdain it. Some think it an easy task and others consider it
tough, demanding labor. The problem, in a nutshell, is that consulting represents an unknown commodity in communication. Although everyone
knows what classroom teachers do and feels what they do has inherent
value to a program, and everyone clearly understands and appreciates the
role of the scholar in a department, no group, it seems, can agree on what a
consultant does or even whether one working in the academy ought to consult. The field of communication is different, in this regard, than most other
academic fields. Psychologists are quick to accept the notion that clinical
faculty may be good teachers, good scholars, and also highly capable of
working with clients on the outside. Top-notch scholars and teachers in
economics, government, history, and art see nothing wrong with lending
their skills to clients, whether they be in the public or private sectors. As-
tronomers, physicists, chemists, and biologists are not the least bit anxious
about offering their learned opinions to public forums and private industry.
Why this hesitation in the field of communication? Probably because many
in the field are not yet confident of the status of the discipline. They think
that our newly won academic respectability might be challenged and that
the floodgates will open to charlatans and their chicanery if consulting were
seen as a viable enterprise for the active scholar-teacher.

Although it is undoubtedly impossible to disentangle all the various issues involved in consulting in a short chapter, I want to describe some basic

issues and concerns about the role of consulting in communication education. I do this by describing what consultants in communication fields do, by offering some advice on how to become a communication consultant, and by addressing some considerations you will face if you are interested in working with nonacademic groups.

Before going any further, let us focus this discussion. This chapter is aimed at those people who want to do consulting on a part-time basis. It does not address the activities, roles, or issues involved in full-time consulting. Some people, after finishing a degree, decide they would rather not work in an academic environment. Nor do they want employment with a single organization. Instead, they opt to become full-time consultants offering their knowledge and skills to any buyer. Although much of what is written here applies to these people, they face many issues that cannot be adequately described in a chapter of this length. Full-length books are available on this career option.

Understand also my bias from the start: Consulting is an important form of education. The setting where it takes place may not be the typical classroom; the students not the traditional 18- to 22-year-old population; the form of assessment not the customary one—there are seldom tests. But in the end, you, as a consultant, can impart vital knowledge to your listeners—knowledge that they might otherwise miss. Organizations, government agencies, businesses, and professional groups can profit from what you, as a person trained in communication, can tell them. You can offer insights, reflections, information, and reactions that can significantly affect their choices and decisions. Consulting represents as valid a form of education as that which occurs in the more traditional college education. Done well, it can have important consequences for the learner as well as for the groups the individual works for or belongs to. Moreover, working outside the environment of the academy can offer the practicing scholar-teacher many opportunities to discover important questions and consequential applications for his or her work.

WHY DO PEOPLE IN COMMUNICATION CONSULT?

Although there are as many different justifications for consulting as there are people, most reasons fall into four major categories.

1. The field of communication has always been (and will continue to be) an applied field. Consulting represents a way of helping people communicate more effectively in their lives. It is a way of applying our knowledge about communication to the problems people face. We, as a discipline, purport two

things: (a) that we are better than others in understanding the processes and complexities involved in communication, and (b) that we are capable of helping people communicate more effectively—that there are skills people can acquire that will aid them in becoming better communicators. Our insight into communication should translate into usable, practical knowledge.

2. Consulting provides communication professionals with unique opportunities to work with people outside the normal classroom. These people may not take notes, their questions are often less theoretical than those encountered in classes, and they seldom have "incentives" such as tests or papers. Instead, you work with people who are listening for answers that will enhance their job performance or life satisfaction. The consultant, first and foremost, is a teacher. For many people who regularly teach college students, working with people in the nonacademic world offers a refreshing opportunity to talk with a seemingly much more varied audience. In addition, as a consultant you can affect, in substantial ways, the directions a company takes or the choices an individual makes in coping with issues. Your advice can have significant and long-lasting consequences. For many who regularly consult, the opportunity to work in the nonacademic world is highly valued. Not only does one do important work, but it is fun! Do not underestimate the fun component. Many people who spend portions of their time working outside the traditional classroom will tell you that the real reason they do it is because it is fun. You are putting on a show, your mind gets challenged, and you are talking to people who, if you do a good job, will reinforce you in many ways that you seldom encounter in the traditional classroom.

3. Consulting provides the academic with a "reality check." It offers the classroom teacher a chance to hear from people who are not in school everyday. People you consult with will ask questions that hint at needed research and offer ideas that may form the corpus of later classroom lectures. They will ask "so what" questions, demand clear thinking, and wonder aloud about issues of relevance, practicality, and sensibility. They will force you, as the teacher-consultant, to directly address practical problems that need solutions. One thing that you will quickly discover is that most people are really quite smart—they have got insightful ideas, see through muddled thinking, and are quick to grasp concepts that are relevant or interesting to them.

4. Academicians consult because it offers them extra money above and beyond what they are paid on their regular jobs. At some schools (particularly business schools), part of the job offer a prospective candidate receives may include a guarantee of a certain number of consulting opportunities. Most people in the field of communication do not, however, receive offers such as this. Moreover, most people who engage in part-time consulting do not make that much additional money. Money is certainly one motivator, but if

money alone is what you want, consulting on a part-time basis is probably not likely to be satisfying. It requires too much work for the amount you will take in.

WHAT KINDS OF CONSULTING DO PEOPLE IN COMMUNICATION DO?

Every consulting job is different, but a quick survey of the sorts of work people in communication do outside of academia suggests that most consulting falls into four clusters.

Giving Talks

Many, many people in the field of communication spend some of their time giving speeches to different businesses, community groups, and professional associations. Those talks range from brief breakfast and after-dinner presentations to hourlong sessions on communication-related topics. Some of these talks are primarily informative, others are motivational, and some, in all truth, are mostly for entertainment. Whatever the focus, the audience expects you to talk about something having to do with communication, your area of expertise. If you want to work outside of the walls of academia you should have one or two general speeches on communication well prepared. They should be relatively short, informative, relevant, and entertaining.

Intervention Consulting

Here, an organization or group needs an expert. As a consultant, you offer your knowledge and skills to solve a particular problem the organization is experiencing. Were you an organizational communication expert, you might be asked to aid a company in communicating a major decision or change. For instance, communication consultants have helped companies cope with problems such as a serious personnel change. You might also be asked to help develop a customer service program, aid in restructuring internal communication, or advise the business on new marketing techniques for products. If your expertise lies in political communication, you may find yourself working with a political candidate assessing public opinion, writing speeches, and designing an effective electoral campaign. In health communication, you may assist in developing a prevention and information campaign, counsel physicians and other health care personnel on ways to improve their communication with patients, or work with administrators on patient information systems. Whatever the issue, the contracting entity seeks out your expertise because you know something that they need.

Personnel Training

The consultant's role in this arena is to develop and refine the communication skills of a group of people. This may include giving informative talks as well as developing workshops that teach participants those skills. In some cases, the training is highly specific (e.g., teaching new recruiters how to effectively interview job applicants, or developing selling skills in a group of beginning salespeople). In other cases, the training is designed to bolster or reinforce already existing skills (e.g., working with a group on meeting or presentation skills).

Research Consulting

An organization may request your services to discover, describe, or confirm some phenomena. You might be asked to assess the level of employee satisfaction with company communication, the impact of a particular communication modality on employee understanding of company policies (e.g., the effectiveness of written materials on company health benefits), or the effectiveness of various internal communication media in an organization. In other settings, you might be asked to evaluate consumer perceptions of product advertising, test methods to achieve greater market share for a radio station, or assess the most effective marketing technique used by salespeople for a company. In the legal arena, you might be called on as an expert witness on topics such as the reliability of eyewitness testimony, be asked to research and assist in jury selection and witness preparation, or be invited to experimentally examine the best ways of presenting a case.

ISSUES YOU NEED TO REMEMBER

Deciding to spend some time working with people in the role of a consultant requires you to reflect about a few important issues. First, and foremost, what do you know about communication that can help others? People hire consultants because of their expertise, because inside their group or organization they lack vital knowledge or critical skills that a consultant can provide. It is important to remember that organizations exist because they are good at what they do and they expect the same from you. One of the most common mistakes people make when they begin consulting is believing they know about every imaginable topic: They do not. Figure out where your expertise lies, and limit your consulting to that arena. Nothing is as embarrassing as purporting to be an expert at something and then having people inadvertently discover that you are not. Being the best at one thing is enough to fill your consulting calendar for years to come.

You need to stay current in your academic specialties. People who hire you want to get "the" expert in the area. If you are working with dated information, you are not going to be effective. You also need to constantly be on the lookout for things that can add to your presentations and consulting work. When you hear a humorous story, read an interesting statistic, or discover a relevant example, make sure you write it down and put it in a handy spot for later reference. You should also regularly browse business periodicals to keep informed of the newest trends in consulting. Fifteen years ago, customer service, as an area of training and consulting, was virtually unknown. Today it is a very trendy topic.

Second, understand that any organization is spending a good deal of money on you when you act as a consultant. It is easy to forget that. The bulk of the money they are spending is not on your fee. Rather, it is the investment they are putting into your program. Work it out for yourself. Suppose some organization offers you $1,000 for a talk on improving communication skills. They bring in 60 of their employees to listen to you for 3 hours. Each of those people are paid, shall we say, on average, $25 per hour. That is $75 per person for the program or, for the 3 hours a total of $4,500. That amount does not include the time the company lost in work, in the availability of personnel, or in the cost of the facilities. In the end, your stipend is only about 20% of the cost to the company of your presentation. This assumes that the organization does not need to pay for travel or rooms for people attending. This means you had better do your best to give them their money's worth.

Third, preparation is key for successful consulting. Never assume that you can "wing it" when addressing or working with a group. In classroom teaching, there is a maxim that for every hour of classroom time, the good instructor spends 5 hours preparing. Let me suggest a corollary: When working as a consultant, double or triple that time. Preparation means working both on the content of the materials and on its presentation. Simply preparing a thorough outline of material you want to cover is not enough. You also need to spend time determining how best to present that material. In organizations today, audiovisual materials are often a must. People like well-done slides and overheads; people expect nicely done, complete written materials they can take home with them. Preparation also means expending time learning about the organization or person you are working with. Find their annual report or press clippings and read them carefully.

Take a tour of the plant and talk to employees. Do anything, in short, that will increase your familiarity. Why? Because when you do start working with the individual or organization, they will want you to address them directly. They are not paying for a "canned" talk or consulting job.

Fourth, remember that people are not listening to you because there is a test scheduled or a grade assigned. You are going to have work very hard to keep them interested and involved. Certainly, what you discuss should directly address their concerns. It is sometimes difficult for academic people to cope with the sort of information that nonacademic people desire. Often, theories, concepts, and methods academicians find fascinating are totally uninteresting to a lay audience. For the most part, people you will work with will want "bottom line" answers that can help them solve pressing—often immediate—problems. Be prepared for numerous "so what" questions. Also be prepared to be challenged by many personal experience stories, anecdotes, and statements of "You have to be here to understand."

You will also have to be entertaining. Remember, people vote with their feet. There is nothing wrong with this. Nowhere is it written that communication professionals need to be tedious and obscure. You, as a consultant (and also, hopefully, as a teacher), need to make people want to listen. Do not misunderstand—you do not need to be a stand-up comedian. You do need to project enthusiasm, excitement, and a sense of humor when you work with groups.

Fifth, you will have to learn how to market yourself. Getting started as a consultant is tough to do. How does one go about it? The most critical thing is to let people know that you exist.

HOW DOES ONE DEVELOP CONTACTS FOR CONSULTING?

Develop Relationships With Continuing Education Programs at Your School

Most colleges and universities offer continuing education programs either independent of particular academic units or within some of those units. Business colleges often have management or executive development programs, pharmacy schools offer continuing education programs, and public affairs schools may provide public education programs. Go over to those offices and introduce yourself. Tell them what you do and ask how you might be included in programs they produce. Most continuing education offices do not pay that much, but they do offer two things. First, they offer a good way to meet people who may later hire you. Impress them here, and they may seek you out for further work. Second, working in continuing education programs gives you an opportunity to try out materials in a semitraditional classroom setting. It is absolutely essential that you recognize that what works in a traditional undergraduate classroom may not work at all in the nonacademic arena. Working in a continuing education program offers you a midway point between classroom and nonclassroom to test materials, content coverage, and audience adaptation.

Make Public Presentations to Community Groups

In every town or city there are many fraternal, professional, and social groups that are always looking for speakers. Most of the time, they are seeking people who can provide an interesting, informative, and perhaps entertaining talk about some topic. Most of the time, they have no money; you will talk for free. The reason you give these talks is to develop contacts and experience. Many of the people in an audience work in businesses or groups. Later, when they need someone with your expertise, they will remember you. Moreover, those talks give you an opportunity to try out material, learn how to adapt information to different audiences, and most importantly, get feedback about your presentation style.

Directly Market Yourself

Many people who want to consult spend some money and time directly marketing themselves. They may put advertisements in the phone book (in big-city Yellow Pages, for instance, there is a category called "public speaking instruction"), they may call on potential clients, and they may send out mass mailings. If you decide on this option, there are two things you need to consider. First, whatever you do, make sure that it is tastefully done. Second, make sure people in your department are aware of your efforts. Colleagues who are not positive about consulting do not want to be surprised to see your picture in the local newspaper as working with some group. If the direct approach to marketing yourself is not palatable to you, some indirect techniques might be useful. In some cities there are agents who try to get consultants work. Find such an agent, and let him or her market you. You might also drop hints whenever you can about your realm of expertise. Get on a local radio or television show, talk about communication, and during the conversation indicate that, in addition to your work at school, you consult. Tell your chairperson that when people call asking for a consultant or speaker that you would like to be recommended. Get in touch with government agencies to ensure that you get every request for proposals for consulting contracts. Keep in touch, as well, with former students and alumni. Let them know that you do work for companies, individuals, and organizations. You never know when a former student might be sitting in a meeting, hear that a consultant is needed, and think of you.

Reinforce Any Contacts You Get

When you do some work for a client, make sure your work is extraordinarily good. Make it a point to measure your success not in money alone, but in whether you get invited back to do further work. Find additional niches for your expertise in the company or organization and then offer yourself for further work in those areas. Ask people you have done work for if you might use them as a reference for other groups. Finally, and most importantly, stay in touch with people who hire you. Visit them, drop them reprints of relevant research, and so on.

CONCLUSION

In the end, the single most important thing you need to remember about consulting and training is that quality always wins out. If you develop true expertise in an area and can communicate that expertise in an informed and interesting way, people will hear about it. Gloss without content can only go so far.

Finally, remember who you are. You are an expert in an important field that is central to humankind. You have knowledge that can be used for many different purposes. Every day, check your ethics and your values. Ethically, do not be a servant to every cause. If you are teaching at a college, university, junior college, or high school, remember that you are first and foremost a teacher at that institution. Do not give your students or colleagues less attention because of your desire to consult. Keep your research program going, continue your thinking, and build your teaching skills.

Effective communication is central to the success of any individual or organization. You, as a consultant, can help people and firms better themselves through your expertise in communication. Done well, consulting is a legitimate, important instructional opportunity for the scholar-teacher in the field of communication.

VI

Exploring Important Professional Issues

37

Ethical Issues In Teaching

Kenneth E. Andersen
University of Illinois

During the 1990s, controversies over ethics and values attracted major public attention. The general public increasingly questioned the ethical practices of those in the professions and focused directly on ethical and value issues in the political process generally and in the actions of politicians specifically. Educators increasingly were questioned about their role and responsibility for teaching values and instilling both ethical awareness and practices. Often, teachers came under fire for their choice of textbooks, assigned or optional; for their treatment of students; and for particular values they endorsed and exemplified or failed to endorse or exemplify.

Not surprisingly, communication teachers are affected in many ways by the increased interest in ethical issues. The central role of communication means that many ethical decisions are tied to communication activity, both the goals sought and the means employed. Teachers confront efforts to remove books from libraries, ban the presentation of certain plays, and prohibit the use of certain topics and approaches to teaching. Teachers find that such matters as fair use of material, plagiarism, acceptability of language, use of particular motivational appeals, or even topics for speeches become sources of difficulty when students, teachers, parents, and administrators do not share common standards. The responsibility and right of educators to develop the curriculum and to teach in what they believe to be the most effective manner often lead to controversy in the community as well as conflicts with individual students or parents.

The communication classroom shares the concern of every classroom about cheating on exams, plagiarized material, fairness in grading, and ensuring responsible use of individual rights. However, the teacher dealing with communication theory and practice inevitably also faces issues that arise out of the subject matter: ethical communication goals; acceptable ethical practices in treatment of content, language use, and motivational appeals; deceptive communication; policies relative to the mass media; practice of critical listening; censorship; and the development of an adequate basis for making communication decisions in one's profession, community activity, and private life.

Teachers have a somewhat unique responsibility in that they inevitably serve as role models for their students. Historically, teachers were held to a higher behavioral standard by the community, often with specific standards of conduct written into their contracts. Today, their position still gives them a degree of "power" not always perceived by teacher or students. Students are often drawn to a particular major in college or to a career choice by the influence of a teacher, and individual students still idolize or develop "crushes" on a particular teacher. In mentoring students and colleagues, educators must be sensitive to the power—wanted or not—that they have. As professional educators they have the responsibility to contribute to the growth of the individual, enriching the potential of that individual to flourish as a human being and have a successful career. Even with the best of intentions and carefully considered actions, it is possible to exploit a student or a younger colleague. Deliberate exploitation of that relationship for personal gain of any sort is a clear ethical violation. Recent controversies about prohibition of personal contact outside the classroom as well as prohibitions of touching and unwanted attention highlight the importance of ethical behavior in interaction with others, particularly in relationships where there is an imbalance of power, authority, or responsibility. Communication teachers who often work one on one with students, direct plays, coach debate and forensics, and travel with students have particular responsibilities for ethical interactions.

The communication teacher must be prepared to deal not only with ethical issues that arise in any classroom, but also with ethical issues relative to the theory and practice of communication, including assisting students in accepting responsibility for their choices in the entire range of communication activities, situations, roles, and purposes.

This chapter is designed to assist the teacher in coping with ethical issues and value questions. The chapter examines the nature of ethics, ethical issues that arise in the classroom, ethical issues that arise in teaching communication, and methods of dealing with ethical issues.

THE NATURE OF ETHICS

Ethics (moral philosophy) is the systematic study of value concepts such as *good, bad, fair, honest, just,* and the application of such terms to actions and intentions and as descriptors of character. Ethical inquiry asks questions about principles of morality, the nature of the morally good or blameworthy. Ethics is concerned with the questions of how one ought to live and what constitutes a good life. In this sense, it is closely tied to our values, to what we esteem and value in our lives and in the lives of others: power, fairness, love, wealth, justice, honesty, freedom, knowledge, and beauty.

Philosophers distinguish three kinds of ethical studies: descriptive, normative, and metaethical. *Descriptive ethics* examines the ethical practices of a particular individual, group, nation, or period. The ethos or image of a communicator is a descriptive judgment that someone makes of the nature or character of an individual. *Normative ethics* is concerned with judgments of what constitutes right or wrong, good or bad behavior, actions, and character. It is concerned with practical decisions such as how one behaves, both in a particular situation and as a general rule. When one speaks of an ethical code, an unethical practice, or a good person, one is typically dealing with questions of normative ethics. *Metaethics* is concerned with questions of the meaning of various ethical terms and with the logical processes involved when making ethical statements and claims.

Communication teachers find themselves making use of all three levels of ethical inquiry; for example, descriptive in distinguishing standards that an audience utilizes for political speakers versus medical doctors; normative in making judgments about the ethical quality of a particular word choice, speech, or speaker, or the point of view taken in reporting an event on a newscast; and metaethical in discussing the requirements of personal or professional ethical codes.

Philosophical inquiry serves many valuable functions: It subjects convictions and beliefs to critical scrutiny, both our own and that of others; it brings to light presuppositions and hidden assumptions; it asks questions about the ultimate worth of actions and goals. Normative ethics calls for judgment or wisdom . Normative ethics is not simply a matter of information and knowledge, although information and knowledge are essential bases from which to proceed.

ETHICS AND THE TEACHER

Questions that involve ethical issues arise naturally in every classroom, whatever the subject matter. Questions concerning clear communication of requirements, testing the material presented, grading standards, time for completion of major assignments, favoritism, and the effects of bias or prejudice involve ethical practice as well as quality of teaching. Many elements of classroom management (protecting students from harassment, limiting intrusions and disruptions, accommodating a range of opinions and points of view, encouraging active participation, avoiding ridiculing or embarrassing students for "wrong answers") are important ethical goals.

Ethical issues cannot be avoided. There will be efforts to cheat on examinations. Students may copy their homework. Test questions may be pirated. Speakers may present material drawn almost verbatim from a magazine, *Cliff Notes*, or some other source given brief acknowledgment for a single direct quotation. Increasingly the Internet provides an array of opportunities for the student to present material that is not his or her own work, material that was not critically examined, compared with other sources, or expressed in his or her own formulation. Students may express religious prejudices, use obscene gestures, or employ sexist language without any sense of impropriety. Students assigned to work in cooperative learning groups may default on their responsibilities, placing others at risk of failure, and be content to let the others do the work. Students may bring an exaggerated concern for fairness, questioning many educational practices such as assigning grades. Students may believe it is more important not to hurt the "feelings" of another than to honestly express their beliefs or emotions.

Such issues cannot be dealt with only after the fact or on a private, individual basis. Students must know what constitutes fair use of material, understand what constitutes plagiarism, and be aware of the limits of cooperative effort. They need to understand the responsibilities associated with the role of student. However, a teacher should not assume students know what constitutes plagiarism. In elementary school my son copied items verbatim from encyclopedias and was encouraged to do so. Despite my warnings he persisted in such practices until an English teacher assigned an F for undue reliance on outside sources: Standards had changed! Evidence from academic standards cases is persuasive: Many students do not understand the nature of plagiarism. Teachers need to be direct, clear, and firm in identifying standards and in defining the various violations of acceptable practice and the penalties that will ensue. Teacher presentations and class discussions of specific examples are particularly helpful.

Where matters of classroom practice are concerned, wise teachers make their standards very clear. Whereas certain ethical norms are open questions that each individual must decide for oneself, and general agreement cannot be expected, on certain issues (such as plagiarism) there is a need to be quite clear that a public, universal standard is mandated. Violations, however, are typically dealt with on a private basis. Often, teachers prefer to handle the matter themselves although they may decide to turn to existing structures as student disciplinary panels or the principal.

Numerous ethical matters are not tied directly to the classroom. Relationships with other teachers, administrators, parents, and the community pose many ethical dilemmas. When does one report the violation of school rules or standard procedures by a peer or superior? Reviewing a colleague for appointment or a merit raise or evaluating teaching effectiveness involves ethical responsibilities. In casting a play, seeking student assistance, or conducting research, there should be an assurance of informed consent and freedom from coercion. What is seen by a teacher as a means of promoting friendship and establishing a good rapport may be seen as harassment by some and favoritism by others. How accurately and precisely does a letter of recommendation reflect one's actual judgment? How free can the teacher be in advocating unpopular causes in the community—a right to free speech—when that may indirectly or directly affect the classroom?

As a member of a profession, an educator is expected to adhere to responsible norms of professional conduct and can be held to those standards by the courts as well as by students, parents, and administrators. Legal liabilities, contracts, social pressure, and professional preparation as well as individual conscience play an important part in guaranteeing a certain minimal standard. However, if individuals as a group meet only the minimal standard, that standard inevitably erodes to be replaced with another standard that is even less demanding.

ETHICS AND TEACHING COMMUNICATION

It is essential to understand the range of ethical issues that arise in teaching communication, whether these involve theory, practice, or criticism of the various forms, purposes, settings, or media. The remainder of this chapter highlights some areas in which ethical issues arise in teaching communication and some ways in which those issues have been resolved, and concludes with some suggested means to enhance students' ability to deal with ethical issues in communication.

Nature of Ethical Issues in Communication

Potentially, ethical issues may arise at any point where a choice, conscious or unconscious, is made or the perception exists that a choice could be made. Aristotle emphasized this point in his doctrine of choices as applied to communication, noting that every choice made by a speaker provides a basis for a judgment of character. It is helpful, however, to note some major areas in which ethical issues arise.

Ethical issues arise in the process of defining the nature of communication, particularly the role and functions that it serves for the individual, the group, the larger community, or humanity as a whole. Justifiable ethical positions and defenses of specific ethical choices are derived from the role and function assigned to communication generally and from the specific function or form of communication being studied. Some ethical positions are grounded in the nature of the communication process itself. Thus, a dialogical approach stressing equality of all participants may yield a different standard than a stress on communication serving the needs of the state, whether democratic or totalitarian. The degree to which communication is to serve the individual versus the state or larger society and the priority of the goals of one over the other have tremendous consequences for determination of what is ethical.

A key issue concerns the locus or place of responsibility for ethical communication. Many approaches to communication place major emphasis on the source, the originator of the communication act. Hence, many ethical standards are focused upon the behavior of the source. One test of successful communication is whether it achieves the purposes or goals of the source. However, if one takes a comprehensive view of communication, one knows that communication must also serve the receivers in terms of their needs and goals. Ultimately, communication must serve the needs of or, at least, not be unduly harmful to the society. Hence, an ethic tied only to the goals and purposes of the source is almost inevitably faulty and will be rejected by other participants if it ignores their interests and society's interests in the communication process. Each individual plays multiple roles in the communication process over time. Is it logical that an ethic should elevate the concerns of the individual in one role over the concerns of those in every other role? Is it true that a politician functioning as a politician should be held to a different standard of "promise keeping" than that same person as salesperson, friend, or mother?

Ethical issues also arise in terms of particular mediums and settings. Does the press have a higher standard for objectivity, completeness, and accuracy of reporting than an individual speaker? Does a person in a face-to-face debate have a different standard for presentation of both sides of an issue than an individual making the only presentation on an issue to a partisan, well-informed audience? Does the standard of the overtness of presentation of erotic material vary for print, photographs, speeches, or film? Should a nation at war restrict information flow to a greater degree than it does in peacetime? Should—must—a government allow criticism of that government? In thinking about the answers to these questions, most individuals have a sense that there are different standards to be met in different situations.

The means and methods employed in communication pose significant ethical issues. Even if the goal of a communication is sound, the means employed may be so detrimental that they corrupt the goal or achieve the goal, but produce other negative consequences such as impairing future communication. Even the most desirable goal does not legitimate every means. Historically writers on communication have focused largely on ethical issues of content. Andersen (1979) found six major categories of ethical shortcomings relevant to the source's treatment of material: inadequate research or a failure to meet logical standards of truth; sacrificing convictions in adapting to the audience; insincerity, trying to be what one is not; withholding and suppressing relevant information; relaying false information; and using motivational materials to hinder the communication of truth.

A seventh category that Andersen (1979) identified focused on a different area of ethical concern: the receivers and their failure to listen critically, a failure to respond to the content in a rational manner, and an insensitivity to ethical dimensions. Many textbooks fail to focus on questions of ethical responsibilities of readers and listeners, the consumers in the communication process. Those concerned with interpersonal and small group communication are more likely to emphasize the active nature and the responsibilities of all participants in communication due to the immediate alteration of roles—the dual interaction that marks such communication. Ethical issues are posed by the failure of individuals to expose themselves to or respond to relevant messages. Further, the way in which individuals respond may be crucial: The receiver may depend on prejudice, stereotypes, authority figures, or blind acceptance; or accept responsibility for testing and weighing communication on more relevant bases; or usually, some combination of the two. Many receivers do not accept responsibility for their reactions or for their failure to act.

Finally, specific topic areas within the study of communication may pose particular ethical issues. Cross-cultural communication, for example, involves participants in a range of ethical dilemmas. Different practices, some of which have ethical considerations, are involved whether in bargaining over an item for sale or in framing an international treaty. Some common ethical ground must be found that permits dialogue and agreement. Even within the same culture, conflicts may arise in defining ethical practice. The guarantee of freedom of speech in the First Amendment is an unlimited source of disputes. The Supreme Court has never satisfactorily (or consistently) defined such terms as *obscenity* and *pornography*. Yet there are increasing pressures to censor books, plays, and classroom materials on such grounds.

Methods of Resolution

How is the classroom teacher to deal with ethical issues including the potential for conflict among the ethical views of students coming from diverse cultural, religious, economic, and linguistic backgrounds? One approach to resolving ethical issues is to depend on the conscience, morality, or ethical standards of the individual teacher. However, in the absence of certainty on ethical issues, a teacher is rightly reluctant to impose personal standards on students. Even if that is attempted, it is often not successful. Typically, students' judgments of what is ethical will vary widely on some issues, minimally on others. Students often have not tested the ethical standards they strongly espouse or oppose. However, to assert that no ethical standards apply is unreasonable. How does one proceed?

First, although there is not universal agreement on ethical standards, the lack of agreement should not be interpreted to mean that any ethical standard is as good as any other. Some standards are more defensible than others, and one responsibility of the teacher is to assist the students in learning how to test and defend standards and to recognize strengths and weaknesses of differing views. A strategy is available for use in assessing actions for their ethicality. First, it is essential that the facts of the case be as clear and complete as possible. Often the solution to a dispute lies in clarifying the factual basis of the matter, for many "ethical" disagreements turn out to be disagreements about factual claims. Once the facts are clear, application of various ethical standards or guidelines can be considered. The relevant ethical criteria or standards should be identified and their application justified. One frequent difficulty is that a single standard is employed when multiple standards may be relevant. Ethical codes typically contain a series of moral articles or standards ordered in terms of priority. Specific situations may demand a reordering of priorities. Ethical standards are not abstract ideals; they need to be practical guides to action. One test of ethical standards is to subject them to intense critical scrutiny, but the ability of ethical standards to direct action and to provide adequate justifications found acceptable by others are major tests as well.

For more than 2,000 years philosophers have offered, tested, refined, and discarded a wide range of approaches to ethics. Their thinking and the experience of societies and individuals are invaluable resources. Although most individuals have not formally studied ethics, they have been influenced by such injunctions as: treat others as you would like to be treated, seek the greatest good for the greatest number, be truthful, avoid doing evil even if not compelled to do what would be most beneficial to others. The idea of testing ethical practices from the point of view of the parties involved as well as the impact on society is widespread.

A number of methods, each with strengths and weaknesses, have been used to determine ethical guidelines for communication. One method is to determine the relevant ethical standards of the audience or relevant group through a process of audience analysis. If communication practices meet the standard held by those to whom the communication is addressed, it is presumably ethical. Several difficulties exist with this view: The analysis may be faulty, the standard may be so low that it is obviously too defective for use, the relevant standard may not be clearly developed or widely shared by the group, and it may conflict with widely held standards.

A second method often used is generalizing a particular religious or moral point of view. However, there are difficulties in agreeing on the interpretation, rejection by those who do not accept that particular view, and difficulty of knowing what the generalized standard dictates in a particular situation. Suppose one takes the standard of not lying as a universal prescription. How should the individual have responded when the Nazi storm troopers knocked on the door and asked, "Is X inside?" if answering truthfully condemns an innocent individual to a concentration camp or gas chamber?

A third approach involves the view that ethical practices should flow from the nature of the political system. A democracy commits itself to an informed citizenry, creating a need for sharing information and for a free exchange of ideas. Although it seems reasonable to accept the idea that certain ethical responsibilities follow from living in a democracy, it is less clear that individuals do not have the right to demand the same ethical standards simply because they live in a dictatorship under a reign of terror. Are the state's rights superior to those of the individual?

A fourth method for deriving ethical standards is to work from the nature of the communication process itself, a basis that I endorse (Andersen, 1983), or from the nature of humanity itself. Representative of such approaches is the stress on dialogical communication of Johannesen (1996). Many have argued that individuals have a right to respect; to fair treatment; to information on which to make a reasonable, informed, and individual decision, simply because one is a fully functioning human being. However, what is appropriate to one communication setting or purpose may not generalize to other settings or purposes. Further, issues of what constitute human nature and the ideal "humanness" seem as problematic as agreeing on a common ethical standard through other approaches.

A final possibility, not inconsistent with any of the preceding approaches, is to set a goal of establishing a personal ethical code consciously held and tested as a result of systematically reflecting on and testing various approaches. This makes individuals responsible not only for coming to hold a clear view of their own ethical code, but also for a willingness to validate that code publicly by justifying it as a basis for action binding self and others until such time as the code or application is shown to be unjustified.

CLASSROOM STRATEGIES

As noted earlier, teachers inevitably face ethical issues in the classroom as well as ethical issues linked to the particular subject matter. Quite spontaneously, students raise a number of ethical issues. Further, the teacher should assist students in recognizing ethical issues and their appropriate importance. The subject matter of communication courses causes a range of value questions to be addressed, although not all teachers emphasize the ethical dimensions in treating those questions. In communication classes dealing with presentations to others, questions concerned with purposes, means, balance of logical and motivational elements, and fair use must receive attention. Courses that deal with communication history; communication theory; or regulation, criticism, and practice of communication should accord ethical considerations a proper role.

Yet for reasons suggested earlier, including the lack of agreement on ethical standards, the ethical dimension is often given minimal attention. Such an approach is unwise. Decisions about ethics affect communication in a wide range of immediate as well as long-term ways. Omitting the ethical dimension leaves students without assistance on important issues that teachers of communication are best prepared to address. Omission of the topic increases the likelihood of attacks on the teacher for failing to deal with value issues. Such attacks often come from those who believe they have the answer and demand that that answer become the orthodoxy of the classroom.

When and how does the teacher treat ethical issues in a course? Some ethical concerns lend themselves to integration throughout the entire course. Certain value positions and ethical presuppositions necessarily play a role throughout any course. In these instances, the ethical dimension becomes an ongoing part of the course.

In many courses, it will be useful to have a unit in which ethical issues are addressed. Typically, units on ethics are offered late in the course on the grounds that substantial knowledge about the communication process is required before the significance of ethical issues can be fully seen and constructively discussed. Although ethical considerations may provide a perspective for integrating the class material, it is essential that the ethical dimension be given its place throughout the course. Thus, the unit on ethics may best be seen as a final effort to rework and refine ethical issues that have surfaced throughout the course.

There are a growing number of sources devoted to communication ethics. Some of the more useful current sources are listed in the References and as Suggested Readings at the end of the chapter.

Although methods and procedures will vary with teacher, subject matter, and nature of the individual class, the following goals drawn from work at the Hastings Center (Rosen & Caplan, 1980) are appropriate in dealing with the ethical dimensions of communication:

1. Stimulating the moral imagination: "Morality matters; it is at the core of human lives."
2. Recognizing ethical issues, which involves a careful, rational effort to identify moral issues.
3. Developing analytical skills to discern and weigh relevant arguments.
4. Developing a sense of moral obligation and personal responsibility.
5. Developing the ability to tolerate disagreement but resisting ambiguity.

CONCLUSION

Ideally, teachers will have had a course in communication ethics, a course in moral philosophy, or have been exposed to the ethical dimension of communication in the various courses they completed. However, preparation is not the major determinant of success in this area. The key to success in dealing with ethical issues is a sensitivity to the ethical dimension so that its presence is felt in course planning and preparation, in classroom presentations of material, in discussion, and in evaluation. Helpful resource material is readily available. Once the ethical dimension is introduced, ethical issues will pop up in the news, be brought to class by students, and appear spontaneously in the classroom. Students often enjoy the challenge of developing and justifying ethical codes for particular settings, forms, or for communication generally. Discussion of these proposed codes demonstrates that the communication process is a valuable means for exploring ethical issues while developing understanding, discouraging ambiguity, and enhancing tolerance. Whatever the means, students find their appreciation and practice of communication is enhanced to the degree they understand the nature and importance of the ethical dimension to and in communication.

SUGGESTED READINGS

Andersen, K. E. (1984, January). A code of ethics for speech communication. *SPECTRA*, pp. 2–3.

Bellah, R. N., Madsen, R., Smith, W. M., Swidler, A., & Tipton, S. M. (1985). *Habits of the heart.* Berkeley: University of California Press.

Bok, S. (1989). *Lying: Moral choice in public and private life.* New York: Vintage Books.

Christians, C. G., & Covert, C. L. (1980). *Teaching ethics in journalism education.* Hastings-on-Hudson, NY: The Hastings Center.

Christians, C. G., Rotzoll, K., & Fackler, M. (1991). *Media ethics: Cases and moral reasoning* (3rd ed.). New York: Longman.

Denton, R. E., Jr. (Ed.). (1991). *Ethical dimensions of political communication.* New York: Praeger.

Goodlad, J. I, Soder, R., Sirotnik, K. A. (Eds.). (1991). *The moral dimensions of teaching.* San Francisco: Jossey-Bass.

Goodwin, H. E. (1983). *Groping for ethics in journalism.* Ames: University of Iowa Press.

Greenberg, K. J. (Ed.). (1991). *Conversations on communication ethics.* Norwood, NJ: Ablex.

Haiman, F. (1981). *Speech and law in a free society.* Chicago: University of Chicago.

Jaksa, J. A., & Pritchard, M. S. (1994). *Communication ethics: Methods of analysis* (2nd ed.). Belmont, CA: Wadsworth.

Johannesen, R. L. (1997). *Ethics in human communication* (5th ed.). Prospect Heights, IL: Waveland Press.

MacIntyre, A. (1981). *After virtue.* Notre Dame, IN: University of Notre Dame Press.

Makau, J. M., & Arnett, R. C. (Eds.). (1997). *Communication ethics in an age of diversity.* Urbana: University of Illinois Press

Nilsen, T. R. (1974). *Ethics of speech communication* (2nd ed.). Indianapolis, IN: Bobbs-Merrill.

Norman, R. (1983). *The moral philosophers: An introduction to ethics.* Oxford, UK: Clarendon Press.

REFERENCES

Andersen, K. E. (1983). *Persuasion theory and practice* (2nd ed.). Boston: American Press.

Andersen, M. K. (1979). *An analysis of the treatment of ethics in selected speech communication textbooks.* Unpublished doctoral dissertation, University of Michigan, Ann Arbor.

Johannesen, R. L. (1996). *Ethics in human communication* (4th ed.). Prospect Heights, IL: Waveland Press.

Rosen, B., & Caplan, A. L. (1980). *Ethics in the undergraduate curriculum.* Hastings-on-Hudson, NY: The Hastings Center.

38

Fitting Into the Department
and the Profession

James C. McCroskey
West Virginia University

Students typically see teachers as the power source in colleges and universities. Many new teachers, particularly graduate assistants serving as teachers for the first time, have similar perceptions. In fact, individual classroom teachers typically have comparatively little control over the environment in which they work.

Teaching is a profession that functions within complex organizations—departments, colleges, universities, and university systems. Virtually all instruction that occurs in today's institutions of higher education is part of a highly coordinated educational system, one in which all of the parts are very much interrelated.

Systems are successful only to the extent that their components are successfully interrelated. Universities are composed of interrelated colleges. Colleges are composed of interrelated departments. Departments are composed of interrelated faculty members. A faculty member who thinks he or she can operate in an autonomous fashion is likely to be viewed by others as a "loose cannon." Such people are viewed as dangerous to the system, and are likely to be "thrown overboard" the first time the opportunity arises.

ACADEMIC FREEDOM

One of the most valued rights of university faculty members is academic freedom. Unfortunately, it is also the most misunderstood. *Academic freedom* is the freedom of a teacher to state the truth about matters related to her or his discipline as he or she sees it, without fear of losing her or his position or otherwise being punished for the views expressed. It also includes the right of a teacher to speak out when he or she sees injustice in society, to support whatever political candidate or position he or she chooses, and to challenge the views of established authority. In short, this is the academic version of the right held by everyone in U. S. society—the freedom of speech.

Unfortunately, many teachers misinterpret this right to mean that they have the freedom to teach anything in any way they please in their classrooms. Academic freedom relates to political issues, not to academic ones. Colleges are regularly forbidden to teach subject matter that is deemed more appropriate for another college. Departments are restricted from teaching content that has been assigned to another department. Within a given department, faculty are restricted from teaching content in one course that is determined to be part of a different course. Such restrictions are necessary. Otherwise, students could be subjected to the same content over and over, never having the opportunity to study things that they may need or want. Of course, anyone who has been a student knows that some needless overlap continues to exist, and some courses include materials that are of interest to no one other than the teacher teaching them. Such problems, however, are not caused by academic freedom; they are a function of one or more people ignoring or abdicating their responsibility to exercise appropriate control in the academic environment.

Control in most academic institutions of today follows a top-down path. Whoever is in control of the purse is in control of the institution. In practice, however, most control as regards individual courses is exercised at the departmental level. This occurs as a function of appropriate delegation of authority from upper levels. Every course must be approved by some unit before it can become a part of a university's curriculum, and the approval authority normally is delegated to some faculty unit—often a group of faculty members elected by their peers. Such groups frequently are known as *curriculum committees*. They may exist at every level of the institution. However, because content specialists generally exist only at the departmental level, this is the level that serves the primary function of screening out inappropriate courses. This function may be performed by a departmental administrator, a faculty committee, or (particularly in smaller departments) by the faculty as a whole.

The new faculty member, then, enters a world not of her or his own making, a world full of special but not yet understood interests, a world with an unknown history, a world that is as likely to be hostile as it is to be friendly. It is a world in which the newcomer is free to say whatever he or she thinks, and propose any changes he or she would like to make. Everyone else is free to support the changes, ignore the suggestions, attack them, or simply shun the newcomer altogether. It is up to the newcomer to fit in.

DEPARTMENTAL GOVERNANCE

If an observer looks at departments in the same field across a number of universities, regardless of the particular academic discipline, he or she most likely will be surprised at how different one department is from another. Some of the differences are obvious—size of the department, median age of the faculty, content that is emphasized, quality of the facilities, and the like. Other factors, such as the department's culture, may be much less obvious but much more important to the new person's success. Near the top of the nonobvious list is the manner in which the department is governed.

The manner in which a department is governed typically is a function of tradition. If one asks why a particular department is operated the way it is, the answer that usually is correct (although often not given) is because it has been operated that way for a long time. Senior faculty tend to dominate most departments and the more senior one gets, the more likely one believes the old maxim "If it ain't broke, don't fix it." Change comes only with considerable difficulty, or in the face of impending disaster, in most departments.

Tradition, then, is a driving force in most departments. What is routine, and has been for a long time, is part of the department's culture. Often, the members of the department may not even be aware that they do some things very differently than a neighboring department. The newcomer must become acquainted with the department's culture as quickly as possible in order to avoid making serious errors in her or his dealings with people who have been in the department for a longer period (Richmond & McCroskey, 1992). The first thing to determine is the basic political system. There are essentially four general systems that may be in place: autocracy, fiefdoms, democracy, and chaos.

Autocracy

An *autocracy* exists when one individual, usually known as a head or a chair, or a small group of faculty members, makes all of the major decisions and judgments in the department. In such systems, the leader(s) may or may not consult with other people prior to making decisions. The decisions may be made with individual faculty members' best interests in mind, or the interests of faculty may not even be taken into account.

Under the autocratic system, rank becomes very important. The head or chair is at the top, followed by the full professors, the associate professors, the assistant professors, the instructors, the doctoral assistants, the masters assistants, and so on. The value of a person's opinions is roughly equal to the rank that person holds in the system. The opinions of new people, particularly those holding graduate assistantships, are viewed with minimum concern.

People brought up with the traditional U. S. values for democracy often react very negatively to an autocratic system, particularly when they first enter. Their instinct is to fight, an instinct that, if not kept under control, will almost certainly result in negative consequences for the newcomer. New people entering an autocratic system should keep in mind that it was the autocrat who decided to allow them to enter, and it is reasonable to assume the autocrat wants to see them do well to demonstrate the wisdom of that decision.

The concept of the benevolent autocrat is an important one to understand. Although autocrats have the power to bring harm to the newcomer, they also have the power to provide many positive rewards. The decision on which path the autocrat will follow usually rests with the newcomer—the one who is supportive of the autocrat receives support in return. Benevolent autocrats are those who use their power to help the people under them. Few autocrats are so altruistic that they help those who choose to attack them. In large measure, then, a new person often has the choice of generating an enemy or a benevolent autocrat. Whether an autocrat is perceived as benevolent or not is a function of the relationship between the autocrat and the individual doing the perceiving.

Fiefdoms

The system of *fiefdoms* is a special case of autocracy. Instead of having one person (or one small collective group) at the top and in control, the department is broken (either formally or informally) into smaller units that have individuals (fiefs) in charge. These individuals are nominally subordinate to a person or persons above them, but in practice do pretty much whatever they want so long as they do not stray too far into some other fief's territory. Typically fiefs are identified by titles such as basic course director, coordinator of graduate studies, head of the division of rhetoric, and associate chair for research.

Fiefs behave mostly like other autocrats. The rule of survival is "Those that go along, get along." It is up to the new person to make peace with the various fiefs with or under whom he or she must work. Getting in trouble with a fief is tantamount to getting in trouble with the head autocrat. When pushed, the person over the fief will almost always support the fief when there is a conflict with a new person.

Within the fief system there is a high sense of territoriality. Each fief has an intellectual or administrative territory over which he or she reigns. The fief approaches the new person with the basic attitude of "I've got mine. You do what you want, but don't mess with my area." Typically, there are areas within the department over which no one appears to reign. These are open to individuals to build on, if they do so carefully.

Democracy

The idealized political system in a department is democracy. Many new teachers assume that all departments are run in a democratic manner—one person, one vote. In practice, that rarely occurs. In most departments it is recognized that some people, by nature of their background, experience, and rank, are "more equal" than others. The closest most departments come to democracy is a consensus system. Formal votes are taken only rarely, but everyone is asked for their input. If significant opposition to a decision emerges, that decision is not made until the opposition is dealt with. The significance of the opposition usually is determined by the status of those expressing opposition.

Democracy is often chosen as a departmental system in revolt against an autocratic system with which people have become dissatisfied. Frequently, the outcome is the replacement of one undesirable system with another. Although democracy is not a bad system, democracy that gets completely out of control can be bad. It is not uncommon for a democratic system in a department to become a dictatorship of the majority. A coalition of faculty within the department simply takes over and votes down anything they do not want, even if it means trampling on the needs of the minority. Even more common is what has been called *rampant democracy*. When this breaks out, people begin to complain about being "committeed" or "meetinged" to death. Some departments literally have a vote on such matters as how many paper clips to purchase or when other people will hold office hours. When faculty spend more clock hours per week in meetings than in classrooms, rampant democracy is present.

For the new person who enters a department with a democratic system, the road ahead poses many pitfalls. It is critical that the new person be supported by a majority of the established people. These are the people who will determine such things as where (maybe even whether) the new person has an office, what that person will teach, when it will be taught, and, most importantly, whether the person will be retained.

Chaos

The last system is, essentially, no system. *Chaos* often results when a powerful person or persons leave the department. This may be the result of promotion (e. g., to associate dean), death, retirement, or resignation. Any relatively sudden departure of powerful people may leave a gap in the system. The time when this typically is felt most is at the beginning of a school year, exactly at the time when a new person is most likely to enter the system.

Whether the system in the past has been autocratic or democratic, specific people have been present to keep the system functioning. Only the fiefdom approach is relatively secure from the loss of a powerful person. In that system, most of the system managers are still in place, and only one needs to be replaced. Under conditions of chaos, struggles for power and control are likely to be common. Unless a new person has been employed specifically to replace a departed person in the same role, a new person has little chance of surviving such battles and emerging on top. The wiser course is to avoid those battles.

Such a choice may be difficult to make, because no one may really know who is in charge. This circumstance often results when a person is appointed interim chair to replace a departed chair. The whole political system is, at least temporarily, up for grabs. There may be pressure on the new person from many quarters and too little information available to permit wise decisions.

The preceding discussion of the various departmental political systems that a new person may encounter is intended to sensitize you to the kinds of problems you may face as a new person in a department. No one of them is inherently easier to survive than another. The key to survival is to recognize what system exists and establish positive relationships with as many of the relevant decision makers in the system as possible. Always remember: The department got along without you before you came. It probably can get along quite well again if it gets rid of you.

THE BASIC COURSE

Almost all departments representing the primary academic disciplines offer "basic" courses in their disciplines. New people are the ones most likely to be assigned to teach such courses. Hence, one's first teaching experience as a faculty member in many disciplines is in the basic course.

In the communication field, it is unusual for a graduate assistant never to have any assignment with a basic course. In excess of 90% of all graduate assistants in most communication departments are involved in the teaching of a basic course. The nature of that involvement varies drastically from department to department.

Basic courses in most communication departments exist primarily to serve students who are majoring in other disciplines. They may be content or skills courses; they may center on public speaking, on interpersonal communication, on mass communication, on communicating in organizations, on rhetorical theory, on communication theory, or on some combination of those—or even something entirely different.

There is no standard for what the basic course in communication will be from department to department. Thus, it is likely that a new person entering a department will be confronted with a different type of basic course than he or she has seen or taken previously. This is particularly problematic if the department has a relaxed approach to the course. Sometimes the new person simply is given a text and told to teach the course. In some cases, there is a common syllabus, but in some there is not. In some cases, the new person is not given either a text or a syllabus—he or she is simply told to teach the course. All that is provided is the course title and catalog description. In contrast, some departments provide a complete package for their basic course as well as extensive training for new people in how to teach it. In general, the degree of freedom in teaching the basic course is inversely related to the degree of assistance one is provided for teaching the course. Generally, the more the department values the basic course, the more assistance is provided and the less flexibility is permitted.

How much a new teacher of the basic course is valued is partially dependent on how much the basic course is valued by the department. Some departments virtually live off of the basic course. For others, the basic course is considered a necessary evil: No one wants it, but someone has to do it. It is not unusual for a department to delegate the basic course to one person (the basic course fief) and turn its collective head away. Researchers may look to the basic course as the source of compliant participants. The university may look at it as a place to put masses of students who must take something. Other disciplines may look at the course as a valuable contributor to their students' education, or as a source of too many high grades. In some places, the basic course is the battle ground for opposing intellectual forces within the department. Will the public speaking or the interpersonal forces reign supreme? Shall we teach the masses about the media or the postpubescents about female–male relationships?

There are probably as many views of the basic course as there are viewers. If there is a right and correct view, it has yet to receive the acclaim it deserves. Nevertheless, as a new person in a department, you are almost certain to be exposed to the truth about the basic course soon after your arrival. To survive, it is best for you to go along with whatever is the prevailing view. As a new person, your chances of introducing significant change in the department's approach to the basic course are nil. However, if you make a significant amount of noise about it, you might be labeled a problem person, and problem people constantly run into problems.

THE CURRICULUM—WHERE DO I FIT?

A department's curriculum is the set of courses that the department offers; but it is more than that. It is the external manifestation of the department's history, philosophy, and culture. It provides the justification for the existence of the department and the individual members of that department. It is the definition of that department both to students and to faculty members of other departments. In many ways, it is the department.

In many instances, a new person is employed explicitly to teach a certain course or courses in that curriculum. Even so, the new person's niche is far from guaranteed. Sometimes, one or more continuing members of the department want to take over those courses, change them, or even abolish them. The new person may almost immediately be put on the defensive by challenges from older department members.

It is not unnatural for a faculty member, new or not, to become possessive of a course he or she has been assigned to teach and to become defensive if that course is attacked. It is easy to forget that no faculty member "owns" any course. As teachers of courses, we are, at most, temporary custodians—even if we created the course. Courses belong to universities. They may be, and sometimes are, moved from one department to another, and even from one college to another.

Assumed ownership of courses causes many problems and conflicts in departments, not the least of which are problems that may be encountered by new people. A person who has taught a course in the recent past, who decided he or she did not want to teach it again, and who participated in the hiring of a new person to handle that responsibility, still may feel possessive of the course. Although all faculty members must take care to avoid undue possessiveness of courses, it is particularly important for the new faculty member to be sensitive to the causes of such responses and to avoid stimulating "ownership" reactions. One of the best ways to do this is to ask the former faculty of the course for advice. New people usually have no knowledge of the problems that have been confronted (and often solved) by their predecessors, so such advice may be extremely valuable. Even if it is not, just being asked for it may help the other person accept the transition with less hostility. One of the worst ways to approach this new responsibility is to criticize how the course was handled previously and profess the intention to make improvements. Such criticism will be heard as criticism of the person who taught the course before. Even if that person is no longer in the department, do not forget that friends of that person most likely still are.

One of the more difficult things for new people to deal with is having someone they feel has less qualifications than they do in charge of a course or program. Almost everyone agrees that the most qualified person is the one who should be in charge. Unfortunately, far fewer people agree on what constitutes "most qualified."

The wise course for the new person is to keep her or his opinions about qualifications private. If the opinions are clearly wrong, this will avoid the embarrassment of being demonstrably wrong. If they are right, it is very likely that others will reach the same conclusions in due course. The key is "in due course," and that almost always represents more time than the new person would prefer to wait. Impatience is a fault that few new people can afford to exhibit. People who have been in systems for some time expect new people to "pay their dues" before they are granted full privileges as a member of the system. Exhibiting an unwillingness to be patient most commonly results in a longer, not a shorter, period of "dues paying" before being accepted as a true member of the system.

At some time or other, everyone in higher education must serve as a new person in a system. For most of us, this experience will be repeated several times over the course of our professional lives. It can be viewed as an opportunity to start afresh, accept new challenges, and make new friends, or it can be seen as knocking down barriers to doing what one really wants to do. Those who take the former view have a very good chance of being accepted into the new system and being successful in it. Those who take the latter view represent a problem waiting to happen. The new person makes the choice of which course to follow.

DEVELOPING AS A PROFESSIONAL

Although most new doctoral graduates are very much aware that they must confront adjustment to a new department when they accept their first post-doctoral position, many are not aware that their professional development is only beginning. They tend to think that their education is now complete, but it is not. In fact, their learning has only begun.

Knowledge is exploding in virtually all fields. It is very difficult to stay up-to-date in most. That is certainly true of the field of communication. This is a young field, and most of the leading scholars in the history of the field are still alive and productive.

Professionals are expected to keep themselves up-to-date in their area(s) of the field. People who do not meet that expectation are often referred to as "dead wood." The PhD is a research degree (and some EdD degrees are also). Society has invested heavily in every individual who achieves a doctoral degree. Thus, it is the responsibility of each doctoral recipient to give back to the society that made it possible for her or him to attain this advanced degree.

Colleges and universities classify such contributions into the categories of research, teaching, and service. Not all institutions have high expectations for contributions in all areas, but some do—principally those who grant advanced graduate degrees, most of which are known as "Research 1" institutions. The vast majority of new knowledge in all fields is generated by faculty in these institutions. Hence, faculty in these institutions must "publish or perish." What this means is they must do the quality of research that will qualify for publication in the field's major journals if they are to meet the expectations of their institution. If they do not, they will be expected to relocate to an institution that does not have such expectations.

Quality teaching is expected by virtually all colleges and universities, although those emphasizing research sometimes are more tolerant of mediocre teaching if the faculty member demonstrates excellence in research. Quality teaching results in high levels of student learning on both the cognitive and affective dimensions. That is, quality teachers produce students who not only understand and can apply the content of the field (cognitive learning) but also view that field in highly positive ways (affective learning). Such students become lifelong learners. To maintain such a high standard of teaching, the individual must stay abreast of the scholarship published in the field and consistently hold the interests of the students at the forefront of her or his concern. Quality teachers must both know and care. The absence of either produces indifferent teaching and little, or even negative, learning.

Service to the general public is expected by most colleges and universities. Service exists when the individual faculty member makes her or his expertise available to the local, regional, and national publics in appropriate forms. This may take the form of publishing information that is useful to readers of specialized publications, presenting programs for groups in need of the information the faculty member can provide, consulting with private or public organizations to assist them in improving their performance, or many other ways in which expertise can be disseminated.

Faculty must continue to grow as professionals or they become the "dead wood" that most faculty never want to be. They must keep up with the research in the field, even if their personal research contributions are limited. They must bring this constantly growing expertise to the students in their classes and to the public through service activities. To be a professional is to be a constantly improving scholar and teacher. In this way the individual not only becomes a valued and respected professional in the department, but also a valued and respected professional in the field.

REFERENCES

Richmond, V. P., & McCroskey, J. C. (1992). *Organizational communication for survival.* Englewood Cliffs, NJ. Prentice-Hall.

Author Index

Subject Index

nonverbal communication, 165, 167
organizational communication,
    148–149
research methods, 220–221
rhetorical studies, 124–125
the basic course, 456
  Preparing students to use, 302
Timing, *see* Course, schedule
Tools, *see* Resources
True–false questions, 436–437
Turn taking, 371–372
Tutoring, 377–378
Two-year colleges
  audiovisuals at, 478
  courses at, 474–475
  curriculum at, 472, 475–478
  functions of, 471–474
  history of, 472
  skills required for graduates of, 476
  students at, 474
  teaching at, 473–479

V

Validity
  definition of, 419
  in evaluation of students, 426, 432–33
  in evaluation of teachers, 419–420
  of research methods, 217
Values, of society, 17–18, 20–21
Videotape, *see* Audiovisuals

W

Wait time, 368
Writing
  assignments, 78–79, 303–306
  de-emphasizing assessment of, 304–306
  evaluation of, 303–306
  goals, 27–29
  in interpersonal communication courses
    96–97
  in personalized system of instruction, 384
  to promote teacher–student dialogue,
    303–306
  use in instruction, 303–306